THE RATIONAL FOUNDATIONS OF ECONOMIC BEHAVIOUR

This is IEA conference volume no. 114

The Rational Foundations of Economic Behaviour

**Proceedings of the IEA Conference
held in Turin, Italy**

Edited by

Kenneth J. Arrow

Enrico Colombatto

Mark Perlman

and

Christian Schmidt

in association with the
INTERNATIONAL ECONOMIC
ASSOCIATION

First published in Great Britain 1996 by
MACMILLAN PRESS LTD
Houndmills, Basingstoke, Hampshire RG21 6XS
and London
Companies and representatives throughout the world

UNESCO subvention 1992/93/SHS/SES/68/SUB/16

This book contains the proceedings of a conference
organized by the International Economic Association
in collaboration with the International Centre for
Economic Research, Turin

A catalogue record for this book is available
from the British Library.

ISBN 0–333–62197–2

First published in the United States of America 1996 by
ST. MARTIN'S PRESS, INC.,
Scholarly and Reference Division,
175 Fifth Avenue,
New York, N.Y. 10010

ISBN 0–312–12708–1

Library of Congress Cataloging-in-Publication Data
The rational foundations of economic behaviour : proceedings of the
IEA conference held in Turin, Italy / edited by Kenneth J. Arrow . . .
[et al.]
p.   cm.
Includes bibliographical references and index.
ISBN 0–312–12708–1
1. Rational expectations (Economic theory)—Congresses.
2. Rational choice theory—Congresses.   3. Economic man—Congresses.
I. Arrow, Kenneth Joseph, 1921–
HB199.R37   1996
330—dc20   95–7828
                                                                              CIP

© International Economic Association 1996

10   9   8   7   6   5   4   3   2   1
05   04   03   02   01   00   99   98   97   96

Printed and bound in Great Britain by
Antony Rowe Ltd, Chippenham, Wiltshire

Contents

The International Economic Association

A non-profit organization with purely scientific aims, the International Economic Association (IEA) was founded in 1950. It is a federation of some sixty national economic associations in all parts of the world. Its basic purpose is the development of economics as an intellectual discipline, recognizing a diversity of problems, systems and values in the world and taking note of methodological diversities.

The IEA has, since its creation, sought to fulfil that purpose by promoting mutual understanding among economists through the organization of scientific meetings and common research programmes, and by means of publications on problems of fundamental as well as of current importance. Deriving from its long concern to assure professional contacts between East and West and North and South, the IEA pays special attention to issues of economies in systemic transition and in the course of development. During its more than forty years of existence, it has organized eighty round-table conferences for specialists on topics ranging from fundamental theories to methods and tools of analysis and major problems of the present-day world. Participation in round tables is at the invitation of a specialist programme committee, but ten triennial World Congresses have regularly attracted the participation of individual economists from all over the world.

The Association is governed by a Council, composed of representatives of all member associations, and by a fifteen-member Executive Committee which is elected by the Council. The Executive Committee (1992–95) at the time of the Turin Conference was:

President:	Professor Michael Bruno, Israel
Vice-President:	Academician Abel G. Aganbegyan, Russia
Treasurer:	Professor Erich Streissler, Austria
Past President:	Professor Anthony B. Atkinson, UK
Other Members:	Professor Karel Dyba, Czech Republic
	Professor Jean-Michel Grandmont, France
	Professor Yujiro Hayami, Japan
	Professor Anne Krueger, USA
	Professor Juan-Antonio Morales, Bolivia
	Professor Agnar Sandmo, Norway
	Professor Amartya Sen, India
	Professor Rehman Sobhan, Bangladesh
	Professor Alan D. Woodland, Australia
	Professor Stefano Zamagni, Italy
Advisers:	Professor Kenneth J. Arrow, USA
	Academician Oleg T. Bogomolov, Russia
	Professor Mohammed Germouni, Morocco
	Professor Luigi Pasinetti, Italy

Secretary-General: Professor Jean-Paul Fitoussi, France

General Editor: Professor Michael Kaser, UK

Professor Sir Austin Robinson was an active Adviser on the publication of conference proceedings from 1954 until his final short illness in 1993.

The Association has also been fortunate in having secured many outstanding economists to serve as President:

Gottfried Haberler (1950–53), Howard S. Ellis (1953–56), Erik Lindahl (1956–59), E.A.G. Robinson (1959–62) G. Ugo Papi (1962–65), Paul A. Samuelson (1965–68), Erik Lundberg (1968–71), Fritz Machlup (1971–74), Edmond Malinvaud (1974–77), Shigeto Tsuru (1977–80), Victor L. Urquidi (1980–83), Kenneth J. Arrow (1983–86), Amartya Sen (1986–89), and Anthony B. Atkinson (1989–92).

The activities of the Association are mainly funded from the subscriptions of members and grants from a number of organizations, including continuing support from UNESCO, through the International Social Science Council.

Acknowledgements

As editors of this volume, we feel particularly grateful to all those who contributed to the organization of the conference, which took place at Villa Gualino (Turin, Italy), where the preliminary versions of the papers were presented; to Frank Hahn, without whom the whole project would not have seen the light; to the members of the Programme Committee (Terenzio Cozzi, Frank Hahn, Amartya Sen, Stefano Zamagni and the four editors); to the International Centre for Economic Research (ICER) and the Chamber of Commerce of Turin, which provided skills and financial support. We also want to thank the French National Centre for Scientific Research (CNRS) and the Singer-Polignac Foundation for supporting a preliminary meeting arranged by Christian Schmidt and held in Paris in December 1992.

We are also indebted to Michael Kaser, who guided us throughout the editorial process, as well as to Kristin Anderson, Alessandra Calosso and Charles McCann, whose patience and hard work have been of great relevance as regards both the conference and the editing of the volume.

List of Contributors

Kenneth J. Arrow, Stanford University, USA
Robert J. Aumann, The Hebrew University of Jerusalem, Israel
Pierpaolo Battigalli, Princeton University, USA, and Politechnico di Milano, Italy
Kenneth Binmore, University College London, UK
Jonas Björnerstedt, Stockholm University, Sweden
Enrico Colombatto, Università di Torino, Italy
Franco Donzelli, Università di Milano, Italy
Massimo Egidi, Università di Trento, Italy
Frank Hahn, University of Cambridge, UK and University of Siena, Italy
Peter J. Hammond, Stanford University, USA
John H. Holland, University of Michigan, USA
Richard C. Jeffrey, Princeton University, USA
Daniel Kahneman, Princeton University, USA
Mordecai Kurz, Stanford University, USA
*Avishai Margalit, The Hebrew University of Jerusalem, Israel
Marco Mariotti, University of Manchester, UK
Bertrand Munier, GRID, École Normale Supérieure de Cachan, France
Mark Perlman, University of Pittsburgh, USA
Charles R. Plott, California Institute of Technology, USA
Alvin E. Roth, University of Pittsburgh, USA
Jean-Louis Rullière, GRID, École Normale Supérieure de Cachan, France
Hamid Sabourian, King's College, University of Cambridge, UK
Pier Luigi Sacco, Università di Firenze, Italy
*Larry Samuelson, University of Wisconsin, USA
Christian Schmidt, Université Paris-Dauphine, France
Amartya Sen, Harvard University, USA
Amos Tversky, Stanford University, USA
Bernard Walliser, CERAS, École Nationale des Ponts et Chausées, France
Jörgen Weibull, Stockholm University, Sweden
Menahem E. Yaari, The Hebrew University of Jerusalem and the Open University
of Israel, Israel
* Co-authors of papers who did not attend the Conference

Abbreviations

a.e.	almost everywhere
AMS	Aggregate monotomic selection
BI	backward induction
CERAS	Centre d'enseignement et de recherche en analyse socio-économique
CKR	Common knowledge of rationality
DELTA	Département et laboratoire d'économie théorique et appliquée
DNA	Deoxyribonucleic acid
DPH	Discovered preference hypothesis
GRID	Groupe de recherche sur le risque, l'information et la décision
IBM	International Business Machines
i.i.d	independent identically distributed
NALP	National Association for Law Placement
NCAM	National Collegiate Athletic Association
NRMP	National Resident Matching Programme
PC	personal computer
PD	Prisoner's Dilemma
PGY1	First year postgraduate
PI	perfect information
STP	Sure Thing Principle
WAMS	Weak asymptotically mean stationary

Preface

Kenneth J. Arrow

1 THE GENERAL NOTION OF RATIONALITY

The concept of rationality is used in economic analysis in three different ways: as a descriptive hypothesis about behaviour, as a normative concept, and as an aspiration, i.e., a way of organizing behaviour which is desirable and to which individuals and societies should be educated. In this conference and this preface, emphasis will be placed on the descriptive aspects. But in fact the three points of view are in perpetual interaction.

Rationality is about choice. Whatever other considerations may enter, the underlying assumption is that, on any given occasion, there is an *opportunity set* of alternatives among which choice must be made. The major meaning of rationality is a condition of consistency among choice made from different sets of alternatives.

Although formally this general statement is valid, it is convenient to distinguish two kinds of rationality for the individual: *rationality of action* and *rationality of knowledge*. Further, modern work shows that it is not sufficient to consider only individuals. There is need for a concept of rationality which takes into consideration the existence of many individuals who are also acting and whose actions affect each other. This has been called *interactive rationality*. Interactive rationality may again be rationality of action or rationality of knowledge.

Let me expand a bit on these concepts. Rationality of actions means roughly that the alternative choices can be ordered in preference, the ordering being independent of the particular opportunity set available on any given occasion. (Consistency conditions weaker than ordering have also been explored.) A more complex formulation, especially appropriate under conditions of uncertainty, distinguishes between *actions* and *consequences*. Choice is over sets of actions, but preference orderings are over consequences. Under certainty, an action leads to a consequence; but under uncertainty, an action may lead to one of many consequences, which one being uncertain. Hence choice requires not only the preferences among consequences, but (uncertain) knowledge of the relation between actions and consequences. Both preference and judgement are needed.

Rationality of knowledge means making the best use of knowledge available to form these judgements. This has its clearest meaning when knowledge is represented by probabilities. Then in effect rationality of knowledge means using the laws of conditional probability, where the conditioning is on all available information. Rationality of knowledge is a special form of rationality of action, when the actions include bets on the outcome of random events.

Interactive rationality is relevant when the payoff to any agent depends on the actions of others. In general, then, the best choice of action by A depends on the actions of B, and vice versa. But how can A know the actions of B? Is it possible to have knowledge (even probabilistic knowledge) of the actions of another?

Competitive equilibrium theory provides on answer to this conundrum, game theory (Nash equilibrium) another, each with its own assumptions. But the deeper logical question is, how do either of these equilibrium concepts come into being? And, of course, the second question is, are the answers empirically convincing?

2 RATIONALITY OF ACTION IN ECONOMIC THEORY

What role has rationality played in economic theory? Let us consider specifically the hypothesis of rationality of action. In classical economics (Adam Smith, David Ricardo, John Stuart Mill), its role is almost confined to the statements that capital and labour flow from low-reward uses to high-reward uses. This led to the proposition that in equilibrium the rate of return to capital is the same in all industries. It also seemed to lead to the proposition that wages are equalized. But since they clearly are not, it was necessary to have a more complicated view. Smith argued that jobs are not equally pleasant; hence, what are equalized are 'net advantages', balancing off wages against job satisfaction. But this is clearly only a partial truth.

Rationality of consumers affects demand, and the classical school denied that demand had any role in determining prices in a competitive setting. To be sure, 'use value' was necessary for the commodity to have 'exchange value', but once there was some use value its extent had no role in determining prices. There was little interest, therefore, in the theory of demand, though Ricardo recognized that demand did matter in monopoly pricing.

Rationality of producers (i.e., profit maximization) is, however, not absent from classical economics. Ricardo may have had nothing to say about profit maximization for firms in general, but he certainly understood the rationality of farms; profit maximization by farmers yielded the surplus which was equal to the land rent under competitive conditions.

In the 1870s, W. Stanley Jevons and Léon Walras recognized that the classical logic was flawed; a coherent theory recognized the multiplicity of final factors and, as a logical implication, the importance of demand in price determination. They introduced the marginal utility theory to explain demand: that is, the maximization of utility subject to the budget constraint. They and others correspondingly developed the theory of the firm as a rational profit-maximizing entity, although here they followed the hitherto-neglected work of Augustin-Antoine Cournot (1838).

Oddly enough, utility maximization had appeared much earlier as an explanation of the demand for gambles, in the famous paper of Daniel Bernoulli (1738). To be precise, he explained the limited willingness to engage even in favourable gambles by the hypothesis of maximizing the expectation of a concave utility function; the same hypothesis explained the purchase of actuarially unfair insurance against losses.

The theories of demand under both certainty and uncertainty have been much developed in the last seventy-five years. The full implications of marginal utility theory for demand were explored by Eugene Slutzky in 1915 and have since been used extensively as a basis for econometric work. Analogous developments in the theory of production have been even more fruitful empirically. Expected-utility theory has been the basis for a theory of portfolio selection in securities markets which has altered not only theory but also practice.

The expected-utility theory is especially rich in testable implications and has given rise to important critical work by cognitive psychologists as well as economists. Questionnaire responses have been a favourite empirical tool, and it was with these that Maurice Allais showed that even scholars advocating expected-utility theory violated its implications. Subsequent work by cognitive psychologists, notably Daniel Kahneman and Amos Tversky, have considerably refined the evidence for the violations and advanced some alternative hypotheses of behaviour.

Methodologically, this work raises an important question. There is a tradition in economics that only prices and quantities derived from actual sales and purchases should be used as evidence, on the grounds that only then is there adequate motivation. However, such restriction of observations means that many questions cannot even be asked, in particular the value of goods that are not traded in markets. This problem has become one of practical policy as well as scientific inquiry in the United States, since estimates of environmental values based on questionnaire surveys (called *contingent valuations*) are used there as a basis for assessing liability for damages as well as for the formation of public policy.

The evidence for failure of rationality creates a need for alternative models of behaviour. Complete rejection of rationality has seemed too extreme to almost every scholar. Somehow we are convinced, by introspection if nothing else, that there is something purposive and consistent about our choices. These considerations have led to hypotheses of 'bounded rationality' or, perhaps more generally, of 'learning'. Put another way, individuals have strategies for gradually improving performance on the basis of experience. It is not always appreciated that learning models do not necessarily lead, even in the limit, to optimal behaviour as standardly defined.

3 RATIONALITY OF KNOWLEDGE

Rationality of knowledge in the usual models is equivalent to Bayesian updating. This is a complex process and is usually too difficult to test directly from market data. However, it does have some testable implications. One is that securities prices ought to be a martingale (today's price is the expected value of tomorrow's price); if not, then there are predictable profits, which is inconsistent with equilibrium. Prices change only because of surprises. A similar argument holds for consumption, as argued by Robert Hall; since consumption, according to rationality theory, depends on the expected present value of future incomes, changes in consumption must constitute a random walk. These implications, while not strictly true, nevertheless hold with a fair degree of approximation, thereby giving some support to the rationality of knowledge.

On the other hand, rationality of knowledge is strongly contradicted in questionnaire studies by cognitive psychologists. For one thing, there is too little reliance on base-line data, which should be used as prior probabilities. Also, market data are not uniformly favourable to the hypothesis of rational expectations; as Robert Schiller has pointed out, stock market prices are more variable than they should be if they are expected present values.

4 INTERACTIVE RATIONALITY IN ECONOMICS: SYMMETRIC INFORMATION

Economists have learned in the last forty years to distinguish different conditions on the distribution of information among many economic agents. The traditional case has been that of *symmetric information*; there are uncertainties in the world, but everyone has the same uncertainties, i.e., the same probability distribution over states of the world. (Although I refer to this case as 'traditional', a clear formulation dates back only about forty years.)

The analysis of interaction is greatly simplified under the assumption of general competitive equilibrium. The need for any one agent to know the strategies of other agents is replaced by the knowledge of prices (actually, this is not quite right). But this apparent simplification is somewhat illusory. The prices are, after all, the result of decisions made by all agents, which in turn require knowledge of prices. The problems of mutual knowledge do not disappear but take the form of the process of achieving equilibrium. The relevance of this issue was already recognized by Walras, who developed a 'supply and demand' dynamics. While the equilibrium of this system is indeed competitive equilibrium, its stability is not in general true.

Departing from competitive equilibrium leads to game-theory formulations. The equilibrium concept is that of Nash, but how is this reached? Cournot introduced what we now call Nash equilibrium for a situation with few rival sellers. He assumed in effect that, at least in equilibrium, each agent knew the strategy of each other agent. He supplemented this argument with a best-reply dynamics, and it is clear that convergence to an equilibrium is not guaranteed.

There are therefore strong similarities in defining interactive rationality in competitive equilibrium and in non-cooperative games, such as Cournot oligopoly. The latter does offer even more difficulties, since even existence of equilibrium is not guaranteed.

In recent years, Robert Aumann, Adam Brandenburger, and others have done a considerable amount of work on the knowledge requirements for Nash equilibrium, some of it still unpublished. There is scope for disagreement as to the very statement of the problem. Clearly, if the (pure) strategies of others are known to each agent, then Nash equilibrium holds if each agent is rational. But can the strategies of other players be known? Suppose instead that the rationality of all agents is common knowledge. Then apparently all that can be deduced is the successive elimination of strictly dominated strategies.

5 INTERACTIVE RATIONALITY: ASYMMETRIC INFORMATION

The notions of rationality and their economic implications take especially complex forms when different agents have access to different information. The point is that their actions can reveal something of their knowledge.

There are several implications even in the case of general competitive equilibrium. First of all, markets are necessarily incomplete because contingent contracts can be made only when all parties know the realization of the contingency (a point first made by Roy Radner). Second, the market outcomes themselves reveal to others information held by some economic agents. As a result, essentially all the relevant private information is (generically) revealed, a result that hardly seems to correspond to reality.

Indeed, one specific implication is sharply contradicted by obvious facts. Economic agents who differ only by the information they have will not trade securities (or other assets) with each other. A new piece of information available to some individuals and not to others will indeed cause securities prices to change, but it will not cause any transactions to take place; the price changes will themselves transmit the information to the previously uninformed. While there are other motives for securities trade (e.g. life-cycle changes), it is hard to explain the enormous volume of trade except in terms of speculation based on an alleged superiority of information. Hence, the hypothesis of common knowledge of rationality seems clearly inconsistent with the volume of trade.

Similar considerations hold in broader game-theoretic contexts. Actions are revealing; rationality then implies that individuals may refrain from seemingly profitable actions in order to avoid revealing knowledge. A classic real-life example was the refusal by British authorities to warn the city of Coventry about an imminent German raid in the Second World War, for to have done so would have revealed to the Germans that their code had been broken.

6 REMARKS ON EVOLUTION AND LEARNING

As remarked at the end of Section 2, there is a reformulation of rationality in which individuals pursue a goal of gradual improvement. This procedural rationality is not necessarily weaker than full rationality, for it presupposes a strategy of improvement, which might itself be fairly complex.

There are variations on this theme. One is the idea of learning by an individual, and the question arises, what is the context in which learning takes place? An alternative which has become very popular in recent years is to draw an analogy with biological evolution. There are no strategies for individual improvement; rather, behaviour which improves performance gains in frequency, while behaviour which is ill-rewarded declines in frequency. This is mathematically and perhaps conceptually similar to the Darwinian 'survival of the fittest', as developed by theoretical biologists (such as R.A. Fisher, J.B.S. Haldane, and, more recently, John Maynard Smith). When applied to game theory, the picture is not of repeated play with the same players but rather play with a random selection of others from the population.

The learning theory also presupposes the increase of frequency of rewarded responses and extinction of unrewarded responses, so that the learning and evolution points of view seem similar. But the outcomes are not; learning theorists have always tended to argue that the steady states of learning are not necessarily optimal.

The Preface is simply intended to set forth one point of view about the rationality hypothesis and its role in economics.

Introduction

Enrico Colombatto and Mark Perlman

Whatever the origins of rationality, one of its major uses has been the employment of its principles in non-violent discourse. Indeed, the hope that rational discussion would be persuasive in the avoidance of violence is to be found in the first chapter of the Book of Isaiah, 'Come let us reason together...' (1:18). Georg Hegel suggested that for those who look upon the world rationally, the world in its turn presents a rational aspect ('Introduction', *Philosophy of History*). Nonetheless, insofar as reason and rationality could be expected to replace fratricidal and larger conflicts, the historic fact is that it has not. Why? Because there is a variety of rationalities, and in their applications considerable differences persist. As it will be seen in this volume, vehement disputation concerning what is rationality and its applications to economics remains to this day.

Often reason is contrasted with creativity. Bertrand Russell pointed to reason in its best light: 'Reason is a harmonising, controlling force rather than a creative one' (*A Free Man's Worship and Other Essays*, 1976, ch. 2). It may well be the case that the explanation for the failure of reason is that in practice it collides with imagination.

Rationality itself may have a number of sources as well as a plethora of purposes. These, too, may interfere with the irrefutability of a reasoned argument.

If for the present the centrality of the role of rationality in economics is commonly accepted, its dominance is less than fully secure. Many argue that rational economic systems are not descriptive of the historical process because exogenous factors ('shocks') have repeatedly interfered with the resolution of choices. Others have, however, pointed out that the rules of rational thought do permit some resolutions, and insofar as exceptions have to be made, they can be made after the 'rational expectation' has been defined and articulated.

Christian Schmidt and Mark Perlman more than a dozen years ago began discussions about the desirability of having a conference comparing the different varieties of rationality in economics. In the course of time, others, including Frank Hahn, Kenneth Arrow and Enrico Colombatto, joined the planning group and the conference took shape. At times the *foci* varied, but in the end four themes were defined:

Rational choice and logical problems
Rationality in game theory
Rational behaviour from an experimental approach
Alternative treatments of rationality in decision-making systems

Fourteen papers were commissioned and accepted, discussants were alerted. What follows in this volume are the revised papers and comments.

The remainder of this Introduction offers our brief summaries of the papers. The conference was held over the long weekend of 15 to 18 October 1993, at the Villa Gualino, under the aegis of the International Economic Association and the auspices of Colombatto's International Centre for Economic Research, Turin, Italy.

In Part I, 'Rational Choice and Logical Problems', the first paper, 'Decision Kinematics', is by Richard C. Jeffrey (Chapter 1). It addresses an important and well-known issue in utility theory: namely that, as a matter of fact, it is hard to maintain that each outcome is associated to a state of nature and that, therefore, decision-making takes place according to the probability distributions which associate each state of nature to each outcome.

In order to provide an alternative solution to this possibly fragile assumption, Jeffrey considers that preferences are also necessarily associated with the means by which results are obtained, that (subjective) probabilities are influenced by past events, and that decision-making is surely biased by the actor's choice of the 'rules of the game' according to which he wants to play. Actually the kinematics of the decision-making process correspond to the (fixed) rules of the game along which decisions are taken, and the choice of these kinematic rules thus defines the state of nature and the results which will follow.

In his Comment to Jeffrey's paper, Christian Schmidt accepts Jeffrey's point about the need to provide an alternative to the 'act-independent state' assumption. Efforts have been made by several authors (including Jeffrey), but doubts have not been cleared. The kinematic approach, however, seems to address (and successfully reject) the idea of counterfactual probability, rather than that of causality in decision theory. Convincing answers are still badly needed.

In 'Consequentialism, Structural Rationality and Game Theory', Peter J. Hammond (Chapter 2) proposes to examine rationality as consequentialism, as opposed to rationality as act-utilitarianism (cf. Kahneman, below). Suggesting an axiomatization that operationalizes 'structural rationality' (rationality from a consequentialist point of view), Hammond also notes that it is neither necessary nor sufficient for 'full rationality'. Consequentialism will maximize utility only if probabilities are objective. He suggests that its principal usefulness is in cases of 'unboundedness of imagination', but that this can be handled with the idea of 'bounded rationality'. Structural rationality therefore in essence has no place, although Hammond thinks it may still be of some derivative use. He does not accept satisficing as a solution to bounded rationality, for such a solution requires optimization. Hammond considers (as does Mariotti, below) that Savage's axioms are useful for *decision* theory, but inappropriate for *game* theory. In decision theory the environment is given; in game theory it is endogenous.

In the Comment to this paper, Bertrand Munier's view of Hammond's contribution is important, for it clearly shows 'that a rational agent may ... violate expected utility'; but Munier does not share Hammond's rejection of structural rationality. According to Munier, justified scepticism follows only from Hammond's own version of consequentialism, where individuals have an extremely limited capacity to recall past actions; whereas structural rationality still holds if a broader characterization of consequentialism is considered.

Christian Schmidt in his essay 'Paradoxes of Rationality in Decision-Making Theory' (Chapter 3) takes issue with the standard economic definition of rationality as utility maximization. Instead, he proposes that economists consider that the proposition 'agents are assumed to act rationally' be rephrased to 'the model builder rationally assumes that agents act rationally'. Schmidt shows that some of the paradoxes that are said to result from the accepted definition of rationality result from a failure of logic, while the majority (such as the Ellsberg Paradox) are the result of a lack of sufficient information. It is not enough to restrict rationality to a type of knowledge, or even as a process, because it is comprised of elements of both.

In his Comment, Franco Donzelli argues that if Schmidt's suggested taxonomy is accepted, one may be led to conclude that no rationality model with prescriptive or predictive purposes can be tested, for all the possible paradoxes would disappear. As such, this new taxonomy would not only be unhelpful for empirical purposes, but even questionable when examined in the light of the traditional paradoxes in the literature on rationality. Schmidt's rejoinder sees that argument as based on a misunderstanding of his propositions.

In 'Rationality and Comprehension' (Chapter 4), Avishai Margalit and Menahem Yaari analyse recent attempts to define a theory of knowledge within the decision-making framework and apply it to explain interactions among the agents. They argue that the factual/analytical concepts, at the basis of the current notion of common knowledge (with the logical-omniscience assumption), are far from satisfactory; the division is misleading, for action on the basis of shared knowledge would be reduced to a minimum. Instead, a new idea of *comprehension* is put forward, according to which agents understand the state they are in despite the absence of purely-sensorial stimuli and/or of purely-analytical abilities. Comprehension is acquired through the physical or virtual reduction of the state space, until the agent 'understands' his actual state.

Amartya Sen (Comment) wonders whether a theory of '*comprehension*' can really be considered a substitute for a theory of knowledge; would it not be more appropriate to define it as a theory of 'belief'? Furthermore, Sen holds that the introduction of comprehension into the theory of knowledge could be a much welcome '*complement*' to factual and analytical perceptions, not necessarily a *substitute*.

Robert Aumann (Reply) also agrees with the need to analyse in great detail the foundations of basic principles of the theory of common knowledge, but remains doubtful about the limited role that the authors attribute to communication among agents. He expresses doubt also about the very existence of a substantial difference between the usual idea of 'knowledge' and the authors' concept of 'comprehension'.

Part II, 'Rationality in Game Theory', begins with 'Rationalizing Backward Induction?' (Chapter 5) in which Ken Binmore and Larry Samuelson criticize Robert Aumann's well-known attempts to justify 'backward induction' in game-theoretic situations. They argue, for instance, that Aumann treats rationality as an attribute of the environment, instead of an epistemological notion. The authors conclude that Aumann's position is unjustified, because in essence he assumes that agents ignore evidence in an effort to cling to Aumann's peculiar definition of rationality; thus agents are rational. As Aumann defines rationality, agents, irrespective of what they may consider their own best interests, never lie, cheat, steal or are duplicitous, because such actions are wrong. Others probably behave in the same way, and further, we expect them always so to behave and never let us down. Taking the Aumann approach seriously would mean that agents never make mistakes; it is the environment that has caused them to take actions which are perceived as irrational; but we cannot, of course, charge them with irrationality, because their actions must be rational. In short, the authors argue for looking at rationality as *reason*, not as something which exists independently from the individual.

The Comment by Bernard Walliser questions the generality of the authors' argument. From an educative standpoint, backward induction can be questioned only if the role of surprise is suitably specified. From an evolutionary perspective, backward induction usually works well in extensive-form games, but the very nature of most economic problems and games makes this kind of experiment rather hard to perform.

Robert Aumann (Reply) argues that the fact that backward induction makes no sense in some perfect-information games has nothing to do with the fact that the common knowledge of rationality implies backward induction, which is indeed the core of the problem and which has not been discussed by the authors.

In 'The Decision-Theoretic Foundations of Game Theory' (Chapter 6) Marco Mariotti argues that the accepted notion that Savage's subjective probability theory is the basis for game theory is mistaken. He argues that the concept of strategic rationality is different from that of classical rationality (i.e., of the von Neumann–Morgenstern variety). This position is very much in line with the argument presented in Kurz's paper (see below). Savage's axioms are held to be inappropriate as the basis for game theory, while von Neumann and Morgenstern's are appropriate and, indeed, are those which have been employed in its foundation. Thus one must reject game theory as having been founded on Bayesian foundations, for the idea of subjective probabilities is not consistent with the formulation of game-theoretic models, although the analysis is at times couched in Bayesian terms.

While Savage's axioms are inappropriate for game theory, they are nonetheless valid for decision theory. It is evident that in game theory, changing the environment changes the basis for the decision, while in decision theory the environment is given (is independent of) the choices made. This point has been neglected in the literature and, when considered, treated as a 'trivial problem'. While the literature has given lip-service to the idea of subjective probabilities, the theory ignores them as irrelevant.

Pierpaolo Battigalli in the Comment agrees on the doubtful suitability of Bayesian probability in a game-theoretic approach, as stated in the orthodox form. In order to avoid the collateral problems that classical probability would raise, Battigalli proposes an interpretation of 'virtual acts as bets of an external observer'. In this form, virtual choices could be maintained, but would not affect the players' outcome – thereby making non-cooperative games consistent with Savage's axioms.

'Nash Equilibrium and Evolution by Imitation' by Jonas Björnerstedt and Jörgen Weibull (Chapter 7) presents an updated analysis of Nash's ' "mass action" interpretation of equilibrium points', where players no longer need to be perfectly aware of the structure of the game. The key issues addressed concern the possibility that the population frequency, from which players are selected, is non-stationary. Population dynamics are therefore modelled by reference to a set of 'evolution-by-imitation' assumptions; its consequences on the nature of the Nash equilibria and on the validity of the mass-action interpretation are then studied in detail.

As expected, the original conclusions of the mass-action interpretation still hold, but their general validity is significantly weakened in a dynamic framework, by reason of the diffusion of learning across society. The speed and quality of the learning process may take different forms, and they do affect the behaviour of the players and hence affect the stability property of the equilibria.

The discussion put forward by Pier Luigi Sacco (Comment) observes that the authors' contribution may well be a promising starting point: (i) for work on a more detailed analysis of when and how an agent decides to imitate another agent and thus proceed along a learning path; (ii) for extending the notion of rationality in evolutionary dynamic frameworks; (iii) for opening new areas of research, so as to describe – say – the role of social relationships and group selection.

In Part III, 'Rational Behaviour from an Experimental Approach', Amos Tversky's 'Rational Theory and Constructive Choice' (Chapter 8) points to the growing awareness in mainstream economic circles of the notion that people *construct* choices instead of *discovering* them, a view consistent with Roth's paper (see below). (It would also be interesting to see in this regard some discussion of the theories of Shackle and Hayek, and even Simon, who have been advocating much the same thing for many, many years, as has Tversky, himself. As a matter of fact, Alvin Roth, in his comment, even believes that the rational model is acceptable only as a useful and general enough approximation of behaviour; it cannot pretend to be an adequate description, for individuals may change their 'references' [and thus their preferences] or – as Tversky suggests – agents may respond to a choice of processes. But we are still waiting for a better alternative).

Next, in 'New Challenges to the Rationality Assumption' (Chapter 9), Daniel Kahneman proposes to expand the definition of rationality to account not only for the *actions* of agents, but for the *consequences* of those actions as well. This is said to expand the set of necessary conditions for rationality. Apparently, he defines away such seeming paradoxes as those listed by Ellsberg and Allais (as discussed by Schmidt and Donzelli). The question so raised is obvious – if rationality is indeed reason, then defining it in terms of consequences reduces it to a triviality. Rationality no longer applies to individual choice, but, rather, the agent is supposed to know and account for the consequences of those choices. Even Savage admitted that the computational problems were immense when limited to *acts*; they are definitely exaggerated when one must also look towards the consequences of those actions. (Again, it seems that the work of Shackle and Simon and Mises and Hayek must be re-examined to provide the philosophical basis for the argument over the definition of rationality, so that it is not misinterpreted or employed haphazardly. That this is a philosophical argument Kahneman apparently accepts, as he invokes the consequentialist arguments of Sen as the basis for his belief that some such redefinition is required. Further, it seems as though the notion of rationality is becoming extended as much to further a political agenda as it is to define behaviour).

Although Charles Plott shares Kahneman's need for a deeper analysis of the procedures which lead to preferences and decisions, his Comment (focused generally on economics) is more prudent regarding the consequences of the current attempts, despite their obvious flaws, to redefine the foundations of rationality for the social sciences.

Chapter 10, 'Rational Individual Behaviour in Markets and Social Choice Processes' by Charles R. Plott, puts forward a new observational theory, called the 'discovered preference hypothesis' (DPH). It is aimed at explaining observed deviations from the general rational-behaviour pattern. According to DPH, behaviour is *irrational* (but not necessarily random) if the agent has accumulated no previous experience in the area in which he must take a decision; and, is *close to rational* if the agent is experienced; becomes *strategic* when other agents are also taken into account. In short, the DPH suggests that preferences are gradually discovered – and responses redefined – as the individual accumulates experience. To support this argument, which implies the need to devote new thoughts to the building-blocks of economic theory, Plott provides a number of examples showing that: (i) the size of the deviations from rationality-theory predictions decreases with experience; (ii) the speed of understanding of other agents' behaviour may be variable and slow; (iii) institutions may play a role in accelerating discovery. Such evidence is thus inconsistent with constructed-preference hypotheses and also defies the common-knowledge idea of rationality.

Daniel Kahneman (Comment) acknowledges Plott's effort to explain observed behaviour as deviations from the rational model, but wonders whether such anomalies are really due to the DPH phenomenon, or as he believes, to the fact that the rational model is inadequate to explain how people ultimately make decisions. Indeed, he believes that Kahneman insists on the supremacy of bounded-rationality processes, in the light of which rationality remains (as Roth also claims) at most a valuable approximation.

Alvin E. Roth's 'Adaptive Behaviour and Strategic Rationality: Evidence from the Laboratory and the Field' (Chapter 11) contrasts the *traditional* uses of the term 'rationality' as employed by economists with the way agents have been found *actually* to behave, and finds considerable dissension. He notes that the 'environments' within which agents act should be examined when we attempt to measure or even discuss conceptually 'rationality' as it applies to the agent, since the environment may itself be a key to what is defined as rational. (The Heisenberg Principle applied to economics.) It may be perfectly reasonable for a person in a given situation to misdirect others as to his true intentions in order to arrive at what he thinks will be a better outcome for himself than would be forthcoming were he to respond honestly to queries as to his desires. (Roth's questioning of the unlimited use of equilibrium theories to explain actions harkens back to the similar positions of Shackle – and others of the Austrian persuasion – and even to Herbert Simon.)

Jean-Louis Rullière in his Comment underlines the nice properties of the author's suggested learning process, which need not assume environmental stability, nor knowledge about the agents' past behavioural patterns (facts will be enough), and the author actually opens the way to a substantial revision of the concept of equilibrium in economic theory.

Part IV, 'Alternative Treatments of Rationality in Decision-Making Systems', begins with John H. Holland's 'The Rationality of Adaptive Agents' (Chapter 12). Quite clearly the term 'rationality' requires a more precise definition. In this paper, rationality is used in two different senses: the environmental and the epistemological. Holland uses the term *perfect rationality* as a mathematical construct identifying the environment within which individuals act. *Human rationality* then refers, one may assume, to the actual reasoning process employed in human action. Rationality in the first instance means arguing from a stipulated set of axioms. *Perfect rationality* implies that 'knowledge of a set of facts or premises (axioms) is equivalent to knowledge of all the consequences (theorems) that the set implies'. This condition is not the same as 'rationality as reasonableness', which appears to be the second meaning. One may be rational and yet choose to act in a way which to all outside observers is completely contrary to the rules of logic or even to the person's best interest as they perceive it. Savage's man is rational because he accepts the decision axioms Savage established. The *'rational'* is then not equivalent to the *'logical'* (in the sense of Descartes and others of the Rationalist or deductivist school), but only *'reasonable'*. While Savage defines rationality in the subjective sense, his subsequent theory mapping acts to consequences effectively reduces to Holland's 'perfect' rationality, with the resulting immense computational difficulties. But while Savage is a *subjectivist*, he is most certainly not a *deductivist*.

Frank Hahn (Comment) provides a general evaluation of the attempts to consider rationality as the equivalent of agents performing algorithms: but is that really consistent with reality? Hahn entertains serious doubts – for the evidence is ambiguous, and the prescriptive value of algorithmic-based procedures (fundamental in the economist's eyes) remains questionable.

In his 'Routines, Hierarchies of Problems, Procedural Behaviour: Some Evidence from Experiments' (Chapter 13) Massimo Egidi argues that routines are procedures which are memorized and then retrieved by individuals who want/need to save time and effort in a decision context. This paper's aim is to study how agents produce and store them, possibly through the decomposition of a problem into a set of relatively simple sub-problems, and to examine the kind of results to which routine-dominated behaviours lead.

Hamid Sabourian (Comment) does not reject the insights possibly provided by the routine version of procedural rationality, but raises some doubts about its usefulness at the present stage of research. For on the one hand, the limited and sometimes ambiguous evidence so far available (including Egidi's) is also consistent with other theories which assume some kind of learning process. On the other hand, economics is not a game of cards; indeed, it is an area where problems are usually quite hard to decompose!

And finally, Mordecai Kurz in his 'Rational Preferences and Rational Beliefs' (Chapter 14) begins by making a fundamental observation (one now gaining general acceptance) that the axiomatization of von Neumann and Morgenstern 'caught on' in economics and decision theory, while the improvement of Savage (which incidentally existed in the earlier works of Ramsey and Borel) did not, not because the Savage version required the mapping of states to consequences, but required no underlying probability distribution function to be specified (Savage in fact insisted on subjective probabilities). The economic models developed by the rational expectationists (among others) required objective distributions which we could know and hence incorporate within these models (in fact, the rational expectations theorists went one step further, equating the subjective with the objective probabilities). Von Neumann and Morgenstern, with their emphasis on cardinality and objective probability distributions, made the task of modelling that much simpler. Here Kurz proposes to supplement the Savage axioms with an objective probability function, albeit one unknown to the agents (thus differing from the Muthian equality of subjective and objective distribution functions). Rationality is defined with respect to the agent's selection of a model consistent with the data.

Thus, the computational questions remain, and even Savage admitted that this was a problem for his own theory. This re-identification makes Savage's framework acceptable to Kurz.

Kenneth Arrow (Comment) draws attention to the constraints that Kurz's model implies in order for rational beliefs to take shape. The idea of an agent having a prior., which is then modified according to an objective-distribution, is surely attractive. But what happens when the objective is not observed? Then guessing may be tempting, but possibly misleading. One may still claim that beliefs remain rational, but then the predictive power of the theory – and much of its appeal – would be lost. Schmidt takes this up in a 'Postface', putting the problem for a decision-maker not as concerned with rationality, but about the rational answer to the expected irrationality of others.

Part I

Rational Choice and Logical Problems

1 Decision Kinematics

Richard C. Jeffrey

PRINCETON UNIVERSITY, USA

1 LOGIC

If adopting options involves adopting particular probability distributions over the states of nature, your preference ranking of options should agree with your numerical ranking of expectations of utility computed according to the corresponding distributions (von Neumann and Morgenstern, 1944, 1947). In fact, von Neumann and Morgenstern took your utilities for states of nature to be the same, no matter which option you choose, e.g., when states of nature determine definite dollar gains or losses, and these are all you care about. This condition may seem overly restrictive, for the means by which gains are realized may affect your final utility – as when you prefer work to theft as a chancy way of gaining $1,000 (success) or $0 (failure). But the condition can always be met structurally, e.g., here, by splitting each state of nature in which you realize an outcome by work-or-theft into one in which you realize it by work, and another in which your realize it by theft. The difference between the work and theft options is encoded in their associated probability distributions, each of which assigns probability 0 to the proposition that (= the set of states in which) you opt for the other. This means taking a naturalistic view of the decision-maker, whose choices are blended with states of nature in a single space, Ω; each point ω in that space represents a particular choice by the decision-maker as well as a particular state of the rest of nature.

Bolker (1965, 1966, 1967) and Jeffrey (1965, 1983, 1990) offer a framework of that sort in which options may be represented by propositions (i.e., in statistical jargon, 'events'), and choice is a matter of truthmaking. For the option of making true the proposition A, the corresponding von Neumann-Morgenstern probability distribution will be the conditional distribution $pr(—|A)$, where the unconditional distribution $pr(—)$ represents your prior probability judgement, i.e., prior to deciding which option-proposition to make true. And your expectation of utility associated with the A-option will be your conditional expectation of utility, $E(u \,|\, A)$ – also known as your *desirability* for truth of A, denoted '*des A*' (Jeffrey, 1965), i.e., in the discrete case:

$$des\,A = E(u \mid A) = \Sigma_{\omega \in \Omega} u(\omega) pr(\{\omega\} \mid A)$$

Now preference (>), indifference ($\sim$), and preference-or-indifference ($\geq$) go by desirability, so that

$$A > B \text{ if } des\,A > des\,B, \quad A \sim B \text{ if } des\,A = des\,B, \quad A \geq B \text{ if } des\,A \geq des\,B$$

Note that it is not only option-propositions that appear in preference rankings; you can perfectly well prefer a sunny day tomorrow (= truth of 'Tomorrow will be

3

sunny') to a rainy one even though you know you cannot affect the weather.

Various principles of preference logic can now be enunciated, and fallacies identified, as in the following two examples. The first is a fallacious mode of inference according to which you must prefer B's falsity to A's if you prefer A's truth to B's:

(Invalid) $$\frac{A > B}{\therefore \neg B > \neg A}$$

Counterexample: Death before dishonour. $A =$ You are dead tomorrow; $B =$ You are dishonoured today. (You mean to commit suicide if dishonoured.) If your probabilities and desirabilities for the four cases tt, tf, ft, ff concerning truth and falsity of AB are as follows, then your desirabilities for A, B, $\neg B$, $\neg A$ will be 0.5, -2.9, 5.5, 6.8, so that the premise is true but the conclusion false.

	case:	tt	tf	ft	ff
pr(case):		.33	.33	.01	.33
des(case):		0	1	-100	10

The second is a valid mode of inference:

(Valid) $$\frac{A > B}{\therefore A \geq (A \vee B) \geq B}$$ (provided A and B are incompatible)

Proof. Given the proviso, and setting $w = pr(A \,|\, A \vee B)$, we find that $des\,(A \vee B) = w(des\ A) + (1 - w)\,(des\ B)$. This is a convex combination of $des\ A$ and $des\ B$ which must therefore lie between them or at an endpoint.

Bayesian decision theory is said to represent a certain structural concept of rationality. This is contrasted with substantive criteria of rationality (Kahneman, 1995) having to do with the aptness of particular probability and utility functions to particular predicaments. With Davidson (1980, 1984), I would interpret this talk of rationality as follows. What remains when all substantive questions of rationality are set aside is bare logic, a framework for tracking your changing judgements, in which questions of validity and invalidity of argument-forms can be settled as illustrated above. A complete set of substantive judgements would be represented by a Bayesian *frame*, i.e., a probability measure *pr* defined on a Boolean algebra of subsets of a space Ω (the 'propositions'), a utility function *u* defined on Ω, and an assignment of elements of the Boolean algebra as values to 'A', 'B' etc.[1] Points in Ω represent 'possible worlds' or 'elementary events' (Kolmogorov, 1933); sets of such points represent propositions (Kolmogorov's 'events'). In any logic, validity of an argument is truth of the conclusion in every frame in which all the premises are true. In a Bayesian logic of decision, Bayesian frames represent all possible answers to substantive questions of rationality; we can understand that without knowing how to determine whether particular frames would be substantively rational for you on particular occasions. So in Bayesian decision theory we can understand validity of an argument as truth of its conclusion in any Bayesian frame in which all of its premises are true, and understand consistency of a judgement, e.g., of the judgement that $A > B$ but not $\neg B > \neg A$, as existence of a non-empty set of Bayesian frames in which it is true. On this view, consistency – bare structural rationality – is simply representability in the Bayesian framework.[2]

2 KINEMATICS

In the design of mechanisms, kinematics is the discipline in which rigid rods and distortionless wheels, gears, etc. are thought of as faithful, prompt communicators of motion. The contrasting dynamic analysis takes forces into account, so that, e.g., elasticity may introduce distortion, delay, and vibration; but kinematical analyses often suffice, or, anyway, suggest relevant dynamical questions. That is the metaphor behind the title of this section and behind use of the term 'rigidity' below for constancy of conditional probabilities.[3]

In choosing a mixed option – say, O_1 or O_2 depending on whether C is true or false – you place the following constraint on your probabilities.

Stable conditional probablities $pr(O_1 \mid C)$ and $pr(O_2 \mid \neg C)$ are set near[4] 1

As choosing the mixed option involves expecting to learn whether C is true or false, choosing it involves expecting your probabilities for C and $\neg C$ to move toward the extremes:

Labile probabilities of conditions $pr(C)$ and $pr(\neg C)$ will change from near 1/2 to near 0 or 1

This combination of stable conditional probabilities and labile probabilities of conditions is analogous to the constraints under which the following is a useful mode of inference; for if confidence in the second premise below is to serve as a channel transmitting confidence in the first premise to the conclusion as well, the increase in pr(first premise) had better not be accompanied by a decrease in pr(second premise).[5]

Modus Ponens
$$\frac{\begin{array}{c} C \\ D \text{ if } C \end{array}}{\therefore D}$$

When unconditional probabilities change, some conditional probabilities may remain fixed; but others will change. *Example*: Set

$$a = pr(A \mid C), \quad d' = pr(A \mid \neg C), \quad o = pr(C)/pr(\neg C)$$

and suppose a and d' both remain fixed as the odds o on C change. Then $pr(C \mid A)$ must change, for[6]

$$pr(C \mid A) = \frac{d'}{d' + ao}$$

Does it seem clear that the only rational way to change probability assignments is by conditioning, i.e., replacing prior probabilities $pr(A)$ by conditional probabilities $pr(A \mid \text{data}) = pr(A \wedge \text{data})/pr(\text{data})$? That would be a mistake, a confusion of the prior/posterior distinction with the unconditional/conditional distinction. The mistake is exposed by the elementary probability calculus, according to which the equation

Conditioning $$pr_{\text{new}}(A) = pr_{\text{old}}(A \mid \text{data})$$

is equivalent to the following two equations, *jointly*:

Rigidity[7]	$pr_{new}(A \mid \text{data}) = pr_{old}(A \mid \text{data})$
Certainty	$pr_{new}(\text{data}) = 1$

The first of these, rigidity, is generally overlooked – perhaps because of a tendency to think that conditional probabilities are always stable. But clearly the second alone, certainty, is not enough. Here are two ways to see that:

(1) If certainty sufficed we would have $pr_{new}(A) = pr_{old}(A \mid A \lor \neg A) = pr_{old}(A)$ for all A, i.e., your probability function could never change.
(2) Consider the case where, with the usual probabilistic attitudes, you draw a card and see that it is an ace or a deuce. Then pr_{new} (ace or deuce) $= 1$, so that if certainty sufficed, $pr_{new}(\text{ace})$ would be $pr_{old}(\text{ace} \mid \text{ace or deuce})$. But since $pr_{new}(\text{ace or deuce or tray})$ is 1 if $pr_{new}(\text{ace or deuce})$ is, if certainty sufficed we would also have $pr_{new}(\text{ace}) = pr_{old}(\text{ace} \mid \text{ace or deuce or tray})$, and the contradiction $1/2 = 1/3$ would follow.

But what alternative is there to conditioning? Must not the rational effect on observation always be certainty of the truth of some data proposition?

Surely not. Much of the perception on which we reasonably base action eludes that sort of formulation. Our vocabulary for describing what we see, hear, taste, smell, and touch is no match for our visual, auditory, etc. sensitivities, and the propositional judgements we make with confidence are not generally tied to our sensory modalities. *Example*: The other day my wife and I saw Mayor Dinkins on Broadway. There were various clues: police, cameramen, etc. We looked, and smiled. He came and shook hands. Someone gave us Dinkins badges. We had known an election was coming and that the candidates were campaigning. At the end we had no doubt it was the Mayor. But there was no thought of describing the sensations on which our progress toward conviction was founded, no hope of formulating sensory data propositions that brought our probabilities up the unit interval toward 1:

$pr_{old}(\text{It's Dinkins})$, $pr_{old}(\text{It's Dinkins} \mid \text{data}_1)$, $pr_{old}(\text{It's Dinkins} \mid \text{data}_1 \land \text{data}_2)$, ...

Of course the people in uniform and the slight, distinguished figure with the moustache might all have been actors. Our visual, auditory and tactile experiences did combine with our prior judgements to make us nearly certain it was the Mayor, but there seems to be no way to represent that process by conditioning on data propositions that are sensory certainties. The accessible data propositions were chancy claims about people on Broadway, not authoritative reports of events on our retinas, palms and eardrums. We made reasonable moves (smiling, shaking the hand) on the basis of relatively diffuse probability distributions over a partition of such chancy propositions – distributions not obtained by conditioning their predecessors on fresh certainties (Jeffrey, 1992, pp. 1–13, 78–82, etc.).

Here are two generalizations of conditioning that are applicable in such cases, provided rigidity conditions hold for a partition $\{C_1, C_2 \ldots\}$ of Ω. In the second, $\text{fac}(A)$ and $\text{fac}(C_i)$ are the factors $pr_{new}(A)/pr_{old}(A)$ and $pr_{new}(C_i)/pr_{old}(C_i)$ by which, in effect, you multiply probabilities to update them.[8]

Rigidity Conditions   If $pr_{new}(A \mid C_i) = pr_{old}(A \mid C_i)$ for all i, then ...
Generalized Conditioning (Probabilities)[9]   ...$pr_{new}(A) = \Sigma_i pr_{new}(C_i) pr_{old}(A \mid C_i)$
Generalized Conditioning (Factors)[10]   ...$fac(A) = \Sigma_i fac(C_i)\, pr_{old}(C_i \mid A)$

Generalized conditioning allows probabilistic response to observations which prompt no changes in your conditional probabilities given any of the C_i but do prompt definite new probabilities or factors for the C_i. (If your new probability for one of the C_i is 1, this reduces to ordinary conditioning.)

Probabilistic judgement is not generally a matter of assigning definite probabilities to all propositions in a Boolean algebra, any more than yes/no judgement is a matter of assigning definite truth values to all of them. Typical yes/no judgement identifies some propositions as true, leaving truth values of others undetermined. Similarly, probabilistic judgement may assign values to some propositions, none to others.

The two sorts of generalized conditioning tolerate different sorts of indefiniteness. The probability version determines a definite value for $pr_{new}(A)$ even if you had no old probabilities in mind for the C_i, as long as you have definite new values for them and definite old values for A conditionally on them. The factor version, determining the probability ratio fac (A), tolerates indefiniteness about your old and new probabilities of A and of the C_i as long as your $pr_{old}(C_i \mid A)$ values are definite. Both versions illustrate the use of dynamic constraints to represent probabilistic states of mind. In the next section, judgements of causal influence are analyzed in that light.

3 CAUSALITY

In decision-making it is deliberation, not observation, that changes your probabilities. To think you face a decision problem rather than a question of fact about the rest of nature is to expect whatever changes arise in your probabilities for those states of nature during your deliberation to stem from changes in your probabilities for options. In terms of the analogy with mechanical kinematics: as a decision-maker you regard probabilities of options as inputs, driving the mechanism, not driven by it. (In other circumstances you might choose to drive the same mechanism using different variables as inputs; the question is about what you take yourself to be doing now.)

Is there something about your judgemental probabilities which shows that you are treating truth of one proposition as promoting truth of another – rather than as promoted by it or by truth of some third proposition which also promotes truth of the other? Here a positive answer to this question is used to analyze puzzling problems in which we see acts as mere symptoms of conditions we would promote or prevent if we could. Such 'Newcomb problems' (Nozick, 1963, 1969, 1990) pose a challenge to the decision theory floated in the first edition of *The Logic of Decision* (Jeffrey, 1965), where notions of causal influence play no role. The present suggestion about causal judgements will be used to question the credentials of Newcomb problems as decision problems.

The suggestion (cf. Arntzenius, 1990) is that imputations of causal influence are not shown simply by momentary features of probabilistic states of mind, but by intended or expected features of their evolution. The following is a widely recognized probabilistic consequence of the judgement that truth of one proposition ('cause') promotes truth of another ('effect').[11]

$$\beta > 0 \qquad\qquad pr(\text{effect} \mid \text{cause}) - pr(\text{effect} \mid \neg\text{cause}) > 0$$

But what distinguishes cause from effect in this relationship? – i.e., a relationship equivalent to

$$pr(\text{cause} \mid \text{effect}) - pr(\text{cause} \mid \neg\text{effect}) > 0$$

with Arntzenius, I suggest the following answer, i.e., rigidity relative to the partition {cause, ¬ cause}.[12]

Rigidity Constancy of $pr(\text{effect} \mid \text{cause})$ and $pr(\text{effect} \mid \neg\text{cause})$ as $pr(\text{cause})$ varies

Both $\beta > 0$ and rigidity are conditions on a variable 'pr' ranging over a set of probability functions. The functions in the set represent ideally definite momentary probabilistic states of mind for the deliberating agent. Clearly, pr can vary during deliberation, for if deliberation converges toward choice of a particular act, the probability of the corresponding proposition will rise toward 1. In general, agents' intentions or assumptions about the kinematics of pr might be described by maps of possible courses of evolution of probabilistic states of mind – often, very simple maps. These are like road maps in that paths from point to point indicate feasibility of passage via the anticipated mode of transportation, e.g., ordinary automobiles, not 'all terrain' vehicles. Your kinematical map represents your understanding of the dynamics of your current predicament, the possible courses of development of your probability and desirability functions.

Jeffrey (1965) used conditional expectation of utility given an act as the figure of merit for the act, *sc.*, its desirability, *des*(act). Newcomb problems (Nozick, 1969) led many to see that figure as acceptable only on special causal assumptions, and a number of versions of 'causal decision theory' were proposed as more generally acceptable. In the one I like best (Skyrms, 1980), the figure of merit for choice of an act is the agent's unconditional expectation of its desirability on various incompatible, collectively exhaustive causal hypotheses.[13] But if Newcomb problems are excluded, then in genuine decision problems *des*(act) will remain constant throughout deliberation, and will be an adequate figure of merit.

In any decision problem whose outcome is not clear from the beginning, probabilities of possible acts will vary during deliberation, for finally an act will be chosen and so have probability near 1, a probability no act had initially. Newcomb problems (Figure 1.1) seem ill-posed as decision problems because too much information is given about conditional probabilities, i.e., enough to fix the unconditional probabilities of the acts. We are told that there is an association between acts (making A true or false) and states of nature (truth or falsity of B) which makes acts strong predictors of states, and states of acts, in the sense that p and q are large relative to p' and q' – the four terms being the agent's conditional probabilities:

$$p = pr(B \mid A), \; p' = pr(B \mid \neg A),$$
$$q = pr(A \mid B), \; q' = pr(A \mid \neg B),$$

But the values of these terms themselves fix the agent's probability for A[14]

$$pr(A) = \frac{q \cdot p'}{q \cdot p' + (1 - q) \cdot p}$$

Of course this formula does not fix $pr(A)$ if the values on the right are not all fixed, but as decision problems are normally understood, values are fixed, once given. Normally, p and p' might be given, together with the desirabilities of the act – state combinations, i.e., just enough information to determine the desirabilities of A's truth and falsity, which determine the agent's choice. But normally, p and p' remain fixed as $pr(A)$ varies, and q and q', unmentioned because irrelevant to the problem, vary with $pr(A)$.

We now examine a Newcomb problem that would have made sense to R.A. Fisher in the late 1950s.

4 FISHER

For smokers who see quitting as prophylaxis against cancer, preferability goes by initial *des*(act) as in Figure 1.1b; but there are views about smoking and cancer on which these preferences might be reversed. Thus, R.A. Fisher (1959) urged serious consideration of the hypothesis of a common inclining cause of (A) smoking and (B) bronchial cancer in (C) a bad allele of a certain gene, possessors of which have a higher chance of being smokers and developing cancer than do possessors of the good allele (independently, given their allele). On that hypothesis, smoking is bad news for smokers but not bad for their health, being a mere sign of the bad allele, and, so, of bad health. Nor would quitting conduce to health, although it would testify to the agent's membership in the low-risk group.

On Fisher's hypothesis, where $\pm A$ and $\pm B$ are seen as independently promoted by $\pm C$, i.e., by presence (C) or absence $(\neg C)$ of the bad allele, the kinematical constraints on pr are the following.[15]

Rigidity	a, b, a', b', defined as follows, are constant as $c = pr(C)$ varies.
	$a = pr(A \mid C)$, $b = pr(B \mid C)$, $a' = pr(A \mid \neg C)$, $b' = pr(B \mid \neg C)$
$\beta > 0$	$pr(B \mid A) > pr(B \mid \neg A)$, i.e., $p > p'$
Indeterminacy	$0 < a, b, a', b' < 1$
Independence	$pr(A \wedge B \mid C) = ab$, $pr(A \wedge B \mid \neg C) = a'b'$

Since, in general, $pr(F \mid G \wedge H) = pr(F \wedge G \mid H) / pr(G \mid H)$, the independence and rigidity conditions imply that $\pm C$ *screens off* A and B from each other, in the following sense.

Screening-off	$pr(A \mid B \wedge C) = a$, $\quad pr(A \mid B \wedge \neg C) = a'$
	$pr(B \mid A \wedge C) = b$, $\quad pr(B \mid A \wedge \neg C) = b'$

Under these constraints, preference between A and $\neg A$ can change as $pr(C) = c$ moves out to either end of the unit interval in thought-experiments addressing the question 'What would *des A* $-$ *des* $\neg A$ be if I found I had the bad/good allele?' To carry out these experiments, note that by the probability calculus we have the first of the following expressions for p, whence the second follows via the kinematical constraints.

$$p = \frac{pr(A \mid B \wedge C)pr(B \mid C)pr(C) + pr(A \mid B \wedge \neg C)pr(B \mid \neg C)pr(\neg C)'}{pr(A \mid C)pr(C) + pr(A \mid \neg C)pr(\neg C)}$$

$$p = \frac{abc + a'b'(1 - c)}{ac + a'(1 - c)}$$

And similarly for p':

$$p' = \frac{(1 - a)bc + (1 - a')b'(1 - c)}{(1 - a)c + (1 - a')(1 - c)}$$

Now final p and p' are equal to each other, and to b or b' depending on whether final c is 1 or 0. Since it is c's rise to 1 or fall to 0 that makes $pr(A)$ rise or fall as much as it can without going off the kinematical map, the (quasi-decision) problem has two ideal solutions, i.e., mixed acts in which the final unconditional probability of A is the rigid conditional probability, a or a' depending on whether c is 1 or 0. But $p = p'$ in either case, so each solution satisfies the conditions under which the dominant pure outcome (A) of the mixed act maximizes *des* $\pm A$. (This is a quasi-decision problem because what is imagined as moving c is not the decision but factual information about C.)

The initial probabilities .093 and .025 in Figure 1.1b were obtained by making the following substitutions in the formulas for p and p' above.

$$a = .9, \quad d' = .5, \quad b = .2, \quad b' = .01, \quad c'(\text{initially}) = .3$$

As p and p' rise toward $b = .2$ or fall toward $b' = .01$, tracking the rise or fall of c toward 1 or 0, the negative difference *des*(continue) $-$ *des*(quit) $= -1.8$ in Figure 1.1b rises toward the positive values $5 - 4b = 4.2$ and $5 - 4b' = 4.96$ in Figure 1.2. Unless you, the smoker, somehow become sure of your allele, neither of the two judgemental positions shown in Figure 1.2 will be yours. The diagram only shows that, for you, continuing is preferable to quitting in either state of certainty about the allele. The kinematical map leads you to that conclusion on any assumption about initial c. And initial uncertainty about the allele need not be modelled by a definite initial value c. Instead, an indefinite initial probabilistic state can be modelled by the set of all pr assigning the values a, a', b, b' as above, and with $c = pr$(bad allele) anywhere in the unit interval.[16]

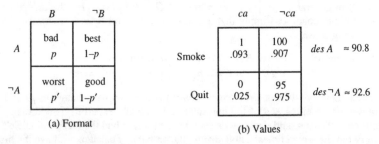

	B	¬B
A	bad	best
	p	$1-p$
¬A	worst	good
	p'	$1-p'$

(a) Format

	ca	¬ca	
Smoke	1	100	*des A* ≈ 90.8
	.093	.907	
Quit	0	95	*des* ¬A ≈ 92.6
	.025	.975	

(b) Values

Figure 1.1   Newcomb problems as decision problems

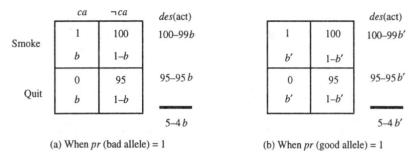

Figure 1.2 caption:
Figure 1.2 Since *b* and *b'* are at most 1, continuing is preferable on either genetic hypothesis

If you are a smoker convinced of Fisher's hypothesis, your unconditional probabilities of continuing and quitting lag behind *pr*(good) or *pr*(bad) as your probability for the allele rises toward 1. In particular, your probability $ac + a'(1 - c)$ for continuing rises to $a = .9$ from its initial value of .62 or falls to $a' = .5$, as c rises to 1 from its initial value of .3 or falls to 0. Here you see yourself as committed *by your genotype* to one or the other of two mixed acts, analogs of gambles whose possible outcomes are pure acts of continuing and quitting, at odds of 9 : 1 or 1 : 1. You do not know which of these mixed acts you are committed to; your judgemental odds between them, $c:(1 - c)$, are labile, or perhaps undefined. This genetic commitment antedates your current deliberation. The mixed acts are not options for you; still less are their pure outcomes. (Talk about pure acts as options is shorthand for talk about mixed acts assigning those pure acts probabilities near 1.) Then there is much to be said for the judgement that quitting is preferable to continuing (sc., as the more desirable 'news item'), for quitting and continuing are not options.

As a smoker who believes Fisher's hypothesis you are not so much trying to make your mind up as trying to discover how it is already made up. But this may be equally true in ordinary deliberation, where your question 'What do I really want to do?' is often understood as a question about the sort of person you are, a question of which option you are already committed to, unknowingly. The diagnostic mark of Newcomb problems is a strange linkage of this question with the question of which state of nature is actual – strange, because where in ordinary deliberation any linkage is due to an influence of acts ±*A* on states ±*B*, in Newcomb problems the linkage is due to an influence, from behind the scenes, of deep states ±*C* on acts ±*A* and plain states ±*B*. This difference explains why deep states ('the sort of person I am') can be ignored in ordinary decision problems, where the direct effect of such states is wholly on acts, which mediate any further effect on plain states. But in Newcomb problems deep states must be considered explicitly, for they directly affect plain states as well as acts (Figure 1.3).

In the kinematics of decision the dynamical role of forces can be played by acts or deep states, depending on which of these is thought to influence plain states directly. Ordinary decision problems are modelled kinematically by applying the rigidity condition to acts as causes. Ordinarily, acts screen off deep states from plain ones in the sense that *B* is conditionally independent of ±*C* given ±*A*, so that while it is

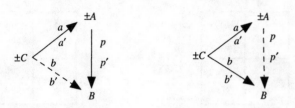

(a) Ordinarily, acts ±A screen off   (b) In Newcomb problems, deep states
deep states ±C from plain states ±B.   screen off acts from plain states.

Figure 1.3 Solid/dashed arrows indicate stable/labile conditional probabilities

variation in c that makes $pr(A)$ and $pr(B)$ vary, the whole of the latter variation is accounted for by the former (Figure 1.3a). But to model Newcomb problems kinematically we apply the rigidity condition to the deep states, which screen off acts from plain states (Figure 1.3b). In Figure 1.3a, the probabilities b and b' vary with c in ways determined by the stable a's and p's, while in Figure 1.3b the stable a's and b's shape the labile p's as we have seen above:

$$p = \frac{abc + a'b'(1 - c)}{ac + a'(1 - c)} \qquad p' = \frac{(1 - a)bc + (1 - a')b'(1 - c)}{(1 - a)c + (1 - a')(1 - c)}$$

Similarly, in Figure 1.3a the labile probabilities are:

$$b = \frac{apc + a'p'(1 - c)}{ac + a'(1 - c)} \qquad b' = \frac{(1 - a)pc + (1 - a')p'(1 - c)}{(1 - a)c + (1 - a')(1 - c)}$$

While C and $\neg C$ function as causal hypotheses, they do not announce themselves as such, even if we identify them by the causal roles they are meant to play, e.g., when we identify the 'bad' allele as the one that promotes cancer and inhibits quitting. If there is such an allele, it is a still unidentified feature of human DNA. Fisher was talking about hypotheses that further research might specify, hypotheses he could only characterize in causal and probabilistic terms – terms like 'malaria vector' as used before 1898, when the anopheles mosquito was shown to be the organism playing that aetiological role. But if Fisher's science-fiction story had been verified, the status of certain biochemical hypotheses C and $\neg C$ as the agent's causal hypotheses would have been shown by satisfaction of the rigidity conditions, i.e., constancy of $pr(- \mid C)$ and of $pr(- \mid \neg C)$, with C and $\neg C$ spelled out as technical specifications of alternative features of the agent's DNA. Probabilistic features of those biochemical hypotheses, e.g., that they screen acts off from states, would not be stated in those hypotheses, but would be shown by interactions of those hypotheses with pr, B, and A, i.e., by truth of the following consequences of the kinematical constraints.

$$pr(B \mid act \wedge C) = pr(B \mid C), \quad pr(B \mid act \wedge \neg C) = pr(B \mid \neg C)$$

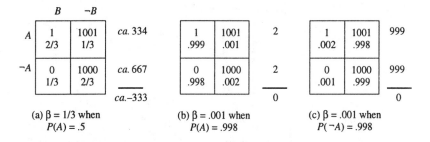

Figure 1.4 As $P(A)$ or $P(\neg A)$ nears 1, β nears 0 and *des A – des ¬A* goes positive

As Leeds (1984) points out in another connection, no purpose would be served by packing such announcements into the hypotheses themselves, for at best – i.e., if true – such announcements would be redundant. The causal talk, however useful as commentary, does no work in the matter commented upon.

5 NEWCOMB

The Flagship Newcomb Problem resolutely fends off naturalism about deep states, making a mystery of the common inclining cause of acts and plain states while suggesting that the mystery could be cleared up in various ways pointless to elaborate. Thus, Nozick (1969) begins:

> Suppose a being in whose power to predict your choices you have enormous confidence. (One might tell a science-fiction story about a being from another planet, with an advanced technology and science, who you know to be friendly, and so on). You know that this being has often correctly predicted your choices in the past (and has never, so far as you know, made an incorrect prediction about your choices), and furthermore you know that this being has often correctly predicted the choices of other people, many of whom are similar to you, in the particular situation to be described below. One might tell a longer story, but all this leads you to believe that almost certainly this being's prediction about your choice in the situation to be discussed will be correct. There are two boxes...[17]

Here you are invited to imagine that some science-fiction story has put you into a probabilistic frame of mind where, in Figure 1.1, desirability of $\neg A$ is greater than that of A because although you think A's truth or falsity has no influence on B's, your β is near 1, i.e., p is near 1, p' near 0. Does that seem a tall order? Not to worry! High β is a red herring; a tiny bit will do, e.g., if desirabilities are proportional to dollar payoffs as in Figure 1.4, then the 1-box option, $\neg A$, maximizes desirability as long as β is greater than .001.

To see how that might go, think of the choice and the prediction as determined by independent drawings by the agent and the predictor from the same urn, containing tickets marked '2' and '1' in an unknown proportion $x{:}1 - x$. Initially, the agent's

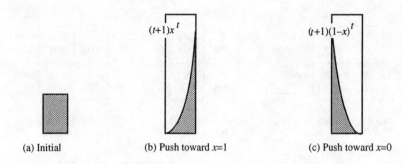

(a) Initial   (b) Push toward *x*=1   (c) Push toward *x*=0

Figure 1.5 Two patterns of density migration. (a) $t = 0$ (b,c) $t \approx 2$

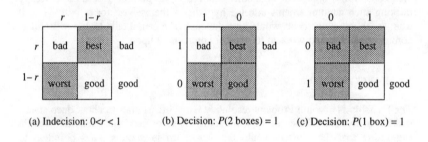

(a) Indecision: 0<*r* < 1   (b) Decision: P(2 boxes) = 1   (c) Decision: P(1 box) = 1

Figure 1.6 Deterministic 1-box solution; P(shaded) = 0; $\beta = 1$ until decision

unit of probability density over the range [0, 1] of possible values of *x* is flat (Figure 1.5a), but in time it can push toward one end of the unit interval or the other, e.g., as in Figure 1.5b and c.[18] At $t = 997$ these densities determine the probabilities and desirabilities in Figure 1.4b and c, and higher values of *t* will make *des A* − *des* ¬*A* positive. Then if *t* is calibrated in thousandths of a minute this map has the agent preferring the 2-box option after a minute's deliberation. The urn model leaves the deep state mysterious, but clearly specifies its mysterious impact on acts and plain states.

The irrelevant detail of high β was a bogus shortcut to the 1-box conclusion, obtained as in Figure 1.6a if β is not just high but maximum, which happens when $p = 1$ and $p' = 0$. This means that the shaded cells in Figure 1.6a have unconditional probability 0, and preference between *A* (bad-for-sure) and ¬*A* (good-for-sure) is clear, as long as *r*, the probability of *A* (taking both boxes), is neither 0 nor 1, and β remains maximum, 1. Here the density functions of Figure 1.5 are replaced by probability assignments *r* and $1 - r$ to the possibilities that the ratio of 2-box tickets to 1-box tickets in the urn is 1 : 0 and 0 : 1, i.e., to the two ways in which the urn can control the choice and the prediction deterministically and in the same way. In place of the smooth density spreads in Figure 1.5 we now have point-masses *r* and $1 - r$ at the two ends of the unit interval, with desirabilities of the two acts constant as long as r is neither 0 nor 1. Now the 1-box option is preferable throughout deliberation until the very moment of decision.[19] But of course this reasoning uses the premise that pr(predict $2 \mid$ take $2) - pr$(predict $2 \mid$ take $1) = \beta = 1$ through deliberation, a premise making formal sense in terms of uniformly stocked urns but very hard to swallow as a real possibility.

6 HOFSTADTER

Hofstadter (1983) saw Prisoners' Dilemmas as down-to-earth Newcomb problems. Call the prisoners Alma and Boris. If one confesses and the other does not, the confessor goes free and the other serves a long prison term. If neither confesses, both serve short terms. If both confess, both serve intermediate terms. From Alma's point of view, Boris's possible actions (B, confess, or $\neg B$, don't) are states of nature. She thinks they think alike, so that her choices (A, confess, $\neg A$, don't) are pretty good predictors of his, even though neither's choices influence the other's. If both care only to minimize their own prison terms this problem fits the format of Figure 1.1a. The prisoners are thought to share a characteristic determining their separate probabilities of confessing in the same way – independently, on each hypothesis about that characteristic. Hofstadter takes that characteristic to be rationality, and compares the Prisoners' Dilemma to the problem Alma and Boris might have faced as bright children, independently working the same arithmetic problem, whose knowledge of each other's competence and ambition gives them good reason to expect their answers to agree before either knows the answer: 'If reasoning guides me to ..., then, since I am no different from anyone else as far as rational thinking is concerned, it will guide everyone to ...'. The deep states seem less mysterious here than in the Flagship Newcomb Problem; here they have some such form as $C_x = We$ *are both likely to get the right answer, i.e., x.*[20] But to heighten similarity to the Prisoner's Dilemma let us suppose the required answer is the parity of x so that the deep states are simply $C = We$ *are both likely to get the right answer, i.e., even,* and $\neg C = We$ *are both likely to get the right answer, i.e., odd.*

What's wrong with Hofstadter's view of this as justifying the cooperative solution?[21] The answer is failure of the rigidity conditions for acts, i.e., variability of pr(He gets $x \mid$ I get x) with pr(I get x) in the decision-maker's kinematical map. It is Alma's conditional probability functions $pr(- \mid \pm C)$ rather than $pr(- \mid \pm A)$ that remain constant as her probabilities for the conditions vary. The implausibility of initial *des*(act) as a figure of merit for her act is simply the implausibility of positing constancy of β as her probability function pr evolves in response to changes in $pr(A)$. But the point is not that confessing is the preferable act, as causal decision theory would have it. It is rather that Alma's problem is not indecision about which act to choose, but ignorance of which allele is moving her.

7 CONCLUSION

Hofstadter's (1983) version of the Prisoner's Dilemma and the Flagship Newcomb Problem have been analysed here as cases where plausibility demands a continuum

[0,1] of possible deep states, with opinion evolving as smooth movements of probability density toward one end or the other draw probabilities of possible acts along toward 1 or 0. The problem of the smoker who believes Fisher's hypothesis was simpler in that only two possibilities $(C, \neg C)$ were allowed for the deep state, neither of which determined the probability of either act as 0 or 1.

The story was meant to be a credible, down-to-earth Newcomb problem; after all, Fisher (1959) honestly did give his hypothesis some credit. But if your genotype commits you to one mixed act or the other, to objective odds of 9:1 or 1:1 on continuing, there is no decision left for you to make. Yet the story persuaded us that, given your acceptance of the Fisher hypothesis, you would be foolish to quit, or to try to quit: continuing would be the wiser move. This is not to say you will surely continue to smoke, i.e., not to say you see a mixed act at odds of 1: 0 on continuing as an option, and, in fact, as the option you will choose. It only means you prefer continuing as the pure outcome of whichever mixed act you are unknowingly committed to. 'Unknowingly' does not imply that you have no probabilistic judgement about the matter – although, indeed, you may have none, i.e., c may be undefined. In fact, with $c = .3$, you think it unlikely that your commitment makes odds of 9:1 on continuing; you think the odds most likely to be 1:1. But whatever the odds, you prefer the same pure outcome: continuing. You don't know which 'gamble' you face, but you know what constitutes winning: continuing to smoke, i.e., the less likely outcome of the more desirable 'gamble'. These scare-quotes emphasize that your mixed act is not a matter of spinning a wheel of fortune and passively awaiting the outcome; you yourself are the chance mechanism.

You think there is an objective, real[22] probability of your quitting, i.e., .9 or .5, depending on whether you have the bad genotype or the good one; there is a fact of the matter, you think, even though you do not know the fact. If the real odds on your continuing to smoke are even, that is because your tropism toward smoking is of the softer kind, stemming from the good allele; you are lucky in your genotype. But how does that work? How does the patch of DNA make you as likely to quit as continue? How do we close the explanatory gap from biochemistry to preference and behaviour, i.e., to things like the relative importance you place on different concomitants of smoking, on the positive side a certain stimulus and sensual gratification, on the negative a certain inconvenience and social pressure? These influences play themselves out in the micro-moves which add up to the actual macro-outcome: continue, or quit. And if the odds are 9 : 1, that will stem from a different pattern of interests and sensitivities, forming a strong tropism toward continuing to smoke, somehow or other rooted in your DNA. What's weird about Fisher's science-fiction story is not its premise, that the mental and physical states of reasoning animals are interconnected, but the thought that we might have the sort of information about the connection that his story posits – information unneeded in ordinary deliberation, where acts screen it off.[23]

The flagship Newcomb problem owes its *bizarrerie* to the straightforward character of the pure acts: surely you can reach out and take both boxes, or just the opaque box, as you choose. Then as the pure acts are options, you cannot be committed to either of the non-optional mixed acts. But in the Fisher problem, those of us who have repeatedly 'quit' easily appreciate the smoker's dilemma as humdrum entrapment in some mixed act, willy nilly. That the details of the entrapment are describable as cycles of temptation, resolution and betrayal makes the history no less believable – only more petty. Quitting and continuing are not options, i.e., $pr\,A \approx 0$ and $pr\,A \approx 1$ are are not destinations you think you can choose, given your present position on your kinematical map, although you may eventually find yourself at one of them. The reason is your conviction that if you knew your genotype, your value of $pr\,A$ would be either a or a', neither of which is ≈ 0 or ≈ 1. (Translation: 'At places on the map where $pr\,C$ is at or near 0 or 1, $pr\,A$ is not.') The extreme version of the story, with $a \approx 1$ and $a' \approx 0$, is more like the flagship Newcomb problem; here you do see yourself as already committed to one of the pure acts, and when you learn which that is, you will know your genotype.

I have argued that Newcomb problems are like Escher's famous staircase on which an unbroken ascent takes you back to where you started.[24] We know there can be no such things, but see no local flaw; each step makes sense, but there is no way to make sense of the whole picture; that's the art of it.[25]

Notes

1. These capital letters function as sentences. Logically equivalent sentences are assigned the same values.
2. See Jeffrey (1987) and (1965, 1983) sec. 12.8. The point is Davidson's (e.g., 1980, pp. 272–3).
3. Here, as in the case of mechanisms, rigidity assumptions are to be understood as holding only within rough bounds defining normal conditions of use, the analogs of load limits for bridges.
4. Near: you may mistake C's truth value, or bungle an attempt to make O_i true, or revise your decision.
5. As it is on the 'material' reading of 'if' as *or not* when the increase in $pr\,(D$ if $C)$ arises from a decrease in $pr\,(C)$. Note that $pr\,(D$ if $C)$ need not equal $pr\,(D \mid C)$ – anyway, not when 'if' is read as *or not*, for $pr\,(D \vee \neg C) = pr\,(\neg C) + pr\,(D \mid C)pr(C)$. But the material reading of 'if' does deliver those goods in the limit as $pr(C) \to 1$, given stability of $pr\,(D \mid C)$, for then final $pr\,(D \vee \neg C)$ will agree with initial $pr\,(D \mid C)$.
6. Derivation: $pr\,(C \mid A) = pr\,(A \wedge C)/pr\,(A) = a'pr\,(\neg C)/[a'pr\,(\neg C) + apr(C)]$.
7. Also known as 'sufficiency' (Diaconis and Zabell, 1982). A sufficient statistic is a random variable whose sets of constancy ('data') form a partition satisfying this condition.
8. *Bayes factors* (Good, 1950) are the corresponding figures for your odds on A against B: fac(A)/fac(B).
9. Proof. With $pr_{old}(A \mid C_i) = pr_{new}(A \mid C_i)$ at the right, this is an identity in the probability calculus.
10. Proof. Divide both sides of the preceding equation by $pr_{old}(A)$ apply Bayes's theorem to $pr_{old}(C_i \mid A)$.
11. The 'regression coefficient' of a random variable Y on another, X, is $\beta = cov(X, Y)/var(X)$, where $cov(X, Y) = E[(X - EX)(Y - EY)]$ and var $(X) = E(X - EX)^2$. If X and Y are indicators of propositions (*sc.*, 'cause' and 'effect'), $cov(X, Y) = pr$ (cause $\wedge$ effect) pr (cause)pr (effect), var(X) $= pr$ (cause)pr ($\neg$cause), and β reduces to the left-hand side of the displayed inequality.
12. For random variables generally, rigidity is constancy of the conditional probability distribution of Y given X as the unconditional probability distribution of X varies.
13. Where there is only one such hypothesis, this reduces to the desirability of the act. Skyrms's figure of merit is $\Sigma_K E(u \mid K \wedge A)pr(K)$ when 'K' ranges over a countable set

of pairwise incompatible, collectively exhaustive hypotheses regarding causal connections among acts and states, hypotheses to which the agent assigns positive probabilities. To obtain Jeffrey's (1965) figure of merit replace $pr(K)$ by $pr(K \mid A)$ in this formula, which then reduces to $E(u \mid A)$.

14. Since $pr(A)/pr(\neg A) = pr(A)pp'/pr(\neg A)p'p = qp'/(1-q)p$. Thanks to David Krantz for this.
15. Thanks to Brian Skyrms for this paragraph.
16. I take it that the values a, a', b, b' given above hold even when c is 0 or 1, e.g. $b = pr(ca \mid \text{bad}) = .2$ even when $pr(\text{bad}) = 0$; the equation $b \cdot pr(\text{bad}) = pr(ca \wedge \text{bad})$ is not what defines b.
17. The being has surely put \$1,000 in one box, and has (B) left the second empty or ($\neg B$) put \$1,000,000 in it, depending on its prediction of whether you (A) take both boxes, or ($\neg A$) take only the second.
18. In this kinematical map, $pr(A) = \int_0^1 x^{t+1} f(x)dx$ and $pr(B \mid A) = \int_0^1 x^{t+2} f(x)dx/pr(A)$, with $f(x)$ as in Figure 1.5b or 1.5c. Thus, with $f(x)$ as in (b), $pr(A) = (t+1)/(t+3)$ and $pr(B \mid A) = (t+2)/(t+3)$. See Jeffrey (1988).
19. At that point the desirabilities of shaded rows in (b) and (c) are not determined by ratios of unconditional probabilities, but continuity considerations suggest that they remain good and bad, respectively.
20. And here ratios of utilities are generally taken to be of the order of 10:1 instead of the 1000:1 ratios that made the other endgame so demanding. With utilities 0, 1, 10, 11 instead of 0, 1, 1000, 1001, indifference between confessing and remaining silent now comes at $\beta = 10\%$ instead of one tenth of 1%.
21. Cf. von Neumann and Morgenstern's (1947, p. 148) transcendental argument, remarked upon by Skyrms (1990, pp. 13–14), for expecting rational players to reach a Nash equilibrium.
22. See the hard-core subjectivist's guide to objective chance in Jeffrey's *The Logic of Decision*, sec. 12, and note that the 'no one chooses to have sacked Troy' passage from the Nichomachean Ethics, used by Skyrms (1980, p. 128) to introduce causal decision theory, also fits the present scepticism about Newcomb problems.
23. Cf. Davidson's (1980, p. 223) conclusion, that 'nomological slack between the mental and the physical is essential as long as we conceive of man as a rational animal'.
24. 'Ascending and Descending' (lithography, 1960), based on Penrose and Penrose (1958); see Escher (1989, p. 78).
25. Elsewhere I have accepted Newcomb problems as decision problems, and accepted '2-box' solutions as correct. Jeffrey (1983, sec. 1.7 and 1.8) proposed a new criterion for acceptability of an act – 'ratifiability' – which proved to break down in certain cases (see Jeffrey 1990, p. 20). In Jeffrey (1988, 1993), ratifiability was recast in terms more like the present ones – but still treating Newcomb problems as decision problems.

References

Arntzenius, F. (1990) 'Physics and Common Causes', *Synthese*, vol. 82, pp. 77–96.

Bolker, E. (1965) 'Functions Resembling Quotients of Measures', Ph.D. dissertation (Harvard University).

Bolker, E. (1966) 'Functions Resembling Quotients of Measures', *Transactions of the American Mathematical Society*, vol. 124, pp. 292–312.

Bolker, E. (1967) 'A Simultaneous Axiomatization of Utility and Subjective Probability', *Philosophy of Science*, vol. 34, pp. 333–40.

Davidson, D. (1980) *Essays on Actions and Events* (Oxford: Clarendon Press).

Davidson, D. (1984) *Inquiries into Truth and Interpretation* (Oxford: Clarendon Press) pp. 125–39.

Diaconis, P. and S. Zabell (1982) 'Updating Subjective Probability', *Journal of the American Statistical Association*, vol. 77, pp. 822–30.

Escher, M.C. (1989) *Escher on Escher* (New York: Abrams).

Fisher, R. (1959) *Smoking, the Cancer Controversy* (London: Oliver & Boyd).

Good, (1950) *Probability and the Weighing of Evidence* (London: Charles Griffin & Co.).

Hofstadter, D.R. (1983) 'The Calculus of Cooperation is Tested Through a Lottery', *Scientific American*, vol. 248, pp. 14–28.

Jeffrey, R.C. (1965, 1983, 1990) *The Logic of Decision* (New York: McGraw-Hill; Chicago: University of Chicago Press).

Jeffrey, R.C. (1987) 'Risk and Human Rationality', *The Monist*, vol. 70, no. 2, pp. 223–36.

Jeffrey, R.C. (1988) 'How to Probabilize a Newcomb Problem', in J.H. Fetzer (ed.), *Probability and Causality* (Dordrecht: Reidel).

Jeffrey, R.C. (1992) *Probability and the Art of Judgement* (Cambridge: Cambridge University Press).

Jeffrey, R.C. (1993) 'Probability Kinematics and Causality', in Hill, D., Forbes. M. and Okruhlik, K. (eds) *PSA 92*, vol. 2 (East Lansing, MI: Philosophy of Science Association, Michigan State University).

Kahneman, D. (1995) 'New Challenges to the Rationality Assumption', in this volume.

Kolmogorov, A.N. (1933) 'Grundbegriffe der Wahrscheinlichkeitsrechnung', *Ergebnisse der Mathematik*, vol. 2, no. 3. Translation: *Foundations of Philosophy* (Berlin: Springer-Verlag) (1950) (New York: Chelsea).

Leeds, S. (1984) 'Chance, Realism, Quantum Mechanics', *Journal of Philosophy*, vol. 81, pp. 567–78.

Nozick, R. (1963) 'The Normative Theory of Individual Choice', Ph.D. dissertation (Princeton University).

Nozick, R. (1969) 'Newcomb's Problem and Two Principles of Choice', in N. Rescher (ed.), *Essays in Honor of Carl G. Hemple* (Dordrecht: Reidel).

Nozick, R. (1990) Photocopy of Nozick (1963), with new preface (New York: Garland).

Penrose, L.S. and R. Penrose (1958) 'Impossible Objects: A Special Type of Visual Illusion', *The British Journal of Psychology* vol. 49, pp. 31–3.

Skyrms, B. (1980) *Causal Necessity* (New Haven, Conn.: Yale University Press).

Skyrms, B. (1990) *The Dynamics of Rational Deliberation* (Cambridge, Mass.: Harvard University Press).

von Neumann, J. and O. Morgenstern (1944, 1947) *Theory of Games and Economic Behaviour* (Princeton: Princeton University Press).

Comment

Christian Schmidt

UNIVERSITÉ PARIS-DAUPHINE, FRANCE

Jeffrey's paper looks like the last but not necessarily the ultimate step of a long intellectual work. From the first edition of his *Logic of Decision* (1965) until now, Jeffrey has continuously refined a Bayesian theory of decision which is different from Savage's Bayesianism on two grounds. Whereas Savage's purpose is dominated by a statistical preoccupation,[1] Jeffrey's aim is to provide a plain logical framework for decision-making. According to Jeffrey, events are logical propositions which can be true or false and the choice of an act is analyzed as 'truth-making' (i.e. a calculation based on truth values). Furthermore, in Savage's formulation, the states of the world are independent of the acts to be chosen by the decision-maker. Jeffrey does not refer to the states of the world, but calculates directly the conditions under which the acts entail the consequences expected by the decision-maker (cf. the probability matrices). These probabilities need not be independent from the chosen act (Jeffrey, 1965, pp. 4–5). Thus, the domain of Jeffrey's theory is broader than the 'small world' primarily investigated by Savage.[2]

This attempt to extend the Bayesian treatment to more general choice situations is a real challenge for an orthodox theory of decision. On the one hand, the Savagian 'acts-dependent states' assumption appears as a very stringent limitation, but on the other hand, its relaxation immediately opens a Pandora's box generating many problems. As Jeffrey has himself pointed out, the core of Savage's framework is summarized in the well-known 'omelette' example (Jeffrey, 1977). The omelette example teaches us that framing rationally a choice situation necessarily implies that the decision-maker knows perfectly the definite consequences of every possible act in each possible state of the world. In other words, the decision-maker must define the states of the world in such a way that the choice situation can be described by the omelette canonic table (Savage, 1954). As soon as this result is obtained, the questions raised by the existence of possible causal relations of dependence between the states of the world and the acts are drastically precluded. Nevertheless, they quickly reappear when the decision-maker does not have a sufficient knowledge to determine the outcomes which can be associated to every consequence of his acts from the beginning of the deliberation. Roughly speaking, either the act-independent state is to be considered as a shadow assumption for framing rationally the choice situations (Schmidt, 1994), and the relevance of the Bayesian machinery is strictly bounded, or the Bayesian rules for computing rationality are to be considered as taking into account various hypotheses about the relationship between acts and states of the world evaluation. Jeffrey deliberately chooses the second option. He has successively proposed two different solutions which will be now discussed.

The problem to be solved can be expressed as follows: how to choose rationally one action among a set of possible acts when subjective probabilities associated to their conditional consequences change with the chosen act. Jeffrey gives 'ratificationism' at the first answer to the question (Jeffrey, 1981, 1983). To be 'ratifiable', the chosen option must maximize the expected outcome of the decision-maker on the grounds of the probabilistic matrix corresponding to the act he thinks he will finally decide to perform (Jeffrey, 1983, p. 5). Ratificationism was introduced as a challenge to the causal decision theories. According to almost all these causal theories, one must start with the hypothesis of a causal dependence of the independence as a special case (Gibbard and Harper, 1978; Skyrms, 1982; Lewis, 1981). Jeffrey claims alternatively that the non-causal formulation of the problem provided by the ratificationism is a generalization of his logic of decision, where the troublesome cases corresponding to such kinds of dependence are taken into account (Jeffrey, 1985, p. 480). Unfortunately, the ratificationism criticism does not always offer a sufficient basis for eliciting an option, as has been shown in many counter-examples.

Jeffrey shifts here from ratificationism to kinematics. Kinematics is a metaphoric name for modelling the general mental dynamics of the decision-maker's conditional probabilities during the deliberation process. One cannot confuse their two components: on the one hand the probabilities for the states of the world to be true or false, the acts being given, noted p on the other hand, the probabilities for the acts to be false, the states of the world being given, noted q. According to Jeffrey's schema, the relevant question for rational choice does not concern the causal interpretation of these conditional probabilities but rather the identification of the values which are fixed from the beginning and the values which vary during the deliberation. The values of q obviously vary from the beginning to the end of the deliberation when the probability of the chosen act approaches 1. Such variations may or may not generate p's variations according to the specific characteristics of the choice situation. The decision-maker's information can even lead to cases where the rational choice is overdetermined, as in the Newcomb example, or underdetermined.

This new version of Jeffrey's logic of decision raises three questions: first, the link between kinematics and ratificationism; second, the way it challenges the causal decision theories; third, the light it puts on Newcomb problems.

At first glance, kinematics seems to be an extension of ratificationism by the generalization of its dynamics. Such an oversimplified interpretation is not entirely correct. With ratificationism, Jeffrey has elaborated a Bayesian criterion for choosing rationally when the independence condition is not satisfied. The purpose of kinematics is to provide a general logical framework for decision problems. Indeed kinematics can be used to frame ratifiable decisions, but the implications of Jeffrey's kinematics go beyond the ratificationist doctrine. One of its most unexpected results is to restore in a more sophisticated version Savage's approach, where the acts are replaced by the probabilities of the decision-maker to make them true or false and the states of the world are replaced by their probabilities to be true or false. As for Savage, choosing rationally implies for Jeffrey that the rational option to be chosen has been described in choice situations rationally framed by the model builder, corresponding to the state-independent act assumption in Savage's canvas. Therefore, Jeffrey argues that the decision problem is ill-posed when the desirabilities of acts – states combinations vary throughout the deliberation as a consequence of p's variations. Thus Newcomb difficulties are not to be understood as the result of a decision problem, because the Newcomb Choice Situation is an ill-posed question from the viewpoint of the logic of decision. Kinematics offers to Jeffrey another line along which he can defend his *logic of decision*.

Kinematics versus causal theories does not meet the point. One must recall the origins of the debate. A suspicion about the existence of a dependence between the states of the world and the acts in specific choice situations has questioned the Bayesian non-causal (or evidential) theories of rational choice. Three directions have been investigated in order to solve the emerging difficulties: (a) different principles of maximization are to be applied according to the interpretation given to the act-independent states assumption in the envisaged situations (see, for example, the distinction between causal and epistemic independence: Gibbard and Harper, 1978); (b) the traditional principle of expected utility maximization is to be revised in order to cover choice situations with act-dependent states (see Jeffrey's ratificationism); (c) the principle for choosing rationally requires appropriate information which does not exist in several choice situations with act-dependent states in the Newcomb style (see Jeffrey's kinematics understood in a Savagian spirit). In addition, the technical translation of each of these options refers to different views on probabilities. For a strict Savagian, the probabilities are unconditional on the grounds of act-independent states of the world. For Jeffrey, the decision-maker uses conditional probabilities where the probability values attached to the outcomes are dependent on the acts which are performed. For most of the causal theoreticians, the probability values are attributed to the counterfactual statements linking the outcomes on the chosen act (counterfactual probabilities).

The real question is about the comparative relevance of these probabilistic treatments to describe the choice situations. The Savagian interpretation of unconditional probabilities necessarily leads one to adopt option (c). Likewise, the counterfactual probabilities used by the theorists of causal decision-making are consistent with option (a). Gibbard and Harper on their side use the distinction between conditional and counterfactual probabilities as foundations for two different principles of utility maximization. As for Jeffrey, the conditional probabilities developed in the kinematic direction are a consequence of his refusal of counterfactual probabilities. Therefore, the kinematic version of Jeffrey's logic of decision is more an alternative to the counterfactual approach to decision theory rather than a challenge to causal theories of decision.

Finally, the role played by the Newcomb Choice Situation in all this story seems surprising. It can be summarized in three rounds. First round: Newcomb's example raises problems for the Bayesian principle of rationality and opens the way to causal theories of decision consistent with option (a). Second round: the examination of features of Newcomb choice situations shows that a casual relation between the occurrence of the states and the chosen action is impossible; thus the causal theories of decision cannot be applied to Newcomb situations. Third round: the cornerstone of Newcomb problems is to be found in too much and irrelevant information for the decision-maker: accordingly Newcomb choice situations are to be considered neither as a decision nor a game-theory problem (Schmidt, 1994), which is consistent with option (c).

The reason why the Newcomb Story remains up to now a fascinating enigma for the decision-making theorists is still stranger. I do not believe that Newcomb problems are like Escher's famous Staircase. The clue to their mystery emerges as soon as the time schedule of the choice situation is reintroduced in the story. In any case, when the decision-maker chooses one of the two options, the providential person has already made a decision, so that in fact the chosen act cannot change the obtained state of the world. But if for one reason or another the providential person never fails in prediction, it means that the time order of the decision sequences does not affect the outcome, which is then independent of the decision-maker (the 'deep state' in Jeffrey's language). Choosing the two boxes is the only rational decision according to the first hypothesis, just as choosing the opaque box is the unique rational decision in the second hypothesis. The puzzling thing is that the time schedule gives here the relevance of Savage's timeless schema in the first case, whereas the fiction-story rubs out the time uncertainty. Following Eells's suggestion, one should attribute to Newcomb many solutions rather than many problems (Eells, 1984).

Notes

1. As pointed out by the title of Savage's book *The Foundations of Statistics*
2. Savage was conscious of this limitation; he himself suggested a general direction to investigate the logical relations between what he called 'small worlds' and the 'great world', Savage, 1954, pp. 82–91).

References

Eells, E. (1984) 'Newcomb's Many Solutions', *Theory and Decision*, vol. 16, pp. 59–105.

Gibbard, A. and Harper, W.L. 'Counterfactuals and Two Kinds of Expected Utility', in Hoocker, C.A., Leach, J.J. and McClennen, E.F. (eds), *Foundations and Applications of Decision Theory* (Dordrecht: Reidel) pp. 125–62.

Jeffrey, R.C. (1965) *The Logic of Decision*, 1st ed. (New York: McGraw-Hill).

Jeffrey, R.C. (1977) 'Savage's Omelet', *Philosophy of Science Association*, East Lancing Mich., vol. 2, pp. 361–71.

Jeffrey, R.C. (1981) 'The Logic of Decision Defended', *Synthèse*, vol. 48, pp. 473–92.

Jeffrey, R.C. (1983) *The Logic of Decision*, 2nd edn (Chicago: University Press of Chicago).

Lewis, D. (1981) 'Causal Decision Theory', *Australian Journal of Philosophy*, vol. 59, pp. 5–30.

Savage, L.J. (1954) *The Foundations of Statistics* (New York: John Wiley).

Schmidt, C. (1994) 'Paradoxes of Rationality in Decision-Making Theory?', Chapter 3 in this volume.

Skyrms, B. (1982) 'Causal Decision Theory', *Journal of Philosphy*, vol. 79, pp. 695–711.

2 Consequentialism, Structural Rationality and Game Theory

Peter J. Hammond

STANFORD UNIVERSITY, USA

1 THREE CONSEQUENTIALIST AXIOMS

In the space allowed to me, I shall try to impart some of the key ideas of the 'consequentialist' approach to rational behaviour. At the same time, I shall try to assess its significance and to explain its limitations.

Consequentialism relies on the presumption that behaviour is rational if and only if it is explicable by its consequences. More specifically, the set of consequences which can result from behaviour should depend only on the set of feasible consequences. And, as the key assumption, this should be true for an (almost) unrestricted domain of finite decision trees whose terminal nodes have specified consequences.

More formally, let Y denote a fixed domain of possible consequences. Let $\mathfrak{T}(Y)$ denote the domain of finite decision trees with consequences in Y.[1] Each member T of $\mathfrak{T}(Y)$ takes the form of a list:

$$\langle N, N^*, X, n_0, N_{+1}(\cdot), \gamma(\cdot) \rangle$$

whose six components are:

(1) the finite set of nodes N;
(2) the subset $N^* \subset N$ of decision nodes;
(3) the complementary set $X = N \setminus N^*$ of terminal nodes;
(4) the initial node $n_0 \in N$;
(5) the correspondence $N_{+1}(\cdot) : N \twoheadrightarrow N$ determining what set $N_{+1}(n)$ of nodes immediately succeeds each node $n \in N$, which satisfies obvious properties ensuring that N has a tree structure with X as the set of terminal nodes because $N_{+1}(x)$ is empty for all $x \in X$;
(6) the mapping $\gamma : X \rightarrow Y$ from terminal nodes to associated consequences.

At any decision node $n \in N^*$, each immediate successor $n' \in N_{+1}(n)$ of node n corresponds to a particular move from n to n' which the agent can make. Thus behaviour at $n \in N^*$ can be described by a non-empty 'chosen' subset $\beta(T, n)$ of the set $N_{+1}(n)$ of all immediate successors of node n.[2] The first assumption is:

Axiom 1 (Unrestricted domain). There is a *behaviour correspondence* β whose values satisfy $\emptyset \neq \beta(T, n) \subset N_{+1}(n)$ at every decision node $n \in N^*$ of every decision tree $T \in \mathfrak{T}(Y)$.

25

It should be noted that Axiom 1 is not entirely innocuous. For example, suppose that the consequences were extended to include a list of what would result from the different actions available to the agent at each moment of time. Then important facts about the structure of the decision tree could be inferred from these extended consequences. So the domain of decision trees on which behaviour is defined would be limited accordingly. Thus, Axiom 1 makes sense only when the consequences themselves do not depend on the structure of the tree.[3] Of course, such independence has been the standard assumption in classical decision theory.

An important and natural property of the behaviour correspondence concerns *subtrees* which take the form

$$T(n) = \langle N(n), N^*(n), X(n), n, N_{+1}(\cdot), \gamma(\cdot) \rangle$$

for some initial node n which is any node of T. Here $N(n)$ consists of all nodes in N which succeed n, including n itself. Of course n becomes the initial node of $T(n)$. Also $N^*(n) = N \cap N(n)$, $X(n) = X \cap N(n)$, while the mappings $N_{+1}(\cdot)$ and $\gamma(\cdot)$ apply to the restricted domains $N(n)$ and $X(n)$ respectively. The relevant property I shall assume is:

Axiom 2 (Dynamic consistency). In every subtree $T(n)$ of each decision tree $T \in \mathfrak{X}(Y)$, and at every decision node n^* of $T(n)$, one has $\beta(T(n), n^*) = \beta(T, n^*)$.

The justification for this second assumption is that both $\beta(T(n), n^*)$ and $\beta(T, n^*)$ describe behaviour at n^*; whether n^* is regarded as a decision node of the full tree T or of the subtree $T(n)$ should be irrelevant. It turns out that, for an agent whose tastes are changing endogenously, even naive behaviour in decision trees is dynamically consistent in this sense; for such an agent the inconsistency will be between plans and actual behaviour.[4]

The most important axiom of consequentialism is the third, which will be stated next. It involves considering, for any tree $T \in \mathfrak{X}(Y)$, the *feasible set* $F(T)$ of all possible consequences which can result from the agent's decisions in T. This set, and the feasible sets $F(T(n))$ for each subtree $T(n)$ in turn, can be constructed by backward recursion. To do so, let $F(T(x))$ be $\{\gamma(x)\}$ when $x \in X$ is any terminal node, and then define

$$F(T(n)) = \bigcup_{n' \in N_{+1}(n)} F(T(n'))$$

for all decision trees $T(n)$ starting at the other nodes of T. Of course, $F(T) = F(T(n_0))$.

The following statement of the third axiom also involves the set $\Phi_\beta(T)$ of all possible consequences which can result from the agent's decisions when they lie in the behaviour set $\beta(T, n)$ at each decision node $n \in N$. This set can also be constructed by backward recursion through the subtrees of T. The construction starts with $\Phi_\beta(T(x)) = \{\gamma(x)\}$ for the trivial subtree $T(x)$ starting at any terminal node $x \in X$, and then proceeds by defining

$$\Phi_\beta(T(n)) = \bigcup_{n' \in \beta(T, n)} \Phi_\beta(T(n'))$$

for all other nodes $n \in NX$, until it arrives at $\Phi_\beta(T) = \Phi_\beta(T(n_0))$.

After these preliminary constructions, I can state:

Axiom 3 (Consequentialist behaviour). On the domain of all non-empty finite subsets of Y there exists a *revealed consequence choice function* C_β which is non-empty valued and satisfies the property that $\Phi_\beta(T) = C_\beta(F(T))$ for all $T \in \mathfrak{T}(Y)$.

This means that the set of possible consequences of behaviour should depend only on the feasible set of consequences, so that behaviour can be interpreted as the pursuit of chosen consequences. The assumption that $C_\beta(F)$ is non-empty for every F in its domain loses no generality. For, given any non-empty finite set of consequences $F \subset Y$, one can construct a tree whose only decision node is the initial node n_0, while each consequence $y \in F$ has a corresponding terminal node x_y for which $\gamma(x_y) = y$. Then, of course, T is a finite decision tree in $\mathfrak{T}(Y)$ for which $F(T) = F$ and $\Phi_\beta(T) = \{y \in F \mid x_y \in \beta(T, n_0)\} \neq \emptyset$.

It is the three 'consequentialist' axioms presented above which have such strong implications, [5] and so play such a crucial role in all that follows. I want to emphasize very strongly that none of the other usual rationality hypotheses are being invoked. There is no presumption that a preference ordering exists. When we come to risk and uncertainty, there will be no assumption of independence or of Savage's sure-thing principle. These standard rationality hypotheses will turn out to be implications of the three axioms set out above, however. That is what is so striking about them.

2 A REVEALED PREFERENCE ORDERING

In simple decision trees without risk or uncertainty, behaviour satisfying Axioms 1–3 must reveal a preference ordering[6] over the consequence domain. Specifically, given the revealed consequence choice function C_β defined on the domain consisting of all non-empty finite subsets of Y, there is a unique corresponding weak preference relation R_β defined by

$$y R_\beta y' \Longleftrightarrow y \in C_\beta(\{y, y'\})$$

This is the preference revealed by behaviour in any decision tree T whose feasible set $F(T)$ consists of a pair of consequence $\{y, y'\}$ – or of a single consequence in case $y = y'$. The relation R_β is complete because $C_\beta(F)$ is non-empty whenever $F = \{y, y'\}$, so either $y R_\beta y'$, or $y' R_\beta y$ or both.

The above definition of R_β already ensures that

$$C_\beta(F) = \{y \in F \mid y' \in F \Longrightarrow y R_\beta y'\} \tag{1}$$

whenever F is a singleton or a pair set. Then $C_\beta(F)$ consists of precisely those members of F which maximize the preference relation R_β. In fact it is not too difficult to prove that (1) also holds for every finite set $F \subset Y$, no matter how large, and also that R_β is a preference ordering. Thus Axioms 1–3 imply:

Ordinal choice. The revealed choice function C_β defined on the domain of all finite non-empty subsets of Y corresponds to a preference ordering R_β defined on the whole of Y.

To save space, however, the proof is not given here – see Hammond (1988, section 5). Instead, I just state:

Theorem 1.   Suppose that Y is any consequence domain. Then:

(a) Any behaviour correspondence β satisfying Axioms 1–3 reveals an ordinal choice function C_β.
(b) Conversely, given any preference ordering R on Y, there exists an associated behaviour correspondence β satisfying Axioms 1–3 whose revealed preference ordering R_β is equal to R.

Thus, one contentious axiom of structural rationality has become an implication of other axioms that may be harder to question. Above all, those who argue that a preference ordering is not necessary for structural rationality owe us an explanation of how they expect agents to depart from the consequentialist axioms, and how they should behave in decision trees.[7] Perhaps the structure of the tree, as well as the set of feasible consequences, should be allowed to affect the set of chosen consequences. But would this really be rational?

Note that Theorem 1 includes the converse of its first part. This is important because it confirms that ordinality is a *complete* characterization of behaviour satisfying the three consequentialist axioms. The converse is easily proved by ordinal dynamic programming arguments, as in section 8 of Hammond (1988).

3   UNCERTAINTY AND THE SURE-THING PRINCIPLE

Formally, let Y denote the consequence domain, and E a fixed non-empty finite set of possible states of the world. A *decision tree with uncertainty* is then defined as a list:

$$T = \langle N, N^*, N^1, X, n_0, N_{+1}(\cdot), \gamma(\cdot), S(\cdot) \rangle$$

Compared to the definition in Section 1, the new features are: (i) N^1 the set of *natural nodes* at which nature's move reveals information; and (ii) the *event correspondence* $S{:}N \twoheadrightarrow E$ specifying what non-empty set $S(n) \subset E$ of states of the world is possible after reaching node $n \in N$. Note that N is now partitioned into the three disjoint sets N^*, N^1 and X. At any natural node $n \in N^1$, nature's move partitions the set $S(n)$ into the collection of pairwise disjoint subsets $S(n')$ ($n' \in N_{+1}(n)$). At any decision node $n \in N^*$, however, the agent's move cannot refine what information there is already about the state of the world, and so it is required that $S(n') = S(n)$ whenever $n' \in N_{+1}(n)$. Finally, the consequence mapping γ takes its value $\gamma(x)$ in the relevant Cartesian product set $Y^{S(x)} {:=} \Pi_{s \in S(x)} Y_s$ at each terminal node $x \in X$, where each Y_s ($s \in E$) is just a copy of the consequence domain Y.[8] Thus terminal nodes are associated with profiles $\gamma(x) = \langle y_s \rangle_{s \in S(x)} \in Y^{S(x)}$ of uncertain contingent consequences rather than with certain consequences $y \in Y$.

An obvious modification of the unrestricted domain Axiom 1 is to require that $\beta(T, n)$ be defined throughout all finite decision trees with uncertainty. Axioms 2–3 (dynamic consistency and consequentialist behaviour) can be applied virtually without change. The revealed consequence choice function, however, should really be replaced by a collection C_β^S of such functions, one for each non-empty set $S \subset E$. The reason is that feasible sets and revealed consequence choice sets will be subsets of different Cartesian product sets Y^S ($\emptyset \neq S \subset E$) rather than just of Y.

The backward recursion construction of Section 1 must also be adapted to treat natural nodes $n \in N^1$. At such nodes, because choices at different later decision nodes can be made independently, it is natural to construct the following Cartesian products:

$$F(T(n)) = \prod_{n' \in N_{+1}(n)} F(T(n')) \subset \prod_{n' \in N_{+1}(n)} Y^{S(n')} = Y^{S(n)}$$

$$\Phi_\beta(T(n)) = \prod_{n' \in N_{+1}(n)} \Phi_\beta(T(n')) \subset \prod_{n' \in N_{+1}(n)} F(T(n')) = F(T(n))$$

Given any non-empty $S \subset E$, consider the restricted domain $\mathfrak{T}^S(Y)$ of finite decision trees with no natural nodes, and with $S(x) = S$ at every terminal node. This restricted domain is effectively equivalent to $\mathfrak{T}(Y^S)$, the domain of finite decision trees with consequences in Y^S. Applying Theorem 1 to this domain establishes the existence of a *conditional preference ordering* R_β^S on Y^S that is revealed by consequentialist behaviour in such trees.

Consequentialism also establishes an important relationship between the different revealed preference orderings R_β^S ($\emptyset \neq S \subset E$). Indeed, let S_1 and S_2 be two non-empty disjoint subsets of E, and let $S = S_1 \cup S_2$. Let a^{S_1}, b^{S_1} be two contingent consequences in Y^{S_1}, and c^{S_2} a contingent consequence in Y^{S_2}. Consider the decision tree illustrated in Figure 2.1, with an initial natural node n_0 whose two successors are: (i) decision node n_1, at which $S(n_1) = S_1$; and (ii) terminal node x_c, at which $S(x_c) = S_2$ and $\gamma(x_c) = c^{S_2}$. Suppose that n_1 offers the choice of going to either of the terminal nodes x_a and x_b, at which $S(x_a) = S(x_b) = S_1$ while $\gamma(x_a) = a^{S_1}$ and $\gamma(x_b) = b^{S_1}$.

In this tree the non-trivial feasible sets are $F(T(n_1)) = \{a^{S_1}, b^{S_1}\}$ and $F(T) = F(T(n_0)) = F(T(n_1)) \times F(T(x_c)) = \{a^{S_1}, b^{S_1}\} \times \{c^{S_2}\} = \{(a^{S_1}, c^{S_2}), (b^{S_1}, c^{S_2})\}$. Using the definition of the revealed preference relations R_β^S on Y^{S_1} and $R_\beta^{S_1}$ on Y^{S_1}, as well as the dynamic consistency assumption that $\beta(T, n_1) = \beta(T(n_1), n_1)$ leads to the following chain of logical equivalences:

$$a^{S_1} R_\beta^{S_1} b^{S_1} \iff a^{S_1} \in C_\beta^{S_1}(\{a^{S_1}, b^{S_1}\}) = C_\beta^{S_1}(F(T(n_1))) \iff a^{S_1} \in \Phi_\beta^{S_1}(T(n_1))$$

$$\iff x_a \in \beta(T(n_1), n_1) \iff x_a \in \beta(T, n_1) \iff (a^{S_1}, c^{S_2}) \in \Phi_\beta^S(T)$$

$$\iff (a^{S_1}, c^{S_2}) \in C_\beta^S(\{(a^{S_1}, c^{S_2}), (b^{S_1}, c^{S_2})\}) \iff (a^{S_1}, c^{S_2}) R_\beta^S (b^{S_1}, c^{S_2})$$

Thus, to summarize, consequentialism implies:

Savage's sure-thing principle. Whenever $S \subset E$ is partitioned into non-empty sets $S_1 \cup S_2$, and a^{S_1}, $b^{S_1} \in Y^{S_1}$ while $c^{S_2} \in Y^{S_2}$, then

$$a^{S_1} R_\beta^{S_1} b^{S_1} \iff (a^{S_1}, c^{S_2}) R_\beta^S (b^{S_1}, c^{S_2})$$

The main result of this section is:

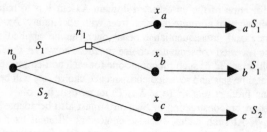

Figure 2.1

Theorem 2. Suppose that Y is any consequence domain and that E is any finite non-empty set of uncertain states of the world. Then:

(a) For any behaviour correspondence β satisfying Axioms 1–3, the hypothesized revealed choice functions C_β^S, defined for all non-empty $S \subset E$ on the domain of finite non-empty subsets of the appropriate Cartesian product set Y^S, must correspond to preference orderings R_β^S which together satisfy the sure-thing principle.

(b) Conversely, given any family of orderings R^S (for all non-empty $S \subset E$) defined on each product set Y^S that together satisfy the sure thing principle, there is an associated behaviour correspondence β satisfying Axioms 1–3 whose revealed preference ordering R_β is equal to R.

Part (a) has already been explained, though not proved formally. Like part (b) of theorem 1, the converse can be proved by ordinal dynamic programming arguments. See Hammond (1988) for complete proofs.

4   UNORDERED EVENTS

One of the principal axioms used by Savage (1954) actually goes back to earlier work by Keynes, Ramsey, de Finetti and others. This is the *ordering of events*. It requires the existence of a weak ordering $\geq$ on subsets of E, with the idea that the associated strong ordering $S_1 > S_2$ should mean that S_1 is more likely, or more probable, than S_2. More specifically, suppose that $\bar{y}$ and $\underline{y}$ are respectively 'good' and 'bad' consequences in Y, and that an agent is given the choice between the following two alternative contingent consequences:

(1) $(\bar{y}\,1^{S_1},\,\underline{y}1^{S_2})$, representing $\bar{y}$ for sure if S_1 occurs, and $\underline{y}$ for sure if S_2 occurs;

(2) $(\underline{y}\,1^{S_1},\,\underline{y}\,1^{S_2})$, representing $\underline{y}$ for sure if S_1 occurs, and $\bar{y}$ for sure if S_2 occurs.

Then $S_1 > S_2$ should be equivalent to $(\bar{y}\,1^{S_1},\,\underline{y}\,1^{S_2})$ being preferred to $(\underline{y}\,1^{S_1},\,\bar{y}\,1^{S_2})$ for all pairs $\bar{y}$, $\underline{y}$; with $\bar{y}$ preferred to $\underline{y}$, because it is always preferable to 'win' a good consequence contingent upon a more likely event.

An important corollary of Theorem 2 is that this ordering of events property is not an implication of the consequentialist axioms, because those axioms imply only the existence of conditional preference orderings satisfying the sure-thing principle, and no more. To establish this, it is enough to exhibit a family of contingent preference orderings satisfying the sure-thing principle but not the ordering of events.

Indeed, suppose that $Y = \{y_1, y_2, y_3\}$. Also let $E = \{s_1, s_2\}$. Then let $v{:}Y \to \Re$ be the real valued utility function defined by $v(y_i) := i - 2$ $(i = 1, 2, 3)$ whose values will be assumed to represent the preference ordering R_β^s on Y for each single state $s \in E$. Suppose too that R^E on Y^E is represented by the utility function $\phi_{s_1}(v(y_{s_1})) + \phi_{s_2}(v(y_{s_2}))$, where

$$\phi_{s_1}(v) = \begin{cases} v & \text{if } v \geq 0 \\ 2v & \text{if } v < 0 \end{cases} \quad \text{and} \quad \phi_{s_1}(v) = \begin{cases} 2v & \text{if } v \geq 0 \\ v & \text{if } v < 0 \end{cases}$$

Because this utility function is additive, it is obvious that the sure-thing principle is satisfied.

In this case the total utility of the pair (y_1, y_2) (meaning y_1 if state s_1, and y_2 if state s_2) is $\phi_{s_1}(-1) + \phi_{s_2}(0) = -2$, while that of the pair (y_2, y_1) is $\phi_{s_1}(0) + \phi_{s_2}(-1) = -1$. Hence (y_2, y_1) is preferred to (y_1, y_2), thus suggesting that s_1 is more likely than s_2. On the other hand, the total utility of (y_2, y_3) is $\phi_{s_1}(0) + \phi_{s_2}(1) = 2$, while that of the pair (y_3, y_2) is $\phi_{s_1}(1) + \phi_{s_2}(0) = 1$. Hence (y_2, y_3) is preferred to (y_3, y_2), thus suggesting that s_2 is more likely than s_1. There is no well-defined ordering of the two events $\{s_1\}$ and $\{s_2\}$.

5 RISK AND UNCERTAINTY COMBINED

Without objective probabilities, consequentialism in decision trees with uncertainty does not imply the ordering of events, and so *a fortiori* does not imply that subjective probabilities are revealed by the agent's behaviour. With objective probabilities, however, and given some additional structural assumptions, it will be true that consequentialist behaviour must maximize expected utility, where expectations are represented by appropriate combinations of objective and subjective probabilities.

The first step is to extend once again the definition of a decision tree to accommodate a set N^0 of *chance nodes* at each of which there is a collection $\pi(n' \mid n)$ $(n' \in N_1(n))$ of *transition probabilities*. Here $\pi(n' \mid n)$ is the probability of reaching n' conditional on having reached n already. Of course $\pi(n' \mid n) \geq 0$ for all $n' \in N_{+1}(n)$ and $\Sigma_{n' \in N_{+1}(n)} \pi(n' \mid n) = 1$ for all $n \in N^0$. For reasons that will emerge in due course, in fact I shall consider only probabilities satisfying $\pi(n' \mid n) > 0$ everywhere. One could argue that parts of the decision tree that are reached with only zero probability should be pruned off anyway, though in game theory this leads to severe difficulties in subgames.

So a finite decision tree becomes a list

$$T = \langle N, N^*, N^0, N^1, X, n_0, N_{+1}(\cdot), \pi(\cdot \mid \cdot), S(\cdot), \gamma(\cdot) \rangle$$

Now N is partitioned into the four sets N^*, N^0, N^1 and X (though any of the first three sets could be empty). It is also appropriate to re-define the range of the consequence mapping γ on X to consist of (simple) probability distributions on the appropriate set $Y^{S(x)}$, rather than single members of $Y^{S(x)}$. Thus probabilities $\gamma(y^{S(x)} \mid x) > 0$ must be defined for each $x \in X$ and $y^{S(x)} \in Y^{S(x)}$. Moreover, it must be true that $\gamma(y^{S(x)} \mid x) > 0$ only for those $y^{S(x)} \in Y^{S(x)}$ in the finite *support* of $\gamma(\cdot \mid x)$.

It is also necessary to modify once again the recursive construction of the two sets $F(T(n))$ and $\Phi_\beta(T(n))$ for the subtree $T(n)$ starting at each node $n \in N$ so as to allow for chance nodes and probabilistic contingent consequences. In fact, it is natural to take

$$F(T(n)) = \Sigma_{n' \in N_{+1}(n)} \pi(n' \mid n) F(T(n')); \quad \Phi_\beta(T(n)) = \Sigma_{n' \in N_{+1}(n)} \pi(n' \mid n) \Phi_\beta(T(n'))$$

at any chance node $n \in N^0$ where the transition probabilities are $\pi(n', n)$ ($n' \in N_{+1}(n)$). Thus each set consists of all possible appropriately probability weighted sums, as n' ranges over $N_{+1}(n)$, of the probability distributions belonging to the succeeding sets $F(T(n'))$ or $\Phi_\beta(T(n'))$. Finally, at natural nodes the appropriate product sets are no longer Cartesian products of sets, but rather sets consisting of all the independent joint probability distributions that can be created by multiplying members of the appropriate sets of probabilities in every way possible.

The consequentialist axioms 1–3 of Section 1, as modified in Section 3, can now be applied to this new extended domain of decision trees. They imply that there exists a conditional revealed preference ordering R_β^S for every non-empty $S \subset E$. The domain of R_β^S is no longer Y^S, however, but the set $\Delta(Y^S)$ of all 'simple' probability distributions over Y^S – i.e., all distributions having finite support. Moreover, the *sure-thing principle* should now be re-stated so that, whenever S_1, S_2 are non-empty disjoint subsets of E, and $\lambda, \mu \in \Delta(Y^{S_1})$ while $\nu \in \Delta(Y^{S_2})$, then

$$(\lambda \times \nu) R_\beta^S (\mu \times \nu) \Longleftrightarrow \lambda R_\beta^{S_1} \mu$$

where $S = S_1 \cup S_2$ and $\times$ denotes the usual product of the probability distributions.

This does not exhaust the implications of consequentialism, however. In this new framework with some objective probabilities, it is also possible to adapt the argument used in Section 3 to derive the sure-thing principle and establish the following:

Independence condition. Suppose that $\lambda, \mu, \nu \in Y^S$ for some non-empty $S \subset E$, and that $0 < \alpha < 1$. Then $\alpha\lambda + (1 - \alpha)\nu \, R_\beta^S \alpha\mu + (1 - \alpha)\nu \Longleftrightarrow \lambda R_\beta^S \mu$.

In fact, were zero probabilities allowed in decision trees, one could prove the same result even when $\alpha=0$. The implication would be that $\nu R_\beta^S \nu \Longleftrightarrow \lambda R_\beta^S \mu$ for all $\lambda, \mu, \nu \in Y^s$. Since the left-hand side of this equivalence is always true, so is the right-hand side, and so there must be universal indifference over Y^S, for every non-empty $S \subset E$! To avoid this absurdity with ordinary probabilities requires either restricting the domain to exclude zero probability moves at chance nodes, as has been done in this paper, or else not imposing the dynamic consistency condition $\beta(T, n') = \beta(T(n), n')$ in decision subtrees $T(n)$ which can only be reached with zero probability. Neither escape is really appropriate in game theory, however, which has led me to consider decision trees embodying non-Archimedean probabilities in Hammond (1994a, 1994b). Here, though, the exclusion of zero probabilities can perhaps be forgiven as a simplifying assumption.

By now the following result, whose proof is once again to be found in Hammond (1988), should come as no surprise:

Theorem 3.   Suppose that Y is a given consequence domain, that E is a given non-empty finite set of possible states of the world. Then:

(a) If behaviour satisfies axioms 1–3 for the domain of finite decision trees with chance and/or natural nodes in which there are no zero probability moves at any chance node, then there must exist a family of revealed conditional preference orderings R_β^S on $\Delta(Y^S)$, one for each non-empty $S \subset E$, satisfying both independence and the sure thing principle.

(b) Conversely, given any family R^S of orderings on the sets $\Delta(Y^S)$ ($\phi \neq S \subset E$) that satisfies independence and the sure-thing principle, there is an associated behaviour correspondence β satisfying axioms 1–3 in all finite decision trees without zero probabilities at any chance node, whose revealed conditional preference ordering R_β^S is equal to R^S for each non-empty $S \subset E$.

6   SUBJECTIVE PROBABILITY

We remain some way short of Anscombe and Aumann's (1963) formulation of subjective probabilities. For one thing, the ratios of those probabilities amount to marginal rates of substitution between expected von Neumann–Morgenstern utilities conditional on different events; so far, we have not imposed any continuity on behaviour in a way that even ensures the existence of a utility function. Another problem is that Anscombe and Aumann assumed that two probability distributions λ, $\mu \in \Delta(Y^S)$ would be equivalent, and so indifferent, whenever the marginal distributions λ_s, $\mu_s \in \Delta(Y_s)$ were equal for all $s \in S$. As pointed out in section 12 of Hammond (1988), this assumption is crucial in ruling out the kind of preference pattern observed in Ellsberg's (1961) 'paradox'. Indeed, such patterns cannot be excluded by the consequentialist axioms on their own without some help from additional plausible assumptions.

The continuity issue is easily treated. Consider a family of finite decision trees T^π which are all identical except for the collection $\pi = \langle \pi(\cdot \mid n) \rangle_{n \in N^0} \in \Pi_{n \in N^0} \Delta^0(N_{+1}(n))$ of strictly positive probability distributions at each chance node. For each common decision node $n^* \in N^*$, there is an induced correspondence $\pi \longmapsto \beta(T^\pi, n^*)$, from the domain $\Pi_{n \in N^0} \Delta^0(N_{+1}(n))$ of allowable transition probability distributions at different chance nodes to the range of non-empty subsets of $N_{+1}(n^*)$. Now, continuity of behaviour generally requires such a correspondence to be upper hemi-continuous. Where the domain and the range are both compact sets, as they are here, upper hemi-continuity is equivalent to the following closed graph property:

Axiom 4 (Continuous behaviour as probabilities vary).   For each decision node $n \in N^*$ the graph $\{(\pi, n') \in \Pi_{n \in N^0} \Delta^0(N_{+1}(n)) \times N_{+1}(n^*) \mid n' \in \beta(T^\beta, n^*)\}$ of the correspondence $\pi \longmapsto \beta(T^\pi, n^*)$ is a relatively closed set.

As is fairly easy to show, it then follows that for each non-empty $S \subset E$, the revealed conditional preference relation R_β^S on $\Delta(Y^S)$ must have the property that the two sets

$$\{\alpha \in [0,1] \mid \alpha\lambda + (1-\alpha)\mu R_\beta^S \nu\} \quad \text{and} \quad \{\alpha \in [0,1] \mid \nu R_\beta^S \alpha\lambda + (1-\alpha)\mu\}$$

are closed, for each triple λ, μ, $\nu \in \Delta(Y^S)$. This continuity property is one of Herstein and Milnor's (1953) three axioms, applied to the binary relation R_β^S. The other two are that R_β^S is an ordering and that the independence condition is satisfied. The implication of their main theorem is the existence, for each non-empty $S \subset E$, of a unique cardinal equivalence class of *conditional von Neumann – Morgenstern utility functions* (NMUFs) v^S such that R_β^S is represented on $\Delta(Y^S)$ by the expected value $Ev^S := \Sigma_{y^S \in Y^S} p^S(y^S) v^S(y^S)$ of v^S, where $p^S(y^S)$ denotes the probability of y^S.

The second issue, regarding the sufficiency of considering only marginal probability distributions, is much less straightforward. In fact, two extra assumptions are generally needed to ensure the existence of subjective probabilities. Of these, the first is:

Axiom 5 (Certainty equivalence). Suppose that T and T' are two decision trees without any natural nodes in which the only differences are in the event sets $S(n)$, $S'(n)$ at each node n of the common set of nodes N, and in the associated consequences $\gamma(x)$, $\gamma'(x)$ which occur at each terminal node x of the common set of terminal nodes $X = X'$. Specifically, suppose that in tree T there exists a single state $e \in E$ such that $S(n) = \{e\}$ for all $n \in N$, while $\gamma(x)$ is a riskless consequence in Y for all $x \in X$. On the other hand, suppose that in tree T' one has $S'(n) = S$ for all $n \in N$, while $\gamma'(x) = \gamma(x)1^S$ for all $x \in X$, where $\gamma(x)1^S \in Y^S$ denotes the particular constant contingent consequence function whose value is $\gamma(x)$ in each state of the world $s \in S$. Then the behaviour sets $\beta(T, n^*)$ and $\beta(T^\pi, n^*)$ are equal at each common decision node $n^* \in N^*$ of the two trees T and T'.

Thus, the decision tree T' in which there is no uncertainty about the consequence at each terminal node, even though there may be uncertainty about the state of the world, is regarded as equivalent to the tree T in which there is not even any uncertainty about the state of the world. In fact, given the special property of tree T', one can regard T as an alternative 'certainty equivalent' decision tree. Because of Theorem 3 it should be no surprise that, together with Axioms 1–3, this new assumption implies the existence of a state-independent revealed preference ordering R_β on $\Delta(Y)$ which is equal to $R_\beta^{\{s\}}$ on $\Delta(Y_s)$ for every $s \in E$, and also equal to the restriction of R_β^S to $\Delta(Y1^S)$ for every non-empty $S \subset E$ (where $Y1^S$ denotes the set of constant contingent consequences of the form $y1^S$, for some $y \in Y$). In particular, Axiom 5 rules out awkward examples such as that presented in Section 4.

The second additional assumption is:

Axiom 6 (Three consequences). There exist at least three consequences y_1, y_2, $y_3 \in Y$ such that $y_3 P_\beta y_2 P_\beta y_1$, where P_β denotes the strict preference relation corresponding to the revealed preference ordering R_β.

Axioms 5 and 6 together rule out rather strange conditional NMUFs such as $V^S(y^S) = \Pi_{s \in S} V_s(y_S)$ or $-\Pi_{s \in S}[-V_s(y_s)]$, and instead imply that $V^S(y^S) = \Sigma_{s \in S} V_s(y_s)$ for a unique co-cardinal equivalence class of state contingent NMUFs $v_s : Y_s \to \Re$ ($s \in E$). Moreover, Axiom 5 in particular implies that there exists a unique cardinal equivalence class of state-independent NMUFs $v^* : Y \to \Re$ with the property that each v_s is cardinally equivalent to v^*. Hence there must exist additive constants α_s and positive multiplicative constants ρ_s (all $s \in E$) such that $v_s(y) \equiv \alpha_s + \rho_s v^*(y)$. In fact, the family of constants ρ_s ($s \in E$) is unique up to a common multiplicative constant, and so there are well defined *revealed conditional probabilities* given by $P(s \mid S) :=$ $\rho_s / \Sigma_{e \in S} \rho_e$ whenever $s \in S \subset E$. Finally, as in Weller (1978), whenever $s \in S \subset S' \subset E$ these revealed conditional probabilities must satisfy

$$P(s \mid S') = \frac{\rho_s}{\Sigma_{e \in S'} \rho_e} \times \frac{\Sigma_{e \in S} \rho_e}{\Sigma_{e \in S'} \rho_e} = P(s \mid S) \, P(S \mid S')$$

The important implication is:

Bayes' rule. Whenever $s \in S \subset S' \subset E$, it must be true that $P(s \mid S')$ $= P(s \mid S')P(S \mid S')$.

These arguments help to justify the following main theorem, also proved in Hammond (1988):

Theorem 4 (Subjective expected utility maximization). Suppose that Y is a given consequence domain, that E is a given non-empty finite set of possible states of the world. Then:

(a) Suppose that behaviour satisfies Axioms 1–6 for the domain of all finite decision trees with chance and/or natural nodes in which there are no zero probability moves at any chance node. Then there must exist a family of revealed conditional preference orderings R_β^S on $\Delta(Y^S)$, one for each non-empty $S \subset E$. Moreover, these orderings must in turn reveal a unique cardinal equivalence class of state independent NMUFs $v^*{:}Y \to \Re$ and unique positive conditional probabilities $P(s \mid S)$ ($s \in S \subset E$) satisfying Bayes' rule, such that R_β^S is represented by the subjective expected utility expression

$$\Sigma_{y^S \in Y^S} p^S(y^S) \, \Sigma_{s \in S} P(s \mid S) v^*(y_s) \equiv \Sigma_{s \in S} P(s \mid S) p_s(y_s) v^*(y_s)$$

where p_s denotes the marginal probability distribution on Y_s generated by p^S on Y^s.

(b) Conversely, given any state independent NMUF $v^* : Y \to \Re$ and family of positive conditional probabilities $P(s \mid S)$ ($s \in S \subset E$) satisfying Bayes' rule, if the associated behaviour correspondence β maximizes subjectively expected utility, then it must satisfy Axioms 1–5 in all decision trees without zero probabilities at any chance node.[9]

7 GAME THEORY AND RATIONALIZABILITY

Of late, the most widespread use in economics of the expected utility model of decision-making under uncertainty has been in non-cooperative game theory. Following prominent works such as Aumann (1987) and Tan and Werlang (1988), most game theorists now take the view that players in a game should have beliefs about other players' strategies described by subjective probabilities, and that they should then choose their strategies to maximize their respective expected utilities. This seems at first to be an entirely natural use of orthodox decision theory. Yet there is an important difference in extensive form games between, on the one hand, natural nodes at which nature moves exogenously, and on the other hand, players' information sets at which moves are determined endogenously by maximizing the relevant player's expected utility. In particular, I have often seen it claimed that, in this game-theoretic context, the existence of subjective probabilities and the maximization of subjectively expected utility are justified by Savage's axioms. Apart from betraying a fondness for Savage's particular set of axioms which may be hard to justify, this overlooks the fundamental issue of whether it makes any sense at all to apply Savage's axioms, the Anscombe–Aumann axioms, or some similar collection such as Axioms 1–6 above, to strategic behaviour in non-cooperative games.[10]

In fact there is one very clear difference between classical decision theory and orthodox game theory. In decision theory, all subjective probability distributions over unknown states of the world are regarded as equally valid and equally rational. Game theory, by contrast, started out by attempting to determine players' beliefs endogenously. Indeed, it appears that the need Morgenstern (1928, 1935) had perceived to close certain economic models by determining expectations was what aroused his interest in von Neumann's (1928) early work on the theory of 'party games'. Much later, Johansen (1982) still felt able to argue that, for games with a unique Nash equilibrium, that equilibrium would entirely determine rational behaviour and rational beliefs within the game.

Since the work of Bernheim (1984, 1986) and Pearce (1984) on rationalizability, and of Aumann (1987) on correlated equilibria, game theorists have begun to pay more careful attention to the question of what rational beliefs players should hold about each other. Aumann follows the equilibrium tradition of Nash in looking for a set of common expectations over everybody's strategies (a 'common prior') that attaches probability one to all players choosing optimal strategies given those common expectations. Bernheim and Pearce relax this condition and look for 'rationalizable' expectations which can differ between players, but must attach probability one to all players choosing strategies that are rationalizable – i.e., optimal given their own rationalizable expectations. Thus, in the work on rationalizability, what becomes endogenous is each player's set of rationalizable strategies, rather than expectations about those strategies.

Rationalizable expectations are especially interesting because of the way in which they, and the associated rationalizable strategies, can be constructed recursively. First-order rationalizable expectations are arbitrary; first-order rationalizable strategies are optimal given first-order rationalizable expectations; second-order rationalizable expectations attach probability one to players choosing first-order rationalizable strategies; second-order rationalizable strategies are optimal given second-order rationalizable expectations; third-order rationalizable expectations attach probability one to payers choosing second-order rationalizable strategies; and so on. The result of this recursive construction is a diminishing sequence of sets of n-th order rationalizable strategies and of associated sets of rationalizable beliefs or expectations. In the end, rationalizable strategies are those which are n-th order rationalizable, for all natural numbers n. What is happening here is that our concept of rationality (or rationalizability) is becoming more refined as n increases and we progress further up the hierarchy.

Though the usual consequentialist axioms cannot be applied to multi-person games, it seems that a variant of them can be. This involves the idea of *conditionally rational behaviour* for each player, based on *hypothetical probabilities* attached to the other players' strategies. Specifically, it is assumed that each player's behaviour satisfies the consequentialist axioms in all decision trees that result from extensive games by attaching specific hypothetical probabilities to all other players' moves at each of their information sets. This implies that each player maximizes expected utility, given these hypothetical probabilities. It then remains to determine, as far as possible, what, if any, hypothetical probabilities represent beliefs that are rational, or at least rationalizable. This, of course, is more or less what non-cooperative game theory has been trying to accomplish since its inception.

At the moment, then, it seems that game theory says that it is irrational to attach positive probabilities to rational players choosing strategies that are not rationalizable. Further restrictions on rational beliefs may emerge from subgame perfection and 'forward induction' arguments.[11] But other restrictions beyond these are hard to motivate, at least in the current state of game theory. Above all, only if rationalizable strategies are unique should we expect rational beliefs to be determined uniquely.

8 STRUCTURAL RATIONALITY VERSUS BOUNDED RATIONALITY

Section 6 concluded by showing that Axioms 1–5 and subjective expected utility maximization are equivalent for a consequence domain satisfying Axiom 6. The behaviour so described satisfies some well-known 'structural' conditions which have often been regarded as required for logical consistency or coherence. Hence I call such behaviour *structurally rational*. It is important to understand that structural rationality is neither sufficient nor necessary for full rationality.

Insufficiency of structural rationality is fairly evident. Maximizing the expected value of *any* utility function with respect to *any* subjective probabilities is structurally rational. So is *minimizing* expected utility! More seriously, a fuller concept of rationality clearly requires the pursuit of appropriate ends and the holding of reasonal beliefs, neither of which is entailed by structural rationality, or by consequentialism.

Less evident is the fact that structural rationality is not necessary for rational behaviour either. I am prepared to claim that it would be necessary if there were no bounds at all on an agent's rationality. If all our decision problems were straightforward, rationality could well entail behaviour satisfying Axioms 1–5, for a suitable domain of consequences. In practice, however, reality confronts us with enormously complex decision problems. Modelling these as decision trees, and then constructing the sets $F(T)$ and $\Phi_\beta(T)$ as in Section 2, is a task which poses horrendous difficulties for the decision analyst, quite apart from any human agent. After all, as has often been noted, it is impossible to model completely even a problem as well structured as how to play chess. Simplification is inevitable.

I shall assume that simplification gives rise to a rather small finite decision tree which models the true decision problem only imperfectly. Many nodes may be omitted, as may many of the possibilities at each node. In this sense there is a *bounded model*. And *bounded rationality* would seem to involve the use of such bounded models. Then there seems no particular reason why an agent's rational behaviour should exhibit structural rationality. After all, behaviour cannot then be explained only by its consequences, but will also depend upon what happens to be included in the agent's decision model.

Nevertheless, consequentialism, together with the structural rationality it entails, still makes sense within whatever model lies behind the agent's decision. In tournament chess it is rational not to analyse so deeply that one loses on time. But rationality does demand appropriate patterns of thought in whatever analysis does get conducted within a limited time. The incomplete plan (or 'variation') chosen by a player should be the best given the possibilities that could be considered within the time which the player felt able to devote to making that plan. A good player will not deliberately make an inferior move; nor probably will a bad player! Bad moves and even blunders may occur, but only because important considerations and possibilities have been 'overlooked' – i.e., omitted from the player's bounded model.

What bounded rationality forces us to consider are *vaguely formulated decision trees*. These will be just like ordinary decision trees, except that both consequences $y \in Y$ and states $s \in E$ will be vaguely formulated – imprecisely described, in effect. It is impossible to distinguish all the consequences of the true decision tree, or all the possible states. Instead, the agent can only analyse a coarsening Y_0 of the consequence domain Y, and a coarsening E_0 of the state space E. The different elements $y_0 \in Y_0$ will determine a partition $\cup_{y_0 \in Y_0} Y^0(y_0)$ of Y into sets of consequences that the agent fails to distinguish. There is a similar partition $\cup_{s_0 \in E_0} E^0(s_0)$ of E. The latter partition is equivalent to Savage's (1954) model of 'small worlds'.

Such coarsenings already imply that the agent can consider only decision trees in the domain $\mathfrak{T}(E_0, Y_0) = \cup_{\emptyset \neq S^0 \subset E_0} \mathfrak{T}^{S_0}(Y_0)$ rather than in the true domain $\mathfrak{T}(E, Y) = \cup_{\emptyset \neq S \subset E} \mathfrak{T}^S(Y)$. But the game of chess, for example, already has very simple consequences – win, lose or draw. Nor is there room for any intrinsic uncertainty. In chess, the necessary coarsening affects the decision tree itself. The domain $\mathfrak{T}(E_0, Y_0)$ gets coarsened to $\mathfrak{T}_0(E_0, Y_0)$, each of whose members T_0 corresponds to an enormous class $\mathfrak{T}^0(E_0, Y_0; T_0)$ of undistinguished complex decision trees. Such coarsening of the set of possible trees can also occur in any other decision problem, of course.

This approach to bounded rationality differs from the well-known one due to Simon (1972, 1982, 1986, 1987a, b), because he appears to allow an agent to 'satisfice' even within his own model. By contrast, I am asking for optimality within the agent's own model, though of course satisficing is allowed and even required in the choice of that model. This seems much more reasonable as a standard for normative behaviour.

9 EXPANDING SMALL WORLDS AND IMPROVING BOUNDED RATIONALITY

The discussion in Section 7 on rationalizability in games suggests, however, that one should go beyond such fixed bounded models. After all, there is a sense in which rationalizable strategies emerge from increasingly complex models of a game. Initially other players' strategies are treated as entirely exogenous, then as best responses to exogenous beliefs, then as best responses to best responses to exogenous beliefs, etc. A strategy is rationalizable if and only if enriched models of the other players and of their models can never demonstrate the irrationality of that strategy.

Similarly, consider a particular bounded model based on the particular coarsenings Y_0 of Y, E_0 of E, and $\mathfrak{T}_0(E_0, Y_0)$ of $\mathfrak{T}(E_0, Y_0)$. One feels that a rational agent who uses this model should have some reason for not using a richer bounded model. Such a richer model would be based on coarsenings Y_1 of Y, E_1 of E, and $\mathfrak{T}_1(E_1, Y_1)$ of $\mathfrak{T}(E_1, Y_1)$ which are refinements of Y_0, E_0 and $\mathfrak{T}_0$ respectively. That is, for each $y_1 \in Y_1$, the class $Y^1(y_1)$ of consequences which the agents fails to distinguish from y_1 should be a subset of $Y^0(y_0)$ for the unique $y_0 \in Y_0$ such that $y_1 \in Y^0(y_0)$. Similarly, for each $e_1 \in E_1$ and $T_1 \in \mathfrak{T}_1(E_1, Y_1)$, it should be true that $E^1(e_1) \subset E^0(e_0)$ where $e_1 \in E^0(e_0)$, and also that $\mathfrak{T}^1(E_1, Y_1; T_1) \subset \mathfrak{T}^0(T_0)$ where $T_1 \in \mathfrak{T}^0(T_0)$.

In fact, as Behn and Vaupel (1982) and Vaupel (1986) have suggested, what one really expects of a *rational* boundedly rational agent are some reasonable beliefs about whether a more refined model would change the decision being made at the current node of life's decision tree, as well as reasonable beliefs about what the consequences of a revised decision are likely to be. It is as though the agent were involved in a complicated game with some other very imperfectly known players – namely, versions of the same agent who use more complicated decision models. Should the agent take the trouble to enrich the decision model and so become one of these other players, or is it better to remain with the existing bounded model?

Note that an agent who does choose a more complicated model then has the same kind of decision problem to face once again – namely, the decision whether to complicate the model still further. In this way the agent can be viewed as facing an uncertain potentially infinite hierarchy of vaguely formulated trees, with increasing refined consequence spaces Y_n, state spaces E_n, and tree spaces $\mathfrak{T}_n(E_n, Y_n)$ $(n = 1, 2, ...)$.

There should then be an associated sequence β_n $(n = 1, 2, ...)$ of behaviour correspondences, each satisfying Axioms 1–5 for the appropriate domain $\mathfrak{T}_n(E_n, Y_n)$ of decision trees. So there will exist increasingly refined NMUFs $v_n:Y_n \to \mathfrak{R}$ and subjective probabilities $P_n(s_n \mid E_n)$ $(s_n \in E_n)$.

At this stage one should look for consistency conditions which it is reasonable to impose on different members of this hierarchy. And consider in more detail the decision when to stop analysing the current decision problem more deeply. Thus, a model of rational behaviour becomes hierarchical, and even self-referential, as in the theory of games. There also seem to be some links, of which I am only dimly aware, with recent developments in the theory of the mind and of self-awareness. This seems to be an inevitable implication of bounds on rationality. Nor should such links be at all surprising. However, this is still largely an unexplored topic, as far as I am aware. In fact, I may be proposing going at least one step further in the hierarchy of more and more complicated collective decision problems concerning how best to describe rational behaviour. If so, who knows what the next enriched models are likely to be?

Notes

1. Of course, it is restrictive in general to consider only finite decision trees. But not when discussing the implications of consequentialism, as is done here. The issue with infinite decision trees is whether behaviour can be well defined in a way that naturally extends consequentialist behaviour in finite trees. Obviously, this will require a technical analysis of compactness and continuity conditions.

2. This formulation does exclude stochastic behaviour, according to which $\beta(T, n)$ is a probability distribution over $N_{+1}(n)$. Under the consequentialist axioms set out below, it turns out that a very strong transitivity axiom – or what Luce (1958, 1959) describes as a 'choice axiom' – must be satisfied. In fact, there must exist a preference ordering over consequences which is maximized by all the consequences that can occur with positive probability given the agent's stochastic behaviour. Thus randomization occurs only over consequences in the highest indifference class of feasible consequences available to the agent. Furthermore, each consequence must have a positive real number attached indicating the relative likelihood of that consequence occurring, in case it belongs to the highest indifference class that the agent can reach.

3. Actually, Prasanta Pattanaik and Robert Sugden tried to convince me of essentially this point many years ago. Jean-Michel Grandmont and Bertrand Munier were finally more successful during the conference. I am grateful to all four, and would like to apologize to the first two.

4. See Hammond (1976) for more discussion of naive behaviour in decision trees, especially the 'potential addict' example, Also, Amos Tversky has suggested that Axiom 2 be called 'subtree consistency'. I am sympathetic, but have not followed this suggestion for two reasons: (i) earlier papers used the term 'dynamic consistency', and I would like to be consistent myself; (ii) subtrees do represent dynamic choice possibilities when the tree models decisions which will be made in real time.

5. For obvious reasons, one does not speak of (logical) 'consequences'.

6. Following the terminology of social choice theory, a 'preference ordering' means a reflexive, complete and transitive binary weak preference relation.

7. Some critics of consequentialism, notably Machina (1989) and McClennen (1990), have offered such explanations, especially for behaviour that maximizes a preference ordering and yet violates the independence condition which, as discussed in Section 5, is one other implication of consequentialism.

8. An important generalization allows the consequence domain Y_s to depend on the state s. As one might expect, it then becomes harder to ensure that behaviour reveals subjective probabilities. However, both the sure-thing principle and independence do still follow from the consequentialist axioms.

9. Evidently Axiom 6 cannot be an implication of expected utility maximization if there are only one or two consequences.

10. A similar point is the main concern of the paper by Mariotti presented to the same conference.

11. The relationship between forward induction and 'conditional rationalizability' is discussed in Hammond (1993).

References

Anscombe, F.J. and R.J. Aumann (1963) 'A Definition of Subjective Probability', *Annals of Mathematical Statistics*, vol. 34, pp. 199–205.

Aumann, R.J. (1987) 'Correlated Equilibrium as an Expression of Bayesian Rationality', *Econometrica*, vol. 55, pp. 1–18.

Behn, R.D. and J.W. Vaupel (1982) *Quick Analysis for Busy Decision Makers* (New York: Basic Books).

Bernheim, B.D. (1984) 'Rationalizable Strategic Behavior', *Econometrica*, vol. 52, pp. 1007–28.

Bernheim, B.D. (1986) 'Axiomatic Characterizations of Rational Choice in Strategic Environments', *Scandinavian Journal of Economics*, vol. 88, pp. 473–88.

Ellsberg, D. (1961) 'Risk, Ambiguity, and the Savage Axioms', *Quarterly Journal of Economics*, vol. 75, pp. 643–69.

Hammond, P.J. (1976) 'Changing Tastes and Coherent Dynamic Choice', *Review of Economic Studies*, vol. 43, pp. 159–73.

Hammond, P.J. (1988) 'Consequentialist Foundations for Expected Utility', *Theory and Decision,*, vol. 25, pp. 25–78.

Hammond, P.J. (1993) 'Aspects of Rationalizable Behavior', in K.G. Binmore, A.P. Kirman and P. Tani (eds) *Frontiers of Game Theory* (Cambridge, Mass.: MIT Press) ch. 14, pp. 277–305.

Hammond, P.J. (1994a) 'Elementary Non-Archimedean Representations of Probability for Decision Theory and Games', in P. Humphreys (ed.) *Patrick Suppes: Scientific Philosopher vol. 1, Probability and Probabalistic Causality* (Dordrecht: Kluwer Academic Publishers) pp. 25–61.

Hammond, P.J. (1994b) 'Consequentialism, Non-Archimedean Probabilities, and Lexicographic Expected Utility', presented to the Second Workshop on 'Knowledge, Belief and Strategic Interaction: The Problem of Learning' at Castiglioncello (Livorno), Italy in June 1992; to appear in the conference proceedings published by Cambridge University Press.

Herstein, I.N. and J. Milnor (1953) 'An Axiomatic Approach to Measurable Utility', *Econometrica*, vol. 21, pp. 291–7.

Johansen, L. (1982) 'On the Status of the Nash Type of Noncooperative Equilibrium in Economic Theory', *Scandinavian Journal of Economics*, vol. 84, pp. 421–41.

Luce, R.D. (1958) 'An Axiom for Probabilistic Choice Behavior and an Application to Choices among Gambles (abstract)', *Econometrica*, vol. 26, pp. 318–19.

Luce, R.D. (1959) *Individual Choice Behavior* (New York: John Wiley).

Machina, M.J. (1989) 'Dynamic Consistency and Non-Expected Utility Models of Choice Under Uncertainty', *Journal of Economic Literature*, vol. 27, pp. 1622–68.

McClennen, E.F. (1990) *Rationality and Dynamic Choice* (Cambridge: Cambridge University Press).

Morgenstern, O. (1928) *Wirtschaftsprognose: Eine Untersuchung ihrer Voraussetzungen und Möglichkeiten* (Economic Forecasting: An Investigation of its Presuppositions and Possibilities) (Vienna: Julius Springer).

Morgenstern, O. (1935) 'Vollkommene Voraussicht und wirtschaftliches Gleichgewicht' (Perfect Foresight and Economic Equilibrium), *Zeitschrift für Nationalökonomie*, vol. 6, pp. 337–57.

Pearce, D. (1984) 'Rationalizable Strategic Behaviour and the Problem of Perfection', *Econometrica*, vol. 52, pp. 1029–50.

Savage, L.J. (1954) *The Foundations of Statistics* (New York: John Wiley).

Simon, H.A. (1972, 1986) 'Theories of Bounded Rationality', in C.B. McGuire and R. Radner (eds), *Decision and Organization* (2nd edn.) (Minnesota: University of Minnesota Press) ch. 8, pp. 161–76.

Simon, H.A. (1982) *Models of Bounded Rationality* (2 vols) (Cambridge, Mass.: MIT Press).

Simon, H.A. (1986) 'Rationality in Psychology and Economics', *Journal of Business*, vol. 59 (Supplement), pp. 25–40.

Simon, H.A. (1987a) 'Bounded Rationality', in J. Eatwell, M. Milgate and P. Newman (eds), *The New Palgrave: A Dictionary of Economics* (London: Macmillan).

Simon, H.A. (1987b) 'Satisficing', in J. Eatwell, M. Milgate and P. Newman (eds) *The New Palgrave: A Dictionary of Economics* (London: Macmillan).

Tan, T.C.-C. and S.R. da C. Werlang (1988) 'The Bayesian Foundations of Solution Concepts of Games', *Journal of Economic Theory*, vol. 45, pp. 370–91.

Vaupel, J.W. (1986) 'Un pensiero analitico per decisori indaffarati' (An Analytical Thought for Busy Decision-makers), in L. Sacconi (ed), *La decisione: Razionalità collettiva e strategia nell'amministrazione e nelle organizzazioni* (Milano: Franco Angeli) ch. 13, pp. 226–38.

von Neumann, J. (1928) 'Zur Theorie der Gesellschaftsspiele' (On the Theory of Party Games), *Mathematische Annalen*, vol. 100, pp. 295–320.

Weller, P.A. (1978) 'Consistent Intertemporal Decision Making Under Uncertainty', *Review of Economic Studies*, vol. 45, pp. 263–6.

Comment

Bertrand Munier

GRID, ÉCOLE NORMALE SUPÉRIEURE DE CACHAN, FRANCE

Professor Hammond has provided us with a construct thanks to which we can put to the test the relationships between instrumental (or substantive, to use Simon's words) rationality hypotheses and some more fundamental hypotheses on behaviour patterns. His basic idea consists in using the framework of extensive games rather than the traditional but more limited framework of games in normal form and to define *behaviour norms* on the decision trees. One then associates to such a behaviour conditions on the choice of payoffs or consequences which result from *theorems* rather than being considered as *axioms*, as is the case in standard utility and decision theory, grounded on the normal form. Professor Hammond has thus developed a major contribution to our understanding of the subject of this conference. Yet his normative conclusion that an agent's behaviour can be regarded as 'structurally rational' if and *only if* the agent maximizes expected utility is not convincing.

Although Professor Hammond claims on a few occasions to resort to 'plausible assumptions' – an expression usually referring to observation – it is fairly clear that he essentially deals with a normative issue in the sense of Bell, Raiffa and Tversky (1988, ch. 1). I thus want to make clear that I shall depart in what follows from considerations on the descriptive value or on the prescriptive value of this model and shall try to concentrate on normative considerations. I claim that Hammond's framework can be used to show that a rational agent may, in many cases, violate expected utility, and therefore that Hammond's important contribution does not consist in what has been regarded as 'the' justification of the independence axiom through his construct. I shall show that this construct should be regarded as a *specific* version of consequentialism, and that an extended version of consequentialism can also be derived from a similar construct within the framework of extensive games. Although comments on Sections 8 and 9 of this chapter would also be called for, I shall refrain here from going into bounded rationality considerations due to time and space limitations.

1 'FULL MEMORY' AND AXIOM 1 OF HAMMOND'S CONSEQUENTIALISM

The main objection one can have to the specific way Professor Hammond axiomatizes and handles consequentialism (Sections 1 to 6 in the above chapter; and Hammond, 1988) is that it essentially excludes what could be termed 'full memory', in the general sense where a decision-maker keeps in mind, when trying to reach a decision, the preceding nodes of the tree, i.e. the opportunities he or she has had to take some steps and the reasons for the choices made as opposed to other possibilities. This 'full memory' – which can be looked at as an extreme version of the 'perfect recall' concept of game theory – is very frequent and regarded as most important in management behaviour, particularly in strategic management

(Wiseman, 1988; Tardieu and Guthmann, 1991). It can also be found in the behaviour of many households and is of course used in a more specific way as a central idea in case-based decision theory (Riesbeck and Schank, 1989; Gilboa and Schmeidler, 1992).

Professor Hammond has of course reflected on this issue (including specific interpretations of it, like regret, etc.) and proof of this fact can be found in several places in his work, particularly in his seminal *Theory and Decision* paper (1988, see especially pp. 26, 34–5, 38). But he had consistently argued that full memory in the above sense would not affect his construct and could be taken care of within his axiomatization by the very simple trick that such considerations could be embedded within the set of possible consequences. Although I am happy with the fact that Hammond, following our discussion at this conference in Turin, has changed his view and included a new appraisal in the final version of his paper (footnote 3 of the above chapter, as well as the paragraph at the end of which the reader is referred to it), it will be helpful for what follows to explain in some detail why the trick invoked in earlier versions of Hammond's paper cannot work, unless changes are introduced in the original construct, which subsequently modify the implications of it.

Let us recall that according to axiom 1, the behaviour correspondence β is defined at *every* decision node $n \in N^*$ of *every* finite decision tree $T \in \tau(Y)$ compatible with the finite subset S of the domain of consequences Y and that a basic assumption of the chapter is that this domain of consequences Y is *fixed* (p. 25).

Let us assume that we now, following Hammond's earlier suggestions, 'extend' the consequences to have them include some memorized account of the decisional situations available to the agent in all non-terminal nodes. In order to model this fact within Hammond's construct, one has to let the mappings γ from the set of terminal nodes X to the set of associated consequences in Y depend on T and the domain of possible consequences Y become, for every terminal node X of a tree $T \in \{T\}$, some set valued function of T. One has then:

$$\forall T, \forall X, \quad \gamma = \gamma(T, X) \text{ and } Y^{S(X)} = Y^{s(x)}(T, X)$$

But then, two ways are open to us. (i) Either we stick to axiom 1 and do not accept any restriction on $\{T\}$. Then, Y not being fixed any more for all T's, theorem 1 cannot be proven, as Lemma 5.1 (Hammond, 1988, pp. 40–2) is now valid only if the tree T considered is *given*. The implication of a transitive binary relation on consequences for *all* trees does not hold any more. (ii) Or we are able to define some partition of the set $\{T\}$ of decision trees T into some proper subsets $\tau_i \subset \{T\}$, in each of which 'full-memory' does not play any role, i.e. induces, for every given X, the same $Y^{s(x)}(T, X)$ for all $T \in \tau_i$, $i = 1, 2, \ldots \ldots, n$. Hammond's theorems could then be proven, but only for the trees *within* each single class τ_i.

How large each class τ_i could be would then be the next interesting question. It would have to be explored. I conjecture that the cardinal of any τ_i would be some (rapidly) decreasing function of the cardinal of the set of nodes N, i.e. that for problems of the size most often encountered in real life, all τ_i's would be of very small size, maybe in some cases would only contain one single tree!

We can then seriously ask the question whether the subsequent results of Hammond's chapter would be maintained, in particular whether independence could still be derived as a theorem, rather than appear as an axiom, except of course within each single τ_i.

2 ARE THERE MORE GENERAL CONSEQUENTIALIST WORLDS THAN HAMMOND'S?

In a world where 'full memory' is accepted, axiom 2 has little meaning, if any, because 'dynamic consistency' (the fact that, at any given node n of a tree, the decision-maker effectively chooses what he had imagined, while still not having made his choice at the initial node of the tree, he would choose at node n) would be necessarily met (Machina, 1989; McClennen, 1988, 1990). It should be underlined that this is a wider and weaker sense of 'dynamic consistency' than the one resorted to by Hammond in his axiom 2. The latter is called in the recent literature the 'separability' condition, and claims that 'dynamic consistency' should be ensured by the rational character of behaviour at any node n subject to ignoring the whole tree other than the subtree having as initial node n and as nodes its successors in the initial tree.

Definitions are left to every one of us, and Hammond has chosen to define *his* consequentialism through the three axioms he has used here. However, is axiom 2 of as great importance as the two others? Certainly not: Hammond states himself that 'the most important axiom of consequentialism is the third'; and we just pointed out that the important property of 'dynamic consistency' can be required in a more general sense than what axiom 2 states.

Suppose we nevertheless keep axiom 2 for the time being. Let us consider the different τ_is. There will be an infinite number of them, in general. $\forall\, i,\ \mid \tau_i \mid$ will be some finite number, as we already have argued, whereas $\mid \tau \mid$ is an infinite one.

As for the set of consequences associated with all terminal nodes, it will become the union over the T's of the sets of consequences associated with each T and all X's, i.e.:

$$C = \bigsqcup_{T \in \tau} \left[\bigsqcup_{X \in X} Y^{S(X)}(T, X) \right]$$

The restriction of this set to each τ_i is finite, by Hammond's hypothesis and our definition of τ_i But if no further assumption can be made, *consequentialism will be only 'locally' true.* The whole world will appear to be endowed with some *locally valid* utility function and some 'generalized' expected utility rule, in a different sense from Machina's (1982), but in a sense which would extend the same sort of idea: *Within* each τ_i indeed, theorem 1 of Hammond will still hold, i.e., there will be a revealed ordering on the domain of consequences, and independence will be recovered through theorem 3 above as a property. But these properties will not hold *across* the different τ_i's.

In general, 'full memory' will admittedly be consistent only with a weakened form of axiom 2, which is then not needed under Hammond's form, for the reasons discussed above. For example, we might restrict axiom 2 to be only valid within each subset τ_i (for a different approach, see Abdellaoui and Ami, 1993). An interesting question is then: What kind of further assumption could we make, in this case, to rescue the basic consequentialist idea? We might make the assumption that the whole set τ has a domain of associated consequences C which, although being the union of sets of consequences which vary with T, is finite.

The total number of possible orderings being then finite, it is inevitable that many

τ_i's will be associated to the same ordering j. To each of at least some of these orderings, there will be a set $\{\tau_i\}j$ associated, with all τ_i's in it being endowed with the same ordering j. In each of these $\{\tau_i\}j$'s, the world will be such that an ordering of consequences (the ordering j) will prevail, but *not* the independence property in general. Such a world would be closely akin to the non-expected utility maximizers one discussed by Machina (1989) and not far either from the non-expected utility world favoured by McClennen (1988, 1990). The rationality of the decision-maker in a world of this type can be characterized by ordering, but not by independence, while such a decision-maker cannot be subject to any money pump. I call such a world an 'extended consequentialist' world.

This is precisely why I think that claiming that the independence axiom is a property 'following from consequentialism' or from 'the' consequentialist axioms does not seem to me to be a *sufficiently qualified* statement. In fact, the independence property follows only from the *particular* consequentialism defined and designed in Professor Hammond's chapter specifically from the chosen versions of axiom 1 and axiom 2. It does *not* follow from the general idea of consequentialism that everyone has in mind before reading Hammond's chapter and which pertains to some form of axiom 3 essentially. In other words, I feel that there are general forms of consequentialism which could be modelled and that what we have in the above chapter is the *specific* model of Hammond's consequentialism. And while I think that one can argue in favour of a normatively compelling *ordering* because it characterizes the more general forms of consequentialism, I think that *independence* follows *only* from Hammond's specific consequentialism, as does expected utility. One cannot argue that the latter concept appears as normatively compelling, even when considering a framework of the *type* put forward by Hammond which, again, is what we really owe to him.

In other words, we can be facing problem structures (we have discussed here the *sequential* structure, but there are other features of the problems to be taken into account) for which expected utility behaviour will be a norm, and structures for which it will not and for which there may exist a more general norm, of the non-expected utility type. Rationality specifications are, to an extent which has not been sufficiently evaluated, *contingent*.

3   THE FUNDAMENTALLY CONTINGENT CHARACTER OF PREFERENCE FUNCTIONALS

Our comments, we hope, show that, as soon as the mappings γ become tree-dependent (as our γ_T above are), there appears what could be called a *tree-contingency* of rationality.

Yet even in the case of theorem 1 above, where no chance nodes, no 'natural' node is being considered, risk appears under the form of lotteries possibly associated to the terminal nodes through the mappings γ. Then, another type of contingency of rationality can appear: risk attitudes vary, even in these static lotteries, according to the structure of the lottery, as a long list of experiments shows, starting with the Allais' Paradox. With a refined methodology (the 'Closing In' method), Abdellaoui and Munier (1994) show experimentally that expected utility is recovered only in a subset of the Marschak–Machina triangle. This is a *different type of contingency of rationality*, about which the construct of Hammond does not and cannot say anything (Hammond's results cannot be derived when the domain is limited to trees with only one initial node immediately succeeded by terminal nodes).

I have not commented on the game-theoretic extension of Hammond's construct. But what has been said here shows that most of the debate is about one-player decision trees. On this, I agree with Hammond's view.

References

Abdellaoui, M. and D. Ami (1993) 'Rationalité devant le risque: quels arguments accepter?', *Note de Recherche-GRID* no. 93–08, November.

Abdellaoui, M. and B. Munier (1994) 'On the Fundamental (Risk-Structure Dependence of Individual Preferences under Risk', *Note de Recherche-GRID*.

Bell, D.E., H. Raiffa and A. Tversky (1988) *Decision Making, Descriptive, Normative and Prescriptive Interactions* (London: Macmillan) see ch. 1, pp. 9–30.

Gilboa, I. and Schmeidler, D. (1992) 'Case-Based Decision Theory', unpublished paper, Northwestern & Ohio State University.

Hammond, P.J. (1988) 'Consequentialist Foundations for Expected Utility', *Theory and Decision*, vol. 25, pp. 25–78.

Machina, M.J. (1982) 'Expected Utility Analysis without the Independence Axiom', *Econometrica*, vol. 50, pp. 277–323.

Machina, M.J. (1989) 'Dynamic Consistency and Non-Expected Utility Models of Choice Under Uncertainty', *Journal of Economic Literature*, vol. 27, no. 5, pp. 1622–68.

McClennen, E.F. (1988) 'Dynamic Choice and Rationality', in B. Munier (ed.), *Risk, Decision and Rationality* (Dordrech/Boston: Reidel) pp. 517–36.

McClennen, E.F. (1990) *Rationality and Dynamic Choice: Foundational Explorations* (Cambridge: Cambridge University Press).

Riesbeck, C.K. and R.C. Schank (1980) *Inside Case-Based Reasoning* (Hillsdale, N.J.: Lawrence Erlbaum Associates).

Tardieu, H. and B. Guthmann (1991) *Le Triangle Stratégique* (Paris: Les Editions d'Organisation).

Wiseman, C. (1988) *Strategic Information System* (Chicago: Irwin).

3 Paradoxes of Rationality in Decision-Making Theory

Christian Schmidt

UNIVERSITÉ PARIS-DAUPHINE, FRANCE

1 INTRODUCTION

Whereas almost all economic models assume that agents act rationally, economists do not devote much time to the investigation of the actual meaning of 'acting rationally' and its implications for economic agents. The following observations render such a situation still more surprising. The conventional formulation of rationality as a utility maximization appears irrelevant or, at least, unnecessary for the understanding of many Keynesian as well as monetarist macroeconomic models (Arrow, 1987; Malinvaud, 1991; Leijonhufjud, 1992). Even some of the better established results in microeconomic theory do not require the maximization of the individual agent's utility function. Let us consider, for example, the clearing of transactions in a competitive economy, where satisfying budget constraints does not imply this assumption (Arrow and Hahn, 1971).

Such a broad formulation of agents' rationality is not sufficient in cases where the assumption plays a central role as, for example, in uncertainty and/or interaction between well-defined decision-makers. Under such circumstances, economists most often share the much more precise formulation of rationality associated with Bayesian and/or games theory. Unfortunately, these models of rational choice generate many counter-examples on the grounds of their application to specific data. We should recall, among others, the problems raised by Allais and Ellsberg for the expected utility model, and the counter-intuitive results exemplified by Selten's Chain Stores and Rosenthal's Centipede for non-cooperative games with perfect information and common knowledge.

Roughly speaking, either the assumption that economic agents act rationally is too vague and, subsequently, most often unnecessary (or even irrelevant), or, if it is more precise, its content must be questioned. A different interpretation of rationality is developed here in order to avoid such an unpleasant conclusion. The sentence 'agents are assumed to act rationally' should be understood as an implicit simplification for the actual proposition 'the economic model-builder rationally assumes that agents act rationally'. In other words, it is rational for the economic model-builder to choose a model where the decision-makers act rationally. This point will be elaborated further. Accordingly, agents' rationality appears intricately embedded in the modeller's own rationality and the meaning of the first necessarily refers to the second. Some of the so-called paradoxes of rationality in decision-making are re-examined in the light of this prospect. They are surveyed in the next part of the chapter (Section 2). This critical examination shows that only a few of them are actually logical paradoxes. Section 3 is devoted to their analysis, where an alternative foundation for the assumption of rationality in economics is derived from the application of counterfactuals.

2   PARADOXES AND SO-CALLED PARADOXES OF RATIONALITY

The label 'paradoxes of rationality' in decision-making covers a large spectrum of heterogeneous cases. The problems raised are often multi-level and differ from one to another. Let us try to organize this *prima facie* chaotic picture by picking up some of their common features. The term 'paradox' is used at large when the implementation of rules derived from a logical model of rational choice to compute a solution in a specific situation leads to unexpected results.

The meaning of such an unexpected result may be very different. A first case occurs when the results empirically observed violate explicitly (or implicitly) one or the other of the assumptions included in the model of rational choice supposed to be used by the decision-makers, as for the independence axiom in the Allais experiment based on the answers to a questionnaire. A second case arises when the results obtained via the computation of the model of rational choice appear counter-intuitive, as for the consequence of using backward induction in the Centipede Game. A third case happens when the results look self-contradictory, as for the necessary irrationality of the rational choice according to the semantic rules of the rational choice model.

In order to clarify the situation, let us consider four items which are necessary for the emergence of the so-called 'paradoxes', namely: (i) the description of a choice situation; (ii) the existence of a reference model of rational choice; (iii) the implementation of the prescriptions derived from the reference model in the choice situation; (iv) the recognition of disharmony between the expected and obtained results. Each of these items leaves room for lack of precision and ambiguity which can lead to the so-called paradoxes which will now be illustrated.

2.1   The Choice Situation

A choice situation is characterized by a set of data and by proposed alternative actions, one of which is to be chosen by a decision-maker according to available information. It must be underlined that this information is generally assumed to be the same for both the decision-maker and the inventor of the choice situation, as well as for anybody considering the choice situation. Such an assumption sounds reasonable as long as the information provided by the data is unambiguous and precise. However, such conditions are often directly, or indirectly, ruled out by the description of the choice situation itself.

Let us consider the following assertion in Newcomb's Choice Situation: x will deposit or not deposit 1 million dollars in an opaque box on the basis of his expectation regarding the decision-maker's choice between the two proposed alternatives: A 'take only the opaque box', and B 'take two boxes, one of which is the opaque box, the other a transparent box containing \$1,000' (Nozick, 1969). The decision-maker knows that x is a highly reliable predictor of his choice. The meaning of x as a 'reliable predictor' remains both imprecise and ambiguous, although this statement is assumed to be common knowledge between x, the decision-maker, any observer and, obviously, the model-builder (Nozick, 1969).

Another example is provided by Ellsberg's Problem (Ellsberg, 1961). An urn containing 30 red balls and 60 black and yellow balls in unknown proportions describes a choice situation which provides imprecise information for the decision-maker. Such an imprecision leads to ambiguity. Another of Ellsberg's examples compares two other choice situations, the examination of which may explain why. In Situation I, the urn contains one hundred red and black balls in a known proportion of half red and half black. In Situation 2, the proportion of red and black balls is unknown. Indeed, although information on data is more precise for the decision-maker in Situation 1 than in Situation 2, nevertheless no rational decision-maker would hesitate in choosing indifferently between red or black in either of the choice situations. This does not imply a similarity between the two situations. On the contrary, the majority of tested people prefer Situation 1 to Situation 2 (Ellsberg, 1961). Let us return to the initial example. The available data mix together precise information (30 red balls) and imprecise information (60 black and yellow balls). Their combination can be organized in different ways to describe the choice situations which, are, for this reason, ambiguous (Levi, 1986).

In many counter-examples called 'paradoxes', the data which describe the choice situation are not precise enough and therefore the information available renders the choice situation ambiguous. The assumption that any decision-maker, as well as any observer, gives the same meaning to the described choice situation on the grounds of available data can easily be argued under these circumstances (see the 'framing effect' Tversky and Kahneman, 1986).

2.2 The Reference Model

To be rational in a choice situation means choosing a proposed option according to an acknowledged model of rational choice. Such a model is assumed to be acknowledged at once by the inventor of the choice situation and by the supposed decision-maker. For this reason, we propose labelling it the 'reference model'.

From a logical point of view, any model of rational choice is derived from a theory which is characterized by two components: a set of axioms and a set of definitions, in order to build up propositions relevant to the choice situations which have definite values of truth. For example, Savage's expected utility model is based on P_1, P_2 ... P_7 postulates and on some basic definitions concerning the 'world' of the decision-maker (acts, states, consequences, etc.) (Savage, 1954). All the propositions derived from Savage's postulates by means of these definitions are then logically consistent and semantically meaningful. A model of rational choice is a reference model, not only because it is acknowledged as such, but also because it can be applied to the choice situation. Any decision-maker must be able to compute the available data corresponding to the choice situation in the machinery of the reference model. Therefore it is implicitly assumed that the data given by the model-builder for describing the choice situation provide sufficient information for using the reference model and hence for choosing rationally between available options. Such a condition is not always satisfied, as many counter-examples show.

One can consider the expected utility model as the reference of the well-known counter-examples of Allais (1952).[1] Indeed Allais associates a probability value and a monetary pay-off to each possible outcome resulting from the option chosen by the decision-maker in the lotteries considered. But these data are not sufficient for the maximization of the determined expected utility function of the decision-maker, because of the lack of information about the utility function of the money (Levi, 1986). Therefore the expected utility model cannot be *sensu stricto* the reference of rational choice in Allais's choice situation. Such an observation does not rule out Allais's result, where no expected utility function is consistent with the revealed decision-maker's preference in Allais experiments. Indeed, the rational person does not use the expected utility as a reference model because it is irrelevant in Allais choice situations. As Allais himself claims, his results do not involve any paradox (Allais, 1987, p. 8).

A simplified and different one-shot version of Selten's Chain Store model (Selten, 1978) provides a more complex illustration. Let us take two decision-makers, a monopolist and a competitor, each of them having only two options. The competitor must choose between A, entering the market controlled by the monopolist, or B deciding not to enter the market. As for the monopolist, the choice is between a, accepting the competitor entering and sharing the market with him, or b, refusing entrance to the competitor and starting a struggle against him; contrary to Selten's example, it is not required that the competitor necessarily moves first. The available data are summarized by the matrix in Figure 3.1 where the numbers attributed by each decision-maker to the outcomes are their preference order indices:

		Monopolist	
		a	b
Competitor	A	(3, 2)	(1, 1)
	B	(2, 3)	(2, 3)

Figure 3.1

The reference model is obviously the strategic rationality of a non-cooperative game with the two Nash equilibria (A, a) and (B, b). According to a first version of the reference model, which we propose calling the 'Competing Game', the situation is pictured in Figure 3.2.

The information provided by the example does not necessarily lead to such a result where (A, a) is the equilibrium reached by the players choosing rationally. The threatened monopolist may assert to the competitor an initial announcement noted b' of the type: 'if you choose A, I shall choose b'. Thus model G1 (Figure 3.2) is transformed into model G' 1 (Figure 3.3).

In model G'1 (Figure 3.3) the competitor will choose rationally B, and (B, b) becomes the reached equilibrium: its relevance as a correct interpretation of the reference model of rational choice still remains questionable. Indeed, b' is a conditional statement which is credible on the grounds of the monopolist's assumed rationality. At first glance, b' has almost the same meaning as b and therefore asserting b' seems to be as irrational as choosing b (Selten's imperfect equilibrium

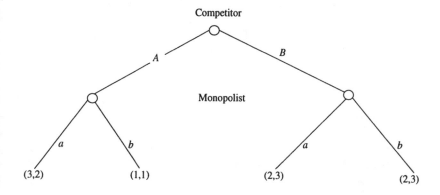

Figure 3.2   Model G1

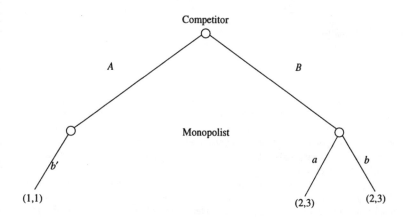

Figure 3.3   Model G'1

argument). But the argument is fallacious here: *b'* cannot be reduced to *b* because it does not have the same meaning; *b'* is a conditional proposition, the implementation of which is determined by the competitor's decision, whilst *b* is an actual proposition, the implementation of which is an immediate consequence of the monopolist's choice. Thus an additional model, G2 (Figure 3.4), is required in order to investigate the rationality of *b'* which determines its credibility in the reference model. We propose to call it the 'Deterrence Game' (Schmidt, 1990, 1991).

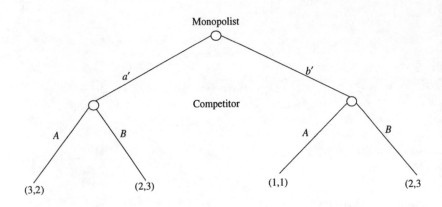

Figure 3.4   Model G2

In model G2, *a* is replaced by *a'*, which means deciding not to threaten the competitor by the deterrence statement. Thanks to the Deterrence Game, the monopolist must choose *b'* consistently with the rational choice reference model. Therefore, and contrary to Selten's view, G'1 as well as G1 is to be considered as a correct representation of the reference model for the given data provided by the exemplified choice situation.

According to G1, i.e. the competing model, (*A*, *a*) is the only perfect equilibrium, which means that the competitor must choose rationally *A* and the monopolist *a*. According to G'1, via the reference to the Deterrence Game G2, (*B*, *b*) is the only perfect equilibrium and, for the same reason as before, the competitor must choose rationally *B* and the competitor *b*. Is the deterrence model to be considered as a component of the reference model? The answer is yes but it does not imply that the deterrence model must necessarily be understood as an enlargement of G1. The question remains open. Incidentally, it must be noted that the pay-offs exhibited in Figure 3.1 to depict the choice situation in the language of the reference model are consistent with the Competing Game as well as the Deterrence Game: an additional source of ambiguity for the reference model.

In several counter-examples labelled conventionally as paradoxes of rationality in the literature, the reference model cannot be used in the choice situation, as described in the first example. Sometimes, it can be used in various ways leading to different results, as in the second example.

Strictly speaking, nobody can choose rationally according to the reference model in the first case, whereas there is no reason for each decision-maker to use the same version of the reference model in the second, according to his or her strategic position. One can argue that, in the second example, the reference to a model of rational choice actually raises a meta-problem *vis-à-vis* the reference model. Indeed, choosing rationally means that, in the second example, the competitor actually chooses the Competing Game and the monopolist the Deterrence Game.

2.3 The Implementation of the Reference Model

The reference model of rational choice is implemented in a specified choice situation as long as the chosen option among the proposed alternatives is directly derived from its prescriptions. Such a statement seems innocuous and true in a trivial manner. More reflexion shows, however, that the conditions of this implementation are actually the cornerstone of many counter-examples. Two different types of questions must be raised. First, the non-implementation of a supposed reference model is often induced by experimental data. Schematically, experimental results show that the options chosen by the decision-makers submitted to experimental tests do not correspond to the solutions which are obtained if these decision-makers had correctly implemented the reference model which is in the experimenter's mind (Kahneman, Slovic and Tversky, 1982; Slovic, Lichtenstein and Fishoff, 1982). Second, implementing a reference model means that the options chosen by the decision-maker are computed on its grounds. But the results of this computation often contradict the intuitive meaning commonly associated with the term 'rational', according to the reference model itself (Rosenthal, 1981; Binmore, 1990; Reny, 1992). The first observations support arguments against the empirical validity of the reference model, the interpretation of which leads to a methodological debate. We propose to quote it as the *revealed non-implementation* of the reference model of rational choice. The second observations are used to question the computational relevance of the reference model. We propose to label it the *computational implementation* of the reference model.

It must be underlined that the distinction between these two facets of the problem of the implementation of the reference model cannot be reduced to the traditional distinction positive/normative. Indeed, prescriptions can be derived from the reference models but such prescriptions must not be understood as norms. For example, the prescriptive interpretation given to P_1 ... P_7 in Savage's expected utility model, simply means that, if the decision-maker maximizes the expected utility relative to a subjective probability distribution, his or her choice is consistent with P_1, P_2 ... P_7. If we accept this evidence, we shall see first that, in observed choice situations, the alleged reference model is not actually implemented by the decision-maker; second, that the implementation of the reference model might raise logical difficulties which are brought to light by specific examples.

The problem of Slovic and Lichtenstein, unfortunately called 'Reversals Preference', provides an illustration of the first type (Slovic and Lichtenstein, 1968, 1971). Let us consider two lotteries A and B, each of them corresponding to a determined amount of money associated to a probability. The decision-makers who are tested have to choose one or the other, and, then, to assess the lowest monetary selling price, they ask for each of them noted $\pi(A)$ and $\pi(B)$. In many cases observed experimentally, $\pi(B) > \pi(A)$, whilst A is chosen against B by the decision-makers. An inconsistency seems to occur between the preference of the decision-maker i

when he chooses A, on the grounds of $A \succ_i B$ and the preference eliciting from the price evaluation where $\pi(B) > \pi(A)$.[2] However no precise interpretation exists of these two statements as long as the reference model is not taken into account.

The implementation of the expected utility model as the reference by the observed decision-makers requires a bridge between the two choice situations. The most common interpretation is provided by the assumption of a certainty equivalence c linking the two alternatives. According to the expected utility model $A = c(A)$ and $B = c(B)$. If π is understood as the monetary expression of the subjective certainty equivalence, $A \succ B$ and $\pi \approx c$ implies $\pi(a) > \pi(b)$ by transitivity. Inconsistency actually means that i's preferences are intransitive. But such an interpretation is bounded. It has been proved that $\pi = c$ if, and only if, the independence axiom of the expected utility model is also satisfied (Karni and Safra, 1986; Holt, 1986). Furthermore if $\pi \neq c$, the transitivity, or the independence axiom, is violated, but not necessarily both. To sum up, implementing the expected utility model in the experiments which showed the preference reversal phenomena requires that $\pi = c$. The observations of $A \succ B$ and $\pi(B) > \pi(A)$ are inconsistent with $\pi = c$, and thus reveal that the expected utility model is not currently implemented by the observed decision-makers. First, the experimental results are not sufficient to prove that the decision-makers implement an alternative reference model, and one can alternatively argue that they simply do not succeed in implementing the experimenter's expected utility reference model. Second, the observed results do not allow the identification of which prescription derived from the axioms of the experimenter's reference model is ruled out by the experiments.

Another interpretation of the 'Preference Reversal' has been proposed (Slovic, Griffin and Tversky, 1990; Tversky, Slovic and Kahneman, 1990). According to them, the cash equivalent $\pi(A)$ and $\pi(B)$ respectively associated with A and B measured in terms of minimum selling price can be considered as a certain equivalent in the previous sense if, and only if, what they call the 'invariance principle' is assumed in the reference model implemented by the observed decision-makers. By 'invariance', Tversky and Kahneman assume that the preference options are independent of their description (Tversky and Kahneman, 1986). Indeed, $\pi = c$ implies this condition. But the rejection of the invariance condition allows $A \succ_i B$ and $\pi(b) > \pi(A)$ to be consistent with the transitivity of the decision-makers' preferences. Therefore the observed results either violate the invariance or the transitivity, both of them being assumed by the expected utility model.

Let us try to synthesize these two interpretations. The experimental results lead to the rejection of at least one of the three following prescriptions inferred from the set of axioms of the theory supporting the expected utility model, namely (i) the preference transitivity, (ii) the independence condition, (iii) the invariance principle. It has been demonstrated by reference to the expected utility model that the rejection of (ii) implies the rejection of (i) (Karni and Safra, 1986). As, in the same reference model, (ii) implies (iii) the rejection of (ii) also implies the rejection of (iii). Therefore one can conclude from a logical point of view that the three prescription inferred from the expected utility model are jointly ruled out and that the question raised by the 'preference reversal' is like the Duhem problems.[3]

In any case, the origin of the failure to implement the expected utility sought to by the experimenters is to be found in the decision-maker's difficulty in eliciting certainty equivalence. Such an observation suggests two different lines of explanation. Either the failure is due to the design of the experiments which interact with the definition of the subject's preferences (Karni and Safra, 1986) or it is the consequence of the irrelevance of the reference model (Tversky, Slovic and Kahneman, 1990). But the set of empirical data derived from the experimental device does not provide a sufficient basis for discrimination between these two conjectures.

Let us move on to the computational aspect of the implementation. As long as the choice situation cannot be reduced to a one-shot decision and necessitates decision trees with many nodes, the implementation of the rational choice reference model requires the use of a computing machine. The aim of the machine is to translate the whole reference model in terms of unambiguous prescriptions to be applied by any decision-maker in the choice situation. Thanks to its programme, the available data are computed according to the model in order to give a relevant prescription for the decision-maker at each node of this choice situation.

The Centipede Game provides a classic example derived from the interpretation of this implementation which disturbs intuition. Let us then consider a two-player non-cooperative sequential game with perfect information, where the players move alternately. At the end of each sequence, the income is increased by a fixed amount but its allocation between the players is reversed. The number of the sequences is finite and the order to move is determined (one player moves first and the other last). It is assumed that Selten's Perfect Sub-Game is the rational choice model reference for both players and that it is common knowledge (Selten, 1975). Following Binmore's suggestion, the Zermelo algorithm provides a suitable programme for implementing the model in the choice situation, the prescription of which is to delete successively every weakly dominated pure strategy at each node back from the terminal node of the game (Binmore, 1990).

Indeed the solution computed by this machine for the first player is to pick up his share at the first node and thus end the game. A very counter-intuitive solution compares the pay-off which can be obtained at the last node. The argument that such a counter-example rules out the operational consistency of the reference model is based on the assumption that the Zermelo algorithm used by backward induction is sufficient to implement Selten's perfect rational choice model in the choice situations described by the Centipede Game. This assumption must be discussed. Let us underline its implications. If this is so, both players are supposed to believe in it and this belief must also be common knowledge for the players. Accordingly, the distinction disappears between the players and the machine they are using, and thus, between the players themselves.

The logic underlying this oversimplified machine can be summarized by two primitive propositions, namely P, 'the node$(\cdot)$ is rationally reached', and Q, 'at the node $(\cdot)$ the rational choice is ... '. Assuming n the finite number of the nodes, the main logical implications of the programmes are the following relations (i) $Q(n-1) \Rightarrow P(n)$; (ii) $P(n) \Rightarrow Q(n)$ and thus (iii) $Q(n-1) \Rightarrow Q(n)$. One can demonstrate that the rationality of the backward induction argument is entirely supported by (i), (ii) and (iii), the validity of which is not controversial. But it does not guarantee the possibility of assessing a true value at each possible proposition computed by the machine.

In order to demonstrate this point, let us consider a 'Centipede' choice situation where $n = 100$. No truth value can be assessed *sensu stricto* to $P^{(1)}$. Thus

$P(1) \Rightarrow Q^{(1)}$ is meaningless. Furthermore, $Q(100)$ is tautologically true, which rules out $Q^{(100-1)} \Rightarrow Q(100)$. The semantic of this machine cannot overlap the domain of the rational choice reference model. Therefore the decision-maker necessarily uses information out of this logical machinery to implement the abstract reference model. There is no reason for the players to use it in the same way as long as they have to choose at different nodes characterized by data which is not identical.

More subtly, the proposition Q contains some ambiguity. 'At node $(\cdot)$' really implies 'to be at node $(\cdot)$'. But 'to be at node $(\cdot)$' can be understood in different ways. Either it simply means to be in the position to explore mentally one of the sub-choice situations of the game, or it means to be actually in the sub-choice situation reached rationally through the process of implementation. This statement can be true for each node according to the first meaning, whilst it is only true for node 1 and false for all the others in the example, according to the second meaning. It can be argued on the grounds of the second meaning that being in a node other than node 1 implies being irrational and thus not implicit in proposition Q. A more general argument has been developed against the acceptance of the subjunctive conditional propositions on the type $Q(\cdot)$. 'If the decision-maker was in the node $(\cdot)$, he would rationally choose ... ' (Spohn, 1978, 1982). It is based on the rejection of a possible interpretation of counterfactuals which will be discussed later. Such a drastic manner of avoiding ambiguity leads to contesting Selten's Perfect Sub-Game as a rational choice model reference.

There is a temptation to link the observations which demonstrate that the reference model is not experimentally implemented and the logical limitations of its computability. In several experimental studies of the 'Centipede' example, the first player most often chooses not to stop the game at the first node (MacKelvey and Palfrey, 1992). This behaviour cannot be related to any logical failure in the prescription provided by the machine, which is unambiguous according to its programme. An argument in favour of a linkage may be developed in the following form. By choosing the programme's prescription at node 1 the first player makes the prescription useless at node 2 for the second player and stops the game. Except for $P(1)$, $P(\cdot)$ is necessarily false. As $P(1)$ has no truth value, a discrepancy appears between the actual dynamics of the choice situation and the computing machinery. Therefore it can be argued that the decision-makers in the experimental situation use this weakness of the model's implementation programme in order to transform the meaning of the initial Centipede Game. To appreciate the rationality of this process requires, once again, going beyond the initial formulation of the choice situation.

2.4 The Unexpected Result

The minimum required for a reference model of rational choice is to predict the option rationally chosen by any decision-maker in every choice situation which belongs to the domain of the model. All the counter-examples point out cases where this self-evident requirement seems to be ruled out. Three situations can be tentatively identified:

(a) a discrepancy between the option experimentally chosen by the presumed rational decision-makers and the option chosen by the implementation of the reference model in the choice situation;

(b) a suspicion about the rational validity of the option chosen by implementing the reference model of rational choice in the choice situation;

(c) a logical deadlock in the implementation of the relevant reference which fails to designate the option to be rationally chosen in the choice situation.

(a), (b) and (c) are not mutually exclusive. Let us recall that the experimental results (a) have been readily associated with the 'Centipede' Game (b). In the same spirit, but longer ago, the Prisoner's Dilemma Game was the subject of repeated experiment. Tested with two decision-makers, each of them knowing the number of the sequences, and also that the other knows them, the results obtained broadly verified (a), insofar as the decision-makers chose to cooperate (Rappoport and Chamma, 1965; Rappoport and Dale, 1973). At the same time, the implementation of strategic rationality by means of backward induction can lead to (b). As far as (c) is concerned, it necessarily induces the unpredictability of the assumed rational decision-maker's choice and, for this reason, verifies (a). An informal illustration can be associated with Newcomb's Problem. The variety of the solutions to the problem proposed by a sample of readers of the *Scientific American* can be considered as an empirical confirmation of its unpredictability (1974).[4]

It is not very surprising that the revelation of (b) may be associated with the observation of (a) but the existence of such a coincidence does not mean that the occurrence of (a) must necessarily be imputed to (b). Very stringent conditions are necessary to validate this inference. Decision-makers must choose their option according to the rational choice reference model of the experimenter and must know exactly how to implement it in the experimental choice situations. Generally speaking, either the tested decision-makers are specialized in decision theory, as in Allais' first experiment, and the observed results do not convey additional information on the logical background of the counter-example, or the sample of the tested decision-makers is selected among actual decision-makers, as in MacCrimmon's experiments (MacCrimmon, 1965, 1967) and one can suspect that these conditions are not satisfied.

To sum up, the recognition of a correspondence between (a) on the one hand and (b) or (c), on the other, is not very significant. As no direct correspondence can exist linking the counter-intuitive results brought out from experiments and the individual axioms of the theory isolated from various and sometimes approximate versions of the expected utility model, there is no real hope for the former to actually reveal paradoxes in the latter.

The fruitfulness of (a) is based on considerations other than (b) and (c). Their investigation can provide a stimulating starting point for inventing other models of rational choice. Either an alternative approach of rational choice is tentatively induced directly from the examination of compared experimental results, as for the 'prospect theory' elaborated by Kahneman and Tversky (1979), or the choice situations, which generate these counter-examples, are utilized in order to test the consistency of an alternative class of models, theoretically derived by extension and transformation of the expected utility model, as in the case of the non-expected utility models promoted by Machina (1987, 1989). Furthermore, (b) and (c) arise most often in dynamic choice situations with several decision-makers characterized by a mutual dependence on the reference model's implementation by each of them.

(a) Dynamic Choice Situations

A choice situation is considered dynamic as long as the information provided by the time order must be taken into account for implementing the reference model, even if the reference model itself is timeless (cf. Savage, 1954, pp. 10, 17 and 23). The comparison between the one-shot version and the finite repeated version of the Prisoner's Dilemma Game is illuminating for the role played by time. In both cases the chosen strategies, according to the model of perfect strategic rationality, are sub-optimal and, thus, troublesome for common sense. In the first case the Nash equilibrium is the pair of best strategic replies, consistent with the strategic rationality of the players and with the available information on the game. Therefore, in spite of its sub-optimality, it does not contain any logical paradox. In the second case indeed the perfect equilibrium solution is also consistent with the strategic rationality of the players, but not with all the available information for its complete implementation. Strictly speaking, backward induction is used in one-shot as well as in repeated games. But according to the information sets of the players, the question of 'forward induction' only appears in dynamics – i.e. as previously suggested, backward induction generates a pragmatic paradox by jumping across the content of the information for the decision-maker at each node actually reached (Pettit and Sugden, 1989). Generally speaking, to implement the reference model of rational choice via backward induction boils down to eradicating time information.

(b) More Than One Decision-Maker

The existence of at least two rational decision-makers does not imply that these choice situations can be framed in a game structure according to the narrow acceptance of game theory. Let us consider, for example, Newcomb's Choice Situation. Following the initial story, the decision-maker has no information about the preferences of the providential person who deposits or does not deposit $1 million in the opaque box. Treating this potential depositor as a player and framing Newcomb's Choice Situation in a two-person non-cooperative game remains questionable. Furthermore, even if game theory supplies a relevant framework for the choice situation, it does not necessarily follow that each decision-maker has sufficient information to know in which game he or she is actually playing in the case of incomplete information of each player on the other's preferences. Such a situation requires the investigation of the solutions derived from all the potential games consistent with the player's information (Schmidt, 1994).

Finally the extension of the choice situation initially studied with only two persons to n decision-makers facilitates the necessary refinement of the mutual knowledge analysis. A good example could be provided by the examination of choice situations closed to the Centipede Game with three interconnected players who decide rationally through various degrees of information. Different alternative assumptions about the information of each player on the game being played by the other players are to be introduced in the initial model in order to study their implications on rational decision-making processes.

Let us assume, for example, that the Centipede Game is played by three players named Mary, Peter and Paul. Mary plays a two-person Centipede Game with Peter and another with Paul. Peter and Paul do not know each other. Mary plays both games and becomes the linkage between the three-player set. Consequently we are not dealing with a three-person game. Furthermore Mary is supposed to choose sequentially her moves in the two games. Each equilibrium can no longer be analyzed *ceteris paribus*. Indeed, knowing that the two other players reached the equilibrium in the first game enables Mary (and indirectly the third player) to reach a better equilibrium according to its pay-offs. Therefore, the equilibrium in the first game provides additional information to the players of the second game which can modify the equilibrium of their own game.

(c) Mutual Dependence Implementation

The implementation of the rational choice reference model is strictly dependent on the knowledge of each decision-maker about its implementation by the others. Therefore, rationality is a mutually embedded notion, most often considered as 'common knowledge'. However, assuming the reference model as common knowledge does not guarantee that its implementation is also common knowledge. Revisiting the Deterrence Game illustrates this difficulty. Let us reformulate in a more elaborated form, as in Figure 3.5.

The monopolist is now Player 1 and the Competitor Player 2, which obliges reversing the pay-offs associated with the outcomes in the initial matrix (Figure 3.1). The deterrence statement of the monopolist *vis-à-vis* the competitor captures the specificity of the game. As previously mentioned, this can be formulated in the following conditional form b', 'If the competitor has chosen to play A, then b would have been implemented'. At node 1, Player 1 has to choose between b' and a', where a' only means the renunciation of the deterrence statement. The rationality of the monopolist's behaviour is dependent on the expected rationality of the

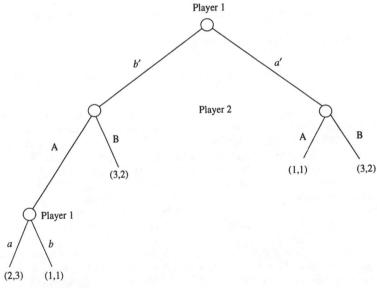

Figure 3.5 Model G3

competitor who will play at node 2. At node 2, the actual alternative is not the same for Player 2 according to the options chosen by Player 1 at node 1. Player 2 rationally chooses A if a' has been chosen by Player 1 on the grounds of Player 1's rational choice at node 3 (backward induction) and B if b' has been chosen. Knowing that Player 2 is rational, Player 1, as he rationally prefers that Player 2 chooses B, must also according to backward induction choose b' at the first node, i.e. the deterrence statement.

However, the knowledge of the competitor about the monopolist's rationality generates some suspicion about the rationality of the monopolist's behaviour in choosing b'. Indeed, Player 2 rationally chooses B at node 2, as long as he believes that the implementation of b by Player 1 is rational, which cannot be true because b is a dominated strategy. So Player 2 rationally infers that Player 1 will not implement b and, therefore, he rationally chooses A at node 2. Thanks to the rationality assumption as common knowledge,[5] the monopolist has known all this since the beginning of the game and, consequently, does not rationally choose b' at node 1. Thus the monopolist cannot rationally deter the competitor (Selten, 1978).

This argument is not quite convincing here, due to the pecularity of the choice situation described by the Deterrence Game (Schmidt, 1991). It does not take into account the distinction between the choice of a conditional strategy and the conditional way in which it is implemented. For the sake of clarification, this distinction will be translated into terms of counterfactuals. A conditional strategy noted b' is to be considered as a proposition p associated to a conditional logical operator. Two main conditional operators may be associated to p, namely the necessity operator noted $\square \rightarrow$ and the possibility operated $\lozenge \rightarrow$ (Lewis, 1973). If b' refers to the necessity operator, its meaning is expressed in the following form:

$\square\, p$: if A were to be chosen by the competitor, b would be implemented.

If b' refers to the possibility operator, its meaning is expressed in the following form:

$\lozenge\, p'$: if A were to be chosen by the competitor, b might be implemented by the monopolist.

Propositions p and p' do not mean the same thing, but, discriminating between p and p' goes beyond the counterfactual theory. According to Lewis's conception, counterfactuals introduce restrictions in possible worlds corresponding to an accessibility relation. In the Deterrence Game, $\square\, p$ implies that only (B, b) has a truth value and consequently must be considered as accessible, whilst $\lozenge\, p'$ implies that either (b, B) or (a, A) is accessible because, if the competitor chooses A, this does not preclude b not being implemented by the monopolist. The *raison d'être* of this restriction is to be derived from outside, either as the consequence of logical consideration (logical necessity) or as a consequence of physical laws (physical necessity).

In addition, choosing b' and conditionally implementing it is one and the same decision in spite of the time schedule, and b' means $\square\, p$ or choosing b' does not preclude the possibility for the monopolist to stop its implementation if the competitor has chosen a, and thanks to the time schedule b' means $\lozenge\, p'$. Choosing b' is a decision which is irrevocable in the first case but may be revoked in the second case. In the first case, the conditional implementation of b only depends on the competitor's decision to choose *a* at the second node. In the second case, the conditional implementation of *b* not only depends on the competitor's decision but also on an additional decision by the monopolist. One can argue that the rationality prescriptions of game theory are satisfied with $\Box$ *p* in the first type of deterrence game as well as with $\Diamond$ *p'* in the second type of deterrence game (but not $\Box$ *p* in the first and not $\Diamond$ *p'* in the second). The failure is not due to rationality prescription but to the laws derived from non-cooperative game theory for building counterfactuals.

3   TOWARDS AN UNDERSTANDING OF PATHOLOGICAL RATIONALITY

The inquiry in Section 2 has shown that only a few among the so-called paradoxes of rationality really correspond to a logical failure. Most of them offer various mixtures of imprecision in the available information, ambiguity in the meaning of prescriptions derived from the reference models and sometimes logical semantic impasses. In some cases, the existence of a deadlock is a direct consequence of imprecise data, as in the Ellsberg situation. In other cases, it is the result of equivocal statements, as in the deterrence situation. Finally, there are cases where the insufficiency of prior information or the ambiguity of prescriptive statements are associated with logical dead-ends. Section 3 is devoted to the investigation of their semantics. For the sake of clarity, the two components of the difficulties will be divided and the following analyses will be focused on the logical background of the observed pathologies of rationality.

Let us come back to the meaning of 'acting rationally' for economic decision-makers. According to a narrow acceptance, 'rationality', as used here, conveys pragmatic knowledge. As for its cognitive dimension, the reference to choice situations must be recalled. Accordingly, 'acting rationally' means choosing a rationally justifiable option among the possible actions consistent with the available data on the choice situation. Its cognitive implications are the following: (i) the decision-maker thinks rationally (or believes he thinks that he chooses rationally), (ii) the observer, who is most often the model-builder himself, knows (or believes he knows) that the decision-maker thinks (or believes he thinks) that he chooses rationally. In addition to (i) and (ii), when several decision-makers are the players of a game, it is assumed that (iii) each decision-maker knows (or believes he knows) that the other decision-makers think (or believe they think) that they choose rationally. In any case, according to (ii) and (iii), the cognitive dimension of any rational choice goes beyond strict individualism.[6]

As for the pragmatic dimension of rationality, let us recall that a rational choice is the result of the implementation of a reference model in a definite choice situation. The existence of a reference model provides the key to '*justifiability*'. Therefore choosing rationally implies believing that the reference model of rational choice is relevant. Apart from such a prerequisite, the implemetation necessitates two types of operations, namely (a) framing rationally the information deduced from the data, as well as from the knowledge of rationality previously listed, and (b) computing this information in a machinery system provided by the reference model to obtain the rational solution. According to the views of Kahneman and Tversky, framing must be considered as an unavailable step linking rationality as knowledge (its cognitive facet) to rationality as a computation (its pragmatic facet). Furthermore, the rational computing solution requires the implementation of a model, a process which cannot be reduced to a careful examination of the presumptive implications of its axioms. Thus, generally speaking, rationality is partly a specific kind of knowledge and partly a particular process to implement this knowledge in a given situation. The logical pathologies may be related to one or the other component. At one extremity, the identified deadlocks belong to the large class of knowledge paradoxes, whatever their denomination in philosophical literature (paradoxes of the knower, Kaplan and Montague, 1967; epistemic paradoxes, Burge, 1984; doxic paradoxes, Koons, 1992). More precisely, the complete understanding of a sentence like 'x knows that y is rational (or irrational) and then ...' generates difficulties for the analysis of a special sub-class of knowledge paradoxes. The statement of the deterrer in the Deterrence Game exemplified them. At the other extremity, logical difficulties occur with the implementation brought up by the machinery which computes programmes of rationality. Such kinds of trouble must be viewed in the light of the Church–Turing machine. The problem raised by the use of 'backward induction' in some finite repeated games like the Centipede Game provides an example. Both are connected because the implementation of rational processes also raises knowledge problems. Between these two extremes remains the crucial but rather informal landscape of framing the information for the computation. This is the main source of the pseudo-paradoxes.

3.1 Rationality and Paradoxes of Knowledge

Binmore observed rather elliptically that the difficulties with rationality which appear in game theory 'are nothing more than the Liar's Paradox and the Newcombe Paradox dressed up in mathematical language' (Binmore, 1990, p. 172). In the same spirit, Koons has theorized that Liar-like paradoxes are at the root of puzzles which emerge from many choice situations based on rational agent models, as in game theory (Koons, 1992, pp. ix–x and ch. 2). Such ideas must be elaborated. Indeed 'rational belief' is in some ways connected to 'thinking the truth' but it does not necessarily entail that the former can be completely reduced to the latter. A logical treatment of rational behaviour in decision-making theory raises two kinds of difficulty. The first refers to the use of propositions for describing actions, choice options and strategies; the second concerns the way of using truth values for understanding the kind of rational knowledge which operates in decision-making. Furthermore, the meaning of rational belief is still more specific and probably more complex in game theory than in individual rational choice theories. Because a game is an interrelated choice situation, rational knowledge is to be formalized hierarchically by order, from mutual first order to second and infinitum order, conventionally labelled 'common knowledge'. In addition, 'rational belief' must not be reduced to rational knowledge. Therefore, (i) shifting from the Liar's Paradox to Newcomb's Paradox and then (ii) from Newcomb's Paradox to game-theory situations requires additional investigations. To clarify the matter, similarities as well as differences between semantic paradoxes such as the Liar's Paradox, on the one hand, and the logical problems generated by rational belief in definite choice situations, on the other, will be set out.

(a) From 'Liar'-Like Paradoxes to Newcomb's Problems[7]

Let us consider the following two situations:

Situation 1[8] There are two boxes: one is empty and the other contains $1,000. A providential person commits himself to place $1 million in one box or the other, if he rationally thinks that the decision-maker chooses irrationally. The decision-maker has to choose between *A* and *B*: *A* = taking the box which is empty and *B* = taking the box which contains $1,000.

The decision-maker is assumed to know that the providential person always keeps his promise. Rationality is assumed to be common knowledge between the providential person and the decision-maker.

Situation 2[9] There are two boxes: one is opaque and empty; the other is transparent and contains $1,000. A providential person commits himself to place $1 million in the opaque box, if he expects that the decision-maker will choose the opaque box. The decision-maker has to choose between *C* and *D*: *C* = taking the opaque box and *D* = taking the two boxes.

The decision-maker is assumed to know that the providential person always keeps his promise, and that his expectation is reliable on the grounds of the decision-maker's rationality. Rationality is assumed to be common knowledge between the providential person and the decision maker. Framed in Savage's canvas, Situation 1 and Situation 2 are 'small worlds'; *S*1 and *S*2 are the two states of the world depending on whether the providential person places or does not place $1 million in the box, the two actions being noted *A* and *B* in Situation 1, and *C* and *D* in Situation 2. The corresponding matrices are identical in both situations (Figures 3.6 and 3.7).

It does not follow, however, that Situation 1 and Situation 2 described by the same matrices for the sake of a rational representation are identical in reality. We should first of all scrutinize Situation 1. As *B* strongly dominates *A*, choosing *B* cannot be irrational, though the irrationality of choosing *A* is questionable. As long as *A* is chosen, the final outcome is $1 million, i.e. $999,000 more than if *B* is chosen. In the end, neither *A* nor *B* can be considered as an irrational choice, and the decision-maker, as well as the providential person who commits himself to offer $1 million, seem to be in a deadlock. It is difficult for the decision-maker to rationally justify irrationality.

Situation 2 leads to a different conclusion. Here, *D*, which strongly dominates *C*, would be chosen rationally. Of course, the providential person, who knows that the decision-maker chooses rationally *D*, does not place $1 million in the opaque box. Nevertheless, one cannot infer from this that choosing *D* becomes irrational and that *C* must be rationally chosen. Indeed, the true state occurs before the decision-maker makes his or her choice and the outcomes associated to *D* are $1,000 more than the outcomes associated to *C*. There is no deadlock in Situation 2 but only the unfortunate occurrence of an incompatibility of rational choice with the optimality, a result of which resembles a Prisoner's Dilemma (Lewis, 1979; Sobel, 1985).

Two major differences emerged from the comparison between Situation 1 and Situation 2. First, in Situation 1 the providential person's self-commitment which determines the choice situation informs the decision-maker who thinks rationally

	S1	S2
A	1M	
B	1M +1000	1000

Figure 3.6 Situation 1

	S1	S2
C	1M	
D	1M +1000	1000

Figure 3.7 Situation 2

that he will choose irrationally. According to the cognitive implication of rationality, acting rationally for the decision-maker means to rationally believe that he or she chooses rationally. Rationally thinking to choose irrationally contradicts this. More generally, there is no evidence that such a proposition is meaningful. The difficulty is almost the same for every proposition asserting its denial, as in the Liar's Paradox. This is not exactly the same in Situation 2 where the providential person's self-commitment requires the predictability of the decision-maker's rationality.

Situation 1 generates a semantic difficulty for rationally justifying an irrational choice which does not exist in Situation 2. Situation 2 reveals a rather troublesome consequence of the strategic definition of the limitation of rationality. Game theorists are perfectly aware that the best strategic answer for a player in a given situation does not preclude the existence of other possible outcomes which would be better for him, but the rationality of players is bound by the rules of the game. Indeed in Situation 2, ($1 million + $1000) is a possible outcome, but it cannot be reached rationally by the decision-maker on account of his specific set of information on the choice situation.

This observation underlines the difference in the description of the two choice situations. Whereas in both cases the self-commitment of the providential person must be understood as a subjective conditional, their content is not identical. In Situation 1, the consequence of its implementation depends only on the acknowledgement that the decision-maker really does choose irrationally. As rationality is common knowledge, no difference exists between the providential person and the decision-maker on these grounds. Therefore the providential person is to be considered as a device. In any case, the commitment is implemented just after the decision-maker has made his choice. Thus the occurrence of $S1$ or $S2$ is causally dependent on choosing A or B in Situation 1, and Savage's approach cannot be used as a reference model.

In Situation 2, the consequence of the implementation does not depend on the actual choice of the decision-maker but on the providential person's expectation concerning his or her choice. Moreover, the commitment is implemented before the decision-maker has made his choice. The occurrence of $S1$ or $S2$ is causally independent from choosing C or D in Situation 2, even if the expectation of the providential person is based on the assumption that the decision-maker will choose rationally, and rationality is common knowledge. At best, the option chosen by the decision-maker ratifies the providential person's expectation.

Let us now move to the solution proposed for solving the Liar-like paradox in Situation 1. The logical background of the problem lies in the sentence 'the decision-maker thinks rationally that he chooses irrationally' which is neither rational nor irrational, as long as it is rational to think something true and irrational to think something false. Such a sentence can hardly be considered as a proposition in the classical logic sense because of a lack of truth values. It does not follow however that its content is meaningless. Indeed, as this sentence is not true, one can infer that it is true to assert that this sentence is not true. Therefore it is rational to think that this sentence is not rational and the contradiction then disappears (Parsons, 1974; Burge, 1979, 1984; Koons, 1992). The general line of reasoning can be summarized as follows for a proposition p, where p_0 and p_1 correspond to different levels of knowledge:

(1) $p_0 = p$ is not true $\Rightarrow$ it is irrational to think that p_0 is true;
(2) $p_1 = $ it is true that p is not true $\Rightarrow$ it is rational to think that p_1 is true; therefore
(3) It is rational to think that p is not true if $p = p_0$ and to think that p is true if $p = p_1$.

Unfortunately this elegant way of solving the semantic paradox does not help the decision-maker in choosing between A and B in situation 1 because he does not have sufficient knowledge to be able to discriminate between p_0 and p_1 to be applied to A and B.

The specific conditions of the choice situation prevent the decision-maker from evaluating the rationality of choosing A or B, because their truth or their falsity are not independent of this evaluation. Let us consider the proposition pA 'choosing A is rationally justifiable'. The truth of pA depends on the providential person's evaluation of the irrationality of *pA*. As rationality is common knowledge between the providential person and the decision-maker, the providential person's evaluation and that of the decision-maker are the same. Therefore, the truth of *pA* depends on the decision-maker's own evaluation. This would not be the same for an observer whose evaluation does not necessarily affect the truth of *pA*. At this stage, solving this kind of paradox seems to be the exclusive privilege of the observer, who may be the inventor of the choice situation (Koons, 1992, pp. 125–6).

A careful examination of the choice situation suggests another solution. The origin of the difficulty lies in the meaning of the providential person's commitment. It can be expressed in the following counterfactual proposition:

☐ *p*1 'If the providential person thought the decision-maker had chosen irrationally between *A* and *B*, then 1 million dollars would be deposited'.

Such a statement requires an investigation of the different levels of knowledge.

Level 1 The reference model provides the framework for understanding the first level. Rationality is assumed to be the maximization of the outcome by the decision-maker. Thus choosing *A* is irrational and, accordingly, *pA* is false, and choosing *B* rational and accordingly *pB* is true. Unfortunately the reference model cannot take into account the content of the providential person's commitment. The domain of the reference model is too narrow to cover the whole semantics of the choice situation, which requires exploring a second level of knowledge.

Level 2 Let us introduce a cognitive operator $T.R._xp$. '*x* thinks it rational that *p* ...' where to think something rational is to think that something is true (cf. above, p. 67). The content of rationality is the same as when it is defined in the reference model, i.e. the maximization of *x*'s outcome (Level 1). Furthermore, rationality is supposed to be common knowledge between the providential person and the decision-maker. Therefore *x* may designate either the providential person or the decision-maker (or both).

According to the reference model and to ☐ *p*1, $T.R._xpA$ and $\sim T.R._xpB$.

$T.R._xpA \Rightarrow p_A$ is not false.
$T.R._xpB \Rightarrow p_B$ is not true.

As previously noted p_A is false (Level 1) and not false (Level 2), whilst p_B is true (Level 1) and not true (Level 2).

It can be argued that Levels 1 and 2 are not sufficient to investigate the semantics of this choice situation and that it is necessary take into account other levels of knowledge. But using additional cognitive operators of order 2 ... *n* does not help, because the original difficulty generated by the coexistence of thinking it rationally (or thinking it rational to think ..., etc.) on the one hand, and choosing irrationally, on the other, remains.

The solution is to be found in another direction. If the knowledge of the providential person and the decision-maker on the choice situation is exactly the same, their actions are different. With the same initial knowledge, the decision-maker has to choose between *A* and *B*, whilst the providential person has to choose between depositing and not depositing $1 million. Due to the epistemic deadlock previously described, the decision-maker cannot choose between *A* and *B*, nor can the providential person choose between depositing and not depositing $1 million. However, this pragmatic feature of the situation provides additional information to the decision-maker. Indeed the providential person is unable to choose whether or not to deposit 1 million dollars. Being aware of this, the decision-maker will rationally choose *B*. Thanks to this pragmatic context, the validity of the reference is restored. For the sake of comparison, let us express the providential person's commitment in Situation 2 by the following counterfactual proposition:

☐ p_2 'If the providential person expected that the decision-maker would choose *C*, then $1 million would be deposited in the opaque box'.

Such a statement is not clear, precisely because the providential person is known as a 'highly reliable predictor'. In fact we need more information to justify the accessibility assignment, i.e. the kind of laws which support the providential person's expectations. It has been suggested that the liability of the providential person's prediction is based on the rationality assumption considered as a common knowledge between the providential person and the decision-maker (Selten and Leopold, 1982). Indeed, if the decision-maker is assumed to choose rationally, the expectation of the decision-maker's behaviour can be reduced from the evaluation of the option to be rationally chosen in the given choice situation. The providential person's commitment can be now understood as follows:

☐ p_2' 'If the providential person rationally thought that the decision-maker would choose *C*, the $1 million would be deposited in the opaque box'.

This interpretation illustrates some similarities between Situation 2 and Situation 1. At a first level, corresponding to the reference model of rational choice shared by the providential person and the decision-maker, choosing *D* is rational and then *pD* is true, whereas choosing *C* is irrational and, then, *pC* is false. Due to ☐ p_2', a second level of knowledge can also be imagined where choosing *C* is thought to be rational and choosing *D* is not thought to be rational. At first glance, the difficulty in Situation 2 seems like the epistemic Liar's Paradox in Situation 1.

However, the specific pragmatic conditions of the choice Situation 2 rules out the relevance of this similarity. For time-schedule considerations, the contradiction between the first level and the second level of knowledge does not exist for the decision-maker. When the decision-maker chooses between *C* and *D*, the providential person has already chosen and his choice has been implemented. The true evaluation of p_C and p_D does not depend on the option he has chosen and the first level reference model is quite sufficient to justify rationally his choice, and using the same formulation as in Situation 1 *T.R.X_pD and ~T.R.X_pC, X being the decision-maker*.

Thanks to rationality as common knowledge, the providential person rationally expects that the decision-maker will choose *D*. Therefore *x* can also designate the providential person who, according to his commitment, has no reason to deposit $1 million in the opaque box.

Is the Liar's Paradox associated to Newcomb's Problem a dummy-window? Selten and Leopold's interpretation of Newcomb's Problem enables us at one and the same time to formulate the question as a counterfactual and to eliminate its paradoxical connotation. In other versions of the Newcomb Story, the providential person is supposed to be a predictor who never fails in his predictions. If so, and whatever the interpretation proposed for the conditional necessity expressed by $\Box \ p_2$, the true evaluation of pC and pB is no longer independent from the chosen option because of the impossibility of discriminating between the choice of the decision-maker and its expectations by the providential person; but it does not lead to a paradox any more because the uncertainty disappears. According to $\Box \ p_2$, choosing C logically implies now that \$1 million has been deposited and D that it has not been deposited; C must be unhesitatingly chosen by the rational decision-maker (Levi, 1975, pp. 172–3).

Two general observations can be inferred from this comparison. First, the paradoxes of rational knowledge occur in relation to conditional statements expressed by counterfactual propositions. These types of paradoxes result from the meaning of their contents which appears self-contradictory, according to the level of knowledge considered by the decision-maker, as in the assertion of the liar in the Liar's Paradox. Therefore the existence of a Liar-like Paradox in decision-making theory is connected to the causal theory of rational choice. Second, the rationality of the decision-maker is strictly limited by his position in the pragmatic context of the choice situation. This kind of cognitive limitation is not inconsistent with the assumption of rationality as common knowledge between different persons in a given choice situation. Two persons may have the same information and assess the same truth value at the different levels of knowledge which are the same for both, whilst their understanding of the choice situation is not necessarily the same, due to their own positions in the decision-making process. The two examples described in Situation 1 and Situation 2 show that such pragmatic constraints on the cognitive conditions of the decision-maker sometimes enable him to solve unexpectedly the paradox of rational knowledge derived from the description of the choice situation.

(b) From Newcomb's Problems to Game-Theory Difficulties

The next question to be raised is the possibility of framing Situations 1 and 2 as games. It must be recalled that the bridge between the Liar's Paradox and the deadlock in the rational decision-making situation is provided by the counterfactual statement of the providential person. Therefore this linkage can be extended to game theory if the providential person can be correctly pictured as the player of a hypothetical game corresponding to the described choice situations.

Of course, the providential person is a decision-maker in a choice situation of more than one decision-maker, but each decision-maker belonging to such a choice situation is not necessarily the player of a game. Contrary to Selten and Leopold's assertion (1982, p. 198), the existence of two decision-makers for characterizing a choice situation is not a sufficient feature to guarantee the relevance of its description as a two-person game.

The player of a game is, at least, identified by (i) a set of pay-offs associated with the outcomes of the game, (ii) a separate set of information, (iii) a set of pure strategies. The providential person in Situation 1 does not satisfy (i) and (ii). Consequently A and B cannot be considered as strategies in the sense of game theory. Situation 1 cannot be pictured as a two-person game. As far as Situation 2 is

	S'1	S'2	S'3	S'4
C	1M	1M	0	0
D	1M 1000	1M 1000	0 1000	0 1000

S'1 =   the providential person places correctly $1M in the opaque box
S'2 =   the providential person places incorrectly $1M in the opaque box
S'3 =   the providential person does not place correctly $1M in the opaque box
S'4 =   the providential person does not place incorrectly $1M in the opaque box

Figure 3.8   The providential person's expectation

concerned, it has been assumed with Selten and Leopold that the providential person was a player on the grounds of the assumption of rationality as common knowledge. The question is to be revisited, starting from the original version of Newcomb's choice situation where this assumption is not required.

Let us first of all clarify the relationship between the original version of Newcomb's Story and the Liar's Paradox. If all available data on the choice situation are effectively supposed to be common knowledge between the decision-maker and the providential person (Nozick, 1969, p. 113), it does not follow that rationality is common knowledge between them. The decision-maker knows that the providential person's decision to place $1 million in the opaque box is based on his own expectations about his personal choice between *C* and *D* and that the providential person knows that the decision-maker knows it and so on ..., but the decision-maker does not know more. The providential person's expectations regarding the option chosen by the decision-maker can be either true or false. Therefore the two initial possible states of the world S_1 and S_2 (see Situation 2 above) must each split into two states according to the correct or incorrect expectation held by the providential person regarding the action chosen by the decision-maker. The choice situation is now framed in Figure 3.8.

Figure 3.8 does not reproduce the standard Savagian format for framing the rational choice situation (Savage, 1954, p. 14 *et seq.*; and Figure 3.6 above). Before the beginning of the decision-making process, the set of possible states of the world corresponding to Savage's definition is composed by S'1, S'2, S'3 and S'4. But as soon as the decision-maker has made his choice, this set is reduced either to (S'1, S'4) or to (S'2, S'3) according to the choice of *C* or *D* by the decision-maker. Strictly speaking, choosing *C* precludes S'2 and S'3 , and choosing *D*, S'1 and S'4 (see the hatched squares in Figure 3.8). The definition of the actual set of the possible states of the world by the decision-maker is not quite independent of his choice. Does this dependence rule out the Savage principle asserting that the states are independent of the chosen action? The relevance of Savage's reference model for framing Newcomb's situation is traditionally discussed in these terms (see the causality problem in decision-making theory: Gibbard and Harper, 1978; Lewis, 1981;

Jeffrey, 1981, 1983; Eells, 1982, 1984).

Let us explain how such a question can be related to the Liar's problem of knowledge. According to Savage's views, every choice situation has to be framed by means of the triplet $\{S, A, C\}$, where S is the set of the possible states of the world, A the set of the available actions for the decision-maker, and C the set of the consequences, i.e. the set of outcomes to be associated to each action. Acting rationally for the decision-maker means choosing a within A maximizing the decision-maker's preference order defined on C. If $s \in S$ is dependent on $a \in A$, the decision-maker cannot choose rationally because the set of consequences actually obtained will not be independent of his preference evaluation. The decision-maker is unable to designate the action to be rationally chosen for the same reason that the truth of the Liar's statement cannot be evaluated. Following Burge's colourful expression, one can speak of an 'incestuous' evaluation (Burge, 1984, p. 277) which generates a logical deadlock in both cases. Therefore, the conditions for the actions to be independent of the states of the world may be understood as a way of escaping the Liar-like paradox of knowledge in rational choice situations.

Let us recall that the occurrence of one of the four initial states of the world (the 'true state') remains all the more independent of the chosen action because it occurs before the decision-maker's choice. A distinction between two kinds of knowledge is thus necessary in order to describe Newcomb's Problem in Savage's terms. The first concerns the definition of the set of the states of the world which refers to the Savagian concept of the 'small world' (Savage, 1954, pp. 82–9). The second concerns the states of the world which will actually be obtained. During his deliberations, the decision-maker does not only ignore which state of the world will actually be obtained but also to which small world it belongs. This second uncertainly disappears as soon as the decision-maker has chosen, but the first uncertainty remains.[10]

To sum up, the origin of the specific problem raised by Newcomb's Choice Situation is not to be found in the content of the providential person's commitment itself, but in the information concerning the reliability which is associated to it, through the given evaluation of the providential person's predictive performance. If the decision-maker knows nothing about this predictive performance, he would rationally choose D on the grounds of the dominance principle (complete ignorance). Likewise, he would rationally choose C if he knew that this predictive performance is perfect, which means that the truth value of the providential person's commitment is 1, dropping any kind of uncertainty. Nevertheless, whatever the reliability of the providential person's prediction, no causal dependence exists between the decision-maker's choice and the providential person's action.

The transformation of Newcomb's Choice Situation in a two-person game may be understood as an attempt to specify the meaning of the information about the reliability of the providential person's previsions. This information is relevant for the decision-maker as long as he is concerned, i.e. it refers to his own choice in the given situation. Let us note x for the decision-maker, y for the providential person and p^* for the proposition which describes the option rationally chosen by the decision-maker.

As the decision-maker is assumed to be rational, $xP^* \Rightarrow T.R._x p^*$. If the providential person knows that the decision-maker is rational, $T.R._y(T.R._x p^*) \Rightarrow T.R._y p^*$. Thus predicting p^* means for y almost the same thing as thinking p^*

rational. Under these cognitive conditions on rationality, *y* maximizes his prediction of *x*'s choice. *y*'s purpose is supposed to be predicting correctly *x*'s choice, and qualitative values noted 1 and 0 can be associated to the outcomes of the game, according to the validity (or the non-validity) of *y*'s prediction. 'Predicting correctly' is then assimilated to 'thinking the truth' Selten and Leopold (1982, p. 199).

The reasoning for justifying the relevance of this game-theoretical framing can be summarized as follows:

(1) *y* is a reliable predictor of *x*'s choice;
(2) *x* will choose rationally in the choice situation;
(3) *y* knows that *x* will choose rationally in the choice situation.

(1), (2) and (3) are information directly provided by Newcomb's Original Story. Selten and Leopold tend to demonstrate that (1), (2) and (3) imply that *y*'s prediction of *x*'s choice is based on rationality and, therefore, that *y* as well as *x* acts rationally. Their argument is developed on the grounds of a counterfactual of the type 'if *y*'s prediction were not based on rationality assumption, either *y* would not be a reliable predictor or *x* would not choose rationally'. The validity of the argument remains questionable on the two points.

The negation of this counterfactual is to be analyzed. If *x* chooses rationally, then *y* is not a reliable predictor but a predictor who cannot fail in predicting *x*'s choice. Thus it does not refer to (1) but to a stronger assumption (*y* never fails in predicting the fact that *x*'s choice leads to the designation of *D* as *x*'s rational choice on the grounds of the solution of the game; on the other hand, if *y* never fails in predicting *x*'s choice, then *C* is the rational choice for *x* (as previously shown on grounds of lack of uncertainty). Therefore the counterfactual is to be revised as follows: 'If *y*'s prediction were not based on the rationality assumption, then *x* would not choose rationally.'

Let us suppose now that *y* chooses to deposit $1 million in the box. Does it necessarily follow that *x* when taking the two boxes will not choose rationally? All to the contrary, one can argue that the assumption of rationality is not violated but that the content of *y*'s initial commitment is ruled out and, consequently, *y* fails in his prediction in spite of (3). The only way to avoid this puzzling case is to assume that the commitment only ratifies in advance *x*'s choice. But, if this is so, *y*'s commitment does not provide any additional information to *x*. Indeed, because of this self-reference hypothesis, the ambiguity disappears and there is no room for a paradox. The problem initially raised by Newcomb's Choice Situation is not solved but transformed.

This example shows that it is not sufficient to assume that *x* is rational and that *y* knows that *x* is rational to guarantee that *y* is also rational when *y*'s decision is closely related to *x*'s choice. There is no smooth continuity from Savage's concept of rationality to game theory's definition of rationality. Knowing that the other players are rational is an intrinsic component of the self-rationality of each player. The definition of each player's own rationality refers to the other players' rationality (and the reverse), so the concept of rationality is self-referential in game theory. Its introduction in order to solve Newcomb's Problem operates as a *deus ex machina*.

Thus, the semantic difficulty of choosing rationally something irrational which can be related to the Liar's Paradox (cf. Situation 1) is now dressed up in a very different way in game theory. The question is no more to think rationally an irrational option but to play rationally vis-à-vis an irrational player. In the first case, every possible action is false or true depending on the level of knowledge considered by the decision-maker; in the second case, there is no possible strategy to be chosen by the player of the game. Therefore, game theorists protect themselves in assuming both rationality as common knowledge and backward induction.

Notes

1. The counter-example imagined by Allais in 1952 is based on the expected utility function derived from the von Neumann and Morgenstern axiomatic formulation of utility theory (Allais, 1979, pp. 445–51). It must be noticed that the von Neumann and Morgensterm axiomatization of utility does not explicitly take into account the independence axiom. This condition was formally expressed later by Savage as the 'sure-thing principle' (Savage, 1954, pp. 21–6) but was anticipated by Nash in the framework of game theory (Nash, 1953).

2. $\succ_i$ symbolizes i's subjective preferences whereas $>$ symbolizes the objective inequality between $\pi(A)$ and $\pi(B)$. The relationship between A and B and $\pi(A)$ and $\pi(B)$ does not necessarily have the same meaning.

3. At the beginning of the century, the French physicist P. Duhem argued that falsifying a theory in physics requires identifying which hypothesis is ruled out by the actual experiment. Such a condition is rarely satisfied because most often several hypotheses are at the same time ruled out by a given experiment (Duhem, 1906 [1981]). This situation, labelled as Duhem's methodological problem, has been extended to economics on the occasion of Allais's counter-example discussion (see Mongin, 1987).

4. The variety of explanations provided by the readers of *Scientific American* for justifying the proposed solutions reveals that Newcomb's Choice Situation has been understood in various ways according to different reference models. These solutions suggest the possibility of framing the situation in alternative reference models of rational choice. For a discussion of the proposed solution, see MacCrimmon and Larsson (1979, p. 393).

5. Rationality as common knowledge is obviously a sufficient condition for supporting this argument but it is not necessary. The argument of rationality only requires that Player 1 knows that Player 2 knows that he is rational.

6. Investigating rational choice requires (i) and (ii) for individual choice situations and (i), (ii) and (iii) for game situations. One can also imagine situations where (iii) is replaced by (iv), another decision-maker knows (or believes he or she knows) the initial decision-maker thinks (or believes he thinks) that he chooses rationally. This other person is labelled as a 'being' or a 'providential person' for underlining the cognitive asymmetry between the initial decision-maker and the other (see Newcomb's Story). Definitely, situations of rational choice where rationality can be understood in a purely individualistic prospect do not exist. But it does not mean that its collective dimension has the same content in each of these three cases.

7. The Newcomb Story brings together various problems. In a provocative paper entitled 'Newcomb's Many Problems', Levi identifies four cases raising different problems (Levi, 1975). We sympathize with Levi's argument, even if we do not share all his conclusions.

8. This is a revised version of a story imagined by Gaifman (1983) and extensively discussed by Koons (1992).

9. One can recognize one of the many versions of the Newcomb Story.

10. Other versions of the Bayesian decision-making theory have been proposed. Jeffrey's

theory is one of the most elaborate. Instead of reasoning in terms of states, Jeffrey prefers to refer directly to a probability matrix of the conditions under which the consequences are obtained. Accordingly the probabilities of these conditions need not be independent of the act (Jeffrey, 1965, 1983). Translated into Jeffrey's terms, Newcomb's Choice Situation necessitates introducing a distinction between the decision-maker's conditional and unconditional probabilities about his own predicament. Jeffrey calls his revised decision theory 'ratificationism' (Jeffrey, 1981, 1983).

References

Allais, M. (1952) 'Fondements d'une théorie positive des choix comportant un risque et critiques des postulats et axioms de l'école américaine', *Econométrie*, vol. XL (Paris: CNRS).

Allais, M. (1979) 'The So-Called Allais Paradox of Rational Decision Under Uncertainty', in *Expected Utility Hypotheses and the Allais Paradox*, M. Allais and O. Hagen (eds) (Dordrecht: Reidel Publishing).

Allais, M. (1987) 'Allais Paradox', in *The New Palgrave Dictionary*, J. Eatwell, M. Milgate and P. Newman (eds) (London: Macmillan).

Arrow, K. and F. Hahn (1971) *General Competitive Analysis* (San Francisco: Holden-Day).

Arrow, K. (1987) 'Economic Theory and the Hypothesis of Rationality', in *The New Palgrave Dictionary*, J. Eatwell, M. Milgate and P. Newman (eds) (London: Macmillan).

Binmore, K. (1990) *Essays on the Foundations of Game Theory* (Oxford: Basil Blackwell).

Burge, T. (1984) 'Epistemic Paradox', *Journal of Philosophy*, vol. 81.

Duhem, P. (1906) [1981] *La théorie physique, son objet, sa structure* (Paris, Vrin).

Eells, E. (1982) *Rational Decision and Causality* (Cambridge: Cambridge University Press).

Eells, E. (1984) 'Newcomb's Many Solutions', *Theory and Decision*, vol. 16.

Ellsberg, D. (1961) 'Risk Ambiguity and the Savage Axioms', *Quarterly Journal of Economics*, vol. 75.

Gaifman, H. (1983) 'Infinity and Self-Applications', *Erkenntnis*, no. 20.

Gibbard, A. and W. L. Harper (1978) 'Counterfactuals and Two Kinds of Expected Utility', in *Foundation and Applications of Decision Theory*, C.A. Hooker, J.J. Leach and E.F. MacClennen (eds) (Dordrecht: Reidel).

Holt, C. (1986) 'Preference Reversals and the Independence Axiom', *American Economic Review*, vol. 76.

Jeffrey, R. (1965) (2nd edn 1983) *The Logic of Decision* (Chicago: Chicago University Press).

Jeffrey, R. (1981) 'The Logic of Decision Defended', *Synthèse*, vol. 48.

Kahneman, D. and A. Tversky, (1979) 'Prospect Theory: An Analysis of Decision Under Risk', *Econometrica*, vol. 47.

Kahneman, D., P. Slovic, and A. Tversky, (eds) (1982) *Judgement Under Uncertainty: Heuristics and Biases* (Cambridge: Cambridge University Press).

Kaplan, D. and R. Montague (1967) 'A Paradox Regained', *Notre-Dame Journal of Formal Logic*, vol. 1.

Karni, E. and Z. Safra (1986) 'Preference Reversals and Observability of Preferences by Experimental Methods', *Economic Letters*, vol. 20.

Koons, R.C. (1992) *Paradoxes of Belief and Strategic Rationality* (Cambridge: Cambridge University Press).

Leijonhufjud, A. (1992) 'Is Macroeconomics Too Rational?', mimeo.

Levi, I. (1975) 'Newcomb's Many Problems', *Theory and Decision*, vol. 6.

Levi, I. (1986) 'The Paradoxes of Allais and Ellsberg', *Economics of Philosophy*, vol. 2, no. 1.

Lewis, D. (1973) *Counterfactuals* (Cambridge Mass.: Harvard University Press).

Lewis, D. (1979) 'Prisoner's Dilemma is a Newcomb Problem', *Philosophy of Public Affairs*, vol. 8, no. 3.

Lewis, D. (1981) 'Causal Decision Theory', *Australian Journal of Philosophy*, vol. 80.

MacCrimmon, K. (1965) *An Experimental Study of the Decision-Making Behavior of Business Executives* (Los Angeles: University of California) mimeo.

MacCrimmon, K. (1967) 'Consistent Choice and the Allais Problem: Theoretical Considerations and Empirical Results', *Western Management Science*, UCLA, Working Paper no. 130.

MacCrimmon, K.R. and S. Larson, (1979) 'Utility Theory: Axioms versus Paradoxes', in *Expected Utility Hypotheses and the Allais Paradox*, M. Allais and O. Hagen (eds) (Dordrecht: Reidel).

Machina, M. (1987) *Economic Theory of Individual Behavior Toward Risk: Theory, Evidence and New Directions* (Cambridge: Cambridge University Press).

Machina, M. (1989) 'Dynamic Consistency and Non-Expected Utility Models of Choice Under Uncertainty', *Journal of Economic Literature*, vol. XXVII, no. 3.

MacKelvey, R.D. and R.T. Palfrey (1992) 'An Experimental Study of the Centipede Game', *Econometrica*, vol. 60.

Malinvaud, E. (1991) *Voies de Recherches Macroéconomiques* (Paris: Odile Jacob).

Mongin, P. (1987) 'Problèmes de Duhem en théorie de l'utilité espérée', *Fundementa Scientiae*, vol. 9, no. 2/3.

Nash, J.F. (1953) 'Two-Person Cooperative Games', *Econometrica*, vol. 21.

Nozick, R. (1969) 'Newcomb's Problem and Two Principles of Choice', in *Essays in Honor of Carl G. Hempel*, N. Resher (ed.) (Dordrecht: Reidel).

Parsons, C. (1974) 'The Liar's Paradox', *Journal of Philosophy*, vol. 3.

Pettit, P. and Sugden, R. (1989) 'The Backward Induction Paradox', *Journal of Philosophy*, vol. 86.

Rappoport, A. and A.M. Chamma, (1965) *The Prisoner's Dilemma*, (Ann Arbor: University of Michigan Press).

Rappoport, A. and P.S. Dale, (1973) 'The "End" and "Start" Effects in the Iterated Prisoner's Dilemma', *Journal of Conflict Resolution*, vol. 11.

Reny, P. (1992) 'Rationality in Extensive Form Games', *Journal of Economic Perspectives*, vol. 6, no. 4.

Rosenthal, R.W. (1981) 'Games of Perfect Information, Predatory Pricing and Chain Store Paradox', *Journal of Economic Theory*, vol. 25.

Savage, L.J. (1954) (2nd edition 1972) *The Foundations of Statistics* (New York: John Wiley).

Schmidt, C. (1990) 'Dissuasion, rationalité et magasins à succursales multiples', *Revue d'économie politique*, vol. 33.

Schmidt, C. (1991) *Penser la Guerre, Penser l'Économie* (Paris: Odile Jacob).

Schmidt, C. (1994) 'Preference, Knowledge Belief and Crisis In the International Decision-Making Process: A Theoretical Approach Through Qualitative Games', in *Game Theory and International Relations*, P. Allan and C. Schmidt (eds) (London: Edward Elgar).

Selten, R. (1975) 'Re-examination of the Perfectness Concept for Equilibrium Points in Extensive-Games', *International Journal of Game Theory* vol. 4.

Selten, R. (1978) 'The Chain-Store Paradox', *Theory and Decision*, vol. 9.

Selten, R. and U. Leopold, (1982) 'Subjective Conditionals in Decision and Game Theory', in *Philisophy of Economics*, Heidelberg; (Springer-Verlag).

Slovic, P. and A. Tversky, (1974) 'Who Accepts Savage's Axiom?', *Behavioral Science*, vol. 19.

Slovic, P. and S. Lichtenstein, (1968) 'The Relative Importance of Probabilities and Payoffs in Risk-Taking', *Journal of Experimental Psychology*, Monography 78, 3.

Slovic, P. and S. Lichtenstein, (1971) 'Reversal of Preferences Between Bids and Choices in Gambling Decisions', *Journal of Experimental Psychology*, vol. 89.

Slovic, P., D. Griffin and A. Tversky (1990) 'Compatibility Effects in Judgement and Choice', in *Insights in Decision-Making: A Tribute to Hillel J. Einhorn*, R.M. Hogarth (ed) (Chicago: The University of Chicago Press).

Slovic, P., S. Lichtenstein, and B. Fishoff (1982) 'Response Mode, Framing and Information Processing Effects in Risk Assessment', in *New Directions for Methodology of Social and Behavioral Science: Questions Framing and Response Consistency*, R.M. Hogarth (eds) (San Francisco: Jossey-Bass).

Sobel, J.H. (1985) 'Not Every Prisoner's Dilemma is a Newcomb Problem', in *Paradoxes of Rationality and Cooperation*, R. Campbell and L. Sowen (eds) (Vancouver: The University of British Columbia Press).

Spohn, W. (1978) *Grundlagen des Entscheidungstheorie* (Kronberg: Springer Verlag).

Spohn, W. (1982) 'How to Make Sense of Game Theory', in W. Stegmuller, W. Balzer and W. Spohn (eds) *Philosophy of Economics*, (Heidelberg: Springer-Verlag).

Tversky, A. and D. Kahneman, (1986) 'Rational Choice and the Framing of Decisions', in *Rational Choice*, R.M. Hogarth and M.W. Reder (eds) (Chicago: University of Chicago Press).

Tversky, A., P. Slovic, and D. Kahneman, (1990) 'The Causes of Preference Reversal', *American Economic Review*, vol. 80.

Comment
Franco Donzelli

UNIVERSITÀ DI MILANO

The two main parts of Professor Schmidt's chapter are Sections 2 and 3. Section 2 is chiefly aimed at drawing a distinction between two types of 'paradoxes of rationality', which, for the sake of brevity, might be called 'genuine' and 'spurious' paradoxes, respectively. Section 3 is instead devoted to a discussion of a few problems concerning those paradoxes that the author deems to be of the 'genuine' type. My comments will mainly focus on the critical arguments developed in Section 2 of the chapter.

Right at the beginning of that Section (p. 50), and again towards the end of it, Schmidt suggests a taxonomy of the phenomena generally labelled as 'paradoxes of rationality' in the literature. According to the proposed classification, the following three cases should be distinguished:

(a) a first case occurs when one can observe 'a discrepancy between the option experimentally chosen by the presumed rational decision-makers and the option chosen by the implementation of the reference model in the choice situation';

(b) a second case occurs when there is room for some 'suspicion about the rational validity of the option chosen by implementing the reference model of rational choice in the choice situation'; and, finally,

(c) a third case occurs when there appears to exist 'a logical deadlock in the implementation of the relevance reference model, which fails to designate the option to be rationally chosen in the choice situation'.

Schmidt explicitly recognizes that, in practice, the boundaries between the three classes of phenomena cannot always be precisely drawn. Yet the whole of his discussion in Section 2 tends to suggest that, at least in principle, one should try one's best to make use of the above classification in order to systematize an otherwise chaotic picture. Precisely, what is suggested is that one should group under (a) all those situations where experimental tests appear to provide negative evidence against the set of axioms on which some specified model of rational choice or behaviour is built. In this context, experimental tests should be taken to mean either laboratory or informal tests involving real-life experimental subjects. Well-known examples of paradoxes falling under this heading are generated, e.g., by Allais' and Ellsberg's classical experiments or by the more recent laboratory tests producing the so-called phenomenon of 'preference reversals'; all these examples are discussed at length in the chapter. Instead, one should group under (b) all those situations where it is the very model-builder (or, more generally, an external examiner or theoretician) who is led by his 'intuition' to call into question the plausibility of the concept of rationality underlying the proposed model of rational choice or behaviour. No public experiment of the type considered under (a) is really needed is this case to prompt the critical scrutiny of the model-builder; but his 'intuition' is almost invariably assisted by some sort of thought experiment, which often simply consists in imagining what his behaviour would be should he find himself in the choice situation described by the model under discussion. A well-known example of a paradox falling under this heading is represented by Selten's Chain-Store Paradox; once again, this example is repeatedly taken up in the chapter. Finally, those situations that give rise to paradoxes or problems of a purely logical character (due, in particular, to some inconsistency in the axioms or definitions underlying the model under question) should be grouped under (c). According to the author, the so-called 'Newcomb Problem' may be taken as a paradigmatic example of this class of paradoxes.

Although the discussion in Section 2 is very broad and touches upon a number of different issues, the main point which is made therein seems to me to be the following: only those situations that are grouped under heading (c) do in effect give rise to 'genuine' paradoxes of rationality; on the contrary, those situations that are categorized under (a) and, probably,[1] under (b) as well, can only give rise to 'spurious' pseudo-paradoxes, whose relevance has consequently to be dismissed.

The central argument goes as follows. Any concept of rationality can only be fruitfully discussed with reference to a well-defined model of rational choice or behaviour; hence, given any concept of rationality which one is willing to critically examine, one is bound to specify the so-called 'reference model' in terms of which the examination has to take place. But, according to Schmidt, in most, if not all, experimental tests which have been proposed in this area the reference model is not clearly specified by the experimenter: specifically, the data provided by the experimenter are insufficient, the choice situation is imprecisely specified or ambiguous, and the rules for implementing the prescriptions of the reference model are not clearly stated, so that in the end the decision-makers who are subjected to the test are not able to uniquely identify the reference model which is in the mind of the person who originally designed the experiment. But, due to this identification problem, whatever evidence can be gathered from the experiment cannot be used against (or, for that matter, in favour of) the characterization of rationality which is implicit in a reference model which cannot be clearly identified. Hence, the many paradoxes of rationality which have emerged over time in connection with experimental situations falling under heading (a) ought really to be regarded as pseudo-paradoxes, which do not deserve all the attention that they have been able to attract in the more or less recent past. A similar criticism is then apparently extended also to the thought experiments on which the paradoxes grouped under (b) ultimately rest.

The above thesis is then illustrated by Schmidt by means of examples drawn from both the field of decision theory strictly speaking (where expected utility theory, and especially the so-called Allais and Ellsberg paradoxes, are discussed at length) and the field of game theory (where some problems connected with backward induction, subgame perfection, as well as other solution concepts characteristic of non-cooperative game theory are examined).

In my opinion, Schmidt's argument, as summarized above, is generally unconvincing. But what seems to me to be definitely wrong is the interpretation of the available experimental evidence which is suggested by him, as well as the reasons he gives for belittling the relevance of such evidence.

Before trying to argue my criticism, I would like to recall a distinction that, though it has been made innumerable times, is sometimes neglected. In building a model of rational behaviour, the model-builder may have one of two different motivations in mind. The first motivation has to do with the possible use of models of rational behaviour in formally characterizing the intuitive concept of rational behaviour; when so understood, the theory is normative or prescriptive in nature. The second motivation, instead, concerns the possible use of models of rational behaviour in explaining and predicting actual behaviour; when so conceived, the theory has of course a positive (or explanatory or predictive) character.

The relevance of this distinction has been repeatedly stressed in the literature. Sen (1987, p. 74), for example, writes: 'We have to make a clear distinction between (1) what type of behaviour might be described as *rational*, and (2) what rational behaviour models might be useful in making predictions about *actual* behaviour. These different questions are not, of course, independent of each other. But the first step in pursuing their interrelation is to recognize the distinction between the two questions.'

What I would like to add, at this point, is that problems (if not paradoxes) concerning rationality may, and indeed do, arise in both respects: there exist situations where the prescriptive value of a given model of rational behaviour can be legitimately questioned, as well as situations where it seems legitimate to scrutinize the predictive power of a given model of rational behaviour. However, the methods of inquiry are necessarily specific to either case.

Laboratory experiments and informal tests involving real-life subjects are characteristically designed with a view to assessing the predictive power of a given model. It is fair to say, however, that if the results of a number of such tests turn out to be systematically negative as far as the predictive power of a certain model is concerned, this may indirectly lead (though by no means invariably leads) to calling into question the prescriptive value of that model as well. As to the prescriptive validity of models of rational behaviour, it is a commonly held view that such dimension of rationality is much harder to test than the former. According to Myerson (1991, p. 22), for example, in order to test the prescriptive validity of a certain model of rational behaviour 'one can only ask whether a person who understands the model would feel that he would be making a mistake if he did not make decisions according to the model'. Hence, according to this view, the characteristic way (or even the only way) by means of which the model-builder or an external examiner can try to assess the prescriptive value of a given model of rational behaviour is to resort to some kind of carefully designed thought experiment.

Now, as we have seen, paradoxes or problems arising in connection with public experimental tests are grouped by Schmidt under heading (a) in his taxonomy; paradoxes or problems arising in connection with thought experiments, aiming to assess the prescriptive validity of a certain model of rational behaviour, are grouped under (b); and, finally, paradoxes or problems of a purely logical character are grouped under (c). But then to suggest that all 'genuine' paradoxes or problems concerning rationality arise in connection with case (c), while only 'spurious' pseudo-paradoxes can arise in connection with case (a) and, probably, case (b) as well, is tantamount to suggesting that neither the predictive nor the prescriptive role of models of rational behaviour can ever be legitimately tested.

This conclusion is sufficiently at variance with all the received view to rouse some suspicion about its validity. But the suspicion grows greater and greater when one considers the examples by means of which Schmidt tries to illustrate and support his thesis.

Take, for instance, the first and best-known example of an experimental test in decision theory, i.e., the test resulting in the so-called Allais paradox. Schmidt suggests that it would be incorrect to interpret the experimental evidence produced by Allais' and similar experiments as demonstrating that the axioms of expected utility theory have been violated by the majority or modal choices made by the experimental subjects. The reason for this is that, according to Schmidt, in this and similar experiments the data provided by the experimenter are insufficient for the subjects of the experiment to be able to identify the reference model which is in the mind of the experimenter, that is, in the case under discussion, expected utility theory. In particular he complains that, while the prizes associated with the lotteries to be ranked are specified in money terms, no utility of money function is specified, so that, within the context of the experiment, it would be impossible for the decision-makers to maximize expected utility, as required by expected utility theory.[2] Thus, so the argument goes, if the decision-makers are not even able to maximize expected utility, given the data of the experiment, how can the result of the experiment be used to assert that the axioms of expected utility theory have been violated?

But, in my opinion, this argument is faulty. Schmidt seems to forget that, according to expected utility theory, a von Neumann–Morgenstern utility function has to be constructed, and can indeed be constructed, starting from preferences over lotteries, in accordance with the axioms of the theory. So a von Neumann–Morgenstern utility function cannot possibly be part of the data of an experiment aiming to test the predictive validity of expected utility theory. Moreover he seems to forget that the chief negative result of Allais' and similar experiments is that *no* such utility function exists which is consistent with the majority or modal choices made by the decision-makers.[3] Hence, one can conclude that in this case (i) the data provided by the experimenters are by no means insufficient, and (ii) the results of the experiments under discussion can be legitimately used to call into question the predictive power of expected utility theory (which, of course, does not mean that such results necessarily undermine its prescriptive appeal; moreover, they have nothing to do with its logical consistency).

Now, do the results of Allais' experiment give rise to a 'genuine' paradox of rationality, or rather to a 'spurious' pseudo-paradox, as is apparently claimed by Schmidt? Here the discussion may tend to degenerate into an empty terminological dispute. In this respect, it may be of some interest to recall that Allais has always consistently refused to regard as a paradoxical result the result which has been named after him. But the reasons why Allais has always rejected the current denomination of the so-called Allais paradox are completely different from those suggested by Schmidt: according to Allais, the result of his experiment is not paradoxical simply because it is not unexpected (to him); from his own point of view, in fact, such a result may appear unexpected, hence paradoxical, only to those theorists (the 'neo-bernoullians', in his own terminology) who wrongly deem the axioms of expected utility theory to be self-evident and are consequently baffled by their manifest violation (cf., e.g., Allais, 1979, 1987). But, whatever name one cares to give to the phenomenon under question, the fact remains that, contrary to what

Schmidt seems to suggest, the results of Allais' experiment do undermine the predictive power of expected utility theory, thereby posing a serious problem to those social scientists who advocate the use of such a theory for explanatory purposes.

Quite similar remarks could be made about Schmidt's discussion of the so-called Ellsberg Paradox (p. 51). Here again the author suggests that, due to the 'imprecise' or 'ambiguous' character of the choice situation, as described by the experimenter, no definite conclusion can be drawn from the results of Ellsberg's or similar experiments as far as the rationality of the decision-makers is concerned. But, once again, Schmidt seems to forget that the basic tenet of strict Bayesianism is that decision-makers are *always* able to form numerically definite and consistent probability judgements; hence, from this point of view, the fact that in Ellsberg-type experiments the probability distribution of some crucial variable is not specified cannot be taken to mean that the data provided by the experimenter are insufficient, nor that the choice situation is 'ambiguous'. Further, the author seems to forget that the main negative result of Ellsberg's and similar experiments is that *no* probability distribution exists which is consistent with the majority or modal choices made by the experimental subjects. Hence, also in this case one can conclude that the results of the experiments under discussion can be legitimately used to call into question the predictive power of expected utility theory and/or the soundness of strict Bayesianism.

Finally, let us turn to a third example, drawn from non-cooperative game theory, by means of which Schmidt tries to support his thesis that not only in real experiments, but also in some (or perhaps most) thought experiments, the misspecification of the reference model prevents the experimenter from drawing any definite conclusion from the results of the experiment.

In Figure 3.1 the author introduces a 2 × 2 payoff bimatrix, inviting the reader to think of it as the 'data' of a thought experiment concerning a two-player non-cooperative game. The two players are supposed to represent a 'competitor' and a 'monopolist', with pure strategies (A, B) and (a, b), respectively. The model itself is said to be 'a simplified and slightly different one-shot version of Selten's Chain-Store model'. The author then suggests that the strategic-form game represented by the specified bimatrix can be given three different interpretations: specifically, he suggests that the strategic form under question can be associated with three alternative extensive-form games, whose trees are given in the immediately following pages.[4] According to Schmidt, the fact that the same strategic form can be thought of as derived from three different extensive forms (to which, moreover, different equilibria or solution concepts are said to apply) is a further instance of the fact that, when the data of an experiment (in the present case, a thought experiment) are insufficiently specified, the reference model cannot be uniquely identified by the decision-makers; from which it would follow that whatever the outcome of the experiment no definite conclusion concerning the rationality of the decision-makers can be reached. In this regard, the following two remarks are in order.

First, it is a well-known fact that a given strategic-form game may be consistent with a number of alternative extensive forms: this simply depends on the fact that, in general, some information is lost in passing from an extensive form to the corresponding strategic form, so that there cannot exist an injective function mapping extensive forms into corresponding strategic forms. So, if this were the central point of Schmidt's example, his argument would be wholly uncontroversial. Unfortunately, however, he seeks to prove much more than this: apparently, what he intends to demonstrate is that many 'paradoxes of rationality' allegedly arising in the context of non-cooperative game theory simply depend on an insufficient specification of the data to be used in the proposed thought experiments. But, to my knowledge, nobody has ever regarded as a 'paradox of rationality' the fact that a given strategic-form game can be associated with a number of extensive-form games, possibly characterized by different solution concepts. In particular, contrary to what might appear from his discussion, Schmidt's problem has nothing to do with Selten's Chain-Store Paradox, even if the latter is said to be the source of inspiration for the former.

Second, of the three extensive forms given by Schmidt at pp. 53–4, only the first one is certainly consistent with the strategic form specified at p. 52, provided that the two decision nodes of the 'monopolist' are assumed to belong to one and the same information set. However, both the second and the third one, as they stand, are definitely inconsistent with the original strategic form. Hence, strictly speaking, no rational player acquainted with the rules of game theory and informed of the data contained in the payoff bimatrix of Figure 3.1 could be engaged in either of the last two extensive-form games of pp. 53–4. This has nothing to do with any 'paradox of rationality' but with comprehension of the theory. Barring any chance move, the strategic form given at p. 52 can be thought of as derived from one or the other of the following three extensive forms: either one of the two equivalent one stage, simultaneous-move, imperfect-information extensive-form games which can always be associated with a two-player strategic form (one of them is in effect the first extensive form given by Schmidt; or the two-stage, perfect-information extensive-form game, where the 'competitor' moves first and if, and only if, he chooses A, then the 'monopolist' can choose between a and b (incidentally, the latter extensive form, curiously neglected by Schmidt, is the only one which can give rise to a situation similar to the one underlying Selten's 'chain-store paradox').

To sum up, Schmidt's claim that the outcome of experimental tests of models of rational behaviour cannot in general be taken to demonstrate the existence of problems (if not paradoxes) concerning the modelling of rationality is ill-grounded. On the contrary, if one considers the results of the many real experiments (laboratory or otherwise) which have been carried out so far in this field, one can legitimately draw the following conclusions:

(1) The available experimental evidence calls into question the predictive power of a number of models of rational behaviour.

(2) While it is true that negative experimental evidence is generally not regarded as a sufficient reason for questioning the prescriptive validity of a given model, it is also true that systematic negative experimental evidence tends to undermine the prescriptive validity of a model as well.

(3) As pointed out by Schmidt, it is often true that the negative experimental evidence generated by a particular experiment is not sufficient to specify which one(s) of the many axioms characterizing a given model has (have) been violated in the experiment concerned. However, it is sometimes possible to design further and finer experiments which help discriminate among the

potentially violated axioms (this has been the case, for example, with the so-called phenomenon of 'preference reversals').

Further, if one considers the thought experiments which have been systematically used over the years in order to assess the prescriptive validity of a number of models of rational behaviour, one is led to conclude that such experiments, imperfect as they are, have been able to bring to the fore a number of issues, problems or paradoxes that would probably have gone unnoticed otherwise.

Finally, it is certainly true that, in itself, the emergence of negative experimental evidence has no implication whatsoever concerning the logical consistency of the set of axioms on which the model is based whose predictive power or prescriptive validity is being tested. But, to my knowledge, nobody has ever held the opposite view.

Notes

1. This qualification is due to the fact that, in my opinion, the discussion developed in the chapter is not so clear as to dispel all possible doubts concerning the real intentions of the author, particularly as far as the situations grouped under (b) are concerned.
2. This is the way in which I interpret the following statement by Schmidt (p. 52): 'But these data are not sufficient for the maximization of the determined expected utility function of the decision-maker because of the lack of information about the utility function of the money... Therefore the expected utility model cannot be *sensu stricto* the reference of rational choice in Allais' choice situation.'
3. This fact is in effect recognized by Schmidt. But then, curiously enough, he apparently refuses to draw the obvious implications of such recognition.
4. One further extensive form, somehow related to the original strategic form of p. 52, is introduced much later in the chapter (pp. 61 ff.). But, since the exact relationship between this fourth extensive form and the original strategic form is by no means clear, the fourth extensive form will be disregarded in the following discussion.

References

Allais, M. (1979) 'The So-Called Allais Paradox of Rational Decision Under Uncertainty', in M. Allais and O. Hagen (eds), *Expected Utility Hypotheses and the Allais Paradox* (Dordrecht: Reidel).

Allais, M. (1987) 'Allais Paradox', in J. Eatwell, M. Milgate, and P. Newman (eds), *The New Palgrave. A Dictionary of Economics*, vol. 1 (London: Macmillan), pp. 80–2.

Myerson, R.B. (1991) *Game Theory. Analysis of Conflict* (Cambridge, Mass.: Harvard University Press).

Sen, A. (1987) 'Rational Behaviour', in J. Eatwell, M. Milgate, and P. Newman (eds), *The New Palgrave. A Dictionary of Economics*, vol. 4 (London: Macmillan), pp. 68–76.

Reply

Christian Schmidt

UNIVERSITÉ PARIS-DAUPHINE, FRANCE

Professor Donzelli's Comment contains detailed observations and radical criticisms. His complaint is aimed at (i) what he supposes to be the thesis of my chapter and (ii) the validity of the alleged arguments to support it. Unfortunately the relationship between the criticized thesis and the core of my chapter appears very weak. As for the arguments sustaining the ideas developed in my chapter, they are largely misunderstood by the commentator. Therefore, Donzelli's contribution takes the form of a parallel piece.

Several preliminary observations provide an estimation of the gap. The two main parts of my chapter are balanced and their content complementary. The purpose of the critical survey developed in the first main part (Section 2) is aimed at preparing the reader to my own analysis which is focused on an *epistemic* paradox in the decision-making theory. Donzelli's Comment is devoted to Section 2, taking no account of Section 3. Consequently, it loses more than half of the complete argumentation. The term 'paradox', which is the central concept, clearly refers in my chapter to a logical presentation. According to the Oxford English Dictionary (1989, p. 189) it means 'A statement or a proposition, which from an acceptable premise and despite sound reasoning, leads to a conclusion that is against sense, logically unacceptable or self-contradictory'. Throughout his Comment, one looks in vain for Donzelli's definition of a paradox. Most often he speaks of 'paradoxes or problems' 'problems or paradoxes' or 'problems (if not paradoxes)' without giving any precision to the kind of problems raised by a paradox. For the sake of such a clarification, the target of his repeated criticisms remains at best fuzzily determined. Indeed, self-contradiction does not much trouble Donzelli. On one hand, the supposed thesis of my chapter is judged at variance with all received views' (p. 80–81) whilst it is claimed in conclusion that 'nobody has ever held the opposite view' (p. 84). It is not clear, what he really means.

While much can be said about the merits of experimental economics, Donzelli seems to entertain an obsessive view of experiments. Testing the descriptive and the predictive statements derived from the models of rational behaviour is his main concern. I do not contest the legitimacy of this topic, except that it does not cover my point in a paper devoted to paradoxes of rationality according to the precise definition previously recalled. Starting from his preconception Donzelli reconstructs the supposed thesis of my chapter and then bravely criticizes it at length.

The following illustrations of Donzelli's method are sufficiently convincing. One short paragraph for Allais and another one for Ellsberg, where their respective 'so-called paradoxes' are briefly evoked in my chapter, become in Donzelli's understanding a discussion at length of their relevance. More serious is the transformation of the aim of my proposed typology. Thanks to Donzelli my three categories support a taxonomy for classifying situations on the grounds of experimental considerations, namely the public experimental tests for (a), the thought experiment for (b), and no experimental basis for (c). Aside from the innate skills of Donzelli's rhetoric, it does lead to a thorough misinterpretation of my thought. The proposed typology is not based on a means by which some problematic results are obtained in decision-making but on the meanings to be associated to various results labelled 'paradoxes of rationality' in the corresponding literature. Incidentally, I never use the term 'thought experiment' because I feel this notion is controversial for the topic. Another distinction between experiments and computations would have been relevant in the matter for Donzelli's purpose, but, rather curiously, he never mentions it.

Thus, and contrary to Donzelli's allegations, I do not argue that the negative results pointed out by experimental evidence do not reveal any serious problems in modelling rational decision-making. I have myself underlined that their investigation can provide a stimulating starting point for inventing other models of rational choice. But before that, the question to be clarified is the nature of the relationship between the difficulties which have been experimentally observed and the structures of logical paradoxes. It goes far beyond a quarrel of terminology. A careful analysis of the different components of those puzzling rational decision-making instances (choice situations, reference models, conditions of implemenation) is the necessary prerequisite for such a clarification. As for the definition of logical paradoxes, the domain is too broad and the matter too complex (Quine, 1976) to be reduced to the inconsistency of a set of axioms as is misleadingly suggested by Donzelli. If simplicity sounds beautiful, oversimplification is counterproductive.

Moving to Donzelli's technical criticisms reinforces the relevance of this observation. His discussion of Allais' counter-examples provides an illustration. I do not contest that there does not exist an expected utility function which is consistent with the majority of the decision-maker's preferences revealed by the experiment: on the contrary (see my chapter, p. 52). These decision-makers obviously do not follow the classical expected utility model in their choices. The actual question is to explain what it means. According to the various interpretations proposed more than forty years ago, the answer is neither trivial nor self-evident. I have just focused on one point previously underlined by Levi (1974, 1986). The expected utility calculation remains indeterminate due to the gap between the payoffs which are specified in money and the utilities which are used in its achievement – a specific difficulty which has nothing to do with the von Neumann and Morgenstern system of axioms. Anyway and whatever the accepted interpretation of Allais' observed phenomenon, Allais, Donzelli and I agree to reject its designation as a 'paradox': an additional reason for reducing its discussion in a paper devoted to paradoxes.

The oversimplification device leads Donzelli to group together Ellsberg's and Allais' results on the grounds of an apparent similarity between the non-existence of a probability distribution in the former and the non-existence of a utility function in the latter consistent with the observed behaviours. But here again the basic question concerns the understanding of Ellsberg's experimental results. Such an investigation requires a much more cautious examination of the cognitive conditions of the information which is available to the decision-makers in this specific choice situation. This quest cannot be satisfied with the Donzelli's simple invocation of the strict Bayesianism 'credo', which incidentally remains rather imprecise.

More generally, I wish to recall my position on the meaning of the experimental counter-examples of Allais, Ellsberg, Slovic and Lichtenberg and others *vis-à-vis* the question of paradoxes of rationality. To say that Allais, as well as Ellsberg's results, for instance, rule out the predictive power of the expected utility model (and not the theory) in the corresponding choice situations, only means that a majority of tested people does not apparently choose the expected utility as a reference model, and nothing else. I argue that two separate investigations are necessary for evaluating the real impact of such observations on possible paradoxes of rationality. The first concerns the experimental conditions: it develops into a confrontation between the perception of the experimental conditions by the tested persons and the experimentator (a much more difficult question than in the natural sciences). The second investigation is devoted to a comparison by the theoretician between the tentative rationalization of the set of data gathered during the experiments of such a model of rationality, including the expected utility model. These investigations are quite independent each one from the other, but the significance of the second operation is highly dependent on the information derived from the first.

Confusion peaks when the commentator discusses one of my game-theory examples. Except for the initial inspiration, the problem raised by the situation which is described by the options to be rationally chosen by a competitor and a monopolist is totally different from the Selten Chain-Store Paradox. First, each agent is supposed to be in a one-shot decision-making situation without any specification of the time sequences. Second, the rationality of a deterrence behaviour in such an hypothetical situation is the actual topic to be studied. Third, the deterrence is considered as a conditional statement, the validity of which is tested through a counterfactual treatment. Accordingly, the matrix in Figure 3.1 which summarizes the information must not be confused with the normal form of a game (and certainly not with the Selten game). Moreover, $G'1$, which is inexplicably identified by Donzelli as the extensive form of this fallaciously misinterpreted game, is only a graph used to introduce the conditional statement for the deterrence purpose (see my chapter, p. 52–53). The new notations (a' and b') are added here to avoid any confusion. It must be noted that b' does not designate a strategy but the conditional proposition (p. 61–62). As for G2, it does not depict the extensive form of an hypothetical normal-form game, but must be understood as an intermediate step for the chosen formalization of the deterrence in a conditional subgame which is developed later in the chapter (see pp. 61–3). Therefore the question of the consistency between the strategic form of a game and the three extensive games supposed to be derived from it, which is the core of Donzelli's argument, misses the point completely *vis-à-vis* the rational validity of deterrence. Once again, Donzelli's oversimplified assertions on consistency between the normal form and the extensive forms of a game are not only irrelevant but still more controversial in a broader context (see Kohlberg and Mertens, 1986, versus Selten); an existent debate involving people other than me.

References

Kohlberg, E. and J.F. Mertens (1986) 'On the Strategic Stability of Equilibria', *Econometrica*, vol. 50.

Levi, I. (1974) 'On Indeterminate Probabilities', *Journal of Philosophy*, vol. 71.

Levi, I, (1986) 'The Paradoxes of Allais and Ellsberg', *Economics and Philosophy*, vol. 2.

Oxford English Dictionary, The (1989) 2nd edn (Oxford: Clarendon Press).

Quine, W.V. (1976) *The Ways of Paradoxes* (Cambridge Mass.: Harvard University Press).

4 Rationality and Comprehension*

Avishai Margalit

THE HEBREW UNIVERSITY OF JERUSALEM, ISRAEL

and

Menahem Yaari

THE HEBREW UNIVERSITY OF JERUSALEM AND THE OPEN UNIVERSITY
OF ISRAEL

1 INTRODUCTION

Economists and game theorists have recently been devoting a great deal of attention
to laying down a theory of knowledge for decision-making units. (We shall often
refer to decision-making units as 'agents'). What does the agent know about 'the
world'? What does the agent know about other agents? And finally, when can we
say that a given fact, event, or proposition is common knowledge among two or
more agents? Some readers may find this kind of exploration rather curious, in view
of the fact that 'decision-making units' are theoretical entities. It should be noted,
however, that the purpose of the exercise is normative rather than descriptive.
Basically, the question being asked concerns the structure of knowledge being
required for the agents, if this or that theory of interaction (e.g., Nash equilibrium) is
to be upheld. A detailed account of the recently developed models of knowledge for
interacting agents may be found in Geanakoplos (1992).

In this chapter, we shall argue that the concept of knowledge that has emerged in
these discussions is unreasonably narrow and confining. The framework which we
criticize and which, we claim, lies at the basis of today's theories of knowledge for
interacting agents, is characterized by the following three principles:

(1) *Dichotomy.* There are two, and only two, types of knowledges: factual and
analytic.
(2) *Factual = Sensory.* Knowledge is factual if, and only if, it is acquired through
the receipt of a sensory signal. The agent's factual knowledge at any given state
is defined to coincide with the sensory signal received by the agent at that state.
(3) *Logical Omniscience.* Analytic knowledge is innate, perfect, and complete. All
tautologies and contradictions are known for what they are; knowing a

---

* We are very much indebted to Kenneth J. Arrow, Kenneth G. Binmore and Amartya K. Sen
for their comments. We also wish to thank Robert J. Aumann for giving us permission to
refer to his unpublished work (1992).

tautology is itself a tautology; knowing p implies knowing all p's logical consequences; if p is not a contradiction, then p is known to be possible.

We regard these three percepts as a vestige of a naive positivist orthodoxy which, for some reason, microeconomists and game theorists have chosen to embrace. Why some of today's finest economic theorists should submit to such an orthodoxy is a fascinating question in the sociology of science. Perhaps it has something to do with the cult of free market economics which tends to view the economic agent as an organism relentlessly engaged in gratification-seeking. Be that as it may, our purpose here is merely to point out that the three principles stated above provide an inadequate basis for the theory of knowledge that is needed in the study of interaction among agents.

2   INTERACTIVE EPISTEMOLOGY

Among the many contributions made recently on this topic of knowledge in rational decision-making, there is as far as we know only one where an attempt is made to develop the decision-makers' information structures from basic principles. This is Robert J. Aumann's remarkable (unfortunately as yet unpublished) essay (1992). Aumann's construction uses the following building-blocks:

(a) There is a (finite non-empty) set of *individuals*. Their number is n.
(b) A *language* is given, where the symbols are letters from a (finite or denumerable) alphabet, to which are added $n+4$ further symbols, viz. $\vee$, $\neg$, (,), k_1, k_2, ..., k_n.

The symbols of the language are given the following interpretations. Each letter in the alphabet is a 'natural occurrence'. The symbol $\vee$ means 'or', the symbol $\neg$ means 'it is not true that...', the symbols (and) have the usual meaning of parentheses, and, for $i = 1, 2, ..., n$, the symbol k_i means 'individual i knows that...'. The *formulas* of the language are given by the rules that each letter of the alphabet is a formula and that, given two formulas f and g, $f\vee g$, $\neg f$, $k_i f$ (for $i = 1, 2, ..., n$) are also formulas. On this basis, a system of modal logic is now constructed, using the axioms of propositional calculus plus $4n$ further axioms, viz.

$$(k_i f) \Rightarrow f$$
$$(k_i(f \Rightarrow g)) \Rightarrow ((k_i f) \Rightarrow (k_i g))$$
$$(k_i f) \Rightarrow (k_i k_i f)$$
$$(\neg k_i f) \Rightarrow (k_i \neg k_i f)$$

where $i = 1, ..., n$, f and g are formulas, and $f \Rightarrow g$ means $(\neg f)\vee g$. A *thesis* (or a *tautology*) is now defined by the conditions:

every axiom is a thesis;
if f and $(f \Rightarrow g)$ are theses, then g is a thesis;
for $i = 1, ..., n$, if f is a thesis, then $k_i f$ is a thesis.

The resulting system is a multi-agent version of the modal logic known as $S5$, originally introduced by Lewis and Langford (1932) in the exploration of possibility and necessity. Aumann now defines a *state of the world* as a list of formulas that contains all the theses and is inference-complete (i.e., if f and $f \Rightarrow g$ are in the list, so is g) such that a formula f is in the list if, and only if, its negation $\neg f$ is *not* in the list. The *signal* received by agent i at state S is the set of all formulas f such that f is not a thesis and $k_i f$ belongs to the list S.

Agent i's signal at a given state S carries two different kinds of information. First, there are the letters α of the alphabet for which $k_i \alpha$ belongs to S. This is what agent i knows at S about what Aumann calls 'natural occurrences'. This part of the signal is clearly sensory. Secondly, agent i's signal contains information about what *other* agents know, i.e., it includes formulas of the form $k_j f$ such that $k_i k_j f$ belongs to S, for some other agent j. How agent i can ever come to possess this kind of information turns out to be a very thorny issue. Note, in particular, that as a consequence of the axioms, the implication $k_i k_j f \Rightarrow k_i f$ always holds; i's sensory knowledge of f is a necessary condition for i's ability to know that j knows f. All this is discussed at greater length in Section 3, below.

Aumann's essay contains a curious distinction between knowledge (without quotation marks) and 'knowledge' (with quotation marks). If at some state S f is a fact (i.e., a *formula* which is not a thesis and belongs to S) then agent i either knows f (this is written $k_i f \in S$) or else agent i does not know f ($\neg k_i f \in S$). This is factual knowledge. For this to be at all meaningful, agent i must 'know' the *language* in which f and $k_i f$ appear as formulas. Knowledge that is embodied in the structure of the language is normally called *analytic*. Aumann calls it 'knowledge' (with quotation marks). Notice that, in Aumann, a great many things are worked into the structure of the language, thus becoming 'known' (with quotation marks) to all agents, as part of their analytic tool-kit. For example, the state space, i.e., the complete account of all the possible states that the world can be in, is 'known' and therefore analytic. Who the other agents are, how many of them, and what their information structures are: all this is 'known' and therefore analytic – to say nothing of all theses, which are (tautologically) 'known', thus obviously analytic. Now, from the point of view of decision-making, knowledge and 'knowledge' are of course equally applicable. In choosing actions, agents will bring to bear all the information they have, whether factual or analytic. The main difference between the two is that factual information possessed by one agent may not become available to other agents (due to differences in signals received), whereas analytic information is common to all agents, and this is itself commonly known. Some simple consequences of all this will now be explored.

3 KNOWLEDGE AT THE LOWEST COMMON DENOMINATOR

In examples of two-agent interactive situations it has recently become fashionable to refer to the two agents as Alice and Bob. Onto this bandwagon we are delighted to jump. Alice and Bob are travelling in a car. Alice is driving and Bob is at her side, in the passenger's seat. They approach an intersection with a traffic light. It is a special kind of traffic light: instead of being made up of three separate lighting elements – one red, one amber and one green – this traffic light is a high-tech job, with a single lighting element that changes colours. When Alice and Bob reach the intersection the light is red, so Alice stops the car. She can do this because she can see the red light for what it is (namely red), i.e., she is colour-cognizant. Bob, on the other hand, is colour-blind. The light changes to green. Alice knows (sees) that now the light is green. Bob is colour-blind, so he does not know this. So far, so good. Now, what does Bob know about what Alice knows? Bob certainly knows that Alice knows the colour of the light, i.e. Bob knows that Alice is not colour-blind, and this knowledge is *analytic*. Indeed, Alice's being colour-cognizant (i.e., her information structure) is part of the 'language'. If Bob had any doubt about whether or not Alice can see colours, he would have to move to a new world, and a new language, with the number of agents increased to include 'Alice$_1$' and 'Alice$_2$' in place of what used to be simply 'Alice', Alice$_1$ being colour-cognizant and Alice$_2$ being colour-blind. He would then have to proceed from some prior probability distribution on who it is that he is driving with (Alice$_1$ or Alice$_2$), which he would have updated, using Bayes' Rule, to take account of the evidence that, whoever it is that he is driving with, this person did in fact stop at the intersection. ('Did she stop because she saw a red light?') So, to keep matters simple, let us go back to just one Alice, good old colour-seeing Alice, and to Bob knowing this. Alice knows that now the light is green and Bob does not. Can Bob know that Alice knows that the light is now green? Absolutely not! While he does know (analytically) that Alice can see colours, he cannot know (factually) that right now she sees green. Why? Because the event 'Alice sees green' is contained in the event 'the light is green', and so if Bob, who is colour-blind, cannot know the latter, he certainly cannot know the former. (In symbols, let g be the formula 'the light is green'. $K_Ag \Rightarrow g$ is a thesis, so $K_B(K_Ag \Rightarrow g)$ is true. It therefore follows from the second axiom that $K_BK_Ag \Rightarrow K_Bg$ and since the consequent is false, so it the antecedent.) Well, you might say, Bob obviously cannot know that Alice knows that the light is green, because Bob, being colour-blind, simply does not know what 'green' *is*. This argument sounds good but it is invalid. For Bob knows *exactly* what 'green' is. Recall that Bob knows Alice's information structure. In fact, he knows Alice's information structure *analytically*, as part of his knowledge of the language. Alice can see colours and Bob knows this. He knows exactly which visual signal Alice receives at every state of the world and, in particular, he knows exactly at which states she receives the signal 'green'. But the set of states at which she receives the signal 'green' is precisely the set *defining* the colour green. This, after all, is the meaning of Alice's being colour-cognizant: she can recognize green for what it is. Hence Bob knows exactly what 'green' means, yet he cannot know that Alice knows that the light is green. Why? Bob cannot acquire the knowledge that Alice knows that the light is green, because knowledge is only acquired through the receipt of a sensory signal.

The problem seems to lie in the fact that people do not have sensory access to what other people know, which, under the sensory/analytic dichotomy, would appear to rule out any possibility for knowledge to be conveyed between individuals. Yet, much of what people know is, in fact, knowledge that had been conveyed to them from other people. Alice cannot arrange for Bob to know what she knows, no matter how hard she might try. Certainly, no oral pronouncement can ever make Bob know that she sees a green light. If she were to utter the words 'I see a green light', all Bob would know would be 'Alice says she sees a green light'.

This newly acquired knowledge may affect Bob's *beliefs* concerning Alice actually seeing a green light, but not his knowledge of it. Bob's beliefs depend, among other things, on Bob's theory regarding Alice's *motives* in making her pronouncement, whereas Bob's knowledge should not.

Things get worse as Alice and Bob prepare to move. (Imagine a dozen or so cars lined up behind Alice and Bob, with the drivers impatiently hooting their horns.) As soon as Alice sees the light changing to green, she can of course put the car in gear and proceed to cross the intersection. But Alice wants Bob to know what she is doing. She wants him to know that the policy 'move when the light is green' has been adopted (or is being considered). To her dismay, she discovers, however, that Bob can never know this policy. For, in order for Bob to know any policy of action, it must be the case that this policy of action is *measurable* with respect to Bob's information structure. The policy 'move when the light is green' does not satisfy this requirement. There are in fact only two policies which Alice can adopt with Bob's knowledge, namely 'move, no matter what colour the light' and 'stay put, no matter what colour the light'. And if both Alice and Bob subscribe to the rule that peril must be avoided, then they will agree that 'stay put, no matter what' is the policy to be adopted. Just imagine the frustration of those drivers in the cars behind.

This is, of course, none other than Aumann's (1976) celebrated 'Agreeing to Disagree' result. Suppose that Alice, after receiving a signal, uses this signal to update her prior probability distribution (i.e., her prior *beliefs*) over some sample space. If Bob is to know Alice's posterior distribution, then Alice must take care not to condition on anything that Bob cannot know. She must, in other words, restrict the evidence to be used for updating her beliefs to publicly known events. So, if Alice and Bob share a common prior and if both use the same decision rule (Bayes' updating rule, say) then restricting the evidence to publicly known events will obviously result in Alice and Bob reaching the same posterior distribution. They cannot agree to disagree. (Note that this coincidence of posteriors is here a consequence merely of Bob's knowing Alice's posterior distribution. This is because we are dealing with the special case where one agent's – Alice's – information structure is a *refinement* of the other agent's – Bob's – information structure. In the more general case, with no such relationship between the information structures, to obtain the coincidence of posteriors one must postulate that these posteriors are *common knowledge* among the agents. The argument, however, is basically the same: in order for the posteriors to be common knowledge, agents must restrict their updating to publicly known events, so agreement on the posteriors follows from agreement on the priors and on the updating rule.)

Where does all this leave us? It leaves us with the awkward conclusion that, under the sensory/analytic dichotomy, the only knowledge that agents can *share* is knowledge at the *lowest common denominator*. If you want me to know that you know something, then you must take care not to know too much. If Alice wants Bob to know what she knows, then she must take care not to know that the light has turned green. This awkward conclusion follows, we maintain, from an uncritical embrace of the principle that knowledge is either sensory or else analytic. How can Bob know that Alice knows that the light is green? Obviously, he cannot know this analytically, as part of the 'language', so this knowledge must in fact be sensory. Bob's information on what Alice knows must be obtained through the receipt of a sensory signal, and this can only happen when that information is consistent with

Bob's capacity for receiving sensory signals.

These remarks apply also to the much-discussed notion of common knowledge of rationality. If you and I are rational, then for our rationality to be common knowledge between us, we must restrict our behaviour in such a way that an observer who can only see public events will know that we are rational. Our rationality must, so to speak, be evident at the lowest common denominator.

All this points to a theory of knowledge which seems to us too confining. Now the obvious retort to this criticism is to say that for a theory to have explanatory power, it must be confining. But this, we maintain, is more a case of embracing a dogma than of seeking reasonable explanatory power. We would argue, following Hintikka (1973), that the possibility of knowledge which is neither analytic nor sensory must be allowed for. Agents must be allowed to possess knowledge which, on the one hand, is knowledge about the world (and in this sense 'factual') but, on the other hand, does not depend on the receipt of a sensory signal. We will maintain, for example, that knowing what states the world can possibly be in – i.e., knowledge of the 'state space' – is necessarily knowledge of this kind. (In our opinion, writing the state-space into the language, thereby making its knowledge analytic, is a ploy that cannot seriously be defended.) We propose that the word *comprehension* be used to designate this kind of knowledge which is neither analytic nor sensory. Thus, Bob, who is colour-blind, should nevertheless be able to *comprehend* the fact that Alice knows that the light is green. Similarly, agent A should be able to *comprehend* that agent B is rational without B's rationality necessarily being measurable with respect to the information structure that arises from writing down the sensory signal received by A at every state of the world.

4 THE BOY-SCOUT VERSION OF THE HANGMAN'S PARADOX

Think of a group of boy-scouts (say n of them) forming a single file, i.e., standing in a straight line one behind the other, each (except the first) facing the back of the boy directly in front. Of course, the boy-scouts in the line all wear caps on their heads. Among these caps, all but one are white and the remaining one – exactly one cap – is red. None of the boys is near-sighted or colour-blind, so each boy can see all the caps worn by the boys who are ahead of him in line, and recognize their colours. He can't see his own cap, nor of course the caps of those behind him. This is, so to speak, the physics of the situation, and we shall assume that all the boys know it. How did they come to know it? In what sense do they know it? How thoroughly do they know it (do they know, for example, the underlying physical and biological laws)? These questions are all relevant and difficult, but we are here following Aumann and saying that the boy-scouts have a common 'language', in which their knowledge of what we have called the physics of the situation is somehow embedded. It should be noted that through knowing the physics of the situation, each boy also knows something about what the other boys know. For example, the boy who is fifth in line knows what it means (physically) to be, say, eighth in line, and in particular what being eighth in line allows one to see. The fifth boy thus knows something about what the eighth boy knows. Basically, this knowledge rests upon *counterfactual* reasoning: If I *were* eighth in line, this is what I *would* see, so says the boy who is fifth. Counterfactual knowledge generally plays a major role in economic and game-theoretic reasoning, and this case is no exception. Note, however, that under the sensory/analytic dichotomy, all counterfactual knowledge is necessarily analytic since the *counter*-factual cannot be factual.

We shall now consider a world with n possible states, defined by who is wearing the red cap. Formally, a state-space Ω may be defined by writing $\Omega = \{1, 2, ..., n\}$, where the i-th state ($i \in \Omega$) is identified by the assertion 'the red cap is on the head of the boy who is i-th in line'. We assume, with Aumann, that all the boys know Ω, and that this knowledge is analytic.

Let $s_i(j)$ be the sensory signal which the i-th boy (i.e., the boy who is i-th in line) receives when the state of the world is j (i.e., when the j-th boy is the one wearing the red cap). We have:

$$s_i(j) = \begin{cases} j & \text{if } j < i \\ \neg(1 \vee 2 \vee \ldots \vee i - 1) & \text{if } j \geq i. \end{cases}$$

The values which the function $s_i(\ )$ can take are sentences (or propositions). When $j < i$, $s_i(j)$ is the sentence 'the red cap is on j's head', i.e., when $j < i$, the signal received by the i-th boy tells him exactly what the state of the world is. When $j \geq i$, i's signal tells him only that the red cap is neither on 1's head, nor on 2's head, ..., nor on $(i-1)$'s head. Note that when $j \geq i$ the values of $s_i(j)$ are constant, i.e., i receives the same signal at all j, so long as $j \geq i$. Let $\Pi_i(j)$ be the set of all states at which the signal received by i would be the same as that received at j. In order words, $\Pi_i(j)$ is the set of those states in Ω which i cannot distinguish from state j:

$$\begin{aligned} \Pi_i(j) &= \{j' \in \Omega \mid s_i(j') = s_i(j)\} \\ &= \begin{cases} \{j\} & \text{if } j < i \\ \{i, i+1, \ldots, n\} & \text{if } j \geq i. \end{cases} \end{aligned}$$

This definition gives rise to the following important remark. In defining the set $\Pi_i(j)$, one uses a condition of the form $s_i(j') = s_i(j)$. Now the values of the function $s_i(\ )$ are *sentences*, so in order to define $\Pi_i(\ )$, one must first settle the question of what it means for two sentences to be equal. In a formal language, sentences are equal when they are logically equivalent, and logical equivalence is well defined within the language. Normally, however, people do not receive signals dressed as formal propositions, nor do they normally have a Robert Aumann on hand to transform for them all facts and all knowledge of facts into formulas in some pre-constructed formal language. People normally receive signals in the form of sentences in some *natural* language. More precisely, the signals which an individual receives, if they are not themselves sentences in some natural language, are *processed* by the receiving individual into sentences in some natural language. In either case, the assertion $s_i(j') = s_i(j)$ is now to be understood as saying that individual i regards (or understands, or comprehends) the two natural-language sentences $s_i(j')$ and $s_i(j)$ as equivalent to each other, i.e., that from individual i's point-of-view the sentences $s_i(j')$ and $s_i(j)$ 'say the same thing'. At this point, one immediately faces a whole host of issues having to do with the status and possible indeterminacy of meaning in natural languages and with how information which is formulated in a natural language is comprehended and conveyed. These are precisely the questions which Donald Davidson (1984) and others (see, e.g., Lewis (1983)) have been discussing under the heading of 'Radical Interpretation'. Thus, going from the function $s_i(\ )$ to the function $\Pi_i(\ )$ is far from a trivial matter.

The set $\Pi_i(j)$ tells us what the i-th boy knows about the state of the world when the true state is j. Specifically, when the true state is j, what the i-th boy knows is that the world is in one of the states in $\Pi_i(j)$. Unlike $s_i(j)$ which is a sensory signal and hence represents *factual* knowledge, $\Pi_i(j)$ spells out knowledge which in general is not factual (or not *merely* factual). In particular, when $j \geq i$ we have $\Pi_i(j) = \{i, i+1, ..., n\}$ which says that i knows the true state to be one of the states i, $i+1$, ..., n. In order to arrive at this knowledge, the i-th boy must reason as follows: (i) I can see (factual knowledge) that none of the boys ahead of me wears the red cap, i.e., that the true state is not in the set $\{1, 2, ..., i\text{-}1\}$. (ii) I know (analytically) that the state-space is Ω, which is given by the set $\{1, 2, ..., n\}$. (iii) From the fact that the true state must be in Ω but is not in $\{1, 2, ..., i\text{-}1\}$ I *deduce* (analytically) that the true state is in $\{i, i+1, ..., n\}$. Thus, in order to arrive at $\Pi_i(j)$, the i-th boy uses both factual and analytic knowledge, plus logical deductions which are also defined to be part of analytic knowledge. Now the logical inference which the i-th boy uses to arrive at $\Pi_i(j)$ is a very primitive one, and it is hard to object to the assumption – and an assumption it is – that he is capable of performing such inferences. Recall, however, that under Aumann's theory, agents are assumed capable of correctly carrying out *all* logical reasoning, no matter how complex. Once the axioms are in the language, so are all the theorems. This is the so-called Logical Omniscience, mentioned briefly in Section 1, above. The questions arising in this connection are extremely difficult. Is a capacity for omniscient logical reasoning a precondition for rationality? If it is, then nobody is rational. If it is not, then one must decide what would be the minimal capacity for logical reasoning required for rationality. For it is not even meaningful, let alone useful, to speak of rationality for an agent who does not possess *some* capacity for logical inference. And what about computational omniscience, which is a consequence of logical omniscience? Does inability to solve a given problem in polynomial time imply that full rationality is unattainable? We do not pretend to have a theory of knowledge for rational decision-making that gives satisfactory answers to these questions. Our claim is merely that going for logical omniscience, as the existing theory does, is not likely to be the right way.

The function $\Pi_i(\ )$ leads us immediately to the i-th boy-scout's information structure. Specifically, since $\Pi_i(j)$ tells us what i knows when the state is j, letting j run through the entire set Ω would give us a description of what i knows at any given state, which is i's information structure. Accordingly, letting Π_i be defined by $\Pi_i = \{\Pi_i(1), \Pi_i(2), ..., \Pi_i(n)\}$, we get

$$\Pi_i = \{\{1\}, \{2\}, \ldots, \{i-1\}, \{i, i+1, \ldots, n\}\}.$$

for $i = 1, 2, ..., n$. The function Π_i, which is indeed referred to as i's *information structure*, is clearly a *partition* of the state-space Ω.

In the previous section there were two agents, Alice and Bob, with information structures such that Alice could always know what bob knows, but Bob could not always know what Alice knows. Alice's information partition was a *refinement* of Bob's. Here the situation is similar, albeit with possibly more than two agents. Each boy-scout in the line knows more than the boys ahead of him and less than the boys behind him. For any two boy-scouts in the file, the information partition of the one who is behind is a refinement of the information partition of the one who is ahead. In particular for the first and last boys we have:

$$\Pi_1 = \{1, 2, \ldots, n\}$$

and

$$\Pi_n = \{\{1\}, \{2\}, \ldots, \{n\}\}$$

The first in line knows nothing (about who is wearing the red cap) and the last in line knows everything, in the sense that no matter who wears the red cap, n knows it.

We are now, at long last, ready to introduce a version of the so-called Hangman's Paradox. (See Sorenson, 1982 for a related discussion.) Suppose that the boy in the t-th place in the line is in fact the one wearing the red cap, i.e., let the state of the world which actually obtains be denoted t ($t \in \Omega$). Consider the condition

$(*)$ $\qquad\qquad\qquad\qquad\qquad \{t\} \notin \Pi_t$

What $(*)$ says is: he who wears the red cap does not know that he is wearing it.

Suppose that $(*)$ becomes known to those poor boy-scouts standing in line. That is, assume that the boys *know* $(*)$ to be true. Obviously, this knowledge cannot be sensory, so we have to assume that the boys know $(*)$ *analytically*, in the same way that they know Ω and the Π_i's. (Note that $(*)$ being known analytically makes $(*)$ *common knowledge* among the boys.) We shall say nothing about how the boys could have come to know $(*)$, even though obviously this is a question of considerable importance.

As soon as $(*)$ is known, the boy who is 17th in line raises his hand and, when given permission to speak, says: 'Making us stand in line like this for hours on end is nothing but a cruel hoax. There's no one here with a red cap on his head!' This proclamation obviously causes some alarm in certain quarters, so no. 17 is ordered to explain. 'Well,' he says, 'the red cap — assuming there is one — cannot possibly be on n's head, because if it were n would know it. Now, $n - 1$ cannot possibly have the red cap on his head, because if he did, he would see all the boys ahead of him wearing white caps so he would know that the red cap is either on his own head or on n's. But $n - 1$ knows that the red cap cannot be on n's head (if it were, n would know it), therefore it must be he, $n - 1$, who is wearing it. Thus, if he himself had a red cap on his head he would know it. Continuing recursively in this manner, we find that if any one of us had the red cap on his head he would know it, and this would be true in particular for the boy t, whoever he might be.' Having thus completed his argument, no. 17 is asked to please take off his cap. 'What colour is your cap?' he is asked. 'Red.' 'Did you know you were wearing the red cap?' 'No.'

Let us examine this story carefully. Checking the condition $(*)$ against the definition of the information partitions Π_i, we find that $(*)$ is true if, and only if, $t < n$. Repeating, for the sake of emphasis, we have that the assertions $\{t\} \notin \Pi_t$ and $t < n$ are *equivalent* to each other. Now suppose that at the outset we were to assume that the boy-scouts somehow came to know $t < n$ instead of assuming, as we had, that what they came to know was $(*)$. Surely, since $t < n$ and $(*)$ are equivalent, there can be no difference between the two settings. Yet think of that smart kid, no. 17. If $t < n$ were the assertion that was known to be true, he would no doubt have held his peace thus sparing himself an embarrassment. There simply is no hope for a recursive argument based on $t < n$, an inequality which says merely that the red cap is not on the last boy's head. Something is amiss.

Note that in recounting no. 17's argument we did not use (*) directly. Instead we used the English sentence 'he who wears the red cap does not know that he is wearing it'. Is it indeed the case that this sentence expresses the same reality that the formula (*) does? Not quite. A formula is only meaningful insofar as the symbols comprising it are well-defined. In particular, both the meaningfulness and the meaning of the formula

$$\{t\} \notin \Pi_t$$

depend on the definitions of the various symbols appearing in it, and primarily on the definitions of the information partitions Π_1, Π_2, ..., Π_n. These, we recall, are defined as follows:

$$\Pi_i = \{\{1\}, \ldots, \{i-1\}, \{i, \ldots, n\}\}$$

for $i = 1$, ..., n. The Π_i are only well defined given the definition of the state-space Ω, i.e. given $\Omega = \{1, 2, \ldots, n\}$. Thus (*) is only meaningful – and only applicable – for this particular state-space and for these particular information structures. The English-language phrase 'he who wears the red cap does not know that he is wearing it' is not so tightly tied down. In fact, what no. 17 did was to use this phrase while constantly *changing* the state-space and the corresponding information structures. Here is exactly what he did:

(1) We all know (*), and (*) is equivalent to $t < n$.

(2) $t < n$ means that n cannot be the true state of the world, so $\Omega = \{1, 2, \ldots, n\}$ is *not* the correct state-space. Rather, the correct state-space is $\Omega^{n-1} = \{1, 2, \ldots, n-1\}$.

(3) If Ω^{n-1} is the correct state-space, then the correct information structures are not Π_1, ..., Π_n but Π_1', ..., Π_n' defined by

$$\Pi_i' = \{\{1\}, \ldots, \{i-1\}, \{i, \ldots, n-1\}\} \quad \text{for } i = 1, \ldots, n-1$$
$$\Pi_n' = \Pi_{n-1}'$$

(4) Letting t be the true state and noting that t can only take on the values 1, 2, ..., $n-1$, we must now re-write (*) for the new setting, as follows:

$$(*)^{n-1} \qquad \{t\} \notin \Pi_t'$$

Translated into English, what $(*)^{n-1}$ says is 'he who wears the red cap does not know that he is wearing it'.

(5) The condition $(*)^{n-1}$ is equivalent to $t < n-1$. If $(*)^{n-1}$ is known to be true, then $n-1$ can never be the state of the world, so Ω^{n-1} is not the correct state space but rather $\Omega^{n-2} = \{1, 2, \ldots, n-2\}$.

and so forth.

What this shows is that in order to obtain a proper version of the Hangman's Paradox (or the Surprise Test Paradox) one needs a condition which is stronger than

(*). Specifically, the condition that will give us the paradox, and provide the proper foundation for no. 17's argument, is this:

(**) Whatever the appropriate state-space and corresponding information structures Π_i, the true state t shall satisfy

$$\{t\} \notin \Pi_t$$

Given (**), no. 17's argument seems flawless: The appropriate state-space keeps shrinking until the empty state-space (no one's got a red cap) is reached, where the condition $\{t\} \notin \Pi_t$ can be said to hold vacuously. Yet, when no. 17 takes a look at his own cap he finds that it is red, admitting that he did not know this when the cap was still on his head. Something must have gone wrong in his reasoning after all.

As we have seen, no. 17's backward induction argument works through the manipulation of the state-space. Well, it turns out that manipulating the state-space is a very tricky business. In order to find out where the crux of the matter lies, let us reconstruct no. 17's argument in such a way that his conclusion will in fact be correct.

We start with $\Omega = \{1, 2, ., n\}$, together with the condition $\{t\} \notin \Pi_t$ which, as we know, is equivalent to $t < n$. At this point, no. 17 makes the following suggestion: 'Since $t < n$, it is certain that the n-th boy cannot be wearing the red cap. So, what is the point of keeping no. n stupidly standing in line like this?' This leads to no. n being told that he can put his cap in his pocket and go to the cafeteria for a cup of hot chocolate. We are now left with just $n - 1$ boys standing in line, the n-th having left for the cafeteria. The new state-space is given (*physically*) by $\Omega^{n-1} = \{1, 2, ..., n - 1\}$ and $\{t\} \notin \Pi_t$ tells us that the red cap cannot be on $(n - 1)$'s head. So, $n - 1$, who no longer has any relevance for who is wearing the red cap, is excused and goes to the cafeteria for hot chocolate. The line has physically shrunk once again, the new state space is $\Omega^{n-2} = \{1, ..., n - 2\}$ and the process can continue. No. 17, who will be completing his argument in the cafeteria, is now absolutely right: the state-space has been reduced to nought and the condition $\{t\} \notin \Pi_t$, if at all meaningful, holds vacuously.

In this version of the story, the shrinking of the state-space is *physical*. It becomes part of what we have called 'the physics of the situation'. In the previous version, with all the boys staying in line with their caps on their heads, the shrinking of the state-space was *virtual*. The very same argument can be sound when the revisions of the state-space are physical, and faulty when these revisions are virtual. It thus becomes a matter of utmost importance for agents to know the precise grounds for admitting a candidate to membership in the state-space or denying it. This kind of knowledge can be neither purely factual nor purely analytic. We call it comprehension.

5 CONCLUSION

The most consistent and eloquent advocate of the view that knowledge must be either sensory or else analytic was, of course, David Hume. From the very start, however, one of the nagging questions which Hume's analysis did not appear to resolve was how to deal with knowledge of 'other selves'. Some critics went so far as to assert that Hume's position must necessarily lead to solipsism. It would not be incorrect, we think, to describe this essay as an echo of that criticism of David Hume: in the study of interaction among agents, the requirement that agents' knowledge be subject to sensory/analytic dichotomy cannot be sustained. Our suggestion for relaxing this dichotomy involves the introduction of what we have called 'comprehension'. Whether or not 'comprehension' can be modelled explicitly remains to be seen.

References

Aumann, R.J. (1976) 'Agreeing to Disagree', *The Annals of Statistics*, vol. 4, pp. 1236–9.

Aumann, R.J. (1992) 'Notes on Interactive Epistemology', version of 17 July 1992, unpublished.

Davidson, D. (1984) 'Radical Interpretation', in D. Davidson, *Inquiries into Truth and Interpretation* (Oxford: Clarendon Press) pp. 125–39.

Geanakoplos, J. (1992) 'Common Knowledge', *Journal of Economic Perspectives*, 6, 4, pp. 53–82.

Hintikka, J. (1973) 'Information, Deduction, and the A-Priori', in J. Hintikka, *Logic, Language-Games and Information*, (Oxford: Clarendon Press) pp. 222–41.

Lewis, C.I. and C.H. Langford (1932) *Symbolic Logic* (New York: Dover) (2nd edn, 1959).

Lewis, D. (1983) 'Radical Interpretation', in D. Lewis, *Philosophical Papers*, vol. 1 (New York: Oxford University Press), pp. 108–22.

Sorenson, R.A. (1982) 'Recalcitrant Variations of the Prediction Paradox', *Australasian Journal of Philosophy*, vol. 60, pp. 355–62.

Comment

Amartya Sen

HARVARD UNIVERSITY, USA

1 INTRODUCTION

This is a paper of much interest and importance for epistemology in general and for the methodology of economics and game theory in particular. It argues against a form of the positivist theory of knowledge, and the use of that theory in providing the epistemic foundations of knowledge – including 'common knowledge' – in economics and game theory. The theory of knowledge under scrutiny relies exclusively on a twofold classification of all knowledge, namely, *factual* (derived from sensory signals), and *analytic* (including the presumption of logical omniscience). Margalit and Yaari argue that this provides 'an inadequate basis for the theory of knowledge that is needed in the study of interaction among agents'.

Aside from showing the *incompleteness* of the twofold categories of knowledge (to supplement which Margalit and Yaari offer an additional category of knowledge which they call 'comprehension'), they also discuss other limitations of the prevailing theory, in particular the *overdemanding* nature of the standard assumption of 'logical omniscience'. The authors provide good arguments to justify their claims.

2 INADEQUACY OF THE TWOFOLD CATEGORIZATION OF KNOWLEDGE

Margalit and Yaari's criticisms are aimed at the positivist theory of knowledge in general, but they apply with particular force to the theory of 'common knowledge', which draws on that general positivist approach. 'Common knowledge' is much used in contemporary game theory and economics, though its philosophical basis is usually left unexamined and implicitly taken for granted rather than being stated or discussed explicitly. One of the few exceptions is that remarkable theorist Robert Aumann, whose pioneering analysis of 'interactive epistemology' provides an explicit formal system which can *inter alia* accommodate the theory of common knowledge – a theory which owes much to Aumann's earlier work. Margalit and Yaari are particularly concerned with the formulation to be found in 'interactive epistemology', which is – as they rightly note – essentially a multi-agent version of a system known as S5, developed by Lewis and Langford in modal logic. The multi-agency aspect is necessary to accommodate common knowledge. Margalit and Yaari's thesis of the failure of the twofold categorization of knowledge is established *within* this framework, and the force of the argument rests to a great extent on their showing a particular feature of common knowledge: 'knowledge at the lowest common denominator'.

In their interesting example involving Alice and Bob, colour-blind Bob can entertain the *belief* that Alice, who moves the car forward after having stopped, knows that the colour of the traffic light has changed from red to green. Though in an informal description we might be inclined to say that Bob has 'inferred' the greenness of the light from Alice's behaviour, Bob cannot really *know* it, *if* his knowledge must be confined to the sensory and analytical categories only. He cannot see the colour of the light himself, and while he can certainly see that Alice is moving forward, or hear her say, 'Green, at last!', the greenness of the light cannot be analytically derived from these and other sensory perceptions. For the same reason, Bob cannot *know* that Alice *knows* that the colour is now green, since that would require Bob to know that the colour is indeed green. So long as Bob's knowledge is necessarily confined to the union of his sensory perception and analytical truths, their common knowledge would be confined to the lowest common denominator and will *not* include knowledge of the colour of that traffic light.

This is not to dispute that various theories of *belief* – used in economics and game theory (among other disciplines) – have invoked categorizations that go beyond the conjunction of analytical beliefs and sensory ones. This would apply, for example, to the 'priors' presumed in behaviour under uncertainty, which cannot be derived only from analytical truths and sensory perceptions. But Margalit and Yaari are concerned with *knowledge* as opposed to *belief*, and in the standard form of the positivist theory of knowledge from which the epistemology underlying the theory of 'common knowledge' is derived, only two categories are, in fact, admitted. The inadequacy discussed is that of a theory of knowledge, not of a theory of beliefs.

To postulate common *knowledge*, another category of knowledge would be needed. Margalit and Yaari propose a category they call 'comprehension'. In the particular case of Alice and Bob, knowledge based on a causal 'understanding' of Alice's behaviour would fall into this category, taking us beyond the conjunction of sensory perception and analytical reasoning. A similar conclusion emerges in the interesting case of Hangman's Paradox, with the need for a 'kind of knowledge' that is 'neither purely factual nor purely analytic'.

3   COMMON KNOWLEDGE AND BEYOND

These arguments on the inadequacy of the twofold categories of knowledge rely on the structure of 'interactive epistemology' and the motivational force of the assumption of 'common knowledge'. That is a momentous enough conclusion, given the commanding hold of the theory of common knowledge in contemporary game theory and economics. But if someone had no truck with common knowledge, he or she would not need – on the basis of the argument presented here – to drop the twofold classification of all knowledge.

It can indeed be argued that the two-category view of knowledge is inadequate *in general*, not just inadequate for carrying the full weight of the demands of common knowledge. Margalit and Yaari are inclined to make this general claim. However, since their reasoning is developed *within* the structure of interactive epistemology, some additional arguments would seem to be needed for the project of debunking the twofold category of knowledge *in general* – even if the elaborate structure of interactive epistemology were not to be adopted.

For this, what is needed is a clear and economic identification of exactly those claims, which belong *inter alia* to interactive epistemology (among much else) and cause problems given the twofold categorization of knowledge. It would, of course, be *sufficient* for this bigger project to *establish first* the need for the presumptions that constitute common knowledge and interactive epistemology, and *then* make those presumptions serve as premises in the argument to follow. But this would be a hard route to try, since that framework is so demanding and overambitious.

It would also be an *unnecessarily* hard route. In fact, Margalit and Yaari can work with the much weaker requirement that acknowledges the *possibility* of such understanding as Bob's knowledge of the colour of the traffic light (and correspondingly his knowledge of Alice's knowledge of that colour). A theory of knowledge that *never* allows Bob to 'know' the colour of the traffic light *through any reasoning whatsoever* would be severely limited *in general*, no matter what we think of the rest of the demands of interactive epistemology and of common knowledge in particular. Similar statements can be made about some of the knowledge that is involved in Margalit and Yaari's account of the Hangman's Paradox, not to mention various bits of 'knowledge' to which Sherlock Holmes lays claim in arguments that go well beyond logical truths and sensory knowledge (even Watson would recognize this).

The two-fold categorization of knowledge into sensory and analytic information produces a very limited domain of knowledge which excludes not only the full force of interactive epistemology and of common knowledge (thereby excluding an extremely ambitious theory), but also various other – more limited – claims about what we can or cannot know. There is a more general argument here, the basis for which is laid by Margalit and Yaari themselves. It would turn on a very weak demand of the *possibility* of knowing more than what they call 'the lowest common denominator', and this is all they need, given the line of reasoning they have already indicated. An explicit pursuit of the general form of that argument may also help us to get a clearer idea of the contents of what they call comprehension, since that is presently serving the purpose of a 'miscellaneous' category – whatever knowledge the positivist twofold classification cannot encompass.

4 KNOWING WHAT ONE KNOWS

This issue of generalization – from a critique of the twofold categorization of the theory of interactive epistemology and of common knowledge, to a more general critique of the twofold categorization in the positivist theory of knowledge – relates to a small tension that runs throughout this engaging chapter. On the one hand, the authors are clearly interested in the limitations of the particular theories now in vogue, and they state their project as: 'we shall argue that the concept of knowledge that has emerged in these discussions is unreasonably narrow and confining' (p. 89). On the other hand, they are, in fact, 'gunning' for the Humean twofold categorization in general, and conclude with the need for 'relaxing this dichotomy' by introducing what they call a third category called 'comprehension' (p. 95). The ambitions of the chapter rise as it proceeds, and this is just right, since their demonstrations not only undermine a prevailing and elaborate theory of knowledge currently used – typically implicitly – in game theory and economics, but also show the failure of the twofold categorization to make sense of *possibilities* of knowledge which we would find hard to do without, *in general*.

Because of their bigger project, they let pass several other limitations of the theory of interactive epistemology and common knowledge which they could have discussed, but chose not to. One can, for example, be deeply sceptical of the claim of the theory of common knowledge that $k_i(f) \Rightarrow k_i k_i(f)$, that is, if a person knows something, she also knows that she knows it. This is a standard part of the prevailing theory, but seems to be particularly difficult to defend. A person who has not swum for fifty years may not know whether she really does not still how to swim, but could well discover, when she tries it, that she does indeed know how to swim, even though she did not know that she knew it. There are limitations of this kind that would be also worth discussing in the specific project of providing a critique of interactive epistemology and common knowledge, but which would have distracted attention from Margalit and Yaari's implicit focus on problems that arise more generally.

5   LOGICAL OMNISCIENCE

Turning to Margalit and Yaari's rejection of 'logical omniscience' (their other line of criticism of the theory of common knowledge), there is perhaps a need here to emphasize that this assumption has two distinct limitations – related respectively to realism and rationality – neither of which entails the other. Logical omniscience is most definitely not a characteristic of the world in which we live: people do frequently fail to draw logical implications of one kind or other. Nor is it a good assumption for rational behaviour – a point that is quite separate from the unrealism of logical omniscience. A person's rationality need not be seen as severely compromised just because he is unable to solve an extrenely complex mathematical puzzle (even though the solution is analytically contained in the puzzle itself).

In the theory of rationality, there is an important issue as to 'how much' logical ability must be presumed for the rationality of a person. An individual's inability to 'get' elementary implications can certainly compromise the presumption of rationality. For example, a person who is informed that a particular light comes *on* if and only if a specific switch is put on the 'on' position, but still cannot figure out that to avoid having the light *on*, he must have the switch in another position, lacks something in rationality. On the other hand, the logical power needed to solve 'the four-colour problem' cannot in general be a requirement of rationality. Where to draw the line is a problem of much importance, and lines would have to be drawn in between the two extremes for an adequate theory of rationality.

6   A CONCLUDING REMARK

Both problems to which Margalit and Yaari draw attention are of great importance – not just for the prevailing theory of common knowledge and the philosophical underpinning provided by 'interactive epistemology', but also for theories of knowledge and rationality in general. We have reasons to be grateful to the authors for showing us what they have explicitly shown. If we still grumble (as I suppose I have done a bit) that we wish they would analyse the implications of their own line of reasoning in a more *general* form, that is, in fact, a reflection of our appreciation of what they have already done. The penalty of excellence can be more work.

Reply to Margalit and Yaari

Robert J. Aumann

THE HEBREW UNIVERSITY OF JERUSALEM, ISRAEL

On the issue of 'logical omniscience' – the assumption that if one knows something, then one knows all its logical consequences – I am in complete agreement with Margalit and Yaari. There is no question that this is an important, far-reaching, and rather unreasonable assumption, and that it would be highly desirable to get rid of it. Unfortunately, I know of no coherent system of epistemic logic that does so, even in the one-agent case. One could take the position that this problem is so central that until it is solved, there is no point in bothering with the epistemic foundations of interactive decision theory at all. In the 'Notes on Interactive Epistemology' (Aumann, 1992) to which Margalit and Yaari refer, I chose not to take that position, but to set forth the epistemic foundations of game theory and rational economics as they appear today, i.e., with the assumption of logical omniscience.

Also, I agree entirely that the 'sensory – analytic dichotomy' is not useful or appropriate. The word 'sensory' does not appear in Aumann (1992): indeed, there is nothing there about the source of an agent's knowledge. The main point of Aumann (1992) is to give a coherent foundation for the representation of non-tautological knowledge that agents may have about each other's knowledge. If, as Margalit and Yaari claim, the dichotomy precludes agents from acquiring such knowledge, I am certainly with them in rejecting it.

On the other hand, the interpretation of 'Agreeing to Disagree' (Aumann, 1976) in Margalit and Yaari misses the whole point of that result. They write that 'Alice must take care not to condition on anything that Bob does not know'. I had hoped to have made it clear – both in the 1992 notes and in the original paper (1976) – that that is not so! The first two sentences of Aumann (1976) read, 'If two people have the same priors, and their posteriors for a given event A are common knowledge, then these two posteriors must be equal. *This is so even though they may base their posteriors on quite different information.* See also section 5 of Aumann (1992).

As for the 'Hangman's Paradox', the paradox seems to have nothing to do with *multiple* periods: it works just as well for one. Suppose one tells a class, 'Our next scheduled meeting will be devoted to an exam, but you will not know this beforehand'. Obviously, this involves a contradiction, so the students will not know what to make of it. At the next scheduled meeting, the exam is given, so the first part of the announcement was correct. The second part was also correct: since the announcement was gibberish, it couldn't be taken seriously, so the students indeed did not know about the exam.

With 17 periods, it is the same: though the announcement is more complicated to think through, in the end it is still (i) gibberish, and (ii) correct.

More precisely, it is not the content of the announcement that is gibberish, but its being an announcement – something that the listeners are meant to know after hearing. Some propositions simply cannot be known, though they may well be true – for example, any proposition of the form 'x and not kx' (of which the one-period Hangman's Paradox is an instance). If we call this f, then kf is equivalent to 'kx and not *kx*', which is tautologically false.

While I agree with Margalit and Yaari on the 'sensory – analytic dichotomy', I must admit to being puzzled as to the nature of the point they are trying to make. If Alice tells Bob that the light turned green, why doesn't he know this? They say that he only knows that she said it: but that sounds like a quibble. If one wishes to go that route, one may as well say that she herself doesn't know that the light is green, only that she sees it as green; perhaps she is hallucinating or dreaming, or has developed a fever that affects her colour perception. Alternatively put, why do Margalit and Yaari not consider hearing as one of the senses? This whole line of argument is unconvincing. In particular, the conclusion that knowledge cannot be conveyed between individuals seems farfetched indeed.

It appears from several places in their chapter (e.g., p. 91, lines 25–31; p. 92, lines 30–32; p. 94, lines 16–18) that Margalit and Yaari have a basic misunderstanding of the construction in Aumann (1992). I *assume* no analytic knowledge other than that which is embodied in the axiom schema of the propositional calculus and of knowledge, and the *modus ponens* rule. All other analytic knowledge is *derived*, not assumed. Given the number of agents, the state space is *categoric*. And if one considers the number of agents an issue, it may be taken to be a denumerable infinity (i.e., a pool large enough to cover all agents); then this, too, is categoric, and there is no substantive knowledge at all in the state space. In a sense, that is the whole point of the construction in Aumann (1992) – to *derive* the state space, so that it need *not* be assumed as analytic. The problems that Margalit and Yaari raise are discussed in section 5 of my 1992 notes; the subsequent construction solves these problems.

One may also think of this in another way: that the state space is not a part of the agent's knowledge at all, but is only in the analyst's mind. All that the agent knows is a list of formulas. The rest is a construction that is useful for the analyst, but that the agent does not need.

Finally, it may be that the disagreement between the authors and me is largely semantic – I use the term 'knowledge' in a more comprehensive way than they, to include what they call 'comprehension'.

There is also a difference in emphasis and direction between us. They are interested in the sources and meaning of knowledge – how things get to be known, and what it 'really means' for them to be known. My approach is less philosophical and more pragmatic; basically, I wish only to provide a coherent formalization of those aspects of knowledge that are relevant to interactive decision theory and related disciplines.

References

Aumann, R.J. (1976) 'Agreeing to Disagree', *The Annals of Statistics*, vol. 4, pp. 1236–9.
Aumann, R.J. (1992) 'Notes on Interactive Epistemology', version of 17 July 1992; available as DP 67 at the Center for Rationality and Interactive Decision Theory, the Hebrew University of Jerusalem, February 1995.

Part II

Rationality in Game Theory

5 Rationalizing Backward Induction?*

Ken Binmore

UNIVERSITY COLLEGE, LONDON, UK

and

Larry Samuelson

UNIVERSITY OF WISCONSIN, USA

'One must imagine Sisyphus happy' (Albert Camus)

1 THE MYTH OF SISYPHUS

Binmore (1987) explains why backward induction in games cannot be justified by assuming only that there is common knowledge of rationality before the game begins. In writing once more on the myth that it can, we feel like Sisyphus rolling his rock to the top of the hill again. However, it is necessary to respond to Aumann's (1993) attempt to revitalize a fallacy which game theorists must abandon if their discipline is to continue to be taken seriously.[1]

For example, backward induction calls for both players always to play *down* in Rosenthal's Centipede Game of Figure 5.1. It similarly requires that both players always defect in the finitely repeated Prisoners' Dilemma. It also calls for an established retail chain never to resist an entrant in Selten's Chain-Store Paradox. These conclusions are not only counterintuitive. As prescriptions to be followed for purely rational reasons, they are *unsound*, as explained at length in Binmore (1987).

If our response to Aumann's (1993) argument is to be understood, it is essential to be clear from the outset that the issue is not mathematical. In presenting his paper at the recent Nobel Symposium on game theory, he predicted that his audience would find his argument either wrong or trivial. But we think the mathematical part of his argument is neither trivial nor wrong. But the character of Aumann's mathematics is beside the point. We focus on the wrong question if we look for an error in how Aumann deduces his conclusion from his hypotheses.[2] An axiom-definition-theorem-proof format is designed to close the mind to irrelevancies so that attention can be concentrated on the issues that really matter. But if an inappropriate formalism is chosen, one necessarily closes one's mind to issues that it is perilous to neglect. The proverb warns us against closing the stable door after the horse has bolted. But an even worse mistake is to bolt the stable door while the horse is still in the yard.

* The support of National Science Foundation grant SES 9122176 is gratefully acknowledged.

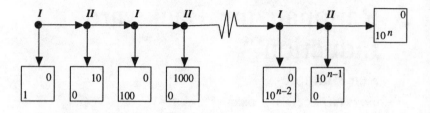

Figure 5.1 Rosenthal's Centipede

Similar considerations bring into question the relevance to actual human behaviour of the whole literature on refinements of Nash equilibrium. Even when the arguments given in favour of the concepts are sound, such an *eductive* approach is worthy of widespread study by economists only to the extent that its prognostications about ideally rational play can serve as approximations to the outcomes that would result if equilibrium were achieved using an appropriate *evolutive* process (Binmore, 1987). For example, in casting doubt on backward induction, one simultaneously casts doubt on the iterated deletion of weakly dominated strategies – one of three principles that Kohlberg and Mertens (1986) list as being fundamental to a sound eductive theory.[3] However, from an *evolutive* standpoint, even *one* round of deleting weakly dominated strategies cannot be justified (Binmore, 1990, p. 75; Samuelson, 1993).

Section 5 follows Binmore, Gale and Samuelson (1993) in using Selten's (1978) Chain-Store Game as a counterexample to the notion that deleting weakly dominated strategies is harmless. The Chain-Store Game is a particularly telling arena in which to set the debate since orthodox game theorists are stuck with predicting that the only rational outcome is the unique subgame-perfect equilibrium, whereas the experimental evidence persistently shows that real people do not play this way in the strategically similar Ultimatum Game – even for high stakes after much experience.

2   BACKWARD INDUCTION

Aumann's formal defence of backward induction in finite games of perfect information[4] is preceded by six statements about the formal ground-rules to which his mathematics applies. The first and second statements are:

(1) Rationality is attributed to 'agents' rather than players, where each vertex of the game tree belongs to a different agent.

(2) All agents choose actions, whether or not their vertices are reached; the action of an agent signifies what he will do *if* his vertex is reached.

If the pun may be excused, the first statement immediately gives Aumann's game away. Critics like myself express doubts about backward induction in games like

Rosenthal's Centipede because it requires players to continue to believe that their opponents are rational whatever evidence to the contrary may be forthcoming. For example, if common knowledge of rationality before the game begins justifies backward induction in the Centipede, then player II knows that she and her opponent will always play *down*. So what conclusion should she draw on finding herself at the fiftieth node of the tree after repeatedly observing the refutation of the hypothesis that her opponent is rational? Proponents of backward induction tell us that 'common knowledge of rationality before the game begins' implies that she should nevertheless continue to act as though she and her opponent were rational. We do not argue that such behaviour should be excluded as a possible recommendation that a game theorist might make – only that one cannot *deduce* that all other behaviour is irrational from the given hypotheses.

Aumann evades this difficulty by following Selten (1975) in pretending that a player in the Centipede is a collection of separate and independent agents. It then becomes possible for the rationality of twenty-five of these agents to be refuted without the need to draw any inference about the irrationality of the remaining twenty-five. However, further comment on this piece of legerdemain will need to be delayed until his second statement has been discussed.

It is significant that Aumann eschews the subjunctive mood in this second statement. Properly, we should therefore interpret its second clause as a *material implication* '$P \Rightarrow Q$' in which P is the statement that a particular vertex is reached, and Q is the statement that the agent who decides at that vertex chooses 'rationally' given his information. But, if Aumann were right, 'common knowledge of rationality before the game begins' would imply that only the first vertex can be reached. The statement P is therefore false in the case of the fiftieth vertex. The corresponding implication '$P \Rightarrow Q$' is therefore true – however one interprets the meaning of Q.[5] It is as though Alekhine were asked how he would play a game of chess on an 8×8 board with 63 squares. *Any* answer would then be rational, because *anything* follows from a contradiction.

The point of being pedantic about material implication is that the final clause of Aumann's second statement needs to be interpreted as a *subjunctive conditional* for the statement to be meaningful in the intended sense. The clause should be restated as, 'The action of an agent signifies what he *would* do, if his vertex *were* reached.' As explained for example by Sandford (1989), a subjunctive conditional 'If P, then Q' is not necessarily true when P is counterfactual. It is not true that, 'If Binmore's Dean were a man, then his salary would be doubled' even though his Dean is actually a woman.

It is idle to pretend that counterfactual reasoning can be evaded in analyzing games. A rational player stays on the equilibrium path because of what he believes *would* happen if he *were* to deviate. C.I. Lewis (1946) revived Leibniz's notion of a 'possible world' in seeking to make sense of such counterfactual assertions. More recently, his namesake, David Lewis[6] (1976) has put together a full-blown theory in which sense is made of a subjunctive conditional 'If P, then Q' in which P is counterfactual, by considering all possible worlds in which P does not hold. The subjunctive conditional is then interpreted as applying to whichever of these possible worlds is 'closest' to the actual world in which we live.

Aumann (1993) is implicitly appealing to some such theory when he tells us that a particular action is rational for player II's twenty-fifth agent *if* the fiftieth vertex is reached. After observing the counterfactual event that all agents at vertices preceding the fiftieth are irrational, Aumann's story makes it overwhelmingly tempting that we assume that the possible world within which his second statement is to be interpreted is that in which agents 1 to 49 are irrational and agents 50 to 100 are rational. But this is just a piece of *interpretation*. We cannot *deduce* that *only* such an interpretation is viable merely from 'common knowledge of rationality before the game begins'. If this hypothesis is refuted in play, we have a *contradiction* from which *anything* can be deduced.

Although we invoke the authority of David Lewis, we do not think that his theory of counterfactuals helps very much with game-theory problems. Everything that matters in addressing practical problems hinges on the topology used to interpret the word 'close', and this is not a subject that it makes much sense to discuss in the abstract. Before returning to Aumann's argument, let us therefore say something about our own (not very profound) attitude to counterfactuals in games.

3 INTERPRETING COUNTERFACTUALS

Consider a husband who explains to his wife that he would not have lost this month's mortgage repayment if he had been dealt the Ace of Diamonds rather than the Queen of Spades in last night's poker game. His wife has no difficulty in interpreting this counterfactual assertion, because the story tells her how Nature chose an actual world from a set of possible worlds that might have been. The actual world in which she is without a roof over her head was realized as a consequence of the shuffle and deal that proceeded the disastrous hand at the poker game. If a different card *had* been dealt, she *would* have retained her home.

To make sense of counterfactuals in games, we think one always needs to find an equivalent of the deal at last night's poker game. Such an equivalent cannot be found by contemplating abstract definitions of rationality, any more than the wife could make sense of her husband's counterfactual by minutely examining the card that he actually was dealt. Just as the Queen of Spades has to be seen as having been drawn from a deck of cards, so a rational player has to be seen as having been drawn from a set of possible players – some of whom are irrational.

Selten's (1975) notion of a trembling-hand equilibrium treats counterfactuals in precisely this manner. No player ever thinks an irrational thought in Selten's story, but irrational actions are taken with some small probability δ by mistake. In the limit as $\delta \to 0$, irrational moves are counterfactual. But if they were observed they would be interpreted as having taken place in a nearby possible world in which $\delta > 0$.

Selten's trembling-hand story provides a means of interpreting subjunctive conditionals that preserves backward induction. With this story, players will always defect in the finitely repeated Prisoners' Dilemma. However, in the well-known Gang of Four paper, Kreps, Milgrom, Roberts and Wilson (1982) offer an alternative story. If irrational play is observed, it is attributed to an irrational type of player who occurs with probability $\delta > 0$ and always plays *tit-for-tat* no matter what. It is shown that rational players will then cooperate for long periods in the finitely repeated Prisoners' Dilemma even though δ may be very small.

Who is right, Selten or the Gang of Four? We hope that it is now evident that this is a badly posed question. The 'rightness' of the interpretation of counterfactuals is not a matter for the propositional calculus. Nor can counterfactuals be evaded in game theory. A rational player stays on the equilibrium path because of what *would* happen if he *were* to deviate. But it is counterfactual that he will deviate. One cannot interpret such a counterfactual without having a view on the kind of mistake that a rational player *would* make, if a rational player *were* to make a mistake. To have a view on this question, it is necessary to follow the advice of Selten and Leopold (1982) in having available a model of a player which is sufficiently rich that it includes both rational and irrational variants. In the limiting case, when irrational types occur with probability zero, certain actions will be impossible. However, in the counterfactual event that such an event occurs, one has a mechanism available for dealing a possible world in which events that are impossible in the actual world can be realized. But there is obviously no 'right' way to construct the necessary models of irrational behaviour. One needs to look at the *context* in which the game is played for inspiration on this score. But this context is precisely what is abstracted away when one adopts the conventional mathematical formalism.

Consider, for example, the context in which chess is normally played. In such a context, it is quite extraordinarily obtuse to propose a trembling-hand interpretation of the counterfactuals that arise during play. If Black repeatedly makes bad moves, is White really to assume that she always thought everything through correctly, but that Nature kept jogging her elbow at the moment of making a move so that she somehow repeatedly found herself lifting her hand having set the wrong piece down on the wrong square? Is White also to explain his *own* mistakes with the same story – even when introspection tells him that the true explanation is that he reasoned badly? When put so baldly, the suggestion is laughable. If a player makes stupid moves in chess, the explanation of first resort must surely be that he or she reasoned badly and therefore will perhaps reason badly in the future.

Aumann (1993) mentions Zermelo's celebrated use of backward induction in 1912 to show that chess has a 'solution'. But Zermelo's argument does *not* say that common knowledge of rationality implies that a player should necessarily use a subgame-perfect strategy. It tells White what to do in order to guarantee his maximin value in every subgame – but such behaviour is not necessarily optimal. Suppose, for example, that Black has missed many opportunities to win in reaching the current position,[7] and White now faces a subgame in which the best he can do against good play by Black is to force a draw. However, White sees a move that will win unless Black responds much more cleverly than she has in the past. However, if she does see the clever response, then White will lose for sure. What should White do? The answer depends on his estimate of the probability that Black will see her clever response. Given her past behaviour, he would be stupid to assign a probability of one to this eventuality. But this is what a trembling-hand story would require him to do.

Notice that we do not deny that Zermelo's use of backward induction demonstrates that common knowledge of rationality before the game begins will indeed result in each player getting his maximin value in chess.[8] What Zermelo claimed is indeed true. Nor do we deny that it would usually be appropriate to use backward induction to analyze the Centipede, if this were *actually* played by Aumann's 100 independent agents.[9] Nor do we deny that evolution will tend to eliminate certain types of irrationality and hence open up the prospect of convergence on a subgame-perfect equilibrium in the long run. We deny only

that backward induction is a *necessary consequence* of common knowledge of
rationality before the game begins.

4 CHAIN-STORE PARADOX

In this section, Selten's (1978) Chain-Store Paradox will now be used as an example
while discussing assumptions under which backward induction can be justified.
Figure 5.2(a) shows a version of the Chain-Store Game. Player II is a chain-store
and player I is a potential rival thinking of setting up a single store that will compete
with the chain in one particular town. Player I must stay out of the market by
playing *H* or enter by playing *L*. In the latter case, player II may acquiesce in the
new situations by playing *Y* or she may initiate a price war by playing *N*.

A backward induction analysis results in the subgame-perfect equilibrium in
which player II chooses *Y* and player I chooses *L*, as indicated by the doubled lines
in Figure 5.2(a). Traditional game theory therefore predicts that the potential rival
will enter and that the chain-store will acquiesce. The chain-store paradox arises
when the Chain-Store Game is repeated 100 times with a new potential entrant at
each repetition. Backward induction again leads to a subgame-perfect equilibrium in
which all potential entrants enter the market and the chain-store always acquiesces
in their entry. The doubled lines in Figure 5.2(b) show the subgame-perfect choices
at each node in the case when the Chain-Store Game is repeated only twice. Selten
(1978) regarded such an outcome as paradoxical, because the chain-store has the
alternative strategy of fighting the first few entrants with a view to establishing a
reputation for toughness that will deter the entry of later potential entrants.

As with the repeated Prisoners' Dilemma, it is not hard to find variants of the
repeated Chain-Store Game in which a traditional analysis does not eliminate the
use of a tough strategy by the chain-store. One may allow the number of repetitions
to be indefinite. Or one may stick with the finitely repeated case and follow Kreps,
Milgrom, Roberts and Wilson (1982) by introducing a small amount of incomplete
information about the type of the chain-store. Even a small prior probability that the
chain-store may be an 'irrational' type who always fights is enough to overturn the
subgame-perfect prediction of the original game. However, this chapter is about the
validity of backward induction rather than the realism of various models. We shall
therefore stick with the finitely repeated case with perfect information.

Even in this case, we argue that no paradox exists, because there are flaws in the
reasoning by means of which Aumann (1993) and others with less formal arguments
deduce the backward induction principle from the assumption that there is common
knowledge of rationality before the game begins. In fact, the next section offers
evolutive reasons why we should not exclude Nash equilibria that fail to be
subgame-perfect even when the Chain-Store Game is played *once and once only*.

Nevertheless, we do not deny that there are eductive assumptions that do justify
backward induction. And we agree very much with Aumann (1993) that, although
the reasoning that deduces backward induction from such assumptions may be
criticized as trivial, it is still worthwhile being explicit about what assumptions are
necessary. However, the two alternative assumptions considered here will not be
nearly as attractive to applied workers as Aumann's suggestion that it suffices to
assume that there is common knowledge of rationality before the game begins.

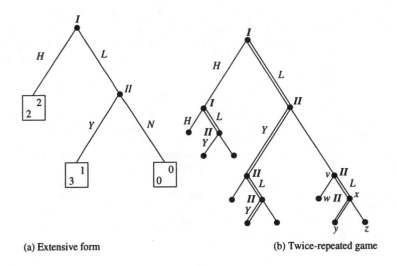

(a) Extensive form   (b) Twice-repeated game

Figure 5.2   The Chain-Store Game

Assumption 1   The first assumption we consider is that it is not only common knowledge before the game begins that all players are rational, but that it would always remain common knowledge that the players would act rationally in the future – regardless of what might have happened in the past. This assumption need not be discussed further since it merely makes explicit the missing assumptions in Aumann's argument.

Assumption 2   The second assumption we consider follows Binmore (1993) in appealing to a very strong form of revealed preference theory. The purpose of the argument is to show that various fallacies that purport to show that it is rational to 'make commitments' cannot possibly demonstrate that backward induction is *necessarily* irrational in certain games. The trivial argument in fact shows that *any* behaviour in a finite game of perfect information can be rationalized as being subgame-perfect if one is free to make whatever assumptions seem convenient about what is going on inside the heads of the players.

Consider, for example, the pattern of behaviour indicated in the twice-repeated, Chain-Store Game of Figure 5.2(b). Let us focus on the node *x* reached after the history *LNL*. Since the action *Y* at this node is doubled, assign a payoff to player II at the node *y* that is reached after the history *LNLY* a higher payoff than at the terminal node *z* reached after the history *LNLN*. Now focus on the terminal node *v* reached after the history *LN*. Since the action *L* is doubled at this node, assign a higher payoff to player III at the terminal node *y* than at the terminal node *w* reached after the history *LNH*. The interpretation that goes with such an assignment of payoffs is the following. It is taken to be common knowledge that player II would choose *Y* if node *x* were reached. It is also taken to be common knowledge that player III would choose H if node υ were reached. Notice that, in the latter case, player III has available information about the nature of player II that will be part of what determines his knowledge about what player II would do if player III were to play L. The information is that player II played N in the past. This is a counterfactual event before the game begins.

Such an extreme use of the theory of revealed preference clarifies certain logical matters. It is even more useful in exposing the fallacies of those who argue that cooperation in the one-shot Prisoners' Dilemma is necessarily rational. However, it should be emphasized that its interpretation of the payoffs in the repeated Chain-Store Game differs markedly from that normally taken for granted in game theory (although not in the one-shot Prisoners' Dilemma). In Figure 5.2(a), for example, the standard assumption is that the payoffs 0, 2 and 3 attributed to player I are von Neumann and Morgenstern utilities that can be elicited by asking player I hypothetical questions about his preferences amongst lotteries in which the prizes are the outcomes represented by the terminal nodes. But such hypothetical questions can be answered without any reference to what player I knows about what player II would choose if player I were to play L.

5 ULTIMATUM GAME

In this section, we abandon the extreme version of revealed preference theory discussed in the previous section. In the Ultimatum Game to be studied next, the payoffs can be taken to be sums of money. Our plan is to use the game as an example in which backward induction goes spectacularly awry in an evolutive context.

The Ultimatum Game involves two players who must divide a dollar. The rules specify that player I begins by making an offer of $x \in [0, 1]$ to player II, who then accepts or refuses. If player II accepts, player I gets $1 - x$ and player II gets x. If player II refuses, both get nothing. Traditional game theory predicts that the play of this game will result in the unique subgame-perfect equilibrium in which player II plans to accept whatever she is offered and player I offers player II nothing.[10]

Although subgame-perfect predictions sometimes perform well in laboratory tests, this is not true of the Ultimatum Game. In the first of many experiments by numerous authors on this and related games, Güth *et al.* (1982) found that the modal offer was one-half and that player I had roughly half a chance of being rejected if he offered about one-third of the sum of money available. Results of this general character have been repeatedly observed under increasingly more challenging conditions, as reported in the surveys of Bolton and Zwick (1993), Güth and Tietz (1990), Roth (1991) and Thaler (1988).

Orthodox game theorists tend to ignore these experimental results, or else express doubts about the validity of the experimental data. However, we suggest that a more realistic attitude is to question a theory whose relevance to actual behaviour is being so firmly refuted. To explore the possibility that the eductive arguments which lead to the subgame-perfect prediction in the Ultimatum Game are irrelevant to behaviour generated by an evolutive process, Binmore, Gale and Samuelson (1993) have run extensive simulations of noisy versions of the replicator dynamics for the Ultimatum Game. Even if the absolute noise levels are very small, they find that,

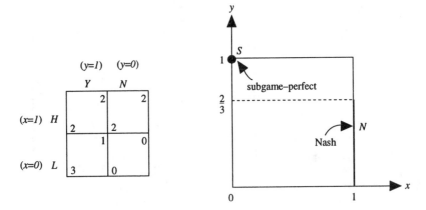

Figure 5.3 The Chain-Store Game again

when the responding population is noisier than the proposing population, a Nash equilibrium that is not subgame-perfect survives as an asymptotic attractor. At this Nash equilibrium, player I offers about 20 per cent of the dollar to player II. Player II refuses all smaller offers with some positive probability.[11]

Space does not allow a discussion of these simulations. Instead, we shall study the version of the Chain-Store Game given in Figure 5.2(a). This can be regarded as a simplified form of the Ultimatum Game. For this interpretation, player I is seen as having the opportunity to make a high offer (*H*) or a low offer (*L*). If he makes a high offer, it is assumed that player II accepts. If he makes a low offer, player II may accept (*Y*) or refuse (*N*). Figure 5.3(b) shows the pairs (*x*, *y*) that represent equilibria in the game, where *x* and *y* are the probabilities with which *H* and *Y* are played. There is a unique subgame-perfect equilibrium *S* at (0,1) in Figure 5.3(b), and a component *N* of Nash equilibria occupying the closed line segment joining (1,2/3) and (1, 0).

Figure 5.4(a) shows the trajectories of the standard replicator dynamics in the Chain-Store Game:

$$\dot{x} = x(1 - x)(2 - 3y) \qquad (1)$$
$$\dot{y} = y(1 - y)(1 - x) \qquad (2)$$

Notice that the subgame-perfect equilibrium *S* is an asymptotic attractor. But there are Nash equilibria which are local attractors without being subgame-perfect. This is true of all the points in the relative interior of *N*.

One may reasonably respond to the observation that Nash equilibria other than the subgame-perfect equilibrium may be attractors of the replicator dynamics by observing that the model artificially excludes the evolutionary pressure against weakly dominated strategies that would otherwise eliminate them. It is therefore necessary to consider models in which small fractions of all possible strategies are continually injected into the population – including those that test the 'rationality' of responders who refuse positive offers. Only if the survival of Nash equilibria that are

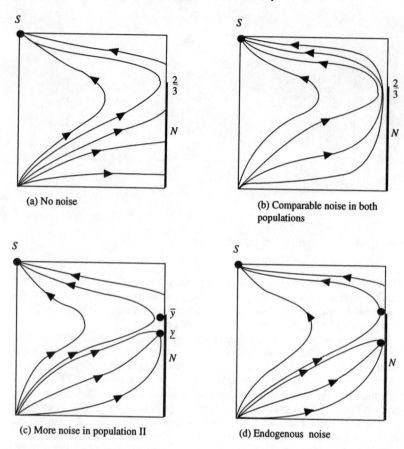

(a) No noise

(b) Comparable noise in both
populations

(c) More noise in population II

(d) Endogenous noise

Figure 5.4   Phase diagrams

not subgame-perfect is robust in the presence of such noise can we realistically argue against the subgame-perfect prediction.

It is natural to see such a noisy model as an evolutionary gloss on Selten's (1975) trembling-hand story. However, caution is necessary before pressing the analogy too far. Samuelson and Zhang (1992) show that adding noise to the replicator and other evolutionary dynamics does not necessarily lead to the elimination of weakly dominated strategies. The question of whether only subgame-perfect equilibria can survive in a noisy evolutionary environment therefore remains open.

To investigate the robustness of the conclusion that a Nash equilibrium which is not subgame-perfect can survive as an asymptotic attractor, Binmore, Gale and Samuelson (1993) study the perturbed replicator equations:

$$\dot{x} = \Delta_1 x(1-x)(2-3y) + \delta_1(\tfrac{1}{2} - x) \tag{3}$$
$$\dot{y} = \Delta_2 y(1-y)(1-x) + \delta_2(\tfrac{1}{2} - y) \tag{4}$$

The case $\Delta_j = 1$ is of special interest, since it represents a situation in which agents in population j die or leave the game at rate δ_j to be replaced by novices who play strategy i with an exogenously determined probability θ_i.

Figures 5.4(b) and 5.4(c) show the trajectories for the perturbed replicator dynamics. Take $\phi = \delta_1 \Delta_2 / \delta_2 \Delta_1$. In Figure 5.4(b), $\phi < 3 + 2\sqrt{2}$. In Figure 5.4(c), $3 + 2\sqrt{2} < \phi$. Since $3 + 2\sqrt{2} \sim 5.8$, responders are therefore appreciably noisier than proposers in the second case.

The striking difference between Figures 5.4(b) and 5.4(c) is that the second has an asymptotic attractor in the set N, whereas only the subgame-perfect equilibrium is an asymptotic attractor in the first. In the case when the responding population is significantly more noisy than the proposing population, we therefore have a substantive argument in favour of retaining a Nash equilibrium that is not subgame-perfect. But when should we expect the responding population to be noisier than the proposing population?

Some intuition on this subject can be obtained by reverting to the full Ultimatum Game. Suppose that noise in this game is caused by players misreading the strategic situation and so acting in a manner that is appropriate to some other game. For example, the Ultimatum Game might be confused with a more commonly occurring type of take-it-or-leave-it game in which the reputation for toughness matters, or with the take-it-or-leave-it game played by retail outlets, which leave a responder free to try her luck at a similar game down the street. A reasonable hypothesis would seem to be that players will be more prone to misreading games the smaller are the payoffs at stake. But, close to the subgame-perfect equilibrium, responders will have very little at stake in the Ultimatum Game. We should therefore anticipate that their behaviour will tend to be much noisier than the behaviour of proposers, for whom an inappropriate choice can be very costly. In the Ultimatum Game, this consideration creates an evolutionary pressure *against* the subgame-perfect equilibrium.

In the Chain-Store Game, matters are not so clear-cut because the subgame-perfect equilibrium always has a substantial basin of attraction even in Figure 5.4(c). However, a natural avenue of investigation is to endogenize the noise. For example, consider the case when $\Delta j = 1 - \delta_j$ and δ_j is related to the current payoff levels at the time t by the formula

$$\delta_i(t) = \frac{\alpha\beta}{\alpha + \lambda_i(t)}$$

where α and β are constant and $\lambda_i(t)$ is the difference between the maximum and minimum expected payoff from each strategy i, given the current opponents' strategies. When this difference is zero, as is the case for responders at the subgame-perfect equilibrium, the noise level takes its highest value of β. If the difference could increase all the way to infinity, $\delta_i(t)$ would decrease to zero.

Figure 5.4(d) shows the trajectories of the perturbed replicator dynamics with such endogenized noise. The immediate point is that Figure 5.4(d) resembles Figure 5.4(c). In particular, when the noise is endogenized, the equilibrium noise levels require the responding population be significantly noisier than the proposing population. The same phenomenon occurs in our simulations of the full Ultimatum Game with even more striking conclusions.

The preceding argument shows backward induction is at best dubious in an evolutive context – even in the very simple Chain-Store Game in which a unique subgame-perfect equilibrium is obtained after only two rounds of deleting weakly and strongly dominated strategies. However, the use of rational expectations equilibria in large models is a staple of macroeconomic theory. Similarly, the successive deletion of weakly dominated strategies is a standard tool in the industrial organization literature when considering complicated games with multiple equilibria. The use of these tools does not lead to successful predictions in laboratory experiments on the Ultimatum Game. Perhaps they fail to lead to successful predictions when applied on the grand scale for similar reasons.

6 CONCLUSION

As noted earlier, Aumann predicted that some of his audience would categorize his paper as wrong and others as trivial. In saying this, he hit an important nail on the head. In treating the eductive argument for backward induction as trivial, game theorists have gone badly wrong. The interpretation of subjunctive conditionals is anything but trivial – otherwise it would not be a subject of controversy among logicians. Game theorists have also gone badly wrong in treating as trivial the fact that the equilibria achieved by evolutive processes will necessarily resemble those achieved by eductive argumentation.

The moral seems quite plain. If the foundations of game theory are to escape the fate of Sisyphus, we have to learn that the interpretation of mathematical models needs as much care and attention as their analysis. However, our guess is that we still have a long time to wait before interpretive issues begin to get the attention that they deserve. In the meantime, that stone will keep rolling down the hill.

Notes

1. Since this paper was written, a new version of Aumann's (1993) paper has been circulated. In addition to the argument criticized here, the new paper contains a different argument for backward induction which Aumann attributes to Samet. Samet's argument fails for much the same reason as Aumann's.
2. Or for errors in the mathematics of Bicchieri (1988), Reny (1985) and others who come to different conclusions from Aumann.
3. Binmore (1987) argues that all three principles are mistaken.
4. With this restriction, a whole class of more general criticisms (Binmore, 1987) about the concept of common knowledge of rationality can be left on the sidelines.
5. Samet made the same point at the Nobel Symposium where Aumann presented his paper. When the entirely rational Samet becomes King of Sweden, his avowed plan is to swap his kingdom for a cup of coffee.
6. The same David Lewis (1969) anticipated Aumann (1976) in saying that an event E is common knowledge if and only if everybody knows E, everybody knows that everybody knows E, and so on. However, David Lewis did not anticipate Aumann's mathematical machinery, which converted a philosophical curiosity into a practical tool.
7. It is not an valid objection to say that common knowledge of rationality before the game begins precludes such an event. Although the event cannot occur given the prior information, we still have to say what White *would* do if the event *were* to occur.
8. To compute a maximin value, one always takes the most pessimistic view of the plans of

the other players. In a two-person, zero-sum game, a player who employs backward induction as recommended by Aumann will therefore come up with a strategy that guarantees his maximin value. But, for the reasons given by von Neumann and Morgenstern (1944), with common knowledge of rationality at time zero in a two-person, zero-sum game, neither player can hope for more than his maximin value.

9. But not always. It may be, as in the Horse Game studied in Binmore (1987), that there are grounds for supposing that some type of irrationality in one player will be correlated with the same type of irrationality in another. (After all, the number of business schools is not so very large and so different agents might well have been taught game theory by the same instructor.)

10. If offers must be made in whole number of cents, other subgame-perfect equilibria also exist, but player II never gets more than one cent in any of these.

11. It is natural to object that player II should realize that it is irrational to choose nothing when something is available without waiting to be taught by evolution. On this subject, it is perhaps instructive to follow Frank (1988) in considering how most of us behave in restaurants that we never expect to visit again. After the waiter gives your change, you can either take it all or return the customary amount. Of course, we tell ourselves little stories about why we do the latter that do not involve irrationality. This section discusses why such stories and the emotional attitudes that accompany them manage to survive.

References

Aumann, R. (1976) 'Agreeing to Disagree', *The Annals of Statistics*, vol. 4, pp. 1236–9.

Aumann, R. (1993) 'Backwards Induction and Common Knowledge of Rationality', paper presented at the Nobel Symposium on Game Theory, to appear in *Games and Economic Behaviour*.

Bicchieri, C. (1988) 'Common Knowledge and Backwards Induction: A Solution to the Paradox', in M. Vardi (ed.), *Theoretical Aspects of Reasoning About Knowledge* (Los Altos, Calif.: Morgan Kaufmann).

Binmore, K. (1987) 'Modeling Rational Players I', *Economics and Philosophy*, vol. 3, pp. 9–55.

Binmore, K. (1990) *Essays on Foundations of Game Theory* (Oxford: Basil Blackwell).

Binmore, K. (1993) *Playing Fair: Game Theory and the Social Contract I*, (Cambridge, Mass.: MIT Press).

Binmore, K., J. Gale, and L. Samuelson, (1993) 'Learning and Subgame-Perfection', University of Wisconsin Discussion Paper.

Bolton, G. and R. Zwick, (1993) 'Anonymity versus Punishment in Ultimatum Bargaining', Pennsylvania State University Discussion Paper.

Frank, R. (1988) *Passions within Reason* (New York: Norton).

Güth, W., R. Schmittberger, and B. Schwarze, (1982) 'An Experimental Analysis of Ultimatum Bargaining', *Journal of Behaviour and Organization*, vol. 3, pp. 367–88.

Güth, W. and R. Tietz, (1990) 'Ultimatum Bargaining Behavior: A Survey and Comparison of Experimental Results', *Journal of Economic Psychology*, vol. 11, pp. 417–49.

Harsanyi, J. and R. Selten, (1988) *A General Theory of Equilibrium Selection in Games* (Cambridge: Mass.: MIT Press).

Kohlberg, E. and J. Mertens, (1986) 'On the Strategic Stability of Equilibria', *Econometrica*, vol. 54, pp. 1003–37.

Kreps, D., P. Milgrom, J. Roberts, and R. Wilson, (1982) 'Rational Cooperation in the Finitely Repeated Prisoners' Dilemma', *Journal of Economic Theory*, vol. 27, pp. 245–52.

Lewis, C.I. (1946) *An Analysis of Knowledge and Valuation* (La Salle, Ill.: Open Court).

Lewis, D. (1969) *Conventions: A Philosophical Study* (Cambridge, Mass.: Harvard University Press).

Lewis, D. (1976) *Counterfactuals* (Oxford: Basil Blackwell).

Reny, P. (1990) 'Common Belief and the Theory of Games with Perfect Information', *Journal of Economic Theory*, vol. 59, pp. 257–74.

Roth, A. (1991) 'Bargaining Experiments', in J. Kagel and A. Roth (eds), *Handbook of Experimental Economics* (Princeton: Princeton University Press).

Samuelson, L. (1993) 'Does Evolution Eliminate Dominated Strategies?', in K. Binmore, A. Kirman and P. Tani (eds), *Frontiers of Game Theory* (Cambridge, Mass.: MIT Press).

Samuelson, L. and J. Zhang (1992) 'Evolutionary Stability in Asymmetric Games', *Journal of Economic Theory*, vol. 57, pp. 364–91.

Stanford, D. (1989) *If P, Then Q* (London: Routledge).

Selten, R. (1975) 'Reexamination of the Perfectness Concept for Equilibrium Points in Extensive-Games', *International Journal of Game Theory*, vol. 4, pp. 25–55.

Sandford, D. (1989) *If P, Then Q* (London: Routledge).

Selten, R. (1978) 'The Chain-Store Paradox', *Theory and Decision*, vol. 9, pp. 127–59.

Selten, R. and U. Leopold (1982) 'Subjunctive Conditionals in Decision Theory and Game Theory', in W. Stegmuller, W. Balzer and W. Spohn (eds), *Studies in Contemporary Economics, Vol, 2: Philosophy of Economics* (Berlin: Springer-Verlag).

Thaler, R. (1988) 'Anomalies: The Ultimatum Game', *Journal of Economic Perspectives*, vol. 2, pp. 195–206.

von Neumann, J. and O. Morgenstern, (1994) *The Theory of Games and Economic Behavior* (Princeton: Princeton University Press).

Comment

Bernard Walliser

CERAS, ÉCOLE NATIONALE DES PONTS ET CHAUSSÉES, PARIS, FRANCE

1 INTRODUCTION

In an extensive-form game with perfect information, the backward induction procedure gives rise to three distinct paradoxes:

(a) a logical one: backward induction, when sustained by common knowledge of rationality, is self-refuting or at least mis-justified;
(b) a theoretical one: backward induction, when looked for by simulation in evolutionary games, is seldom obtained asymptotically;
(c) an empirical one: backward induction, when tested in laboratory experiments, is not adopted by players in several games.

Binmore and Samuelson's paper deals essentially with the first two, respectively from an eductive and evolutionary point of view.

2 THE EDUCTIVE APPROACH

2.1 The Modeller's Point of View

For the modeller, with a qualitative definition of common knowledge of rationality, it seems rather obvious that such an assumption cannot be kept (other assumptions being unchanged) if a player really deviates from the backward induction path in a game. This was clearly stated informally by Binmore (1987) and more formally by Reny (1992), for instance on the Centipede example. But the situation is not so clear when reasoning at the beginning of the game and trying to justify the backward induction procedure. In fact, it is necessary to consider what the players would do at nodes that are not reached by the backward induction equilibrium (technically obtained by iterative deletion of weakly dominated strategies).

The main problem here concerns the more or less strong definition of the common knowledge assumption, discussed by game theorists as well as by epistemic logicians. At one extreme, one has 'common knowledge' CK, where knowledge obeys both 'internal' axioms (positive and negative introspection) and 'external' axioms (truth axiom), the last implying that knowledge is true. At the other extreme, one has 'common belief with probability one' CB_1, where the beliefs are subjectively considered as certain, but may be false and refuted by messages acting as 'surprises'. In order to have only external axioms, Stalnaker (1993) proposes two intermediate concepts. In the first CK', there is CB_1 in the 'real world' that what the players believe with probability one is true, so that no surprise can arise, even if beliefs may be violated in other worlds. In the second CK'', each knowledge is belief with probability one and is robust with respect to truth, i.e. would be confirmed should the player get a message which is true in the considered world, so that surprises become possible even in the real world.

With these concepts, it is possible to show that backward induction is justified with CK (Aumann, 1993) and CK' (Stalnaker, 1993), but that some indeterminacy happens with CK'' (Stalnaker, 1993) or CB_1 (Ben Porath, 1992). The result by Aumann (1993) stems partially from the heavy truth assumption, which implies that the intended actions have to be implemented (Pettit and Sugden, 1985); but it follows essentially from some sort of 'cognitive conquentialism', which states that the past messages have no influence on the present action, and is embedded in the fact of considering at each period a 'new' player (Binmore–Samuelson). The first result by Stalnaker (1993) arises because no surprise can be expected to intervene in the deliberation phase, although it may occur in the implementation phase. The result by Ben Porath (1992) is that all 'strongly rationalizable equilibria' (technically obtained by one deletion of weakly dominated strategies and then iterative deletion of strongly dominated strategies) are possible; it stems from the fact that a surprise may be accounted for in different ways (revised beliefs being only compatible with game history).

2.2 The Player's Point of View

For the player, the problem is to define a belief updating scheme when an unexpected message occurs. For instance, in the AGM system (Gärdenfors, 1988), syntactical axioms are first defined in order to transform the initial set of believed propositions H into a revised set H^*_x, when message X is obtained, especially when X contradicts H. These axioms are equivalent to an 'epistemic entrenchment' order on propositions such that, observing X, the less entrenched propositions in contradiction with X are alleviated until restoring the consistency of the belief system H^*_x accepting X. In the 'possible worlds' semantics, the epistemic entrenchment order is similar to a qualitative 'possibility distribution' on events, itself reflected by embedded spheres centred on H, corresponding to decreasing degrees of belief on worlds; the updated set of worlds H^*_x is then the intersection of X with the nearest sphere around X. This framework is in agreement with the theory of counterfactuals initiated by Lewis and Stalnaker; according to the 'Ramsey test', proposition 'if X, then Y' is acceptable if, in the nearest worlds from H where X is true, Y is equally true.

Coming back to games, if a player assumes the other to deviate from the backward induction path, he can consider such an event as the premise of a classical conditional (the deviation is plausible) as well as of a counterfactual conditional (the deviation is unexpected) ; but in any case, he has to call into question one assumption at least which justifies it. The first one concerns the automatic translation of intentions into actions; it is violated by the 'trembling-hand' assumption (Selten, 1975) which considers possible uncorrelated errors in implementing plans. The second one concerns the common knowledge of the game structure; it is circumvented by uncertainty on players' types (Kreps *et al.*, 1982) on their utilities as well as on their structural beliefs (and revision rules). The third one concerns the common knowledge of rationality; it is bypassed by considering a weaker form of crossed knowledge such as n-common knowledge (Bicchieri, 1989) or ε-common knowledge (Monderer and Samet, 1989); it is also bypassed by considering a weaker form of rationality such as bounded rationality (Simon) or even resolute choice (McClennen).

The first justification of deviation confirms the backward induction procedure because it is meaningless for the other player; the others lead to a larger set of equilibria because they allow for many more interpretations. But the fundamental problem for the player is to build an epistemic entrenchment hierarchy with the preceding assumptions; if Selten considers apparently that the first assumption is the less entrenched, Binmore–Samuelson state that it is the most entrenched and should be doubted only in last resort. But such a hierarchy must be exogenously affected to each player by the modeller, as well as the player's preferences; the point is that this hierarchy is probably more contextual to the class of games considered than other players' characteristics.

3 THE EVOLUTIONARY APPROACH

3.1 The Framework's Relevance

In order to test empirically the backward induction procedure, the Ultimatum Game studied by Binmore–Samuelson is probably not well fitted because numerous side effects can explain the observed unexpected behaviours. On the one hand, the backward induction equilibrium assumes that the proposing player is offering an infinitesimal amount of money to the responding one, which may distort the relation between money and utility, through perception as well as edge effects. On the other hand, fairness considerations may be very influential in this distribution problem.

In fact, if considering the extensive-form games, backward induction is problematic for only few of them, especially the Ultimatum Game. More precisely, when considering all 18 possible two-person games (with ordinal utilities and no ties), where player 1 has two moves, and player 2 responds to one by two moves, only a couple of games may have an equilibrium which is not trivially the backward induction one. The first is the reduced Centipede Game, isomorphic to an adapted version of the Prisoner's Dilemma and of the Newcom Problem and showing the non-credibility of a promise. The second is precisely the Ultimatum Game, isomorphic to the Chain-Store Paradox, and showing the non-credibility of a threat (Figure 5.5).

A more general limit is that a genuine evolutionary process cannot, in general, be

Figure 5.5 The Reduced Centipede Game and Ultimatum Game

considered as a realistic one. On the one side, some drastic conditions have to be satisfied in order to converge towards an asymptotic stable state. The players keep their rigid behaviour all along the process, the context in which the game is played is stationary for a long period of time, and the game considered is isolated from all other games the players play simultaneously. On the other side, the precise support of the evolutionary process is badly defined and appears different in economics than in biology. The variation mechanism is less stochastic (Darwinian) and more oriented (Lamarckian), the transmission mechanism is less deterministic and more symbolic, and the selection mechanism is similar only when assimilating utility to fitness.

3.2 The Robustness of Results

In fact, the eductive and the evolutionary process are two extremes, where the agents are respectively guided by a 'Lewisian hand' and a 'Darwinian hand'. But some intermediate and more realistic processes have to be designed in order to build a whole spectrum, where the work of cognition (perfect at the beginning and absent at the end) is progressively replaced by the work of time (from statics to long-term dynamics). An 'epistemic learning process' considers that the agents have imperfect beliefs on the others' characteristics and update them when observing others' actions, thus guided by a 'Bayesian hand'. A 'behavioural learning process' considers that the agents only observe the utility they got through their past actions, and reinforce the good actions or inhibit the bad ones, thus guided by a 'Skinnerian hand'; this last process can be extended to imitation when players mimic the others' actions that succeeded.

These processes give rise to results that are yet rare, local and dispersed, for extensive-form games even more than for normal-form games. In an evolutionary process, Samuelson and Zhang (1992) have shown that weakly dominated strategies are not necessarily eliminated, even in a noisy context. In a cognitive learning process, Nöldeke and Samuelson (1993) have shown that, for a game where each player plays only once on each path, a locally stable state (when existing) is a perfect equilibrium; however, when considering a locally stable set (which always exists), it contains the perfect equilibrium, but many others too.

But the results with dynamic processes seem not very robust to the numerous assumptions which sustain them: the players' bounded behaviours, the players' meeting mechanisms, the updating or ameliorating or reproducing rules, the asymptotic states considered. For the moment, the demarcation line between contexts in which backward induction is justified and those in which it is not is far from being delineated. Moreover, even if different types of dynamic processes are sometimes formally identical, they are semantically very different and correspond to different practical situations. It then has to be made explicit why the results obtained in one field sustain a concept in another: the backward induction procedure can be justified by learning arguments, but is harder by strict evolutionary arguments.

Coming back to 'the myth of Sisyphus' emphasized by Binmore-Samuelson, the comparison of Sisyphus' stone with the backward induction problem is perhaps more positively expressed in the following sentence: 'each grain of that stone, each mineral splinter of that mountain full of night, forms a world by itself' (A. Camus).

References

Aumann, R. (1995) 'Backwards Induction and Common Knowledge of Rationality', *Games and Economic Behavior*, vol. 8, pp. 6–19.

Ben Porath, E. (1992) 'Rationality, Nash Equilibrium and Backward Induction in Perfect Information Games', mimeo, Department of Economics, Tel Aviv University.

Bicchieri, C. (1980) 'Self-Refuting Theories of Strategic Interaction: A Paradox of Common Knowledge, *Erkenntnis*, vol. 30, pp. 69–85.

Binmore, K. (1987) 'Modeling Rational Players I', *Economics and Philosophy*, vol. 3, pp. 179–214.

Gärdenfors, P. (1988) *Knowledge in Flux* (Cambridge, Mass.: MIT Press).

Kreps, D., P. Milgrom, J. Roberts, and R. Wilson, (1982) 'Rational Cooperation in the Finitely Repeated Prisoner's Dilemma, *Journal of Economic Theory*, vol. 27, pp. 245–52.

Monderer, D. and D. Samet, (1989) 'Approximating Common Knowledge with Common Beliefs', *Games and Economic Behavior*, vol. 1, pp. 170–90.

Nöldeke, G. and L. Samuelson, (1993) 'An Evolutionary Analysis of Backward and Forward Induction', *Games and Economic Behavior*, vol. 5, pp. 425–54.

Pettit, P. and R. Sugden, (1985) 'The Backward Induction Paradox', *Journal of Philosophy*, vol. 86, pp. 169–82.

Reny, P. (1992) 'Rationality in Extensive-Form Games', *Journal of Economic Perspectives*, vol. 6, no. 4, pp. 103–18.

Samuelson, L. and J. Zhang, (1992) 'Evolutionary Stability in Asymmetric Games', *Journal of Economic Theory*, vol. 4, pp. 364–91.

Selten, R. (1975) 'Reexamination of the Perfectness Concept for Equilibrium Points in Extensive Games', *International Journal of Game Theory*, vol. 4, pp. 25–55.

Stalnaker, R. (1993) 'Knowledge, Belief and Counterfactual Reasoning in Games', paper presented at a workshop of the Stanford Institute of Theoretical Economics (August).

Reply to Binmore and Samuelson

Robert J. Aumann

THE HEBREW UNIVERSITY OF JERUSALEM, ISRAEL

I heartily agree with many of the points made by Binmore and Samuelson. First, that the evolutionary approach to game theory is very important, though perhaps not to the exclusion of all other approaches. Second, that in perfect information (PI) games, backward induction (BI) may yield choices that are not only unwise and unreasonable, but quite simply irrational. Third, that interpretational issues are very important in these matters, and that in discussing them, one cannot rely exclusively on mathematics. Fourth, that in game theory and decision theory in general, and in the matter at hand in particular, one cannot restrict oneself to material implication, but must use what Binmore and Samuelson call 'subjunctive conditionals'. Fifth, that deleting weakly dominated strategies is not 'harmless'. Sixth, that in considering equilibria, one should not restrict attention to those that are 'trembling hand' perfect. Seventh, that the experimental results in the Ultimatum Game constitute an important phenomenon that cannot and should not be ignored or dismissed, and on which game theory has much of importance to say. And I could go on, listing many more points of agreement with their positions.

These positions are argued by Binmore and Samuelson at great length, with fervour and flair and even some reasoned arguments. I have promoted many of them myself – some in the very paper they are attacking (Aumann, 1995) and others previously (Aumann, 1985, 1987, 1992a, 1992b). Indeed, the point about 'subjunctive conditionals' is absolutely central to my position (see Aumann, 1995, section 4b). I am delighted to have Binmore and Samuelson on my side in this matter, as well as in the others listed above.

The one cardinal point on which I disagree with them is my contention that common knowledge of rationality (CKR) implies backward induction. Wisely, they have made their position on this impregnable. Their arguments cannot be refuted, as they make no arguments. To be sure, they do *assert* in one place that CKR does not imply BI, and in another that there are flaws in my reasoning. But nowhere do they *show* that CKR does not imply BI, or even attempt a reasoned argument to that effect; and nowhere do they point to a single flaw, either logical or conceptual, in *my* argument.

To challenge the result that CKR implies BI, one must either find a logical flaw in my demonstration, or challenge my formulations of the underlying concepts – rationality and knowledge. Binmore and Samuelson do neither. Instead, they devote all their energy to arguing that in certain PI games, the BI choices may be (or are) unreasonable. That is correct; but it does not preclude CKR implying BI. You cannot discredit 'p implies q' by questioning q; perhaps p is also questionable. People who chide others – wrongly! – for confusing subjunctive conditionals with material implications should not themselves fall into the much more elementary error of confusing an implication with its consequent. Physician, heal thyself!

The fact of the matter is that there is a big difference between rationality and CKR, a point that Binmore and Samuelson consistently slur over. CKR is a very strong assumption, much stronger than simple rationality, and in some situations may just be too much to ask for (Aumann, 1992b). It is this, and this only, that accounts for the strangeness of the BI outcome in some PI games.

There is nothing more to say; I cannot defend myself against an attack that has no substance – is all smoke and no fire. A more detailed discussion of the issues may be found in Aumann (1995). As for the question in Binmore and Samuelson's title – 'Rationalizing Backward Induction?' – my answer is 'no; showing that CKR implies BI'.

References

Aumann, R.J. (1985) 'What Is Game Theory Trying to Accomplish?', in K. Arrow and S. Honkapohja (eds), *Frontiers of Economics* (Oxford: Basil Blackwell) pp. 28–76.

Aumann, R.J. (1987) 'Game Theory', in J. Eatwell, M. Milgate and P. Newman (eds), *The New Palgrave, A Dictionary of Economics* (London: Macmillan) vol. 2, pp. 460–82.

Aumann, R.J. (1992a) 'Perspectives on Bounded Rationality', in Yoram Moses (ed.), *Theoretical Aspects of Reasoning About Knowledge*, Proceedings of the Fourth Conference, TARK, 1992 (San Mateo, Calif.: Kaufmann) pp. 108–17.

Aumann, R.J. (1992b) 'Irrationality in Game Theory', in P. Dasgupta, D. Gale, O. Hart and E. Maskin (eds), *Economic Analysis of Markets and Games* (Essays in Honor of Frank Hahn) (Cambridge, Mass.: MIT Press) pp. 214–27.

Aumann, R.J. (1995) 'Backward Induction and Common Knowledge of Rationality', *Games and Economic Behavior*, vol. 8, pp. 6–19.

6 The Decision-Theoretic Foundations of Game Theory

Marco Mariotti*

UNIVERSITY OF MANCHESTER, UK

1 INTRODUCTION

In current game theory there is a wide consensus on the idea that it is possible to derive solution concepts for non-cooperative games from more primitive principles of individual decision theory under uncertainty. This view has been consolidated in the last fifteen years, when several theorists (e.g. Aumann, 1987; Bernheim, 1984, 1985; Brandenburger and Dekel, 1986, 1987; Borgers, 1993; Harsanyi, 1977; Nau and McCardle, 1990; Pearce, 1984; Tan and Werlang, 1988) have studied various ways in which this can be done. Others (e.g. Harsanyi and Selten, 1988; Kreps and Wilson, 1982; Cho and Kreps, 1987; to name but a few) have firmly grounded the study of *refinements* of Nash equilibrium on the notion of subjective beliefs. Binmore (1991, 1992) is perhaps the most notable exception to this approach.

The aim of this chapter is to question the view that classical decision theory can provide an adequate foundation for game theory. I will try to convince the reader that rationality in a strategic context is not equivalent, and cannot be reduced, to classical rationality in an isolated problem of decision under uncertainty. In order to clarify the type of approach under criticism, here are two quotations from authorities in the field:

> our theory of rational behaviour in game situations will be a direct generalization of the Bayesian theory of rational behaviour under uncertainty. Following the Bayesian approach, we shall assume that any player *i* will express his expectations about the behaviour of another player *j* by assigning *subjective probabilities* to various alternative actions that player *j* may possibly take. (Harsanyi, 1977, p. 11; italics in the original)

> The logical roots of game theory are in Bayesian decision theory. Indeed, game theory can be viewed as an extension of decision theory (to the case of two or more decision makers), or as its essential logic fulfilment. (Myerson, 1991, p. 5).

The standard axioms in the theory of decision under uncertainty are those stated by

* I wish to thank Pierpaolo Battigalli, Hamid Sabourian and Bob Sugden for their detailed comments. Participants at a 'Quaker' meeting at the University of Cambridge and at a 'Rationality Group' meeting at the University of East Anglia also provided very useful comments, as well as my PhD examiners, Luca Anderlini and Ken Binmore. Of course I am alone responsible for the paper.

133

Savage (1954) (or some equivalent set of axioms). Many of the authors quoted in the opening paragraph explicitly invoke these axioms. They allow one to express the uncertainty faced by a player in any situation by means of a subjective probability distribution. Subsequently one constructs a utility function on the basis of these probabilities. The basic tenet of the Bayesian approach to game theory is that a player should be able to attach a probability distribution to any variable whose value is now known to him or her with certainty. These variables are the 'state of nature' of Savage's framework. In particular, then, the possible ways the game can be played by the rivals is regarded by each player as a collection of states of nature (see the quotation from Harsanyi, 1977, above).

One may note that, historically, such a view runs against the 'classical' approach to game theory, according to which every probability distribution defined on the strategy set of a player should derive either from long-run frequencies or from an objective randomization on the part of the player. In that case, utility is constructed on the basis of these objective probabilities. For example, von Neumann and Morgenstern (1947), in analysing a two-player game, claim that

> from the point of view of player 1 who chooses a variable ... the other variable *can certainly not be considered as a chance event*. The other variable ... is dependent upon the will of the other player, which must be regarded in the same light of 'rationality' as his own. (p. 99; my italics)

And Luce and Raiffa (1957) answer the question 'what does it mean to select a mixed strategy?' with

> we shall take the point of view that the selection of a pure strategy by means of a mixed strategy is equivalent to performing an experiment. (p. 74)

The fact that the originators of game theory did not apply Bayesian reasoning to the discipline is helpful to remind one that the current obsession with providing 'Bayesian foundations' to solution concepts is not to be accepted without questioning. But here the intention is not so much to defend this 'classical' view against the subjectivist approach. Less ambitiously, I would rather like to tackle the question: how *exactly* are the Savage axioms to be applied in a game theoretic context?[1] No answer seems to be found in the literature. The only answer I was able to come up with is, unfortunately, a negative one. The axioms not only seem inappropriate in games, but lead to contradictions. To enhance clarity of presentation, a brief description of the general argument of this chapter follows.

There is a crucial difference between states of nature as meant by Savage and the strategies available to a player in a game. The difference, loosely speaking, is this. The process leading to the realization of one of the states of nature, in the Savage sense, is independent of the course of action taken by the decision-maker. But the strategies which are played in a game cannot be considered independent of each other. A link between them is established by the fact that a strategy is decided upon by a rational player and not by an objective and independent 'nature', together with common knowledge of rationality. For instance, Harsanyi (1977), writes:

> the point is precisely that he [a player] *cannot* regard the other players' strategies as given independently of his own. (p. 113; italics in the original)

This should not be controversial. What may be controversial is the extent to which this undermines the current foundations of game theory. Game theorists seem to take the matter rather lightheartedly, being satisfied to look for the *restrictions* on beliefs implied by the interdependence, rather than looking for the implications on the *possibility of existence* of personal probabilities in games. One should realize that it is even impossible to *describe* the strategy of a player in a game in a way which is independent of the strategies available to the other players. Any complete description of one of, say, Row's strategies should consist of a 'physical' description of the strategy plus a qualification regarding the *game as a whole*, like 'in the game where Column can choose in the set S_i of strategies'. However, it is well known that the Savage formulation demands that we should be able to carry out 'thought experiments' on the choice behaviour of the agents with regard to 'conceivable' acts (as Schmeidler and Wakker, 1989, call them). But allowing a player to choose between 'conceivable' strategies in a game changes the nature of the other players' strategies. That is, it changes the description of the states of nature. Whilst this has no bearing in an individual decision problem, it makes a crucial difference in a strategic context.

I will show (i) that there is a direct contradiction between the Savage axioms when common knowledge of them is assumed, where common knowledge will be meant to have at least the implication of iterated elimination of *strongly* dominated strategies; and (ii) that common knowledge of the Savage axioms is not compatible with iterated elimination of *weakly* dominated strategies, even in simple cases where weak domination is invoked only in a two-by-two game and for only one strategy, so that none of the usual perplexities about this procedure apply (see Section 2.2 for the precise definitions of the procedures).

The argument supporting (i) turns on a special conceptual point. The application of the Savage axioms to games is not straightforward. One has to know how to interpret in the context of a game the ordering of what Savage calls 'acts'. Since this point is likely to be controversial, and since Bayesian game theorists provide no insight on this when invoking Savage's axioms, I will deal with it in more than one place in the chapter: first, in Section 2.1; then in Section 4.3; and finally in Section 5.2. However, the argument showing that common knowledge of dominance is not compatible with Savage rationality (Section 3.2) *does not* depend on this conceptual point and should therefore not be controversial.

2   THE BAYESIAN VIEW OF EQUILIBRIUM IN GAMES AND THE QUESTION OF 'PRIVATE BETS'

This section contains a brief reminder of the Bayesian approach to game theory. The readers who are familiar with the Savage axiom system may skip subsection 2.2, but are encouraged to pay attention to subsection 2.1, where the question of 'private bets' is discussed. There are two general premises in the Bayesian approach:

(1) the situation of a player in a game can be formally represented as an individual decision problem under uncertainty, where the states of nature which are the objects of uncertainty are, or include, the strategies of the other players;

(2) the axioms of rationality that a player is supposed to obey are those stated by

Savage (or any other set of axioms allowing an expected utility representation of preferences over actions: e.g., Anscombe and Aumann's (1963) 'horse-races' and 'lottery-wheels' formulation).

We now turn to a closer analysis.

2.1 'Private Bets and Virtual Acts'

In the Savage framework, probabilities are derived by imposing consistency requirements on the agent's 'betting' behaviour. When the states of nature are the moves of an opponent in a game, this amounts to imposing consistency requirements on a player's choice of strategies when faced with changes in the outcomes of the game associated with the various strategy combinations. But when we step out of the individual decision-making context, one problem arises. Should such bets be *private*, i.e. only known to the player who is taking them? The point of view taken here is that this would be *impossible* in a game. Payoffs are part of the description of the game itself, and this *must be common knowledge*. Bets cannot be independent of the play, since they do affect a player's evaluation of his or her own strategies. If a player was perceiving utility from the choice of a strategy without the other player knowing this, we simply would be throwing away the common knowledge assumption. Formally, let an n-person game be denoted by $G = (S_i, c_i)$, $i = 1, ..., n$, where S_i is the (finite) strategy space of player i and c_i is a consequence function attaching a consequence (a member of a given set of consequences C) to any strategy profile.[2] The uncertainty faced by player i in a game $G = (S_i, c_i)$, $i = 1, ..., n$, is the choice of strategy on the part of the other players. So the set of states of nature in player i's decision problem is simply $S_{-1} = \chi\, S_j$, $j \neq i$, the Cartesian product of the strategy spaces of the players other than i.

But the space of acts for player i, in the Savage sense, is not simply the space of strategies S_i. It is a set A_i including S_i and other 'conceivable' strategies that it is necessary to consider in order to check the consistency of a player. A_i coincides with the set of all the possible mappings from S_{-j} to C. Savage asks the decision-maker to be able to rank all these objects. Here is where the interpretational problem mentioned above arises. A virtual act is 'virtual' because it cannot be performed in a certain game. But then, *what does it mean to say that it belongs to the domain of a player's preferences*? This is a question that presumably should have been answered by those who espouse the Bayesian approach; but, to the best of my knowledge, this has not been done. The common knowledge of the structure of the game seems, however, to leave us with only one answer: that the preferences on virtual acts are the preferences on these acts should they become strategies effectively playable in a game. Suppose this was not the case. Then player i's ranking of acts in A_i will include acts which yield her payoffs different from those of any strategy s_i in G, on the assumption that player j, $j \neq i$ believes he[3] is playing game G. This type of situation is another game, say G'. So, while i knows she is playing game G' j believes he is involved in game G. This makes G' a game in which there is no common knowledge of the same structure.[4] We do not have a clear theory of how such games may be played. Here it is enough to notice that player i would play in the extensive form of G' in a way which may even appear absurd to player j (see Section 4.3 for an example). Given that G' is not a game in the usual sense of the word, there is no relationship between the beliefs i holds on j's behaviour in G' and those he holds on j's behaviour in G's, and this would automatically defy Savage's framework. I will thus proceed on the interpretation of Savage's bets as 'public' bets. I will, however, return to this issue in Section 4.3 and 5.2.

2.2 The Axioms

Here are some of the Savage postulates (for player i; I will omit some i-subscripts for ease of notation).

P1 (Ordering) There exists a complete ordering $\geq$ on A_i (and an induced complete ordering on consequences given by the ordering on strategies with a constant consequence).

P2 Let $S_{-i} \supset K$. Let $s_i, s_i', t_i, t_i' \in A_i$, let $c(s_i, s_{-i}) = c(s_i', s_{-i})$, and $c(t_i, s_{-i}) = c(t_i', s_{-i})$ for all $s_{-i} \in S_{-i} \backslash K$, and let $c(s_i, s_{-i}) = c(t_i, s_{-1})$ and $c(s_i', s_{-1}) = c(t_i', s_{-i})$ for all $s_{-i} \in K$. Then, $s_i \geq s_i'$ implies $t_i \geq t_i'$.

Definition: $s_i \geq s_i'$ given K, with $S_{-i} \supset K$, iff $t_i \geq t_i'$ for any t_i and t_i' such that $c(t_i, s_{-i}) = c(s_i, s_{-i})$ and $c(t_i', s_{-i}) = c(s_i', s_{-i})$ for all $s_{-i} \in K$, and $c(t_i, s_{-i}) = c(t_i', s_{-i})$ for all $s_{-i} \in S_{-i} \backslash K$. A subset K of S_{-i} is *null* if $s_i \geq s_i'$ given K for any s_i and s_i'.

P3 Let $c(s_i, s_{-i}) = c$ and $c(s_i', s_{-i}) = c'$ for all $s_{-i} \in K$, with K a non-null subset of S_{-i}. Then $s_i \geq s_i'$ given K iff $c \geq c'$.

P4 (Revealed Likelihood) Let $S_{-i} \supset H, K$. Let $s_i, s_i', t_i, t_i' \in A_i$. Let $c, d \in C$ with $c > d$, and let $c(s_i, s_{-i}) = c$ for $s_{-i} \in H$ and $c(s_i, s_{-i}) = d$ for $s_{-i} \in S_{-i} \backslash H$, $c(t_i, s_{-i}) = c$ for $s_{-i} \in K$ and $c(t_i, s_{-i}) = d$ for $s_{-i} \in S_{-i} \backslash K$. Let $c', d' \in C$ with $c' > d'$, and let $c(s_i', s_{-i}) = c'$ for $s_{-i} \in H$ and $c(s_i', s_{-i}) = d'$ for $s_{-i} \in S_{-i} \backslash H$, $c(t_i', s_{-i}) = c'$ for $s_{-i} \in K$ and $c(t_i', s_{-i}) = d'$ for $s_{-i} \in S_{-i} \backslash K$. Then, $s_i \geq t_i$ iff $s_i' \geq t_i'$.

P5 $c > d$ for some $c, d \in X$.

P1–P5 enable one to represent the uncertainty of player i over S_{-i} by means of a qualitative (subjective) probability distribution p_i over S_{-i}.[5]

Player i will then maximize her expected utility calculated using the probability measure p_i. If there is common knowledge of Savage-rationality, the appropriate Bayesian solution concept is rationalizability (correlated or not correlated) in the Bernheim – Pearce sense. By imposing further restrictions on the beliefs of the players, it is possible to obtain further solution concepts like Nash or correlated equilibria (see, for example, Tan and Werlang, 1988; Aumann, 1987; Brandenburger and Dekel, 1986, 1987).

Before proceeding further, three consequences of P1–P3 (note that P4 is not necessary) should be emphasized for future reference.[6]

Partition Dominance: let $\{H_k\}$ be a partition of S_{-i} and let $s_i \geq s_i'$ given H_k for all k, then, $s_i \geq s_i'$ given S_{-i}. Moreover, if strict inequality holds for some H_k, then $s_i > s_i'$.

Dominance: if $c(s_i, s_{-i}) \geq c(s_i', s_{-i})$ for all $s_{-i} \in S_{-i}$, then $s_i \geq s_i'$. Moreover, if strict inequality holds for some non-null s_{-i}, then $s_i > s_i'$.

Sure Thing Principle (STP): let $c(s_i, s_{-i}) = c(s_i', s_{-i})$ for all $s_{-i} \in B$, $c(t_i, s_{-i}) = c(t_i', s_{-i})$ for all $s_{-i} \in B$, $c(s_i, s_{-i}) = c(t_i, s_{-i}) = c$ for all

$s_{-i} \in S_{-i} \backslash B$, and $c(s'_i, s_{-i}) = c(t'_i, s_{-i}) = c'$ for all $s_{-i} \in S_{-i} \backslash B$; then, $s_i > t_i$ iff $s'_i > t'_i$.

The following principle is not a direct consequence of the Savage axioms but will be invoked later:

Weak Dominance: if $c(s_i, s_{-i}) \geq c(s'_i, s_{-i})$ for all $s_{-i} \in S_{-i}$, then $s_i \geq s'_i$. Moreover, if strict inequality holds for some s_{-i}, then $s_i > s'_i$.

In the examples I will present it will be assumed that the players:

(1) know each other's preferences over consequences (i.e., constant acts);
(2) do not know whether the others regard as null a particular state of nature, unless this is a consequence of the other axioms (see below);
(3) obey P1–P5 defined above:
(4) have common knowledge of (1), (2) and (3).

Assumption (1) is simply part of the description of a complete information game. Assumption (2), if contradicted, would imply an *a priori* knowledge, on the part of the players, of at least some of the beliefs of the others, which is not a feature of the usual description of a game. Assumption (3) defines Savage rationality. Assumption (4) is ambiguous, since common knowledge has not been formally defined. However, it is enough for my purposes to assume that it has at least the following implication:

Iterated Elimination: for all i, let $S_i(0) = S_i$ and let $S_i(k) = \{s_i \in S_i(k\text{-}1) |$ there is no $s'_i \in S_i(k\text{-}1)$ such that $c(s'_i, s_{-i} > c(s_i, s_{-i})$ for all $s_{-i} \in S_{-i}(k\text{-}1)\}$. All states not in $S(\infty)$ must be considered null.

For future reference, I also state the following principle:

Weak Interated Elimination: for all i, let $S_i(0) = S_i$, and let $S_i(k) = \{s_i \in S_i(k\text{-}1) |$ there is no $s'_i \in S_i(k\text{-}1)$ such that $c(s'_i, s_{-i}) \geq c(s_i, s_{-i})$ for all $s_{-i} \in S_{-i}(k\text{-}1)$ and strict inequality holds for some $s_{-i}\}$. All states not in $S(\infty)$ must be considered null.

Weak Interacted Elimination is a principle common to many refinements of solution concepts in games, and although it does not derive from common knowledge of the Savage axioms, it seems to represent an essential component of a game-theoretic definition of rationality. Even if in some games weak iterated elimination presents some problems (see, e.g., Myerson, 1990, p. 60), it will not do so in the simple examples I will construct (Sections 3 and 4).

3 FORMAL ANALYSIS

3.1 Using STP and Revealed Likelihood

In this subsection we will use STP and Revealed Likelihood to state two impossibility results. Probably no axiom in decision theory has faced so much criticism, from both the theoretical and the empirical front, as STP. I personally consider STP a very intuitive decision-theoretic postulate, at least from a normative viewpoint, embodying the notion of independence across states. The criticism here will therefore be of a different nature.

Revealed Likelihood, on the other hand, embodies the 'prizes do not affect probabilities' principle, and seems to have attracted fewer challenges than STP even at the individual decision-making level.

We can state the following two results (proofs in appendix).

Proposition 1: *suppose there are at least seven consequences. Then P1–P5 are not consistent with Iterated Elimination.*

Proposition 2: *suppose there are at least six consequences. Then P1–P3 and P5 are not consistent with Weak Iterated Elimination.*

What drives these results is the fact that the precise amount that a decision-maker will earn in a certain state of nature affects the 'probability' attached by her to that state of nature. This is because in this case the 'state of nature' is a matter of choice on the part of another intelligent decision-maker, who understands the dominance relations within the strategy set of his opponent; and, by the common knowledge assumption, the first decision-maker is aware of this.

3.2 Dominance

Here we concentrate on dominance alone. Elimination of dominated strategies and the related dominance principle may look at first sight like unquestionable postulates of rational behaviour. Indeed, Fishburn (1987) claims that

> the normative appeal of the dominance principle is not seriously challenged by anyone, including Allais ... It is also reported as descriptively valid when its states' alignment for s_i versus s_i' is clear. (p. 829, with inessential changes in notation and terminology)

And Marschak (1986), even more strongly, maintains that

> Dominance is a simple and persuasive norm; one need only think of the violator as a player of Russian roulette. (p. 132)

However, upon reflection on the fact that STP can be seen as a dominance principle, and that yet it has been so sharply criticized, one may begin to suspect that even dominance ought not be taken for granted in all circumstances.

A powerful case against dominance comes from the possibility of the outcomes being themselves games (which is not surprising since in this case dominance becomes very similar to STP), a situation whose consequences do not seem to have been explored so far. Remember that in games such a situation occurs relatively often: at an information set of an *extensive-form game* a player may be in fact deciding which of two subgames to play, so that she must be able to express a preference ordering over these games. Consider the game G of Figure 6.1.

	L	R	
T	e, b	a, c	Game G
B	b, c	b, b	

Figure 6.1

The ordering over consequences, for both players, is

$$e > d > c > b > a$$

Now suppose G is treated as a consequence in itself, and player 1 is asked whether she prefers to obtain consequence c for sure or to play game G. Notice that *no restriction can be imposed a priori on this type of preference*. The restrictions imposed by means of decision-theoretic axioms concern the acts *within* a game, not the game itself. Then, the prospect of getting e in the game may well prompt the player to choose G. So assume that her ordering is

$$G > c$$

With this assumption, in the game of Figure 6.2, OUT is a strongly dominated strategy for player 1, and therefore it has to be IN > OUT.

	IN	OUT
IN	G, G	d, a
OUT	c, d	c, c

Figure 6.2

However, the normal form of the extensive forms describing this strategic situation is represented in Figure 6.3 (the notation should be self-explanatory).

	INLEF	INRIG	OUT₂
INTOP	e, b	a, c	d, a
INBOT	b, c	b, b	d, a
OUT₁	c, d	c, d	c, c

Figure 6.3

At this point apply iterated elimination of *strongly* dominated strategies, removing in succession OUT_2 and INBOT. We are left with a two-by-two game where INLEF is weakly dominated. If we eliminate INLEF, INTOP is *strongly* dominated. Thus, the strategy profile $(OUT_1, INRIG)$ is uniquely determined by this procedure: OUT_1, dominated in the presentation of the game given in Figure 6.2, is the unique rational strategy in the more explicit presentation of Figure 6.3!

This example shows that a player who is rational in the sense of applying iterated elimination of weakly dominated strategies is not indifferent between playing a 'composite' game in different stages or directly. Note well: we have resorted to weak domination only at one round and for only one strategy, so that *none of the usual problems with weak domination arises*.

We can interpret the interative procedure with an appealing extensive-form story. Suppose that, after playing IN and having been called on to move a second time, player 2 is wondering whether he should play LEFT or RIGHT. Then, he must reason thus:

'Player 1 had the opportunity of getting c for sure by playing OUT, but she didn't. She played IN instead. Now, if she played BOTTOM, she would get $b > c$ for sure. Then she could have fared better for sure by playing OUT at the outset. So the only reason for her to play IN is to continue with TOP at her second node, in the hope of getting the best outcome d. Therefore, I am sure of which node of my information set I am at, and the optimal action for me is RIGHT.'

But then Player 1 knows that should she play IN and then TOP, she would get b for sure, and in the light of this she has to play OUT, getting $c>b$.

'Speeches' of this type are standard fare in game theory. In general, one can observe the difference between these two situations:

(1) player i prefers to play a game G rather than getting c for sure;
(2) player i prefers to play a game strategy that allows one to play in turn a subgame G, rather than playing a strategy which yields her c for sure.

The difference is that when G is the whole game (situation (1)), player j does not need to know i's preference for G over c; he only needs to know i's ranking over consequences in G. But when G is a subgame, i's preference for G over c is *revealed* by i's play, j acts on the basis of this knowledge, and i acts on the basis of her knowledge of j's knowledge. This casts serious doubts on the universal applicability of the dominance principle: a move by an opponent is not a state of nature.

4   SIMPLE ORDERING

4.1   Problems with the Notion of Ordering

While the idea that there exists a rational way (or several rational ways) to play a game constitutes the foundation of the theory of solution concepts, the assumption that a player should form a complete and transitive preference ordering on his strategy set, as would be demanded by Savage's axioms, goes a long way beyond that idea. As a matter of fact, even at the pure decision-theoretic level, the ordering axiom has failed to convince many critics. For instance, Shafer (1988) claims: 'In general, the practical problem will be to choose one act. Why is it normative to go further and rank all acts?' (p. 204). And much earlier on, and more vividly, Wolfowitz (1962) so expressed himself: 'When a man marries he presumably chooses, from among possible women, the one whom he likes best. Need he necessarily be able also to order the others in order of preference?' (p. 476).

In games, these doubts are enhanced. The main conceptual difficulty is related to the normative aspect of Savage's theory. for it is not even clear what it *means* for a player to express a preference ranking between two strategies neither of which is 'a rational way to play the game' (an equilibrium strategy). In a decision-theoretic context, one possible way out is to embed preferences in choices. But this will not do in game theory. It may be acceptable to interpret the choice, in the whole game, of an equilibrium strategy instead of a non-equilibrium strategy as an expression of preference for the former. However, in order for the player to compare two non-equilibrium strategies, she must in some way be able to consider the choice between them in a hypothetical reduced game where the 'rational' strategy is not available. Since the Bayesian approach to game theory is inspired by Savage's work, it is perhaps appropriate to remember that Savage's own view is that preferences are to be interpreted in terms of choice:

> I think it of great importance that preference, and indifference, between *f* and *g* be determined, at least in principle, by decisions between acts and not by response to introspective questions. (Savage, 1954, p. 17)

Unfortunately, though, as soon as we try to derive a player's preference ordering from her choices out of subsets of her strategy set, it may turn out that the preference relation that rationalizes ('is revealed by') such choices has some undesirable properties. Indeed, it might not even be an ordering at all.

4.2 An Example

The next example, illustrated in Figure 6.4, follows those of the previous section in that it points out a clash between strategic rationality meant as elimination of weakly dominated strategies, and the Savage postulates. Suppose that players strictly prefer a non-dominated strategy to a weakly dominated one, and there is common knowledge of this. Preferences are $f > e > d > c > b > a$.

Consider the game obtained by removing T. Then R weakly dominates L, so that for Row strategy M is chosen over B. A similar reasoning shows that she must choose T over M in the game where B is not available.

	L	R
T	e,c	a,b
M	d,c	d,c
B	f,b	c,c

Figure 6.4

However, in the whole game, B strongly dominates T. Therefore, the preference relation rationalizing Row's choices is cyclic and thus is not a simple order, contradicting Savage's P1.

4.3 A Possible Objection Related to the Question of 'Conceivable' Choices

There is one possible objection to the method I have used to derive the choice behaviour of the agent. I have implicitly assumed that choosing between a subset of strategies means playing the subgame obtained by removing from the game all the other strategies. In this way the players whose choice behaviour is not being tested are aware of the fact that the player whose choice behaviour is being tested cannot use certain strategies. Another method would be to inform only the latter of the restriction on her strategy set, and let the other players play the game as if no modification has been made. But this method is not viable for reasons analogous to the ones given in the discussion on bets being private. First of all, and more important, it plainly contradicts the idea that the description of the game must be common knowledge between the players. Secondly, from a more operational point of view, when the normal form of the game is obtained from some extensive form, the restriction of some player's choices could force this player to play the game in a way that in the eyes of the other, uninformed, players is irrational. Take the game of Figure 6.5.

	L	R
T	c, c	c, c
M	a, a	b, b
B	a, b	b, a

Figure 6.5

Suppose that this normal form is obtained as a description of this situation: Row chooses whether to play *T*, thus determining a payoff *c* for both players, or to give the move to Column who chooses between *L* and *R*. Then, in ignorance of Column's choice, Row chooses between *M* and *B*. If Row's choice were to be restricted to {*M,B*} without Column knowing this, what should the latter, upon discovering he's been given the move, make of the fact that Row has not used a dominant strategy?

5 CONCLUDING REMARKS

5.1 The Relationship with the Purely 'Decision Theoretic' Attacks on Savage

I have already emphasized that my criticisms are of an entirely different nature from the usual criticisms of Savage's theory. The STP, for instance, has been criticized from a theoretical viewpoint mainly with concern for the possibility that outcomes can be themselves lotteries, but its force as a dominance principle when outcomes are simple is harder to reject in a decision-theoretic framework. Similarly, in a decision-theoretic framework the axiom of ordering would be surely much more acceptable than in a game-theoretic one, where it poses extra conceptual problems. The dominance principle, on the other hand, could be considered as safe as in decision theory only as long as one restricted the consequences to 'simple' ones, i.e. not themselves games. This is an impossible thing to do, however, for games in extensive form.

5.2 The Question of 'Conceivable Acts' and 'Private Bets'

In the proof of propositions 1 and 2, in order to show the desired inconsistency, I have replaced some pairs of strategies in the game with other, equivalently ordered, pairs (see Appendix). So, I am assuming that the Savage 'bets' are not private. A common reaction to this procedure has been to claim that I am cheating because 'I am changing the game'. To this I can reply as follows:

(1) Formally, I am doing to the game *exactly* what Savage does to a decision problem in order to prove his representation theorem. If this looks odd in the context of a game, it can only be evidence against the reduction of games to decision problems à la Savage. The point is that, because in a decision problem the states of nature are independent of choice, it is relatively easy to make sense of the following statement: 'if I could choose between them, I would rank two acts *a* and *a'* in the same way I rank two acts *b* and *b'* that I can choose'. But in a game, changing the strategy sets of the players affects the choice of strategy of the others. It is true then that 'I am changing the game', at least in this sense: suppose that my opponent can choose 'left' or 'right'. Then a complete description of her strategy 'left' would be, for example, either 'left in the game where the opponent can choose between *a* and *a'*' or 'left in the game where the opponent can choose between *b* and *b'*'. But *this change of description would also have to be done for the states of nature in a decision problem*. The reason why this is not done is that we believe it is irrelevant: whether a coin will land heads or tails is independent of the bets one can take. Now there are two possibilities. Either it is claimed that this independence holds also in the game, in which case I am not 'cheating' in my proof. Or it is claimed that such independence does not hold in a game, in which case I would indeed be cheating, but *it would be impossible to apply the Savage theorem in the context of a game*.

(2) Examples of the type constructed in Figure 6.5 seem to provide a rather compelling reason to think that bets can only be public. Once we have private bets we are in fact making the payoff description private rather than common knowledge. This not only *contradicts the assumption of common knowledge* of the game, but moreover *may generate seemingly absurd behaviour* (from the point of view of the other players) in an extensive-form game.

(3) It was suggested to me that one could make 'private bets' with player *i* by preventing player *j*'s payoffs from being affected by player *i*'s choice among the conceivable acts. So we would have player *i* playing the game, and simultaneously ranking 'tokens' representing conceivable acts. But how can player *i* rank these tokens unless she imagines herself really playing the game?. And, otherwise, what is she ranking?

There is really no third way: as a matter of logic, bets can only be either private or public!

(4) The analysis of dominance in Section 3.2 of the chapter stands independently of criticisms on bets being private in conceivable acts.

5.3   Relevance of this Chapter

Of those who have been exposed to previous versions of this paper, a minority of enthusisatic approvals was offset by a majority of strong objections. On some occasions I have more or less explicitly been accused of trying to make an irrelevant point into a big foundational issue. The curious phenomenon is that the objections fall neatly into two categories. One group has said it is *wrong* because 'I am cheating'; the other that it is *trivial* because everybody is aware of the problems it raises. Both things cannot be true, but surely this is a proof of the difficulty of getting across the central message of the chapter (due partly, no doubt, to my lack of ability, but also to the sensitive subject-matter). I hope in this version to have argued exhaustively on the 'cheating' part (*ad nauseam*, see Sections 2.1, 4.3 and 5.2), and to have made clear that in any case Section 3.2 stands independently of whether I am cheating or not. As for triviality, it is true that everybody knows that changing payoffs affects players' beliefs, and so does forward induction. But I do not think that enough attention has been paid to the relevance of this for the use of subjective probabilities in games. In chapter 1 of leading game-theory books we find either Savage's or Anscombe/Aumann's theories. The next chapter usually starts by saying that since the moves of the opponents in a game are unknown, one can attach subjective probabilities to them on the basis of the previous chapter's discussion. The present contribution has been to analyse the missing link between chapter 1 and chapter 2, and to show that in fact there is no justification for such a link.

APPENDIX

Proposition 1: Suppose there are at least seven consequences. Then P1–P5 are not consistent with Iterated Elimination.

Proof:
Notice, first of all, that since $\geq$ is a binary relation on A_i one may derive its restriction to a subset H of A_i by considering the set H separately. Now consider the game in Figure 6.6. Let the consequences be ranked as follows *by both players*:

$$g > f > e > d > c > b > a$$

Denote Row's acts by listing their consequences in the three states s_2', s_2'', s_2'''. So s_1' will be denoted by *fde*, s''_1 by *dfe* and so on.

	s_2'	s_2''	s_2'''
s_1'	f,d	d,f	e,d
s_1''	d,d	f,f	e,d
s_1'''	d,f	c,d	f,f

Figure 6.6

By STP,

$$fde \geq def \text{ iff } fdg \geq dfg$$

But in the game obtained by replacing *fde* with *fdg* and *dfe* with *dfg*, *dcf* is a strongly dominated act, so that by Iterated Elimination it must be considered null. Applying Iterated Elimination again makes null also s_2', s_2''', and by Dominance (notice that s_2'' cannot be null) it has to be $dfg > fdg$, that is

$$dfe > fde.$$

However, by P4,

$$fde \geq dfe \text{ given } \{s_2', s_2''\} \text{ iff } bae \geq abe \text{ given } \{s_2', s_2''\}$$

so that, by Partition Dominance,

$$fde \geq dfe \quad \text{iff} \quad bae \geq abe$$

Now, replacing *fde* with *bae* and *dfe* with *abe*, *dcf* dominates both *bae* and *abe*. By Iterated Dominance, consequently, s_2'' must be null. By Partition Dominance, $bae \geq abe$ (remember that, since s_2'' is null, $abe = bae$ given s_2'), that is

$$fed \geq dfe$$

contradicting the previous conclusion that *dfe* > *fde*.

Proposition 2: suppose there are at least six consequences. The P1–P3 and P5 are not consistent with Weak Iterated Elimination.
Proof:
Take the three-player game in Figure 6.7. Player 1 chooses rows, player 2 chooses columns and player 3 chooses matrices. The payoffs of the player for each combination of strategies are listed in this order. Suppose that the consequences are ranked, by all three players, as follows:

$$f > e > d > c > b > a$$

	s_2'	s_2''	s_2'''	s_2''''	
s_1'	d,a,a	a,d,a	c,a,a	b,a,a	
s_1''	$a,a,a,$	d,d,a	c,a,a	b,a,a	s_3'
s_1'''	a,a,d	$a,d,d,$	d,a,d	a,a,d	
s_1''''	a,d,a	a,a,a	a,d,a	d,d,a	
s_1'	a,a,a	d,d,a	$c,a,a,$	b,a,a	
s_1''	$d,a,a,$	a,d,a	c,a,a	b,a,a	
s_1'''	a,a,a	a,d,a	$d,a,a,$	a,a,a	s_3''
s_1''''	a,a,d	a,d,d	a,a,d	d,a,d	

Figure 6.7

Define the following additional acts for player 1:

$s'1 \backslash f$ is the same as s_1' with the consequence *c* replaced by *f*.
$s'1 \backslash e$ is the same as s_1' with the consequence *b* replaced by *e*.
$s''1 \backslash f$ is the same as s_1'' with the consequence *c* replaced by *f*.
$s''1 \backslash e$ is the same as s_1'' with the consequence *b* replaced by *e*.

Then, by P2,

$$s_1' \geq s_1'' \text{ iff } s_1' \backslash f \geq s_2'' \backslash f \text{ iff } s_1' \backslash e \geq s_1'' \backslash e$$

But it is easy to see, by a repeated application of Weak Iterated Elimination, that, replacing s_1' with $s_1' \backslash f$ and s_1'' with $s_1'' \backslash f$ yields

$$s_1' \setminus f > s_1'' \setminus f$$

and, similarly, replacing s_1' with $s_1' \setminus e$ and s_1'' with $s_1'' \setminus e$ yields

$$s_1' \setminus e < s_1'' \setminus e$$

This contradiction establishes the desired inconsistency result.

Notes

1. It should be made clear at the outset that no criticism on the validity of these axioms as decision-theoretic axioms *per se* is formulated. This is an entirely separate, if important, question (see e.g. Fishburn, 1987, 1988; Gardenfors and Sahlin, 1988; and Sugden, 1987, for excellent surveys and critical views). I shall limit myself to pointing out what seems to me a serious clash between the idea of rationality they imply and a game-theoretic definition of rationality, of which common knowledge of rationality is an essential ingredient.

2. Since we are dealing with the most primitive description of a game, such consequences are physical, and not utility representations of them; they are probably best thought of as amounts of money.

3. We use the convention that i is a woman, j is a man.

4. Since j is completely unaware of the true situation, he cannot even attach a probability distribution of 'states of nature': this is not an incomplete information game either.

5. A further axiom on the 'divisibility' of the state space makes p_i into an additive probability measure. Another 'sure thing'-type axiom permits the construction of a cardinal utility index over consequences. I shall have nothing to say on these two axioms.

6. In order to avoid confusion, a little clarification is needed on a point of terminology. In the original Savage (1954), the Sure Thing Principle is actually P2; while Partition Dominance is the verbal justification Savage uses to justify *his* Sure Thing Principle. However, in the literature, STP is usually characterized as above.

References

Anscombe, F.J. and R.J. Aumann (1963) 'A Definition of Subjective Probability', *Annals of Mathematical Statistics*, vol. 34 pp. 199–205.

Aumann, R.J. (1987) 'Correlated Equilibrium as an Expression of Bayesian Rationality, *Econometrica*, vol. 55 pp. 1–18.

Bell, D.E., H. Raiffa, and A. Tversky (eds) (1988) *Decision Making. Descriptive, Normative and Prescriptive Interactions* (Cambridge: Cambridge University Press).

Bernheim, D. (1984) 'Rationalizable Strategic Behaviour', *Econometrica*, vol. 52 pp. 1007–28.

Bernheim, D. (1985) 'Axiomatic Characterizations of Rational Choice in Strategic Environments', *Scandinavian Journal of Economics*, vol. 88 pp. 473–88.

Binmore, K. (1991) 'Debayesing Game Theory', UCL Discussion Paper 91–16.

Binmore, K. (1992) 'Foundations of Game Theory', in J.J. Laffont (ed.), *Advances in Economic Theory. Sixth World Congress*, vol. 1, Econometric Society Monographs (Cambridge: Cambridge University Press).

Borgers, T. (1993) 'Pure Strategy Dominance', *Econometrica*, vol. 61 pp. 423–30.

Brandenburger, A. and E. Dekel, (1986) 'On an Axiomatic Approach to Refinements of Nash Equilibrium', Economic Theory Discussion Papers, University of Cambridge, no. 104.

Brandenburger, A. and E. Dekel (1987) 'Rationalizability and Correlated Equilibria', *Econometrica*, vol. 55 pp. 1391–402.

Cho, I.K. and D.M. Kreps (1987) 'Signalling Games and Stable Equilibria', *Quarterly Journal of Economics*, vol. 102 pp. 179–221.

Ellsberg, D. (1961) 'Risk, Ambiguity and the Savage Axioms', *Quarterly Journal of Economics*, vol. 75 pp. 643–69.

Fishburn, P. (1970) *Utility Theory for Decision Making* (New York: John Wiley).

Fishburn, P. (1987) 'Reconsiderations in the Foundations of Decision under Uncertainty', *Economic Journal*, vol. 97 pp. 825–41.

Fishburn, P. (1988) 'Normative Theories of Decision Making under Risk and under Uncertainty', in Bell *et al.* (1988).

Gardenfors, P. and N.E. Sahlin (eds) (1988) *Decision, Probability and Utility* (Cambridge: Cambridge University Press).

Harsanyi, J. (1977) *Rational Players and Bargaining Equilibrium in Games and Social Situations* (Cambridge: Cambridge University Press).

Harsanyi, J. and R. Selten (1988) *A General Theory of Equilibrium Selection in Games* (Cambridge, Mass.: The MIT Press).

Heller, W.P., Starr, R.M. and D.A. Starrett (eds) (1986) 'Uncertainty, Information, and Communication' (volume 3 of Essays in Honor of Kenneth J. Arrow) (Cambridge: Cambridge University Press).

Hey, J.D. and P.J. Lambert (eds) (1987) *Surveys in the Economics of Uncertainty* (Oxford: Basil Blackwell).

Kreps, D.M. and R. Wilson (1982) 'Sequential Equilibria', *Econometrica*, vol. 50 pp. 863–94.

Luce, D. and H. Raiffa (1957) *Games and Decisions* (New York; Wiley).

Mariotti, M. (1992) 'Three Essays on Credibility and Beliefs in Game Theory', Ph.D. dissertation, Cambridge University, UK.

Marschak, T. (1986) 'Independence versus Dominance in Personal Probability Axioms', in Heller *et al.* (1986).

Myerson, R.B. (1990) *Game Theory. Analysis of Conflict* (Cambridge, Mass: Harvard University Press).

Nau, R.F. and K.F. McCardle (1990) 'Coherent Behaviour in Noncooperative Games', *Journal of Economic Theory*, vol. 50 pp. 424–44.

Pearce, D. (1984) 'Rationalizable Strategic Behaviour and the Problem of Perfection', *Econometrica*, vol. 52 pp. 1029–50.

Savage, L.J. (1954) *The Foundations of Statistics* (New York: John Wiley).

Schmeidler, D. and P. Wakker (1989) 'Expected Utility', in J. Eatwell, M. Milgate, and P. Newman (eds) 'Utility and Probability', *The New Palgrave: A Dictionary of Economics* (London: Macmillan).

Shafer, G. (1988) 'Savage Revisited', in Bell *et al.* (1988) (original version in *Statistical Science*, 1986, vol. 1 pp. 463–85.

Sugden, R. (1987) 'New Developments in the Theory of Choice Under Uncertainty', in Hey and Lambert (1987).

Tan, J.C.C. and S.R.C. Werlang (1988) 'The Bayesian Foundations of Solution Concepts in Games', *Journal of Economic Theory*, vol. 45 pp. 370–91.

von Neumann, J. and O. Morgenstern, (1947) 'Theory of Games and Economic Behaviour' (Princeton, NJ.: Princeton University Press).

Wolfowitz, J. (1962) 'Bayesian Inference and Axioms of Consistent Decision', *Econometrica*, vol. 30 pp. 470–9.

Comment

Pierpaolo Battigalli

POLITECNICO DI MILANO, ITALY

1 INTRODUCTION

Marco Mariotti has rendered a valuable service to the profession, making us aware of the problems arising when we try to develop a unified view of decision theory and non-cooperative game theory. Unlike von Neumann and Morgenstern (1944), the so-called Bayesian approach regards probability distributions over a player's strategies as opponents' subjective beliefs, which must be coherent with the implications of common knowledge of the game and of players' rationality. But formal theories yielding subjective probabilities, such as Savage (1954), have only been developed for one-person decision problems where consequences of choices are affected by an unknown state of nature. Mariotti argues that opponents' strategies cannot be interpreted as states of nature. He concludes that the decision-theoretic foundation of game-theoretic solution concepts is therefore undermined.

Mariotti's basic argument is the following. Savage-like theories of decision-making under uncertainty derive subjective probabilities of states from preferences over lotteries or *acts*. These preferences do not only concern actually possible actions in the given decision situation, but also *virtual* choices in hypothetical decision situations where the state of nature affects the consequences of an action in different ways. The underlying assumption is that the relative likelihood of different states is the same in all these situations. But this assumption cannot be maintained if the decision-maker is a player considering her choices in different games against a fixed set of opponents with a fixed set of possible strategies/acts. Indeed one should expect that the opponents' behaviour in different games be different, even though their payoff functions are fixed, as long as the game to be played is common knowledge.

This argument seems quite compelling, but it only shows that the extension of classical decision theory to multi-person decision situations is problematic. It does not show that such an extension is impossible. The core of this argument is that virtual acts in hypothetical decision situations should be identified with strategies of the decision-maker in hypothetical games. I will argue that a different interpretation of virtual acts as bets of an *external observer* eliminates the above-mentioned conceptual problem and is consistent with the Bayesian approach to non-cooperative game theory.

The remainder of this Comment is organized as follows. Section 2 presents a formal restatement of Mariotti's main proposition in order to further clarify the nature of the problem. Section 3 proposes an alternative interpretation of virtual acts in situations of strategic interaction.

2 ITERATED DOMINANCE AND SAVAGE POSTULATES: AN IMPOSSIBILITY RESULT

Mariotti presents two impossibility results concerning the inconsistency of Savage's postulates with iterated strict dominance and iterated weak dominance. Although the logic behind these results is basically the same, I think that the one concerning iterated strict dominance is more interesting.

Iterated *weak* dominance is a very controversial solution concept. It well known that the final solution may depend on the order of elimination, but this unpleasant fact is only a consequence of more fundamental theoretical problems (see, e.g., Samuelson, 1992; and Börgers and Samuelson, 1992). It has been recently pointed out that non-Archimedean preferences (Blume *et al.*, 1991) can justify the elimination of weakly dominated strategies in strategic environments where actions are chosen intentionally and there is complete information. But even this is not enough to justify the *iterative* deletion of weakly dominated strategies (see, e.g., Blume, *et al.* 1991). Strong and controversial assumptions about 'infinitesimals of different orders' of non-Archimedean probability measures are needed in order to provide a theoretical foundation to this algorithm (see, e.g., Stahl, 1991; Battigalli, 1993; and Rajan, 1993).

It can be reasonably argued that also the examples considered by Mariotti (including extensive games where forward induction arguments can be obtained by iterated weak dominance) display the controversial features of iterated weak dominance. Since the intrinsic difficulties of this solution concept could blur the main point to be discussed, here I focus on iterated *strict* dominance.

Since in the present context players' attitudes toward risk are not given, we consider an 'ordinal' normal form game, i.e. a game in strategic form specifying the consequences of each strategy profile and each player's ordinal preferences about consequences (see, e.g., Börgers, 1993). Formally, an n-person non-cooperative ordinal game is given by the following elements:

$C = \{a, b, c \ldots\}$: set of *consequences*
$N = \{1, 2, \ldots, n\}$: *players'* set; for each $i \in N$
S_i : player i's set of *strategies*
$S_{-i} = X_{j \in N \setminus \{i\}} S_j$: set of i's *opponents'* strategy profiles
$c_i : S_i \times S_{-i} \to C$: player i's *consequence function*
$\geq_i \subseteq C \times C$: player i's (complete, transitive) *preference relation*

It is informally assumed that the given ordinal strategic game and players' rationality are common knowledge. A minimal implication of this assumption is that the players do not choose interatively strictly dominated strategies. More formally, for all $i \in N$, $k = 1, 2, \ldots$, let

$$S_i(k) := S_i \setminus \{s_i \in S_i \mid \exists t_i \in S_i, \forall s_{-i} \in s_{-i}(k-1), c_i(t_i, s_{-i}) >_i c_i(s_i, s_{-i})\}$$

be i's set of k-undominated strategies. Note that $S_i(k) \subseteq S_i(k-1)$ for all k. By an obvious introspection argument no player i would choose a strategy outside the iteratively undominated set $S_i(\infty) := \cap_k S_i(k)$. Therefore each player i should be indifferent between two strategies s_i' and s_i'' such that $c_i(s_i', s_{-i}) \simeq_i c_i(s_i'', s_{-i})$ for all $s_{-i} \in S_{-i}(\infty)$. This suggests that opponents' profiles $s_{-i} \in S_{-i} \setminus S_{-i}(\infty)$ should be

1 \ 2	L	R
U	a / a	a / b
M	b / c	c / c
D	c / b	b / b

1 \ 2	L	R
U	a / a	a / b
M	b / b	c / b
D	c / c	b / c

Figure 6.8 Two ordinal games.

Savage-null from the point of view of i.

Now fix a player, say player i, and interpret S_{-i} as the set of states of nature for decision-maker i. According to this interpretation the set of *acts* is $\mathscr{A}_i := \{a_i \mid a_i : S_{-i} \to C\}$. Note that i's strategies in the given game correspond to the following subset of acts:

$$\mathscr{A}_i(c_i) := \{a \in \mathscr{A}_i \mid \exists s_i \in S_i, \forall s_{-i} \in S_{-i}, a(s_{-i}) = c_i(s_i, s_{-i})\}$$

But the decision-maker's subjective probability distribution is recovered from her preference relation over the whole $\mathscr{A}_i$. Preferences concerning acts outside $\mathscr{A}_i(c_i)$ are interpreted as virtual choices in hypothetical ordinal games $G(c_i')$ obtained by replacing i's consequence function c_i with another consequence function c_i'.

Note that i's opponents' consequence functions do not change. Nonetheless each player j's set of *iteratively* undominated strategies in each game $G(c_i')$ depends on i's consequence function c_i'. Consider, for example, the games in Figure 6.8 where both players' ranking of consequences is $a < b < c$. In the left game M is strictly dominant for player 1. Thus player 2's iteratively undominated strategy is R. In the right game D is strictly dominant and player 2's interatively undominated strategy is L. The set of player j's iteratively undominated strategies in the game corresponding to c_i' is denoted $S_j(\infty, c_i')$.

In this formal framework Mariotti's main result (proposition 2.1) can be restated as follows:

Proposition. Consider the class of ordinal games $\{G(c_i') \mid c_i' : S_i \times S_{-i} \to C\}$. Let $\mathscr{R}_i$ be the set binary relations $\leq \cdot$ on $\mathscr{A}_i$ satisfying the following properties:

(SA) axioms P1–P5 in Savage (1954);
($\leq_i$) for every pair of constant acts (a_i', a''_i) where $a_i'(s_{-i}) \equiv c'$ and $a_i''(s_{-i}) \equiv c''$, $a_i' \leq \cdot a_i''$ if and only if $c' \leq_i c''$;
(ID) for all $c_i : S_i \times S_{-i} \to C$, $s_i \in S_{-i'}$, if $s_{-i} \in S_{-i} \backslash S_{-i}(\infty, c_i')$
then s_{-i} is $\leq \cdot$ –null (i.e. two acts are $\leq \cdot$.- equivalent if they yield the same consequences for all $s_{-i} \in S_{-i}(\infty, c_i')$)

Then, for some specifications of $\{G(c_i') \mid c_i' : S_i \times S_{-i} \to c\}$, $\mathscr{R}_i$ is empty, i.e. (S), ($\leq_i$) and (ID) are mutually inconsistent.

Remark. Property ($\leq_i$) says that the preference relation $\leq \cdot$ concerning acts must be consistent with the given preference relation $\leq_i$ concerning consequences. Property (ID) says that, for every game $G(c'_i)$, $\leq$. must 'reveal' a zero probability for opponents' strategies which are iteratively dominated. This is justified by the informal assumption that the decision-maker bets must be 'public'. Since such bets correspond to hypothetical games $G(c'_i)$, the player/decision-maker should take into account the implications of common knowledge of $G(c'_i)$ and of players' rationality.

Proof. Consider again the games in Figure 6.8. Applying (ID) to the left game we obtain $(a, b) \simeq .(b, b)$, while applying (ID) to the right game we obtain $(a, b) < .(b, b)$. (I am maintaining Mariotti's notation where acts are identified by ordered *tuples* of consequences.)

As the simple example used in the proof makes clear, once it is appropriately formalized, Mariotti's impossibility result is quite trivial. This, however, does not mean that the result is not interesting. (Actually one could argue that quite a few famous impossibility results are trivial, if triviality is identified with simplicity of the proof). This result makes crystal clear that, if we want to take a Savage-like approach to decision-making in a situation with strategic interaction, we cannot identify hypothetical decision situations with hypothetical games where the decision-maker's choices affect her opponents' consequences.

3 SUBJECTIVE PROBABILITIES AND BETS OF AN EXTERNAL OBSERVER

Orthodox game theory offers two kind of solutions for non-cooperative games: (i) set-valued solution concepts such as *rationalizability*, whereby the players may have heterogeneous probabilistic expectations, but they share a common view about 'strategically irrational' choices, and (ii) point-valued solution concepts such as the Nash equilibrium whereby the players have common probabilistic expectations (for a review see, e.g., Myerson, 1991, ch. 3). In both cases the solution concept is meant to describe the behaviour of rational and intelligent players where

> We say that a player in the game is *intelligent* if he knows everything that we know about the game and he can make any inferences about the situation that we can make. (Myerson, 1991, p. 4)

An intelligent player analyzes a game from the point of view of an *external observer*. This suggests an interpretation of states of nature, acts, and preferences over acts that is very different from the one considered in the previous section.

Consider player/decision-maker i in a given n-person game G with a set of virtual acts $\mathscr{A}_i := \{a_i \mid a_i : S_{-i} \to C\}$. Her preference relation over $\mathscr{A}_i$ should represent her choices in hypothetical $(n + 1)$-games where i is in the role of player $n + 1$, the 'observer', the consequence functions of players 1, ..., n are constant with respect to the observer's choice and correspond to game G, and the observer consequence function c_{n+1} is constant with respect to the choice of player i (a copy of player/ decision-maker i in the actual game G).[1] Note that the set of iteratively undominated strategies of players 1, ..., n in G and in all $(n + 1)$-extensions of G is obviously the same. Therefore Savage axioms are no longer inconsistent with the requirement that

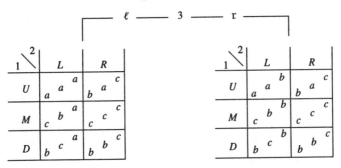

Figure 6.9 A 3-person extension of the left game in Figure 6.8.
Player 3 is an 'observer'.

iteratively dominated opponents' strategies should be Savage-null.

For example, let G be the left game of Figure 6.8 and consider the 3-person extension depicted in Figure 6.9. According to (ID), player 3 is indifferent between L and R_i, i.e. $(a,c) \simeq . (b,c)$ and L is $\geq$.-null.

The fact that a transitive preference over $\mathscr{A}_i$ is recovered from virtual choices in such hypothetical games relies on the natural assumption that the player\decision-maker regards the other players' behaviour in each $(n+1)$-extension as independent of the consequence function c'_{n+1} and there is no relevant distinction between these games as far as players $1, ..., n$ are concerned.[2] Analogously, i's preferences over S_i in G are recovered from preferences over $\mathscr{A}_i$ because there is no relevant distinction between G and its $(n+1)$-extension as far as i's opponents are concerned.

The decision-maker's choices in the $(n+1)$-extension of G can be interpreted as isolated bets about the outcome of separate games identical to G. Mariotti argues that, according to the common knowledge assumption of orthodox game theory, bets should be public. But it is easy to see that in the present context the difference between private and public bets is immaterial, since the players of the hypothetical games are not concerned with the observer's behaviour.

Mariotti has convincingly argued that game theory cannot be regarded as a mere extension of decision theory to a multi-person setting. But in my opinion he goes too far when he claims that Savage-like representation theorems are not applicable to a game-theoretic context. On the contrary, I have just argued that there is no intrinsic inconsistency between decision theory and classical game theory.

Notes

1. The latter assumption is not really necessary, but it simplifies the comparison with Mariotti's framework.

2. Of course this would not be true if side payments were possible. But side payments are excluded in non-cooperative games.

References

Battigalli P. (1993) 'Strategic Rationality Orderings and the Best Rationalization Principle', Rapporto Interno 93.014, Dipart. Economia e Produzione, Politecnico di Milano.

Blume, L., A. Brandenburger, and E. Dekel (1991) 'Lexicographic Probabilities and Choice under Uncertainty', *Econometrica*, vol. 59, pp. 61–79.

Börgers, T. (1993) 'Pure Strategy Dominance', *Econometrica*, vol. 61, pp. 423–30.

Börgers, T. and L. Samuelson (1992) 'Cautious Utility Maximization and Iterated Weak Dominance', *International Journal of Game Theory*, vol. 21, pp. 13–25.

Gul, F. (1991) *Rationality and Coherent Theories of Strategic Behaviour*, Research Paper no. 1990, Graduate School of Business, Stanford University.

Myerson, R. (1991) *Game Theory. Analysis of Conflict* (Cambridge Mass.: Harvard University Press).

Rajan, U. (1993) *Non-Archimedean Probabilities, Equilibrium Refinements, and Rationalizability*, mimeo, Department of Economics, Stanford University.

Samuelson, L. (1992) 'Dominated Strategies and Common Knowledge', *Games and Economic Behavior*, vol. 4, pp. 284–313.

Savage, L. (1954) *The Foundations of Statistics* (New York: John Wiley).

Stahl, D. (1991) *Lexicographic Probabilities, Common Knowledge, and Iterated Admissibility*, mimeo, Department of Economics, University of Texas.

von Neumann, J. and O. Morgenstern (1944) *The Theory of Games and Economic Behavior* (Princeton: Princeton University Press).

7 Nash Equilibrium and Evolution by Imitation*

Jonas Björnerstedt[†] and Jörgen W. Weibull[‡]

DEPARTMENT OF ECONOMICS AND INSTITUTE FOR INTERNATIONAL
ECONOMIC STUDIES, STOCKHOLM UNIVERSITY, SWEDEN

1 INTRODUCTION

The Nash equilibrium criterion is usually justified on rationalistic grounds, in terms of the involved players' 'rationality', and, in some way or other, shared knowledge or beliefs about each other's rationality and/or strategies etc. (see, e.g., Tan and Werlang, 1988; and Aumann and Brandenburger, 1991).

1.1 Nash's Rationalistic Interpretation

In his unpublished Ph.D. dissertation, John Nash provided the following rationalistic interpretation of his equilibrium criterion:[1]

> We proceed by investigating the question: what would be a 'rational' prediction of the behaviour to be expected of rational playing the game in question? By using the principles that a rational prediction should be unique, that the players should be able to deduce and make use of it, and that such knowledge on the part of each player of what to expect the others to do should not lead him to act out of conformity with the prediction, one is led to the concept of a solution defined before.
>
> If S_1, S_2, ..., S_n were the sets of equilibrium strategies of a solvable game, the 'rational' prediction should be: the average behaviour of rational men playing in position i would define a mixed strategy s_i in S_i if an experiment were carried out.
>
> In this interpretation we need to assume the players know the full structure of the game in order to be able to deduce the prediction for themselves. It is quite strongly a rationalistic and idealizing interpretation. (1950, p. 23)

Nash used the phrase *position i* as we today would use the phrase 'player i'.

* An earlier version of this paper was presented at the conference. We are grateful for comments from the discussant and from participants in this conference, as well as from participants in the Roy seminar, Paris, December 1993.
† Björnerstedt's research was sponsored by the Wallander Foundation for Research in the Social Sciences.
‡ Weibull's research was sponsored by the Industrial Institute for Economic and Social Research (IUI), Stockholm. He thanks DELTA, Paris, for its hospitality during part of the writing of this paper.

Hence, 'playing in position *i*' here means 'choosing from the *i*-th player's strategy set with accompanying payoffs'.

Note the restriction to *solvable* games. Nash defines a game to be such if all its (Nash) equilibria are *interchangeable* in the sense that if *s* and *s'* are equilibria, then also the strategy profile *s"* in which some player *i* plays according to *s* but all other according to *s'*, is an equilibrium. All two-person constant-sum games are solvable in this sense. However, many relevant games for economics are not solvable, in which case Nash suggested something in the spirit of set-wise refinement:

> In an unsolvable game it sometimes happens that good heuristic reasons can be found for narrowing down the set of equilibrium points to those in a single sub-solution, which then play the role of a solution. (1950, p. 23).

Here a *sub-solution* is a maximal set of interchangeable equilibria (1950, p. 10). For instance, a strict Nash equilibrium, i.e., a strategy profile *s* in which every strategy s_i is the *unique* best reply to *s*, viewed as a singleton set, is a sub-solution in this sense.

1.2 Nash's 'Mass Action' interpretation

In fact, Nash also provided a quite distinct 'as if' interpretation, which he called the *mass-action* interpretation:

> We shall now take up the 'mass action' interpretation of equilibrium points. In this interpretation solutions have no great significance. It is unnecessary to assume that the participants have full knowledge of the total structure of the game, or the ability and inclination to go through any complex reasoning processes. But the participants are supposed to accumulate empirical information on the relative advantages of the various pure strategies at their disposal.
>
> To be more detailed, we assume that there is a population (in the sense of statistics) of participants for each position of the game. Let us also assume that the 'average playing' of the game involves *n* participants selected at random from the *n* populations, and that there is a stable average frequency with which each pure strategy is employed by the 'average member' of the appropriate population.
>
> Since there is to be no collaboration between individuals playing in different positions of the game, the probability that a particular *n*-tuple of pure strategies will be employed in a playing of the game should be the product of the probabilities indicating the chance of each of the *n* pure strategies to be employed in a random playing. (1950, pp. 21–2)

Nash notes that if s_i is a population distribution over the pure strategies available to the *i*-th player position, then $s = s_i$ is formally identical with a mixed strategy profile, and the expected payoff to any pure strategy in a random matching between individuals, one from each player population, is identical with the expected payoff of the pure strategy when played against the mixed strategy profile *s*. With $p_{i\alpha}(s)$ denoting the *i*-th player's expected payoff when using pure strategy α against a mixed-strategy profile *s*, Nash continues:

> Now let us consider what effects the experience of the participants will

produce. To assume, as we did, that they accumulated empirical evidence on the pure strategies at their disposal is to assume that those playing in position i learn the numbers $p_{i\alpha}$ (s). But if they know these they will employ only optimal pure strategies, i.e., those pure strategies... such that $p_{i\alpha}(s) = \max_\beta p_{i\beta}(s)$. Consequently, since s_i expresses their behavior s_i attaches positive coefficients only to optimal pure strategies, ... But this is simply a condition for s to be an equilibrium point.

Thus the assumption we made in this 'mass-action' interpretation led to the conclusion that the mixed strategies representing the average behavior in each of the populations form an equilibrium point. (1950, p. 22)

Actually, of course, we can only expect some sort of approximate equilibrium, since the information, its utilization, and the stability of the average frequencies will be imperfect. (1950, p. 23)

Hence, in the 'mass-action' interpretation, Nash argues that stationarity in population frequencies over pure strategies implies that the corresponding frequency distribution constitutes a Nash equilibrium. Although Nash did not discuss the matter, this approach presumes that there is no issue of strategically influencing the future behaviour of other individuals. One could imagine that the populations are so large that unilateral deviations cannot be detected by others.

1.3 Difficulties with the 'Mass Action' Interpretation

There are a few problems with this interpretation, though.

First, if the frequency distribution is indeed stationary but not completely mixed, i.e., does not involve *all* pure strategies in the game, then how can an individual know the payoffs of unused pure strategies? One way out would be to make the stronger assumption that all individuals know their whole payoff *function*, as well as the current population state, and can *deduce* the payoff associated with any deviation. But this would seem to run against the very spirit of the 'mass action' interpretation which emphasizes that the participants need not know much about the game or be able to make complex calculations, but instead base their strategy choice on *empirical* information about the 'relative advantages' of different pure strategies. Alternatively, one could assume that every now and then individuals 'experiment' by momentarily using some unused strategy in order to learn the payoffs of unused strategies. But in order to obtain precise information about the *expected* payoffs to such alternative strategies, a substantial amount of aggregate experimentation is needed, which would perturb the population frequency distribution and hence reduce the informational value of experimentation (at fixed rates of interaction and strategy revision). It is also not clear what *incentives* individuals would have to experiment.

Secondly, the 'mass action' interpretation does not say what would happen if the population frequency were not stationary but changed over time. The only suggestion in this direction is that we should only expect an 'approximate equilibrium' if the 'stability of the average frequency is imperfect' (see quote above). But this is not entirely convincing, since small fluctuations in frequencies (for example due to individuals' experimentation) may trigger a 'mass movement' away from the current 'approximate equilibrium'. (Think, for example, of population frequencies near those of some weakly dominated Nash equilibrium.)

In order to handle non-stationary population frequency distributions we need a model of population *dynamics* in which robustness properties of stationary distributions with respect to small frequency perturbations can be examined; in other words a dynamic stability analysis is called for.

Thirdly, the postulated behavior in the 'mass action' interpretation, to play optimally against the observed population distribution, implicitly involves some form of inertia, even in the context of a stationary and completely mixed Nash equilibrium. For even if all frequencies and payoffs are common knowledge, and the frequency distribution constitutes a Nash equilibrium, 'rationality' does not imply that all individuals will *continue* to play according to this equilibrium. First, such players are by definition completely indifferent between all pure strategies in the support of the Nash equilibrium in question, which in a completely mixed Nash equilibrium is the full pure-strategy space, and hence may without any payoff loss change pure strategy within this support. Hence, implicit in Nash's interpretation is a notion that indifferent individuals in the aggregate do not change strategy. Secondly, and more profoundly, even if a certain stationary Nash-equilibrium frequency distribution has been observed for any amount of time, this does not imply that the only 'rational' expectation is that this distribution will prevail. In fact, 'rational' players may 'rationally' believe that a certain equilibrium will be played up to a certain time, whereafter another equilibrium will be played, etc.[2] Nash's presumption, namely that individuals who have observed a stationary frequency distribution will not use any strategy which is sub-optimal against this distribution, thus implicitly involves some form of inertia. Indeed, from a behavioural viewpoint, some form of inertia appears natural.

1.4 Towards a Behavioural Model of Population Dynamics

Rather than developing a learning model, the present chapter examines in some detail the implications of the 'mass-action' interpretation in the context of a class of population dynamics based on 'evolution by imitation'. Indeed, prominent social scientists and biologists argue that adaptation by way of imitation of successful behaviours is a fundamental driving force shaping human behaviour and intelligence (see, e.g. Ullman-Margalit, 1978; and Dawkins, 1976).

As will be seen, if a population frequency distribution has full support over the pure strategies and is stationary in such an imitation dynamics then the distribution indeed constitutes a completely mixed Nash equilibrium, just as the above reasoning did suggest. Since there is no explicit 'experimentation' in the dynamics considered here, population distributions other than Nash equilibria can also be stationary, namely, precisely those distributions which are such that all pure strategies in the support of each player-population distribution earn the same payoff. In a sense, such a population distribution constitutes a Nash equilibrium *relative* to the pure strategy subsets which constitute its support. However, one can show that any such non-Nash stationary distribution is dynamically unstable, since by definition some unused *better* pure strategy is then available to some player population.[3]

The above implication is true even for the relatively weak notion of *Lyapunov stability*, which, in essence requires that a small perturbation of the population distribution does not trigger a movement *away* from the distribution. For predictive purposes, however, the more stringent notion of *asymptotic stability* is more reliable;

a population distribution has this stability property if it is Lyapunov stable and, moreover, attracts nearby population distributions *towards* itself. Only under asymptotic stability are predictions robust against occasional perturbations of the population state, e.g. due to 'experimentation', 'mistakes', 'random mutations' etc. Unfortunately, however, many, if not most, relevant games possess *no* asymptotically stable population distribution *at all*.

For instance, a Nash equilibrium which does not reach all the information sets in an underlying extensive-form representation of the game is in general not asymptotically stable in any of the considered population dynamics. The reason is simply that local strategies at unreached information sets can be changed without affecting payoffs. In a generic extensive-form game, the Nash equilibrium in question will for this reason belong to a non-trivial connected set of Nash equilibria, and, since all Nash equilibria are stationary in the studied population dynamics, there is no dynamic force 'pulling' the population distribution back towards the Nash equilibrium in question within the set to which it belongs, and hence the Nash equilibrium in question is *not* asymptotically stable in any such population dynamics.

Moreover, it has been shown that even an *isolated* Nash equilibrium, i.e., one which has a neighbourhood without other Nash equilibria, is asymptotically stable in 'bench-mark' populations dynamics if, and *only* if, it is *strict*. Many games of interest lack strict Nash equilibria, so again one cannot hope to find asymptotically stable population distributions.

These observations suggest that the 'mass-action' interpretation may have quite limited validity when used to predict *individual* strategy profiles, and, indeed, that the very criterion of Nash equilibrium may not have so strong 'as if' foundations as could be hoped. This had led some researchers instead to consider set-valued predictions.

Here, we will reformulate Nash's 'mass-action' interpretation in terms of asymptotically stable *sets* of strategy profiles. A set-valued prediction of this type simply means that once the population distribution has entered such a set, it will remain there, and, moreover, if the distribution is perturbed to fall slightly outside the set, then the dynamics will bring it back towards the set over time. Existence of asymptotically stable sets is no problem (just make the set sufficiently large), and, as will be seen, set-wise asymptotic stability does have a *set-valued* implication for Nash equilibrium play.

2 THE MODEL

2.1 The Game

Consider a finite n-player game in normal (or strategic) form. Let $I = \{1,...n\}$ be the set of *player positions* in the game, A_i the pure-strategy set of player position i, S_i its mixed-strategy simplex, and $S = \times_{i \in I} S_i$ the polyhedron of mixed-strategy profiles. For any player position i, pure strategy $a \in A_i$ and mixed strategy $s_i \in S_i$, let s_{ia} denote the probability assigned to a. The *support* or *carrier* of a mixed strategy $s_i \in S_i$ is the subset $C_i(s_i)$ of pure strategies to which s_i assigns positive probability, i.e. $C_i(s_i) = \{a \in A_i : s_{ia} > 0\}$. A strategy profile s is called *completely mixed* or *interior* if *all* pure strategies are used with positive probability, i.e., if $C_i(s_i) = A_i$ for all player positions $i \in I$. In contrast, a strategy profile is *pure* if only *one* pure strategy in each player position is assigned positive probability, i.e., if $C_i(s_i)$ is a singleton for each player position $i \in I$.

The expected payoff to player position i when a profile $s = (s_1, \ldots, s_n) \in S$ is played will be denoted $u_i(s)$, and $u_{ia}(s)$ denotes the payoff to player position i when the individual in this position uses pure strategy $a \in A_i$ against the profile $s \in S$. The pure-strategy best-reply correspondence for player position i is denoted $\beta_i : S \to A_i$. Hence, a strategy profile $s \in S$ is a *Nash equilibrium* if and only if every pure strategy in its support is a best reply to s, i.e., if $C_i(s_i) \subset \beta_i(s)$ for all i, or, more explicitly, $s_{ia} > 0 \Rightarrow a \in \beta_i(s)$.

2.2 The Transmission Mechanism

A *population state* is formally identical with a mixed-strategy profile $s \in S$, but now each component $s_i \in S_i$ represents the distribution of pure strategies in player population i, i.e., s_{ia} is the probability that a randomly selected individual in population i will use pure strategy $a \in A_i$.

At each play of the game, n individuals are randomly drawn, one from each player population. We assume that no individual ever randomizes but always uses some pure strategy in every play of the game. However, every now and then each individual reviews her pure-strategy choice. Let $r_{ia}(s)$ denote the average *time-rate* in population state $s \in S$ at which an individual in player-population i, who currently uses strategy $a \in A_i$, reviews her strategy choice. Likewise, let $p_{ia}^b(s)$ denote the probability that such a reviewing individual will choose strategy $b \in A_i$. We write $p_{ia}(s)$ for the induced probability *distribution* over A_i; formally this is a mixed strategy for player position i: $p_{ia}(s) \in S_i$. Note that $p_{ia}^a(s)$ is the probability that the reviewing individual decides not to change strategy.[4]

In a finite population one may imagine that the review times of an a-strategist in population i constitute the arrival times of a Poisson process with average (across such individuals) arrival rate $r_{ia}(s)$, and that at each such arrival time the individual instantly selects a pure strategy according to the conditional probability distribution $p_{ia}(s)$ over S_i. Assuming that all individuals' Poisson processes are statistically independent, the probability that any two individuals happen to review simultaneously is zero, and the aggregate of reviewing times in the i-th player population among a-strategists is a Poisson process with arrival rate $s_{ia}r_{ia}(s)$ when the population is in state s. If strategy choices are statistically independent random variables, the aggregate arrival rate of the Poisson process of individuals who switch from one pure strategy $a \in A_i$, to another, $b \in A_i$, is $s_{ia}r_{ia}(s)p_{ia}^b(s)$.[5]

2.3 The Induced Dynamics

Since we consider large (technically speaking infinite) populations, we invoke the law of large numbers and model these aggregate stochastic processes as deterministic flows, each such flow being set equal to the expected rate of the corresponding Poisson arrival process.[6] Rearranging terms, one obtains the following population dynamics

$$s_{ia} = \sum_{c \in S_i} r_{ic}(s) p_{ic}^a(s) s_{ic} - r_{ia}(s) s_{ia} \qquad (1)$$

In order to guarantee that this system of differential equations has a unique solution through every initial population state $s^0 \in S$, we hence forth assume that the involved review functions $r_{ia} : S \rightarrow R_+$ and choice-probability functions $p_{ia} : S \rightarrow S_i$ are Lipschitz continuous. Under this hypothesis, the equation system (1) induces a well-defined dynamics on the state space S (by the Picard–Lindelöf Theorem; see, e.g., Hirsch and Smale, 1974). In particular, a solution trajectory starting in S never leaves S, and a solution trajectory starting in the interior of S remains for ever in the interior (but may of course converge to a limit point on the boundary of S).

3 IMITATION DYNAMICS

3.1 Definition

A population dynamics of the form (1) will be called *imitative* if more prevalent strategies are more likely to be adopted by reviewing individuals, *ceteris paribus*. More precisely, if two pure strategies b, $c \in A_i$ currently have the same expected payoff, but b is currently more popular than c in the sense that more individuals in player population i currently use b, then the choice probability for b, $p_{ia}^b(s)$ should exceed that of c, $p_{ia}^c(s)$. Technically this can be expressed as the requirement that each choice probability $p_{ia}^b(s)$ be strictly increasing in s_{ib}, the population share of the potential 'target' strategy b.

Of course, such an imitative feature does not preclude that individuals also are sensitive to payoffs. For instance, the behaviourally plausible notion that individuals with less successful strategies are, on average, more inclined to review their strategy choice than individuals with more successful strategies can be formalized by having the average review rate $r_{ia}(s)$ non-increasing in the current expected payoff $u_{ia}(s)$. The likewise plausible notion that more successful strategies are, on average, more prone to being adopted than less successful ones can be formalized by letting each choice probability $p_{ia}^b(s)$ be non-decreasing in the expected payoff $u_{ib}(s)$ of the potential 'target' strategy b. These possibilities will now be illustrated in a few examples.

3.2 Pure Imitation by Failing Individuals

As a model of 'pure', or 'unbiased' imitation, assume that a reviewing individual adopts the pure strategy of 'the first man in the street'. Hence, independently of which strategy the reviewing individual has used so far, it is as if he or she were to draw an individual at random from her player population, according to a uniform probability distribution across individuals, and adopt the pure strategy of the individual she happened to sample. Formally:

$$p_{ia}^b(s) = s_{ib} \qquad (2)$$

for all population states s and pure strategies a, b $\in$ A_i. In a sense, one could say that a reviewing individual then decides to 'just do what others are doing' in her player population.[7]

If, moreover, the average review rates within each player population are independent of the current strategy of the potential reviewer, i.e. $r_{ia}(s) = r_{ib}(s)$, for every state s, player population i, and pure strategies a, b, then this form of pure imitation leads to no change at all in the population state; all states are stationary. In particular, Nash's contention that a stationary frequency distribution in his 'mass-action' interpretation necessarily constitutes a Nash equilibrium, is not valid. But this is no surprise, since by assumption payoffs are here completely irrelevant both for review propensities and choice probabilities.

More plausibly, suppose instead that individuals with less successful strategies review their strategy at a higher average rate than individuals with more successful strategies, i.e., let

$$r_{ia}(s) = p_i[u_{ia}(s), s] \tag{3}$$

for some positive function $\rho_i : R \times S \rightarrow R_+$ which is strictly decreasing in its first argument.

Note that this monotonicity assumption does not presume that an a-strategist in population i necessarily *knows* the expected value $u_{ia}(s)$ of her current pure strategy, nor that she knows the current state s. For instance, some or all such individuals could have some noisy empirical data on their own current payoff and perhaps also on some alternative pure strategies or, say, the current average payoff u_i (s) in their player population. The only informational assumption in (3) is that, on average, the review rate of a-strategists is higher if their expected payoff is lower, *ceteris paribus*.

Under assumptions (2) and (3), the population dynamics (1) becomes

$$\dot{s}_{ia} = \left(\sum_{c \in A_i} \rho_i[u_{ic}(s), s]s_{ic} - \rho_i[u_{ia}(s), s] \right) s_{ia} \tag{4}$$

Note that the *growth rate* $\dot{s}_{ia}/s_{ia}$ of the population share of a-strategists by assumption is higher than that of the population share of b-strategists if and only if the current payoff $u_{ia}(s)$ to strategy a exceeds that of strategy b.

Despite this monotone connection between payoffs and growth rates, it is still not true that stationarity implies Nash equilibrium. For instance, any *pure* strategy profile is a stationary state in (4), for the simple technical reason that the dynamics does not allow any population share s_{ia} to increase from zero. The intuitive explanation is simply that all reviewing individuals imitate 'the first man in the street', and in a population state with (at least) one pure strategy absent, *no* 'man in the street' uses that pure strategy, and so no reviewing individual will adopt that strategy. In particular, any *pure* population distribution, whether it be a Nash equilibrium or not, is stationary.

However, stationarity in the *interior* of the state space S *does* imply Nash equilibrium. For in such a population state *all* pure strategies in the game are used by some individuals, and so all pure strategies available to each player position must earn the same payoff, by stationarity in (4), and hence the population state constitutes a Nash equilibrium. To see the intuition for this, suppose, on the contrary, that some pure strategy $a \in A_i$ earns more than another, $b \in A_i$. Then a-strategists would on average abandon their strategy at a lower time rate than b-strategists, while both types of strategist would be equally likely to be imitated (by (2)). Hence, the share of a-strategists would grow at a higher rate than that of b-strategists. In particular, both growth rates could not be zero, and so the population state would not be stationary.

In sum, this sort of imitation process does lend some support to completely mixed Nash equilibria. Unfortunately, though, such equilibria turn out to have poor stability properties, and hence are not likely to be observed (see Section 4 below).

Note, finally, that if the function ρ_i is *linear* (or, more exactly, *affine*) in the payoff argument, i.e., $\rho_i(z, s) = \alpha_i(s) - \beta_i(s)z$ for some positive functions α_i, β_i, then (4) boils down to the following simple expression

$$\dot{s}_{ia} = \beta_i(s)[u_{ia}(s) - u_i(s)]s_{ia} \tag{5}$$

In other words, then the growth rate of the share s_{ia} of a-strategists in player population i is proportional to the difference between the payoff to a-strategists, $u_{ia}(s)$, and the average payoff in player population i, $u_i(s)$. But this is merely a player-specific rescaling of time in the so-called *replicator dynamics*, studied in evolutionary biology! That dynamics is derived from particular assumptions about biological asexual reproduction, and takes the form (5) with $\beta_i(s) = 1$ for all $i \in I$ and $s \in S$.[8]

3.3 Imitation of Successful Individuals

While the transmission mechanism in the preceding sub-section is 'purely' imitative in the sense of being independent of the payoffs of potential 'target' strategies, it seems behaviourally more plausible to assume that more successful individuals are more likely to be imitated than less successful ones.

An example of such a 'success-oriented' imitation dynamics will here be outlined. In order to isolate this 'pull' effect from the above studied 'push' effect away from less successful strategies, we now set all average review rates equal to one:

$$r_{ia}(s) = 1 \tag{6}$$

for all population states s, player positions i and pure strategies $a \in A_i$. Instead, now let the choice probabilities $p_{ia}^b(s)$ be increasing both in the target population share s_{ib} and in the target payoff $u_{ib}(s)$, as follows

$$p_{ia}^b(s) = \frac{\theta_i[u_{ib}(s), s]s_{ib}}{\sum_{c \in A_i} \theta_i[u_{ic}(s), s]s_{ic}} \tag{7}$$

where $\theta_i : R \times S \to R_+$ is strictly increasing in its first argument. In other words, the 'pull' towards a pure strategy $b \in A_i$ is proportional to its 'popularity' s_{ib}, where the proportionality factor may depend on the reviewing individual's current pure strategy a and on the current population state s, and, most important, is an increasing function of the current expected payoff of the 'target' strategy b.

As in the earlier case of differentiated review rates, the informational assumption behind choice probabilities of the form (7) is *not* that an a-strategists in population i necessarily knows the current expected payoffs $u_{ib}(s)$ of all available pure strategies *b*, nor does she have to know the current population state *s*. It is sufficient that some individuals have some, perhaps noisy, empirical information about some available payoffs, and, on average, move more towards those with higher current expected payoffs than towards those with lower. In fact, some individuals may, due to observational noise, change to strategies which perform worse than the strategy they abandoned.

Conversely, (7) allows for the opposite possibility that virtually all reviewing individuals adopt one of the currently optimal (pure) strategies, by making the 'attraction' function θ_i sufficiently 'payoff sensitive'. For instance, suppose each function θ_i is exponential, $\theta_i(z, s) = e^{\sigma_i z}$ for some $\sigma_i > 0$.[9] The boundary case $\sigma_i = 0$ then corresponds to 'pure' imitation as discussed above, and the limit case $\sigma_i \to \infty$ corresponds to 'pure' best-reply behaviour at interior states *s*, in the sense that all reviewing individuals then switch to currently optimal pure strategies.[10] Hence, choice probabilities of the form (7) span a whole range of myopic choice behaviours from pure imitation to pure optimization. In particular, individuals with very high *individual* review rates (given the overall unit average rate) can be made to move virtually instantaneously to a currently optimal strategy, and hence almost always play optimally against the current population strategy *s* even if this fluctuates over time.

Choice probabilities of the form (7), combined with the assumption (6) of unit review rates, result in the following population dynamics:

$$\dot{s}_{ia} = \left(\frac{\theta_i[u_{ib}(s), s]}{\sum_{c \in A_i} \theta_i[u_{ic}(s), s] s_{ic}} - 1 \right) s_{ia} \tag{8}$$

Just as in the above case (4) of pure imitation combined with payoff-dependent review rates, pure strategies *a* with higher expected payoffs $u_{ia}(s)$ have higher growth rates in (8) than pure strategies with low expected payoffs. Again, and essentially for the same reasons, it is still *not* true that stationarity implies Nash equilibrium, while stationarity in the *interior* does.

Similarly as in the pure imitation dynamics (4), we note that if the 'attraction' functions θ_i are *linear* (strictly speaking *affine*) in the 'target' payoff, i.e., $\theta_i(z, s) = \lambda_i(s) + \mu_i(s)z$ for some positive functions λ_i and μ_i, then (8) boils down to the following player-specific rescaling of time in the replicator dynamics:[11]

$$\dot{s}_{ia} = \frac{\mu_i(s)}{\lambda_i(s) + \mu_i(s)u_i(s)} [u_{ia}(s) - u_i(s)] s_{ia} \tag{9}$$

4 DYNAMIC STABILITY AND NASH EQUILIBRIUM

All population dynamics in the preceding section can be written in the form

$$\dot{s}_{ia} = g_{ia}(s) s_{ia} , \tag{10}$$

for some growth-rate functions $g_{ia} : S \to R$ which are Lipschitz continuous and such that $\sum_a g_{ia}(s) s_{ia} = 0$ for every player position $i \in I$ and strategy profile $s \in S$. (This identity is equivalent to saying that the sum of population shares remains constant over time.) Such growth-rate functions will be called *regular*.

4.1 Monotonicity Properties

As noted above, the studied imitation dynamics (4) and (8) also satisfy the following monotonicity condition with respect to payoffs:

$$u_{ia}(s) > u_{ib}(s) \Longleftrightarrow g_{ia}(s) > g_{ib}(s) \tag{11}$$

Such growth rate functions, and their induced dynamics, are usually called *monotonic* in the evolutionary game-theory literature (see Nachbar, 1990; Friedman, 1991; and Samuelson and Zhang, 1992).

Moreover, in some special cases, more precisely in equations (5) and (9), we found that each growth rate $g_{ia}(s)$ was *proportional* to the strategy's payoff excess $u_{ia}(s) - u_i(s)$. In the terminology of Samuelson and Zhang (1992), such growth-rate functions, and the induced dynamics, are called *aggregate monotonic*.

$$g_{ia}(s) = \omega_i(s)[u_{ia}(s) - u_{ia}(s)] \tag{12}$$

for some positive function ω_i.

A special case of aggregate monotonicity is evidently the *replicator dynamics* (see, e.g., Hofbauer and Sigmund, 1988):

$$\dot{s}_{ia} = [u_{ia}(s) - u_i(s)]s_{ia} \tag{13}$$

4.2 Stability Properties

Turning now to stability concepts, suppose some population dynamics is given in the form of a system of autonomous ordinary differential equations, such as, for example (10).

A population state $s^* \in S$ is called *Lyapunov stable* if small perturbations of the state do not lead it away, in the precise sense that every neighbourhood Θ of s^* contains a neighbourhood Θ^o of s^* such that all solution orbits starting in Θ^o remains in Θ forever.[12]

A more stringent stability notion is that of asymptotic stability, which essentially requires that the population also returns towards the state after any small perturbation. Formally, a population state $s^* \in S$ is called *asymptotically stable* if it is Lyapunov stable *and* has a neighbourhood Θ' from which all solution orbits converge to s^* over time.[13]

Both these stability concepts are analogously defined for non-empty and closed *subset* $S^* \subset S$. Just let a *neighbourhood* of such a set S^* mean an open set containing it. Then Lyapunov stability means that every neighbourhood Θ of S^* contains a neighbourhood Θ^o such that all solution orbits starting in Θ^o remains in Θ forever, and asymptotic stability means that, in addition, there is a neighbourhood Θ' of S^* from which all solution orbits converge to S^* (in the sense that the distance to the set S^* shrinks towards zero over time).

4.3 Results for Monotonic Dynamics

We first note that *all* monotonic population dynamics (10) have the same set of stationary states, namely, those states in which all non-extinct pure strategies in each player position have the same expected payoff. Formally, this is the set $S^o = \times_{i \in I} S_i^o$, where

$$S_i^o = \{ s_i \in S_i : u_{ia}(s) = u_i(s) \text{ for all } a \in A_i \text{ with } s_{ia} > 0 \}$$

It follows immediately from this observation that every Nash equilibrium s is a stationary state in all monotonic population dynamics, and that every interior stationary state s is a (completely mixed) Nash equilibrium. As noted earlier, a non-interior population state s may be stationary without being a Nash equilibrium. However, such states are not Lyapunov stable in any monotonic population dynamics, and are thus not likely to be observed in 'practice':

Proposition 1 (Bomze, 1986; Nachbar, 1990; Friedman, 1991): *If $s \in S$ is Lyapunov stable in some monotonic population dynamics (10), then s is a Nash equilibrium*

It is easily established that every *strict* Nash equilibrium is asymptotically stable in any monotonic population dynamics. However, as mentioned in the introduction, the 'typical relevant' case is that the game has *no* strict Nash equilibrium at all. This is the motivation behind set-valued stability approaches. In particular, a set-valued connection has been established between, on the one hand, certain asymptotically stable *sets* of population states and, on the other hand, *sets* of Nash equilibria which meet the requirement of *strategic stability* in the sense of Kohlberg and Mertens (1986). A (closed) set $S^* \subset S$ of Nash equilibria is strategically stable if it (a) is robust with respect to any sequence of small 'trembles' of the strategies, and (b) contains no proper subset with this property. This robustness criterion was designed with the intention to meet certain 'rationalistic' desiderata. However, it so happens that there is a connection between set-wise asymptotic stability in population dynamics of the type studied here (in fact in a larger class of dynamics) and strategic stability. The connection takes the form of set-wise inclusion:

Proposition 2 (Swinkels, 1993): *Suppose $S^* \subset S$ is non-empty, closed and convex. If S^* is asymptotically stable in some monotone population dynamics (10), then S^* contains a strategically stable set of Nash equilibria.*[14]

Hence, *if* we (a) have a monotonic population dynamics defined on the mixed-strategy space S of some game, and (b) have found a (closed and convex) subset S^* which is asymptotically stable in this dynamics, then we are sure that S^* contains some subset S' of Nash equilibria which meets the stringent requirement of strategic stability. In some cases the set S' might be much smaller than S^* while in others these two sets may even coincide. Likewise, in some cases S^* will correspond to only one payoff outcome, while in others S^* may involve many different payoff outcomes. Hence, the *precision* of the evolutionary prediction may differ between games and between subsets within games.

4.4 Results for Aggregate Monotonic Dynamics

From an operational viewpoint, the above result has the drawback that it may be hard to verify asymptotic stability in a given population dynamics. Moreover, the modeller may not be so sure of which exact specification of the dynamics is appropriate to the application at hand, and hence may want to focus on sets which are asymptotically stable in a fairly wide range of population dynamics.[15] In the special case of aggregate monotonic dynamics, there is some headway in these directions – both towards operationality and towards robustness with respect to the dynamics.

We saw above that only for *interior* population states is it true that stationarity implies Nash equilibrium. However, as indicated above, such states have poor stability properties. For instance, Hofbauer and Sigmund (1988) show that *no* interior population state is asymptotically stable in the replicator dynamic (13). The proof of this claim is based on an important observation by Amann and Hofbauer (1985), namely that the replicator dynamics induces the *same* solution orbits in the interior of the state space *S* as a certain volume-preserving dynamics.[16] Such a dynamics has no asymptotically stable state, and since the solution orbits are the same as for the replicator dynamics, the latter has no asymptotically stable state in the interior of the strategy space.

A slight generalization of this result leads to the conclusion that no *interior* closed set *S** is asymptotically stable in the replicator dynamics. Moreover, since the restriction of the replicator dynamics to any sub-polyhedron of the polyhedron *S* of mixed strategy profiles is the replicator dynamics for the associated 'subgame', no closed set *S** which is contained in the relative interior of *S* or any of its sub-polyhedra is asymptotically stable in the replicator dynamics (13). Hence, if we search for sets which are asymptotically stable in a class of population dynamics including the replicator dynamics, then we have to discard all such relatively interior subsets.

Formally, first note that the strategy space *S* is the Cartesian product of *n* simplexes, one for each player, so *S* is a polyhedron. More generally, the set of possible randomizations over any non-empty subset of pure strategies for some player *i* defines a *sub-simplex* of mixed strategies for that player, i.e., a subset $S'_i \subset S_i$ which also is a simplex of mixed strategies. The Cartesian product of such sub-simplexes constitutes a polyhedron of mixed strategy profiles, a *sub-polyhedron* $S' = \times S'_i$ of *S*. In particular, each *pure* strategy profile, viewed as a singleton set, is a minimal sub-polyhedron, and the full set *S'* is the maximal sub-polyhedron.

A closed set $S^* \subset S$ will here be called *relatively interior* if it is contained in the interior of some sub-polyhedron *S'* of *S*. Clearly every sub-polyhedron is a closed and convex set.

Having thus defined the relevant mathematical concepts, the negative result mentioned above, on dynamic stability, can be summarized as follows:[17]

Proposition 3 (Hofbauer and Sigmund, 1988): *Suppose S* is a non-empty and closed subset of S. If S* is relatively interior, then it is not asymptotically stable in the replicator dynamics (13).*

It turns out that, for subsets $S^* \subset S$ which are themselves sub-polyhedra of *S*, the property of asymptotic stability in aggregate monotonic population dynamics can be concisely characterized in terms of a certain correspondence on *S*, called the '*better reply*' correspondence (Ritzberger and Weibull, 1993). This 'new' correspondence γ assigns to each mixed-strategy profile $s \in S$ those pure strategies *a* for each player *i* which give him at least the same payoff as he obtains in *s*. Formally, the image γ(s) of any profile $s \in S$ is the Cartesian product of the subsets

$$\gamma_i(s) = \{a \in S_i : u_{ia}(s) \geq u_i(s)\} \tag{14}$$

one such set for each player $i \in I$. The pure strategies in $\gamma_i(s)$ are thus weakly *better* replies to s than s_i is.

Clearly all pure strategies which are *best* replies are *better* replies in this sense, so the image $\gamma(s)$ of any strategy profile s under the better-reply correspondence γ always contains the image $\beta(s)$ of the best-reply correspondence β. In particular, if $s \in S$ is a Nash equilibrium, then the set of weakly better pure replies coincides with the set of best pure replies, i.e., $\beta(s) = \gamma(s)$. Although $\gamma(s)$ by definition is a subset of pure strategy profiles, it will be notationally convenient to identify it with the associated subset of ('degenerate') mixed strategies (vertices of the polyhedron S).

Ritzberger and Weibull (1993) call a sub-polyhedron S' *closed under the better-reply correspondence* if it contains all its weakly better replies, i.e., if $\gamma(s) \subset S'$ for all $s \in S'$, or, more concisely, $\gamma(S') \subset S'$. For instance, a singleton set $S' = \{s\}$ is closed under γ if and only if s is a *strict* Nash equilibrium, and the full polyhedron S is trivially closed under γ. Moreover, there always exists at least one *minimal* sub-polyhedron which is closed under γ (there are only finitely many sub-polyhedra).[18]

Closedness of sub-polyhedra $S' \subset S$ under the better-reply correspondence γ *characterizes* asymptotically stable in aggregate monotonic population dynamics:

Proposition 4 (Ritzberger and Weibull, 1993): *In any aggregate monotonic population dynamics: a sub-polyhedron $S' \subset S$ is asymptotically stable if and only if it is closed under γ.*

It follows from Swinkels' (1993) result above, Proposition 2, that any sub-polyhedron S' which is asymptotically stable in some monotonic population dynamics contains a set of Nash equilibria which is strategically stable in the sense of Kohlberg and Mertens (1986). However, for aggregate monotonic dynamics, the implication is even stronger: every sub-polyhedron S' which is asymptotically stable in some *aggregate* monotonic population dynamics contains an *essential component* of Nash equilibria.[19] Moreover, an essential component contains a strategically stable set (Kohlberg and Mertens, 1986).

This slightly stronger implication of asymptotic stability follows from Proposition 3 combined with the following result:

Proposition 5 (Ritzberger and Weibull, 1993): *If a sub-polyhedron $S' \subset S$ is closed under γ, then it contains an essential component of Nash equilibria, and hence also a strategically stable set.*

Just as in the case of Proposition 2 above, the cutting power of this result on the connection between evolutionary selection and Nash equilibrium play is game dependent.

The games under consideration being finite, also the set of sub-polyhedra $S' \subset S$ is finite. Hence, it is immediate that there exists at least one *minimal* such sub-polyhedron set S' which is closed under the better-reply correspondence γ, and every strategically stable set of Nash equilibria is contained in some such set. In particular, since a generic extensive form game has at least one strategically stable payoff *outcome* (Kohlberg and Mertens, 1986), the associated strategy set is contained in a minimal sub-polyhedron which is closed under γ, and hence is asymptotically stable in all aggregate monotonic population dynamics.

5 CONCLUSIONS

The discussed dynamic models of evolution by imitation do lend some support to the 'mass-action' interpretation of Nash equilibrium. However, the analysis also suggests that evolutionary predictions may be context dependent. The social, cultural, institutional etc. environment in which the interaction takes place presumably shapes the transmission mechanism by which behaviours spread in society. And different transmission mechanisms induce different population dynamics, and hence possibly different dynamically stable sets. However, the discussed set-valued approach suggests that some, perhaps less precise, predictions can be made with only some qualitative knowledge about the dynamics in question. More exactly, if one requires that predictions be valid for all aggregate monotonic population dynamics – which we saw appeared as 'first order' approximations of the studied imitation dynamics – then one can identify the relevant sets directly by means of the better-reply correspondence, which relies only on the data of the game.

Many directions for further research in the broad area of behavioural foundations for non-cooperative solution concepts appear highly relevant. Rather than sketching here a few such possibilities we advise the interested reader to consult the special issues on evolutionary game theory and game dynamics in *Journal of Economic Theory* (August 1992) and *Games and Economic Behaviour* (vols 4 and 5, 1993).

Notes

1. For a discussion of the context of Nash's work, see Leonard (1993). We are grateful to Harold Kuhn for showing that study and for providing a copy of Nash's dissertation.
2. There is also the further possibility that a certain non-stationary time pattern of frequency distributions is common knowledge.
3. There are games in which the unique Nash equilibrium is unstable but a whole *set* of strategies, containing the Nash equilibrium, constitute an attractor in the dynamics (see Swinkels, 1993; and Ritzberger and Weibull, 1993).
4. Alternatively, one could reinterpret what we here call reviewing as the 'exit' of one individual who is instantaneously replaced by a new 'entrant'.
5. A *Poisson process* is a stochastic point process in continuous time, the points usually being called *arrival times*. The probability distribution of arrival times is given by a function $\lambda : R \to R$, called the *intensity* of the process, such that $\lambda(t)dt$ is the probability for an arrival in the infinitesimal time interval $(t, t + dt)$. Superposition of independent Poisson processes is again a Poisson process, and its intensity is the sum of the constituent intensities. Likewise, statistically independent decomposition, such as at the strategy switchings above, of a Poisson process also result in Poisson processes. See, e.g., Çinlar (1975) for details.
6. Such deterministic approximations are not always innocent; see Boylan (1992) for a critical analysis.

7. This 'pure' form of imitation may alternatively be thought of in terms of 'naïve entrants', i.e., an 'old' individual being replaced by an uninformed 'newcomer'.

8. In an alternative formulation, the replicator dynamics is written on the form (5) with $\beta_i(s) = 1/u_i(s)$. See, e.g., Hofbauer and Sigmund (1988).

9. Cf. the logit model of discrete choice, see, e.g., McFadden (1974).

10. Some technical subtleties arise in the limit: the limit vector field is (i) Lipschitz continuous only on the interior of each of a class of geometrically well-behaved subsets which together partition the state space, and (ii) does not define a *monotonic* dynamics in the sense defined above.

11. If one combines linearity of the 'attraction' functions θ_i with linearity of the review functions ρ_i (as done above), one obtains a dynamics of the same form as (9), but with the nominator $\mu_i(s)$ replaced by the more general expression $\alpha_i(s)\mu_i(s) + \beta_i(s)\lambda_i(s)$. Stability properties of equation (8) can be studied by way of local linearizations. The resulting approximation is a rescaled version of the replicator dynamics.

12. By a *neighbourhood* of a point is here meant an *open* set containing the point.

13. See, e.g., Hirsch and Smale (1974) for definitions and discussions of stability concepts.

14. Swinkels' result (his Theorem 1), is more general both with respect to the dynamics and with respect to the shape of the set S^*.

15. Note, however, that asymptotic stability in one population dynamics implies asymptotic stability in all 'nearby' population dynamics, so the predictions according to the above result are at least 'locally' robust in the space of dynamics.

16. The *divergence* of a dynamic $x = f(x)$ at a state x is the trace of the Jacobian of f at x, i.e., $div[f(x)] = \Sigma_i \partial f_i(x)/\partial x_i$. The dynamics is called *volume preserving* if $div[f(x))] \equiv 0$. Such a dynamics behaves like water flowing under constant temperature and pressure, and can hence have no asymptotically stable state.

17. Hofbauer and Sigmund (1988) state this result only in the special case of an interior singleton in a two-player game. For details concerning its present generalization, see Ritzberger and Weibull (1993).

18. Cf. *curb* sets, i.e., sets closed under the best-reply correspondence, a notion introduced in Basu and Weibull (1991).

19. The set of Nash equilibria is a finite union of connected sets, or *components*, and such a component is called *essential* if it is robust with respect to perturbations of payoffs. See van Damme (1987).

References

Amann, E. and J. Hofbauer (1985) 'Permanence in Lotka-Volterra and Replicator Equations', in W. Ebeling and M. Peschel (eds), *Lotka-Volterra Approach to Cooperation and Competition in Dynamic Systems* (Berlin : Akademie-Verlag).

Aumann, R. and A. Brandenburger (1991) 'Epistemic Conditions for Nash Equilibrium', mimeo., Hebrew University.

Basu, K. and J. Weibull (1991) 'Strategy Subsets Closed Under Rational Behavior', *Economics Letters* vol. 36, pp. 141–6.

Bomze, I. (1986) 'Non-Cooperative Two-Person Games in Biology: A Classification', *International Journal of Game Theory*, vol. 15, pp. 31–57.

Boylan, R. (1992) 'Laws of Large Numbers for Dynamical Systems with Randomly Matched Individuals', *Journal of Economic Theory*, vol. 57, pp. 473–504.

Çinlar, E. (1975) *Introduction to Stochastic Processes* (New York: Prentice Hall).

van Damme, E. (1987) *Stability and Perfection of Nash Equilibria* (Berlin: Springer Verlag).

Dawkins, R. (1976) *The Selfish Gene* (Oxford: Oxford University Press).

Friedman, D. (1991) 'Evolutionary Games in Economics', *Econometrica*, vol. 59, pp. 637–66.

Hirsch, M. and S. Smale, (1974) *Differential Equations, Dynamical Systems, and Linear Algebra* (New York: Academic Press).

Hofbauer, J. and K. Sigmund, (1988) *The Theory of Evolution and Dynamical Systems* (Cambridge: Cambridge University Press).

Kohlberg, E. and J.-F. Mertens (1986) 'On the Strategic Stability of Equilibria', *Economica*, vol. 54, pp. 1003–37.

Leonard, R. (1993) 'Reading Cournot, Reading Nash', University of Québec at Montréal, mimeo.

McFadden, D. (1974) 'Conditional Logit Analysis of Qualitative Choice Behavior', in P. Zarembka (ed.), *Frontiers in Econometrics* (New York: Academic Press).

Nachbar, J. (1990) 'Evolutionary' Selection Dynamics in Games: Convergence and Limit Properties', *International Journal of Game Theory*, vol. 19, pp. 59–89.

Nash, J. (1950) 'Non Cooperative Games', PhD thesis, Princeton University.

Ritzberger, K. and J.W. Weibull (1993) 'Evolutionary Selection in Normal-Form Games', The Industrial Institute for Economic and Social Research, Stockholm, WP 383.

Samuelson, L. and J. Zhang, (1992) 'Evolutionary Stability in Asymmetric Games', *Journal of Economic Theory*, vol. 57, pp. 363–91.

Swinkels, J. (1993) 'Adjustment Dynamics and Rational Play in Games', *Games and Economic Behavior*, vol. 5, pp. 455–84.

Tan, T. and S.R. Werlang, (1988) 'The Bayesian Foundations of Solution Concepts of Games', *Journal of Economic Theory*, vol. 45, pp. 370–91.

Ullman-Margalit, E. (1978) 'Invisible-Hand Explanations', *Synthèse*, vol. 39, pp. 263–91.

Comment[*]

Pier Luigi Sacco

UNIVERSITY OF FLORENCE

1 INTRODUCTION

The evolutionary approach to game theory is probably one of the more rapidly expanding areas in current research in economics. Initially, one of its main reasons of interest seemed to be its usefulness as a source of equilibrium selection processes that didn't rely too heavily on the computational abilities of players. However, as contributions have grown in number and scope, it has become pretty clear that this literature may pursue a more ambitious aim: namely, laying the foundations of a new positive theory of social and economic dynamics with boundedly rational agents.

There is, however, a major difficulty. The origin of evolutionary game-theoretic models is to be found in the biologically motivated literature. They were aimed at providing a rigorous mathematical foundation of Darwinian natural selection processes (see, e.g., Maynard Smith, 1982; Hofbauer and Sigmund, 1988), through a detailed characterization of the dynamics of competition for limited resources, leading to survival of the 'fittest' individuals only. In this context, the relevant consequences of strategic behaviour are not 'payoffs' as commonly meant in economically motivated game theory, but rather 'fitnesses', i.e. ability to reproduce one's genetical endowment. The physical replication of individuals with common genetic traits is clearly of limited interest for most social scientists, and for economists in particular. However, these latter soon understood the potential of this framework: what is needed is to rephrase the model in terms of the replication of *behaviours* rather than individuals, and consequently in terms of standard payoffs rather than fitnesses. Just as fitter traits have access to larger offspring, more rewarding behaviours will spread over the population of 'host' individuals as these learn to recognize them. Some sort of learning process then substitutes for the biological transmission mechanism, namely reproduction. This constructive reinterpretation of the biological metaphor looks then like an appealing starting point for a theory of the birth and evolution of social conventions and norms competing for favourable 'niches' in socio-economic settings ('ecosystems'). As an additional source of interest, all this seems to be a rigorous analytical framework for testing the old 'Chicago' claim that no less than rational behaviour will ever survive in market settings in the long run.

In recent times, a good deal of work has been devoted to a reformulation of the evolutionary paradigm along the lines just described. Economically motivated

[*]I wish to thank Antonio Gay and Domenico Menicucci for several useful conversations, while retaining full responsibility.

evolutionary processes typically involve many agents interacting impersonally, so these dynamics are to be meant as the aggregation of a large number of individual behaviours driven by some form of adaptive learning. Unlike the biological literature, there is however no clear indication as to the appropriate equations of motion describing the relevant social dynamics. One of the main challenges for the theory is therefore finding 'microfoundations' for specific aggregate dynamics in terms of the decision and learning processes that are consistent with them once generally adopted by individual players. Work in this vein is still in its infancy. The small but growing set of papers devoted to the issue generally focuses attention on finding economically motivated analogues for one of the most popular 'biological' specifications: the so-called replicator dynamics. Whether economists should pay special attention to the replicator dynamics is an open point. The general orientation seems to regard it as an analytically convenient representative of the more general class of evolutionary processes known as aggregate monotonic (selection) dynamics (AMS) (see Samuelson and Zhang, 1992). AMS are an interesting theoretical option for economists as a model of 'competitive' social dynamics such that relatively more rewarding (i.e. more rational?) behaviours spread over at a rate that is proportional to their competitive advantage, at the expense of less rewarding ones.

Björnerstedt and Weibull are among those following this orientation. They consider a standard setting with several large players' populations in a continuous time framework, where one player is drawn at random from each population at each stage game. At the beginning of the story, each player has a 'default' strategy choice. What characterizes a specific evolutionary dynamics is how and when people are assumed to reconsider their actual choice ('type'), given the current distribution of choices ('types') across players. Players' behaviour, therefore, does not simply boil down to how they play; it also depends on their 'reaction patterns', i.e. on the frequency of revisions and on the criteria that rule them. These two factors are quantified by a set of population- and type-specific parameters: the average time rates at which strategy choices are revised and the (conditional) probabilities of adoption of feasible strategies (including the one actually chosen).

Revision rates are modelled as arrival rates of mutually independent Poisson processes, implying that the aggregate reaction pattern is strongly asynchronous, i.e. it is never the case that two players are reviewing at the same time. This is a powerful smoothing factor for the aggregate dynamics since it rules out the possibility of massive shifts to, and from, any strategy at any time. Both review rates and adoption probabilities depend (in a 'well behaved' way) on the (expected) performance of the current strategy and therefore on the current population state. More specifically, 'better' (that is, relatively more rewarding) strategies will be reconsidered less often than 'worse' ones; moreover, better strategies are more likely to be adopted once revision occurs. On the other hand, in order to learn the relative profitability of the various strategies players have to sample the behaviours of others, and clearly more frequent strategies will be more likely to be sampled. Thus, the (conditional) probability of adoption of a given strategy basically depends on two features: (a) how widespread, and (b) how good it is with regard to the other feasible ones. Dynamics are calibrated by choosing the relative weights to be assigned to (a) and (b). A (population's) strategy will spread if and only if the net flow toward that strategy is positive, i.e. if and only if, overall, adoptions exceed quits.

Insofar as likelihood of adoption of a strategy is positively related to how widely adopted it is, it can be said that the social dynamics are driven by imitation; Björnerstedt and Weibull show that (i) even naive imitation (i.e. copying the strategy of the first 'passer-by' no matter how good or bad it is) can be enough for reinforcing better strategies at the aggregate level provided that worse strategies are revised more often. Alternatively, (ii) even if average review rates are fixed and thus do not depend on performance, aggregate reinforcement of better strategies can be obtained provided that better strategies are imitated more frequently. In other words, the social dynamics will 'reward' better strategies at the expense of worse ones if a link, however weak, between strategy revision procedures and performance can be established. To obtain the replicator dynamics from this general framework one must simply postulate that review rates (in case (i)) or probabilities of adoption (in case (ii)) are affine functions of performance.[1] More general families like aggregate monotonic dynamics are also easily characterized.

In this comment, three major points related to the issues raised in the authors' chapter will be discussed:

(a) relationships with other results on the 'microfoundations' issue provided by the recent literature;
(b) stability properties of imitative dynamics and their implications in terms of individual players' rationality;
(c) what sort of further developments may be hoped from, and must be required for, this analytical framework.

2 TOWARD A 'MECHANICS' OF STRATEGIC INTERACTION?

In making a case for the weakness of the informational requirements needed to implement their imitative dynamics, Björnerstedt and Weibull argue, in Sections 3.2–3.3 of their chapter, that it is not necessary that players really know exactly their strategy's performance (remember that performance is defined in expected terms). What players need is 'some, perhaps noisy, empirical information about some available payoffs' so that, on average, they are able to 'move more towards those [strategies] with higher current expected payoffs than towards those with lower' (Section 3.3 of their chapter). Such knowledge should induce players using less profitable strategies to revise their choice more often than others and/or to move toward better choices; they are more likely to move the better alternative choices are. The authors do not provide an explicit formal argument to support this claim, but it is certainly reasonable insofar as the performances of alternative strategies are sufficiently far apart. If on the other hand they are close to each other, the claim seems much less innocuous and a formal proof would not sound superfluous: there may be an upper bound to the precision of players' perception of payoffs under limited information (see Sacco, 1994, for an example in a somewhat related context). This latter case is far from irrelevant: indeed, whenever the dynamics are converging to some ω-limit, the payoffs of non-vanishing strategies must be quite similar though unequal in general. But if the discriminatory ability of players is limited and payoff differentials do not accurately translate, albeit on average, into different review rates and/or probabilities of adoption, the payoff-monotonicity condition breaks down and the by-now fairly well-known stability properties of the imitative dynamics (see Section 3 below) could be altered to some extent.

Although interesting and quite useful, Björnerstedt and Weibull's results therefore meet our desiderata on microfoundations only in part: what is lacking is a clear theoretical description of the 'microstructure' of strategic interaction, i.e. what players really observe, how they process these data, how information is translated into behavioural routines, etc. A first, somewhat preliminary attempt at this is Blume (1993), but the bulk of the issue is still there to a large extent; it is far from excluded that at least part of the required mathematical techniques is still to be developed.

Despite these caveats, it may be instructive to compare Björnerstedt and Weibull's theoretical framework and results with those of the related literature, namely Börgers and Sarin (1993), Binmore and Samuelson (1994), and Binmore *et al.* (1993).[2]

Börgers and Sarin (1993) consider a classical learning process with reinforcement à la Bush and Mosteller (1955).[3] Unlike Björnerstedt and Weibull and most of the literature, they assume that, at each stage game, players can choose any feasible strategy with positive probability rather than committing to one. Payoffs are constrained (strictly) between zero and one; when one particular strategy is chosen, it is 'reinforced' in the player's mind with weight equal to the realized payoff. More precisely, the (future) probability of adoption of the chosen strategy is increased according to performance. Non-negativity of payoffs implies that the chosen strategy is always reinforced to some extent however little. On the other hand, being payoffs strictly less than one, no unused strategy ever becomes extinct no matter how rewarding the chosen strategy. The Börgers and Sarin approach is then atypical in at least two respects: the restriction on payoffs and the fact that the competition among strategies occurs within each player's mind, and not within the population of players.[4] Börgers and Sarin prove that both features are indeed necessary to generate the replicator dynamics in this specific learning context. More precisely, they start from a two-player discrete time model and show that (stochastic) learning with reinforcement is actually equivalent (in expectation) to the discrete time replicator dynamics, i.e., in *expected* terms, the probability of adoption of a given strategy will increase if and only if it yields a payoff that is larger than the average one. Moreover, Börgers and Sarin show that for an arbitrary but finite selection of times, the trajectories of the former are close to those of continuous time replicator dynamics in the continuous time limit. However, as is well known (see, e.g., Cabrales and Sobel, 1992; Dekel and Scotchmer, 1992), this does not imply any relationship between asymptotic behaviour for the two dynamics, that will in general be much different.

The equivalence result, however, cannot be carried over to a context of two multi-player populations where everybody has in mind the full set of competing strategies. The reason is very simple. The learning dynamics of each player has the 'replicator' structure; however, being non-linear, the replicator dynamics cannot be aggregated: the social dynamics of 'replicator' players will not have a 'replicator' structure. On the other hand, the non-negativity constraint on payoffs is also quite binding: allowing for negative payoffs means that some previously adoptable strategies may become extinct in case of 'failure', a possibility that is ruled out by the replicator dynamics. Sarin (1993) goes on to show that, within a large class of learning processes, the above-discussed reinforcement scheme is the only one leading, under the stated limitations, to the replicator dynamics.

The main advantage of the Börgers and Sarin result over the Björnerstedt and Weibull one concerns informational requirements. In the Börgers–Sarin framework, players need only know their own actions and payoffs; indeed, they ignore the strategic interaction of their choices with those of other players. Moreover, the relationship between observed data, information processing activities and actions is more explicitly modelled. On the other hand, the Börgers–Sarin framework is much more restrictive than Björnerstedt and Weibull's, the main shortcoming being its limited relevance: if the replicator structure is to be taken only as an instance of an individual learning scheme among others, it loses much of its interest.[5] Seen in this perspective, the implications of the Börgers–Sarin results are mainly negative: if one believes in the (analytical and/or practical) relevance of learning schemes with reinforcement at the individual level, the resulting social dynamics cannot be modelled as a replicator process.

Another alternative framework is that of Binmore *et al.* (1993) and Binmore and Samuelson (1994) who work with a quite general stochastic framework that allows for mutations and noisy selection. They consider a one-population, 2×2 game (with special reference to the case with two strict Nash equilibria) and random matching. As in the Börgers–Sarin approach, the starting point is a discrete-time setting. The learning mechanism followed by players has the following characteristics. Within each period, players are repeatedly drawn to play the game; in every period, everybody plays at least once with probability one. At the end of every period, players are called to revise their 'default' strategy choice with fixed (small) probability. If this is the case, players evaluate their average realized reward in the round of play just ended against a fixed aspiration level. If realized reward falls below aspiration, the current strategy is abandoned. The player's evaluation, however, is subject to noise: what she actually observes is realized reward plus an idiosynchratic random shock whose distribution is given. Once strategy change is decided, the player samples an individual at random and copies her strategy. Copying succeeds with fixed probability; therefore the player mistakenly chooses the other strategy with the complementary probability (in which case a 'mutation' is said to occur). The presence of the random shock altering the player's perception of rewards drives a wedge between fitness and payoffs: it is now possible that less rewarding strategies are not dropped because of a large 'favourable' shock and that, for the opposite reason, more rewarding strategies are. Therefore, better strategies sometimes 'die' whereas worse ones don't because of 'bad luck'. Binmore–Samuelson–Vaughan show that this framework yields the continuous time replicator dynamics (with mutations) if it is progressively specialized by taking suitable limits in the proper order. More specifically, the replicator dynamics is obtained through the following sequence: (i) time is made continuous by shrinking period length to zero; (ii) the number of players goes to infinity. At this point one obtains a replicator dynamics with mutations; by letting (iii) time go to infinity one gets the asymptotics of replicator dynamics perturbed by mutations. One could then obtain deterministic predictions by letting (iv) the mutation rate go to zero. The order of limits at points (iii) and (iv) depends on the authors' concern with what they call the ultra-long run dynamics, i.e. the stochastic dynamics whose asymptotics do not depend on a specific choice of initial conditions:[6] if the possibility of mutations is ruled out too early, the dynamic could get stuck before reaching the ultra-long run equilibrium. Taking (iv) before (iii), the deterministic replicator dynamics will emerge.

The Binmore–Samuelson–Vaughan characterization is still rather precise as to the micro 'mechanics' leading to the social dynamics. What seems especially valuable is the embedding of the deterministic evolutionary dynamics in a broader framework in which the role of stochastic factors is carefully specified and the implicit hierarchy of limiting assumptions underlying the large population, continuous time dynamics is clearly spelled out. However, as for Börgers–Sarin, and although for different reasons, the result is obtained in a very restrictive context: one population, two strategies, and it is not obvious that analogous results can be reproduced at the level of generality of Björnerstedt–Weibull. Also, the one-population assumption is especially restrictive in view of the fact that stability properties for this special case are much different than those for the general n-populations case. Further, there is at least one sense in which the Björnerstedt–Weibull framework is more general than the Binmore–Samuelson–Vaughan one: if deciding to change strategy, players in the latter framework learn through simple imitation, disregarding profitability of the available strategies. The Björnerstedt and Weibull scheme allows this possibility, but also much more.

To sum up, this short comparative survey seems to suggest that Björnerstedt and Weibull's results represent a quite valuable compromise between analytical accuracy and generality, given the present state of knowledge. Moreover, their characterization of the social dynamics in terms of imitation-driven individual learning processes (so that players are aware, to some degree, of the strategic interaction with others) seems especially appealing from the point of view of a positive theory of the birth and evolution of social norms.

3 'WHAT' RATIONALITY?

In the second part of the chapter, Björnerstedt and Weibull discuss stability properties of AMS (and more generally of monotonic) dynamics. It is an established result (see Ritzberger and Weibull, 1993) that, in multi-population AMS dynamics, the set of asymptotically stable states coincides with that of strict Nash equilibria. Several games do not possess any strict Nash equilibrium, however. As a consequence of this, Ritzberger and Weibull have introduced a set-wise extension of point asymptotic stability, namely asymptotically stable sets, showing that they coincide with sub-polyhedra of the strategy simplex that are closed with regard to the so-called better reply correspondence, and that moreover they always contain a strategically stable set in the sense of Kohlberg and Mertens.[7] This latter property may lead one to think of set-wise asymptotic stability as a generalization of point asymptotic stability that is consistent with the 'as if' approach to adaptive processes: despite players' bounded rationality, their interaction leads to the same states that would have been chosen by perfectly rational players (see, e.g., Lucas, 1986). However, this claim is not entirely correct: if the strategically stable set is a 'small' subset of the attractor, the dynamics could stay 'away' from it most of the time, thus leaving no room for 'as if' reasoning. Think for example of 'matching pennies' games for two-population dynamics. For these games, the strategically stable set is just the complete mixed strategy Nash equilibrium, whereas the asymptotically stable set coincides with the whole strategy simplex. The corresponding evolutionary dynamics always cycle around the strategically stable set, at a distance that depends on the choice of the initial condition; more specifically, the dynamics will stay close to the strategically stable set only if the initial condition is close. To be fair, however, one must observe that the time average of trajectories coincides with the mixed Nash equilibrium.

The example is a somewhat robust one for two-population dynamics, in that Jansen *et al.* (1990) have shown that for two-player bimatrix games the strategically stable set is always finite; therefore, the strategically stable set will always be a measure zero subset of any non-trivial asymptotically stable set and the dynamics will be away from it most of the time at least. Moreover, to our knowledge no example of an infinite strategically stable set in *n*-player games is available, so it is reasonable to conjecture that this property holds more generally, if not always. Moreover, upon reflection one sees that, for the case of non-singleton strategically stable sets, no particularly clear implications in terms of 'as if' rationality would obtain even if the dynamics kept bouncing around the set in some complex way.

If the evolutionary approach is to be meant as supporting some notion of individual rationality, it is then hardly the case that such notion has, in general, anything to do with traditional forms of game-theoretic rationality. It is perhaps more sensible to speak of rationality in dynamic terms, e.g. in terms of ability of understanding not only how rewarding strategies are at a given time, but also, and above all, what are the strategies with the biggest 'potential' in the long run. This means, for example, that best-reply players are not necessarily rational in an evolutionary sense, if, say, it is valuable for players of a given type to prevent asymptotic survival of certain other player types. If this motivation is important for players, they will be more interested in strategies that 'hurt' the player types they like least rather than in strategies that are good for them. In particular, it is relatively easy to construct examples where 'hurting' strategies are strictly dominated but are nevertheless selected by the evolutionary dynamics when such 'nasty' player types are present (see Sacco and Scarpa, 1994b; Menicucci and Sacco, 1994). Also, if changing strategy entails some cost, being able to learn where the wind blows not just now but tomorrow becomes important: late movers might discover that switching to better strategies has become too expensive once convergence towards equilibrium causes expected benefits to fall below costs, so they get trapped into inferior choices (see, e.g., Sacco and Scarpa, 1994a). On the other hand, some degree of inertia seems necessary to obtain a predictable social dynamics; if too many players tend to overreact to outplay others or simply understand the global structure of the selection process, the latter will break down and no theoretical prediction will be possible (cf. Morgenstern, 1972).

To sum up, much is still to be done in understanding what picture of individual rationality emerges from the evolutionary approach.

4   WHERE FROM HERE?

Of course, every interesting research project is open to countless potentially interesting developments. In spite of this, it is often the case that some of them play a critical role in the eventual success or failure of the project. In this final section we will briefly comment on some open points that, in our opinion, are (among others) likely to play that crucial role at a later stage.

4.1 Social Relationships

Granovetter (1978, 1985) observes that a satisfactory account of the social dimension of individual choices cannot dispense with an explicit modelling of the social network of relationships in which individuals are embedded. The current generation of evolutionary models postulates that interaction is impersonal, i.e. players have no real reason to be interested in the identity of any specific other player. Consequently, if learning through imitation, players will not be likely to copy any specific player. On the other hand, realistic social relationships are much more structured: if I am willing to imitate someone, it is more likely that I will copy a parent or relative or kin rather than the first man I meet in the street. Likewise, if I am trying to learn the relative profitability of strategies, I will presumably be able to collect detailed information about my relatives' performances and only partial information from casual passers-by. Once this sort of effect is brought into the picture, we are likely to observe localized patterns of behaviour, i.e. behaviour within social groups (as defined by the social 'topology') will be more uniform than behaviour across social groups.

4.2 Group Selection

In some settings it might be valuable for individuals to put some weight on the performance of a larger group in addition to own performance. Insofar as this brings about a large evolutionary advantage, group incentives should sooner or later play a role in individual motivations. Think for example[8] of a Prisoner's Dilemma setting where the marginal benefit of defecting relative to the cooperative payoff is negligible (e.g. one cent over a million dollars), whereas both the loss for a cooperative player meeting a defector and the Pareto loss when both defect rather than cooperate are substantial (e.g. from one million dollars to zero and from one million dollars to one, respectively). Is it reasonable to believe that a player will defect once she knows with reasonable certainty that the other will cooperate? A 'reasonable' social dynamic should perhaps select the cooperative strategy here: after all, we normally expect that other people are not going to stab us in the back for one dollar even if they are sure they can get away with it. The current generation of models does not allow for this sort of consideration, but future ones should.

4.3 Birth and Evolution of Norms

All societies develop some set of social norms that constrain individual choices to some extent. Actual evolutionary models can incorporate given sets of norms into the theoretical description (this simply amounts to suitably restricting choice sets or respecifying payoff functions: see, e.g., Basu, 1992) but are unable to explain with reasonable depth how norms are born and how they evolve, especially when competing sets of norms happen to interact due to migrations, geographical explorations etc. It is *a fortiori* an open point whether there exist clear relationships between social norms and collective welfare and, if so, between the latter and robustness against 'invasion' of competing norms.

Notes

1. In this latter case an additional normalization of players-specific parameters is also needed.
2. We are also aware of another relevant contribution by Schlag (1993), but unfortunately we cannot elaborate on it, because we did not have access to it at the time of writing.
3. See Holland *et al.* (1987) and Arthur (1993) for other applications of this learning paradigm.
4. A somewhat close approach is taken in Sacco (1994).
5. Moreover, Börgers and Sarin only consider the special case of two players/populations, rather than the general *n*-populations case.
6. Quite interestingly, Binmore–Samuelson–Vaughan point out that the ultra-long run dynamics is sensitive to 'strategically equivalent' transformations of payoffs in the sense of Harsanyi and Selten. Therefore, even if fitness 'agree' with payoffs in a strategical sense, i.e. if they are simply taken to be affine functions of payoffs, the ultra-long run equilibrium may depend on how payoffs are actually rescaled by the transformation.
7. Swinkels (1993) proves an analogous but more general result for the class of payoff-monotonic dynamics.
8. I owe this example to Antonio Gay.

References

Arthur, B. (1993) 'On Designing Economic Agents that Behave Like Human Agents', *Journal of Evolutionary Economics*, vol. 3, pp. 1–22.

Basu, K. (1992) 'Civil Institutions and Evolution', Institute for International Economic Studies Seminar Paper no. 523, Stockholm.

Binmore, K. and L. Samuelson (1994) 'Muddling Through: Noisy Equilibrium Selection', mimeo, Dept. of Economics, University of Wisconsin.

Binmore, K., L. Samuelson and R. Vaughan (1993) 'Musical Chairs: Modelling Noisy Evolution', mimeo, Dept. of Economics, University of Wisconsin.

Blume, L. (1993) 'The Statistical Mechanics of Strategic Interaction', *Games and Economic Behavior*, vol. 5, pp. 387–424.

Börgers, T. and R. Sarin (1993) 'Learning Through Reinforcement and Replicator Dynamics', mimeo, University College London.

Bush, R.R. and F. Mosteller (1955) *Stochastic Models for Learning* (New York: Wiley).

Cabrales, A. and J. Sobel (1992) 'On the Limit Points of Discrete Selection Dynamics', *Journal of Economic Theory*, vol. 57, pp. 407–19.

Dekel, E. and S. Scotchmer (1992) 'On the Evolution of Optimizing Behavior', *Journal of Economic Theory*, vol. 57, pp. 392–406.

Granovetter, M. (1978) 'Threshold Models of Collective Behavior', *American Journal of Sociology*, vol. 83, pp. 1420–43.

Granovetter, M. (1985) 'Economic Action and Social Structure: The Problem of Embeddedness', *American Journal of Sociology*, vol. 91, pp. 481–510.

Hofbauer, J. and K. Sigmund (1988) *The Theory of Evolution and Dynamical Systems* (London: Cambridge University Press).

Holland, J.H., K.J. Holyoak, R.E. Nisbett, and P.R. Thagard (1987) *Induction: Processes of Inference, Learning and Discovery* (Cambridge: MIT Press).

Jansen, M., D. Jurg and P. Borm (1990) 'On the Finiteness of Stable Sets', Report 9012, Dept. of Mathematics, Catholic University, Nijmegen.

Lucas, R.E. Jr. (1986) 'Adaptive Behavior and Economic Theory', *Journal of Business*, vol. 59, pp. S401–26.

Maynard Smith, J. (1982) *Evolution and the Theory of Games* (Cambridge: Cambridge University Press).

Menicucci, D. and P.L. Sacco (1994) 'Evolutionary Dynamics with λ-Players', mimeo, Dept. of Economics, University of Florence, in preparation.

Morgenstern, O. (1972) 'Descriptive, Predictive and Normative Theory', *Kyklos*, vol. 25, pp. 699–714.

Ritzberger, K. and J.W. Weibull (1993) 'Evolutionary Selection in Normal Form Games', mimeo, Stockholm University.

Sacco, P.L. (1994) 'Can People Learn Rational Expectations? An "Ecological" Approach', *Journal of Evolutionary Economics*, vol. 4, pp. 35–43.

Sacco, P.L. and C. Scarpa (1994a) 'Adoption of Flexible Technologies in an Evolutionary Environment', preprint.

Sacco, P.L. and C. Scarpa (1994b) 'The Evolutionary Importance of Being Aggressive: Delegation in an Oligopoly with Quantity-Setting', mimeo, Dept. of Economics, University of Bologna, in preparation.

Samuelson, L. and J. Zhang (1992) 'Evolutionary Stability in Asymmetric Games', *Journal of Economic Theory*, vol. 57, pp. 363–91.

Sarin, R. (1993) 'An Axiomatization of the Cross Learning Dynamic', mimeo, Dept. of Economics, University of California, San Diego.

Schlag, K. (1993) 'Why Imitate, and If So, How?', mimeo, Department of Economics, University of Bonn.

Swinkels, J. (1993) 'Adjustment Dynamics and Rational Play in Games', *Games and Economic Behavior*, vol. 5, pp. 455–84.

Part III

Rational Behaviour from an Experimental Approach

8 Rational Theory and Constructive Choice

Amos Tversky

STANFORD UNIVERSITY, USA

1 INTRODUCTION

From its very beginning, early in the eighteenth century, decision theory sought to reduce the tension between normative and descriptive considerations. Bernoulli's nonlinear utility function for wealth attempts to reconcile the principle of mathematical expectation with the psychological intuition of diminishing marginal value, and much of the recent theoretical work on decision under uncertainty attempts to reconcile rational choice with observed violations of expected utility theory. Although such attempts have enriched the theory of choice, the psychological analysis of preference and belief indicates that it is not possible in general to reconcile normative and descriptive accounts of individual choice. The reason for this conclusion – which may be regarded by some as pessimistic or even negative – is that decision-making is a constructive process. In contrast to the classical theory that assumes consistent preferences, it appears that people often do not have well-defined values, and that their choices are commonly constructed, not merely revealed, in the elicitation process. Furthermore, different constructions can give rise to systematically different choices, contrary to the basic principles that underlie classical decision theory.

The rational theory of choice is based on two sets of assumptions: *coherence* and *invariance*. The coherence assumptions include axioms such as intransitivity, stochastic dominance, and independence. These axioms are used, in conjunction with more technical assumptions (e.g., continuity or solvability), to ensure the existence of a utility function with the desired properties that represents the preference relation. Invariance encompasses two requirements: *description invariance* and *procedure invariance*. Description invariance demands that preferences among options should not depend on the manner in which they are represented or displayed. Two representations that the decision maker, on reflection, would view as equivalent descriptions of the same problem should lead to the same choice – even without the benefit of such reflection (Arrow, 1982; Tversky and Kahneman, 1986).

Procedure invariance demands that strategically equivalent methods of elicitation will give rise to the same preference order. For example, the standard theory assumes that an individual's preference between x and y, say, can be established either by offering that individual a direct choice between x and y, or by comparing their reservation prices. Furthermore, the theory assumes that the two procedures yield the same order. It is noteworthy that description invariance and procedure invariance are rarely stated explicitly, although they are an essential part of the rational theory of choice. In some cases, invariance is 'built into' the primitives of the model. For example, if gambles are represented as random variables, then any two realizations of the same random variables must be mapped into the same object. Similarly, if both choice and pricing are assumed to express preference, then the two procedures must give rise to the same ordering.

A third requirement that can be viewed as an invariance condition is the assumption of context independence, or the related principle of independence of other alternatives. This principle demands that the preference order between x and y should not depend on the availability of other alternatives. Context independence follows from the standard maximization model, which assumes that the decision-maker has a complete preference order, and that, given an offered set, the decision-maker selects the option that is highest in that order.

The assumptions of description invariance, procedure invariance, and context independence are routinely assumed in practically all applications of rational choice models. These assumptions are highly compelling from a normative standpoint because they capture elementary requirements of rationality. Unfortunately, they are not descriptively valid. Alternative descriptions of the same choice problems lead to systematically different preferences; strategically equivalent elicitation procedures give rise to different choices; and the preference between x and y often depends on the choice set in which they are embedded. (For recent reviews of the empirical evidence, see Payne, Bettman and Johnson, 1992; Camerer, 1994.) This chapter illustrates these phenomena and the psychological principles that underlie them, and then discusses the relation between normative and descriptive models of choice.

2   DESCRIPTION INVARIANCE AND FRAMING EFFECTS

The first example comes from a study of hypothetical choice between medical treatments (McNeil, Pauker, Sox and Tversky, 1982). Respondents were given statistical information about the outcomes of two treatments of lung cancer, taken from the medical literature. The same statistics were presented to some respondents in terms of mortality rates and to others in terms of survival rates. The respondents then indicated their preferred treatment. The information was presented as follows; the percentage of respondents who chose each option is given in brackets.

Problem 1 (survival frame, $N = 247$)

Surgery: of 100 people having surgery 90 live through the post-operative period, 68 are alive at the end of the first year and 34 are alive at the end of five years. [18%]

Radiation therapy: of 100 people having radiation therapy all live through the post-operative period, 77 are alive at the end of the first year and 22 are alive at the end of five years. [82%]

Problem 2 (mortality frame, $N = 236$)

Surgery: of 100 people having surgery 10 die during surgery or the post-operative period, 32 die by the end of the first year and 66 die by the end of five years. [44%]

Radiation therapy: of 100 people having radiation therapy none die during treatment, 23 die by the end of the first year and 78 die by the end of five years. [56%]

The difference in formulation produced a marked effect. The overall percentage of respondents who favoured radiation therapy rose from 18 per cent in the survival frame to 44 per cent in the mortality frame. The advantage of radiation therapy over surgery looms large when stated as a reduction of the risk of immediate death from 10 per cent to 0 per cent rather than as an increase from 90 per cent to 100 per cent in the rate of survival. This effect was no smaller for experienced physicians or for statistically sophisticated business students than for a group of clinic patients.

This problem illustrates what has come be known as a *framing effect*: equivalent formulations of the same decision problem yield systematically different preferences. Evidently, people choose between descriptions of options rather than between the options themselves. These preferences, which violate the assumption of description invariance, are difficult to justify on normative grounds. Moreover, in the absence of description invariance, the coherence assumptions are all called into question. In fact, any failure of description invariance can induce a violation of dominance. For another demonstration of the framing effect in the context of decision-making under risk, consider the following problems (taken from Tversky and Kahneman, 1986).

Problem 3 ($N = 126$): Assume yourself richer by $300 than you are today. You have to choose between
a sure gain of $100 [72%]
50% chance to gain $200 and 50% chance to gain nothing [28%]

Problem 4 ($N = 128$): Assume yourself richer by $500 than you are today. You have to choose between
a sure loss of $100 [36%]
50% chance to lose nothing and 50% chance to lose $200 [64%]

As implied by the value function of prospect theory (Kahneman and Tversky, 1979), the majority choice is risk-averse in problem 3 and risk-seeking in problem 4, although the two problems are essentially identical. In both cases one faces a choice between $400 for sure and an even chance of $500 or $300. Problem 4 is obtained from problem 3 by increasing the initial endowment by $200 and subtracting this amount from both options. This variation has a substantial effect on preferences. Additional questions showed that variations of $200 in initial wealth have little or no effect on choices. Thus, preferences are quite insensitive to small changes of wealth but highly sensitive to comparable changes in reference point. These observations indicate that the effective carriers of values are gains and losses, or changes in wealth, rather than states of wealth as implied by the rational model. Problems 3 and 4 also indicate that gains and losses are subject to framing effects. Thus, the same outcome can be described as a gain or a loss depending on the induced reference point (see Tversky and Kahneman, 1991).

Schelling (1981) has described a striking framing effect in a tax policy context. He points out that the tax table can be constructed by using as a default case either the childless family (as is in fact done) or, say, the modal two-child family. The tax difference between a childless family and a two-child family is naturally framed as an exemption (for the two-child family) in the first frame and as a tax premium (on the childless family) in the second frame. This seemingly innocuous difference has a large effect on judgements of the desired relation between income, family size, and tax. Schelling reported that his students rejected the idea of granting the rich a larger exemption than the poor in the first frame but favoured a larger tax premium on the childless rich than on the childless poor in the second frame. Because the exemption and the premium are alternative labels for the same tax differences in the two cases, the judgements violate invariance. Framing the consequences of a public policy in positive or in negative terms can greatly alter its appeal.

The analysis of framing effects sheds new light on the classical violations of expected utility theory, devised by Allais (1953). Consider the following choice problems (taken from Tversky and Kahneman, 1986).

Problem 5 ($N = 77$): Which of the following options do you prefer?
A. a sure gain of $30   [78%]
B. 80% chance to win $45 and 20% chance to win nothing   [22%]

Problem 6 ($N = 81$): Which of the following options do you prefer?
C. 25% chance to win $30 and 75% chance to win nothing   [42%]
D. 20% chance to win $45 and 80% chance to win nothing   [58%]

Note that problem 6 is obtained from problem 5 by reducing the probabilities of winning by a factor of four. In expected utility theory a preference for A over B in problem 5 implies a preference for C over D in problem 6. Contrary to this prediction, the majority preference switched from the lower prize ($30) to the higher one ($45) when the probabilities of winning were reduced by the same factor. We called this phenomenon the *certainty effect* because the reduction of the probability of winning from certainty to .25 has a greater effect than the corresponding reduction from .8 to .2.

The following problem illustrates a related phenomenon, called the *pseudocertainty effect*, that cannot be explained by eliminating the independence or the substitution axiom because it involves the violation of description invariance.

Problem 7 ($N = 90$): You draw blindly a ticket from a bag containing 25 tickets numbered 1 to 25, and 75 blank tickets. If you draw a blank ticket, you win nothing. If you draw a numbered ticket, you have the following choice.

E. a sure gain of $30, regardless of the number you draw.   [72%]
F. if your number is between 1 and 20 (i.e., 80%) you win $45; if your number is between 21 and 25 (i.e., 20%) you win nothing   [28%]

Your choice must be made before you draw the ticket.

It is easy to see that problem 7 is logically equivalent[1] to problem 6. In both cases, one faces a choice between a 25 per cent chance to win $30 or a 20 per cent chance to win $45. However, many more subjects made a risk-averse choice in problem 7 than in problem 5. We called this phenomenon the *pseudocertainty effect* because an outcome that is actually uncertain is weighted as if it were certain. Indeed, the preferences in problem 7 are in agreement with those in problem 5, as implied by expected utility theory. It is noteworthy that generalized utility models can account for the violation of substitution in the comparison of problems 5 and 6, but not for the violations of description invariance in problems 6 and 7.

3 PROCEDURE INVARIANCE AND PREFERENCE REVERSALS

In axiomatic theories of choice, the preference order appears as an abstract relation that is given an empirical interpretation in terms of specific methods of elicitation, such as choice or pricing. Procedure invariance demands that normatively equivalent elicitation procedures should give rise to the same preference order. Procedure invariance plays an essential role in measurement theories. For example, the ordering of objects with respect to mass can be established either by placing each object separately on a scale, or by placing both objects on the two sides of a pan balance; the two procedures yield the same ordering, within the limit of measurement errors. Analogously, the classical theory of preference assumes that each individual has a well-defined preference order (or a utility function) that can be elicited either by offering a choice between options, or by observing their reservation price. Procedure invariance provides a test for the existence of a measurable attribute. It would have been difficult to attribute mass to objects if the ordering of these objects with respect to mass were dependent on the measuring device. Similarly, it is difficult to defend the proposition that a person has a well-defined preference order (or equivalently a utility function) if different methods of elicitation give rise to different choices.

Despite its normative appeal, people commonly violate procedure invariance: different methods of elicitation give rise to systematically different choices. This phenomenon, called *preference reversal*, was first demonstrated more than three decades ago by Sarah Lichtenstein and Paul Slovic (1971, 1973). They presented subjects with two prospects having similar expected values. One prospect, the *H* bet, offers a high chance of winning a relatively small prize (e.g., 8 chances in 9 to win $4); whereas the other prospect, the *L* bet, offers a lower chance to win a larger prize (e.g., a 1 in 9 chance to win $40). When asked to choose between these prospects, most subjects choose the *H* bet. Subjects were also asked to state the lowest price at which they would be willing to sell each bet if they owned it. Surprisingly, most subjects put a higher price on the *L* bet. (In a recent study that used this particular pair of bets, for example, 71 per cent of the subjects chose the *H* bet, while 67 per cent priced *L* above *H*.) Numerous experiments replicated this phenomenon, using different bets, monetary incentives, and even a market setting. What is the cause of preference reversal? Why do people charge more for the low probability bet that is chosen less often?

Recent work suggests that the major cause of preference reversal is the compatibility between the response mode and the attributes of the prospects. Psychological evidence indicates that an attribute of an object is given more weight when it is compatible with the response mode than when it is not (Tversky, Sattath and Slovic, 1988). Because the cash equivalence of a bet is expressed in dollars, compatibility implies that the payoffs, which are expressed in the same units, will be weighted more heavily in pricing than in choice. Consequently, the *L* bet is overpriced relative to the *H* bet, which gives rise to the observed preference reversals. This account has been supported by several additional studies. For example, Slovic, Griffin and Tversky (1990) presented subjects with *H* and *L* bets involving non-monetary outcomes, such as a one-week pass for all movie theatres in town, or a dinner for two at a local restaurant. If preference reversals are due primarily to the compatibility of prices and payoffs, which are both expressed in dollars, their incidence should be substantially reduced by the use of non-monetary outcomes. Indeed, the prevalence of preference reversal was reduced by one-half.

Note that the compatibility hypothesis does not depend on the presence of risk. Indeed, it implies a similar discrepancy between choice and pricing for riskless options with a monetary component, such as delayed payments. Let (x, t) be a prospect that offers a payment of x dollars, t years from now. Consider a long-term prospect L, which pays $2,500 five years from now, and a short-term prospect S, which pays $1,600 in one-and-a-half years. Tversky, Slovic and Kahneman (1990) asked subjects to choose between L and S and to price both prospects by stating the smallest immediate cash payment for which they would be willing to exchange each delayed payment. In accord with the compatibility hypothesis, subjects chose the short-term option 74 per cent of the time but priced the long-term option above the short-term option 75 per cent of the time. These observations indicate that the preference reversal phenomenon is an example of a general pattern, not a peculiar characteristic of choice between bets.

Another psychological mechanism that gives rise to preference reversal involves the notion of relative prominence. In many choice problems, subjects agree that one dimension is more prominent than another. For example, people agree that safety is 'more important' than cost. Recent research has supported the hypothesis that the more prominent dimension looms larger in choice than in pricing or matching (Tversky, Sattath and Slovic, 1988). For example, consider two programmes designed to reduce the number of fatalities due to traffic accidents. Each programme is characterized by the expected reduction in the number of casualties and its estimated cost. Since human lives are regarded as more important than money, the prominence hypothesis predicts that this dimension will be given more weight in choice than in pricing. Indeed, when offered a choice between two such programmes, the great majority of respondents favoured the more expensive programme that saves more lives. However, when asked to determine the cost of one programme so as to make it as desirable as the other, nearly all the subjects assigned values that imply a preference for the less expensive programme that saves fewer lives. Thus, human lives were weighted more heavily in choice than pricing, in accord with the prominence hypothesis.

Further demonstrations of preference reversal, based on the prominence hypothesis, have been reported by Kahneman and Ritov (1995). They selected several pairs of public goods where one element of the pair yields only 'existence' value, and the other element involves health or safety. One group of subjects was given a direct choice between the two goods, and another group was asked to determine the largest amount they were willing to pay for each good. The results reveal substantial preference reversals of the type predicted by the prominence hypothesis. For example, Kahneman and Ritov presented subjects with the following pair of problems.

Problem: Skin cancer from sun exposure is common among farm workers.
Intervention: Support free medical checkups for threatened groups.

Problem: Several Australian mammal species are nearly wiped out by hunters.
Intervention: Contribute to a fund to provide safe breeding areas for these species.

When faced with a direct choice between these options, the great majority favoured an intervention concerning skin cancer rather than an intervention concerning Australian mammals. However, subjects were willing to pay more, on average, for safe breeding of Australian mammals than for free checkups for skin cancer. The juxtaposition of the two goods, side by side, led to different preference ordering from that obtained by considering each separately, contrary to procedure invariance. These data are inconsistent with the standard assumption that people have a well-defined preference order that can be elicited using strategically equivalent procedures.

4 CONTEXT DEPENDENCE AND TRADEOFF CONTRAST

The third cluster of empirical observations that are inconsistent with classical rationality involves the effect of the context, defined by the set of options under consideration. One of the basic assumptions of the rational theory of choice is that each alternative has a utility or subjective value that depends only on that alternative. Given a set of options, the decision-maker always selects the alternative with the highest value. If you prefer salmon to steak in a binary choice, for example, you should not select steak from any menu that includes salmon – unless the other entrées provide some information about the relative quality of the steak or the salmon. Thus, a non-preferred option cannot be made preferred by adding new alternatives to the choice set. Despite its simplicity and intuitive appeal, there is a growing body of evidence showing that people's preferences are influenced by the choice set, and that the attractiveness of an option can be increased by enlarging the offered set.

Contrast effects are ubiquitous in perception and judgement. For example, the same circle appears large when surrounded by small circles and small when surrounded by large ones (see Figure 8.1). Similarly, the same product may appear attractive on the background of less attractive products and unattractive on the background of more attractive products. I suggest that contrast effects apply not only to a single attribute, such as size or attractiveness, but also to the tradeoff between attributes. Consider, for example, products that vary on two attributes; suppose x is of higher quality but y has a better price. The decision between x and y, then, depends on whether the quality difference outweighs the price difference, or equivalently on the price/quality tradeoff. I propose that the tendency to prefer x over y will be enhanced if the decision-maker encounters other choices in which a comparable improvement in quality is associated with a larger difference in price. This is the *tradeoff contrast hypothesis*. As illustrated in Figure 8.2, it applies to the

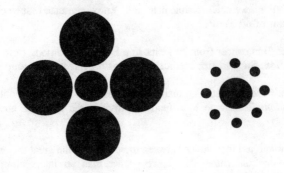

Figure 8.1   The right circle appears larger than the left due to contrast

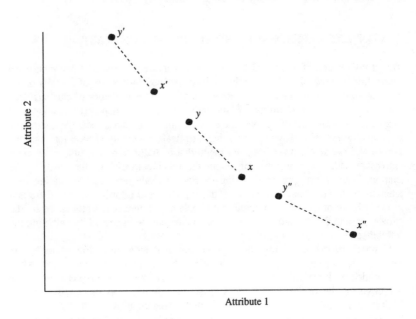

Figure 8.2   A test of background tradeoff

local context defined by the offered set, as well as to the background context, defined by options encountered in the past.

Perhaps the simplest demonstration of the tradeoff contrast hypothesis involves manipulation of the background context; see Simonson and Tversky (1992). In this experiment, half the subjects were given a choice between options x' and y', whereas

Table 8.1 Background contrast

Category: Tyres

Warranty	Price	Background set B' (n = 111)	Background set B'' (n = 109)
x': 55,000 miles	$85	12%	
y': 75,000 miles	$91	88%	
x'': 30,000 miles	$25		84%
y'': 35,000 miles	$49		16%

Warranty	Price	Target set	
x: 40,000 miles	$60	57%	33%
y: 50,000 miles	$75	43%	67%

Category: Gifts

Cash	Coupons	Background set B' (n = 51)	Background set B'' (n = 49)
x': $52	3	92%	
y': $22	5	8%	
x'': $77	4		40%
y'': $67	6		60%

Cash	Coupons	Target set	
x: $47	5	47%	77%
y: $37	6	53%	23%

the second half chose between x'' and y'' (see Figure 8.2). Following the initial choice, all subjects were given a choice between x and y. The tradeoff contrast hypothesis implies that the tendency to prefer x over y will be stronger among subjects who first chose between x' and y' than among those who first chose between x'' and y''. Table 8.1 presents the results for two categories: tyres that vary in warranty and price, and gifts consisting of a combination of cash and coupons. Each coupon could be redeemed for a regular book or compact disk at local stores. Subjects were informed that some of them, selected randomly, would actually receive the gift that he or she had selected.

Table 8.1 shows that the background influenced subsequent choice in the predicted direction. The results for tyres indicate that subjects exposed to Background B', in which a small difference in price ($91 versus $85) was associated with a large difference in warranty (75,000 versus 55,000 miles), were more likely to select from the target set the less expensive tyre than those exposed to Background B'', in which a relatively large difference in price ($49 versus $25) was associated with a small difference in warranty ($35,000 versus 30,000 miles). The same pattern was observed for gifts, as seen in the lower part of Table 8.1. Here the rate of exchange was $15 per coupon in Background B', $5 per coupon in Background B'', and $10 per coupon in the target set. The data again show that subjects exposed to the background in which coupons were fairly expensive were significantly more likely to select from the target set the gift with more coupons than subjects exposed to the background in which coupons were relatively inexpensive.

It could be argued that the observed choices can be justified in terms of the information provided by the context. I wish to make two points in response. First, regardless of whether the observed pattern of preferences can or cannot be rationalized, the data are inconsistent with the standard maximization model. If people commonly rely on the set of alternatives under consideration in order to assess the value of an option, then the standard theory of the consumer should be thoroughly revised to accommodate decisions based on such inferences. Second, an account based on rational inference can explain some examples (e.g., tyres but not others (e.g., gifts). A consumer who is uncertain about the price of a warranty may use the information provided by the background to evaluate whether paying $15 for 10,000 miles of warranty is a good deal or not. The background contrast effect observed in this problem, therefore, can be interpreted as rational inference based on the information provided by the context. This account, however, cannot explain the background contrast effect in the choice between gifts. Suppose you are just willing to trade $10 in cash for one book coupon. Why should you change your mind after observing gifts in which the corresponding tradeoff is $5 or $15? Note that the effect of the background was no stronger for tyres than for books (see Table 8.1). It appears that people's choices exhibit tradeoff contrast whether or not it is normatively justified.

Another implication of the tradeoff contrast hypothesis is that the 'market share' of x can be increased by adding to $\{x, y\}$ a third alternative z that is clearly inferior to x but not to y. Violations of utility maximization based on this pattern were first demonstrated by Huber, Payne and Puto (1982). The following example is taken from Simonson and Tversky (1992). One group ($N = 106$) was offered a choice between $6 and an elegant Cross pen. The pen was selected by 36 per cent of the subjects and the remaining 64 per cent chose the cash. A second group ($N = 115$) was given a choice among three options: $6 in cash, the same Cross pen, and a second less attractive pen. The second pen, I suggest, is dominated by the first pen but not by the cash. Indeed, only 2 per cent of the subjects chose the less attractive pen, but its presence increased the percentage of subjects who chose the Cross pen from 36 per cent to 46 per cent.

Similar effects have been observed in the marketplace. For example, Williams-Sonoma, a mail-order and retail business located in San Francisco, used to offer one bread-baking appliance priced at $275. Later they added a second bread-baking appliance, which was similar to the first but was somewhat larger. The price of this item was $429, more than 50 per cent higher than the original appliance. Not surprisingly, perhaps, Williams-Sonoma did not sell many units of the new item. However, the sales of the less expensive appliance almost doubled, as implied by tradeoff contrast. To the best of my knowledge, Williams-Sonoma did not anticipate this effect. In other situations, salespeople intentionally exploit context effects. A common tactic used to convince consumers to purchase a given product is to present another product and argue that the former is a bargain in comparison with the latter.

The violations of context dependence demonstrated above indicate that people do not maximize a precomputed preference order. Rather, they use the offered set to construct their choices. As a consequence, variations in the offered set produce decisions that are inconsistent with simple utility maximization. It is noteworthy that, unlike some normative models that require enormous memory and difficult computations, the principle of value maximization – as employed in the classical theory of the consumer – is extremely simple: it only requires an ordering of options with respect to preference. It is hard to conceive of a simpler model; any descriptive model of these data is bound to be considerably more complicated (Tversky and Simonson, 1993). The systematic failure of the standard model, I suggest, is not due to its complexity, but rather to the fact that people often do not have a global preference order and, as a result, they use the context to identify what appears to be the 'best buy'.

The analysis of context effects, in perception as well as in choice, provides numerous examples in which people err by complicating rather by simplifying the task; they often perform unnecessary computations and attend to irrelevant aspects of the situation under study. For example, in order to judge which of two circles is bigger (see Figure 8.1), it seems simplest to evaluate the critical figures and ignore the 'irrelevant' circles in the background. Similarly, it appears that the easiest way to decide which of two options is preferable is to compare them directly and ignore the other options. The fact that people do not behave in this manner indicates that many departures from classical models of rational choice cannot be easily explained merely as an attempt to reduce computational complexity.

5 DISCUSSION

The studies reviewed in the preceding sections indicate that human behaviour is often inconsistent with the basic tenets of the standard rational model. The evidence suggests that people often do not have a well-articulated preference order and that their choices are constructed, not merely revealed, in the elicitation process. Moreover, these constructions depend on the framing of the problem, the method of elicitation, and the context of the choice. Because the assumptions of description invariance and procedure invariance are normatively unassailable but descriptively inadequate, it is not possible to reconcile normative and descriptive accounts of individual choice (Tversky and Kahneman, 1986).

The rational theory of choice appears to provide a much better account of people's normative intuition than of their actual behaviour. Indeed, when faced with violations of dominance, transitivity, or description invariance, people often modify their behaviour in accord with the rational model. This observation indicates that people's choices are often in conflict with their own normative intuitions. Both normative and descriptive accounts, I suggest, are essentially empirical, although they refer to different data. The descriptive analysis of choice is concerned with human intuitions about what constitutes reasonable behaviour. Description invariance, transitivity, and stochastic dominance are generally endorsed by people as criteria for rational choice, but this endorsement does not ensure that people's choices will generally satisfy these criteria.

An analogy with ethics may be instructive. A normative ethical account is concerned with the principles that underlie moral judgements. A descriptive ethical account is concerned with human conduct. Both enterprises are essentially empirical, but the first refers to people's moral intuitions whereas the second refers to people's actual behaviour. The two analyses, of course, are interrelated, but they do not coincide. People generally agree that one should pay income tax or contribute to worthy causes, even if they do not always do so. Similarly, people may accept the normative force of description invariance, even though it is often violated in their own choices. Although the separation between normative and descriptive analyses has been widely accepted in ethics, it is somewhat controversial in decision theory. I suspect that the reason for this double standard has to do with the fact that the discrepancy between normative and descriptive theories in ethics stems primarily from motivational considerations, whereas the analogous discrepancy in choice stems primarily from cognitive limitations. It is apparently easier to accept violations of norms that stem from self-interest than violations of norms that result from fallible reasoning.

It is sometimes argued that non-optimal choices are likely to disappear if the decision-makers are offered sufficient incentives and opportunities to learn from experience. The existing evidence, however, does not support this claim (see Camerer, 1994 for a review). Although monetary incentives improve performance in certain situations, the reported violations of the rational theory have been observed even in the presence of contingent payoffs. Regarding learning, the data show that while performance can be greatly improved by repeated experience with effective feedback, such learning does not always generalize to other situations. It is noteworthy that experience is often not the most effective method for improving performance. For example, there is evidence that the incidence of preference reversal is reduced – but not eliminated – when subjects repeatedly evaluate and choose between risky prospects. However, when subjects are made aware that their choices and their evaluations are inconsistent, they generally revise their preferences, even without the benefit of outcome feedback. Thus, it appears that incentives and learning can improve performance, but they do not ensure invariance or coherence.

What are the implications of the present discussion to the relations between normative and descriptive analyses of choice? I have proposed that both enterprises are essentially empirical, that they are both parts of a comprehensive treatment of choice, and that they cannot be readily reconciled although they are closely interrelated. This position by no means precludes the use of normative models to explain observed behaviour. I have only argued that descriptive applications of normative models should be viewed as testable hypotheses that are likely to work in some contexts and fail in others. The existing data show that the assumptions of coherence and invariance cannot be taken for granted. The fact that these assumptions are normatively compelling does not mean that they are automatically satisfied. I have suggested (Kahneman and Tversky, 1992) that the reluctance to depart from the rational model, despite considerable contradictory evidence, is due to the belief that non-optimal behaviour cannot survive in a competitive environment, and that such behaviour is necessarily chaotic and intractable. Both arguments are questionable. First, it appears that people can spend a lifetime in a competitive environment without acquiring a general ability to avoid violations of invariance or coherence. Second, and perhaps more important, human choices are orderly, although not always rational in the traditional sense of the word.

Note

1. This version does not involve the reduction of compound lotteries.

References

Allais, A.M. (1953) 'Le comportement de l'homme rationel devant le risque, critique des postulates et axiomes de l'école americaine', *Econometrica*, vol. 1, pp. 503–46.

Arrow, K.J. (1982) 'Risk Perception in Psychology and Economics', *Economic Inquiry*, vol. 20, pp. 1–9.

Camerer, C. (1994) 'Individual Decision Making', in J. Kagel, and A. Roth, (eds), *Handbook of Experimental Economics* (Princeton: Princeton University Press).

Huber, J., J.W. Payne, and C. Puto, (1982) 'Adding Asymmetrically Dominated Alternatives: Violations of Regularity and the Similarity Hypothesis', *Journal of Consumer Research*, vol. 9, pp. 90–8.

Kahneman, D. and I. Ritov (1995) 'Determinants of Stated Willingness to Pay for Public Goods: A Study in the Headline Method', *Journal of Risk and Uncertainty*, vol. 9, pp. 5–31.

Kahneman, D. and A. Tversky (1979) 'Prospect Theory: An Analysis of Decision Under Risk', *Econometrica*, vol. 4, pp. 263–91.

Kahneman, D. and A. Tversky (1992) 'Advances in Prospect Theory: Cumulative Representation of Uncertainty', *Journal of Risk and Uncertainty*, vol. 5, pp. 297–323.

Lichtenstein, S. and P. Slovic (1971) 'Reversals of Preference between Bids and Choices in Gambling Decisions', *Journal of Experimental Psychology*, vol, 89, pp. 46–55.

Lichtenstein, S. and P. Slovic (1973) 'Response-Induced Reversals of Preference in Gambling: An Extended Replication in Las Vegas', *Journal of Experimental Psychology*, vol. 101, pp. 16–20.

McNeil, B.J., A.S. Pauker, H. Sox, Jr. and A. Tversky (1982) 'On the Elicitation of Preferences for Alternative Therapies', *New England Journal of Medicine*, vol. 306, pp. 1259–62.

Payne, J.W., J.R. Bettman, and E.J. Johnson (1992) 'Behavioral Decision Research: A Constructive Processing Perspective', *Annual Review of Psychology*, vol. 43, pp. 87–131.

Schelling, T.C. (1981) 'Economic Reasoning and the Ethics of Policy', *Public Interest*, vol. 63, pp. 37–61.

Simonson, I. and A. Tversky (1992) 'Choice in Context: Tradeoff Contrast and Extremeness Aversion', *Journal of Marketing Research*, vol. 14, pp. 281–95.

Slovic, P., D. Griffin and A. Tversky (1990) 'Compatibility Effects in Judgment and Choice', in R.M. Hogarth (ed.), *Insights in Decision Making: Theory and Applications* (Chicago: University of Chicago Press).

Tversky, A. and D. Kahneman (1986) 'Rational Choice and the Framing of Decisions', *Journal of Business*, vol. 59, no. 4, part 2, pp. 251–78.

Tversky, A. and D. Kahneman (1991) 'Loss Aversion in Riskless Choice: A Reference Dependent Model', *Quarterly Journal of Economics*, vol. 107, pp. 1039–61.

Tversky, A., S. Sattath and P. Slovic (1988) 'Contingent Weighting in Judgement and Choice', *Psychological Review*, vol. 95, pp. 371–84.

Tversky, A. and I. Simonson (1993) 'Context-Dependent Preferences', *Management Science*, vol. 39, pp. 1179–89.

Tversky, A., P., Slovic and D. Kahneman (1990) 'The Causes of Preference Reversal', *American Economic Review*, vol. 80, pp. 204–17.

Comment

Alvin E. Roth

UNIVERSITY OF PITTSBURGH

1 INTRODUCTION

Professor Tversky presents a quick overview of an ever-growing body of experimental evidence, to which he has been one of the most influential contributors. This evidence demonstrates that human behaviour deviates in systematic ways from the idealized behaviour attributed to expected utility maximizers in particular, and to 'rational economic man' in general. One of the most striking things about this substantial body of evidence is that, starting at least as early as the work of Allais (1953) and May (1954), it has been collected over the same period of years in which expected utility theory has come to be the dominant model of individual behaviour in the economics literature. This adds force to the question Tversky raises in his concluding remarks: what accounts for economists' 'reluctance to depart from the rational model, despite considerable contradictory evidence'?

I shall attempt to outline a two-track answer to this question. First, I shall argue that there are quite defensible reasons for a reluctance to abandon theories of rationality in favour of psychological theories. In particular, I think most economists view the rational model as a useful approximation, rather than as a precise description of human behaviour. Experimental demonstrations that people deviate from the model do not strike at the heart of the belief that the approximation is a useful one, since all approximations are false at some level of detail. In view of this, some kinds of evidence, and alternative models, are likely to be more successful than others in attacking the central role of rationality assumptions in the economic literature.

Second, I shall note that, in fact, there is a growing attempt by economists to move away from an overdependence on idealized models of hyper-rationality. My own paper in this volume (Chapter 11) deals with aspects of this, as do those presented here by Binmore and Samuelson (Chapter 5) and Björnerstedt and Weibull (Chapter 7).

2 RATIONAL MODELS AS USEFUL APPROXIMATIONS

Tversky identifies the essence of the rationality model to be the assumption that an individual can be modelled as having preferences over outcomes. To appreciate the scope of what is being criticized, it will be helpful to consider several increasingly general examples of this kind of model.

The first of these might be called *risk neutral economic man*. This individual chooses among risky outcomes strictly according to their expected value. He is different from real people in many ways: he never buys insurance, but would be willing to pay any finite amount to participate in Bernoulli's (1738) St Petersburg Paradox (if only he could be convinced that the resources exist to pay off any possible winnings). This model remains a useful, and much used, approximation, although economists mostly agree that it is not a precisely true description of all (or even most) individuals in all, or even most situations.

The more general, conventional model of rational economic man, is that of *expected utility maximizing man*. Unlike his risk neutral kin, he buys insurance. But, unlike real people, he ignores sunk costs, he always evaluates probabilities in an actuarial way, and is in general the kind of solid citizen admired by economic theorists. This model has by and large replaced that of risk neutral economic man as economists' 'canonical' model of individual choice behaviour. The reason is that economists became convinced that the phenomena that *could not* be explained by the approximation that individuals maximize expected value were of central importance, and justified a model with unobservable personal parameters of risk aversion. (The phenomena that cannot be captured by the risk neutral model include whole industries, like insurance, and large markets, such as the futures markets for commodities and currencies.) There is every reason to doubt that expected utility theory would have made such inroads into economics only on the strength of anomalies (from the expected value point of view) like the St Petersburg Paradox (for which Bernoulli in fact proposed a kind of expected utility theory as a resolution).

We should also include in this brief catalogue of rationality models a representative example of *almost rational economic man*, who deviates systematically from expected utility maximization in some ways, but who still has preferences. For example, Kahneman and Tversky's (1979) 'Prospect Theory' models an individual who may not always ignore sunk costs, e.g. because he is sensitive to framing which influences his reference point, and who does not handle probabilities like an actuary, but tends to overestimate small probabilities (but sometimes underestimates them, due to 'editing'). Nevertheless, once his reference point has been fixed, and his probability curve pinned down, he has preferences. So although he might be comfortable making non-utility-maximizing choices such as those seen in the Allais Paradox, he would eschew preference reversals.

In contrast to these models of rational choice, Tversky proposes that we direct our attention to models of what we might call *psychological man*. Psychological man does not have preferences, at least not in the sense that economists customarily think of them. Rather he has a collection of mental processes. And different descriptions of options, different frames and contexts, and different choice procedures elicit different processes (so he may sometimes exhibit preference reversals because choosing and pricing elicit different mental procedures.) Furthermore, it may be profitable to understand how his different mental processes are elicited, as in Tversky's anecdote about the bread-baking appliances in the Williams-Sonoma catalogue.

To understand why economists have not abandoned rationality models for psychological models of this sort, it may be helpful to consider for a moment the class of models of individual choice that seem to be suggested by recent research in brain science and clinical pharmacology. *Neurobiological man* does not (even) have a fixed collection of mental processes, in the sense of psychological man. Instead, he has biological and chemical processes which influence his behaviour. Different blood chemistry leads to different mental processes; e.g. depending on the level of lithium (or Valium or Prozac) in his blood, he makes different decisions (on both routine matters and matters of great consequence – even life and death). An understanding of how chemistry interacts with mental processes has proved to be very useful, for instance in treating depression.

One can then pose the neurobiologist's question: what accounts for the (psychologist's) reluctance to abandon the (psychological) model, despite considerable contrary evidence? The psychologist's answer (as imagined by this economist) might go something like this: 'No one really supposes that an individual's mental processes are fixed and never change. But this is a useful approximation. It breaks down for people who have lithium deficiency, and who (therefore) exhibit abrupt cycles of manic and depressive behaviour. But it helps us explain a lot of the phenomena which concern us, without requiring blood tests of our subjects. And while we are fully persuaded that real people have blood chemistry and brain processes, the compelling evidence that the neurobiologists have assembled on this point does not address the question of how often decisions are affected by normal variations in blood chemistry, and therefore does not address the usefulness of our approximation that people call on fixed sets of mental processes in ways that can be predicted without reference to blood chemistry. (We note that even analysis at the level of blood chemistry is only an approximation to the underlying quantum mechanical processes of the brain.) Finally, the blood chemistry model does not seem to bring a lot of explanatory or predictive power to bear on the questions we try to study, like why people exhibit preference reversals.'

My point, of course, is that with the natural substitution of terms, an economist's answer to this question could look a lot like the psychologist's. That being said, it should be obvious that evidence about where approximations break down is enormously useful, even when it is not the sort of evidence that causes the approximations to be abandoned. To know that utility maximization may be a weak guide to choices among alternatives with 'similar' expected values, or to choices involving probabilities near zero or one, can only enhance the actual (as opposed to the apparent) usefulness of the approximation.

Of course, as more evidence of different kinds accumulates, and as alternative models are developed, the situation may change. It therefore seems appropriate to end this discussion with some remarks on the growing role of non-rational models in economics.

3   THE POTENTIAL FOR NON-RATIONAL MODELS IN ECONOMICS

There has been increased exploration of a variety of 'almost rational' models of choice (of which prospect theory is an early example), which generalize expected utility theory but are 'plug compatible' with it, in the sense that they are meant to replace it but do the same job, and fit into strategic and market theories in the same way. Experimental comparisons of such theories with each other and with utility theory are reviewed by Camerer (1995). It remains an open question whether any of these theories organizes all of the data in a way that is clearly superior to utility theory, when the costs of adding additional unobserved personal parameters are counted in. But these theories are not non-rational in the way that Tversky proposes in his chapter here.

The same criticism cannot be levelled at the adaptive models of behaviour which economists increasingly explore. Whether motivated by simple models of learning, or by biological processes involving natural selection (as in the work of Maynard Smith or Holland), these models treat individuals as entirely non-rational automata who make no conscious choices at all, but whose behaviour becomes adapted to their experience. It seems safe to say that most economists also apply these models to human behaviour only as approximations. What makes them potential competitors of utility theory is that in some environments it appears that they may lead to the same kind of equilibria as are predicted by standard (rational) game theory. So, to the extent that economists' reluctance to dispense with rational models of individual choice has to do with the fact that their primary interest is in strategic and market phenomena, and that the rational model helps produce useful predictions about such phenomena, these adaptive models indicate that at least some of these predictions may not depend in a critical way upon rationality assumptions. But these models too are quite different from the models of mental processes which Tversky suggests.

What then are the prospects that models of the kind Tversky proposes, which incorporate approximations of particular mental processes, will gain a substantial foothold among economists? It seems to me that proponents of such models have at least two worthwhile avenues to pursue.

The first of these would be to conduct experiments which show not merely that individuals are sometimes systematically non-rational, but which would start to give us some feeling for how important this phenomenon might be. For example, I do not think that any of the preference reversal experiments have yet given information that would allow us to graph the frequency of preference reversals as a function of the difference in expected value (in, say, percentage terms) between the two gambles with which subjects are presented. While this information might not dramatically affect how investigators with very different theoretical dispositions evaluated the data, it would help address the issue of whether we are seeing a phenomenon likely to play an important role in natural environments. Undoubtedly there are more informative experiments to be done than this one; my point is only that investigators who are aiming to assess the size of the disparity between utility theory and observed behaviour, rather than merely to show that there is one, might better address the usefulness of the utility maximization approximation.

Second, there is no substitute for careful studies of natural environments. Just as expected utility maximization would not have replaced expected value maximization as economists' typical approximation if it were not for the importance of explaining insurance and related phenomena, economists are likely to find most persuasive those attacks on rational models which produce examples of how psychological phenomena are reflected and exploited in, and shape aspects of, important economic activities. It seems likely to me that advertising, and marketing in general, are areas of economic activity in which this approach will prove fruitful. It is hard to imagine that the volume of advertisements with which we (Americans, at least) are bombarded serve only information purposes. Rather, advertisements and other marketing tools may shape preferences in ways that cannot be accounted for by rational models of individual choice.

Consequently, I feel optimistic that economics has much to gain from the diversity of approaches that are beginning to flourish.

References

Allais, M. (1953) 'Le comportement de l'homme rationnel devant le risque: critique des postulats et axiomes de l'école américaine', *Econometrica*, vol. 21, pp. 503–46.

Bernoulli, D. (1738) 'Specimen Theoriae Novae de Mensura Sortis', *Commentarii Academiae Scientiarum Imperialis Petropolitanae*, vol. 5, pp. 175–92. English translation in *Econometrica*, vol. 22, 1954, pp. 23–36.

Camerer, C. (1995) 'Individual Decision Making', in J. Kagel and A.E. Roth (eds), *Handbook of Experimental Economics* (New Haven: Princeton University Press) pp. 587–703.

Kahneman, D. and Tversky, A. (1979), 'Prospect Theory: An Analysis of Decision under Risk', *Econometrica*, vol. 47, pp. 263–91.

May, K.O. (1954) 'Intransitivity, Utility, and the Aggregation of Preference Patterns', *Econometrica*, vol. 22, pp. 1–13.

9 New Challenges to the Rationality Assumption*

Daniel Kahneman

PRINCETON UNIVERSITY, USA

1 INTRODUCTION

The assumption that agents are rational is central to much theory in the social sciences. Its role is particularly obvious in economic analysis, where it supports the useful corollary that no significant opportunity will remain unexploited. In the domain of social policy, the rationality assumption supports the position that it is unnecessary to protect people against the consequences of their choices. The status of this assumption is therefore a matter of considerable interest. This chapter will argue for an enriched definition of rationality that considers the actual outcomes of decisions, and will present evidence that challenges the rationality assumption in new ways.

The criteria for using the terms 'rational' or 'irrational' in non-technical discourse are *substantive*: one asks whether beliefs are grossly out of kilter with available evidence, and whether decisions serve or damage the agent's interests. In sharp contrast, technical discussions of rationality generally adopt a *logical* conception, in which an individual's beliefs and preferences are said to be rational if they obey a set of formal rules such as complementarity of probabilities, the sure-thing principle or independence of irrelevant alternatives. In the laissez-faire spirit of modern economics and decision theory, the content of beliefs and of preferences is not a criterion of rationality – only internal coherence matters (Sen, 1993). The methodology of the debate reflects this concern for consistency: in the classic paradoxes of Allais and Ellsberg, for example, two intuitively compelling preferences are shown to be jointly incompatible with the axioms of expected utility theory, though each preference is unobjectionable on its own. Irrational preferences are diagnosed without having to observe anything that is not a preference.

Some authors have been dissatisfied with the exclusive focus on consistency as a criterion of rationality. Thus, Sen (1990, p. 210) has written:

* Also published in *Journal of Institutional and Theoretical Economics*, March 1994 (as presented at the 11th International Seminar on the New Institutional Economics Wallerfangen/Saar, Germany, June 1993). A different version was presented at a Political and Economic Analysis Workshop in Honour of P. Zusman, in Rehovot, Israel, June 1993. I am greatly indebted to Amos Tversky for many discussions of the issue of rationality over the years, and for insightful comments on drafts of this paper. He should not be assumed to agree with all I say. Alan Schwartz provided helpful editorial assistance.

Rationality may be seen as demanding something other than just consistency of choices from different subsets. It must, at least, demand cogent relations between aims and objectives actually entertained by the person and the choices that the person makes. This problem is not eliminated by the terminological procedure of describing the cardinal representation of choices as the 'utility' of the person, since this does not give any independent evidence on what the person is aiming to do or trying to achieve.

This chapter will ask whether there exists a cogent relation between a person's choices and the hedonic consequences of these choices.

In spite of occasional attempts to broaden the scope of the rationality debate in decision theory, the patterns of preference discovered by Allais and Ellsberg have been at the centre of this debate for several decades. It is often implied that if these paradoxes can be resolved, then economic analysis can safely continue to assume that agents are rational. The focus on paradoxes has indirectly strengthened the rationality dogma: if subtle inconsistencies are the worst indictment of human rationality, there is indeed little to worry about. Furthermore, the preferences that Allais and Ellsberg described do not appear foolish or unreasonable, and lay people as well as many theorists believe they can be defended (Slovic and Tversky, 1974). Indeed, the ambiguous normative status of the Allais and Ellsberg patterns has inspired many attempts to reconcile observed preferences with rationality by adopting a more permissive definition of rational choice (Tversky and Kahneman, 1986).

More recent challenges to the rationality assumption do not lend themselves to such attempts at reconciliation. Numerous experiments illustrate beliefs and preferences that violate a fundamental requirement variously labelled extensionality (Arrow, 1982), consequentialism (Hammond, 1985) or invariance (Tversky and Kahneman, 1986). The same choice problem may evoke different preferences, depending on inconsequential variations in the formulation of options (Tversky and Kahneman, 1986) or in the procedure used to elicit choices (Tversky, Slovic and Kahneman, 1990). The main method of this research still involves the documentation of pairs of preferences, each acceptable in its own, which jointly violate an axiom of invariance. These inconsistencies are more difficult to rationalize than the classic paradoxes, because invariance is a more compelling axiom of rational choice than cancellation or independence (Tversky and Kahneman, 1986). Some examples of this research will be presented below.

The present treatment attempts to supplement the logical analysis of preferences by introducing substantive criteria of rationality. Unlike the logical analysis, a substantive criterion is external to the system of preferences. It requires some way of assessing outcomes as they occur, not only as they are conceived at the time of decision. The substantive question on which we focus here is whether choices maximize the (expected) utility of their consequences, as these consequences will actually be experienced. Accurate prediction of future tastes and accurate evaluation of past experiences emerge as critical elements of an individual's ability to maximize the experienced quality of his outcomes. Demonstrated deficiencies in the ability to predict future experiences and to learn from the past emerge as new challenges to the assumption of rationality. More provocatively, the observed deficiencies suggest the outline of a case in favour of some paternalistic interventions, when it is plausible that the state knows more about an individual's future tastes than the individual knows presently. The basis of these developments is an analysis of the concept of utility, which is introduced in the next section.

2 MULTIPLE NOTIONS OF UTILITY

The term 'utility' can be anchored either in the hedonic experience of outcomes, or in the preference or desire for that outcome. In Jeremy Bentham's usage, the utility of an object was ultimately defined in hedonic terms, by the pleasure that it produces. Others have interpreted utility as 'wantability' (Fisher, 1918). Of course, the two definitions have the same extension if people generally want that which they will eventually enjoy – a common assumption in discussions of utility. Economic analysis is more congenial to wants and preferences than to hedonic experiences, and the current meaning of utility in economics and decision research is a positivistic version of wantability: utility is a theoretical construct inferred from observed choices. This definition has been thoroughly cleansed of any association with hedonistic psychology, and of any reference to subjective states.

The present analysis starts with two observations. The first is that the methodological strictures against a hedonic notion of utility are a relic of an earlier period in which a behaviouristic philosophy of science held sway. Subjective states are now a legitimate topic of study, and hedonic experiences such as pleasure, pain, satisfaction or discomfort are considered open to useful forms of measurement. The second observation is that it may be rash to assume as a general rule that people will later enjoy what they want now. The relation between preferences and hedonic consequences is better studied than postulated.

These considerations suggest an explicit distinction between two notions of utility. The *experienced utility* of an outcome is the measure of the hedonic experience of that outcome. This is similar to Bentham's awkward use; the first footnote of his book was properly apologetic about the poor fit of the word 'utility' to pleasure and pain, but he found no better alternative. The *decision utility* of an outcome, as in modern usage, is the weight assigned to the outcome in a decision.

The distinction between experienced utility and decision utility opens new avenues for the study of rationality. In addition to the syntactic criterion of consistency, we can now hope to develop a substantive/hedonic criterion for the rationality of a decision: does it maximize the expectation of experienced utility? Of course, this criterion is not exhaustive, and its adoption implies no commitment to hedonistic philosophy. As Sen has often pointed out (e.g., Sen, 1987), the maximization of (experienced) utility is not always 'what people are trying to achieve'. It is surely the case, however, that people sometimes do try to maximize pleasure and minimize pain, and it may be instructive to drop the assumption that they perform this optimization task flawlessly.

Errors in the assignment of decision utility to anticipated outcomes can arise from inaccurate forecasting of future hedonic experience. Correct prediction of future tastes is therefore one of the requirements of rational decision-making (March, 1978). Kahneman and Snell (1990) defined the *predicted utility* of an outcome as the individual's beliefs about its experienced utility at some future time. Two sets of empirical questions arise: (i) How much do people know about their future tastes? Is it likely that an objective observer (or a government) could make more accurate predictions than individuals would make on their own behalf? (ii) Do people adequately consider the uncertainty of their future tastes in making decisions? Are decision utilities adequately informed by reasoned beliefs about experienced utility?

Additional issues arise because of possible disparities between memory and actual hedonic experience. Outcomes are commonly extended over time, and global evaluations of such outcomes are necessarily retrospective – and therefore subject to errors. Examples of substantial discrepancies between *retrospective utility* and *real-time utility* are discussed below.

The restoration of Bentham's notion of utility as an object of study evidently sets a large agenda for theoretical and empirical investigation. The following sections summarize highlights of what has been learned in early explorations of this agenda. Decision utility, predicted utility, and the relations between real-time and retrospective utility are discussed in turn. The final section reviews possible implications of the findings for the rationality debate.

3 SOME CHARACTERISTICS OF DECISION UTILITY

Decision utility has long been a topic of study, and much is known about it. The following discussion selectively addresses three research conclusions that are of particular relevance to the issue of rationality, as it is construed in this chapter. (i) *Carriers of utility.* The main carriers of decision utility are events, not states; in particular, utility is assigned to gains or losses relative to a reference point which is often the status quo (Kahneman and Tversky, 1979). (ii) *Loss aversion.* Losses loom larger than corresponding gains (Kahneman and Tversky, 1979; Tversky and Kahneman, 1991). (iii) *Framing effects.* The same objective outcomes can be evaluated as gains or as losses, depending on the framing of the reference state (Tversky and Kahneman, 1986).

An early observation that illustrates points (i) and (iii) above was labelled the isolation effect (Tversky and Kahneman, 1986).

Problem 1. Assume yourself richer by $300 than you are today.
You have to choose between
  a sure gain of $100
  50% chance to gain $200 and 50% chance to gain nothing

Problem 2. Assume yourself richer by $500 than you are today.
You have to choose between
  a sure loss of $100
  50% chance to lose nothing and 50% chance to lose $200

It is easily seen that the two problems are extensionally equivalent in terms of wealth: both offer a choice between a state in which wealth is increased by $400 and a gamble with equal chances to increase current wealth by $300 or by $500. If people spontaneously evaluate options in these terms they will choose the same option in the two problems – but observed preferences favour the 'sure thing' in Problem 1 and the gamble in Problem 2. Because the equivalence of the two problems is intuitively compelling when it is pointed out, the difference between the

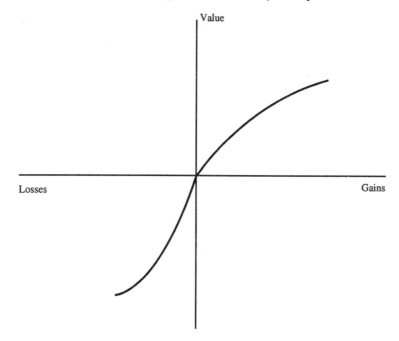

Figure 9.1   A typical value function

responses they elicit is a framing effect: an inconsequential feature of the formulation strongly affects preferences. Most important in the present context, the experiment demonstrates that people are content to assign utilities to outcomes stated as gains and losses, contrary to the standard assumption that the carriers of utility are states of wealth.

Figure 9.1 exhibits loss aversion in a schematic value function: the function is steeper in the domain of losses than in the domain of gains. The ratio of the slopes in the two domains, called the loss aversion coefficient, has been estimated as about 2:1 in several experiments involving both risky and riskless options (Tversky and Kahneman, 1991, 1992). Figure 9.2 (from Kahneman, Knetsch and Thaler, 1991) illustrates the role of a reference point in the evaluation of a transaction. The choice illustrated in this figure is between a state (Point *A*) with more of Good *Y* and a state (Point *D*) with more of Good *X*. The hypotheses about the carriers of utility and about framing effects entail that the preference between *A* and *D* could differ depending on the current reference point – contrary to a substantial body of economic theory. Consider the choice between *A* and *D* from *C*. This is a positive choice between two gains, in Good *X* or in Good *Y*. If the reference is *A*, however, the two options are framed quite differently. One possibility is to retain the status quo by staying at *A*. The alternative is to accept a trade that involves the conjunction of a loss in Good *Y* and a gain in Good *X*. The *C-A* interval is evaluated as a gain in the first frame (from *C*), but the same interval is evaluated as a loss from *A*. Because of loss aversion, the impact of the *C-A* difference is expected to be greater in the

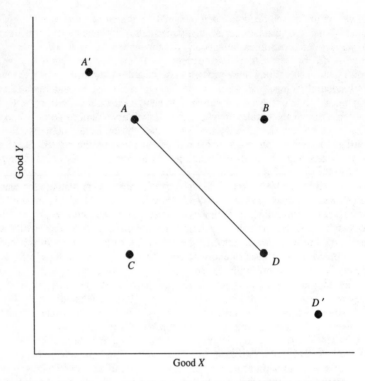

Figure 9.2   Multiple reference points for the choice between A and D

latter case than in the former. We therefore predict a systematic difference between
the preferences in the two frames: If people are indifferent between *A* and *D* from *C*,
they should strictly prefer *A* over *D* from *A* (Tversky and Kahneman, 1991).

The predicted result, known as the endowment effect (Thaler, 1980), has been
confirmed in several laboratories. Subjects in one condition of an experiment by
Kahneman, Knetsch and Thaler (1990) were offered a choice between a decorated
mug (worth about $6 at the university bookstore) and a sum of money; they
answered a series of questions to determine the amount of money at which they
were indifferent between the two options. Other subjects were first given a mug;
they answered similar questions to indicate the amount of money for which they
would just agree to exchange it. The subjects had no strategic incentive to conceal
their true values. A critical feature of the study is that the choosers in the first group
and the mug-owners in the second group faced objectively identical options: they
could leave the experimental situation owning a new mug, or with extra money in
their pockets. The analysis of Figure 9.2 applies, however. If the mug is Good *Y*, the
C-A interval (the difference between having a mug and not having one) is evaluated
as a gain by the choosers, and as a loss by the mug owners. As predicted, the
average cash value of a mug was much larger for the owners ($7.12 in one
experiment) than for choosers ($3.50). A significant (but somewhat smaller)

difference between owners and choosers was observed in a replication by Franciosi *et al.* (1993).

Implications of the endowment effect for various aspects of economic and legal theory have been discussed extensively elsewhere (Ellickson, 1989; Hovenkamp, 1991; Hardie, Johnson and Fader, 1993; Kahneman, Knetsch and Thaler, 1991). The effect is relevant to the present treatment because it implies that decision utilities may be extremely myopic. The subjects in the mugs experiment made a decision that was to have consequences over the relatively long term: a coffee mug is an object that one may use daily, sometimes for years. The long-term states between which the subjects had to choose – 'own this mug' or 'not own this mug' – were the same for all subjects. The large difference between the preferences of owners and choosers indicates that these enduring states were not the main object of evaluation. The effective carriers of utility were the transitions that distinguished the experimental treatments: 'receive a mug' or 'give up your mug'. In this experiment, and perhaps in many other situations, people who make decisions about a long-term state appear to use their evaluation of the transition to that state as a proxy.

The results of the mugs experiment present two overlapping challenges to the assumption of rationality. The logical notion of rationality is violated by the inconsistent preferences observed in different representations of the choice between a mug and money. A substantive condition of rationality is violated if the endowment effect is viewed as a costly manifestation of extreme myopia. An agent who routinely uses transient emotions as a proxy for the utility of long-term states is manifestly handicapped in the achievement of good outcomes.

4 PREDICTED UTILITY: DO PEOPLE KNOW WHAT THEY WILL LIKE?

Although the constancy of underlying tastes is a matter of theoretical debate, the following proposition will not be controversial: the hedonic experience associated with a particular stimulus or with a particular act of consumption is susceptible to large changes over time and over varying circumstances. Some cyclical changes of experienced utility are regular and readily predictable: ingesting the same food may evoke delight in a state of hunger, disgust in satiation. At the other extreme, radical changes of circumstances produce adaptations and changes of experienced utility that violate common expectations. A well-known psychological study showed that most paraplegics adapt far better than most people would predict, and that lottery winners are generally less happy in the long run than the common fascination with lotteries might suggest (Brickman, Coates and Janoff-Bulman, 1978).

Many decisions explicitly or implicitly involve predictions of future consumption and of future utility (March, 1978). An encyclopaedia may not be worth buying if one will not use it, the premium paid for a house with a view may be wasted if the view ceases giving pleasure after a time, and a medical procedure that improves survival chances should perhaps be rejected by a patient who is likely to find life without vocal cords intolerable.

How accurately do people predict their future utility? Most of the evidence about this question is indirect. Thus, it is suggestive that some important results of hedonic research are generally considered counter-intuitive. The surprises include the striking increase of liking by mere exposure to initially neutral stimuli, and some effects of dissonance on tastes (Kahneman and Snell, 1990). A study of people's intuitions about possible ways to induce a child to like or to dislike a food showed a similar lack of collective wisdom about the dynamics of taste. Dynamic inconsistency may be another manifestation of inaccurate hedonic prediction. For example, Christensen-Szalanski (1984) documented the incidence of cases in which women in labour reversed a long-standing preference for delivery without anaesthetics. The reversals could be due to improper discounting of the pain in the initial preferences; they could also reflect an error in the initial prediction of the intensity of labour pains.

Simonson (1990) reported a result that illustrates a failure of hedonic prediction – or perhaps a failure to make such a prediction. Simonson's students were given an opportunity to select from a choice set of snacks at the beginning of a class meeting; they received their selections at the end of the class. Subjects in one experimental condition made one choice each week for three weeks. In another condition subjects made choices for all three weeks at the first session. The choices made by the two groups were strikingly different. Subjects who chose a snack on three separate occasions tended to choose the same snack or a closely similar one every time. In contrast, subjects who chose in advance for three weeks tended to pick different items for the different occasions. It is reasonable to view these variety-seeking choices as erroneous: the subjects apparently failed to realize that their current preferences would be restored after a one-week interval. A further study clarified the nature of the error. Anticipatory choices were less variable when subjects were asked, before indicating a decision, to predict the preferences they would actually have on the subsequent occasions of testing. This finding suggests that the subjects were in fact able to predict their future preferences accurately. In the absence of a special instruction, however, they did not take the trouble to generate a prediction of their future taste before making a decision about future consumption.

Kahneman and Snell (1992) reported an exploratory study of the accuracy of hedonic prediction. They examined predictions of future liking for a food item or a musical piece, under conditions that made a change of attitude likely. In an initial experiment the subjects consumed a helping of their favourite ice cream while listening to a particular piece of music, at the same hour on eight consecutive working days under identical physical conditions. Immediately after each episode they rated how much they had liked the ice cream and the music. At the end of the first session they predicted the ratings they would make on the following day, and on the final day of the experiment. This experiment was intended to test the accuracy of hedonic predictions under relatively favourable conditions. We reasoned that student subjects have not only had much experience consuming ice cream and listening to music; they have had experience with repeated consumption of these items, and could therefore be expected to anticipate the effect of frequent repetition on their tastes. Other experiments in the series used a stimulus that is less familiar and less popular than ice cream in the student population – plain low-fat yogurt.

The accuracy of hedonic predictions was generally quite poor. A comparison of the average of predictions to the average of the actual ratings revealed some shared failures to anticipate common trends in the hedonic responses. For example, most subjects predicted, after tasting one spoonful of plain low-fat yogurt, that they would assign the same rating to a 6 oz helping on the next day. In fact, the larger helping was a much worse experience. Most subjects also failed to anticipate the considerable improvement in the attitude to plain yogurt which occurred (for most of them) with further exposure to that substance. There apparently exists a lay theory of hedonic changes, of mediocre accuracy, which most of our subjects accepted. Another analysis was concerned with individual differences in predictions and in actual hedonic changes. There was substantial variability in both measures, but the correlation between them was consistently close to zero. The data provided no indication that individuals were able to predict the development of their tastes more accurately than they could predict the hedonic changes of a randomly selected stranger.

The results of these studies suggest two conclusions. (i) People may have little ability to forecast changes in their hedonic responses to stimuli (Kahneman and Snell, 1992). (ii) Even in situations that permit accurate hedonic predictions, people may tend to make decisions about future consumption without due consideration of possible changes in their tastes (Simonson, 1990). If supported by further research, these hypotheses about the accuracy of predicted utility and about its impact on decision utility would present a significant substantive challenge to the assumption of rationality.

The properties of predicted utility have implications for other domains. Consider the issue of informed consent to an operation that will change the patient's life in some significant way. The normal procedure for consent emphasizes the provision of objective information about the effects of surgery. However, truly informed consent is only possible if patients have a reasonable conception of expected long-term developments in their hedonic responses, and if they assign appropriate weight to these expectations in the decision. A more controversial issue arises if we admit that an outsider can sometimes predict an individual's future utility far better than the individual can. Does this superior knowledge carry a warrant, or even a duty, for paternalistic intervention? It appears right for Ulysses' sailors to tie him to the mast against his will, if they believe that he is deluded about his ability to resist the fatal call of the sirens.

5   REAL-TIME AND RETROSPECTIVE UTILITY: DO PEOPLE KNOW WHAT THEY HAVE LIKED?

Retrospective evaluations of the experienced utility of past episodes are undoubtedly the most important source of predictions of the hedonic quality of future outcomes. The experiences of life leave their traces in a rich store of evaluative memories, which is consulted, apparently automatically, whenever a significant object or experience is brought to mind (Zajonc, 1980). The system of affective and evaluative memories may be independent of any ability to recall the incidents that produced an attitude. Thus, people often recognize that they like or dislike a person they have met before, without knowing why. Evaluative memories are immensely important because they contain the individual's accumulated knowledge of stimuli that are to be approached and of others that are to be avoided. Indeed, the only form of utility that people could possibly learn to maximize is the anticipated utility of future memories. Every individual has the lifelong habit of trusting memories of past episodes to guide choices among future outcomes. As we shall see, however, trusted evaluative memories are sometimes deceptive.

Although retrospective evaluations and affective memories define what is learned from the past, they are not the ultimate criterion of experienced utility. Hedonic or affective quality is an attribute of each moment of experience; the sign and intensity of the experience may vary considerably even over the course of a brief episode, such as drinking a glass of wine. The retrospective evaluation of an extended episode necessarily involves two operations: the recollection of the momentary experiences that constituted the episode, and an operation that combines the affect of these moments into a global evaluation. Because both operations are fallible, retrospective evaluations should be viewed with greater distrust than introspective reports of current experience. The effects of defective memory are sometimes painfully obvious: people who care for an elderly parent often observe that they accept their parent's immediate responses to the current situation with normal respect, even as they dismiss most retrospective evaluations as unreliable. The difficulties that arise in summarizing an episode by a global evaluation are more subtle, but no less significant.

There are strong normative intuitions about the correct way to combine the utilities of a series of experiences into a global evaluation. A principle of *temporal integration* has considerable appeal: the utility of an episode extended over time is the integral of momentary hedonic value over the duration of the episode. The justification for temporal integration is the assumption that successive selves should be treated equally, an assumption so compelling that a general case for utilitarianism has been built on it (Parfit, 1984). Even more appealing than temporal integration is the principle of *temporal monotonicity*. Consider two episodes that are preceded and followed by a steady state of hedonic neutrality. Assume that the second episode is obtained by adding an unanticipated period of pain (or pleasure) to the first, prior to the return to the neutral state. The monotonicity principle asserts that the hedonic quality of the added period determines whether the longer episode has higher or lower global utility than the shorter. In other words, adding pain at the end of an episode must make it worse; adding pleasure must make it better.[1]

Several recent studies indicate that retrospective evaluations obey neither temporal integration nor temporal monotonicity. The studies conducted so far have dealt with episodes that were uniform in the sign of the hedonic experience, either non-negative or non-positive throughout. Several experiments involved controlled exposure to affect-inducing stimuli (films of pleasant or unpleasant content; loud unpleasant sounds; immersion of a hand in painfully cold water). Subjects used an 'affect meter' to provide a continuous record of their momentary hedonic response during some of these episodes. Later they also provided retrospective global evaluations of the 'overall discomfort' or 'overall pleasure' of the episodes, and in some cases chose an episode to which they would be exposed again. In one non-experimental study (Redelmeier and Kahneman, 1996) patients undergoing a colonoscopy for medical reasons provided reports of pain every 60 seconds, as well as subsequent global evaluations and measures of preference for the entire episode.

The results of these studies support two empirical generalizations. (i) *'The Peak & End Rule'*: global evaluations are predicted with high accuracy by a weighted combination of the most extreme affect recorded during the episode and of the affect recorded during the terminal moments of the episode. Here again, as in the context of decision utility, the evaluation of particular moments appears to be used as a

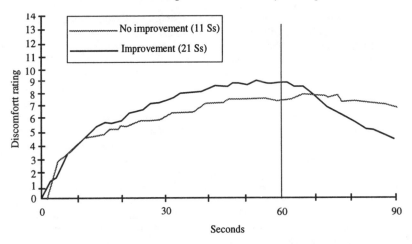

Figure 9.3 Mean of real-time discomfort measure on Long trial, for 11 subjects who indicated little or no decrease of discomfort when temperature changed (grey line), and for 21 subjects who indicated decreased discomfort (black line)

proxy for the evaluation of a more extended period of time. (ii) *Duration Neglect*: the retrospective evaluation of overall or total pain (or pleasure) is not independently affected by the duration of the episode. In the colonoscopy study, for example, the duration of the procedure varied from 4 to 69 minutes in a sample of 101 patients. Surprisingly, these variations of duration had no significant effect on retrospective evaluations. The ratings of both patients and attending physicians were dominated by the intensity of pain at its worst, and by the intensity of discomfort during the last few minutes of the procedure. Duration neglect is not immutable, of course: people can judge the duration of episodes with fair accuracy, and will treat this attribute as relevant when their attention is explicitly drawn to it (Varey and Kahneman, 1992). In general, however, affective peaks and endings are more salient than duration in the cognitive representation of events.

Figure 9.3 is taken from a study that examined violations of the rule of temporal monotonicity in a choice between painful episodes (Kahneman *et al.*, 1993). Paid volunteers expected to undergo three experiences of moderate physical pain during an experimental session. In fact they only had two trials. In the Short trial the subject held one hand in water at 14°C for 60 seconds, then immediately dried his hand with a towel. In the Long trial, the subject held the other hand in water for a total of 90 seconds. During the first 60 seconds of the Long trial the temperature of the water was 14°C, just as in the Short trial; during the extra 30 seconds the temperature of the water was gradually raised to 15°C, still unpleasant but for most subjects a clear improvement over the initial state. The order of the two trials was varied for different subjects. A few minutes after the second trial, the subjects were reminded that they were due to have another trial and were asked which of the two preceding experiences they chose to repeat.

The curves shown in Figure 9.3 present average momentary ratings of discomfort for the Long trial, separately for two groups of subjects who showed different patterns of response: the majority who indicated decreasing discomfort as the temperature of the water was raised, and a minority who reported little change of discomfort. The choices of which trial to repeat were markedly different in these two groups: 17 of the 21 subjects whose discomfort diminished preferred to repeat the Long trial, in violation of temporal monotonicity; only 5 of the 11 subjects whose discomfort did not change preferred the Long trial. The results of both groups conform to the Peak & End rule and exhibit duration neglect. For the minority whose pain did not diminish, the peak and the end of the pain were at the same level (see Figure 9.3), and were the same in the Short and in the Long trials. The Peak & End rule predicts that these subjects should evaluate the two trials alike, a prediction that is confirmed by the nearly even split of preferences. For the larger group of subjects whose pain diminished at the end of the Long trial, the Peak & End rule predicts that this trial should be less aversive than the Short one, and the choice data again confirm the prediction. Overall, about two-thirds of subjects violate dominance in this situation, a robust result that has been replicated with numerous subjects under slightly different conditions.

Additional analyses clarify the mechanism that produces these violations of temporal monotonicity: most subjects erroneously believed that the coldest temperature to which they had been exposed was not the same in the two trials: their memory of the worst moment of the Long trial was mitigated by the subsequent improvement. Our evidence suggests that episodes are evaluated by a few 'snapshots' rather than by a continuous film-like representation (Fredrickson and Kahneman, 1993). The snapshots are in fact montages, which may blend impressions of different parts of the experience. The overall experience is judged by a weighted average of the utility of these synthetic moments.

Other experiments showed that subjects who are only given verbal descriptions of the trials generally prefer the Short one, in accordance with the principle of temporal monotonicity. Telling these subjects that their memory of the Long trial will be more favourable does not diminish their preference for the Short trial. This observation indicates that the participants in the original experiment did not deliberately apply a policy of selecting the experience that would leave them with the most pleasant memory. However, subjects who have had personal experience of the two trials are quite reluctant to abandon their preference for the Long trial even when the nature of the two trials is carefully explained after the fact. It is evidently not easy to overcome a lifetime habit of trusting one's evaluations of personal memories as a guide to choice.

The studies reviewed in this section have documented a consistent pattern of violations of a compelling normative rule. The axiom of temporal monotonicity is a substantive principle of rationality, a variant of 'more is better' formulations of dominance. The violations of this principle have been traced to basic cognitive processes that produce representations and evaluations of episodes. The requirements of substantive rationality are apparently not compatible with the psychology of memory and choice.

The results of the 'cold-water' study illustrate an ethical dilemma that was extensively discussed by Schelling (1984). The history of an individual through time can be described as a succession of separate selves, which may have incompatible preferences, and may make decisions that affect subsequent selves. In the cold-water experiment, for example, the experiencing subject who records momentary affect and the remembering subject who makes retrospective evaluations appear to have conflicting evaluations. Which of these selves should be granted authority over outcomes that will be experienced in the future? The principle of temporal monotonicity assigns priority to the experiencing subject. In the normal conduct of life, however, the remembering subject assumes the all-important role of laying out guidelines for future actions. Is there an ethical justification for favouring one of these evaluations over the other? This question has immediate implications for the application of rules of informed consent in medical practice. Imagine a painful medical procedure that lasts a specified number of minutes and ends abruptly with pain at its peak. We have seen that the physician could probably ensure that the patient will retain a more favourable memory of the procedure by adding to it a medically superfluous period of diminishing pain. Of course, the patient would probably reject the physician's offer to provide an improved memory at the cost of more actual pain. Should the physician go ahead anyway, on behalf of the patient's future remembering self? This dilemma illustrates a class of problems of paternalism that are likely to arise in many policy debates, if considerations of experienced utility are assigned the weight they deserve in these debates.

6   GENERAL DISCUSSION

The standard theory of choice provides a set of conditions for rationality that may be necessary, but are hardly sufficient: they allow many foolish decisions to be called rational. This chapter has argued that it is generally useful and sometimes possible to supplement the logical analysis of decisions by substantive criteria. A substantive analysis provides a more demanding definition of rationality, which excludes some preferences that would pass a test of coherence. The core of a substantive analysis is an independent assessment of the quality of decision outcomes.

The line between logical and substantive analyses is often fuzzy. For example, the 'more is better' rule of dominance is a substantive rule that has the force of a logical principle. A substantive judgement is also implicitly invoked in experimental studies of invariance, where decision-makers express conflicting preferences in choice problems that are said to be 'the same', 'extensionally equivalent', or 'not different in any consequential respect'. In the mugs experiment, for example, it appears unreasonable for owners and choosers to set very different prices for the same object, because the long-term consumption they will derive from it is presumably the same, and because long-term considerations carry more weight than the transient affect associated with giving up an object. A criterion of utility experienced over time is implicit in this argument.

The research reviewed in earlier sections was explicit in evaluating decisions by a criterion of experienced utility. Various proxies were used to measure this subjective variable. For example, choices made near the moment of consumption were the criterion in evaluating earlier commitments (Simonson, 1990). In other studies, the adequacy of retrospective evaluations and of the decisions they support was assessed by applying normative rules (e.g., temporal monotonicity) to real-time records of hedonic experience.

The correspondence of experienced utility and decision utility is often casually assumed in treatments of choice. Contrary to this optimistic assumption, two obstacles to the maximization of experienced utility have been identified here. First, preliminary findings suggest that people lack skill in the task of predicting how their tastes might change. The evidence for this conclusion is still sketchy, but it significance is clear: it is difficult to describe agents as rational when they are prone to large errors in predicting what they will want or enjoy next week. Another obstacle to maximization is a tendency to use the affect associated with particular moments as a proxy for the utility of extended outcomes. This peculiarity in the cognitive treatment of time explains the importance that people attach to the emotions of transactions, and may cause other forms of myopia in decision-making. The use of moments as proxies entails a neglect of duration in the evaluation of past episodes, which has been confirmed in several studies. These results illustrate one particular form of distortion in evaluative memory; there may be others. Observations of memory biases are significant because the evaluation of the past determines what is learned from it. Errors in the lessons drawn from experience will inevitably be reflected in deficient choices for the future.

The rules that govern experienced utility emerge as an important subject for empirical study. For example, research could address the question of how to maximize experienced utility under a budget constraint. Scitovsky (1976) offered an insightful analysis of this problem in his *Joyless Economy*, where he took the position that the maximization of pleasure is a difficult task, which is performed with greater success in some cultures than in others. The process of hedonic adaptation played a central role in his treatment of 'comforts', which suggests that it is pointless to invest resources in objects that quickly lose their ability to give pleasure. Expenditure should be directed to goods and activities that provide recurrent pleasures when appropriately spaced over time. In this light, money may be better spent on flowers, feasts and vacations than on improved durables. A systematic empirical study of the issues that Scitovsky raised is both possible and necessary.

A deeper understanding of the dynamics of the hedonic response is needed to evaluate the welfare consequences of institutions. For example, the course of income changes over a standard academic career appears designed for a pleasure machine that responds well to gradual increments, and treats any losses as highly aversive (Frank, 1992; Loewenstein and Sicherman, 1991; Varey and Kahneman, 1992). Another institution that probably delivers improving outcomes over time is the penal system: the well-being of prison inmates is likely to improve in the course of their sentence, as they gain seniority and survival skills. This arrangement is humane, but perhaps less than efficient in terms of individual deterrence. Suppose, for the sake of a provocative example, that prisoners apply a Peak & End rule in retrospective evaluations of their prison experience. The result would be a global evaluation that becomes steadily less aversive with time in prison, implying a negative correlation between sentence length and the deterrence of individual recidivism. This is surely not a socially desirable outcome. Should shorter periods of incarceration under conditions of increasing discomfort be considered? As this speculative example illustrates, detailed consideration of experienced utility can yield quite unexpected conclusions.

The hedonic criterion of experienced utility is appropriate for some decisions, but it is neither universal nor exhaustive. Rational people may have other objectives than the maximization of pleasure. As Sen has noted, the rationality of decisions is best assessed in the light of 'what the person is aiming to do or trying to achieve'. At least in principle, a substantive evaluation of individual decisions can be extended to other criterial objectives, such as the achievement of increased personal capabilities, or of a good reputation. As the example of experienced utility illustrates, the investigation of any proposed criterion for decision-making must involve three elements: (i) a normative analysis; (ii) development of measurement tools for the evaluation of outcomes; and (iii) an analysis of ways in which decisions commonly fail, by this criterion. Experienced utility is an obvious subject for such a programme, but it need not be the only one.

From the point of view of a psychologist, the notion of rationality that is routinely invoked in economic discourse is surprisingly permissive in some respects, surprisingly restrictive in others. For example, economic rationality does not rule out extreme risk aversion in small gambles or radical discounting of the near term future, although these attitudes almost necessarily yield inferior aggregate outcomes. On the other hand, rationality is often taken to be synonymous with flawless intelligence. Thus, a critic of the rationality assumption faces the following well-fortified position: (i) a definition of rationality which appears to be overly permissive in some important respects; (ii) a willingness of choice theorists to make the theory even more permissive, as needed to accommodate apparent violations of its requirements; (iii) a methodological position that treats rationality as a maintained hypothesis, making it very difficult to disprove; (iv) an apparent readiness to assume that behaviour that has not been proved to be irrational is highly intelligent.

In contrast to the many recent attempts to relax the definition of rational choice, the argument of this chapter has been that the definition should be made more restrictive, by adding substantive considerations to the logical standard of coherence. There is compelling evidence that the maintenance of coherent beliefs and preferences is too demanding a task for limited minds (Simon; 1982; Tversky and Kahneman, 1986). Maximizing the experienced utility of a stream of future outcomes can only be harder. The time has perhaps come to set aside the overly general question of whether or not people are rational, allowing research attention to be focused on more specific and more promising issues. What are the conditions under which the assumption of rationality can be retained as a useful approximation? Where the assumption of rationality must be given up, what are the most important ways in which people fail to maximize their outcomes?

Note

1. The temporal monotonicity principle does not apply if the addition of pain or pleasure to the episode alters hedonic after-effects, such as relief, after-glow, or the effect associated with subsequent recollection. More generally, the analysis of experienced utility becomes difficult to apply where the consumption of memories plays an important role (Elster and Loewenstein, 1992).

References

Arrow, K.J. (1982) 'Risk Perception in Psychology and Economics', *Economic Inquiry*, vol. 20, pp. 1–9.

Brickman, P., D. Coates and R. Janoff-Bulman (1978) 'Lottery Winners and Accident Victims: Is Happiness Relative?', *Journal of Personality and Social Psychology*, vol. 36, no. 8, pp. 917–27.

Christensen-Szalanski, J.J. (1984) 'Discount Functions and the Measurement of Patient's Values: Women's Decisions During Childbirth', *Medical Decision Making*, vol. 4, pp. 47–58.

Ellickson, R. (1989) 'Bringing Culture and Human Frailty to Rational Actors: A Critique of Classical Law and Economics', *Chicago-Kent Law Review* vol. 65, no. 23, pp. 23–55.

Elster, J. and G. Loewenstein (1992) 'Utility from Memory and Anticipation', in: J. Elster and G. Loewenstein (eds), *Choice over Time* (New York: Russell Sage Foundation) pp. 213–34.

Fisher, I. (1918) 'Is "Utility" the Most Suitable Term for the Concept It Is Used to Denote?', *American Economic Review*, vol. 8, pp. 335–7. Reproduced in A. N. Page (ed.), *Utility Theory: A Book of Readings* (New York: Wiley, 1968).

Franciosi, R., P. Kujal, R. Michelitsch and V. Smith (1993) 'Experimental Tests of the Endowment Effect', Economic Science Laboratory Working Paper, University of Arizona.

Frank, R. H. (1992) 'The Role of Moral Sentiments in the Theory of Intertemporal Choice', in J.Elster and G. Loewenstein (eds), *Choice over Time* (New York: Russell Sage Foundation) pp. 265–86.

Fredrickson, B.L. and D. Kahneman (1993) 'Duration Neglect in Retrospective Evaluations of Affective Episodes', *Journal of Personality and Social Psychology*, vol. 65, pp. 45–55.

Hammond, P. (1985) 'Consequential Behaviour in Decision Trees and Expected Utility', Institute of Mathematical Studies in the Social Sciences Working Paper no. 112, Stanford University, Palo Alto, California.

Hardie, B.G.S., E.J. Johnson, and P.S. Fader (1993) 'Modeling Loss Aversion and Reference Dependence Effects on Brand Choice', *Marketing Science*, Fall, pp. 378–94.

Hovenkamp, H. (1991) 'Legal Policy and the Endowment Effect', *Journal of Legal Studies*, vol. 20, pp. 225–47.

Kahneman, D. and J. Snell (1990) 'Predicting Utility', in R. M. Hogarth (ed.), *Insights in Decision Making* (Chicago: University of Chicago Press).

Kahneman, D. and J. Snell (1992) 'Predicting a Changing Taste', *Journal of Behavioral Decision Making*, vol. 5, pp. 187–200.

Kahneman, D. and A. Tversky (1979) 'Prospect Theory: An Analysis of Decisions Under Risk', *Econometrica*, vol. 47, pp. 313–27.

Kahneman, D., J. Knetsch and R. Thaler (1990) 'Experimental Tests of the Endowment Effect and the Coase Theorem', *Journal of Political Economy*, vol. 98, no. 6, pp. 1325–48.

Kahneman, D., J. Knetsch and R. Thaler (1991) 'The Endowment Effect, Loss Aversion, and Status Quo Bias', *Journal of Economic Perspectives* vol. 5, pp. 193–206.

Kahneman, D., D.L. Fredrickson, C.A. Schreiber and D.A. Redelemeier, (1993) 'When More Pain is Preferred to Less: Adding a Better End', *Psychological Science*, no. 4, pp. 401–5.

Loewenstein, G. and N. Sicherman (1991) 'Do Workers Prefer Increasing Wage Profiles', *Journal of Labor Economics*, vol. 9, no. 1, pp. 67–84.

March, J. (1978) 'Bounded Rationality, Ambiguity, and the Engineering of Choice', *Bell Journal of Economics*, vol. 9, pp. 587–608.

Parfit, D. (1984), *Reasons and Persons* (Oxford: Oxford University Press).

Redelmeier, D. A. and D. Kahneman (1996) 'Memories of Painful Medical Treatments: Real-time and Retrospective Evaluations of Two Minimally Invasive Procedures', *Pain*, p. 212.

Schelling, T.C. (1984) *Choice and Consequence* (Cambridge, Mass: Harvard University Press)

Scitovsky, T. (1976) *Joyless Economy: An Inquiry into Human Satisfaction and Consumer Dissatisfaction* (Oxford: Oxford University Press).

Sen, A. (1987) *On Ethics and Economics* (Oxford: Basil Blackwell).

Sen, A. (1990) 'Rational Behaviour', in J. Eatwell, M. Milgate, and P. Newman (eds), *The New Palgrave: Utility and Probability* (London: Macmillan) pp. 198–216.

Sen, A. (1993) 'Internal Consistency of Choice', *Econometrica* vol. 61, no. 3, pp. 495–521.

Simon, H. (1982) *Models of Bounded Rationality* (Cambridge, Mass: MIT Press).

Simonson, I. (1990) 'The Effect of Purchase Quantity and Timing on Variety-Seeking Behavior', *Journal of Marketing Research*, vol. 27, no. 2, pp. 150–62.

Slovic, P. and A. Tversky (1974) 'Who Accepts Savage's Axiom?' *Behavioral Science*, vol. 19, pp. 368–73.

Thaler, R. (1980) 'Toward a Positive Theory of Consumer Choice', *Journal of Economic Behavior and Organization*, vol. 1, pp. 39–60.

Tversky, A and D. Kahneman (1986) 'Rational Choice and the Framing of Decisions', *Journal of Business*, vol. 59, S251-78.

Tversky, A. and D. Kahneman (1991) 'Loss Aversion in Riskless Choice: A Reference-Dependent Model', *Quarterly Journal of Economics*, vol. 106, pp. 1039–61.

Tversky, A. and D. Kahneman (1992) 'Advances in Prospect Theory: Cumulative Representation of Uncertainty', *Journal of Risk and Uncertainty*, vol. 5, pp. 297–323.

Tversky, A., P. Slovic and D. Kahneman (1990) 'The Causes of Preference Reversal', *American Economic Review*, vol. 80, pp. 204–17.

Varey, C. and D. Kahneman (1992) 'Experiences Extended Across Time: Evaluation of Moments and Episodes', *Journal of Behavioral Decision Making*, vol. 5, pp. 169–86.

Zajonc, R.B. (1980) 'Feeling and Thinking: Preferences Need No Inferences', *American Psychologist*, vol. 35, no. 2, pp. 151–75.

Comment

Charles R. Plott

CALIFORNIA INSTITUTE OF TECHNOLOGY, USA

Professor Kahneman's chapter is a useful integration of research that he has conducted with several co-authors. The phenomena of individual decisions is a source of nagging curiosity for many sciences, applications of sciences, and philosophy. What he has to say should be of great interest to a very large research community. In discussing his chapter I will narrow the perspective to economics and to a lesser extent political science, in the hope of facilitating better and more complete understanding of the fundamental and important perspective that he and his co-authors bring to those particular sciences.

At the outset I should say that I do not like the word 'rationality' used in the title. Consequently, I am not particularly sympathetic with Kahneman's overall purpose to 'argue for an enriched definition of rationality'. The concept lacks scientific precision and as a result is a source of needless controversy and misunderstandings. Many theoreticians have attempted to eliminate the inherent vagueness by defining types. Aizerman *et al.* (1985) for example, connects the concept of rationality to notions of 'optimality' and then produces vastly different concepts of optimality and substantially generalizes classical scalar optimization and the associated use of binary relations over states. The concept of rationality can be connected with notions of logic or it can be connected with notions of specific purpose. The word 'rationality' can be emotionally charged by social philosophy and the connotations of equality and justice that are carried implicitly in the consistency (or lack thereof) of social decisions. Rationality is a very broad term that engenders disagreements where enough disagreement exists already. I will return to this issue later.

Interest in Kahneman's work need not be tied to any particular view of the status of concepts of rationality or the definition of the word. The results stand on their own. The substance of reported research is to develop a theory of human (and perhaps non-human) decisions that rests on four laws. The first three reflect years of previous work and the fourth law is the primary focus of Kahneman's chapter. The laws can be summarized as follows:

Law 1. Decisions are a reflection of decision utilities that are carried by changes to situations and not situations themselves. That is, in the context of decisions the items valued are changes from state to state and not the states themselves, as is generally supposed in decision theory.

Law 2. Changes are relative to a special state called a 'reference point' that is determined by the cognitive 'frame' that exists in the decision environment.

Law 3. Decision utilities foster risk seeking in the loss domain (loss aversion).

Law 4. Decision utilities are influenced by beliefs about hedonic experiences that are determined by states.

The background interpretation of these four laws is in terms of decisions as a process as opposed to a single act. The purpose is to provide a theoretical framework that captures a merging of possibly conflicting attitudes and perceptions into an overall choice. Laws 1-3 are clearly beginning to take a structure from which behavioral propositions can be deduced. For example, the existence of an 'endowment effect' can be deduced from the first three laws. Similarly, the existence of differences in willingness to pay and willingness to accept can be deduced from the first three laws as a corollary to the endowment effect.

The fourth law, the new addition and the major subject of Kahneman's chapter, is an attempt to capture the relationship between decisions and internal states – hedonic experiences, as Kahneman calls them. The ideas are based on reports of cardinal measures of sensations such as pain that one might naturally assume is associated with a disutility or, in terms of the awkward language of preference theory, one would assume is associated with states that an individual would prefer to avoid. The striking result is that the reported preferences over experiences are not related to the integral or the duration of pain experienced. Instead, preferences are based on the peak levels of pain and the pain experienced at the end of an episode. Kahneman theorizes that the decision process that produces this striking result is one that operates through a memory geared to record peaks of experiences more than duration or exposure. That memory process then produces a cognitive representation of events that is used for decisions.

The experiments stimulate many new questions. One wonders if this memory capacity is only cognitive, or is typical of the other types of memory capacities of animals. Would non-cognitive learning, perhaps of the sort detected by galvanic skin responses, obey the 'peak and end' rules and be related to choices? The attempt to associate something so complex as a decision with an internal state could be an important step to understanding the physiological bases for decisions. New technological developments when joined with new theory could provide a completely new dimension to our understanding of decisions and the role of cognition in decisions. It is easy to share Kahneman's enthusiasm for his work.

There is, however, another aspect of Kahneman's chapter: a sense of complaint that needs to be addressed. The chapter contains remarks of a type sometimes encountered in psychologically oriented literature. The remarks suggest a belief that there is a fundamental problem in economics. His title for the chapter is 'New Challenges to the Rationality Assumption' and the body of the chapter is where 'theoretical and practical implications of these challenges to the assumption of economic rationality are discussed'. Of the Allais and Ellsberg paradoxes he says 'It is often implied that if these paradoxes can be resolved, then economic analysis can safely continue to assume that agents are rational. The focus on paradoxes has indirectly strengthened the rationality dogma.' The tone of the chapter is that economics is based on a faulty assumption of rationality supported by an unjustified but 'well fortified position' and that the assumption should be discarded and replaced by the laws listed above. That issue and perspective is in need of exploring.

The first question that one might ask is whether or not economics is built on a rationality assumption of the type that Kahneman presupposes. I think that it is not. Economics is full of assumptions of irrationality. For example, in the competitive model agents are assumed to be price takers. They are assumed to believe that they have no influence at all on price even though within the model itself there is substantial evidence to the contrary that is irrationally ignored. A similar irrationality appears in the reaction functions of the Cournot model (or reaction functions in almost any game model) that have agents continuously overlooking the fact that their decisions are always systematically wrong. The individuals irrationally react, never learn and never think about the problem. The Cobweb model is an additional example. A monopolist, or any imperfect competitor for that matter, in a general equilibrium framework never works through the income effects and other feedback that lead their pricing decisions to influence their own costs and future demand. In public sector models voters irrationally go to the polls to cast their ballots even though they have no return from doing so. In several different game-theoretic models an agent could react in any fashion whatsoever if he/she encountered another agent that was not following an equilibrium strategy. Dynamic models frequently contain *ad hoc* learning and adjustment features that are, in essence, postulating an agent that always makes mistakes and never realizes it. It is well known that the competitive model does not require transitivity at the individual level. Many models involve agents that have random utilities but in making long-term decisions do not know that their utilities are random or might change. Models exist that postulate the existence of people who are tied to a decision rule regardless of evidence or consequences of following the rule. The list of irrationalities in economics models is very long. Almost any applied model in economics will have some aspects of irrationality incorporated. Even models of rational expectations have irrational or incomplete features. The word 'rational' has no single meaning in economics. The word 'The' that appears in the chapter's title and in a similar context throughout the chapter, is inappropriate. Thus, it is not exactly clear what it is about economics models that Kahneman is advocating should be changed.

The message of the chapter is that economists should stop whatever it is that they are doing and adopt laws 1–4. If that is not the message, it will nevertheless be interpreted that way by non-economics readers, and so should be discussed. In either case the message and any such recommendation for economics suffers from substantial problems. Economics is about markets, price formation, entry, the behaviour of systems of possibly strategically interacting agents and related social phenomena. Economics is related to but is not the same as decision theory from which Kahneman draws his observations. The notion of a decision plays a special role in the modelling effort in economics and in game theory as well. The individual as it appears in economics, typically is characterized by only such axiomatic structure that is needed for coherence of a model of system behaviour. There is no need to capture the complete behaviour of an individual in all of its complexity, although if it could be done everyone would be happy.

Given the nature of the phenomena and the purpose of economic science, the model of the individual must be adequate to produce predictions about systems level behaviour. If the model cannot do that then it cannot do the work that motivates the modelling effort in the first place. From the four laws can one derive the standard models of economics and game theory? Do the four laws impose substantial restrictions on market and group behaviour? Are the four laws reliable in that they are manifest in wide-ranging economic activity? If a revolution is needed at the foundations of economics and if Kahneman's research and the research of his co-authors point the way, then the answers to all three questions should be yes. As of this date, that is not the case.

Can one deduce the standard economics model from the four laws? The standard models are known to work reasonably well in predicting behaviour, so, if the new set of laws is going to replace the old then one would expect models deduced from the new laws to perform at least as well as established tasks. For example, can one deduce from the four laws alone, the equilibrium properties of the law of supply and demand and predict the ultimate prices that will evolve in a market? I cannot see how it is possible to deduce an equilibrium price without resort to traditional modelling techniques. The problems for the new laws become compounded when games are contemplated. How can the four laws be used to formulate a model with strategically interacting individuals? What type of strategies might be employed against an individual that places values on changes in states and not on states? Indeed, how would those valuing changes even formulate their own strategies or does the individual even have the capacity to do such a thing? What type of equilibrium concepts might be employed? How, for example could one formulate the bid functions derived from first price auction theory? With the new laws the whole framework needed to apply models from game theory seems to be lacking. The problems do not stop there. Economic models of multiple markets and general equilibrium are powerful. How would such notions be deduced from the four laws without reverting to the standard economics machinery that the new laws are supposed to replace? Rational expectations models are known to produce amazingly accurate models of systems. If the four laws are used how can any agent know what might be expected of other agents whose decisions would depend upon a subjectively perceived reference point? The core under majority rule has strong predictive power. How could one derive similar predictions from the four laws? Briefly put, I think that phenomena of interest to economics cannot be captured by models that are deduced from the four laws given their current state of development.

Do the four laws place significant restrictions on models of phenomena that are of interest to economics? It appears that anything that might be observed in a social context would be consistent with the four laws. If beliefs, for example, are allowed to wander too much, all patterns of behaviour can be described as equilibrium behaviour in a game (Ledyard, 1986). By just relaxing the belief structure and retaining everything else from game theory, a model results that is not refutable. If the four laws are going to produce models that can be applied to conflicts and if the models are to have empirical content, then much more structure must be added. As the laws stand as a group, they do not appear to have the power to do the job that is needed.

Are the four laws generally reliable? Experiments described in the chapter are focused on special types of phenomena as opposed to the broad substance of economics. It seems legitimate to ask if a preponderance of evidence exists in market situations that requires the need of the four laws. In this respect it is easiest to focus on the third law, the propensity of individuals to be risk-averse in gains and risk-seeking in losses. While many examples exist, a natural place to look for such phenomena would be markets in which some sort of speculation is taking place in which agents have a potential for making losses. When this is done one discovers that individuals that engage in the risky behaviour by purchasing something for resale, do so only at prices within the bounds of risk-averse behaviour. With the item purchased they now face losses that risk-seeking behaviour would have them assuming risks in order to avoid. This risk-seeking behaviour is not observed. In other words, the third law does not describe phenomena that is so pervasive and so pronounced in markets that its presence can be easily detected. The reliability of the laws, when applied to commonly observed economic situations, can be called into question.

I suspect that Kahneman does not intend his position to be interpreted as I have done and that I have taken many too many liberties with his arguments. He could be advocating only slight changes in models as opposed to a revolution. However, even if this is the case there are still poblems in appending the proposed laws to economic models. The force of the observations in the paragraphs above still applies. With an economic/game-theoretic model so altered can it still be used to produce results of the sort required of economic models? Will it still place restrictions on data? Until this has been demonstrated the complaints are not justified.

I think that Kahneman's chapter should be read as outlined in my first remarks. The complaints in the chapter should be ignored and the tools that he offers should be accepted on their own terms. The foundations of economics are not yet ready to be replaced by the four laws but I personally think that Kahneman and co-authors are on a productive course. That they have something of value to offer economics is obvious since the challenging phenomena that they have identified would never have been identified by researchers focused by an economic perspective alone. It is not even clear that the theory as it has evolved through economics is capable of pointing researchers in the right direction. While I disagree with the way that he casts his research relative to economics, I fully agree with the words 'New Challenges', used in his title. Economics would be badly mistaken to ignore the results that he is reporting.

References

Aizerman, M.A. (1985) 'New Problems in the General Choice Theory. Review of a Research Trend', *Social Choice and Welfare*, vol. 2, no. 4, pp. 235–82.

Ledyard, J.O. (1986) 'The Scope of the Hypothesis of Bayesian Equilibrium', *Journal of Economic Theory*, vol. 39, pp. 59–82.

10 Rational Individual Behaviour in Markets and Social Choice Processes: the Discovered Preference Hypothesis*

Charles R. Plott

CALIFORNIA INSTITUTE OF TECHNOLOGY, USA

1 INTRODUCTION

The focus on individual behaviour in economics is derived from an interest in the behaviour of groups as they are found in markets, committees, and social choice processes. For the most part, economists have not been interested in what goes on inside the heads of individuals. Thought or thought processes are seldom considered as part of the phenomena to be studied as a part of the science. Economics is primarily a study of choice behaviours and their properties as they become manifest in the context of specific organizational units. By contrast, psychological focus on the individual is derived from a long history of research on the nature of thought and thought processes. In contrast to economics, psychological research does not seem to have been defined by any particular social, institutional, or organizational constraints.

This chapter is an attempt to integrate data and perspectives from these two, substantially different traditions, by introducing an observational theory that I will call the 'discovered preference hypothesis'. With the introduction of such a theory, two disclaimers are necessary at the very outset. Firstly, the perspective of the chapter is distinctively economics. The objective is to improve models of economic and social choice processes. Contributions to psychology are neither attempted nor claimed. Secondly, the discovered preference hypothesis is more of a philosophy, or interpretation of data, than a clearly articulated theory from which precise quantitative propositions can be deduced. It is offered as a means of imposing some understanding on a very complex body of theory, and data generated by experimental economists and by psychologists.

Because of differences in the nature of data, as well as differences in scientific objectives, it would seem to be important to make a clear statement of what is known, and not known, by way of modelling. On one hand, there seems to be little

*The support for this project, provided by the National Science Foundation, is gratefully acknowledged.

debate about the power of models built on principles of rational choice, or on related concepts of purposeful choices, to predict the behaviour of groups of people, such as committees and markets. Models based on such principles are not free of error, which critics of economics are quick to reference, but the success of rationality based models in explaining what is observed in experimental markets and committees cannot be denied. No model, theory, or concept, from any other branch of science yields models with comparable breadth and accuracy when applied to the behaviour of groups of humans. Other models and theories might have the capacity to explain deviations of the data from predictions of the rational choice model. Other models might have the capacity to explain choice behaviour after patterns of decisions are observed; but no other model has the demonstrated ability to produce the predictions in the first instance. Price formation in a market, the strategic behaviour induced by market institutions, the power of an agenda, or the attractiveness of the equilibrium in committees operating under majority rule, cannot be explained by an appeal to principles of psychology. An understanding of supply and demand, and the nature of game-theoretical choices, seem to be indispensable for the task. If principles of psychology have a role to play in explaining social choices, it must be to explain deviations from the general tendencies explained by the rational choice models.

On the other hand, with that strong endorsement of rational models out of the way, the remaining parts of this essay will be devoted to some strategically chosen paradoxes that exist if the endorsement is accepted. The 'deviations from the general tendencies explained by the rational choice models' can be substantial. The problems involve much more than simply placing a period at the end of a sentence written by economic theory. Examples of the paradoxes (or problem areas) seem to be of two types. The first type consists of situations in which the choosing individual has little or no previous experience with the choice/decision task. In economics and in political science, practical examples abound and range from a decision to buy a house, choose a wife, or support a new form of political constitution. The class of such examples, which will be called 'new tasks', abound in economics and they are precisely the type of phenomena on which psychologists have focused. The second class of examples encompasses situations in which the behaviour of another individual is important to a given individual. Again, examples are numerous in economics and political science, and include phenomena like the stock market, problems of coordination, etc. This second class will be called 'other agent' examples.

The purpose of the chapter is, in part, to identify an observational theory that is lurking in the background of the behaviour observed in the two classes of examples. For purposes of discussion, I will call it the *discovered preference hypothesis*. I think this hypothesis is often believed, but seldom stated, and thus it should be brought into the light where it can be examined and criticized. The theory is that rational choices evolve through three stages reflecting experience and practice. Stage one occurs when experience is absent. Untutored choices reflect a type of myopia. The individual is purposeful and optimizing, but exhibits limited awareness about the immediate environment or the possible longer-run consequences of any acts that might be taken. Responses are 'instantaneous' or 'impulsive', reflecting whatever may have been perceived as in self-interest at the instant. To an 'outsider', such behaviour could appear to have a substantial random component because inconsistencies among choices may be present. Systematic aspects of choices might exist, reflecting attention and perceptions, but they might not make sense when viewed from the perspective of a preference based model. Stage two is approached as repeated choices, practice, incentives (feedback), provide sobering and refocusing experiences. Problems of the type found in the first class of examples are no longer present in the data. Choices begin to reflect and incorporate an awareness of the environment, and can be recognized by an 'outsider' as a stable form of 'strategy' or 'decision'. The full constancy of the rational model begins to find support in the data. However, problems of the sort contained in the second class of examples can still be detected. Stage three, the final stage, is one in which choices begin to anticipate the rationality reflected in the choices of others. The fact that others might be acting rationally, and the consequences of that rationality, as it works through the interdependent fabric of social institutions, become reflected in the choices of each agent.

The observational theory might not be as empty as it would seem on first glance. A little closer look suggests that it could be filled with enough substance to alienate everyone. The hypothesis suggests that attitude like expectations, beliefs, risk-aversion and the like, are *discovered*, as are other elements of the environment. People acquire an understanding of what they want through a process of reflection and practice. In a sense, they do not know what they want and it may be costly, or even unpleasant, to go through the process of discovery. Attitude discovery is a process of evolution which has a direction, and in the final stage results in the 'discovery' of a consistent and stable preference. Thus, while the final product of the process may be a preference-like object that is very familiar to economic theory, economists seem to have very little to say about decisions that are made while it is coming into existence. So, economists have little reason to be happy with the observational theory because it suggests that the basic model has only limited applicability. Economists have a need to look elsewhere, or at least a need to look deeper into the decision process.

On the other hand, the discovered preference hypothesis seems to be inconsistent with philosophy that is being used by psychologists, but there seems to be no inconsistencies with the data produced by psychologists. Psychologists tend to distinguish their work from what they call a 'philosophy of articulated values', as opposed to a 'philosophy of basic values', which psychologists tend to embrace. The former, sometimes attributed to economists by the psychologists, would hold that people have well-formed preferences or values.[1] Choices are then made by reference to these values, which themselves are stable. By contrast, psychologists see themselves as operating under a philosophy of basic values from which preferences might be viewed as 'constructed'. The construction depends upon the mode in which a response is called. Task and context are thought to influence the construction and, as a result, preferences are thought to be labile if, indeed, they can be said to exist at all. Of course, if no preferences exist, then there is no foundation for a theory of optimization and no foundation for a theory of strategic behaviour and game theory. The idea of constructed preferences would seem to leave very little room for economics and seems to be substantially contradicted by the existence of economic models that are so powerful in applications.

If preferences are considered as having been 'discovered', rather than 'constructed', then room exists in the philosophy for the process of discovery to be influenced by the perceptions, attention, and the focus of individuals. The path of discovery could be influenced by the context of the situation, the initial conditions so to speak. Tversky, Sattath and Slovic (1988) articulate the paradox created by constructed preference theory well. 'If different elicitation procedures produce different orderings of options, how can preferences and values be defined? And in what sense do they exist?' (p. 383). The message suggested by the examples to be reviewed in the first section below is a possible answer to the question they pose. The effect of different problem frames is not so much to call forth different means of constructing attitudes, as it is to focus perceptions and attention to different features of the environment. The framing effects would then be interpreted as a filter, operating through attention and perception, which effects the information on which otherwise rational choices are made. In terms of the rational model, the framing effects would be the consequences of different information conditions and not the consequences of differently constructed preferences. Individuals' decisions (attitudes) might be labile at first; reflecting only a limited perception of the immediate environment. With practice and experience, under conditions of substantial incentives, and with the accumulating information that is obtained from the process of choice, the attitudes stabilize in the sense of a consistent decision rule, reflecting the preferences that were 'discovered' through the process. The final preferences show no evidence of being labile.

Now, there are four facts that seem to go against the discovered preference hypothesis, as refined by the above paragraphs. (i) The stages of rationality are a property of an individual. Whether or not the stages exist at all may differ from individual to individual. Furthermore, the myopia of the first stage can return if the environment changes. (ii) Some types of rationality may never be acquired naturally. In particular, the rationality that comes from an understanding of the rationality of others might be difficult for some people to comprehend without some help. (iii) Help in acquiring one type of rationality (knowledge of the rationality of others) can come in the form of special social institutions. But, if one type of rationality can be fostered by social institutions, the other types might be fostered that way as well. So, the fact that market institutions are specifically involved in the examples to be discussed might be critical to the fact that rationality/stable attitudes/ preferences evolve (or are discovered) in the first place.

Section 2 of the chapter is an elaboration of the first and second classes of behaviour. The section consists of four examples in which the rationality of other agents is not important or difficult to understand. Section 3 consists of examples of problems of the third class in which common knowledge of rationality becomes important to the functioning of the economic situation or the social process. Section 4 contains examples in which social institutions play a special role in conveying the nature of rationality of other agents in the economy. Together, these three sections describe a pattern of evidence that demonstrates a need to modify standard economic theory. They also suggest why a hypothesis of discovered preference might be more applicable than a hypothesis of constructed preference.

2   NEW TASKS AND FAMILIAR TASKS: THE BEGINNING AND THE END OF AN EXPERIMENT

Under conditions of 'substantial' incentives,[2] how does choice with an unfamiliar task compare with the choices of a familiar task? A natural setting is the beginning and the end of an experiment. The first part of an experiment almost always involves decisions with an unfamiliar task. It is not uncommon for a subject to turn to the experimenter and ask 'what am I supposed to do?' The incentives are present, but frequently the subject has never done the task before. The experimenter simply reads the relevant portion of the instructions again. After the experiment has operated for a while, the people are familiar with the task. So, a comparison of behaviour at the beginning and end of an experiment provides the data of interest.

Four examples are studied. The first three can be interpreted as 'games' with dominant strategies. Therefore, according to pure theory, the choice should be the same, independent of any experience or familiarity with the task. The fourth example is taken from a more complex setting in which a subject is operating in a continuous market, but the behaviour studied has a commonsense element of simplicity.

The behaviour exhibited in each of the examples can be interpreted as involving rather fundamental violations of rationality – at first. However, with experience, the behaviour becomes transformed into patterns that are more recognizable through the lens of preference and decision theory. If the early choices are interpreted as having been influenced by framing, then framing effects go away under the proper circumstances. The patterns of behaviour ultimately look similar across individuals and are understandable in terms of theory. Thus, the framing in these examples could also be interpreted as reflecting a type of myopia, fostered by limited information, conditioned by the nature of perceptions and attention which, with experience under suitable incentives, does not persist. Thus, according to the observational theory, the discovered preference hypothesis, the violations of rationality might be more attributable to information and search rather than how a process of cognition works.

2.1 The Preference Reversal Phenomena

The preference reversal phenomena can be most easily understood by reference to Figure 10.1. Consider an individual faced with the possibility of playing one of the

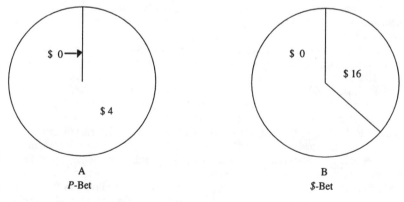

A
P-Bet

B
$-Bet

Figure 10.1 Lottery choice

two lotteries represented by the pie charts. Lottery A yields a payoff of $4.00 with almost certainty, and a payoff of $0 with the small probability, as shown. Lottery B yields a payoff of $16.00, with a payoff of a little more than .33, and a payoff of $0, otherwise. Lottery A is frequently called the P bet, because the probability of winning something is large, and lottery B is called the $ bet, because the amount is large.

When individuals are asked to choose, a large percentage will choose lottery A. However, when asked how much they would pay for the right to play the lotteries, the same individuals will pay more for the right to play lottery B. The inconsistency of the behaviour is apparent. When the individual is asked to state a preference in one way (Which would you choose?), lottery A is preferred but when asked to state preference in another way (Which is of greatest value to you?), lottery B is preferred.

This inconsistency is what psychologists have called the preference reversal phenomenon. It has been an important example of what many believe to be the labile nature of preferences and how preferences are systematically influenced by the context of decision. The inconsistency is systematic, in the sense that reversals one way (P bet is preferred when choice is the response mode, and $ bet is preferred when values are the response mode) are observed with substantially greater frequency than the opposite reversal ($ bet preferred under choice, and P bet valued higher). The preference reversal phenomenon is the *asymmetry* of the switching between the dollar bet and the P bet. The behaviour is not simply random as it might be if individuals were only making mistakes.

Recent experiments conducted by Cox and Grether (1993) inquired whether the preference reversals could be observed in market settings. They implemented an experimental design that had elements of both experimental economics and psychology. The experiments involved measuring the preferences for individuals for lotteries that have been used many times in the psychology literature. The methods of preference elicitation were those that have been used by psychologists, but Cox and Grether used experimental market situations as well. In addition, they paid off on every decision, so no decision was made on hypothetical values. The levels of incentives were on the order of those typically used in economics, as opposed to experiments found in the psychology literature, where incentives have tended not to be as large as the incentives that have been used in economics and in social choice experiments. Thus, the conditions of the experiments contained elements that are usually present in experimental markets where the rational models are observed working well.

Cox and Grether first used methods of preference elicitation that have been used in the preference reversal literature. Choice data was acquired from pairwise choices of individuals. Preference data was acquired by application of the Becker, DeGroot and Marschak procedure.[3] In addition, they used a second price auction (a market institution explained in the next section of this chapter) to obtain pricing data and they used an English clock auction (at first glance it has essential features of the Dutch clock auction) to obtain choice data. Cox and Grether describe this auction as follows: 'In this auction, the price clock starts at the amount of the win state payoff in a bet and then decreases by five cents every second. Each subject must decide whether to choose to play the bet by exiting from the auction at the price showing on the clock, or to remain in the auction. The last subject remaining in the auction receives the amount of money on the price clock when the next-to-the-last subject chooses the bet. All of the other subjects play the bet.' Thus, at each stage of the process, the individual has a choice between the money shown on the clock or the bet. When the bet is preferred to the money the individual removes himself/herself from the auction.[4]

The striking result of Cox and Grether is that the preference reversal phenomenon is clearly observed at first under all experimental conditions (markets and incentives). Then, after replication and experience under conditions of incentives and market institutions, the reversal phenomenon goes away. It is not the market setting alone that removes the reversals since reversals appear when people first participate in the markets. It is also not repetition alone (without incentives) that makes the reversals go away, since the reversals persist in the market settings when the incentives are absent. However, a combination of the repetition in a market setting with incentives will provide an environment in which the preference reversal phenomenon no longer exists. Furthermore, with repetition, the (stochastic) element of choices decreases in the sense that the number of intransitivities[5] in general goes down.

Briefly put, the Cox and Grether experiments exhibit the pattern suggested by the theory advanced in the opening section. The classical preference reversal can be seen as a product of inexperience and lack of motivation, and it goes away with experience in a market setting.

2.2 The Second Price Auction

The second price auction is a special auction in which the object is awarded to the highest bidder, but the price paid is the bid of the second highest bidder. If multiple units are sold, the bids are arrayed from the highest to the lowest. If K units are to be sold they are given to the K highest bidders, but all of the winners pay a price equal to the $K+1$ bid. If it is a selling auction, then the bids are arrayed from lowest to the highest, and the K winners all sell at a price equal to the $K+1$ bid.

From a game-theoretic perspective the optimal strategy in a second price auction is obvious. Under a wide class of environments (independent private values) the optimal strategy is to bid the individual private value. That is, the optimal strategy is to 'reveal' in the bid the 'true' willingness to pay or 'true' willingness to sell. Revelation is a dominant strategy. Yet, when confronted with the task, individuals typically do not choose the optimal. Bidding the value is a dominant strategy and not only is the logic clear, it should be clear at an intuitive level. But the obvious is not necessarily reflected in behaviour when individuals are first confronted with the task. However, after experience, as is the case with the other examples in this section of the chapter, choices converge in the direction of the choices predicted by theory to be the optimum.

The data to be viewed are generated from a typical multiple unit second price auction as it is used in applications.[6] Values are drawn independently for each agent from a uniform distribution with support [0,250]. If the value V is drawn for an individual then that individual can redeem the item for a value V with the experimenter and keep as profit the difference between the price paid for the unit and the value. In the Cox and Grether research, discussed in the previous section, the items sold were lotteries so the 'true' values are not known to the experimenter except perhaps through comparative measurements. In the example discussed in this

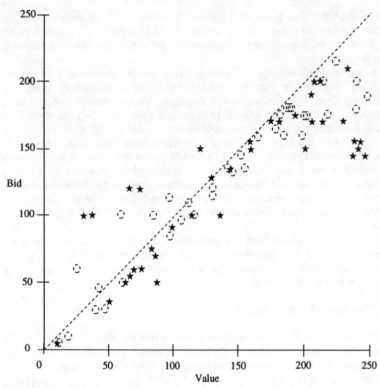

Source: Cason and Plott, 1994

Figure 10.2 Values and bids in a second price auction

section the values are known to the experimenter so deviations from true revelation can be observed.

Figure 10.2 displays the (V, bid) pairs. The ★ are data from the first three periods of the experiment, and the ☉ are the data from the last three periods. Theory (essentially) maintains that all data should be on the 45° line. Data above the line are 'irrational' by any concept in economics. Data below the line could have some interpretations, but for purposes of discussion here are not important. The important thing to observe is that the movement of the data between the first three and last three periods is toward the line. That is, the behaviour of the agents exhibits increasing rationality over the course of the experience. The model is not a perfect predictor of what people do. For example, there is ample room for speculation about why people might have bid more than the value and why such phenomena should persist even so late in the experiment as the 17th period. Nevertheless, the model does predict the exact form of the responses and not only is the movement of the data in that direction, no other model generates predictions that are of equal accuracy.

One is tempted to claim that the evolution of behaviour observed in the experiments is simply one in which subjects adopt an obvious rule-of-thumb. Is it the case that individuals are simply adopting a 'linear rule of thumb' and reflect no rationality or strategic behaviour at all? Existing data suggests that such a hypothesis can be rejected. The data are of two sorts. First, if the rules are changed from a second price auction to a first price auction then behaviour changes accordingly and in ways predicted by game theory. Secondly, experimentation exists with cases in which the predictions of game theory are decidedly nonlinear. Chen and Plott (1992) inquired about the degree of complexity that must be present in rules-of-thumb in order that they be an improvement over the nonlinear rules that are deduced from the optimization principles of game theory. Analysis shows that if (piece-wise) linear rules are going to be an improvement over the complex rules that are predicted by game theory, then the piece-wise rules must be rather complex (have several strategically chosen 'pieces'). None of the simple linear rules perform as well as does the game-theoretic model. It seems fair to say that individuals are not adopting some simplistic rule, like a markdown rule, or a rule that would 'guarantee' some profit level.

In summary, the second price auction data suggests that individual behaviour in an unfamiliar task exhibits aspects of lability and randomness. With experience and incentives, the behaviour takes a form that is more recognizable from a rational choice perspective. The example explored in the next section is a continuation of this thesis. The example is a little more complex and the nature of the 'optimal' strategy is open to more questions but the general pattern, reported so far, will be reported there as well.

2.3 Contributions to Public Goods Provision

Experiments with public goods provision take the following form. Each individual in a group is given a function in the form of a table or graph that indicates the dollar payoff to him/her as a function of the group decision regarding the magnitude of some variable X. That is, each individual i is given a payoff function $f^i(X)$ and is tested on his/her ability to understand the function. If the group chooses a level of X, say $X = 10$, then individual i receives a dollar payment from the experimenter equal to $f^i(10)$. The group choice of X is made by anonymous contributions to a fund to pay for the level of X. That is, if the contribution of individual i to the fund is x_i and if the per unit cost of the variable X is C, then the level chosen by the group is $X = (\Sigma_i x_i)/C$. The amount of dollars that individual i receives is the payoff from the level of public good provided, minus the amount of his/her own contribution to the provision. That is {net dollar payoff to i} $= f^i(X) - x_i$. The cases of interest are those in which the experience is repeated a number of times. With each repetition, the members of the group may or may not be the same, depending upon the purposes of the experiment.

The classical public goods problem, articulated by Samuelson, suggested that individuals have a dominant strategy not to voluntarily contribute to the provision of public goods. That is, the 'rational' strategy is $x_i = 0$ for all i. The situation is not unlike the Prisoner's Dilemma in which the dominant strategy Nash equilibrium is not Pareto optimal. Experimenters desiring to explore the situation carefully, chose parameters for public goods experiments such that the dominance existed.

The data from experiments indicate that substantial contributions can be observed occurring during the first part of the experiments. With replication of periods and incentives the contributions do drop off, but the data from the initial periods in which contributions occur stand in sharp contrast to a theory of rational choice which holds that the level of voluntary contributions should be zero.

An attempt to save the rational model took the form of a theory that gives preferences themselves an endogenous component. The theory is that individuals have a 'cooperative' nature. Their first instincts are to be 'truthful' about what they want. According to this revised theory of rational choice, individuals 'truthfully reveal' their most desired outcome and do what they can to make it happen. One could say that the 'frame' is one in which cooperation through giving is an obvious thing to do, so people do it. For several years the data were accepted as having been explained by this theory of endogenous, or 'home grown' attitudes.

It appears now, that the apparent support of this theory of truthful revelation is a consequence of the randomness of initial choice behaviour supported by an artifact of the experimental design. All of the early experiments were similar. In particular, the optimal strategic (Nash) response under the parameters studied was a choice of zero contribution to the public good. Choices below zero were not permitted by virtue of the structure of the strategy space, and choices above zero were interpreted as reflecting cooperative/truthful responses. Stated this way, the potential for a misinterpretation of the behaviour is obvious. Any pure randomness of responses, resulting from confusion, or lack of reflection, would show up as a positive contribution to the public good and would, thus, be counted as evidence of cooperation and truthful response. Thus, an alternative theory that the data reveal Nash response with an error, has emerged as a competitor to the theory that people are naturally cooperative.

The data from the older literature cannot be used to untangle the two theories. However, the newer literature is more successful. The data from new public goods experiments suggests the hypothesis that the behaviour of people, when initially confronted with the task, is neither cooperative nor truthful. Instead, the behaviour first exhibited by people is consistent with the hypothesis that it reflects large random components derived from lack of decisiveness as an individual works his/her way through the information. As an individual gains experience with the task, considered decisions begin to emerge.

Unfortunately, there are not many papers to review. The possibility that random behaviour could be misinterpreted as cooperative behaviour has not gone without notice,[7] but the problem has not been a high priority among experimentalists.

The relevant experiments are those in which the Nash equilibrium is not on the lower boundary of the strategy set. In two papers Nash equilibria on the upper boundary of the strategy set are studied (Saijo and Yamaguchi, 1996; Palfrey and Prisbrey, 1993a and 1993b). Under such parameters the Nash strategies are also the strategies that would be chosen under a cooperative strategy, or an 'other regarding' strategy. Choices of contributions less than the Nash contribution must result from some other process of choice. In the first study (Saijo and Nakamura), the contributions are below the Nash (self-interested) responses, starting with the first period. While the choices are interpreted by the authors of the study as being 'spiteful', the data also support the interpretation that the choices reflect a fundamental randomness. Of course, random elements would look virtually the same, so the two interpretations of the data cannot be separated. In the second study in which the Nash equilibrium is on the upper boundary (Palfrey and Prisbrey), the data are near the Nash equilibrium from the very first period. As a result, little changes in individual behaviour are observed over the course of the experiment.

In two additional papers (Walker, Gardner and Ostrom, 1990; Andreoni, 1993) the Nash equilibrium was placed strictly on the interior of the strategy set. Random behaviour could be on either side of the Nash response. Presumably, initial attempts to be cooperative would result in choices that begin with contributions above the Nash and then coverage toward Nash with replication of the experience. In both studies decisions are on the non-cooperative side of Nash at first, and then converge toward the Nash response after replication of experience.

Thus, all four studies suggest that responses have a substantial variance during the first periods. The variance can result in choices on either side of Nash and thus can appear as either cooperative or as spiteful behaviour. The variance falls over time and settles near the Nash response with repetition of the experience. The exception is the Palfrey and Prisbrey study in which the responses are near Nash from the start, do not have such a large variance at first, and do not change with repetition. Briefly put, none of these studies support the idea of 'truthful' revelation as an overriding and general property of the initial responses of people in a public goods experiment.[8] Instead, the studies support the idea that what has appeared to be a tendency toward truthfulness is actually something else. The initial choices of individuals have a random component. With experiences and incentives, game-theoretic principles tend to emerge.

2.4 The Continuous Double Auction and the *Hvatat* Phenomena

The next example is taken from markets that operate in continuous time. From a theoretical point of view, optimal behaviour is unknown, but behaviour is observed that is both systematic and difficult to rationalize with any concept of optimality other than what might result from a type of myopia. The example is particularly interesting because it demonstrates how market-level phenomena can be affected by the decision behaviour of one or two individuals who seem to be deviating from the ordinarily accepted rules of rationality.

As part of a process of establishing a programme of experimental economics in Moscow, researchers began with a project of attempting to replicate phenomena that have been widely observed in laboratory economics in the west (Menshikov, Menshikova and Plott, 1993). The project involved several different subject pools from Moscow, which participated in classical computerized multiple-unit double auctions. The basic choice of parameters also involved a single upward shift of demand and supply that was not anticipated by the subjects. The purpose of the shift was simply to document the ability of the model to predict the actual time path of the market. The parameters also involved an asymmetry between demand and supply of a sort that ordinarily causes the observed prices to converge to equilibrium from above, and the experimental design also called for an occasional imposition of non-binding price ceilings that are known to affect market dynamics.

The markets converged to the competitive equilibrium, but the surprising result from the experiments was that the price variance in some experiments was much

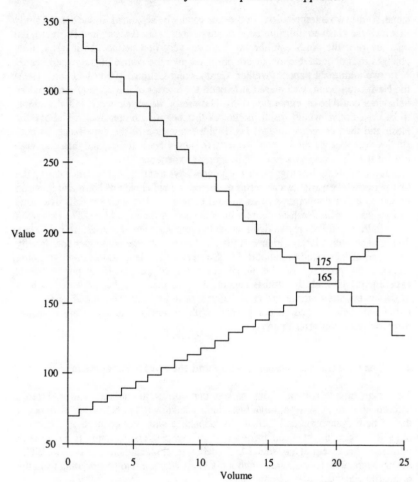

Figure 10.3 Demand and supply

higher than has been observed in the west. Furthermore, the expected features of market dynamics, the direction of convergence and the reaction to price ceilings, were not observed. Close scrutiny of the data resulted in the discovery of types of individual subject behaviour that, upon reflection, has been observed in the west but not to such a pronounced extent.

Hvatat in Russian means 'to grab'. The individuals in these experiments had no experience with market economies and with the related rules. They grew up in an economy in which prices were frequently fixed at levels that were too low and, as a result, shortages were a part of daily experience. The habits of the population included a propensity to acquire anything of value at any time that it was

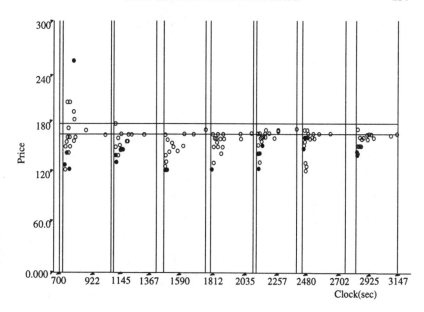

Figure 10.4 All contracts

encountered, in the hope that it could be used or traded for something else. If the act of acquisition was not quick (*hvatat*) someone else would have it and the opportunity would be gone. The term *hvatat* became applied to behaviour in experiments because the Russian scientists saw the behaviour in the experiments as analogous to behaviour they observed in the society around them. The behaviour is by no means irrational, but it does reflect a special type of training or expectation on the part of the subjects.

Once the proper patterns of behaviour had been identified, one naturally looked for similar patterns in data from the western markets and, once attention was so directed, examples were easy to find. The example to be considered here is a double auction experiment that was conducted with students from the California Institute of Technology. This market experiment is the same as many that have been conducted in the west and, except for a few details of the parameters, it is the same as the experiments that were conducted in Moscow.

The induced demand and supply functions are shown in Figure 10.3. The time series of contract prices is shown in Figure 10.4. The vertical axis is the price of the contract, and the horizontal axis measures clock time in seconds so the figure shows the seconds at which contracts took place. The horizontal lines represent the upper and lower bounds of the set of competitive equilibria for this simple market that are shown in Figure 10.3, at the intersection of the demand and supply curves.

Even an untrained eye will notice that the prices tend to converge to near the competitive equilibrium. This is the power of the double auction that is observed universally. What the untrained eye might not notice is the variance of the market prices. The reader is asked to take on faith that the variability of prices in this market

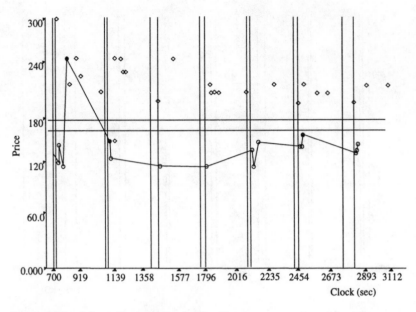

Figure 10.5   Asks and contracts of seller 10

is high relative to most market experiments, whether conducted in the east or the west. Close examination of the data suggests that the variability seems to be due to the actions of a select few people. In particular, the contracts of seller number 10 in Figure 10.4 are filled in with black.

Figure 10.4 shows clearly that seller 10 managed to sell at the lowest prices almost every period. In fact, a study of the figure will show that all the sales of seller 10 are below the average of the prices that existed in the market in any period. Relative to other sellers, and relative to the prices that existed in the market, seller 10 is performing poorly at making profits.

The pattern of behaviour that leads to this relatively unprofitable behaviour can be interpreted as having resulted from a type of myopia. First, this individual tends to react to the environment as opposed to acting on it. In order to see this property, examine Figure 10.5 which contains the activities of seller 10. In the double auction sellers are free to send asks to the market which they hope some buyers will take and buyers send bids to the market. A contract can be made by the seller accepting the bid of a buyer or a buyer accepting the ask of some seller. The asks and the contracts of seller 10 are shown in the figure at the time when they occurred. The asks tendered by seller 10 are the diamonds and the contracts are the circles. A circle filled with black is a contract in which an ask of seller 10 was accepted by some bidder and the open circles are contracts in which seller 10 accepted a bid of some buyer. As is clear, seller 10, for the most part, accepts bids offered by buyers. In the entire experiment seller 10 had only three of his asks taken by a buyer. On all other occasions seller 10 accepted bids.

Secondly, the individual does not seem to understand how to be successful in

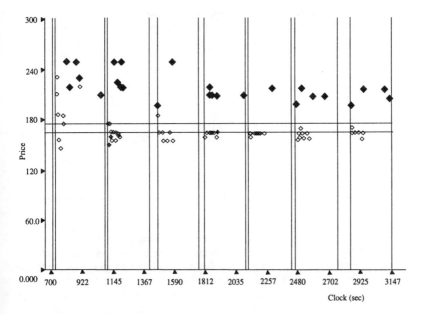

Figure 10.6   Asks of sellers 9 and 10

acting within the environment. From Figure 10.5, the reader can see that the asks of seller 10 have a tendency to be 'away from the market'. This seller's asks, represented by the diamonds in the figure, are much too high to be accepted with any reasonable frequency. The asks tend to be unrealistic above the levels at which trades are taking place, and no well-placed asks are tendered by the individual. In order to see this, study Figure 10.6 which displays the asks of seller 10 as black-filled diamonds, along with the asks of seller 9 whose pattern of asks are typical for the sellers and are shown as open diamonds. As can be seen, the asks of seller 9 are close to the competitive equilibrium and are strategically chosen to be close to the market, with a realistic expectation that one would be accepted. By contrast, the asks of seller 10 are all well removed above all the market activity.

Third, seller 10 tends to act quickly to 'grab' opportunities with little regard to the opportunity cost or the possible consequences if considered over a 'long' horizon. It is as if the individual sees an opportunity to make an instantaneous gain and grabs it with little regard for the benefits that might accrue to a more considered action. This type of quickness tends to be reinforcing because it prevents the individual from surveying what is happening in the environment and thereby tends to deflect attention from information that might result in a change in the behaviour.

The quickness can be seen in all the figures. Seller 10 tends to make trades in the first parts of all periods. Table 10.1 provides some descriptive statistics for sellers 6 and 10, both of whom have a tendency to trade at the low prices. The table gives the number of trades that occurred in the first thirty seconds of a (six-minute) period and the number of trades that occurred in the whole (six-minute) period, for all sellers

Table 10.1   Units traded by period by segment of period: select individuals

Period								
	1	*2*	*3*	*4*	*5*	*6*	*7*	*Total*
1st 30 seconds total volume	5	8	9	6	8	10	7	53
6, 10 volume	4	5	4	2	4	5	5	29
Period total volume	22	19	21	21	22	20	19	144
6, 10 volume	7	6	5	6	8	6	7	45

and for sellers 6 and 10 considered as a pair. On average, 31 per cent of the total market volume occurs in the first 30 seconds of the six-minute period. About 55 per cent of the total volume of the six sellers that occurs in the first thirty seconds is due to two sellers alone, sellers 6 and 10 who sell 64 per cent of their volume in these opening seconds. These two sellers are quick to unload their volume even though this is the time when prices are lowest, as can be seen by a return to Figure 10.4.

The pattern described is the following. The seller is quick to act. The seller accepts the terms offered by a buyer and is not aggressive in offering terms himself in the form of asks, and seldom places a successful ask. The individual reacts quickly to take what is offered without 'negotiating' or considering what alternatives might be presented. It is interesting to note that this behaviour is a consistent property of an individual and is not a property of a group, or the random behaviour of members of a group. The Russians have called such individuals 'rabbits' and theorize that people who are not so myopic develop characteristics of 'wolves' who anticipate rabbit behaviours and set traps with selective bids. An attempt to identify 'wolf' behaviour would involve an excessive deviation from the general theme of this chapter and so the idea will drop here. With or without the wolves, the rabbits tend to act less impulsively as time and experience take place. The price patterns tend to lose the variance and the whole system tends to converge to the equilibrium as predicted by the competitive model.

3   OTHER AGENTS AND THE PROBLEM OF KNOWLEDGE OF RATIONALITY

From time to time, over the years, complicated experiments have been conducted that did not work out exactly as expected, in theory. The perplexing aspects of the experiments were frequently reported as a curiosity, along with the other results that were understandable. Looking back over these experiments, in the light of the advance and refinements of experimental techniques, and a growing number and types of experiments, general patterns tend to suggest themselves. One such pattern seems to be due to a lack of understanding on the part of some agents, of the motivations, intentions, and behaviour of other agents that are participants in the process. Formally, within the context of game-theoretic models, the patterns seem to be due to the possibility that rationality is not common knowledge. Six examples of possible cases can be listed that may prove to be cases.

3.1 Mixed Strategies

The observed lack of independence in mixed strategies is the first example. The aggregated choices of agents participating in conflicts, for which the game-theoretic model has no pure strategy equilibrium, are well approximated by the mixed strategy equilibrium of the game. However, the strategies of an individual do not have the property of independence that is crucial for the security property that the mixed strategy is supposed to provide. If other players are believed to be fully rational, then the independence is necessary.

3.2 Agendas and Voting

The second example comes from agenda theory and the operation of committee processes. An agenda can be imposed as a partitioning of the options into subsets for discussion and voting. For example, if the options were indexed by the letters of the alphabet, then a motion could be that the group choose a vowel. If the motion passes then further motions are restricted to the set $\{(a,e,i,o,u)\}$. If the original motion fails, then (depending upon the exact wording of the original motion) the deliberations are restricted to the set of consonants, and additional motions will be to restrict that set. As the motions continue, sets are removed from further consideration until only one option is left. The agendas are usually applied to a finite set of options that are not labelled with letters or numbers, so the actual motions are typically something that would make sense to an ordinary human. The example is intended only to carry the intuition that an agenda is a refinement of partitions of a finite set, such that at the end of each branch is a single element. The committee process is then a series of votes, each of which will eliminate a set of options until only one option remains as the committee choice.

The influence of the agenda on committee decisions is well documented. It is possible to design agendas that can get the group to choose almost anything that the designer desires. This phenomenon is not related to the classical cyclical majorities. Even if all members of the group have the same preference, the agenda designer can still have considerable power.

The power of the agenda seems to depend on tight control of the information that individuals in the group have, and it depends on aspects of 'myopia' that the theory presupposes exists in individuals in the group. First, the theory assumes that the individual chooses randomly among three decisions rules: (i) vote for the set that contains the most preferred option; (ii) vote against the set that contains the least preferred option; (iii) vote for the set that contains the highest average 'payoff' of options. The data show that if individual decisions are restricted to these three rules then individuals are using different rules at each of the different stages of voting. Second, the theory assumes that the probability with which a decision rule is used is independent of past votes. That is, the theory treats individuals as if they have random features of behaviour and that individuals completely ignore the behaviour of others. The fact that others might be behaving rationally, and that the rationality of others has consequences for one's own voting behaviour, is not part of the model. Now, the agenda model was not developed to study rationality, or the lack of it in individuals or in groups. It was developed as a tool to manipulate groups and to help individuals understand the subtle ways that they might be manipulated by others. The model operates by letting the agenda designer deduce a probability over the outcomes that depends upon the agenda (and the behavioural probabilities used). Thus, the agenda designer can find the agenda that maximizes the probability that the group chooses some option that the designer wants chosen. Whether or not the lack of rationality in the model is aesthetically pleasing is not particularly important because the model works. It is an effective tool for the job for which it was invented. The assumed myopia on the part of voters is simply part of the machinery that helps it do its job.

3.3 Winner's Curse

The Winner's Curse is another example in which knowledge of the rationality of others seems to be a missing element of individual decisions. The Winner's Curse, first observed by Kagel and Levin (1986), occurs in what are called common value, first price auctions. Briefly put, and contrary to theory, in these auctions the winners repeatedly lose money. Furthermore, it does not seem to go away with experience.

A value of an object is randomly determined. For example, a value is drawn from $0 to $300 and the individual who buys the object can resell it to the experimenter for the value drawn. Suppose the value of the object is $V = \$150$. The value is unknown to all bidders at the time that bids must be tendered, but each individual is given a personal 'clue' to the value. That is, for each individual a clue is drawn from a uniform distribution with support $[V - E, V + E]$ where E is some constant known to all individuals. For example, suppose $E = \$30$. If individual i is given the clue $170, then the individual knows that the true value of the object is somewhere in the interval [$170 − $30, $170 + $30] and must formulate a bid for the object based on that formation, together with the knowledge that other individuals are receiving clues that are independently drawn from the same distribution.

The winner is the person that bids the highest and, almost without exception, the winner pays more for the object than the object is worth. The theory of bidding requires that the individual must realize that people with the highest clues are going to be the ones that bid the most. This follows from rationality. But, this means that the person with the highest clue will be the winner and, almost certainly, the person with the highest clue will have a clue that lies above the true value of the object. Thus, in bidding the individual must 'scale back' the bid to condition on an appropriate order statistic. The individual must realize that if he/she has the highest bid, then he/she also has a clue that is greater than the value of the object. Kagel and Levin postulate that the winner's curse results from an inappropriate scaling back, if not a complete neglect of the consequences of the rationality of others.

3.4 Lemons in Markets

A fourth example comes from experiments that are designed to explore the possibility of markets for 'lemons' – as in used cars, not fruit (Lynch, Miller, Plott, and Porter, 1991). In these experiments, sellers of an object have an option of delivering two different qualities of the thing. A seller can deliver a 'super' grade, which is valued highly by the buyers, but also is costly to the sellers, or, the seller can deliver a 'regular' grade that is less desirable to the buyers, but the cost is much less to the sellers.

Given the parameters chosen for the experiment, only supers would be produced and sold in the market if the quality of the commodity was known to the buyer at the time of the sale. The regulars are the lemons. Several different conditions of information have been studied but, for purposes of the discussion here, the interesting experiments are those in which the quality was unknown to the buyer at the time of the sale. The quality was determined after the sale by the seller. Furthermore, there were never discussions between the buyer and the seller, and the buyer did not know the identity of the seller at the time of the sale or at any time after that.

The incentives of the seller under such conditions is clear, at least from the point of view of the theory. The seller has an incentive to offer at a high price hoping that the buyer will think that the seller will deliver a super and take the deal, and then the seller will deliver a regular. Buyers, understanding the motivation of the sellers, will never assume that the seller will deliver a super and only engage in deals that will be profitable if a regular is delivered. The net result should be that only regulars are delivered at prices that fully reflect the fact that only regulars will be delivered. The market will be filled with 'lemons' and sold at prices that reflect the fact that the buyers know that they are buying lemons.

When the buyers first encounter the situation, many pay the high prices as if they were buying a super quality and knew it. This phenomenon occurred in all subject pools of the experiments. The buyers did not apply the rationality logic contained in the paragraph above. On the other hand, sellers responded as anticipated by theory. Only regulars were delivered by the sellers. The experience after the first period or two fostered a dramatic change of behaviour in the buyers. Buyers would find caution immediately and prices would drop. In some subject pools the prices would cave immediately after the first period to near the price that would exist if buyers knew for certain that a regular would be delivered. However, in one subject pool, the prices would drop after the first period but, even after eight periods, prices were still too high, suggesting that the buyers really did not understand the seller's motivations. Buyers were simply treating the market as a lottery in which some probability of a super existed. After several experiences in such markets, and different days of experimentation – each involving several periods – the behaviour of the buyers began to reflect an understanding of the motivations of the sellers. Such an understanding was not immediate by virtue of buyers having reasoned their way through the situation. For some subjects it took a lot of experience and time. The rationality was not common knowledge.

3.5 The Centipede Game

The Centipede Game is a process in which two individuals participate in a finite sequence of moves. The options at each move include two amounts of money (x, y) with $x > 2y$. The chooser can take one (the highest) of the amounts of money, leaving the other amount for the other person and, thereby, ending the game; or, he/she can pass the choice back to the other person. If the choice is passed back, both amounts of money double and the second person has the choice. The game

Table 10.2   Decisions in Centipede Game

$ Amounts of money	.40 .10	.80 .20	1.60 .40	3.20 .80	6.40 1.60	12.80 3.20	25.60 6.40
Choosing individual	1	2	1	2	1	2	1
Trials 1–5							
No. of people choosing	145	145	137	112	64	16	4
No. of terminations	0	8	25	48	48	12	
Probability of termination	0	.06	.18	.43	.75	.81	
Trials 6–10							
No. of people choosing	136	134	124	93	33	10	1
No. of terminations	2	10	31	60	23	9	
Probability of termination	.01	.07	.25	.65	.70	.90	

Source: McKelvey and Palfrey (1992).

continues for a finite and known number of stages.

The only game (perfect information, Nash) theoretic solution is for the first chooser to take the money and stop the game. If both individuals are rational, then the logic of backward induction can be applied. Working backward at each stage, the logic is that if the game reaches that stage then it should stop there. The logic works back from the end of the game to the beginning of the game.

The Centipede Game shown in Table 10.2 was studied by McKelvey and Palfrey (1992). The game started with the amount {$.40, $.10} and if it continued to the final stage the amounts would have grown to {$25.60, $6.40} The data are partitioned into two sets according to the experience that the subject had with the game. Each subject played the game ten times with ten different people. The results of the first 5 games are at the top of the table and the results of the second 5 games are at the bottom.

Each game could have involved seven choices. The table indicates the number of games that had terminated at a given stage. For example, in the first five games no game terminated at the first choice. The probability of termination goes up as the stage increases. For example, if a game reached the 4th stage the probability of termination at that stage was .43. However, in the second five games, after individuals had experienced the first five, the probability of termination if the game reached the 4th stage was .65.

Notice that even in the second ten games, only 1 per cent of the games terminated at the first move. The tendency to terminate moves forward as individuals gain experience, but it would appear that the presumption of common knowledge of rationality cannot be supported by these results.

3.6   Bubbles in Assets Markets

The final example in this section is from experiments motivated by financial markets. Consider an asset with a fifteen-period life. Each period of its life it pays a

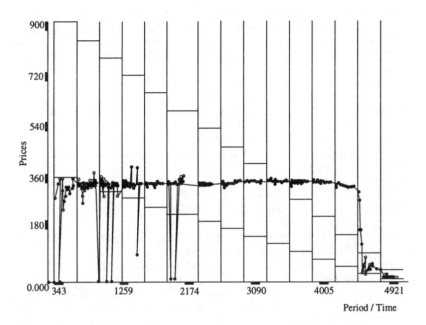

Figure 10.7 Asset market price time series

dividend drawn with equal probability from the set {$.60, $.28, $.08, $.00}. Since the expected value of the dividend is $.24 each period, the draws are independent and the life is fifteen periods, the fundamental value of a unit of the asset is $3.60 before the first dividend is paid. The fundamental value then drops by $.24 each period because of the payment of the dividend and the consequent reduction in the number of dividends left to be paid.

The dividend structure is common knowledge. Each subject is tested for understanding and has a chart in front of him/her from which the fundamental values can be read. The charts are explained publicly. Furthermore, at the end of each period the individuals record the fundamental values when computing the value of what they hold. There should be no misunderstanding about the values of the dividends or the fundamental value of the asset.

At the beginning of the experiment each individual is given an endowment of the asset and/or cash, so securities can be bought or sold as the individual might want. The market was a computerized double auction at the California Institute of Technology and the subjects were knowledgeable about the operations of an electronic market.

The time series of trades are contained in Figure 10.7. The prices are on the vertical axis and time in seconds is on the horizontal. The two lines sloping from upper left to lower right bound the possible values. The lower line is the fundamental value that starts at $3.60 and falls by $.24 each period. The upper line represents the maximum possible dividends. That is, the line represents the value of the asset if it paid the maximum possible each period of the remaining periods of its life.

The time series of trades is dramatic. Prices move quickly through the fundamental expected value and stabilize with a slight inflation. The high prices continue until the fourteenth period when a violent market crash occurs. Prior to the crash, prices were above even the maximum that could be paid by dividends. This behaviour is in stark contrast to a very natural theory which maintains that by applying backward induction, depending on the rationality of all people at each step, the price should have been approximately the fundamental value in each period. However, if an individual thinks that the price will stay high across any two periods it will pay to buy the asset, collect the dividend, and sell the asset back for what was paid for it. The dividend will thus be obtained for free.

If people do not think that all other people are rational then it might pay to speculate. According to Smith, Suchanik, and Williams (1988), the backward induction tends to work after subjects have experience with each other. They maintain that common knowledge of rationality is acquired by observation and experience. The problem is directly related to the 'swing back hypothesis' that was first observed by Forsythe, Palfrey, and Plott (1982).

The problem with other minds and other people is beginning to surface as economic theory and experiments begin to explore deeply into situations of asymmetric information. Social processes have the capacity to integrate information that is known only privately and is disbursed throughout the economy. Common knowledge of rationality is a cornerstone of how such processes might work. Experimental work suggests that this is the most difficult level of rationality and cannot be found reliably in many people and may be acquired only through experience.

On the other hand, perhaps rationality is not common knowledge because rationality is not a fact. Some people may behave in strange ways for the reasons outlined in this chapter. If that is the case, then how can the models be modified to account for it? Experimentalists have begun to explore the implications of the idea advanced by Kreps, Milgrom, Roberts, and Wilson (1982). The hypothesis that irrationalities exist, and that a known probability exists that you may be involved with such a type, has begun to be systematically integrated into the behavioural models. The probability is then treated to the complete menu of rationality in a striking and analysis by El-Gamal, McKelvey, and Palfrey (1993, 1994b).

4   SPECIAL INSTITUTIONS AND THE SOCIAL FORMATION OF RATIONALITY

Economists and political scientists typically study social behaviour in a framework of institutions. The special role that these institutions play in shaping rational choice may be more important than is commonly understood. It could be that the social institutions reflect, and may even be built from internal processes that shape outward forms of rationality. The thesis advanced here is that social institutions must help individuals, as a group, overcome three problems: (i) myopia, (ii) a problem of perception that is closely related to myopia, and (iii) a problem related to the public nature of rationality. The instruments that work, in the sense of fostering efficient interactions, have solved or contribute to the solution of those three problems.

Four examples of such institutions are closely related to the examples explored in the section above. Each institution calls attention to the information that it contains.

There is nothing subtle about the signal that is conveyed. Each institution carries information about the preferences of some other agent, or group of agents, in the system. Each institution involves a complete account of the fact the individual whose preferences are suggested is prepared to act on those preferences. If the institution is functioning properly, little is left to the imagination about what might be going on in the other person's mind.

In agenda process and committee, in the absence of the possibility of a caucus, or other institutions that allow meetings of subgroups, a critical institution is the straw vote on issues that are scheduled to be voted upon later. Now, straw votes can involve cheap talk, but under conditions in which information about the preferences are restricted to no other source, the talk is not cheap. If the agenda is tightly controlled, then committee members have no opportunity to form coalitions, or even to determine if other people exist who might be willing to coordinate strategies. Straw votes are a way in which individuals can find each other and signal intent. In committee experiments straw votes are thought to undo much of the power of the agenda. The advice to those who are using the agenda for purposes of manipulation is to avoid straw votes. In essence, the straw vote changes the order of the agenda by letting people know now what will happen when the subsequent stage of decision is reached. The straw vote helps the individual solve the backward induction problem, but because of the possibility of cheap talk, it is not an ideal vehicle.

The 'lemons' problem, described as the fourth example in the section above, can be solved by the institution of enforceable warranties. Express warranties, if offered by the seller, and if enforceable, will do the trick. The seller guarantees that if a lemon (a 'regular' in the language of the experiment) is delivered, it will be replaced by a high-quality item (a 'super') at no cost to the buyer. The buyer, seeing the precommitment by the seller and knowing the interest of the seller is to deliver a non-lemon, will buy as if the quality of the item is known. In effect, the buyer is accepting the rationality of the seller and is using that knowledge to form his/her own decisions. The prices will reflect the certainty. The sellers will not deliver lemons and the system will be removed from the inefficient lemons equilibrium. Thus, the express warranty performs a function in the system of changing the strategy of the seller and letting the buyer know that it is in the interest of the seller to change.

Two examples of special institutions can be taken from financial markets. The first example is a futures market which addresses the problem of bubbles and crashes, demonstrated in the section above. The bubble seems to be due to an incapacity of the system to support a process of backward induction. If some individual is 'confused', then he/she might buy in one of the final periods, even if prices are 'too high'. That possibility, at any stage, will circumvent the backwards induction process. A futures market solves that problem. The purchase and sale of futures contracts signals intent and commitment at the later stages of the game. An individual participating in the early periods of the market, who sees that the futures market is low for the later periods, knows that the spot price will be low when the future time arrives.[9] Thus, the information about futures prices or, more specifically, information about the plans of other agents in the market, that would otherwise not become known until the future date arrived, are brought to the present by the instrument. The futures price is prominent and calls attention to itself. The meaning of the futures price is not difficult to ascertain. It is a sale now for delivery in the future. There is no speculation about what people might do in the future because they have already precommitted to those decisions. The rationality is revealed.

The second example from finance is technical but it is worthy of mention. It is known that compound securities can have difficulties in achieving 'state revealing' rational expectations equilibria. Decomposition of the compound security into state contingent, 'Arrow–Debreu' securities solves the problem. Under conditions of a single compound security, market prices do not necessarily reveal the state. However, if the compound security is decomposed into equivalent Arrow–Debreu securities the state is revealed almost instantaneously. The problem of state revelation with a single compound security can also be solved if adequate preference information about agents in the economy is publicly available, and if the agents have adequate experience. The process of revelation is slow as experience is accumulated. Whereas, if the state contingent commodities are used, the system moves to efficiency almost immediately. Since the state contingent securities are similar to options, the result leads to a renewed interest in the functions of options in financial markets.

5 CONCLUDING REMARKS

The general thesis of this chapter is that rationality can be understood as a process of discovery, the discovered preference hypothesis. Behaviour seems to go through stages of rationality that begin with a type of myopia when faced with unfamiliar tasks. With incentives and practice, which take the form of repeated decisions in the experimental work (but might include play, banter, discussions with others, stages of commitment, etc.), the myopia gives way to what appears to be a stage of more considered choices that reflect stable attitudes or preference (as opposed to the labile attitudes identified by psychologists). Social institutions are seen as playing an important role in the attainment of a third stage at which individual decisions might incorporate the rationality of others, or the lack of it.

The dialogue that has been taking place in the literature has involved a search for a manifestation in markets of the effects of preference lability that psychologists have identified in the study of individual choices. In Sections 2 and 3 several such effects were identified. Even the behaviour of the double auction market process contains elements of the effects of idiosyncratic features of individual choices. The *hvatat* phenomenon does effect the market. However, these labile aspects of choice seem to yield to another mode of behaviour and suggest that the lability is due more to perception and information processing, as opposed to some fundamental aspect of the way that cognition works.

The final stage of rationality can be facilitated by special institutions. But, if institutions can play such a role in forming rationality at the market, or at the group level, a possibility exists that institutions operating at the level of the individual could be important, as well. Perhaps the stability of market processes themselves are heavily dependent on institutions of one sort or another. The striking results of Gode and Sunder (1993), who demonstrate that markets populated with randomly behaving agents, still contain elements of convergence and efficiency. In other words, in the context of the double auction institution, with the supporting institutions of a budget constraint and equal access to the market, agents can act with substantial arbitrariness and the process will still maintain power to exhaust much of the gains from trade. For some purposes, the minimal addition of institutional constraint might be adequate to foster acceptable economic and political behaviour, even in the absence of the full rationality contained in models of such processes.

Notes

1. This attribution is not correct. The economic literature contains many references to basic preferences, including preferences over attributes, from which other preferences are derived. The whole field of decision theory is devoted to a study of deductions from primitive notions of preferences to complex spaces of alternative acts.
2. 'Substantial' typically means that the individual has an opportunity to make about twice the amount that would be made in the individual's ordinary job.
3. For a detailed account of how this incentive compatible preference elicitation procedure is used, see Grether and Plott (1979).
4. Some question always exists about whether the response mode was a 'choice task' or a 'pricing task'. The fact that Cox and Grether replicate the reversal phenomenon seems to remove controversies of this nature. The data produced by the clock modes are those that are supposed to be produced by the choice modes.
5. The measure of the number of intransitivities is the same as that used by Tversky, Slovic and Kahneman (1990).
6. This means that the conditions of the theory are not faithfully imposed in this experiment. In particular, the buyers are acquiring more than one unit and a variable number of units is being sold. Thus, if one wants to see a clear test of the theory these data are not appropriate. Nevertheless, except for the 'near extra marginal units' which should be those with the lowest values, the optimal strategy is to bid value. Bids should never be above value.
7. The most recent review of the public goods experimental literature has a special section on this issue. See Ledyard (1994).
8. The work of Isaac and Walker (1988a, 1988b) with very large groups, stands as a stark counter-example to this general proposition. Some speculation exists that experimental control (or the lack of it), over very large groups, is a contributing factor to the results. Isaac and Walker are continuing a research programme designed to investigate all such possibilities.
9. Analysis of institutions, like futures markets, must be sensitive to special features that might exist with some variations of the institution. In some markets, futures contracts must be covered. An individual cannot be 'short'. Speculation that the short position is too large can itself be a source of speculation and will interact with the market in ways that will prevent the backward induction process.

References

Andreoni, J. (1993) 'An Experimental Test of the Public Goods Crowding-Out Hypothesis', *American Economic Review*, vol. 83, pp. 1317–27.

Cason, T.N. and C.R. Plott (1994) 'EPA's New Emissions Trading Mechanism: A Laboratory Evaluation', California Institute of Technology SSWP 863, Pasadena, CA. *A Journal of Environmental Economics and Management* (forthcoming).

Chen, K-Y. and C.R. Plott (1992) 'Nonlinear Behaviour in Sealed Bid First Price Auctions', California Institute of Technology SSWP 774, Pasadena, CA. Submitted to *Games and Economic Behavior*.

Cox, J.C. and D.M. Grether (1993) 'The Preference Reversal Phenomenon: Response Mode,

Markets and Incentives', California Institute of Technology SSWP 810, Pasadena, (A. *Economic Theory* (forthcoming).

El-Gamal, M.A., R.D. McKelvey and T.R. Palfrey (1994) 'Learning in Experimental Games',. *Economic Theory*, vol. 4, pp. 901–22.

El-Gamal, M.A., R.D. McKelvey and T.R. Palfrey (1993) 'A Bayesian Sequential Experimental Study of Learning in Games', *Journal of the American Statistical Association*, vol. 88, pp. 428–35.

Forsythe, R.E, T.R. Palfrey and C.R. Plott (1982) 'Asset Valuation in an Experimental Market', *Econometrica*, vol. 50 pp. 537–67.

Gode, D.K. and S. Sunder (1989) 'Human and Artificially Intelligent Traders in Computer Double Auctions', Carnegie-Mellon, GSIA Working Paper.

Gode, D.K. and S. Sunder (1993) 'Allocative Efficiency of Markets with Zero Intelligence Traders: Market as a Partial Substitute for Individual Rationality', *Journal of Political Economy* vol. 101, pp. 119–37.

Grether, D.M. and C.R. Plott (1979), 'Economic Theory of Choice and the Preference Reversal Phenomenon', *American Economic Review*, vol. 69, pp. 623–38.

Isaac, R.M. and J.M. Walker (1988a) 'Communication and Free Riding Behaviour: The Voluntary Contribution Mechanism', *Economic Inquiry* vol. 26, pp. 585–608.

Isaac, R.M. and J.M. Walker (1988b) 'Group Size Effects in Public Goods Provision: The Voluntary Contributions Mechanism', *The Quarterly Journal of Economics*, vol. 103, pp. 179–99.

Kagel, J.H. and D. Levin (1986) 'The Winner's Curse and Public Information in Common Value Auctions', *American Economic Review*, vol. 76, pp. 894–920.

Kreps, D.M., P. Milgrom, J. Roberts and R. Wilson (1982) 'Rational Cooperation in the Finitely Repeated Prisoners' Dilemma', *Journal of Economic Theory*, vol. 27, pp. 245–52.

Ledyard, J.O. (1994) 'Public Goods: A Survey of Experimental Research', California Institute of Technology SSWP 861, Pasadena, August 1993. Forthcoming in A.E. Roth and J.H. Kagel (eds), *The Handbook of Experimental Economics*.

Lynch, M., R.M. Miller, C.R. Plott and R. Porter (1991) 'Product Quality, Informational Efficiency and Regulations in Experimental Markets in R.M. Isaac (ed.) Research in Experimental Economics, vol. 4 (Greenwich, Conn. JA1 Press) pp. 269–318.

McKelvey, R.D. and T.R. Palfrey (1992) 'An Experimental Study of the Centipede Game', *Econometrica*, vol. 60 pp. 803–36.

Menshikov, I., O. Menshikova and C.R. Plott (1993) 'From Non Market Attitudes to Market Behavior: Laboratory Market Experiments in Moscow' (Mimeo).

Palfrey, T. and J. Prisbrey (1993a) 'Anomalous Behavior in Linear Public Goods Experiments: How Much and Why?', California Institute of Technology SSWP 833, Pasadena, CA.

Palfrey T.R. and J.E. Prisbrey (1993b) 'Althuism, Reputation and Noise in Linear Public Goods Experiments, California Institute of Technology SSWP 864, Pasadena, CA., *Journal of Public Economics* forthcoming.

Saijo, T. and T. Yamaguchi (1992) 'The "Spite" Dilemma in Voluntary Contribution Mechanism Experiments', *Journal of Conflict Resolution*, forthcoming.

Smith, V.L., G.L. Suchanek and A.W. Williams (1988), 'Bubbles, Crashes and Endogenous Expectations in Experimental Spot Asset Markets', *Econometrica*, vol. 56, pp. 1119–51 (1988).

Tversky, A., S. Sattath, and P. Slovic (1988) 'Contingent Weighting in Judgement and Choice'. *Psychological Review*, vol. 95 pp. 371–84.

Tversky, A., P. Slovic and D. Kahneman (1990) 'The Causes of Preference Reversal', *American Economic Review*, vol. 80 pp. 204–17.

Walker, J.M., R. Gardner, and E. Ostrom (1990) 'Rent Dissipation in a Limited-Access Common-Pool Resource: Experimental Evidence', *Journal of Environmental Economics and Management* vol. 19 pp. 203–11.

Comment

Daniel Kahneman

PRINCETON UNIVERSITY, USA

It is a troublesome fact of life that the attribution of rationality to economic agents yields predictions that are (i) strikingly accurate in many situations; (ii) systematically inaccurate in others. Plott's chapter is a welcome effort to come to grips with this fact; it aims to advance economic science by incorporating anomalous findings from experimental economics into a conception that is broadly compatible with the prevalent model of the rational economic agent. The chapter consists of a section that introduces Plott's idea of discovered preferences, followed by a series of experimental results that appears to challenge the rational model. My comments focus on the general approach that Plott sketches in his introduction.

Plott's strategy is to use different explanatory mechanisms to explain outcomes when the rational model succeeds and when it fails. The rational model is retained wherever it works, but special mechanisms are invoked as needed to account for anomalies in the behaviour of markets or individuals. The assumption of rationality is not given up: the rationality of agents is supposed to be latent when it is not manifest in the behaviour of the moment. Like Socrates' students who only learned from him what they had always known, economic agents are led to their latent rationality by the Socratic hints of market outcomes.

The hypothesis of *discovered preferences* invokes a 'process of evolution which has a direction'; it eventually 'results in the "discovery" of a consistent and stable preference' (p. 226). This process overcomes problems with 'new tasks' and 'other agents' that may cause cause early deviations from rational behaviour. The metaphor of discovery is an important part of Plott's argument. The critical difference between discovery and invention or construction is that the object of discovery exists while it waits to be discovered. Plott applies the image of discovery both to the individual's underlying preference order and to the individual's rationality. Thus, a futures market does not merely protect people against the errors to which they are prone; it causes rationality to be revealed (p. 248). This is Plott's way of retaining the basic assumptions of the standard economic model, while acknowledging systematic failures of this model under some circumstances.

In addressing the relation between economics and the psychological study of decision-making, Plott identifies a possible task for my discipline: 'If principles of psychology have a role to play in explaining social choices, it must be to explain deviations from the general tendencies explained by the rational choice models' (p. 226). The hypothesis that people have significant problems with new tasks and with other minds is offered as Plott's own account of these deviations. It is worth noting that in this view neither rationality nor the underlying preference order need explaining in psychological terms. For most purposes of economic modelling, they are simply assumed to exist, whether revealed or not.

I do not object to the restricted role that Plott assigns to psychology – among economists he is in fact exceptionally welcoming! However, the sharp distinction that he implies between the treatment of rational and of other-than-rational behaviour is deeply problematic. An analogy from another field of psychology will illustrate the reason for my resistance to this idea. Consider the study of visual perception, in which scientists try to work out the rules that govern how people see shapes, recognize objects and identify their position in three-dimensional space. Visual perception is remarkably accurate, but it is also prone to systematic illusions and biases. An extension of Plott's strategy would partition the topic of visual science into the study of accurate perception and the study of errors and illusions. The former would be considered normal and self-explanatory; explanation would only be required for illusions and biases. In contrast, modern visual science assumes as a matter of course that accurate perception and illusions both need explaining, and that the *same* perceptual mechanisms should explain them. Indeed, illusions are of interest to the student of perception mainly because they shed light on the laws of normal, accurate vision. For example, the distance of landmarks tends to be overestimated on foggy days; the illusion is due to the use of blur as a cue to distance – a cue that is normally helpful yields a predictable bias under particular conditions. An analysis that takes accurate perception for granted and only explains illusions is not good psychology. The relevant question for Plott is whether this strategy is the only way to do good economics.

To facilitate the discussion of this issue, it may be useful to sketch two competing models of the individual agent, which might serve as building blocks in economic theorizing. Model *R* is Plott's proposal. Model *P* is a possible alternative, which contains more imported psychological content.

The main features of Model *R* are the following:

- When functioning properly it is fully rational, i.e., infinitely clever.
- Its motivation is simple, and mainly monetary.
- It has an underlying coherent preference order.

But Model *R* does not always function properly; Plott lists some limitations:

- It is initially confused by new situations or new tasks.
- It may need to discover its preferences in a new context.
- It is initially susceptible to framing effects.
- It is weak on problems involving other agents and other minds.

The limitations can usually be overcome by the ability of Model *R* to benefit from market experience:

- It learns the broadest possible lessons from experience.
- It learns quickly in market situations.

Plott's version of Model *R* will do what he designed it to do: it will account for a restricted set of experimentally observed anomalies, while leaving economic theory untouched. An agent of type *R* is prone to predictable errors in particular situations, but these errors are soon eliminated by the discipline of the market. In most situations of interest to economic theory Model *R* simplifies to the standard rational model.

Model *P* is a composite drawn from research in psychology, behavioural decision research and behavioural economics. It has the following features:

- Its ability to see through complicated situations is limited – for example, it will use backward induction only in the most transparent situations.
- It identifies obvious opportunities, and does not violate dominance when options are easily compared.
- It comes equipped with attitudes, not with a coherent preference order.
- It constructs 'new' preferences when a decision is required. These preferences are labile; they depend on the context of elicitation and are susceptible to framing effects.
- It draws preferences from the memory of previous choices in recurrent situations. Its choices in any given context eventually stabilize.
- It is myopic and tends to attach value to changes rather than to states.
- It is loss-averse, assigning more weight to losses than to opportunity costs, or to gains.
- It adjusts to obvious feedback.
- It can learn to follow explicit rules.
- It is motivationally diverse, affected by intangibles such as envy, indignation and loyalty, as well as by financial incentives.
- It expects other agents to reciprocate cooperative actions.
- It comes in several versions; individual differences in ability and motivation are significant.

There are two questions to be asked about the competing models: Which presents a more plausible sketch of the individual human agent? And which is more useful to economic research? Although Plott may not agree, I believe that the answer to the first question must favour Model *P*. This model is obviously closer to the commonsense view of human agents, the view held by people who are neither economists nor psychologists. More important, its specific features are supported by a considerable body of systematic research. Finally, it has an advantage of internal coherence: rational and less rational behaviours are explained by the operation of the same mechanisms under different circumstances. However, these advantages of Model *P* are hardly decisive. The relative simplicity of Model *R* could make it more attractive and more useful for economic analysis even if Model *P* is a better description of individual economic agents.

Plott's hypothesis of discovered preferences is presented in the context of an emphatic rejection of the notion of constructed preferences which is at the core of Model *P*: 'The idea of constructed preferences would seem to leave very little room for economics and seems to be substantially contradicted by the existence of economic models that are so powerful in applications' (p. 227). This statement includes two distinct charges: that the idea of constructed preferences is useless to economics, and that it is incompatible with the facts revealed by economics research – presumably the frequently successful predictions of market equilibria that Plott has hailed here and in other writings.

Plott's second claim appears implausible. Model *P* describes boundedly rational agents, who respond appropriately to obvious cues and sometimes to subtle ones, can follow rules, and are capable of acquiring adaptive behaviours under favourable conditions of transparency and feedback. The model is surely compatible with efficient market outcomes, and will not be defeated by the observation of great foresight by some agents in some circumstances.

Plott's first claim poses a more difficult problem. His position appears to be that Model *P* is fundamentally incompatible with the model and conceptual approach of economics. This strong stance invites some questions. Is the whole machinery of unbounded rationality necessary to derive the basic results of economic theory? Plott himself appears not to think so. Would it really be disastrous to economics if the standard rational model were treated as a first approximation rather than as a maintained hypothesis? Model *P* could then serve as a source of ideas for more refined theoretical analyses. Is it necessary to wait for anomalies? A proactive alternative would explore the economic implications of specific assumptions about individuals and their preferences. For example, loss aversions and myopia may affect how the unemployed search for jobs; expectations of reciprocity in interactions could affect the functioning of organizations, and so could the existence of agents of diverse types, including some who are *not* best described as opportunistic and guileful. One could imagine a cumulative research programme that investigates the economic hypotheses suggested by a changing model of the human agent. The strategy that Plott favours is distinctly more conservative.

Although I am intrigued by the possibility, I must acknowledge that there is at present not enough evidence to convince a sceptic that the progressive refurbishing of Homo Oeconomicus with items from Model *P* would yield significant benefits to economics. It is good to know that the sceptics that Plott represents take empirical evidence seriously and will change their mind if they eventually need to do so.

11 Adaptive Behaviour and Strategic Rationality: Evidence from the Laboratory and the Field

Alvin E. Roth

UNIVERSITY OF PITTSBURGH, USA

1 INTRODUCTION

The question I will attempt to address here is: What are the prospects that a theory of rationality can serve as a useful approximation of observable behaviour in strategic situations? I will present some empirical evidence that bears on the question, and will also consider the extent to which theories of strategic rationality may be somewhat independent of traditional, idealized assumptions about individual rationality.

Economists traditionally model *individual* rationality by the assumption of utility maximization (either ordinal or cardinal), and often add assumptions about the ability to form correct expectations. *Strategic* rationality is modelled by the assumption that equilibrium (of some kind) will be achieved. (Various particular notions of rationality are embodied in the many different equilibrium 'refinements' which were an active part of the game-theoretic literature until very recently.) One connection between the assumption of individual rationality and the assumption that equilibrium will be achieved traditionally appears in the (sometimes implicit) assumption that equilibrium among rational agents will occur *immediately*, without any period of disequilibrium. Recently, however, there have been many theoretical contributions to the theory of equilibration, sometimes in the context of learning, and sometimes in the context of biological evolution.

Empirical observation, both in the laboratory and the field, suggests that learning and adaptive behaviour are important elements of equilibration. That is, behaviour is seldom observed to be in equilibrium before the actors have some opportunity to gain experience, which suggests that an understanding of what kinds of equilibria (if any) we can expect to see will depend on an understanding of disequilibrium dynamics. Furthermore, behaviour in some kinds of environments is observed to converge relatively quickly to very 'rational looking' equilibria, whereas in other environments such convergence is not apparent. Thus the answer to the question posed in the first paragraph may depend on the kind of environment we are looking at, and one of the tasks of proponents (and critics) of theories of rationality may be to delineate environments on which rationality is or is not a good approximation.

To the extent that we are observing adaptive behaviour (rather than forward-looking optimizing behaviour), we can ask on which environments will observed behaviour be well approximated by the assumption of stationary equilibrium? The *speed* at which behaviour converges to an equilibrium will be important, because for some games, even if behaviour would eventually converge to equilibrium, the speed of convergence may be sufficiently slow so that the game and its equilibria may fundamentally change (due to changes in the general economic environment) before equilibrium is reached. So most observations of such games would be out of equilibrium. And the degree to which initial conditions determine which (if any) equilibrium is reached is important because for environments in which observed behaviour quickly becomes independent of initial conditions, it may be possible to make accurate predictions which do not depend on data about the individuals involved (e.g., about their initial expectations), while for games in which the path of play is highly sensitive to initial conditions, this may not be possible.

Section 2 reviews some experimental evidence showing that in some games subgame perfect equilibrium very quickly becomes a good approximation to observed behaviour, while in other games with similar equilibrium predictions it is not a good approximation at all. It also discusses how the observed behaviour can be modelled by very simple adaptive dynamics, which involve no maximization or forecasting of any sort.

Section 3 reviews historical evidence concerning the evolution of institutions in a number of markets (chiefly entry-level labour markets for professionals) which shows that behaviour in some markets converges to stable outcomes, while in other markets unstable (and inefficient) outcomes persist for many years. So in field data also we see that convergence to certain kinds of equilibrium may be observed in some markets but not in other, apparently very similar markets.[1]

The experimental evidence comes from relatively simple and well controlled laboratory environments which allow us to test particular hypotheses about how play evolves over time. The field data is necessarily more complex and less well controlled, but allows us to see that the convergence to equilibria in some environments but not in other, similar environments, is not a laboratory artifact due to small incentives or insufficient time, but can occur in natural markets with large incentives, over periods approaching a century.

2 EXPERIMENTAL EVIDENCE

The data I discuss here come from two papers: Roth, Prasnikar, Okuno-Fujiwara and Zamir (1991); and Prasnikar and Roth (1992). The first paper compares the behaviour observed in a two-player Ultimatum Bargaining Game and a ten-player Market Game played under comparable conditions in four countries.[2] The games and the general environment in which they were played are described as follows (Roth *et al.*, 1991, pp. 1068–9):

> The two-player bargaining environment we look at is an ultimatum game: one bargainer makes a proposal of how to divide a certain sum of money with another bargainer, who has the opportunity to accept or reject the proposed division. If the second bargainer accepts, each bargainer earns the amount proposed for him by the first bargainer, and if the second bargainer rejects, then each bargainer earns zero. To allow us to observe the effects of experience,

subjects in the bargaining part of the experiment each participate in ten bargaining sessions against different opponents. Although different pairs of bargainers interact simultaneously, each bargainer learns only the result of his own negotiation.

The multi-player market environment we examine has a similar structure: multiple buyers (nine, in most sessions) each submit an offer to a single seller to buy an indivisible object worth the same amount to each buyer (and nothing to the seller). The seller has the opportunity to accept or reject the highest price offered. If the seller accepts then the seller earns the highest price offered, the buyer who made the highest offer (or, in case of ties, a buyer selected by lottery from among those who made the highest offer) receives the difference between the object's value and the price he offered, and all other buyers receive zero. If the seller rejects, then all players receive zero. Each player learns whether a transaction took place, and at what price. To allow us to observe the effects of experience, subjects in the market part of the experiment each participate in ten markets, with a changing population of buyers.

In both the market and bargaining environment, the prediction of the unique subgame perfect equilibrium (under the auxiliary assumption that subjects seek to maximize their monetary payoffs) is that one player will receive all the wealth (or almost all, if payoffs are discrete).

The data for each game are thus from subjects who played the game ten times, against different opponents each time (in order to preserve the one-shot character of each game). Subjects gained experience with the game at the same time as they encountered other subjects who had gained a similar amount of experience. (Subjects played the same role in all rounds – e.g. a subject who was a player 1 in the Ultimatum Game would be a player 1 in all ten rounds.)

All transactions were carried out in terms of '1,000 tokens', convertible into local currency, with a smallest divisible unit of 5 tokens. Note the similarity in the equilibrium structure of the two games: at the perfect equilibria of both the Ultimatum and Market Games, one player's payoff is either 995 or 1,000, but for both games the player can receive any payoff at a non-perfect Nash equilibrium. Nevertheless, the behaviour observed in the two games is different. Figures 11.1a and 11.1b show the distribution of market offers for rounds 1 and 10 in the four countries (the equilibrium offer is 995 or 1,000), while Figures 11.2a and 11.2b show the distribution of bargaining offers (the equilibrium offer is 0 or 5).[3]

For the Market Game, Figures 11.1a and 11.1b show that offers made in round 1 are dispersed, but that by round 10 equilibrium has been reached in all four countries, with from almost 40 per cent to over 70 per cent of all offers being at the highest feasible prices in the different subject pools. (The lowest bar in the graphs includes offers of both 995 and 1,000. Note that perfect equilibrium is achieved in a given market whenever two or more offers of 1,000 are made, so that no prediction is made about the dispersal of lower offers.)

For the Bargaining Game, the situation is very different, as shown by Figures 11.2a and 11.2b. In round 1, the same modal offer, of 500, is observed in each country. But in round 10, the modal offers are still 500 in the US and Slovenia, while in Japan there are modes at 450 and 400, and in Israel there is a mode at 400. These differences in the modes reflect significant differences in the distributions. That is, unlike the Market Game, tenth round offers in the Ultimatum Game have

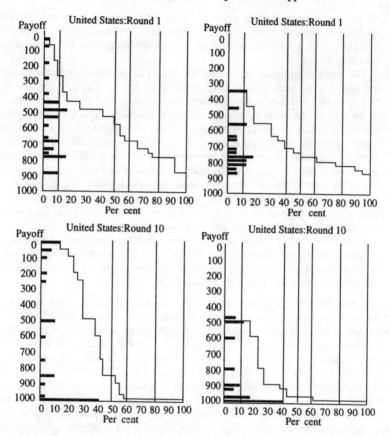

Experimenters: Left side Prasnikar; Zamir; $10; 32 observations. Right side Okuno; $30; 18 observations

Figure 11.1a Distribution of market offers

not begun to approach the perfect equilibrium, and there are significant differences among the subject pools.

The paper by Prasnikar and Roth compared ultimatum and market games with a third game called a 'Best Shot' Game. The Best Shot Game is a two-player game whose rules are that player 1 states a quantity q_1, after which player 2, informed of q_1, states a quantity q_2. An amount of public good equal to the *maximum* of q_1 and q_2 (the 'best shot') results, and each player i receives a payoff which is a function of that quantity of public good ($q = \max\{q_1, q_2\}$) minus $0.82 times q_i. (In particular, each player i receives 0 if $q = 0$, $1 if $q = 1$, $1.95 if $q = 2$, $2.85 if $q = 3$, and $3.70 if $q = 4$, from which is subtracted $.82q_i$.) The perfect equilibrium prediction is that player 1 will choose $q_1 = 0$ and player 2 will choose $q_2 = 4$, giving player 1 a profit of $3.70 and player 2 a $0.42 profit.[4] Prasnikar and Roth observed these

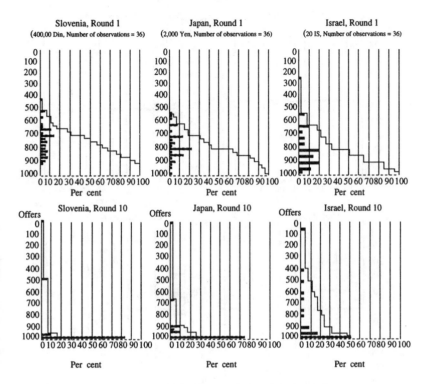

Experimenters: Slovenia Prasnikar; Japan Okuno; Israel Zamir

Figure 11.1b Distribution of market offers

games under two information conditions. Subjects in the full information condition knew that both players had the same payoffs, while subjects in the partial information condition knew only their own payoffs – they did not know how the other player's payoffs were determined. As in the Ultimatum and Market Games, each subject participated in ten one-shot games against different opponents, always in the same position (player 1 or player 2). The results are given in Figure 11.3a and 11.3b.[5] In both information conditions the players learned quickly not to *both* provide positive quantities (so that there are no interior points in Figure 11.3a after round 4, or in Figure 11.3b after round 5). In the full information condition (but not the partial information condition) every player 1 learned to provide $q_1 = 0$ (note in Figure 11.3a that no player 1 provides a positive quantity from round 6 on). And in both conditions the perfect equilibrium outcome $(q_1, q_2) = (0, 4)$ was the modal outcome by round 10, although convergence towards the perfect equilibrium was faster in the full information condition than in the partial information condition.

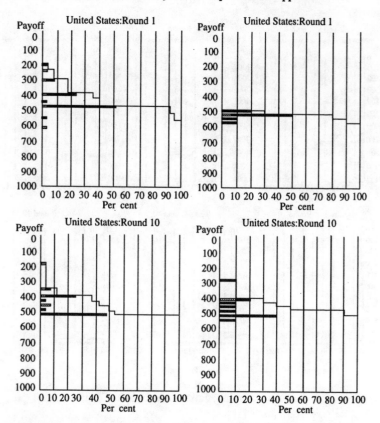

Experimenters: Left side Prasnikar; Zamir; $10; 27 observations. Right side Okuno; $30; 10 observations

Figure 11.2a   Distribution of bargaining offers

Thus all of these three games have extreme perfect equilibrium predictions, and the experimental results (nevertheless) show quick convergence to the perfect equilibrium in the Market Game and Best Shot Game in the full information condition, somewhat slower convergence in the Best Shot Game with partial information, and no apparent approach to perfect equilibrium at all in the Ultimatum Game. We turn next to see what insight into this behaviour we can derive from a family of very simple learning models.

2.1   A Family of Adaptive Models

Roth and Erev (1995) considered whether the evolution of behaviour from round 1 to round 10 in the data from these experiments could be tracked by a simple model

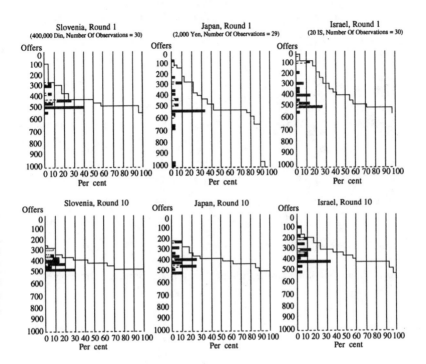

Experimenters: Slovenia Prasnikar; Japan Okuno; Israel Zamir

Figure 11.2b   Distribution of bargaining offers

of learning. We considered a family of adaptive models designed to be consistent with two of the most robust properties observed in the large experimental psychology literature on both human and animal learning, namely the following:

Choices that have led to good outcomes in the past are more likely to be repeated in the future.[6]

and

Learning curves tend to be steep initially, and then flatter.[7]

The models we considered are all variations on the following basic model.

At time $t = 1$ (before any experience has been acquired) each player n has an initial propensity to play his kth pure strategy, given by some real number $q_{nk}(1)$. If player n plays his kth pure strategy at time t and receives a payoff of x, then the propensity to play strategy k is updated by setting

$$q_{nk}(t+1) = q_{nk}(t) + x, \tag{1}$$

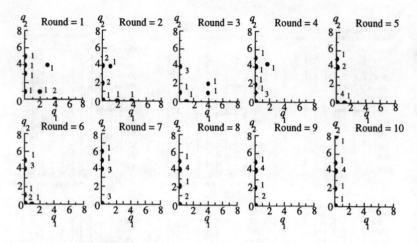

Source: Prasnikar and Roth, 1992.

Figure 11.3a   Best-Shot Game, full information, distribution of outcomes

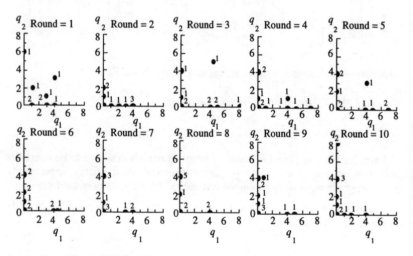

Source: Prasnikar and Roth, 1992.
* In Round 1 there was one additional outcome of $(q_1, q_2) = (7, 21)$
* In Round 2 there was one additional outcome of $(q_1, q_2) = (11, 0)$

Figure 11.3b   Best-Shot Game, partial information, distribution of outcomes

while for all other pure strategies j,

$$q_{nj}(t+1) = q_{nj}(t). \tag{2}$$

The probability $p_{nk}(t)$ that player n plays his kth pure strategy at time t is

$$p_{nk}(t) = q_{nk}(t)/\Sigma q_{nj}(t), \tag{3}$$

where the sum is over all of player n's pure strategies j.

So pure strategies which have been played and have met with success tend over time to be played with greater frequency than those which have met with less success, and the learning curve will be steeper in early periods and flatter later (because $\Sigma q_{nj}(t)$ is an increasing function of t, so a payoff of x from playing pure strategy k at time t has a bigger effect on $p_{nk}(t)$ when t is small than when t is large).

These learning dynamics have a certain resemblance to evolutionary dynamics (cf. Maynard Smith, 1982) even though they are not the 'replicator' dynamics customarily associated with evolutionary models. (In fact this basic model was proposed as an approximation of evolutionary dynamics by Harley, 1981). The chief point of similarity is that the influence of other players' past behaviour on any player n's behaviour at time t is via the effect that their behaviour has had on player n's past payoffs.

The particular models explored in Roth and Erev (1995) were all variations on this basic model, chosen so as to influence their convergence properties. One important variation was to allow 'local experimentation' by modifying equations (1) and (2) so that when player n plays his kth pure strategy and earns a payoff of x,

$$q_{nk}(t+1) = .999(q_{nk}(t) + .95x), \tag{1'}$$

and

$$q_{nj}(t+1) = .999(q_{nj}(t) + .025x) \text{ if } j \text{ is a strategy adjacent[8] to } k, \text{ and}$$
$$q_{nj}(t+1) = .999q_{nj}(t) \text{ otherwise.} \tag{2'}$$

Multiplication by .999 prevents the sum $\Sigma q_{nj}(t)$ for each player n from growing without bound, and thus speeds up learning in the very long term, while distributing .05 of the payoff among propensities to play strategies adjacent to the one played reduces the chance that the process will become stuck at some inferior strategy k because of a run of early choices of k.

Roth and Erev (1995) reported two kinds of analysis of the three experimental games using this model.[9] The first approach involved simulating the play of the game starting from randomly chosen initial propensities to play different pure strategies. The second approach involved trying to predict the round 10 observations in the experiments by using the learning rule to simulate the subjects in each subject pool, starting with initial propensities to play each pure strategy estimated from the data of the first round of play of each game. The random simulations tell us something about how sensitive the outcome of this learning process is to the initial propensities. The data driven simulations tell us something about how much the differences observed between subject pools in round 10 (subject pools in different countries for the Ultimatum and Market Games, and with different information for the Best Shot Game) may be due to adaptive behaviour starting from differences already present in round 1.

The random simulations of the Best Shot and Market Games move quite close to the perfect equilibrium prediction very quickly.[10] The random simulations of the Ultimatum Game, in contrast, do not even come close to the perfect equilibrium prediction in anything remotely comparable to the order of magnitude of the 10 periods for which the data were gathered: the model outlined above converges to the perfect equilibrium only after one million periods. Instead, the simulations of the Ultimatum Game for intermediate term periods (of from 10 to 10,000 periods) have modal demands by player 1 falling in the range of 500 to 800 (and thus bounded well away from the perfect equilibrium prediction that player 1 makes the maximum feasible demand), with the specific distribution of demands sensitive to the initial propensities.

The reason the Ultimatum Game simulations do not approach the perfect equilibrium predictions is that player 2's who are faced with high initial demands (i.e. low initial offers) learn only slowly, no matter what they do, since the difference in payoff between accepting and rejecting a small offer is small. So player 2's who have some initial propensity to reject small offers do not quickly learn to accept them. However, the difference in payoff to a player 1 when he makes a high demand (low offer) and has it rejected, compared to when he makes a moderate demand and has it accepted is large, as is the difference in payoff to players 2 when they reject or accept a moderate demand. So player 2's learn not to reject large offers before they learn not to reject small offers, and player 1's learn not to make very small offers before player 2's learn not to reject them.

In contrast, in the Best Shot Game player 2's quickly learn to free ride if player 1's do not, so player 1's learn to free ride, after which player 2's learn to provide $q_2 = 4$ in response to $q_1 = 0$. And in the Market Game, only the maximum bid is successful, so bidders learn to move their bids steadily upward.

The simulation of the experiments, starting with initial propensities estimated from the data, suggest that the simple learning model described above captures a great deal of what was observed in the experiments. For the Ultimatum Game, the modal offer in round 1 is 500 in all four countries, but in the experiments the distributions of offers became more dissimilar as experience was accumulated. The same thing happens in the simulations from the data, with the simulated American and Slovene offers at round 10 staying at a mode of 5, while the Japanese and Israeli simulations move to a modal offer of 4, as in the experiments.

In contrast, in the Best Shot Game, the data simulation from the full information condition moves quickly towards perfect equilibrium play, while the simulation of the partial information condition moves in the same direction, but more slowly.[11] And the market simulations also move steadily to the perfect equilibrium. To make them move as quickly as in the experiments, however, it is necessary to allow the players to learn from the experience of the winning bidder, and not just from their own experience. (This ability to learn from others' success will also be important in the adaptation observed in the field data described in Section 3.)

To sum up this section, we have considered three games whose perfect equilibrium predictions involve a large payoff disparity between the two sides of the game.[12] Nevertheless, experimental observation shows the perfect equilibrium prediction is a good approximation to behaviour after ten rounds of experience in two of the games, but not in the third. Simulation with a simple learning rule shows that the behaviour in all three games – both the two in which the perfect equilibrium appears, and the one in which it does not – can be well approximated without recourse to highly rational models of individual behaviour.

We turn now from the laboratory to the field.

3   HISTORICAL EVIDENCE

Table 11.1 adapted from Roth and Xing (1994), lists several dozen markets and sub-markets which have in common that, at some stage in their history, they experienced a period in which transactions became earlier and earlier, year after year. Most of these markets are entry level professional labour markets, in which this 'unravelling' of transaction time meant that entry-level jobs were being filled long in advance of the time when employment would begin. For example, in the early 1940s, American hospitals which wished to employ graduating medical students as interns were in many cases hiring them a full two years before employment was due to begin, i.e. when they still had two years of medical school to complete. And the same thing is happening today in one of the markets for law school graduates: American judges in Circuit (appeals) courts are hiring their clerks almost two years in advance. In both cases, there is a considerable loss of information in having to hire so far in advance, and this creates many potential inefficiencies. In different markets, the resulting problems have led to the development, over many years, of a variety of market institutions designed to deal with them. Roth and Xing (1994) describe these markets in some detail. However, for ease of comparison, Table 11.1 classifies the markets as being in one of four stages, according to the following somewhat idealized description also taken from Roth and Xing. (There is no implication that all markets must go through all four stages. Figure 11.4 shows the transitions between stages that have been observed in the markets listed in Table 11.1. Only stage 1 is common to all of these markets.)

Stage 1 begins when the market comes into being (e.g. when a few hospitals begin offering internships, or when federal court clerkships are created by legislation) and the relatively few transactions are made without overt timing problems. By the middle of stage 1 the market has grown, and some appointments are being made rather early, with some participants finding that they do not have as wide a range of choices as they would like – students have to decide whether to accept early job offers or take a chance and wait for better jobs, and some employers find that not all of the students they are interested in are available by the time they get around to making offers. The trade journals start to exhort employers to wait until the traditional time to make offers, or at least not to make them any earlier next year than this year. Towards the end of stage 1, the rate of unravelling accelerates, until offers are being made so early that there are serious difficulties distinguishing among the candidates. There is no uniform time for offers to be made nor is there a customary duration for them to be left open, so participants find themselves facing unnaturally thin markets, and on both sides of the market a variety of strategic behaviours emerge, many of which are regarded as unethical practices. Various organizations concerned with the market may have proposed guidelines intended to regulate it, without notable success. As stage 1 ends, influential market participants are engaged in a vigorous debate about what can and should be done. From

Table 11.1 A selection of markets with timing problems

Market	Organization	Stage
Post-season college football bowls	National Collegiate Athletic Assoc. (NCAA)	1 and 3
Entry-level legal labour markets:		
Federal court clerkships	Judicial conferences	2,1
American law firms	National Association for Law Placement (NALP)	1
Canadian articling positions	Articling Student Matching Programme	
Toronto		4S
Vancouver		3S or 4S
Alberta (Calgary and Edmonton)		3S
Entry-level business school markets:		
New MBAs		occasional stage 1
New marketing professors		1
Other entry-level labour markets:		
Japanese university graduates	Ministry of Labour, & Nikkeiren	2
Clinical psychology internships	Assoc. of Psychology Internship Centres	2
Dental residencies	Postdoctoral Dental	
(3 specialties + 2 general programmes)	Matching Programme	3S
Optometry residencies	Optometric Residency Matching Services	1 & 3
Other two-sided matching:		
Fraternity rush		1
Sorority rush	National Panhellenic Conference	3
Entry-level medical labour markets:		
American first year postgraduate (PGY1) position	National Resident Matching Programme (NRMP)	3S
Canadian first year positions	Canadian Intern & Resident Matching Service	3S
UK regional markets for pre-registration positions:	Regional health authorities	
Edinburgh		3S
Cardiff		3S
Birmingham		4,1
Newcastle		4,1
Sheffield		3 or 4,1
Cambridge		3
London Hospital		3
American specialty residencies:		
Neurosurgery	Neurological Surgery Matching Programme	4S
Ophthalmology	Ophthalmology Matching Programme	3S
Otolaryngology	Otolaryngology Matching Programme	3S
Neurology	Neurology Matching Programme	3S
Urology	AUA Residency Matching Programme	3
Radiation oncology	Radiation Oncology Matching Programme	1 and 3
other specialties[a]	NRMP	3S & 4S

continued

Table 11.1 A selection of markets with timing problems – *cont'd*

Market	Organization	Stage
Advanced specialty positions:		
12 (primarily surgical) specialties[b]	Specialties Matching Service	3S
3 medical subspecialties[c]	Medical Specialties Matching Programme	3S
4 ophthalmology subspecialties	Ophthalmology Fellowship Match	3S
Plastic surgery	Plastic Surgery Matching Programme	3S

Notes:

[a] Anaesthesiology, Emergency Medicine, Orthopaedics, Physical Medicine, Psychiatry, and Diagnostic Radiology.

[b] Colon/Rectal Surgery, Dermatology, Emergency Medicine, Foot/Ankle Surgery, Hand Surgery, Ophthalmic Plastic and Reconstructive Surgery, Paediatric Emergency Medicine, Paediatric Orthopaedics, Paediatric Surgery, Reproductive Endocrinology, Sports Medicine, and Vascular Surgery.

[c] Cardiovascular Disease, Gastroenterology, and Pulmonary Disease.

———

beginning to end, stage 1 may have covered a period of more than fifty years, or fewer than ten.

In *stage 2*, either an existing market organization or a new one created for the purpose attempts to establish a uniform date before which offers should not be made, and often an earlier date before which interviews should not be conducted, and a later date (or time) before which candidates who have received offers should not be required to respond. Sometimes this is hardly successful at all, with many market participants ignoring or circumventing the rules, and those who obey them quickly finding that this puts them at a disadvantage. And even when uniform dates are successfully established and maintained, the market often experiences a great deal of congestion and chaotic behaviour, as the deadlines for accepting or rejecting offers grows near. A firm is eager to know in good time if its offers will be accepted, so that if it has unfilled positions it may approach its most preferred alternative candidates before they have had to accept any offers they have received. And candidates who have received offers, but not from their first-choice firm, are intent upon waiting until the last allowable moment before accepting any offer, in the hope of receiving a better one. Just before the deadline expires many transactions still remain to be made. Firms whose first-choice candidates reject them may now find that their next dozen candidates have already accepted offers, and candidates may receive preferred offers moments after making a verbal commitment to accept an earlier offer. In some markets such verbal commitments are virtually always honoured, and in others they are not. In either event, in the aftermath, many firms and candidates have just missed making connections they would have preferred. The result is that the following year witnesses a resurgence of strategic behaviours designed to avoid being caught short at the end of the market. Often new rules are formulated to prohibit the more brazen of these, and new adaptations are made. While some markets have persisted for many seasons in this fashion, systems of formalized dates are often abandoned, with the market either reverting to stage 1, or moving on to stage 3.

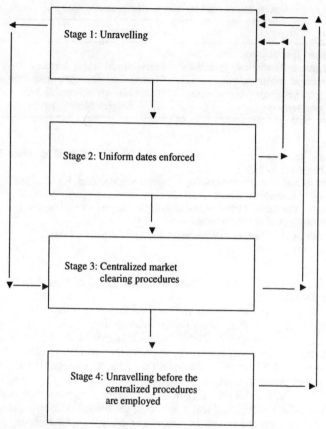

Figure 11.4   Stages and transitions observed in the markets of Table 11.1

Stage 3 begins when centralized market clearing procedures are instituted, either on a voluntary basis or with an attempt to compel participation. Participants normally make initial contacts with each other in a decentralized way, but then participate in the centralized procedure instead of making offers to one another directly. In some markets the centralized procedure is scheduled to significantly reverse prior unravelling, while in other markets it serves simply to halt further unravelling. We observe at least three distinct classes of centralized procedures. The most common, and the only one I will discuss here, are the 'matchmaker' mechanisms employed in many entry-level health-care labour markets, and in the entry-level markets for Canadian lawyers. Under these procedures, firms submit rank-order lists of students and students submit rank-order lists of firms, and the centralized mechanism then produces a matching of students with firms. Centralized mechanisms are not always successful, and so stage 3 sometimes ends with the abandonment of the mechanism and the reversion to stage 1. There are many examples of mechanisms which have proved quite long-lasting, however, and for many of these markets stage 3 may be the final stage in the market's evolution. However, some of these markets go on to stage 4.

In *stage 4*, with centralized procedures in place, unravelling begins (or continues) in the period before the mechanism is employed, as firms and students attempt to gather information about one another and/or gain advantage over their competitors before participating in the market clearing procedure. The markets in which we have observed this kind of unravelling employ matchmaking mechanisms, and the unravelling has often taken the form of recruiting students for summer internships (or in the case of some medical specialties for 'audition electives'), which amount to extensive interviewing opportunities in which the student spends a period of weeks or even months at the firm. Because the percentage of new employees hired by each firm who were previously summer interns there sometimes becomes quite high, these internships can become a way of moving the recruiting process before the centralized matching mechanism, and the process of recruiting summer interns may start to resemble the stage 1 unravelling discussed above. However such unravelling prior to the central market clearing mechanism does not eliminate all its benefits. A matchmaking mechanism still ensures for example that a desirable firm which ultimately wishes to fill five new positions can do so. This contrasts with the situation which existed in stage 1, when employment offers were made in a decentralized way, when it might have been that such a firm would have had to make ten offers to have a good chance of filling five positions, and that it might have ended up in any given year with fewer than five new employees, or more.

An important attribute of many of the stage 3 or stage 4 centralized market mechanisms is whether they produce matchings that are (pairwise) *stable*, in the sense that no firm and worker who are not matched to each other would both prefer to be. For our purposes a matching mechanism will be called stable if the matching it produces is stable with respect to the rank orderings submitted by the agents.[13] In the matching markets observed to date, although many centralized mechanisms have been adopted and then subsequently abandoned, no stable matching mechanism has been adopted by a majority of the active firms in a market and then subsequently abandoned. So stability is a natural equilibrium notion for such markets (although possibly not the only one: see Roth and Xing, 1994).

Table 11.1 lists next to each market the most recently observed stage, and if this stage has been reached from a higher stage then that is shown also – e.g. the 2,1 next to Federal court clerkships indicates that a uniform offer date (stage 2) was tried and abandoned, and that the market has reverted to stage 1. If a stage 3 or 4 centralized mechanism is known to be stable, it is listed as 3S or 4S. Note that Table 11.1 identifies seventeen different markets that have come to be organized by stable matching mechanisms. Thirteen of these are medical labour markets, which reflects that imitation has played a large role in how many of these markets have evolved.

However, imitation in these markets is not a simple matter, as is evidenced by the seven regional markets in the United Kingdom listed in the table. In the late 1960s and early 1970s these markets all attempted to imitate the American market, but since nothing was then known about the stability of the American matching mechanism (which was not studied until Roth, 1984), stability was not a goal (see Roth, 1991).

Overall, the adaptation observed in stage 1 of these markets has a good deal in common with the adaptation observed in the experimental market games discussed in Section 2. In the Market Game, subjects learned to bid steadily higher, while in stage 1 of the labour markets in Table 11.1, participants learned to move steadily earlier. But the subsequent adaptation in these labour markets is much more complex, and involves coordinating the actions of many parties. So it will not be a simple task to model the processes of adaptation which lead to stable outcomes in so many – but not all – of these markets. Here too, therefore, a notion of rational equilibrium, in this case stability, has great organizing power, but much remains to be learned about why some markets converge to stability while other apparently similar markets do not.

4   CONCLUSIONS

Both the laboratory and field evidence presented here suggests that there are environments for which the predictions of appropriate notions of stationary equilibrium provide useful approximations to observed behaviour. At the same time, there appear to be other, similar environments, for which the same equilibrium notions do not capture the observed behaviour. One of the tasks facing both proponents and critics of rational, equilibrium theories of behaviour, will be to learn which environments are which. The work of Roth and Erev (1995) discussed in Section 2 suggests that models of learning may have something to offer in this regard.

It may be natural to ask at this point why, if we think learning is going on, should we bother with stationary equilibrium theories? The discussion of the experimental evidence in particular raises this question, since it supports the hypothesis that even very simple adaptive models may be able to track the evolution of strategic behaviour – both when it leads to equilibrium and when it does not.

The answer, I think, is that because a detailed understanding of the *actual* adaptive behaviour employed by subjects will likely admit both substantial complexity and substantial individual variation, the good correspondence observed between simple models and observed behaviour most likely reflects properties of the games being played at least as much as it reflects attributes of the players (i.e., it is likely that a wide class of adaptive models would produce similar results on these games.) This in turn suggests that the extent to which we may expect 'rational' theories to be good predictors may be a property of the *environment* and not exclusively a property of the individual players. So in the absence of detailed and general theories of learning in strategic environments, theories of equilibrium seem likely to have predictive power on many environments. And even when such learning theories may become available, it seems likely that in the absence of detailed data about individual participants, the most useful predictions about strategic environments on which behaviour converges quickly and robustly to equilibrium would still come from equilibrium theories. And there is reason for optimism that there are many strategic environments which will exhibit such convergence.[14]

I will close by saying that the recent interest in learning models in the game-theory literature makes me feel optimistic about the prospects for productive interplay between the theoretical literature *per se* and more empirically directly investigations.[15] Nevertheless, empirical investigation suggests some differences in approach from those presently emphasized in the theoretical literature on learning. One such difference, emphasized in the present chapter, is the domain on which learning should be expected to approach equilibrium. Where many of the recent theoretical papers have concentrated on dynamics which can be shown always to converge to equilibrium, the empirical evidence suggests that we may want to explain why we see equilibrium in some games and not in others. This is related to the second difference in emphasis, which concerns the time horizon. Many recent papers concentrate on proving theorems about asymptotic convergence to equilibrium – i.e. convergence in the very long term, as time goes to infinity. But, both because many strategic environments do not remain unchanged in the very long term, and also because learning models are probably most informative when the learning curve is steep, the predictions of learning models for the intermediate term are in many cases likely to be the most interesting for empirical purposes.[16]

Notes

1. In both Sections 2 and 3 I concentrate on evidence collected in the course of my own work. This is for reasons of expedience in compactly presenting evidence which bears on the arguments about rationality which are the subject of the present chapter. Similar evidence can be gathered from the work of others, but comparing a diverse collection of evidence would require more space than is available here.
2. Many Ultimatum Game experiments have been reported since the initial work of Guth, Schmittberger and Schwarz (1982). For a survey of these and other bargaining experiments, see Roth (1995).
3. These figures report data gathered in multiple games under the same conditions – the unaggregated data are reported in Roth *et al.* (1991). Observations in Pittsburgh were made for transactions worth $10 and $30, in order to establish a baseline to help control for different currency values at other locations.
4. Thus the ratio of predicted payoffs to the two players is nine to one, which is a much more unequal distribution of payoffs than we observe at agreements of the ultimatum game. Note there is one other outcome, $q_1 = 4$, $q_2 = 0$, which can occur at a Nash equilibrium (but not at a perfect equilibrium).
5. There were twenty subjects in the partial information condition and sixteen in the full information condition. Harrison and Hirshleifer (1989) and earlier reported experimental results for the Best Shot Game under the partial information condition, similar to those reported here.
6. This result, known as the 'Law of Effect', has been observed in a very wide variety of environments at least since Thorndike (1898).
7. This observation is known as the 'Power Law of Practice', and dates back at least to Blackburn (1936).
8. For each game, the simulations were run on a slightly simplified games with a discrete set of offers. In the Ultimatum Game an adjacent strategy for player 1 was taken to be an adjacent discrete offer to the one just made; for player 2 strategies were modelled as minimal acceptable offers and adjacent strategies were adjacent cutoff points. Local experimentation was modelled similarly for the other two games: see Roth and Erev (1995) for details.
9. Roth and Erev (1995) also compared the performance of several other variations of the learning rule, but these differ primarily in their very long-term predictions, and not in their predictions for time comparable to the length of the experiments discussed here.

10. On the equilibrium path. For the Best Shot Game, the fact that players 1 quickly learn not to offer $q_1 = 4$ means that players 2 may persist in a non-equilibrium response to $q_1 = 4$, since such offers are virtually never seen after some learning has taken place. But since players 1 soon give high probability to $q_1 = 0$, players 2 eventually learn to reply to such moves with $q_2 = 4$.

11. Note again that the learning model is so simple that it admits no difference in the learning which goes on when players know each other's payoffs and when they do not. The results of the data simultations suggest that much of what players do differently in the two conditions may already be captured by what they do differently in the first period of play.

12. And previous experimental work suggests that achieving equilibria with large payoff disparities between subjects may be more difficult than achieving equilibria with equal payoffs.

13. Stable matching mechanisms are not incentive compatible, and so agents may have incentives to submit other than their true preferences, but there are nevertheless equilibria at which the resulting outcome is stable not only with respect to the stated preferences but also to the true preferences. See Roth and Sotomayor (1990) for an account of the relevant theory. The notion of pairwise stability in matching models was introduced in Gale and Shapley (1962).

14. Although my topic here has been strategic and not individual rationality, I cannot resist noting that similar conclusions may prove to be justified about theories of individual rationality. Although we have now accumulated an impressive body of work documenting ways in which utility maximization, for example, can be systematically violated, there have been few experiments designed to tell us to what extent, and on what environments, it may nevertheless prove to be a useful approximation. (However, an important and substantial initial step in this direction is taken in Prasnikar, 1993.)

15. See, for just a few examples, Fudenberg and Kreps (1995), Kalai and Lehrer (1993) and Milgrom and Roberts (1991). (It was more difficult to muster such optimism when equilibrium refinement was the current fashion.)

16. This point was emphasized in Roth and Erev (1995), as follows:

> First, we believe that much of the economic phenomena we observe in the world is intermediate term in nature ... Second, even when we identify economic phenomena with sufficient longevity and stationarity so that it is reasonable to believe they are yielding long term behaviour, there is reason to be cautious about the long term behaviour of any *models* we create. This is because every model includes some elements of the situation being modeled while ignoring others. And when the learning curve becomes flat, there is room for unmodeled factors to become important – factors that may be present at every stage of the learning process, but are unimportant when the learning curve is steep.

References

Blackburn, J.M. (1936) 'Acquisition of Skill: An Analysis of Learning Curves,' IHRB Report No. 73.

Fudenberg, D. and D.M. Kreps, (1995) 'A Theory of Learning, Experimentation, and Equilibrium in Games', mimeo.

Gale, D. and L. Shapley (1962) 'College Admissions and the Stability of Marriage', *American Mathematical Monthly*, vol. 69, no. 1 pp. 9–15.

Guth, W., R. Schmittberger and B. Schwarz (1982) 'An Experimental Analysis of Ultimatum Bargaining', *Journal of Economic Behaviour and Organization*, vol. 3, pp. 367–88.

Harley, C.B. (1981) 'Learning the Evolutionarily Stable Strategy', *Journal of Theoretical Biology*, vol. 89, pp. 611–33.

Harrison, Glenn W, and J. Hirshleifer (1989) 'An Experimental Evaluation of Weakest Link/ Best Shot Models of Public Goods', *Journal of Political Economy*, vol. 97 pp. 201–25.

Kalai, E. and E. Lehrer (1993) 'Rational Learning Leads to Nash Equilibrium', *Econometrica*, vol. 61, pp. 1019–45.

Maynard Smith, J. (1982) *Evolution and the Theory of Games* (Cambridge: Cambridge University Press).

Milgrom, P. and J. Roberts (1991) 'Adaptive and Sophisticated Learning in Normal Form Games', *Games and Economic Behaviour*, vol. 3, pp. 82–100.

Prasnikar, V. (1993) 'Binary Lottery Payoffs: Do They Control Risk Aversion?', Center for Mathematical Studies in Economics, Northwestern University, USA, Discussion Paper 1059.

Prasnikar, V. and A.E. Roth (1992) 'Considerations of Fairness and Strategy: Experimental Data From Sequential Games', *Quarterly Journal of Economics*, vol. 107, pp. 865–88.

Roth, A.E. (1984) 'The Evolution of the Labor Market for Medical Interns and Residents: A Case Study in Game Theory', *Journal of Political Economy*, vol. 92, pp. 991–1016.

Roth, A.E. (1991) 'A Natural Experiment in the Organization of Entry Level Labor Markets: Regional Markets for New Physicians and Surgeons in the UK', *American Economic Review*, vol. 81, pp. 415–40.

Roth, A.E. (1995) 'Bargaining Experiments,' in J.H. Kagel and A.E. Roth (eds) *Handbook of Experimental Economics* (Princeton NJ: Princeton University Press) pp. 253–348.

Roth. A.E. and I. Erev (1995) 'Learning in Extensive-Form Games: Experimental Data and Simple Dynamic Models in the Intermediate Term', *Games and Economic Behavior*, vol. 8, pp. 164–212..

Roth, A.E., V. Prasnikar, M. Okuno-Fujiwara and S. Zamir (1991) 'Bargaining and Market Behavior in Jerusalem, Ljubljana, Pittsburg, and Tokyo: An Experimental Study', *American Economic Review*, vol. 81, pp. 1068–95.

Roth, A.E. and M. Sotomayor (1990) *Two-Sided Matching: A Study in Game-Theoretic Modeling and Analysis*, Econometric Society Monograph Series (Cambridge: Cambridge University Press) (paperback edition, 1992).

Roth, A.E. and X. Xing (1994) 'Jumping the Gun: Imperfections and Institutions Related to the Timing of Market Transactions', *American Economic Review*, vol. 84, pp. 992–1044

Thorndike, E.L. (1898) *Animal Intelligence: An Experimental Study of the Associative Processes in Animals*, Psychological Monographs, 2.

Comment

Jean-Louis Rullière

UNIVERSITÉ LUMIÈRE LYON 2, FRANCE

The chapter by A.E. Roth raises many interesting issues which a book on rationality in economics should definitely not leave aside. More specifically, it deals with the question of whether any equilibrium concept could be sufficient to model strategic rationality. We know that individual rationality can be correctly modelled by some maximization principle (see, for instance, the ordering property which is beyond 'consequentialism' as has been discussed in P. Hammond's chapter). But is equilibrium a correct substitute in the case of strategic interaction?

Roth suggests that the path to equilibrium should, in an environment characterized by interaction, become the focus on the rationality scheme. Namely, two considerations have to enter into the picture at this point:

- On the one hand, the speed with which equilibrium is being achieved is an important characteristic, for if it is too low, equilibrium can either never be reached, or only be reached once after prevailing conditions in the environment have changed to such an extent that this 'equilibrium' has become meaningless, i.e. that it is no longer an equilibrium *sensu stricto*.
- On the another hand, progress towards equilibrium should not depend too heavily on initial conditions if one wants the rationality scheme to have a general enough significance.

Roth argues that the concept of perfect subgame equilibrium performs well in the Market Game, as well as the so-called Best Shot Game with respect to the two criteria just put forward. This contribution expands upon his previous work in identifying adaptive learning functions in both games. Historical evidence in the realm of some professional labour markets supports Roth's views. After this general presentation, some comments should now be raised which might disturb such a nice-looking picture of strategic rationality.

The first remark deals with the type of learning expressed by Roth. He assumes that 'the influences of other players' past behaviour on any player n's behaviour at time t is via the effect that their behaviour has had on a player's past payoffs. But one can observe in real life other types of learning procedures: in particular, learning procedures where the influence of the other players is via the beliefs of player n. For example, there are cases where agents realize that their best expectation depends on the expectations of others, who in turn are also attempting to form the best expectation. The learning process should then reach a Nash equilibrium, but the stability of that expectation equilibrium is a dimension which would also have to be explored. In some cases, there are conditions under which the learning process is seriously endangered: at the limit, chaotic situations (which may appear on the path of respective expectations) make any kind of learning simply impossible.

This type of learning process models the Nash equilibrium as an acquired standard of behaviour which is well-founded by a system of consistent beliefs

274

among the players. As Roth noted in his conclusion, these learning models, (Fudenberg and Levine, 1993; Kalai and Lehrer, 1993) characterize the Nash equilibrium as the result of an asymptotic convergence ('i.e., convergence in the very long term, as time goes to infinity'). This condition therefore assumes the game's environmental stability over the infinite time period. The learning process via payoff, as conceived by Roth, has the advantage of not being subjected to this objection.

This mechanism of learning also possesses another interesting property: this very simple model of learning assumes a lack of sophistication on the part of the game's players. 'Choices that have led to good outcomes in the past are more likely to be repeated in the future.' Since this rule implicitly assumes common knowledge among the players, the observation of past actions is sufficient for learning to be achieved. It becomes useless for each player to learn how the other players learn that each one learns that...and so forth and so on. This principle introduces, in fact, a hypothesis of symmetry in the learning functions of the players: in other words, they cannot be distinguished by their learning mechanisms. This type of hypothesis is particularly well-suited for studying the choice of a Nash equilibrium in a game of coordination, as demonstrated by Crawford and Haller (1990). In a such limiting case, everybody's interest is to reach the same equilibrium as, for example, in the famous Telephone Game, because there is a synergetic effect on payoffs. Yet there are cases, at the other end of the spectrum, where the opposite holds and where congestion effects arise when everyone is heading towards the same equilibrium. For example, Pareto optimality can only be reached when drivers have heterogeneous expectations as to which route they should take when given a choice if a specific itinerary risks becoming congested (see Haltiwanger and Waldman, 1985). Thus, learning functions have to be heterogeneous so that a meaningful equilibrium can be reached. Could Roth's results be extended towards this type of situation? More specifically, what can be said about the first principle on which the chapter rests, namely that 'choices that have led to good outcomes in the past are more likely to be repeated in the future'?

The comparison of results among the three types of games under study (i.e., Market Game, Best-Shot Game and Ultimatum Bargaining Game) warrant a second set of comments.

Among the three experimental conclusions, those concerning the Best-Shot Games are the least surprising. The experimental evidence coincides with theoretical characterization of perfect equilibrium: the accuracy of the 'free-rider behaviour' hypothesis in the consumption of a public good has been confirmed. This game corresponds to a variant of Rousseau's famous 'Stag Hunt' parable (1755) where the 'stag hunt' is a collective activity requiring a high level of coordination among hunters, whereas the 'rabbit hunt' is a private activity not requiring any coordination.

Let q_i be the action taken by player i, where $i = 1, \ldots, n$; players i's payoff function is $\Pi_i(q_i; q_{-i})$. In the Best-Shot Game, each player i receives

$$\Pi i(q_i; q_{-i}) = \max \{q_j; j, j = 1, \ldots, n\} - b.q_i \text{ with } b > 0$$

In the Stag Hunt Game, each player I receives

$$\Pi i(q_i; q_{-i}) = a.\min\{q_j; j, j = 1, \ldots n) - b.q_i \text{ with } a > 0 \text{ and } b > 0$$

van Huyck, Battalio and Beil (1990) arrived at the game experimental proof in the case of the Stag Hunt Game, from the 'free-rider behaviour' hypothesis.

The structural comparison of the Market Game and Ultimatum Bargaining Game could provide an explanation as to why in the latter game the difference between the theoretical result and the experimental data is so great. It could be assumed that these two games are almost similar when the number of buyers in the Market Game is equal to one. In this case, if the assumption that the lone buyer and the seller play as in the Ultimatum Bargaining Game is accepted, the stability of result observed in the Ultimatum Bargaining Game could be effectively analyzed.

Let us assume that in the Market Game, a buyer and a seller converge on the transaction (500, 500). This convention (see Lewis, 1969), which does not correspond with Nash's perfect equilibrium (995, 5) or (1000, 0), is nonetheless unstable. Yet at the same time, the experimental results of the market game with n ($n > 1$) buyers show that only Nash's perfect equilibrium is stable.

This difference could be interpreted in terms of knowledge; the reasoning is as follows: if, in the Market Game, each buyer preferred the transaction (500, 500), he still wouldn't know that all the other buyers also preferred (500, 500). This element is not common knowledge among the players. Here is the reason that the observed convention (500, 500), in the case of the Ultimatum Bargaining Game, is distinct from the prediction of the unique subgame perfect equilibrium and also from the experimental and theoretical result in the case of the Marketing Game.

This possible interpretation emphasizes the role of common knowledge among the players in their conventional disequilibrium behaviour. Rubinstein (1989) demonstrated that this predicted behaviour is very different between a situation of 'almost common knowledge' and 'common knowledge'. The quality of stability of an equilibrium is distinctly stronger than that of convention, as had already been observed by Keynes when he wrote (1937, p. 24): 'Knowing that our own individual judgement is worthless, we endeavour to fall back on the judgement of the rest of the world which is perhaps better informed. That is, we endeavour to conform with the behaviour of the majority of the average. The psychology of a society of individuals each of whom is endeavouring to copy the others leads to what we may strictly term a conventional judgement.'

The third and last comment refers to the particular type of modelling selected by Roth. The situation examined in the chapter is modelled as matching games on professional labour markets. But this conflict of interest can be modelled as a pre-emption game (under the hypothesis of continuous time).

Indeed, employers have two opposing interests:

- on the one hand, their collective interest is to delay to the greatest extent possible the date at which they will make a hiring decision, in order to obtain a better selection of employees,
- on the other hand, their individual interests tell them to be alert and pre-empt their competitors, in order to attract the best people.

In reasoning over a continuous time interval, let t, $t \in [0; 1]$. If t is the ending date of the game, the payments of the employer i at date t could be considered within the three following configurations:

- $L_i(t)$ corresponding to the case where the employer i is the first to hire;
- $F_i(t)$ in the case where the employer does not hire first;
- $S_i(t)$ in the case where the employer hire simultaneously.

The preceding conditions imply the assumptions that:

(1) $L_i(t) \geq S_i(t) > F_i(t)$ for all t, $t \in [0; 1]$.
(2) $L_i(t)$ is strictly increasing over the interval $[0; 1]$.
(3) $L_i(t)$, $S_i(t)$, $F_i(t)$ are continuous over the interval $[0; 1]$.

These two opposing interests result in multiple equilibria:

- One equilibrium sits at the very beginning of the period (the alert pre-emption equilibrium).
- Another equilibrium is to be found a the very end of the period (the long patience equilibrium).
- Between these two limiting equilibria, there are at least several 'conventional equilibria' in the sense of Lewis (1969). For example, on the market for semi-conductors, this conventional equilibrium which refers to the timing of the marketing of an innovation, is traditionally called Moore's law. And there is no objective reason whatsoever for this particular timing, except that every industry leader believes there are good reasons for it.

The pre-emptive gain for the employer can be highlighted as the difference for any date t, $L_i(t) - F_i(t)$. This discrepancy, variable over time, could correspond to a measurement of the risk of convention's instability (see Hendricks and Wilson, 1989). This type of theoretical model could overlap partially with Roth's conclusions, through a clarification of the functions $L_i(t)$, $S_i(t)$ and $F_i(t)$. The time-series comparison of these three functions could also justify why some markets converge towards a stable convention (that is an equilibrium or not), whereas others are doomed to instability.

In conclusion, Roth suggests 'that the extent to which we may expect rational theories to be good predictors may be a property of the environment and not exclusively a property of the individual players'. This expectation that Roth's chapter addresses provides a conception of game theory as a theory of equilibrium and not simply as one of equilibrium. The preceding comments have concurred with this conclusion by emphasizing the role of social knowledge of the game's environment and thereby of the game's rules, as noted recently by Arrow (1994, p. 5): 'The rules of the game are social. The theory of games gets its name and much of its force from an analogy with social games. But these have definite rules which are constructed, indeed, by a partly social process. Who sets rules for real-life games?'

References

Arrow, K.J. (1994) 'Methodological Individualism and Social Knowledge', *American*

Economic Review, Papers and Proceedings vol. 84, pp. 1–9.

Crawford, V.P. and H. Haller (1990) 'Learning How To Cooperate: Optional Play in Repeated Coordination Games', *Econometrica*, vol. 58, pp. 571–96.

Fudenberg, D. and D.K. Levine, (1993) 'Steady State Learning and Nash Equilibrium', *Econometrica*, vol. 61, pp. 547–75.

Haltiwanger, J. and M. Waldman, (1985) 'Rational Expectations and The Limits of The Rationality: An Analysis of Heterogeneity', *American Economic Review*, vol. 85, pp. 326–40.

Hendricks, K. and C. Wilson (1989) 'Equilibrium in Preemption Games with Complete Information', mimeo, State University of New York, Stony Brook.

Kalai, E. and E. Lehrer (1993) 'Rational Learning Leads to Nash Equilibrium', *Econometrica*, vol. 61, pp. 1019–47.

Keynes, J.M. (1937) 'The General Theory of Employment', *Quarterly Journal of Economics*, vol. 52, pp. 209–23.

Lewis, D.K. (1969) *Convention: A Philosophical Study* (Cambridge, Mass: Harvard University Press)

Rousseau, J.J. (1755) *Discours sur l'origine et le fondement de l'inégalité par les hommes.*

Rubinstein, A. (1989) 'The Electronic Mail Game: Strategic Behavior Under "Almost Common Knowledge"', *American Economic Review*, vol. 79, pp. 385–91.

van Huyck, J., R.C. Battalio and R.O. Beil (1990) 'Tacit Coordination, Strategic Uncertainty, and Coordination Failure', *American Economic Review*, vol. 80, pp. 234–48.

Part IV

Alternative Treatments of Rationality in Decision-Making Systems

12 The Rationality of Adaptive Agents

John H. Holland

UNIVERSITY OF MICHIGAN, USA

1 INTRODUCTION

Neoclassical models in economics look toward the equilibria that result when agents of perfect rationality interact. This approach opens the study of economics to powerful mathematical tools, such as fixed-point theorems and allied techniques, and much of our current understanding of economic processes is a direct consequence of this mathematics. Despite these advances, there remain real economic processes that exhibit complexities not anticipated by perfect rationality models. Processes that destroy equilibria, such as innovation, emergent organizations, changes produced by speculations based on partial knowledge, and the like, play a pivotal role in contemporary economics. To understand the dynamics of these processes we must increase our understanding of non-equilibrium processes mediated by agents of limited rationality.

The usual view of rationality focuses on deductive inference – the ability to derive consequences from facts – and perfect rationality extends this view by setting aside computational limitations. Under the assumption of perfect rationality, knowledge of a set of facts or premises (axioms) is equivalent to knowledge of all the consequences (theorems) the set implies. Human rationality is both more and less limited. It is more limited, because computational limitations can place solutions of problems, even simply defined problems, beyond human reach. For example, the game of chess can be defined with a dozen rules, yet hundreds of years of study of chess have not uncovered an optimal strategy for playing chess. Computer augmentation of human rationality has not substantially altered the outlook. Human rationality is less limited than perfect rationality because humans can often step right around the limitations of deductive inference, going from particulars to useful general-purpose models, a process called *induction*. In chess, despite the lack of an optimal strategy, we do have principles of good play that suggest both strategy and tactics in novel situations.

The objective of this chapter is to explore the extent to which we can capture human rationality, both its limitations and its inductive capacities, in computationally defined adaptive agents. Simulations based on computationally defined agents open the possibility of exploring analogues of a wide range of economic processes under completely controlled conditions. This, in turn, opens the possibility of discovering patterns that are invariant under changes in parameters and initial conditions. A mathematics based upon such invariants, if we can discover them, would enable us to deal rigorously with the complexities attendant upon

281

disequilibria and limited rationality.

A few words of caution occasioned by conversations with Frank Hahn: it is important to distinguish the algorithms that agents use to mediate their interactions – here called *performance algorithms* – from the algorithm(s) that modify the agents' performance algorithms – here called the *learning mill* (Hahn, 1993). The performance algorithms of an adaptive agent change over time, even in a single agent, whereas, in this approach, the learning mill is a given, operating at a meta-level. In this paper I do not address the broader question of why one should, or should not, view a learning mill as an evolutionary process. There are several different ways of specifying algorithms for learning, and it is not at all clear that these different ways lead to similar constraints on rationality. Perhaps the evolutionary approach to learning proposed here *is* general enough to generate the kinds of performance changes we observe in real agents in real situations. Perhaps not.

I will address one argument that would seem to militate strongly against an evolutionary approach to learning: economic agents anticipate, whereas evolutionary processes seem to be backward looking. However, any experience-based process of induction must be backward looking. Rather, for the evolutionary approach to learning, the question centres on whether or not the performance algorithms generated employ anticipations based on past experience. In the adaptive agents defined here, these anticipations are incorporated in bidding processes mediated by changing, experience-based anticipations of future payoffs.

In trying to choose among different approaches to bounded rationality, two criteria come to mind: (i) there is an advantage, as always in science, if a single framework can encompass separate well-established models and observations, and (ii) there is an advantage in being able to show that certain well-defined mechanisms are adequate to generate phenomena not encompassed by previous models. At this early stage, the objective should be to see just how far the proposed approach can go beyond its initial successes. How much *can* we account for in this way? More important, where do we get blocked?

The chapter now proceeds in three steps. Section 2 outlines a computationally-based definition of an *adaptive agent* (with suitable references for those who would like to fill in the details). Section 3 expands on the inductive apparatus employed by these agents, developing some of the relevant mathematics and relating that mathematics to processes of innovation. One objective of this part of the chapter is to give some suggestion of the kinds of invariants that could lead to a productive theory. Finally, Section 4 explores characteristics of systems composed of many interacting adaptive agents, concentrating on effects of learning and experience-based anticipation. This section concludes with an effort to embed the particulars in a broader perspective.

2 ADAPTIVE AGENTS

I shall define an *adaptive agent* via the computation-based implementation of two processes: (i) a *performance system* that specifies the agent's capabilities at a given point of time, and (ii) a *learning mill* that uses inductive apparatus to modify the performance system as experience accumulates. The next two sub-sections treat each of these processes in turn; the resulting system, called a *classifier system*, provides a rigorous definition of an adaptive agent of bounded rationality (Holland *et al.*, 1986, ch. 4).

2.1 The Performance System

A formal description of a performance system requires, first of all, specification of the system's ways of interacting with its environment (most of which consists of other agents). I will adopt the common view that the state of the environment is conveyed to the performance system via a set of detectors (e.g., rods and cones in a retina, neurons in the cochlea, etc.) and that the system acts upon its environment via a set of effectors (e.g., muscles). I will also adopt the view that the detectors present the performance system with standardized packets of information called *messages*. With these conventions, we can say that the performance system processes messages from the detectors to determine effector settings that act upon the environment.

There is one further channel of interaction with the environment that must be considered: under some circumstances the environment provides the agent with payoff (reward, reinforcement, resource acquisition). That is, from a game-theoretic point of view, some situations amount to overt 'wins' or 'losses', with associated payments. The rate at which the agent acquires payoff is a measure of its performance, and is a vital element in any careful discussion of learning or adaptation (see the discussion of the learning mill).

The detailed definition of the performance system is conveniently carried out in terms of a set of *condition/action rules*. The condition part of each rule 'looks for' certain kinds of messages, and when those messages are present, the action part of the rule posts a message in turn. The rules take a particularly simple form if the messages are all of a standard length (say a binary encoding of a certain number of bits, as for a computer register); it is easily established that this restriction does not affect the agent's computational power. Many rules can be active simultaneously, so many messages may be present at a given time. These messages determine both the internal (rule) and external (effector) activity of the performance system. It is convenient to think of the messages as collected in a list that changes under the combined impetus of the environment and the rules. All rules simultaneously check the message list, and active rules add new messages to the list.

It may be helpful to think of the performance system as a kind of office wherein the message list is a bulletin board holding the memoranda that must be handled that day. Each rule corresponds to a 'desk' that has responsibility for certain kinds of memos. At the beginning of a day, each desk collects the memos for which it is responsible, processes them, and then, at the end of the day, posts the memos that result from its processing. At the beginning of each day, memos come either from the previous day's work (messages produced by the rules) or from outside the office (messages produced by the environment). Some memos cause actions outside the office (messages that control effectors). The possibilities for concurrency and coordination – *parallelism* – are obvious.

Parallelism, in particular, makes it possible for the performance system to combine rules into clusters that model the environment. This offers clear advantages over using monolithic structures to handle each possible situation. When a separate rule is required for each possible combination of inputs, the torrent of relevant and irrelevant data impinging upon an agent generates a combinatoric explosion. If, instead, we use different rules to describe different aspects of the current situation, we gain two important advantages:

(1) Combinatorics work for the system instead of against it. The advantage is similar to that obtained when one describes a face in terms of components, instead of treating it as an indecomposable whole. If we select, say, 8 components for the face – hair, forehead, eyes, nose, mouth, chin, and the like – and allow 10 alternatives for each, then one hundred million faces can be described by combining components, at the cost of storing only 80 individual components.

(2) Experience can be transferred to novel situations. A given rule can be used as a building block in many combinations, just as a single alternative for a facial component, say a particular nose shape, can be used with alternatives for each of the other components (ten million possibilities). If the rule proves useful in a fair sample of these contexts, it is at least plausible to believe it will prove useful in similar combinations not yet encountered.

To exploit these possibilities, the rules must be organized in a way that permits facile reorganization of the system. The first step in this direction is to adopt the tenet that rules serve as hypotheses rather than is incontrovertible facts. As experience accumulates, rules are progressively confirmed or disconfirmed (see the discussion of the learning mill). The agent's reliance upon a rule is based upon its average usefulness in the contexts in which it has been tried previously. This rating is summarized in a quantity called the rule's strength (see the discussion of credit assignment).

To foster coordination and easy reorganization, we add the requirement that all rules with satisfied conditions at time t enter a competition for the right to post their messages. The competition is based on a bidding process: each satisfied rule makes a bid based upon its strength and the specificity of its conditions. A rule that has been useful to the agent in the past (high strength) and uses more information about the current situation (high specificity) will make a higher bid. Higher bidders have a higher probability of winning the competition. Usually there will be many competitors and several winners; only the winners actually post messages. Thus, the competition between rules determines which cluster of rules is active at a given time.

Competition provides a simple, situation-dependent means of resolving conflicts when sets of concurrently active rules attempt to generate responses. Instead of attempting to maintain the consistency of the full-rule repertoire, the system treats contradictory satisfied rules as alternative hypotheses about the current situation. When such alternatives are presented, the system uses competition (and local consistency) to decide which rules to favour, even though the particular combination of rules satisfied may not have been encountered before. The result is a flexible procedure for bringing previous experience to bear on a current, possibly novel, situation.

(Chapters 3 and 4 of Holland *et al., Induction: Processes of Inference, Learning and Discovery* (1986) provide details concerning condition specificity, emergent default hierarchies, support provided by partial information, and the like.)

2.2 The Learning Mill

We are now ready to discuss the ways in which experience modifies the performance system. Experience acts upon classifier systems in two ways. First, via a process called *credit assignment*, it modifies the strengths of rules already present in the performance system, and second, via a process called *rule discovery*, it generates new rules (hypotheses) to be tried. I will discuss these processes in order.

(a) Credit Assignment

Credit assignment is not particularly difficult when the system receives payoff from the environment for a particular action – the system simply strengthens all the rules active at that time (a kind of conditioning). Credit assignment becomes difficult when credit must be assigned to early-acting rules that set the stage for a sequence of actions leading to payoff. Then the system must decide which of the rules active along the way actually contributed to the outcome. Parallelism adds to the difficulty. Only a few of the rules active along the way may contribute to the favourable outcome, while others are ineffective or, even, obstructive. Somehow the credit assignment algorithm must sort this out, modifying rule strengths appropriately.

Classifier systems use the performance system's bidding process as the vehicle for credit assignment. To do this, each rule is treated as a 'middleman', buying and selling messages via its bids and postings. A rule's 'suppliers' at any instant are those rules that have posted messages satisfying its conditions; its 'consumers' are those rules that have conditions satisfied by the message it posts. Under this regime, we treat the strength of a rule as an asset that can be cashed. When the rule wins a bidding competition, it must draw down on its strength to pay the amount of the bid to its current suppliers. (A rule only pays when it wins the bidding process.) As a result, the winning rule's strength is reduced by the amount of the bid, and the strengths of the suppliers are increased in proportion.

A winning rule can recoup its payment in two ways: (i) through payments made to it, in turn, by its consumers, or (ii) through a share of a payoff from the environment. In case (ii) we reach the point, alluded to in the initial discussion of interactions with the environment, where payoff affects the performance system. Because payoff is shared only among rules active at the time of payoff, the system must rely on the 'middleman' exchanges to reward stage-setting rules. The overall credit assignment process that implements these exchanges is called a *bucket brigade algorithm*.

In broad outline, the bucket brigade algorithm works because rules become strong only if they are coupled into sequences leading to payoff. To see this, note first that rules consistently active at times of payoff tend to become strong because of the payoff they receive. As these rules grow stronger, they make larger bids because, as noted earlier, bids are proportional to strength. Consider now a rule that consistently sends a message activating one of the 'payoff' rules – a supplier of the 'payoff' rule. The increased bids of the payoff rule means that this supplier receives larger payments, and becomes stronger in turn. Subsequently, the suppliers of the suppliers begin to benefit, and so on, back to the early stage-setting rules. The whole process, of course, takes repeated 'plays of the game'.

The bucket brigade algorithm is an important component of the limited rationality of agents based on classifier systems. The algorithm requires no overt memory of the long and complicated sequences leading up to payoff; it only requires knowledge of the immediate suppliers and consumers of each rule. The alternative, a complete memory of all transactions and interactions between payoffs, would involve teasing out relevant strands from a tangled mass of strands that includes unnecessary detours and incidentals. Even for modest parallel systems acting in environments with sporadic payoff, this teasing-out process quickly exceeds computational capacity. The bucket brigade algorithm avoids these complications. Chapter 3 of *Induction* provides details of the workings of the bucket brigade algorithm (Holland *et al.*, 1986).

(b) Rule Discovery

The second process employed by the learning mill is rule discovery. Because rule discovery is the *sine qua non* for an adaptive agent, it constitutes the centrepiece of this chapter. In a rule-based system, the whole process of induction succeeds or fails in proportion to its efficacy in generating plausible new rules. However, plausibility is not an easy concept to pin down. It implies that experience biases the generation of new rules; but how?

The starting point is the proposal that plausibility is closely linked to the 'building-block' approach set forth earlier in the discussion of parallelism. Applied to an individual rule, the building-block approach requires that the rule be viewed, not as something monolithic, but as an entity constructed from well-chosen parts. If a part appears in several rules, then those rules constitute samples drawn from the set of all rules that can be constructed from the part. By calculating the average strength of the rules observed to contain the part, we can estimate the usefulness of the part. Though estimates are subject to error, they do provide an experience-dependent guideline. Both the possibility of error and role of experience are consonant with the term 'plausibility'. By treating parts of rules as building-blocks we can approach the generation of plausible rules directly.

Note that a rule can be divided up into component parts (potential building-blocks) in a great many ways. That is, even a single rule constitutes a sample point for a great many possible building-blocks. *A fortiori*, an agent defined by a few hundred rules provides samples for a vast array of building-blocks. Many building-blocks will appear in a dozen or more different rules, and different building-blocks will appear in different subsets of rules. Each such subset is large enough to provide an estimate of the corresponding part's average usefulness in rule formation. So, an adaptive agent quickly accumulates enough information to make good estimates of the relative usefulness of multitudes of building-blocks.

If the learning mill can extract this information, it can bias the rule generation process so that above-average building blocks are favoured in the construction of new rules. However, there is a difficulty. The large numbers of building-blocks involved make an explicit calculation of all the relevant averages a computationally infeasible task; and even if the calculations could be made, the biasing procedure would be difficult to implement. Fortunately, there is a way of achieving the effect of these calculations without carrying them out explicitly. We shall examine this 'shortcut' in the section on genetic algorithms that follows the recapitulation of this section.

2.3 Recapitulation

An adaptive agent, to be effective, must continually balance exploration (acquisition of new information and capabilities) against exploitation (the efficient use of information and capabilities already available). As formulated here, the adaptive agent is described in terms of a rule-based performance system. Rules are assigned strengths that are modified by a credit assignment algorithm to reflect past usefulness to the agent. Two mechanisms help the agent to balance exploration and exploitation:

(1) *Parallel execution* of rules allows transfer of experience to novel situations by the combined activation of relevant rules – building-block rules – that describe aspects of the situation.
(2) *Competition*, based on rule specificity and strength, allows rules to be treated as hypotheses to be marshalled and progressively confirmed (by strength revision under credit assignment) as required by the changing environmental situation.

If an agent is to be able to expand its scope as experience accumulates, it must be able to generate plausible new rules (hypotheses) by discovering and recombining building-blocks for rules themselves. The next section shows how this complex task can be accomplished with limited computational resources.

3 GENETIC ALGORITHMS

The 'shortcut' for biasing rule production towards the use of above-average building-blocks can be explained by resorting to a metaphor from genetics: the learning mill selects high strength rules from the agent's repertoire to serve as 'parents', then it producers new 'offspring' rules by exchanging parts between the parents. The offspring replace low-strength rules in the repertoire. Though it is not obvious, new rules generated by this procedure do indeed incorporate above-average building blocks with ever-increasing frequency. This procedure, when implemented as a computer program, is called a *genetic algorithm*. (A wide range of papers on genetic algorithms can be found in the *Proceedings of the International Conference on Genetic Algorithms, 1991* (Belew and Booker, 1991)). This section shows how genetic algorithms discover and exploit building-blocks.

To make the metaphor from genetics precise, we need a formal counterpart of the building-block concept. The starting point is the observation that a building-block can be formally identified with the set of *all* objects that have the building-block as a component. Here, the set of *all possible* objects is just the set C of all rules (strings) in the classifier language, so that a particular building-block corresponds to a particular *subset* of C.

Abstractly, C can be taken as the set of all binary strings of some length k; that is $C = \{1,0\}^k$. (It is not difficult to deal with arbitrarily long strings of different lengths, but the same points can be made with strings of fixed length.) The subsets of C corresponding to building-blocks are defined with the help of a 'don't care' symbol '*'. Let $C^* = \{1,0,*\}^k$ be the set of all strings of length k over the three-letter alphabet $\{1,0*\}$. Each string s in $C*$ can be used to designate a particular *subset* of C as follows: let c_i designate the bit at the ith position of $c \in C$, and let s_i designate the letter from $\{1, 0,*\}$ at the ith position of $s \in C*$. Then $c \in s$ if, and only if, for each position i, (1) if $s_i \neq *$, then $c_i = s_i$, otherwise (2) c_i can equal either 1 or 0. For example, the string $1****$ from $\{1,0,*\}^5$ designates the *set* of all binary strings of length 5 that start with a 1, namely the set $\{1000, 1001, ..., 11111\}$. The building-blocks (subsets of C) designated by the strings in $C*$ are called *schemata*.

The genetic algorithm does not directly manipulate schemata (building-blocks); it only manipulates strings (rules). To express this point formally, let $R(t)$ designate the set of rules used by the performance system at time t. $R(t)$ can be looked upon as a sample set drawn from C. The genetic algorithm uses the strongest rules in $R(t)$ as 'parents' to generate new elements from C. These new elements replace some elements in $R(t)$ to form $R(t + 1)$. In forming these new rules, the genetic algorithm implicitly recombines schemata common to the better elements of $R(t)$. As we will see, the best way to understand what a genetic algorithm *does* is to understand its effects upon schemata.

To proceed, in assigning a strength $u(c)$ to each rule $c \in R(t)$, the bucket brigade algorithm implicitly defines a utility function $u: C \to$ reals. The genetic algorithm uses the information $u(c)$, $c \in R(t)$, to act on $R(t)$ as follows (details are provided in Holland, 1992, ch. 6):

(1) A probability distribution $P(t)$ is assigned to $R(t)$, with the constraint that $P(c_1, t) > P(c_2,t)$ if $u(c_1) > u(c_2)$.

(For example, $P(c) = u(c)/\Sigma_j u(c_j)$, where the sum is over all $c_j \in R(t)$.)

(2) A set of n pairs is drawn, with replacement, from $R(t)$ using the probability distribution $P(t)$, where $2n$ is less than or equal to the number of rules in $R(t)$, $2n \leq M$.

(These pairs serve as 'parents', generating new trials to be drawn from C.)

(3) The strings in each pair are *crossed* by randomly selecting a different position i for each pair, $1 < i < k$, and exchanging between the strings in the pair the portions of the strings to the left of i.

(For example, if the pair is (01010, 11100) and $i = 2$ for that pair, the result would be the pair (11010, 01100)).

(4) Each bit in the resulting pair of strings has a small probability p_m of being *mutated* to the opposite value; typically $p_m < .01$.

(For example, if the second bit in the string 11010 were mutated the result would be 10010).

(5) $R(t + 1)$ is formed from $R(t)$ by using the strings just formed by crossover and mutation to replace $2n$ strings drawn with uniform probability, without replacement, from $R(t)$.

(If $2n$ is substantially smaller than M, the 'offspring' strings are unlikely to replace the parent strings; instead they replace strings of lower utility. Thus, the new population retains (most of) its information about the better strings it has previously uncovered in the space C of possibilities).

(6) Increment t to $t + 1$ and return to step (1) for the next iteration.

3.1 The Schema Theorem

Though the *crossover* operation in step (3) of the genetic algorithm seems rather strange as a mathematical operator, it actually produces a sophisticated search that exploits useful building-blocks. The schema theorem makes this point rigorously. It shows that a genetic algorithm increases the rate of use (the sampling rate) of *all* (sufficiently compact) schemata of above-average utility, biasing the sampling of the space of possibilities *C* accordingly. This is unexpected because the number of distinct schemata in a single binary string of length *k* is easily shown to be 2^k, so that the number of distinct building-blocks with instances in a set of size *M* is somewhere between 2^k and $M2^k$. That is, the number of building-blocks being tested and exploited is of order 2^k. If *k* is at all large, this greatly exceeds the number *M* of strings being processed. For example, if $k = 20$ and $M = 1000$, the ratio exceeds 1000 to 1. This property of trying out and exploiting many more schemata than the number of strings being processed is called *implicit parallelism* (née *intrinsic parallelism* in the original 1975 edition of Holland, 1992).

The following notation provides for a precise statement of the schema theorem:

$M(s, t)$ = the number of instances of schema *s* in $R(t)$.
   (For example, if $s = 1****$, then $M(s, t)$ gives the number of strings in $R(t)$ that start with a 1).
$P(s, t) = M(s, t)/M$.
$u(s, t)$ = the average utility of the instances of *s* in $R(t)$.
$u(t)$ = the average utility of all strings in $R(t)$.
$d(s)$ = the number of defining bits (non-*letters) in the string from C^* defining the schema *s*.
$L(s)$ = the number of possible crossover points between the outermost defining bits in the string defining the schema *s* (the 'compactness' of *s* is $1/L(s)$; if *s* has only one defining bit, $L(s) = 0$.

Theorem (Schema Theorem). $P(s, t + 1) \geq [1 + \Delta(s, t)]P(s, t)$

   where $\Delta(s, t) = ([u(s, t)/u(t)][1 - L(s)/(k - 1)][1 - p_m]^{d(s)} - 1)(2n/M)P(s, t)$.

From left to right, the factors on the right-hand side of the equation for $\Delta(s, t)$ have the following interpretation:

   $[u(s, t)/u(t)]$ is the expected rate of increase (or decrease) of instances of *s* in the absence of crossover and mutation;
   $[1 - L(s)/(k - 1)]$ sets an upper bound on the probability that schema *s* will be 'broken up' by crossover – it is the probability that a pair of strings will be crossed outside of the outermost defining bits of *s*, using $L(s)/(k - 1)$ as an upper bound on the probability that an instance of *s* will be broken up by the crossover operator;
   $[1 - p_m]^{d(s)}$ is the probability that the schema *s* will not be destroyed by mutation;
   $(2n/M)P(s, t)$ is the probability that a given string in $R(t)$ will be in the set of $2n$ samples drawn from $R(t)$, multiplied by the probability that string is an instance of the schema *s*.

(Because the genetic algorithm is stochastic, this equation only provides a bound on expectations. In the terminology of mathematical genetics, the equation corresponds to a deterministic model of the algorithm. The interested reader can find a proof, with $2n = M$, as theorem 6.2.3 in *Adaptation in Natural and Artificial Systems* (Holland, 1992, ch. 6)).

Schemata that consistently appear in above-average rules are used in exponentially increasing numbers as the performance system develops under the genetic algorithm. (Eventually, when a schema comes to occupy a large proportion of $R(t)$, there is an asymptotic 'slowdown' in the rate of increase, as shown by the schema theorem.) In this process, crossover's most important effect is to generate new combinations of schemata already in $R(t)$. That is, crossover forms strings that contain schemata not previously on the same string. It does this with increasing efficiency and probability for schemata that occupy large portions of $R(t)$. Crossover also acts to generate instances of schemata not before observed. Acting in concert with the implicit parallelism established by the schema theorem, crossover provides a sophisticated, experience-based rule discovery process.

3.2 Innovation

Much that goes on in generating innovations parallels speciation in genetics, particularly speciation in the context of an ecosystem. Each device (genotype) tried amounts to a simultaneous test of all of its component building-blocks. Marketing of variants of a profitable prototype assures that above-average building-blocks are repeatedly tried in new, related contexts. This, in turn, assures that the observation of above-average return, from devices using the building-block, is not a statistical fluke, while simultaneously exploiting the building-block in new contexts. Innovations produced by recombination are exemplified by things as different as the chimera of medieval bestiaries, the combustion engine (which combines the geared wheels of a water mill, the pistons of Watt's water pump, Volta's sparking device, and Venturi's vaporizer), and the digital computer (originating with Babbage's combination of geared wheels, Jacquard's loom control cards, and Gauss's arithmetic). On occasion, new building-blocks are discovered, sometimes by rearrangement of still more elementary building-blocks; new building-blocks usually give rise to technological revolutions. The abstract version of this process is a search through an enormous space of possibilities, biased toward intersections of tested regions (that is, rearrangements of tested parts).

The genetic algorithm serves as a rigorous, simplified prototype of the process. Innovation, so described, seems so straightforward that one wonders why innovation is not more common (though it is common enough in contemporary economies). A closer look at the action of the genetic algorithm provides a hint of the impediment. The difficulty centres on what, at first sight, seems an unblemished advantage: the exponential increase in the number of instances $M(s, t)$ of any above-average schema s. This rapid 'rise time' of above-average schemata entails a hidden reduction in overall search rate called *hitchhiking*.

(a) Hitchhiking

To see this effect, consider what happens when the first instance of a schema s, call it c_s, is uncovered. As the genetic algorithm produces new copies of c_s, the particular bit values at *loci other than the defining bits of s* will also appear in the replicas of c_s. Indeed, were it not for the actions of crossover and mutation; all of the 'offspring' of c_s would be copies of c_s. These bit values at other loci 'hitchhike' as the number of instances of s increases. The resulting 'lock-in' of these bits has an effect much like superstition, producing a bias toward detrimental incidentals that accompany a useful outcome. The lock-in greatly reduces the probability of discovering other schemata disjoint from s.

A rigorous examination can be carried out by concentrating on a defining locus l_i of a schema s' disjoint from s. If exact replicas of c_s should come to occupy the whole of $R(t)$, then all strings in the population would have the bit value at l_i that had hitchhiked along during the 'growth' of s. If this value were different from the one required by s' at that locus, then there would be no samples of s' in $R(t)$. $R(t)$ would be 'locked-in' to a configuration that did not allow any samples of s'. The lock-in would hold sway until mutation switched the value at l_i in some future generation $R(t + t'), t' > 0$. Hitchhiking therefore tends to neutralize implicit parallelism.

Setting the mutation probability p_m to a high value, so the bit values at all loci are frequently changed from generation to generation, is one way to deter hitchhiking, but it is *not* a good way. The factor $[1 - p_m]^{d(s)}$ in the schema theorem makes it clear that a high mutation rate interferes with the exploitation of schemata already discovered. More generally, mutation is a history-independent operation that does not make use of the system's knowledge or past experience.

Rather, the objective should be to balance the effects of replication and mutation, using a low mutation rate, to retain implicit parallelism while deterring hitchhiking. To examine this possibility, I shall use the following additional notation: let $P^*(t)$ be the proportion of strings in $R(t)$ that are *free* of hitchhiking bits at one or more of the d defining loci of schema s' disjoint from s; let $u + b$, $b > 0$, be the average utility of strings that are instances of s, where u is the average utility of strings that are *not* instances of s.

Make the 'worst case' assumption that the offspring of instances of s all carry a complete set of hitchhiking bits at the d defining loci of s', except for strings that undergo a mutation at one of those loci. This sets a lower bound on $P^*(t)$. Using the schema theorem (without the crossover factor), the expected number of such mutated offspring of instances of s is given by

$$2nP[(u + b)/u_{av}][1 - (1 - p_m)^d], \tag{1}$$

where $u_{av} = P(u + b) + (1 - P)u = u + Pb$.

Assume that the offspring of *free* strings are free; that is, assume that the probability is negligible that the d bits at the defining loci of s' mutate 'back' to the particular combination of hitchhiking bits. Then the expected number of free offspring of the free strings is given by

$$2nP * [u/u_{av}]. \tag{2}$$

The random draw, from $R(t)$, of strings that are to be replaced by offspring, reduces the expected number of free strings by the amount

$$-2nP^*. \tag{3}$$

Summing (1), (2) and (3) gives the net change Δ in the number of free strings following one iteration of the genetic algorithm:

$$\Delta \cong 2n[P(p_m d)(u + b)/(u + Pb) + P^* u/(u + Pb) - P^*],$$

using the approximation $[1 - (1 - pm)d] \cong p_m d$ when $p_m \ll 1$. Setting $\Delta = 0$ yields an approximation to the non-zero fixed point at which the proportion of free strings is no longer changing,

$$0 \cong P(p_m d)(u + b)/(u + Pb) + P^* u/(u + Pb) - P^*.$$

Solving gives an approximate value for P^* at the fixed point,

$$P^* \cong p_m d(1 + u/b).$$

In this equation for P^*, the ratio u/b gives the relative advantage of schema s. This relative advantage can be controlled by scaling b in the genetic algorithm. That is, when an instance of s is first discovered, it can be assigned the value $u + b$ by fiat (assigning $u + b$ rather than the value $u(s)$ directly observed) using the average value, u, calculated for the other strings in $R(t)$.

In a biological setting, a typical value for b would be of the order $0.2u$, and a typical value for p_m might be 0.005. With $b = 0.2u$ and $p_m = 0.005$, we see that, for a schema s' defined over $d = 10$ loci, $P^* \cong 0.3$. That is, because of the hitchhiking effect, about 1 sample in 3 will provide new information about the 2^{10} bit combinations possible at the 10 defining loci for schema s'. Stated another way, about $3 \cdot 3 \cdot 2^{10}$ strings will have to be processed by the genetic algorithm to locate an instance of s'. At these same values, instances of s occupy a proportion of $R(t)$ given by

$$P(s, t) \cong (1 - P^*) = 0.7.$$

Thus, with an appropriate setting for b and p_m, it is possible to limit the hitchhiking effect (lock-in) while exploiting useful schemata already discovered. These proportions are closely approximated in actual simulations (Mitchell, 1993).

There is one last problem: schemata with fewer defining bits than the d_{min} used to set a lower bound P^* on the sampling rate will have a sampling rate $P < P^*$. This difficulty can be managed by setting the size M of the initial, randomly generated, population large enough that schemata s' of length $d(s') < d_{min}$ have an expectation of several instances in that initial population. Setting $M > c2^d{}_{min}$, where c is a small integer, will accomplish this; for example, with $d_{min} = 9$ and $c = 5$, the initial population should have size $M > 2560$. With this provision, *all* variants of *all* schemata with $d < d_{min}$ defining loci are present in the initial population, with an average of c copies, making discovery of such schemata a *fait accompli*.

Summing up: if a newly discovered schemata has a value substantially above the population average, $u + b \gg u$, then that schema will quickly come to occupy a large part of the population. But this comes at the cost of a substantial hitchhiking effect, which lowers the chances of finding additional above-average schemata. Scaling b to very small values deters hitchhiking, but then new schemata only slowly come to occupy a substantial portion of the population, and they must be lost along the way because of mutation or crossover. The results just given show that b can be scaled, in conjunction with the mutation rate, so that new schemata can be discovered *and* above-average schemata already discovered rapidly come to occupy a large proportion of the population. Moreover, the results suggest it takes only a small amount of random local variation ($p_m = .005$) to provide a sufficient 'insurance policy', sustaining implicit parallelism in the face of hitchhiking effects.

(b) Broader Considerations

Though the mathematical arguments here are based on particular definitions and algorithms, I think the results offer useful guidelines for more general studies of innovation. The arguments turn on the use of schemata as the formal counterpart of 'building-blocks', but even this restricted definition has direct interpretations in any domain in which the objects of interest can be usefully represented as strings. Schemata can readily be interpreted, for instance, as co-adapted sets of alleles in genetics, active sites on antibodies in immunology, or rule components for agents in economics. Even when there is no easy interpretation of schemata, many of these results can be reinterpreted for building-blocks more broadly interpreted. Consider, for example, the formal operators used in the arguments: sampling biased by observed utility, recombination (crossover), and local variation (mutation). Each of these operators has counterparts in broader domains. It is commonplace to recombine building-blocks to arrive at *plausible* innovations – as mentioned earlier. We generate everything from unicorns and gryphons to new jet engines in this way. Moreover, we tend to favour building-blocks that have worked in the past in similar contexts (sampling biased by observed utility). It is a way of transferring past experience to new situations.

4 INTERACTIONS BETWEEN ADAPTIVE AGENTS

With these preparations we can begin to look at the interactions of agents that are capable of innovation, though they be of limited rationality. I would submit that such interactions are a common aspect of modern economies and worth direct, rigorous investigation. Indeed such a theory would be of help in understanding a broad range of complex adaptive systems (treated on different time-scales), including ecosystems, the immune system, and cognitive aspects of the central nervous system.

For performance systems described in terms of rules, meaningful interaction means that the rules of one agent must be able to apprehend characteristics of other agents. One way to accomplish this is to make one or more of the messages on an agent's message list available to other agents. That is, if agents 'display' some of their messages, informed interactions between agents become possible. Such displayed messages, which I will call *tags*, proclaim characteristics of the agent's internal state, serving much like antigen markers in the immune system, phenotypic markers of an organism, or even political slogans and banners.

A population-based version of the Prisoner's Dilemma (PD) provides a simple example of the effects of such 'surface' tags in a population of interacting agents. (For a good introduction to studies of the PD using genetic algorithms, see Axelrod's paper in *Genetic Algorithms and Simulated Annealing* (Axelrod, 1987).) In the simplest version, each agent displays a single message, which is held constant throughout the agent's existence. Agents in the population come into contact via random pairings, and when two agents do come into contact each is given the option of deciding whether or not it wants to execute one play of the PD. If both agents decide to play, then one play of the game is executed, otherwise no interaction takes place. In this simple version, each agent has only a single rule sensitive to the displayed message of the other agent, and the execution decision is made by that rule. If the condition of that rule is satisfied by the displayed message of the other agent, then the agent offers to execute one play of the PD. If an interaction does take place, each agent determines its particular move ('cooperate' and 'defect' are the two options) according to a strategy determined by its other rules.

The four possible outcomes of an interaction (cooperate–cooperate, cooperate–defect, defect–cooperate, defect–defect) set a payoff for each agent determined by one of the standard payoff matrices for the PD (say [3, 3], [5, 0], [0, 5], [1, 1] in the given order of outcomes). The rate at which a given agent collects payoff determines the probability that it will be selected as a parent under the genetic algorithm. This, in turn, determines the frequency with which its building-blocks appear in the overall population. In particular, it determines the frequency with which various displayed tags appear in the population. As the frequency of a given kind of tag increases, the frequency of interactions involving that tag also increases.

Earlier experiments with selective mating based on tags are relevant here (Perry, 1984). In those experiments, an early, accidental association of a tag with a trait conferring a reproductive advantage is rapidly amplified because of the higher reproduction rate of the tag's carriers. For example, such an advantage is conferred by a tag associated with 'compatible' mates that produce fewer lethal offspring under crossover. The tag, originally meaningless, takes on a meaning. It comes to stand for a particular kind of compatibility. By developing selective mating conditions based on the tags, the agents can react to this compatibility, thereby increasing their fitness.

In the population-based Prisoner's Dilemma, payoff-biased reproduction provides a similar tag amplification. This, in turn, makes it possible for agents to make useful distinctions. For example, an agent developing a condition that identifies tags associated with 'cooperators' will prosper from the increased payoff that results. As in the selective mating experiments, there is strong selection for combinations of tags and conditions that favour profitable interactions. In effect, the agents develop tacit models, anticipating the effects of interacting with agents having certain kinds of tags.

Agents without tags, under random pairing, execute plays of the PD with random unidentified opponents because there is no basis for implementing conditional interactions. The productive 'tit-for-tat' strategy never evolves in this regime; interactions settle on the disadvantageous minimax defect–defect mode. On the other hand, agents with tags evolve along an entirely different path. At some point, as the strategies evolve, an agent appears that (i) employs tit-for-tat and (ii) has a conditional interaction rule based on a tag carried by a sub-population that is susceptible to tit-for-tat. That is, the agent restricts its interactions to agents having strategies that (often) produce a cooperate–cooperate result under tit-for-tat. The resulting higher reproduction rate causes both this agent and its cooperating partners to spread through the population. Subsequent recombinations provide agents that play tit-for-tat *and* restrict their interactions to other agents playing tit-for-tat. Once established, such a sub-population is very resistant to invasion by other strategies. In biological terms, these agents with their conditional tag-mediated interaction have found an Evolutionarily Stable Strategy (Maynard Smith, 1978).

Rick Riolo has carried out experiments comparing the evolution of adaptive agents with tags (displayed messages) against the evolution of adaptive agents without tags (Riolo, 1992). They confirm the expectations that tags provide an advantage.

Even in the limited confines of the population-based PD, the evolutionary opportunities for adaptive agents with tags go considerably beyond the Evolutionarily Stable Strategy just discussed. For example, mimicry becomes possible. An agent can present the tag associated with tit-for-tat, while pursuing a different strategy. Thus, the presence of an agent with a tag that has a well-defined functional meaning – the tag 'means' tit-for-tat in this case – opens new niches for other agents. It is interesting that these niches are usually constrained in size, depending as they do on the continued presence of the 'founding' agent. In the case of mimicry, as biological studies suggest, the mimic can only occupy a small proportion of the overall population relative to the agents being mimicked. This is because other agents begin to adjust to the deception as the proportion of mimics increases. This negative feedback sets a limit on the mimic's expansion. It is typical that tags provide niches of limited 'carrying capacity', leading to highly diverse systems with no 'super-individual' that outcompetes all comers.

5 A BROADER PERSPECTIVE

Even a cursory look at natural agents uncovers many examples wherein tags encourage diversity and complexity. The studies of chemotaxis in the slime mould initiated by Bonner (Bonner, 1947; and for a review of recent work, Kessin and Campagne, 1992) and the studies of cell adhesion molecules initiated by Edelman (Edelman, 1988; see also Sharon and Lis, 1993) provide two sets of examples of chemical messages and receptors interacting to provide sophisticated organizations. Selective mating based on phenotypic characteristics (Hamilton, 1964), and complex interactions in social insects mediated by pheromones (Hölldobler and Wilson, 1990) provide examples of tag-mediated interactions at a more macroscopic level. If these examples are typical, and I think they are, tags play a critical role in the phylogeny of complex adaptive systems.

To go a step further, I think that tags play a central role in the genesis of the fundamental characteristic of complex adaptive systems: a diverse array of agents that interact in an integrated way. Even a small ecosystem can involve hundreds of thousands of distinct species, a mammalian immune system involves like numbers of antibodies, and a municipality involves thousands of distinct kinds of aggregate social interactions. The diversity is not just a randomly derived conglomeration; rather it is a complex web of interdependent interactions, where the persistence of any agent depends directly on the context provided by the other agents. In the population-based PD, tags make diversity possible by breaking the unexploitable symmetry of random pairing. This observation can be elevated, I think, to a general principle governing complex adaptive systems: tags break symmetries, providing opportunities for diversity.

The most general point I would make is that wherever innovation plays an important role it is important to redirect attention from optimality and equilibrium to improvement and preparation for change. This redirection offers insights even in the simply defined, completely deterministic strategic situations typified by games like chess and Go; it offers still more in the complex, stochastic situations prevailing in modern economies. In chess or Go, it is unlikely that we will ever be able to spell out an optimum strategy (say minimax); instead we search for building-blocks that can be put together to describe board configurations (pawn formation, control of centre, tempo, etc.). Then we try to find improvements in (incomplete) strategic rules that exploit these descriptions. (The history of chess strategies since the Middle Ages nicely illustrates the point.) The same point holds *a fortiori* in the much more complex strategic situations that prevail in modern economies. Provision for sustained exploration in innovative systems is much like making provisions for depreciation: it slows down current exploitation in order to prevent future catastrophes. As in evolutionary biology, rewards go to those that manage to locate improvements.

It will be interesting to see if these points can be confirmed in broader contexts. My own attempt in this direction has been to construct a class of models, the Echo models, that constitute a rigorous cartoon drawn from a broad range of systems that show innovation and learning (Holland, 1992, ch. 10). The focus is on complex adaptive systems such as economies, ecosystems, immune systems and the like. An Echo model employs simplified counterparts of mechanisms common to these systems, such as trade, competition, and interactions conditioned on identification. Under particular settings of the parameters, subsystems in Echo specialize to interactions exhibited by well-studied canonical models, including Wicksell's Triangle, Overlapping Generations models, Prisoner's Dilemma games, Two Armed Bandits and biological arms races. The object is to translate Bohr's correspondence principle to these nascent studies of complex adaptive systems. (The studies of Marimon *et al.*, 1990, provide an excellent example of this kind of correspondence.) Then the evolutionary behaviours observed in Echo can be bridged to well-studied rigorous models. Though the work is still in its early stages, Echo does provide a general framework for thought experiments on innovations generated by the interactions of adaptive agents of limited rationality. With good fortune, the correspondences to canonical models will enable us to start on a useful analytic theory.

References

Axelrod, R. (1987) 'The Evolution of Strategies in the Iterated Prisoner's Dilemma', in L.D. Davis (ed.), *Genetic Algorithms and Simulated Annealing* (Los Altos, Calif.: Morgan Kaufmann) ch. 3.

Belew, R.K. and L.B. Booker (eds) (1991) *Proceedings of the Fourth International Conference on Genetic Algorithms* (Los Altos, Calif.: Morgan Kaufmann).

Bonner, J.T. (1947) 'Evidence for the Formation of Aggregates by Chemotaxis in the Development of the Slime Mold *Dictyostelium discoideum*', *Journal of Experimental Zoology*, vol. 106, pp. 1–26.

Edelman, G.M. (1988) *Topobiology* (New York: Basic Books).

Hahn, F. (1993) Personal communication (Professor Hahn is Professor of Economics at Cambridge University).

Hamilton, W.D. (1964) 'The Genetical Evolution of Social Behaviour' *Journal of Theoretical Biology*, vol. 7, pp. 1–52.

Holland, J.H., K.J. Holyoak, R.E. Nisbett and P.R. Thagard (1986) *Induction: Processes of Inference, Learning and Discovery*, (Cambridge, Mass.: MIT Press).

Holland, J.H. (1992) *Adaptation in Natural and Artificial Systems*, 2nd edn (Cambridge, Mass.: MIT Press).

Hölldobler, B. and E.O. Wilson (1990) *The Ants* (Cambridge, Mass.: Harvard University Press).

Kessin, R.H. and M.M. Van Lookeren Campagne (1992) 'The Development of social Amoeba', *American Scientist*, vol. 80, no. 6, pp. 556–65.

Marimon, R., E. McGratten and T.J. Sargent (1990) 'Money as a Medium of Exchange in an Economy with Artificially Intelligent Agents', *Journal of Economic Dynamics and Control*, vol. 14, pp. 329–73.

Maynard Smith, J. (1978) *The Evolution of Sex* (Cambridge: Cambridge University Press).

Mitchell, M. (1993) Personal communication (Dr Mitchell is Resident Director of the Adaptive Computation Program at the Santa Fe Institute).

Perry, Z.A. (1984) *Experimental Study of Speciation of Ecological Niche Theory Using Genetic Algorithms* (Ann Arbor: University of Michigan Ph.D. Dissertation).

Riolo, R. (1992) Personal communication (Dr Riolo is a post-doctoral researcher at the University of Michigan).

Sharon, N. and H. Lis (1993) 'Carbohydrates in Cell Recognition', *Scientific American*, vol. 268, no. 1, pp. 82–9.

Comment

Frank Hahn

UNIVERSITY OF CAMBRIDGE, UK, AND UNIVERSITY OF SIENA, ITALY

Professor Holland has given us a brief account of the work he and others are, and have been, doing on classifier systems and genetic algorithms. He himself is a distinguished innovator in this field, and he has contributed some crucial theorems. No doubt many readers of his brief survey will be keen to read further on this subject, not least Holland's own book.

It is clearly not appropriate to concentrate my comments on the technicalities. We are discussing rationality with particular reference to economics. Most of us are uneasy with the present picture of the agent optimizing over a given set of constraints once and for all. There is much talk of 'bounded rationality' although I shall argue that this is a misnomer for what we have in mind. In any event I shall devote these comments to an evaluation of Holland's contribution to the well-known concerns of economists concerning rationality.

It is plain that if an agent does not perform an act which it is impossible for it to perform it would be silly to regard this as a sign of irrationality or bounded rationality. If you cannot fly you cannot fly. No human agent is capable of knowing all the economic acts open to him now and over the indefinite future, nor is he capable of forming beliefs (probabilities) over those possibilities. An agent acting under this constraint is neither irrational nor boundedly rational: the agent can do no other. Much of economics has simply ignored these simple facts as any microeconomic textbook will testify. Simon (1976) did not, but in my view stopped short of providing a well-founded theoretical alternative. Of course, with the recent attention which has been given to informational constraints and attempts to learn from evolutionary theory, things have begun to change. However, game theory, until just the other day, has remained a stronghold of all knowing and computationally unlimited agents.

What we seem to be looking for is an account of 'procedural rationality'. This invites us to consider the agent as an algorithm. There are many possible algorithms. Presumably the rational agent is the algorithm which on average has the highest payoff. This raises what might be called a 'meta question': do agents know the set of algorithms available, and if so, are they capable of choosing between them? For instance, does one want to make 'parallelism' a necessary element of procedural rationality? After all, agents may not have heard of it or may not have 'figured it out'. To this must be added as the caveat that, not all knowledge can be gained algorithmically. Take for instance, the truth of Godel's theorem that is beyond doubt but cannot be proved algorithmically.

Holland does not address the question of whether his proposals are to be understood as part of a definition of procedural rationality. He discusses how parallelism in rules and the genetic algorithm can deliver high average payoffs. Certainly one is much impressed by the ingenuity displayed and by the attention given to various non-obvious subtleties – for instance to 'hitchhiking'. But while there are a number of side remarks and illustrative allusions, there is no direct discussion of how this work should fit into a reconstruction of the theory of agents' rationality.

At this stage one must take note of an ambiguity in what is aimed at. The adoption of a notion of rationality or of procedural rationality in the first instance tells one how an agent should be advised to act. It is prescriptive, and if rational actions are thought desirable, normative. But in economics we aim at a theory which has descriptive and perhaps also predictive powers. If economic theory is the aim and not prescription, then we must hope that if theory becomes based on a new concept of rational actions, the concepts, halfway, pass empirical scrutiny. And here clearly one can have doubts concerning Holland's proposed procedure. Of course it may be that Holland's algorithm is not the one with highest average payoffs in the set of algorithms. Holland makes no claim that it is, and so perhaps no claim that it is a necessary feature of a rational agent's decision-making. But I suppose that such a claim can indeed be made, for otherwise there is nothing to discuss other than technicalities.

There are several known ways in which to reconcile the prescriptive and descriptive here. One is of course the lazy man's friend, namely an appeal to 'as if'. It may be that no observed actions of any agent are the outcome of algorithmic computations, but nonetheless they are of the sort we would expect from such computations. It is 'as if' the agent engaged in these calculations. There is a very simple objection to this device in economics, even though it may not apply in other areas. Evidence in economics, whether econometric or experimental, is never clear-cut and never beyond doubt. The 'as if' procedure may have merit in rationalizing well-defined observations, for instance that plants have arranged leaves to maximize the surface area exposed to sunlight. We do not have such well-defined and unambiguous observations in economics. In particular we do not have them when it comes to processes of adaptation, learning and innovating.

Take for instance the exercise in the use of classifiers. This was designed to show that the 'artificially intelligent agents' would come to use money as a medium of exchange. We know that money is used as a medium of exchange, so the evidence is not in dispute here. But how do we decide whether the classifier theory really is an explanation? For that, one would naturally be led to ask whether other models of a process leading to monetary exchange are available. They are. So how do we choose? Only by extending the range of problems to be studied by this method and where the evidence will be less sharp.

The other promising route now much in vogue is by way of evolutionary theory. Agents who behave *à la* Holland will have a higher average payoff, while those that do not, on my present hypothesis, will have a lower average payoff. We now add one of two, or both, further hypotheses. One is that higher average payoff is visible and acts as an inducement to imitation by the non-Hollanders. The other is that the low-payoff agents do not survive economically. If this can be spelled out rigorously and with suitable restrictions, then it may be that 'in the long run' only Hollanders, or mostly Hollanders, will be found in the population. Here, if I may exaggerate, the prescription is a matter of life or death. It not only pays to be a Holland agent but in the long run it is vital. Hence the prescriptive is seen to have turned into the descriptive.

I do not know if this evolutionary scenario can be carried out in anything but the artificial examples we now have. But suppose that it can and that in the long run agents are predominantly Hollanders. Then it is important to understand that this 'long run' is not the traditional 'stochastic' long-run equilibrium of economics. For instance it will be a state with possibly continuous learning and innovations. From what I could gather it would not be a situation in which expected payoffs were maximized by choice of actions but at best by choice of rules of action and of rules for changing rules of action. This invites a new view of equilibrium, and that is one of the challenges the Holland chapter presents. (He himself seems to believe that he is dealing with disequilibrium phenomena. But a set of rules and rules for changing rules which give those adopted by other agents, such that no individual agent has an inducement to change, would certainly fit into a traditional equilibrium concept.)

So it may be that the evolutionary approach is a way in which the prescriptive and descriptive can be reconciled. But a lot of work is needed. In particular we need to be able to classify various algorithms by their average payoffs if the evolutionary story is to be possible. The advantage of the evolutionary approach is that we would not need to assume that agents know the different algorithms. They may hit on particular ones by choice and later by imitation. But for all this we do require the means of ranking algorithms. Holland has only shown us a very good one.

I shall conclude this with a number of remarks.

If one is asked to characterize our current concept of rationality, it is by saying that the agent knows what he wants and he knows how to get it. The first part of this is formalized by the notion of complete, reflexive and transitive preferences, the second by the axiom of revealed preference (or, if one likes, utility maximization). If one includes uncertainty, then the first part is amplified by 'the agent has coherent beliefs' which then leads to Savage. The question is this: is there a comparably satisfactory axiomatic structure for procedural rationality? It seems that by suggesting the particular bidding mechanism for subsets of rules, Holland would wish to continue with the first part of the characterization. (Although a critic may suggest that one also needs to know what one wants.) It is the second part, however, which is the difficulty. I do not know whether Holland would wish to argue that the answer to 'how to get it' is his procedure. He does not say so. As far as practical advice to business etc, is concerned, this does not much matter. But for a theory of procedural rationality it does.

The next remark returns me to evolution. I admit to having considerable reservations about the application of the biological paradigm to human affairs. The important point here is that humans can and do act in response to expected events while genes and DNA cannot. Biologists are hostile to teleological interpretation of evolution, and rightly so. But when applied to humans, some teleology may not only be good but unavoidable in a plausible theory. Hollanders are always looking backwards; many humans look forward. The rules we are given are rules for action, not rules for arriving at beliefs. Could one insinuate Bayes into the story?

Lastly I think one must note that artificial-intelligence research has not been conspicuously successful. I confess to a certain romanticism. When I read mathematics at university I plodded from A to B to C etc. A friend of mine many times went straight from A to Z. (There is a story about von Neumann of the same sort.) These are deep waters, and I leave others to get their feet wet. But I for one confess to considerable scepticism that we can capture inventions, innovations and new insights purely algorithmically.

I conclude with an obvious caveat. None of what has just been said detracts in the slightest from Holland's achievement. The question is simply: will it suffice?

Reference

Simon, H.A. (1976) 'From Substantive to Procedural Rationality', in S.J. Latsis (ed.) *Method and Appraisal in Economics* (Cambridge: Cambridge University Press).

13 Routines, Hierarchies of Problems, Procedural Behaviour: Some Evidence from Experiments*

Massimo Egidi

UNIVERSITÀ DI TRENTO, ITALY

'I still believe that, by what is implicit in its reasoning, economics has come nearer than any other social science to an answer to that central question of all social sciences: How can the combinations of fragment of knowledge existing in different minds bring about results which, if they were to be brought about deliberately, would require a knowledge on the part of the directing mind which no single person can possess? To show that in this sense the spontaneous actions of individuals will, under conditions which we can define, bring about a distribution of resources which can be understood as if it were made according to a single plan, although nobody has planned it, seems to me an answer to the problem which has sometimes been metaphorically described as that of the "social mind".' (Hayek, 1980, p. 54)

1 INTRODUCTION: PROCEDURAL RATIONALITY, ORGANIZATION ROUTINES AND PROBLEM SOLVING

The idea that the learning activity plays a central role in human decision-making derives from the pioneering work of Simon, March and Newell. In 1956, in a path-breaking article which constituted a first crucial step in analyzing rationality within organizations, Cyert, Simon and Trow (1956) carried out an empirical analysis of managerial decisions which revealed an evident 'dualism' of behaviour: on the one

*The present paper is based on a laboratory experiment which has been built as a replication of the original one created by M. Cohen and P. Bacdayan at Michigan University. The experiment would never be realized without the careful assistance and generous help of Michael Cohen. I am very grateful to him and to the group of researchers who actively cooperated at the organization of the experiment in Trento: Nicolao Bonini, Alessandro Narduzzo, Salvatore Traina, Paolo Patelli, Riccardo Pereira. They carefully implemented all the steps of the experiment, and critically discussed with me the principal findings. Of course the responsibility for the findings is entirely mine.

hand, a coherent choice among alternatives; on the other, a search for the knowledge required to make the choice. For several months, an observer monitored the decisions made by the executives in a particular firm and recorded a number of features entirely at odds with the prescriptions of the decision theory then current. The principal finding was that when decisions are made in condition of high uncertainty – conditions, that is, poorly structured in terms of knowledge, beliefs, information – their outcomes are not easily assessed. This activates a *search* process intended to frame all the elements involved in the decision.

A dichotomy between types of decision consequently arises, in relation to the different level to which the problems involved are cognitively structured:

> Decisions in organizations vary widely with respect to the extent to which the decision-making process is programmed. At one extreme we have repetitive, well-defined problems (e.g., quality control or production lot-size problems) involving tangible considerations, to which the economic models that call for finding the best among a set of pre-established alternatives can be applied rather literally. In contrast to these highly programmed and usually rather detailed decisions are problems of non-repetitive sort, often involving basic long-range questions about the whole strategy of the firm or some part if it, arising initially in a highly unstructured form and requiring a great deal of the kinds of search processes listed above. (Cyert, Simon and Trow, 1956, p. 238)

What are the features of decisions taken in a highly programmed decision context? Many field observations of human behaviour in organizations show that in well-structured conditions, where subjects must implement sequences of choices *vis-à-vis* alternatives well known to them, their behaviour becomes *routinized*. The sequence of choices confronted by individuals performing an organizational task constitutes a repetitive *procedure* which is memorized, becomes familiar to those executing it, and presents well-defined alternatives codified according to the variants arising from changing external circumstances. Most human activity within economic organizations takes the form of this procedural and routinized behaviour.

If individuals are able to memorize repeated sequences of decisions deriving from their interactions with others, and then execute at least parts of them 'automatically', the role of routines becomes clear: they enable individuals to save on 'rational computation' and radically reduce the complexity of individual decisions. This narrowly restricts the area in which substantive rationality needs to be exercised, and therefore reduces decision 'errors'.

It must be emphasized that this role of routinized behaviour within the decision process – in order to reduce the need for rational computation – is only a working hypothesis, and must be analyzed carefully in order to understand its consequences and to find empirical evidence for it. An effort to explore more precisely how routinized behaviour reduces the need for 'rational computation' has been made by Nelson and Winter (1982), on the basis of the methodological principles enunciated by M. Polanyi in *Personal Knowledge* (1958). They note that some behaviourial sequences consist of actions which are often partially inarticulate, i.e. they are not expressed linguistically, and need not be transmitted in the form of messages. This feature leads Nelson and Winter to the problem of how *tacit knowledge* is formed, transferred and stored in memory. This is an interesting starting point for exploring how cognitive skills, which arise through experience and cooperation, are stored in memory and consequently become building-blocks for subjects who have to solve problems. Along this line of research, Cohen and Bacdayan (1991) suggest that routines are stored as *procedural* memory; following Squire's (1987) distinction between procedural and declarative memory they claim that *procedural* memory appears to be the form that stores the components of individual skilled actions – for both motor and cognitive skills. It is distinguished from *declarative* memory, which provides the storage of facts, propositions, and events (1991, p. 5). They use a laboratory experiment to analyze the emergence of procedural behaviour by two subjects involved in a game which requires coordination and cooperation, and its 'sedimentation' in memory. I will return later to the specific issues raised by their article, because the present chapter is based on a replication of their experiment. The general point at issue here is how the acquisition and memorization of cognitive skills takes place, and how its transfer is possible, i.e. how skills can be re-used. Unfortunately, as Singley and Anderson show (1989), the range of transfer of procedurally encoded skills seems to be very restricted; the two authors demonstrate that progress in this domain has been very limited and further progress is required before we can adequately understand the phenomenon. It is clear that any future success along this direction will progressively shed light on the unsolved aspects of the process of skills acquisition and the creation of new routines.

My purpose here is to explore some of the features of human problem-solving, skills creation and the emergence of routines by conducting careful analysis of the results yielded by replication of Cohen and Bacdayan's experiment.

To clarify the question, let us frame the problem of skills creation in relation to decision-making processes. When a decision is highly unstructured, we are in the situation that Cyert and Simon called non-programmed decisions, where the predominant role is played by the search for the knowledge required to solve a problem. In this situation, not only must subjects gather information, they must also be able to select the information and knowledge that is effectively relevant to their purposes and to assimilate it into the system of knowledge that they already possess. To do so, they must have a 'level of competence' adequate to the situation of choice; they must, that is, implement skills of learning and problem-solving. The core of the decision-making process is therefore the activity of search and learning that furnishes actors with the information and knowledge they require to achieve their goals.

The conditions for standard choice theory to be applied are entirely lacking, because the preferences orderings are highly incomplete, decisions are inter-temporally inconsistent and choices are largely ineffective in relation to the goals to be pursued. The most important part of the process is driven by the ability of the subjects to formulate and solve problems. The problem is how to model this kind of situation.

One way of tackling the problem is based on the idea that the solution to a task can be found by recursively decomposing it into a set of simpler interrelated tasks. This idea, now widely used in the problem-solving theoretical domain, originates from March and Simon's book *Organizations* (1958). To better understand its origin, let us distinguish between two different aspects of routines: on the one hand, there is the aspect that I have emphasized above, i.e. their relationship to the cognitive structures and decision processes of individuals; on the other, routines can be regarded as elementary units which form the basic structures internal to organizations.

Within the organization, we can consider as *routine* any procedure which provides for the execution of a specific task; it is therefore a procedure which solves a set of problems internal to the organization. A procedure can be described as a set of instructions determining the actions to be taken when dealing with a particular circumstance. It seems natural, therefore, to model a procedure as a *program*, in the specific sense given to the term by computation theory, as a list of instructions in an artificial language. This enables us to represent procedures formally and model *procedural rationality* (March and Simon, 1958, ch. 6).

Of course, if we try to describe the functioning of an organization as governed by a hierarchy of procedures, we *cannot* attribute to individuals the ability to memorize, routinize and execute them with precision: if we assume that individuals behave like automata endowed with unlimited memory, we fall into an error similar to that committed by the proponents of 'Olympian' rationality when they attribute to economic agents unlimited computational skills. In reality, individuals do not usually possess precise and detailed knowledge of organizational procedures; they have 'incomplete' knowledge, and they are able to complete it by *recreating its missing components*.

The last observation sums up the central problem of the present chapter: how to explain the ability of individuals to create procedures or recreate missing parts of them while they are coordinating their skills and intellectual efforts to achieve a given goal.[1] As I have said, an important approach used in the cognitive sciences adopts the idea that individuals solve problems by decomposing them into a set of interrelated sub-problems. The methodological status of this approach is twofold: on the one hand, the approach originates from empirical observation of *real human behaviours*; on the other, it is the outcome of careful analysis of the *nature of problems* (mainly in games and other formalized contexts) and therefore is normative in character. As usual, the normative and descriptive aspects of this approach cannot be separated: the models based on the decomposition of problems – like Laird, Newell and Rosembloom's (1987) 'Soar' – do not pretend to be accurate replications of the deep psychological mechanisms behind human behaviour; they merely seek to replicate human behaviours or at least successfully to compete with them. By consequence, an implicit 'as if' hypothesis is presupposed by this approach. It is my purpose to try to reduce the domain of validity of the 'as if' hypothesis and to verify – by means of laboratory experiments – to what extent the problem-decomposition approach can be considered as providing a good explanation of human learning process, at least in playing games.

I will examine how individuals learn to identify the sub-goals, to link them to each other, and to build 'production rules' and procedures for solving elementary sub-goals. On this basis I will explore the emergence of behavioural rules – which involve cooperation – and their relationship with routinized behaviours.

One of the most interesting results which emerge from the experiments is this: if a problem to be solved has a variety of different aspects, as happens in card games when there is a large number of different initial configurations, the learning process dominates the actors' activity. To achieve their goals, players make sequences of moves which depend on the configurations of the game; these sequences are *organizational routines*, which cannot be memorized by players because of their variety and number. Players do *not* keep all knowledge and information they need to play stored in memory: they create and memorize a set of simple 'meta rules'[2] which allow them to generate the organizational routines. These rules are elementary 'production rules' (in the standard sense of cognitive sciences), which are the result of sub-goals identification and allow players to recreate the missing knowledge at any particular moment.

2   TRANSFORM THE TARGET

The game 'Transform the Target' described here was first devised by Michael Cohen and Paul Bacdayan for the experimental study of the development of behaviourial routines in a cooperative context. It is a card game in which two players must cooperate in order to achieve a pre-established goal. A fixed payoff is awarded to each pair of players when the tournament is finished. This payoff is the greater the more rapidly the players complete their games, and it is awarded to the pair, not to the individual, so that both players have an incentive to cooperate.

The game is played on the computer rather than with cards. The players move the cards they see on the computer screen using the mouse. The two players' moves and all the movements of the mouse are recorded, thus providing a detailed information base on the games. A tournament of 40 games involving 32 pairs of players was organized and recorded, replicating the original tournament by Cohen and Bacdayan. I give below the rules of the game as described by the two authors.

The game is played by two players using six cards: the 2, 3 and 4 of a red suit, and the 2, 3 and 4 of a black suit. The players are called respectively Numberkeeper (NK) and Colorkeeper (CK). When the cards are dealt, each player can see only the card in his hand, the card on the target and the card in 'Up' position. The board is illustrated in Figure 13.1. Colorkeeper cannot see the card that Numberkeeper has in his hand and *vice versa*.

In each hand that is played, the ultimate object is to put the red two into the area

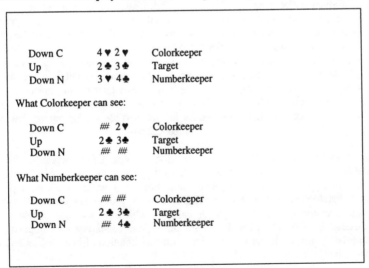

Down C	4 ♥ 2 ♥	Colorkeeper
Up	2 ♣ 3 ♣	Target
Down N	3 ♥ 4 ♣	Numberkeeper

What Colorkeeper can see:

Down C	## 2 ♥	Colorkeeper
Up	2 ♣ 3 ♣	Target
Down N	## ##	Numberkeeper

What Numberkeeper can see:

Down C	## ##	Colorkeeper
Up	2 ♣ 3 ♣	Target
Down N	## 4 ♣	Numberkeeper

Figure 13.1   The board of 'Transform the Target'

marked 'Target'. A move in the game is an exchange of the card in a player's hand with one of the cards on the board (or a 'Pass', making it the other player's turn).

Each player is subject to a restriction on moves: Colorkeeper may make exchanges with the target area only if the colour in the target is preserved. Numberkeeper may exchange with the target only if the action preserves the number in the target area. Exchanges with board areas other than the target are not restricted (Cohen and Bacdayan, 1991). Colorkeeper moves first.

Summarizing, during the game a player can make one of the following moves:

U – exchange his card with the card Up
C – exchange his card with the face-down card on the left of Ck's card
N – exchange his card with the face-down card on the left of Nk's card
T – exchange his card with Target
P – pass

A state of the game is defined by the distribution of the cards on the board. Players do not have full and direct information about the current state of the game, because there are covered cards. Their knowledge of the situation is incomplete, and they must conjecture on the state of the game. The more the game proceeds, the wider is the information collected by players (if they use information in an intelligent way).

Each of the 32 pairs of players played the tournament using the same distribution of cards as all the others. Figure 13.2 shows the sequence of the games played by the 32 pairs with an initial configuration of 4H 2H 2C 3H 4C (nH here denotes card n of Hearts, and mC denotes card m of Clubs). This sequence represents the initial board of the game according to the following convention: the cards placed on the board are treated as the elements of a matrix with three rows and two columns $B(i,j)$, ($i = 1..2$, $j = 1..3$). Figure 13.2 gives an example.

For a given initial distribution of cards, each player has a wide set of possible strategies at his disposal. To find a strategy (and if it exists the best one) a player can follow the standard von Neumann – Morgenstern procedure: he can build the game tree by applying in order all the rules to the possible initial states. However, whereas in the case of (perfect) information games like chess where the initial state is known to both players, so that a tree of strategies can be constructed right from the unique initial state, in this game the initial state is unknown to the two players. At the starting configuration of a hand, each of the two players ignores the three covered cards: each player must therefore deduce the six possible configurations that may occur (counting the disposition of the three unknown cards in the three covered positions, we have six possible configurations).

At the beginning of the game neither of the players knows which of the six possible configurations is the 'real' one. This they can only discover by acquiring further information as they play their hand. For every initial board each player should therefore prepare a strategy. This manner of proceeding obviously would require a memory and a computing capacity which far exceeds normal *non-specialized* human capacities. These are the typical conditions of computational complexity which highlight the relevance of the assumption of bounded rationality.

Moreover, the experiment shows that individuals do not proceed in the manner suggested by the classic model of Olympian rationality. The players are unable to

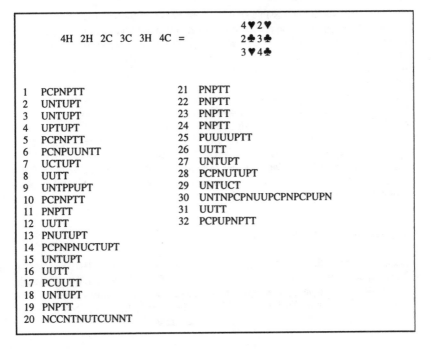

1	PCPNPTT	21	PNPTT
2	UNTUPT	22	PNPTT
3	UNTUPT	23	PNPTT
4	UPTUPT	24	PNPTT
5	PCPNPTT	25	PUUUUPTT
6	PCNPUUNTT	26	UUTT
7	UCTUPT	27	UNTUPT
8	UUTT	28	PCPNUTUPT
9	UNTPPUPT	29	UNTUCT
10	PCPNPTT	30	UNTNPCPNUUPCPNPCPUPN
11	PNPTT	31	UUTT
12	UUTT	32	PCPUPNPTT
13	PNUTUPT		
14	PCPNPNUCTUPT		
15	UNTUPT		
16	UUTT		
17	PCUUTT		
18	UNTUPT		
19	PNPTT		
20	NCCNTNUTCUNNT		

Figure 13.2 Sequence of games played by 32 pairs of players starting from the configuration 4H 2H 2C 3C 3H 4C (experimental data)

use all the information available, and in many cases they are not able to memorize all of it. This depends on the constraints imposed by two types of memory – i.e., the ability to process a little information instantaneously, and the ability to process a lot of information but only through storage in the long-term memory – which make it impossible to adopt a plan which incorporates all six possible configurations (Cohen and Bacdayan, 1991). The experimental data (see below) confirm the fact that the players do not use all the available information. This is because they cannot memorize all of it simultaneously, and because they do not conduct a thorough search of all the rules space.

If each player is unable to memorize all the configurations and to discover the best strategy available, what kind of search process can he activate to find a (good) strategy? The classic analysis of the process of strategic search – Nilsson (1980), Pearl (1984), Newell (1990) – is based on the idea that to each state of the tree can be assigned an evaluator which enables the player to choose among the different local strategies which appear (locally) optimal. The problem with this approach is that the evaluators are supposed to be 'given' exogenously; there is no method by which the evaluators can be generated endogenously.

A different approach is based on the idea that I discussed in the Introduction, namely that the solution to a task can be found by decomposing it into a set of simpler interrelated tasks. As we shall prove experimentally, players do not normally explore all the possible strategies, but move on the space of strategies and sub-strategies, solving local problems and using them as building blocks with which to solve further problems. We shall see that the search in the space of sub-problems is a highly uncertain and conjectural process. In fact when a problem has been decomposed into a set of sub-problems, generally not all of the sub-problems will be immediately solvable. The main goal – at this stage of the exploration – is to understand the relations among sub-problems. During their attempts to understand the connections among problems, players do not focus their attention immediately on the existence of procedures which allow the sub-problems to be solved. The problem space is explored in the sense that new sub-problems and new connections among the sub-problems are discovered; the aim being to reduce recursively complex problems to simpler ones and to understand their reciprocal relationships. This exploration, however, does not require that the solutions of the 'simpler' problems should be known.

3 THE SPACE OF THE SUB-GOALS

Let us see how the space of the sub-problems for the game described above (henceforth Transform the Target) can be constructed. As I have said, the problem is to put 2♥ in the Target. At the beginning of the card game any other card may be in the Target. Reasoning 'backwards' and using the rules of the game, one finds that 2♥ can be put into the Target area only if (see Figure 13.3):

(1) 3♥ or 4♥ is in the Target and the player with 2♥ in his hand is the Colorkeeper;
(2) 2♣ is in the target and the player with 2♥ in his hand is the Numberkeeper.

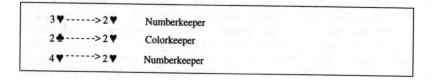

3♥ ------> 2♥	Numberkeeper
2♣ ------> 2♥	Colorkeeper
4♥ ------> 2♥	Numberkeeper

Figure 13.3

The problem can therefore be solved if at the beginning of the game one of the three cards 4♥, 3♥, 2♣ is in the Target area. Let us instead suppose that one of the remaining cards, i.e. 3♣, or 4♣, is in the Target. In this case, the game can be solved if we are able to reduce it to the situation above, i.e. to put one of the cards 4♥, 3♥, 2♣ in the Target. Applying the rules we see that this is effectively possible, and by reasoning backwards as before we obtain relations shown in Figure 13.4.

We have therefore decomposed the problem into its sub-goals. Of course, this is only one of the possible decompositions that could be performed, and takes account

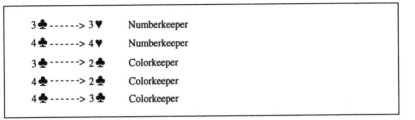

Figure 13.4

only of the situation in the Target. As we shall see from experimental examination of the sequences, there are good grounds for considering it of particular importance.

If we combine these relations among sub-goals we obtain the diagram in Figure 13.5. The nodes of the diagram represent the cards that can be in the Target position of the game board. The nodes adjacent to a given node indicate the cards that can be placed by Nk or by Ck on the Target to replace the card currently on it. For example, if 4♣ is in the Target area, the rules allow its exchange with 4♥, with 3♣ or with 2♣. If we concentrate only what happens on the Target during the game, we find that the sequence of cards follows the connections in Figure 13.1.

Of course, the rules state that certain moves can only be made by Nk and others only by Ck. Figure 13.5 is arranged so that all the horizontal lines represent permissible moves by the Numberkeeper *but not* by the Colorkeeper. Conversely, all the vertical and oblique lines represent moves that Ck is permitted to make but Nk is not.

It is possible to reconstruct the sequences of cards in the Target during a game. This can be done by following the paths in the diagram which begin with the card

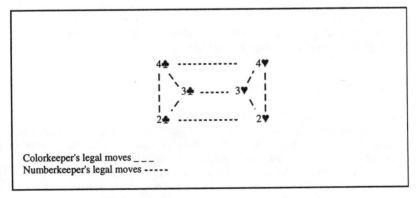

Figure 13.5   Diagram of sub-goals

1	-	4♣	4♥	2♥			
2	-	4♣	2♣	2♥			
3	-	4♣	3♣	3♥	2♥		
4	-	4♣	3♣	2♣	2♥		
5	-	4♣	3♣	3♥	4♥	2♥	
6	-	4♣	3♣	3♥	4♥	4♣ 2♣	2♥
7	-	4♣	....				

Figure 13.6　Paths and Hamiltonians in the sub-goals space

that was on the Target at the beginning and finish with the card on the Target at the end. For example, if the initial card in the Target was 4♣ and the final card is 2♥, then we have the paths as in Figure 13.6

Figure 13.6 therefore represents the space of the sub-goals that the players may – fully or partially – figure out in order to solve the game. Different paths represent different decompositions of the final goal into partial goals.

One notes immediately that the first five paths pass only once through a given node. Every longer path passes more than once through at least one node. In case 6 in Figure 13.6, for instance, the path passes twice through node 4♣.

The situation that arises when 4♣ is on the Target is of particular interest for its complexity, and I shall therefore use it as an example. In Figure 13.6 the paths in the diagram which begin with 4♣ are ordered according to the (increasing) number of nodes that are passed through. Paths 1 and 2 are equivalent because they both compose three nodes, while the others contain a larger number of nodes. It is usually possible to find the minimal path (or paths) connecting two nodes in the diagram, and in our case it is indeed a trivial undertaking: they are the two paths 4♣ 2♣ 2♥ and 4♣ 4♥ 2♥, which are therefore optimal.

The final goal of putting 2♥ into the Target can be achieved with one move if the card on the Target at the beginning of the game is 3♥, 2♣ or 4♥. These are the cards adjacent to node 2♥ in Figure 13.6. In all other cases intermediate goals must be accomplished before the final goal is achieved.

4 CONJECTURAL STRATEGIES

The diagram of the sub-goals (Figure 13.5) can be used to formulate the following working hypothesis: the players do not learn and memorize a game strategy which enables them to behave optimally. Instead, they learn and memorize the diagram of sub-goals, or a part of it, and then use it to devise their own game strategy. Since a strategy must enable a player to decide the move to be made at every state of the game, the problem is whether there exists a concise way of representing the strategy, or whether the player must remember the entire tree of moves of which it is composed. Only if there exists a set of rules which are sufficiently short and simple to be memorized by the player can we assume that he is able to learn it and use it.

In Transform the Target this set of simple rules exists, and it derives from the conjectural decomposition of the problems space. The players generate a fraction of strategy at each stage of the game on the basis of whichever sub-goal is important at the time. I would stress that this is a *conjectural* search (Egidi, 1992) by pointing out that the existence of a given path in the diagram (Figure 13.5) indicates that the problem *admits* to a solution, but that it does not *constructively* provide a solution. The players realize that the problem can be solved, i.e. that there is a procedure which if adopted by them will lead to the desired outcome, but they do not know what this procedure is.

For example, suppose that the card initially on the Target is 4♣. In this case one solution is the sequence 4♣ 2♣ 2♥, and it is reached as follows: Ck puts 2♣ on the Target and Nk puts 2♥ on the Target; 2♣ and 2♥ are the 'key-cards' in this sequence, otherwise they will have to search for the key-cards and then lay them on the Target. Because the two players can always find the two hidden cards, a solution certainly exists.

Accordingly, a solution to the problem exists, but we have not yet specified it in detail. We know that a sequence of key-cards can be put on the Target in order to achieve the goal. But we do not know exactly what sequence of moves Ck and Nk must perform. This manner of proceeding is entirely different from strategy identification in traditional game theory. In the latter case, in fact, to identify a strategy it is necessary to construct the game tree, and therefore to construct the sequences that lead to the desired outcome, but this is not necessary in the scheme analyzed here.

A simple analogy shows that this is an issue with a general bearing on learning and discovery processes. Consider the discovery of theorems in a formalized theory. On the one hand, we have theorems of pure *existence*, which show that the problem is capable of solution. On the other, there are *constructive* theorems which indicate how to find the solution; i.e. ones derived from an algorithm (or procedure) which leads to the solution.

The experimental results discussed below show that this distinction is reflected in the behaviour of the two players, since for the majority of players it is much easier to explore the space of the sub-problems and find the correct paths than it is to identify the procedures required to accomplish these paths.

5 COORDINATION AND SIGNALS

Once both players have identified a path in the diagram, i.e. a sequence of key-cards that must be put on the Target, the problem is that they cannot communicate to each other which path they want to follow. Each player can understand which path the other intends to pursue only by observing the moves that his partner makes. If there is only one optimal path, as happens for example when there is a hearts card on the Target (see Figure 13.5), the interaction between the two players is very simple, and coordination can straightforwardly take place because each player has only one task to perform. If there are two optimal paths, as happens when the 3 or 4 of clubs is on the Target, the players may find coordination extremely difficult, given that the

Conjectural strategy	Card on Target at the beginning	Numberkeeper's sub-strategy	Colorkeeper's sub-strategy	
1	3♥	Reveal 2♥	Seek 2♥	
2	4♥	Reveal 2♥	Seek 2♥	
3	2♣	Seek 2♥	Reveal 2♥	
4	3♣	Seek 3♥	Reveal 3♥	Goto 1
5	3♣	Reveal 2♣	Seek 2♣	Goto 3
6	4♣	Seek 4♥	Reveal 4♥	Goto 2
7	4♣	Reveal 2♣	Seek 2♣	Goto 3

Seek X means: look for card X and put it into the Target area.
Reveal X means: put card X on Up so that your partner can use it.

Figure 13.7

information that each of them obtains from watching the first moves of the other is normally not enough to discover which path has been chosen. In this case, the goals that the two players set themselves may be incompatible, and the game will require ad adjustment of goals after a certain number of moves. This therefore raises a first kind of coordination problem: the coordination of goals.

In the case in which the two players' goals are compatible – that is, both of them have chosen to follow the same path in the diagram – in order to implement their strategy they must acquire the key-card for that path. To do this, they must conduct a search that can proceed in many different ways, both because of the distribution of the cards and because of the different forms that cooperation between the two players can take. Here a second form of coordination takes place: the coordination of procedures.

In order to examine the features of the two kinds of coordination, we must first clarify how a player decides which move to make. As an example, assume that at the beginning of a hand the card on the target is 4♣. If players are able to signal to each other that they want to follow the path 4♣ 2♣ 2♥, their actions will be the following:

Ck looks for 2♣ and, if he has 2♥ in his hand, he reveals it to Nk. When he finds 2♣, he keeps it in his hand and puts it in the target.

If Nk has 2♣ in his hand, he reveals it to Ck. He then looks for 2♥ and, when he finds it, he keeps it in his hand, and waits until Ck puts 2♣ in the target. He finally puts 2♥ in the target.

Of course the problem is how the players can signal to each other the sub-goal they wish to pursue. Before discussing this crucial point, let us generalize the example above. If we extend the analysis to the other minimal paths in the diagram (Figure 13.5), we obtain Figure 13.7.

We have thus identified the strategies that the players must adopt on the basis of minimal paths for each of the possible initial situations of the Target. Figure 13.7

requires some comment. The original task (putting the 2♥ into the Target) has been divided into independent tasks each of which must be completed by a different player.

To understand better how players may coordinate themselves, it is convenient to classify the hands into two orders of difficulty, in relation to the different 'distances' between the card on the target at the beginning of the hand and the final position (2♥ on the Target). This distance is easily measured in terms of the number of sub-goals which compose the problem to be solved: looking at the diagram of sub-goals (Figure 13.5) and counting the number of branches which connect the 2♥ with the card in the Target at the beginning, gives us the number of the sub-goals.

In cases 1, 2, 3 in Figure 13.7 there is only one branch connecting 2♥ with the card in the Target. I classify this kind of hand as being at a 'low' level of difficulty; in cases 4, 5, 6, 7 (Figure 13.7) there are two branches connecting 2♥ with the card in the Target, and I will consider hands of this kind as being at a 'high' level of difficulty.

There are good reasons for this classification. In the case of configurations with a low level of difficulty, in fact, in order to achieve their goal the players must perform actions which require a very elementary kind of goal coordination, one which does *not* require signalling. One of the players – the action leader – must search for the key-card and place it in the Target. The role of the other player is simply to reveal the key-card if he has it in his hand. Consequently, if the players have a clear idea of their elementary goal, they can accomplish it without any further information. In the opposite case of hands with a high level of difficulty, the players must choose between two different paths (at least), and therefore each player must understand the sub-task chosen by his partner in order to move consistently with him.

To coordinate their tasks, the players must use the information arising from the board regarding the status of the cards and eventually the moves which have been made. Let us see how the board status and the moves can be considered as a signalling system which enables the players to coordinate their goals.

Note that in hands with a high level of difficulty (cases 4, 5, 6, 7 in Figure 13.7) the sequences of actions to perform have been divided into two stages according to the two sub-goals pursued. For example, suppose that the card initially in the Target is 4♥ and that the players adopt strategy no 7. This strategy consists of a first phase in which Nk must search for 4♥. When Nk has placed 4♥ in the Target, Ck must search for 2♥ (the second phase of the strategy) in order to put it in the Target.

In each of these two phases there is a 'Leader' player who must *search* for key-card, and a 'follower' who must *reveal* to him that card if he has it. The follower may even help the leader in his search, and if this happens the problem arises of coordinating the search for the key-card. Involved here is *procedural coordination*, which only appears when it is clear to both players which key-card they must search for. As we shall see below, the helping behaviour of the follower is usually inefficient: the move effective course of action, in fact, is one in which the follower only *reveals* the key-card if he has it in his hand, instead of trying to help the leader in his search.

To return to our example, if during the first phase the follower does not have the leader's key-card (4♥) in his hand, instead of waiting until the leader finds 4♥ and puts it in the Target he can immediately start searching for his own key-card, the 2 of Hearts. In this way the second phase is anticipated and performed in parallel with the first, since the two players search *simultaneously* for their key-card: the Colorkeeper for 2♥ and the Numberkeeper for 4♥.

This obviously raises a serious problem of *sub-goal coordination*: how, in fact, can the two players know the card that the other is searching for? Since they cannot signal their intentions, they can only act according to the information yielded by the board, that is, on the moves that have been made. The question is this: is the information rich enough to allow players to understand unambiguously each other's intention and therefore to coordinate their action?

I discuss this crucial point in Section 8; in the section which now follows I go deeper into the distinction between procedural coordination and sub-task coordination.

6   CONJECTURAL STRATEGIES AND PROCEDURAL COORDINATION

Let us return to the analysis of the nature of the strategies listed in Figure 13.7. Each strategy can be realized by executing a set of rules, like 'Search for 2♥' or 'Reveal 4♣'. I shall call 'conjectural strategy' the set of rules which, if followed by the player, lead to completion of the task. Note that these are not strategies in the traditional sense of the term until the *generic* terms 'Seek' and 'Reveal' are transformed into precise *procedures*. At this stage, we can be sure that the game can be successfully played because we know that the players can always successfully conduct their search for the key-cards, even if we do not know the procedures which allow the effective sequence of moves to be made. This is why I use the term 'conjectural': a conjecture must be made in order to assume that the procedures which solve the elementary problems (e.g. 'Seek 2♥') exist and are viable.

To take the final step and transform conjectural strategies into a true procedure (i.e. with a set of rules which state unequivocally the moves that the players must make at every moment of the game), the procedures corresponding to 'Seek' and 'Reveal' must be fully specified. This can be done in many different ways as regards the 'Seek' procedure, depending on how the two players decide to coordinate their actions during the search.

It is obvious that every conjectural strategy identifies a single path. But the relation does not hold in reverse: to each path, in fact, there usually corresponds several strategies. Let us assume that, in order to implement a strategy, the two players decide to acquire the key-cards of the particular path. To do this, they must conduct a search which can take different forms – both because of the arrangement of the cards and because of the different ways in which cooperation between the two players can take place. The problem is therefore to discover the relations between each path and the possible solutions it leads to; that is, the strategies which, if adopted by the two players, enable them to follow the desired path.

The difference between the path and the strategy that realizes it can also be viewed in procedural terms. In fact, the existence of a specific path in the diagram shows that the problem admits a solution, but it does not constructively provide one. The players realize that the problem can be solved, i.e. that there is a procedure which if adopted by them will lead to the desired outcome, but they do not know the procedure(s). On the basis of this observation we can distinguish between substantive coordination and procedural coordination. Substantive coordination is coordination which derives from choosing consistent paths. Procedural coordination derives from jointly devising or discovering a procedure with which plans can be implemented.

Obviously the substantive coordination problem takes very different forms depending on the card in Target. In the first three cases in Figure 13.7, each player has only one possible strategy (optimal or satisficing) available. Hence the substantive coordination can take place as long as each of the two players is aware of the (only) strategy available to the other. The most interesting cases are those in which 3♣ or 4♣ is in the Target area, because the two players have two entirely different strategies available to them. This raises the problem of understanding which of the two strategies the other player intends to use, and therefore of coordinating their actions.

The problem of procedural coordination arises instead in all cases, whatever the card in the Target area may be. In fact, what do 'Reveal' and 'Seek' mean?

'Reveal' may assume slightly different meanings. It is given a 'minimalist' interpretation when a player has a card in his hand which the other is looking for, and which he must reveal by putting in position Up (if he does not have the card in his hand he 'passes', and the other player must perform the search). A stronger interpretation is when a player realizes what card his partner is looking for and seeks it himself in order to reveal the card to him when he has found it. This stronger version entails a procedural coordination problem in the search. The two players may hinder each other if they are both simultaneously seeking the same card. The same holds for the meaning of 'Seek': players can adopt a procedure (UUPT) which involves joint information or a procedure (PCPN) which allows one player only to gather information (see Cohen and Bacdayan, 1991).

Note that if the players move into the diagram of goals (Figure 13.5) while they search for a path connecting the goal (2♥) with the card in the Target (4♣ for example), if they discover the two minimal paths 4♣ 4♥ 2♥ and 4♣ 2♣ 2♥, they find the two optimal solutions not as a consequence of an exhaustive search in the diagram, but because these two solutions are 'easier' to discover. The discovery of the minimal path is therefore not the consequence of choice optimally performed, as the traditional rational choice model suggests: as we will see below, players do not try to make an exhaustive search in the space of the possible procedures before choosing: more 'practically' they identify the minimum path simply by making the minimum effort during their exploration. In this kind of game, in fact, the shortest path between the goal and the card in the target is also the easiest to discover.

7 THE EMERGENCE OF META-RULES

The main point I want to clarify at this stage of the analysis is whether players, after an initial period of learning, behave in a routinized way. We need therefore to define what the routinized behaviour is expected to be in this specific context, and then experimentally check if it emerges from players' actions.

A first possible routinzed behaviour would consist in a fixed choice of one only among the different possible paths connecting two nodes in the diagram of sub-goals (Figure 13.5). If players discover only a part of the diagram of subgoals, they can be tempted to use only this subset. More specifically, we must check if players discover one only of the two alternative conjectural strategies which can be chosen in order to put 2♥ on the Target when the hand is of a high level of difficulty (3♣ or 4♣ on Target).

If we observe only the sequence of cards which appear on the Target during a hand, we see sequences 4♣ 4♥ 2♥ and 4♣ 2♣ 2♥ (the two minimal paths), or more complex ones, like 4♣ 3♣ 3♥ 2♥. To be brief, hereafter I shall call respectively 442 and 422 the two minimal paths 4♣ 4♥ 2♥ and 4♣ 2♣ 2♥. Analogously, I shall use 332 and 322 instead of 3♣ 3♥ 2♥ and 3♣ 2♣ 2♥ (Figure 13.8).

Suppose that the card initially on the Target is 4♣. In this case the two minimal paths are 422 and 442, and the key-cards are 4♥, 2♣, 2♥. Note that whatever path is followed by the players to reach the final goal, only Colorkeeper can make use of 2♣ and only Numberkeeper can use 4♥, while 2♥ can be utilized by both the players. The same holds if 3♣ is initially on the Target. Therefore it is convenient to call 4♥ or 3♥ 'the key-card of Numberkeeper', to call 2♣ 'the key-card of Colorkeeper', and finally to call 2♥ the 'double key-card'.[3]

Assume that during the first hands the players progressively learn to identify some of the different sub-goals and the elementary relations which link them together. In other words, assume that they discover a part (at least) of the sub-goals space represented in Figure 13.5. Suppose for example that they become progressively aware of one of the paths connecting 4♣ with 2♥, the 442 path. We can say that they behave in a routinized way if, after discovery of path 442, they decide to stick to this solution for every hand starting with 4 clubs on the Target (the same holds for hands starting with 3♣).

If the great majority of players behaved as if they were routinized, we might observe a large number of couples following either the 442 or the 422 path, and a small number of players choosing the two optimal paths indifferently.

Figure 13.8 sets out the empirical results. On the horizontal axis we have the times that the path 442 has been chosen (the total number of hands where either 442 or 422 strategy can be applied is 15). On the vertical axis we have the number of couples who have played a given mixed path. It is clear that the players who

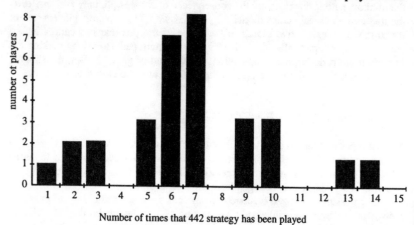

Number of times that 442 strategy has been played

Figure 13.8

	Hand Number	Path 442 and 332	Path 422 and 322	Total
1	1	13	13	26
2	2	18	13	31
3	3	3	29	32
4	4	20	11	31
5	6	2	29	31
6	7	13	17	30
7	9	6	26	32
8	11	3	29	32
9	13	23	9	32
10	14	2	30	32
11	16	1	31	32
12	20	19	13	32
13	22	4	28	32
14	23	30	2	32
15	24	3	29	32
16	25	22	10	32
17	26	18	12	30
18	27	13	19	32
19	28	0	31	31
20	29	25	6	31
21	33	4	28	32
22	34	0	32	32
23	35	4	28	32
24	36	0	32	32
25	37	28	4	32
26	39	2	30	32
27	40	20	12	32

Figure 13.9

followed one path only are a minority (they are represented on the two extreme sides of the statistical distribution) while the great majority adopt the 442 path about 50 per cent of times, and 422 the remaining 50 per cent.

The conclusion is striking: most of the players do *not* react in a routinized way to the situations that arise when the 3 or 4 of clubs is on the Target, in the sense that they do not use the same set of rules to reach the goal whatever the initial configuration of card is on the board: they do not use only one of the two alternative conjectural strategies that can be activated – they use both, depending on the further information arising from the board. There is a normal distribution around a central type which is characterized by a choice for about 50 per cent of times of path 442 and for 50 per cent of path 422. This is a very flexible behaviour in term of goals achievement. To adopt this kind of behaviour, individuals must understand how the space of the sub-problems is structured. At the two extremes of the statistical distribution lie extremely routinized behaviours, in the sense of the rigid choice of

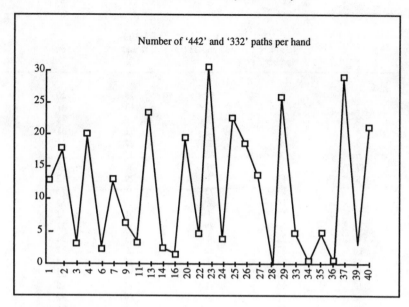

Figure 13.10

one path only (either 442 or 422). Players who adopt this behaviour are subject to a *high* number of procedural errors, a greater number of errors compared with 'flexible' players. The same occurs for 332.

This phenomenon can be explained by the difficulty which arises from the attempt to apply the same set of rules (442, 332 or 422, 322) to every kind of cognitive and informative situation: in fact, not all of the initial card distributions give rise to the same amount of information for the players, and they therefore represent very different cognitive situations. This cognitive difficulty is clearly illustrated by the great difference in the number of players who choose 442, 332 (or the complementary 422, 322) strategy across hands. This number changes radically, as Figures 13.9 and 13.10 show.

In order to explain the variety of behaviours exhibited across hands, we must understand how the information arising from the game can determine the moves of the players, and more generally the choice of a path in the sub-space. For simplicity I define as *static information* that which derives from the board status, and as *dynamic information* that which derives from the partner's (present or possibly past) moves

Looking at the starting configurations of the 40 hands, we can select the ones in which only one key-card appears. In this way we have 'pure' configurations, which show us the reactions of the players more clearly.

These configurations can be classified as follows:

(1) Colorkeeper has his key-card (2♣) in his hand: hands 3, 6, 28.
(2) Colorkeeper's key-card (2♣) is in the Up position: hands 14, 33, 34.
(3) Colorkeeper has the double key-card (2♥) in his hand: hands 4, 23, 29.

---

1. If Ck has his key-card (2♠) in hand then his goal is to put it the Target; the path that players follow is 422 (95 per cent)
2. If the key-card of Ck (2♠) is in the Up position then his move is to pick it up and the path that players follow is 422 (94 per cent)
3. If Ck has the double key-card (2♥) in his hand then his goal is to pass until Nk has put his key-card (4♥) on the target. The path that the players follow is 442 (80 per cent)
4. If the double key-card (2♥) is in the Up position then Ck's goal is either to pick it up (50 per cent and the path followed is 442) or to search (50 per cent and the path followed is 422) for his key-card.
5. If Ck has the partner's key-card (4♥) in his hand, then his goal is to search for his key-card 97 per cent (and the path followed is 422)

Figure 13.11

(4) The double key-card (2♥) is in the Up position: hands 1, 26.
(5) Colorkeeper has the Numberkeeper's key-card (4♥ or 3♥) in his hand: hand 35.

It is easy to verify (Figures 13.9 and 13.10) that within each of the four groups in cases (1), (2), (3), (5), the players behave in a very regular manner: the majority of the players choose the 422 path in cases (1), (2), (5) and the majority choose the 442 in case (3). Accordingly, in Figure 13.10 to the cases (1), (2), (5) correspond a minimum and to case (3) a maximum.

Take case (1) as an example. Here 95 per cent of the players follow the 422 path (the number of players who choose the complementary path 442 corresponds to a minimum point in the graph of Figure 13.10). Note that in this case corresponding to the 422 path is always the same first move to Ck (to put his key-card on the Target). In this 'pure' case, the first move is closely correlated with the path on the graph; this suggests that we should see whether this property is more general, i.e. if in the pure cases there is an univocal correspondence between the status of the board and the move chosen by the players. Figure 13.11 gives the experimental result of the five 'pure' cases.

On the basis of Figure 13.11 we may try to associate either a move or a set of

---

1. If Ck has his key-card (2♠) in his hand then his move is T (put it in the Target)
2. If the key-card of Ck (2♠) is in the Up position then his move is U (Ck picks it up)
3. If Ck has the double key-card (2♥) in his hand then his move is P
4. If the double key-card (2♥) is in the Up position then the Ck's goal is either U (he picks it up) or C,N (search)
5. If Ck has the partner's key-card (4♥) in hand, then his move is C, N (search)

Figure 13.12 Mapping between the space of pure configurations and the space of moves (experimental data)

alternative moves for Ck with each of the five pure configurations (and obviously to do the same for Nk). Figure 13.12 sets out the mapping configurations – moves based on the empirical data.

Note that some of the rules in Figures 13.11 and 13.12 (such as nos 3 and 5), are very 'naive'. In particular, contrary to expectations, the players seem unable to recognize configurations such as 5 in Figure 13.12, where the obvious move to make is U (Ck reveals the card he has in hand to his partner). The same cognitive difficulty arises with hands of low level (i.e. starting with 3, 4 of hearts or 2 of clubs on the Target) when one of the players must reveal to the other the key-card he has in hand. As we will see below, a learning process arises, and very slowly the players become aware of the need to reveal the key-card of their partner.

If we look at the remaining hands, where none of the starting configurations is 'pure', it is evident that more than one of the rules in Figure 13.12 can be applied: a possible conflict among rules emerges, and therefore players must explore the space of the combinations among rules and decide what move to make for every 'mixed' combination. In fact consider as an example a configuration in which Ck has the double key-card in his hand *and* his key-card is in Up position (hands 2, 7, 27): two rules (nos 2 and 3) which prescribe two different moves (U and P respectively) are simultaneously activated. Figure 13.13 shows all the mixed configurations, and the corresponding hands.

In order to solve the conflicts among the different prescriptions arising from the simultaneous application of two rules, and in order to allow players univocally to decide a move for every board configuration, the players may mentally explore the mixed configurations space. To cover exhaustively any possible configuration of key-card, their mental exploration would require great cognitive and memory effort.

As we will see, there is evidence that generally the players do *not* explore all the rules combinations *in advance*. On the contrary they realize the existence of conflicts and ambiguities only during the game, when they directly experiment with the mixed configurations. This behaviour is evidenced – as is clear from Figure 13.13 – by the fact that the reactions of the players to the same configuration change over time in relation to the progress of the learning process.

In cases 4 and 5 of Figure 13.13, in particular, the players modify their reaction to the configurations very slowly: they have noticeable cognitive difficulty in focusing

Ck has in Hand	there is in Up	Hands	choice of path 442 (Figure 13.11)
1 – his Key-card	the Double Key-card	24,39	Min
2 – "	the partner's key-card	36	Min
3 – the Double Key-card	his Key-card	2,7,27	about 50%
4 – "	the partner's Key-card	4,13,29	Max
5 – the partner's Key-card	the Double Key-card	20,25,37	Max (trend)
6 – "	his Key-card	9,22	Max

Figure 13.13 The space of mixed configurations

their attention on the role of the partner key-card and therefore in realizing that it is convenient to 'Reveal' to the partner his key-card.

Summing up, there is a clear evidence that players map between the key-configurations of the game and the moves in such a way as to decide precisely the move to make for every key-configuration. Up to this point, however, the mapping between configurations and moves is not perfectly univocal, because players modify their reactions to the key-configurations (pure and mixed) very slowly. The question is whether this process converges or not on a set of rules which define univocally the move to make for every key-configuration. In order to answer this question we need a model of a boundedly rational player; an artificial player which can display all the possible 'rational' solutions. This is the task of the next section.

8   AN ARTIFICIAL PLAYER

How can we build 'rational' strategies, and assume them as the cornerstone for evaluating the human strategies which emerge from the empirical data? To answer this point we must build a model of procedurally rational action, generate rational strategies and compare them with the experimental data. As will become clear, not only is rationality involved in the construction of the model, but also expectations and rational expectations.

To build an artificial player, we simply use the set of rules of 'Transform the Target' and assume that the artificial player has been able to explore the space of the rules in such a way as to create the diagram of goals. Therefore the artificial player is based only on the division of goals into sub-goals that we have already discussed in detail. His behaviour will be described by a set of 'production rules', i.e. rules of the form 'If <condition> then <action>', which are typical of problem solving and machine learning.

As before, I will discuss only the configurations which are 'difficult' because they admit more than one solution on the diagram of sub-goals. If a player is supposed to be able to explore the sub-goals diagram, he must be able to choose a path in the diagram. We assume he is able to choose the minimal path, reminding the reader of the previous *caveat* concerning the difference between the choice of a minimal path and the traditional optimal choice of a strategy. When there are two minimal paths the problem is which of the two possible paths to choose. Is the information available from the cards disposition on the board sufficient to decide a 'rational' move univocally?

Remember that *static rules* are those arising from application of the decomposition of goals to the information deriving only from the board status. The static rules impose a set of restrictions on the possible actions of the players.

A model based on these rules describes players as reacting only to information provided by the board: players try to apply the set of static rules on the basis of information available from the cards on the board, and if a rule matches the information, they will move accordingly. Figures 13.14 and 13.15 show the set of static rules which arise from the choice between the two possible minimal paths. They have been built simply by using the diagram of sub-goals in the extended form (Figure 13.7).

Note that the Nk's rules are perfectly equivalent to the Ck's ones. Of course these rules do *not* make a correspondence between pure configuration and moves: to any pure configuration there correspond a couple of possible moves, depending on the path that has been chosen on the sub-goals diagram.

The S-rules on page 325, if applied, do *not* uniquely determine a move; they simply reduce the number of possible alternative moves. If we want to build an artificial player which adopts only static rule, we must then further restrict the set of possible actions which stem from the application of a given rule. The restrictions must be applied in such a way that only one move is generated by a rule. One way of doing this is to set the probabilities AA[i] to 0 or 1 values only. Let us therefore assign to probabilities AA[i] only the values 0 or 1. Three different situations can arise.

(1) one rule only matches the information provided by the board;
(2) more than one rule can be applied: a possible conflict among rules emerges;
(3) no rule matches the information on the board; information is not sufficient to decide the move to make.

In the first case a rule can be applied, and consequently a goal is univocally established. The second case has a set of consequences which must be discussed in depth. I therefore anticipate discussion of the third case, which is simpler.

In this case, the set of static rules does not allow players to decide a move for a given card configuration. We cannot hope to solve this situation by adding a set of dynamic rules, for the simple reason that dynamic rules, being based on the partner's moves, can be applied only after the first move of any hand. Consequently, if none of the key-cards is 'visible' at the start of a hand, we cannot use either static or dynamic rules.

This situation is temporary: if we focus our attention, as usual, on the most 'difficult' hands, which start with 3 or 4 clubs on Target, we realize that there are three key-cards, so that at least one of the two players must have a key-card in his control (either one of them has a key-card in his hand, or a key-card is in position U and therefore both players can see it). Therefore only one of the players at most suffers from a temporary lack of information: but even if the situation is 'temporary', the player does not have a rule for deciding his goal. To solve this point, I simply assume that players, in the absence of any information, will search for a key-card. By consequence I add a new rule (search) which covers any card situation which previously did not match the static information. This assumption is largely confirmed by the experimental data.

Now let us turn to the second case, when more than one rule can be simultaneously applied to the board. Here a conflict arises. The conflict must be resolved by providing a specific new rule which decides the priority among the conflicting rules. But how is it possible to select a new rule which allows players to move in a coordinated way? Note that if players behaved on the basis of the static rules only, they would not be able coordinate their goals. The only way to solve the conflict is therefore to use additional information from the game: this means that since the board configurations are insufficient for a coordinated set of actions, (rational) players must use the information arising from past configurations and their partner's moves.

To clarify this point, consider the vector of AA of probabilities distribution under

---

Static rules for Nk (X♣ in Target, X = 3,4)

S-Rule 1 – If I have my key-card (X♥) in hand then my goal is either to put it in the Target
(with probability p = AA[1] (442) or to search for 2♥ (422) with
probability = 1-AA[1]

S-Rule 2 – If my key-card X♥ is on the Up position then my goal is either to pick up X♥
(with probability p = AA[2](442) or to search for 2♥ (422) with
probability = 1-AA[2]

S-Rule 3 – If the double key-card 2♥ is in my hand then my goal is either to wait until my
partner puts his key card 2♣ in the Target (with probability p = AA[3](422)
or to search for X♥(442) with probability = 1-AA[3]

S-Rule 4 – If the double key-card 2♥ is in the Up position then my goal is either to take it
(with probability p = AA[4](422) or to search for my key-card X♥ (442)
with probability p = 1-AA[4]

Figure 13.14

Static rules for Ck (X♣ in Target, X = 3,4)

S-Rule 5 – If I have my key-card 2♣ in my hand then my goal is either to put it in the Target
(with probability p = AA[5] (422) or to search for the double key-card 2♥
(442) with probability = 1-AA[5]

S-Rule 6 – If my key-card 2♣ is in the Up position then my goal is either to pick it up (with
probability p = AA[6] (422) or to search for the double key-card 2♥ (442)
with probability =1- AA[6]

S-Rule 7 – If the double key-card 2♥ is in my hand then my goal is either to Pass until my
partner puts his key-card X♥ in the Target (with probability p = AA[7]
(422) or to search for my key-card 2♣ (442) with probability = 1-AA[7]

S-Rule 8 – If the double key-card 2♥ is in the Up position then my goal is either to pick it up
and Pass until my partner has put X♥ on the Target, (with probability
p = AA[8] (422) or to search for my key-card 2♣ (442) with
probability = 1-AA[8].

Figure 13.15

the assumption that AA[i] can only be 0 or 1, depending on the goal that the players
want to pursue.

AA[1] = 1 means: If Nk has 4♥ in his hand then his goal is to put 4♥ in the Target.
His move is T and the expected path on the diagram is (442)

AA[2] = 1 means: If 4♥ is in the Up position then Nk's goal is to pick up 4♥. His move is therefore U and the expected path on the diagram is (442)

... and so on.

Having attributed to AA[i] a value 0 or 1 for all the arguments from 1 to 8, we have fully defined a one-to-one mapping between rules and moves. This implicitly defines the features of coordination between the two players.

Distribution AA = (1100–0011) represents a 442 path and distribution AA = (0011–1100) represents a 422 expected path. Any different distribution implies a *non-coordinated* sequence of choices. In fact, for example, for the distribution (1100–1100) Nk's goal is 4♥, and Ck's goal is 2♣, which are incompatible.

As an example, Figure 13.16 shows the different behaviours which arise from different 0/1 probability distributions. Note that if the two players follow a couple of goals which are inconsistent, as in the (1100–1100) distribution, they may simultaneously be self-consistent: in fact, in our context, the self-consistency of a player consists in the ability to pursue a given goal in a coherent way. In the (1111–0000) distribution, the two players are inconsistent with themselves. Therefore two possible kinds of behaviour arise: the player's consistency with himself and with his partner. It is important to note that it is possible to identify the player's consistency by analyzing the game's sequences, as shown in Figure 13.16.

I have shown that the great majority of couples do not follow the same fixed path for all different hands. We therefore can identify only a very small number of couples as characterized by a given, fixed distribution of 0–1 probabilities.

This means that the couples which follow – for example – the 442 path in hand no. 11, and are characterized by the sequence of static rules 1100–0011, will not

Nk's goal	Ck's goal	Play:	Paths	Nk's rules	Ck's rules
		Consistent			
				1 2 3 4	5 6 7 8
4♥	2♥	CUUTT	442	1 1 0 0	0 0 1 1
		NUUTT	442	1 1 0 0	0 0 1 1
		Consistent			
2♥	2♣	CPTT	422	0 0 1 1	1 1 0 0
		NPCPTT	422	0 0 1 1	1 1 0 0
		Inconsistent			
2♣	4♥	NUCTUPT	442	1 1 0 0	1 1 0 0
		CUTUPT	422	1 1 0 0	1 1 0 0
2♥	2♥	NPCPPP		1 1 0 0	1 1 0 0
		CPNPCP		1 1 0 0	1 1 0 0

Figure 13.16 Strategies to play hand no. 11 2♣ 3♥ 4♥ 4♣ 3♣ 2♥

D-Rule 1	If Ck's key-card (2♣) was in Up position *and* Ck took it in the last move then Nk searches for the double key-card (2♥)
D-Rule 2	If Ck's key-card (2♣) was in the Up position and Ck did *not* take it (either Ck looks for the double key-card or keeps it in his hand) then Nk searches for his key-card (4♥)
D-Rule 3	If double key-card (2♥) was in the Up position and Ck did take it in the last move, then Nk searches for his key-card (4♥)
D-Rule 4	If the double key-card (2♥) is in Up position and Ck did put it the last move, or did not take it the last move (Ck probably is looking for his key-card or keeps it in his hand), then Nk takes it

Figure 13.17　Dynamic rules concerning Numberkeeper's decisions

follow the same sequence for all remaining hands. Players (slowly) learn to coordinate their sub-goals, i.e. to choose either AA = (1100–0011) or AA = (0011–1100) across hands, in relation to the positions of the key-cards on the board. In consequence, the path to follow on the goals diagram is not fixed in advance but depends on the initial distribution of cards.

The problem now is to establish whether information from the board is sufficient to allow either players to understand his partner's intention, and consequently to choose his moves in a coordinated and consistent way. In other words, we must see whether there are signals sufficient for both players to set the distribution of probabilities either to AA = (1100–0011) or to AA = (0011–1100) in a univocal way, avoiding the inconsistent distributions.

Note that when a configuration on the board is mixed, i.e. when more than one key-card appears simultaneously on the board, more than one rule matches the configuration. Here we are in the situation summarized by Figure 13.13; readers can verify that these situations do not restrict the choice in such a way as to permit players to make univocally one move. By consequence, in both cases, pure and mixed configurations, players need additional information in order to coordinate their goals.

The players decide the most convenient path in relation to the available information: since the information provided by the cards distribution on the board is not sufficient to coordinate their goals, each player must also use information about his partner's past moves.

As a consequence, we must take the dynamic rules into account. These rules allow players to coordinate their goals as they play the hand. Figure 13.17 lists a set of dynamic rules which simply map the key-configuration *plus* the past move *on to* the set of moves. Figure 13.17 sets out Nk's dynamic rules. Likewise, we can build the dynamic rules concerning Ck's decision, by simply exchanging Nk and Ck and Nk's key-card with Ck's key-card in the figure.

It is very important to note that by memorizing the past moves and recursively using the dynamic rules, the artificial player can use all the available information, and therefore can be fully rational, moreover, if the artificial player attributes to his partner the ability to use all available information, he would interpret the partner's moves as rational: in this case, the artificial player would have *rational expectations*.

Even if rational expectation behaviours can be checked in a limited number of hands, the evidence shows that this kind of behaviour is very rare. As is clear from the data that I set out in the next section, the great majority of players do not use all available information, and they do not attribute this kind of ability to their partner.

9   SOME EVIDENCE ON LEARNING

The initial card distributions in the first five hands have been replicated, in the same order, in the five hands after the 25th of the tournament (26 to 30). We consequently have a clear idea of the effects of the learning process, which are given in Figure 13.19. The first left column lists the sequences of moves played by the artificial player using static and dynamic rules. The artificial player uses all available information but does *not* assume rational expectations: this means that he decides the move to make by looking at the configurations, plus the move made by his partner, without pretending to interpret the partner's move as rational. The tabulation requires very little comment: in fact the improvement in the players' ability is very clear.

Comparing the game conduct of the same couple faced with the same distribution (hands 1 and 26, 2 and 27, and so on), we have further confirmation that the couples who choose a goal path for a given cards distribution at hand X (X = 1,...5) do not maintain the same path after 25 hands, i.e. they do not routinize a specific path on the goal diagram.

An issue that must be raised at this point, even though I cannot discuss it in depth, is this: how do the static and dynamic rules of the artificial player emerge? A tentative answer is the following: at the beginning of the tournament players create a set of rules by associating a move to every pure key-configuration. They do this in a very naive way, without fully exploring the space of the sub-goals. Then slowly they are forced by the emergence of mixed configurations to compare the rules-of-thumb and to modify them. Static and dynamic rules are thus gradually generated by comparing the rules of the game against the sub-goals. The evidence from the experiment confirms this description too, although more experimental data and analysis is required to give a careful description of this learning process.

A second aspect of behaviour which concerns procedure formation must be emphasized. If for a large number of hands the card on the Target is the same, the paths that the players must consider to solve the problem do not change for a period of time. This persistence allows players to routinize, i.e. to react to the configurations by 'automatically' deciding the move to make; they follow the sets of static and dynamic rules in a very precise and quick way. If the sequence of hands which starts with the same card on the Target is suddenly interrupted by a simpler distribution (for example, when 2♣ occurs in the Target) the persistence of routinized behaviour prevents the players from reacting in a correct way, and is therefore the cause of numerous errors. This aspect is clearly evidenced by the reduced number of errors and deviations from satisficing behaviour recorded when hands are homogeneous in terms of the Target, and by the high increase of errors when suddenly a different, even if easy, initial distribution appears on the board.

Artificial hands		Experimental data	
	Goals	Hand 1	Hand 26
4H 3C 2H 4C 2C 3H			
UCPTT	442	1	7
NUTT	422	2	1
CUNPTT	422	3	6
UNPCPTT	442	4	8
		10	22
		31.25%	68.75%
		Hand 2	Hand 27
3H 2H 2C 4C 4H 3C			
PCPNPTT	442	2	2
UUTT	422	7	15
PNPTT	442	7	9
		16	26
		50%	81.25%
		Hand 3	Hand 28
3H 2C 4C 3C 2H 4H			
TNPT	322	2	12
TCPNPT	322	1	6
NCPNPNPTT	332	0	0
CNNCCNPTT	332	0	0
NNPCPTT	332	1	0
CCNNPTT	332	0	0
CNNPCPTT	322	0	0
		4	18
		12.5%	56.25%
		Hand 4	Hand 29
2C 2H 4H 3C 3H 4C			
PNPTT	332	7	12
PCPNPTT	332	4	4
NNCPTT	322	0	0
NNCCTCPT	322	0	0
CNTCPT	322	0	0
NCCNNPTT	322	0	0
PNPCPCPTT	332	0	0
CCTT	322	0	0
		11	16
		34.38%	50%
		Hand 5	Hand 30
3C 3H 4C 4H 2C 2H			
NUUPT	42	3	5
CUUPT	42	6	17
		9	22
		28.13%	68.75%

Figure 13.18 The learning effect after 25 hands

10   FINAL REMARKS

This search relies on the ability to learn. I have attempted to use the experimental data which emerge from Cohen's game replication to verify some of the current assumptions about routines emergence and procedural rationality.

Much has been written over the last twenty years about the experimental study and analytical modelling of learning processes. I can recall only three main lines of enquiry: the first began with the pioneering research by Simon (1957), March and Simon (1958) and Newell and Simon (1972), and analyses the learning process as a search in problem space; the second, which originates from McCulloch and Pitts (1943), Hebb (1949) and von Hayek's (1952)[4] ideas, develops models based on neural networks; and the third originates with the invention of genetic algorithms by Holland (1975) and subsequent work on classifier systems (Holland *et al.*, 1988; Goldberg, 1989).

These approaches have been very successful in the machine learning area, but have rarely been compared with the empirical results on human learning by means of laboratory studies. Even though I have focused on the approach based on the problem decomposition, it becomes clear, after analysis of the experimental data, that there are connections with the approaches based on 'production rules', which I wish now briefly to discuss.

To summarize some of the previous findings: the consequences of the assumptions of bounded and procedural rationality, if taken seriously, give rise to a model of human decision-making which is quite different from the traditional picture of decision as unbounded rational choice: cognitive and memory limitations engender a process of search which is highly asymmetric and path dependent. Players move (conjecturally) in the space of sub-problems as they try to connect the local goals to each other in order to achieve their specific goals. Each of them focuses his attention and forms his beliefs differently. Thus the coordination of beliefs becomes a crucial factor in decision-making, which requires cognition and learning.

Each strategy can be realized by executing a set of *production rules*, of the form 'if Condition then Action', where action is, for example, 'Search for 2♥' or 'Reveal 4♣'. I have called 'conjectural strategy' the set of rules which, if followed by the player, lead to completion of the task. Note that these are not strategies in the traditional sense of the term until the *generic* terms 'Seek' and 'Reveal' are transformed into precise *procedures*.

Players discover very slowly a set of production rules, which allow the generation of routines. They start from generating a set of naive rules-of-thumb which maps key-configurations of the game on to moves. The simultaneous matching of these rules, which happens when on the board a mixed configuration appears, gives rise to a process of learning (adaptation) which allows players to substitute conflicting rules and provide new rules for the ambiguous signals. The speed of convergence to a set of stable rules depends on the 'story', i.e. on the order of the sequence of boards (with different cognitive difficulties).

What is the relationship between these findings on learning at micro-behaviour level and the emergence of organizational routines?

I wish to emphasize that on a micro-behaviour level, the cognitive 'atoms' are the elementary production rules (if Condition then Action) which by adaptation to the goals and sub-goals give rise to sequences of action procedurally rational. These sequences are the organizational routines, which are *not* memorized by players. Players do not have to keep all knowledge and information they need to play stored in memory: they only have to remember the cognitive 'atoms' which allow the generation of the organizational routines. This means that they are able to explore and 'recreate' missing knowledge, as I have suggested at the beginning of the present chapter.

We therefore must recognize that the notion of organizational routine should be considered as synonymous with 'not completely specified procedure'. This assumption is confirmed by field studies of the behaviour of individuals in organizations which have evidenced the open and incomplete nature of routines. Incompleteness gives flexibility to the realization of routines and facilitate their change; a flexibility made possible precisely by the fact that agents are able to complete procedures by means of their ability to learn and to solve problems.

Notes

1. These two abilities are quite different from one another: the first concerns the design and planning ability, while the second concerns adaptation and learning. The combination of the two activities suggests a description of the organizational evolution as a 'punctuated equilibria' process, with discontinuities: the planner, or a hierarchy of planners, suddenly modifies the organizational structure, and the employees adapt the 'informal' organization to the new plans; while the idea of organizational learning as the result of the interaction (coordination) among local forces driving the local solution of problems, leads to a Darwinian vision of the organization, characterized by a continuous process of internal evolution.
2. The experiment design does not allow one to verify if players are aware of the meta-rules they use, and consequently if these rules can be considered as *tacit* ones.
3. I am indebted to Ricardo Pereira for this useful distinction.
4. De Vries (1994) writes 'Hayek's *The Sensory Order* is an intriguing book ... Hayek was an outsider. Therefore he did not know D.O. Hebb's *Organization of Behaviour* (1949) until the final version of his own book was practically finished. Hebb's vision was in so many respects similar to his own that Hayek doubted for a while whether he should publish it. However, Hebb was more concerned with physiological details and less with general principles, which were Hayek's main interest.'

References

Allais, M. (1953) 'Le comportement de l'homme rationel devant le risque: Critique des postulats et axiomes de l'école américaine', *Econometrica*, vol. 21, pp. 503–46.

Arrow, K.J. (1971) 'Economic Welfare and the Allocation of Resources for Invention', in F. Lamberton (ed.), *Economics of Information and Knowledge* (London: Penguin Books).

Arrow, K.J. (1974) *The Limits of Organizations* (New York: Norton).

Arrow, K.J. (1978) 'The Future and the Present in Economic Life', *Economic Inquiry*, vol. 16, pp. 157–70.

Axelrod, R. (1984) *The Evolution of Cooperation* (New York: Basic Books).

Cohen, M.D. (1991) 'Individual Learning and Organizational Routine: Emerging Connections', *Organization Science*, vol. 2 pp. 135–9.

Cohen, M.D. and P. Bacdayan (1994) 'Organizational Routines Are Stored as Procedural Memory: Evidence From a Laboratory Study', *Organizational Science*, vol. 5, pp. 554–68.

Cyert, R.M., H.A. Simon and D.B. Trow (1956) 'Observation of a Business Decision', *Journal of Business*, vol. 29, pp. 237–48.

de Vries, R.P. (1994) 'The Place of Hayek's Theory of Mind and Perception in the History of Philosophy and Psychology', in J. Birner and Van Zijp (eds), *Hayek, Co-ordination and Evolution* (London: Routledge).

Egidi, M. (1992) 'Organizational Learning and the Division of Labour', in M. Egidi and R. Marris (eds), *Economics, Bounded Rationality and the Cognitive Revolution* (Aldershot: Edward Elgar).

Goldberg, D.E. (1989), *Genetic Algorithms in Search, Optimization and Machine Learning* (Reading, Mass: Addison-Wesley).

Hayek, F.A. (1952) *The Sensory Order* (London: Routledge & Kegan Paul).

Hayek, F.A. (1980) 'Economics and Knowledge', in *Individualism and Economic Order* (reprint of 1948 first printing) (Chicago: University of Chicago Press).

Hebb, D.O. (1949) *The Organization of Behaviour* (London: Wiley).

Holland, J.H. (1975) *Adaptation in Natural and Artificial Systems* (Ann Arbor: University of Michigan Press).

Holland, J.H., K.J. Holyoak, R.E. Nisbett and P.R. Thagard (1988) *Induction – Processes of Inference, Learning, and Discovery* (Cambridge, Mass.: MIT Press).

Holyoak, K.J. (1990) 'Problem Solving', in N. Osherson and E.E. Smith (eds), *Thinking*, vol. 3 (Cambridge Mass.: MIT Press).

Laird, J.E., A. Newell and P.S. Rosembloom (1987) 'Soar: An Architecture for General Intelligence', *Artificial Intelligence*, vol. 33, pp. 1–64.

March, J.G. (1988) *Decisions and Organizations* (Oxford: Basil Blackwell).

March, J.G. and H.A. Simon (1958) *Organizations* (New York: John Wiley).

McCulloch, W.S. and W. Pitts (1943) 'A Logical Calculus of Ideas Immanent in Neural Nets', *Bulletin* of Mathematical Biophysics, vol. 5, pp. 115–37.

McGuire, C.B. and R. Radner (1972) *Decision and Organization* (Amsterdam: North-Holland).

McLelland, J.L. and D.E. Rumelhard (1988) *Parallel Distributed Processing – Explorations in the Microstructure of Cognition* (Cambridge, Mass: MIT Press).

Nelson, R.R. and S. Winter (1974) 'Neoclassical vs. Evolutionary Theories of Economic Growth: Critique and Prospectus', *Economic Journal*, vol. 84, pp. 886–905.

Nelson, R.R. and S. Winter (1982) *An Evolutionary Theory of Economic Change* (Cambridge Mass.: Belknap Press of Harvard University Press).

Newell, A. (1990) *Unified Theories of Cognition* (Cambridge, Mass.: Harvard University Press).

Newell, A. and H.A. Simon (1972) *Human Problem Solving* (Englewood Cliffs, N.J.: Prentice Hall).

Nilsson, N. (1980) *Principles of Artificial Intelligence* (Palo Alto, Calif.: Tioga).

Pearl, J. (1984) *Heuristics* (Reading, Mass.: Addison-Wesley)

Polanyi, M. (1958) *Personal Knowledge: Towards a Post-Critical Philosophy* (London: Routledge & Kegan Paul).

Simon, H.A. (1957) *Models of Man* (New York: Wiley).

Simon, H.A. (1963) 'Problem Solving Machines', *International Science and Technology*, vol. 3, pp. 48–62.

Simon, H.A. (1972a) 'From Substantive to Procedural Rationality', in McGuire and Radner (1972).

Simon, H.A. (1972b) 'Theories of Bounded Rationality', in McGuire and Radner (1972).

Simon, H.A. (1979) 'Rational Decision Making in Business Organization', *American Economic Review*, vol. 69, pp. 493–513.

Simon, H.A. and A. Newell (1972) *Human Problem Solving* (Englewood Cliffs, N.J: Prentice-Hall).

Singley M.K. and J.R. Anderson (1989) *The Transfer of Cognitive Skill* (Cambridge, Mass.: Harvard University Press).

Squire, L.R. (1987) *Memory and Brain* (Oxford: Oxford University Press).

Winter, S.G. (1982)'An Essay on the Theory of Production', in S.H. Hymans (ed.), *Economics and the World around It* (Ann Arbor: Michigan University Press).

Comment

Hamid Sabourian

UNIVERSITY OF CAMBRIDGE, UK

I find the aims of Egidi's chapter appealing. It tries to go beyond criticizing models based on rationality and tries to contribute to a positive theory. Many experimental works only establish inconsistencies between the results of experiments with some of the implications of the 'rationality' axioms. Egidi instead tries to explore and explain the features of human problem-solving, skill creation and emergence of routines in terms of the processing capabilities of individuals. The method advocated is that of Newell and Simon (1972) based on search and learning.

The modern formulation of a general theory of problem-solving as search is due to Newell and Simon. In their formulation a problem is represented by a set of all states (including the initial state at which the problem begins and a goal state) and a set of actions which serve to change the current state of the problem. A solution is a sequence of actions that can transform the initial state into the goal state in accordance with some constraints. Problem-solving is thus viewed as search: a method of finding a solution among all possible paths joining the initial state to the final path. Due to limited short-term memories, it is impossible to search all possible sequences of moves even in the simplest games. Instead, people consider only a small number of alternatives that seem likely to yield a reasonable outcome. Although such 'heuristic' search methods rarely come up with the first best outcomes, such methods do reasonably well – they are consistent with the 'satisficing' approach.

The process of problem-solving as a search in this approach involves some planning combined with a process of problem decomposition, in which the overall problem is recursively broken into sub-problems, such that each sub-problem can be solved separately. The sub-problems are tackled by setting sub-goals and applying the method of search to each separately. This approach has been closely associated with the production system model in which the sub-problems are solved by production rules of the forms 'if Condition then Action' (Newell, 1973).

Egidi tries to provide some support for this general approach to problem-solving by constructing an artificial player who plays the card game, first introduced by Cohen and Bacdayan (1991), by recursively devising sub-goals and (conjectural) sub-strategies. Egidi's main result seems to be that the actual behaviour of players appears to mimic well the possible play of the artificial player as the game is repeated. Thus the results seem to support the process of learning to solve the game in a manner à la Newell and Simon.

Clearly, the approach of decomposing a problem into sub-problems and solving each simple sub-goal in some orderly (rational) manner is appealing. It is consistent with behaviour in many other games (including chess). The question that arises is what do we learn from the results of experiments such as that performed by Egidi and where do we go from here – how should we introduce these procedural aspects of decision-making into our economic models?

Although it is encouraging to see that players' behaviour tends to become largely consistent with those of the possible artificial players constructed by Egidi, it may also be consistent with other theories. Firstly, notice that there are many strategies (plans) which are consistent with any given outcome path. Secondly, there are a large number of outcome paths which are consistent with the theory based on fully rational agents. For example, when the cards are dealt according to (3H 2H 2C 4C 4H 3C) the sequence of moves by the artificial hands are PCPCPTT, UUTT and PNPTT (see Figure 13.19 in Egidi's chapter). The results of Egidi's experiment are here reproduced (Table 13.1) when the cards are distributed as above.

Table 13.1

	Hand 2	Hand 27
PCPNPTT	2	2
UUTT	7	15
PNPTT	7	9

For different distributions of cards, clearly the game has many (Bayesian) Nash equilibria. It is easy to show that both UUTT and PNPTT (the second and the third play in Table 1) can be sustained as a (Bayesian) Nash equilibrium of the card game if the cards are distributed according to the distribution in Table 1 dealt in hands 2 and 27. Egidi's results demonstrated that the number of times the subjects play these two paths increases from 14 to 24 between the second hand and the twenty-seventh. Moreover, the number of times the non-equilibrium outcome path PCPNPTT is played remains constant at 2. In Figure 13.19 of Egidi's chapter, there are other sequences of plays by artificial hands for different distribution of initial cards. It is not difficult to show that many of these sequences of play are also consistent with (Bayesian) Nash equilibrium of the game. Thus, one may also be able to argue that the experimental result in Figure 13.19 is largely consistent with players learning to play the game according to standard game theory.

The point here is not that players learn to behave rationally according to the theory of games. It is merely to demonstrate some of the data presented by Egidi may be consistent with many different theories including that which says that players learn to behave according to the equilibria of standard game theory. The experimental results of this chapter may also be consistent with other procedural approaches. Egidi's artificial hands are constructed by decomposing the problems into sub-problems and recursively solving them backwards starting with the final goal of playing 2H on the target. One could also do a decomposition and solve the problem forward starting from the initial state. Also, in constructing the dynamic rules, Egidi's artificial player conditions his action on the last move of his partner in the same game. One could also compare the experimental results with more complex dynamic rules which condition actions on other kinds of information. For example, it could be that each player forms expectations about his partner's future play and when they are proved false the player may change behaviour radically in future games. The problem is that although the experimental results seem to be consistent with Egidi's approach, it is difficult to draw any conclusion without considering the predictions of other models of behaviour and problem-solving and without further data analysis.

The second point to consider is the relevance of the specific card game in Egidi to actual economic problems. The game in Egidi's chapter is a team problem (requires coordination) with imperfect information. To play the game in a reasonable way requires memory and computational ability (to search), as well as the ability to signal/reveal and coordinate. Each of these may require different cognitive ability. Although some games may be decomposable into sub-problems which can be solved separately and serially, many realistic problems are rarely decomposable into parts which can be solved independently. In such cases, setting sub-goals and solving them recursively may turn out to be very inefficient (or impossible) relative to a global and/or parallel procedure for solving problems. In many problems (in particular, in those problems in which goals are not so well-defined), people do not establish a representation of a problem and then perform search: rather behaviour in many of these cases involves changes in their representations. Such restructuring is often associated with parallel information processing (as opposed to Newell and Simon's theory in which each problem is mainly solved one-by-one). When sub-problems are highly interdependent and a solution to some sub-problem imposes constraints on other sub-problems, it may not be efficient or even feasible to solve each problem separately and check that all constraints are satisfied. In such cases it may be more efficient to solve all the sub-goals incrementally and in parallel (see Holyoak, 1990 for further discussions of this point).[1]

One needs a great deal more experimental data and analysis to develop a convincing theory of the procedural method of solving a problem such as the card game in Egidi's chapter. I have already mentioned the need for comparing the predictions of different theories. Another exercise might be to ask the players to 'think aloud' and explain their moves. Despite the inherent difficulties involved in assessing the explanations offered by players,[2] this approach might shed some light on the procedural and coordination ability of the players as well as on how sub-goals and rules become established. For example, one could ask the players if they actually decompose the problem into sub-goals, test their understanding of the relationship between different sub-goals and find out if players have any meta-plans.[3] It is often claimed that individuals solve problems by analogy (similarity) between the problem at hand and some other situation. One may be able to develop some understanding of this by asking the subjects in the experiments about possible analogies.

More information on the card game may also help to clarify further some aspects of the subjects' decision-making. For example, Figures 13.9 and 13.10 demonstrate that the subjects do not always follow the same set of rules 422 (322) or 422 (332). A majority of the players do not react in a routinized way, and follow different rules (e.g. both 422 and 442) in different games.[4] One explanation for this (provided by Egidi) is that players use both the information on the card game and past moves of their partners to decide what rule to follow. As a result, in different games with different information, players might follow different rules. More data on the information players had when they chose one rule (e.g. 422) as compared to that available to them when they chose the other rule (442) might shed further light on how the information which the players receive influences their sub-goals and thereby their decision rules.

Finally, one would like to go further than considering an artificial player in a specific game and try to develop a more formal or even an axiomatic approach of procedural decision-making (of the artificial hand). In game theory, a strategy is a plan of what to do at every contingency. One may be able to capture an element of Egidi's meta-plan and the decomposition approach by assuming that players behave 'as if' they choose an optimal plan among a restricted set of strategies which map some fixed *partition* of the set of all contingencies to the set of actions. For example, the recent literature on modelling players as machines in game theory (Abreu and Rubinstein, 1988; Kalai and Stanford, 1989; and Anderlini and Sabourian, 1995, to name a few) tries to provide a formal model of computational/memory constraint by considering equilibria of games played by automata. Although this approach does not model the process of search and decomposition, limiting strategies to those with bounded complexity captures an element of Egidi's artificial behaviour. Moreover, such an approach may provide a formal explanation for the existence of routines and for the existence of meta-plans involving 'heuristic' search (where only a number of alternatives are examined). Another formal approach is the literature on neural computation (see Hertz *et al.*, 1991) and genetic algorithms (see Goldberg, 1989). None of these models have been compared to empirical results on human learning.[5] At this stage, it is difficult to imagine in a foreseeable future an axiomatic model of procedural rationality which captures the many different faces of search and learning. Thus the approach of explaining individual cases of human behaviour in terms of a specific procedural approach seems appealing. Nevertheless, one should recognize the limitation of such an exercise, especially when applied to a card game.

Notes

1. Formal models of parallel processes are used extensively in perception: see Rumelhart *et al.* (1986).
2. In some cases players may not be able to explain their moves (Cohen and Bacdayen, 1991, argue that an important aspect of routine behaviour is that agents often could not explain their own behaviour) and in some other cases 'thinking aloud' influences the actual decisions that agents make.
3. For example, Metcalfe and Wiebe (1987) ask subjects how close they believe they were to finding a solution. They used this kind of result to explain the importance of sudden insights in solving certain problems.
4. This is in sharp contrast to the original card-game experiment in Cohen and Bacdayen (1991) in which they use the result of the same card game experiment as Egidi's to show that individuals follow routines with the same action sequences being repeated many times.
5. Holland classifiers (Holland *et al.* 1986) and some multi-player learning systems such as *Soar* (Laird *et al.*, 1987) could be compared with experimental data.

References

Abreu, D. and A. Rubinstein (1988) 'The Structure of Nash Equilibrium in Repeated Games with Finite Automata', *Econometrica* vol. 56, pp. 1259–81.
Anderlini, A. and H. Sabourian (1995) 'Cooperation and Effective Computability',

Economic Theory Discussion Paper no. 167, University of Cambridge and Econometrica, forthcoming.

Cohen, M.D. and P. Bacdayan (1991) 'Organizational Routines are Stored as Procedural Memory: Evidence from a Laboratory Study', University of Michigan, mimeo.

Goldberg, D.E. (1989) *Genetic Algorithms in Search, Optimization and Machine Learning* (Reading, Mass.: Addison-Wesley).

Hertz, J., A. Krogh and R.G. Palmer (1991) *Introduction to the Theory of Neural Computation* (Santa Fe: Institute Studies in the Science of Complexity, and Addison-Wesley).

Holland, J.H., K.J. Holyoak, R.E. Nisbett and P.R. Thagard (1986) *Induction: Processes of Inference Learning, and Discovery* (Cambridge, Mass.: MIT Press).

Holyoak, K.J. (1990) 'Problem Solving', in N. Osherson and E.E. Smith (eds), *Thinking*, vol. 3 (Cambridge, Mass.: MIT Press).

Kalai, E. and W. Stanford (1989) 'Finite Rationality and Interpersonal Complexity in Repeated Games', *Econometrica*, vol. 65 pp. 397–410.

Laird, J.E. (1984) *Soar User's Manual: Version 4.0*, Intelligent Systems Laboratory, Xerox Palo Alto Research Center, Palo Alto, California.

Metcalfe, J. and D. Wiebe (1987) 'Intuition in Insight and Noninsight Problem Solving', *Memory and Cognition*, vol. 15, pp. 238–46.

Newell, A. (1973) 'Production Systems: Models of Control Structures', in W.G. Chase (eds), *Visual Information Processing* (New York: Academic Press).

Newell, A. and H.A. Simon (1972) *Human Problem Solving* (Englewood Cliffs, N.J.: Prentice Hall).

Rumelhart, D.E., P. Smolensky, J.L. McClelland and G.E. Hinton (1986) 'Schemata and Sequential Thought Processes in PDP Models', in J.L. McClelland, D.E. Rumelhart and the PDP Research Group, *Parallel Distributed Processing: Explorations in the Microstructure of Cognition*, vol. 2, *Psychological and Biological Models* (Cambridge Mass.: MIT Press).

14 Rational Preferences and Rational Beliefs*

Mordecai Kurz

STANFORD UNIVERSITY, USA

1 INTRODUCTION

Preferences are usually taken in economics to be subjective primitives. Yet there seems to be a difference between the subjectivity of preferences over bundles of spot commodities and those of risky prospects. One would hardly challenge our choice of a dinner out of a menu as 'irrational' if we claim that it is our 'favourite' dinner. The same cannot be said for the purchase of a portfolio of securities or an investment programme in risky prospects. Feasible portfolios may be viewed as 'inefficient' and an investment programme as 'unwise'. It is a generally held view that the statement that one 'likes' an investment programme is not sufficient to justify it: the acceptability of such a programme is normally judged by the inherent wisdom and the soundness of the reasoning employed in support of it. This means that choice under uncertainty contains an *objective* component of evaluation which is not present in the subjective choice of an optimal bundle of spot consumption goods.

The objective component mentioned above appears to be reflected in the institutional structures which we observe. One notes the vast literature published by investment advisors, brokers and other professionals supporting or opposing different investment programmes. Most of these writings take an analytical, objectivist, viewpoint in the sense that the argument given is an 'assessment' rather than a purely subjectivist outlook reflecting the preference of the writer. We also note the fact that a very large fraction of our privately owned national wealth is being 'managed' by professional managers who are expected to use objective analysis to justify their investment strategies. A final example points out the fact that a significant part of our private wealth is managed by employers' designated pension funds. It is almost universal that employers restrict their retiring employees to receive only income flows (such as annuities) from their retirement assets but not the assets themselves. This is despite the fact that the employees 'own' these assets due to the vesting conditions of the funds. The common justification for these limitations is the need to prevent the retiring employees from deploying the assets in an irrational manner.

---

*This research was supported by the Lady Davis Fellowship Trust and by the Center for Rationality and Interactive Decision Theory, The Hebrew University, Jerusalem, Israel. The author thanks Kenneth Arrow, Horace Brock, Ho-Mou Wu and Menahem Yaari for helpful comments.

339

How can we then characterize the difference between a purely subjectivist view of preferences over certaint commodity bundles and the less than purely subjectivist view of preferences over risky prospects? The terminology which is usually employed to capture this difference is 'risk assessment'. Its use is based on the premise that choice over risky prospects is a composition of two distinct parts: the first is a purely subjective preference over risky flows *when the risks are known and fully understood* and the second is an assessment of the nature of the risks which the prospects at hand entail. The first part consists of a subjective preference over commodity bundles and the purely subjective expression of risk aversion. The second part of this composition requires more than just 'taste'. Risk assessment involves the objective application of human rationality.

The purpose of this chapter is to explore the above composition and give it a more precise formulation. We shall first show that the composition is only partially recognized in the theory of choice under uncertainty because it insists on the pure subjectivity of preferences. In the next section we explore the von Neumann–Morgenstern (1944) and Savage's (1954) theories in terms of this composition. We examine the reasons why the von Neumann–Morgenstern (1944) theory has had a profound impact in economics while the Savage (1954) theory has had only a limited impact on economic thinking. Next we shall outline the theory of Rational Beliefs developed in Kurz (1994a) and use it to formulate, in conjunction with the von Neumann–Morgenstern (1944) framework, a theory of 'Rational Preferences'. We explore one example in the Appendix.

2 PREFERENCES AND PROBABILITY BELIEFS

The von Neumann–Morgenstern (1944) theory addresses exactly the question of choice among probability distributions over consequences when these probabilities are explicitly specified. In the terminology of Anscombe and Aumann (1963), this theory addressed the 'roulette problem': the risk-taker is assumed to know exactly the nature of the mechanism which generates the risk and this understanding takes the form of an exact knowledge of the probabilities. Under these circumstances there is no risk assessment and individual preferences can be taken as the subjective primitives. This is so since 'risk assessment' is the process of evaluating the risky nature of a prospect *without a complete and precise knowledge of the mechanism which generates the consequences*. When you are given an unbiased roulette you are provided with exact 'structural knowledge' about the mechanism which generates the consequences. The von Neumann–Morgenstern (1944) theory applies when individuals are given such structural knowledge. It is a well-known fact that agents may perceive these probabilities subjectively but this does not alter our view that it is useful to draw a distinction between subjective perception of a specified probability and the process of forming probability beliefs without complete structural knowledge. We may note that the lack of structural knowledge does not necessarily lead to complete ignorance which entails what Anscombe and Aumann (1963) call the Horse Race Problem.

The expected utility theory of von Neumann–Morgenstern has had a profound impact in economics. This success is not necessarily due to the particular set of axioms employed. Rather, it is a result of the fact that the theory provided the scientific framework within which markets for risk, situations of strategic interaction and institutions for risk sharing could be studied. One could hardly begin to understand game theory and all its applications without the von Neumann–Morgenstern utility; the theories of risk aversion, stochastic dominance, optimal portfolios and optimal auctions are examples of major developments which grew out of the von Neumann–Morgenstern framework of analysis. This great success was achieved despite the enormous literature which challenged the specific von Neumann–Morgenstern assumptions.[1]

Empirical and experimental evidence has suggested that the 'Independence Axiom' is often violated, and even when presented with precise probabilities, individuals perceive them in a subjective manner which violates the axioms. This chapter cannot review the very large amount of evidence available. However, we do want to point out that the extensive debate ended up strengthening what we earlier called the von Neumann–Morgenstern *framework*. To explain this statement recall that the specific axioms adopted by von Neumann–Morgenstern (1944) implied the existence of a function $u: X \to R$ over sure consequences (where X is the space of consequences) such that preference among probabilities P on X is represented by a functional which takes the very sharp form

$$U(P) = \int u(x)dP(x). \tag{1}$$

Most of the critical reviews of the theory were directed against the strong form of (1). A careful examination of many of the alternative axiom systems which were developed shows that they preserved the *spirit* of the theory but changed the strong form of (1) in such a way that the new forms were free of all the essential experimental criticism against the theory. To illustrate, we consider three examples of alternative axiom systems.

The 'weighted utility theory' (see, for example, Chew and MacCrimmon, 1979; Chew, 1983; Fishburn, 1983; and Dekel 1986) implies the existence of a 'weight function' $w(x)$ such that the utility functional takes the form

$$U(P) = \int \frac{u(x)w(x)dP(x)}{\int w(x)dP(x)} \tag{2}$$

A second class of axioms implies the 'expected utility with rank dependent probabilities' (see, for example, Edwards, 1962; Handa, 1977; Karmarkar, 1978; and Yaari, 1987). This theory is developed for monetary consequences allowing the ranking by cumulative distributions on an interval. Hence take X to be a compact interval and let F_p be the cumulative distribution induced by P. Then the axioms imply the existence of a function $u: X \to R$ as in (1) but, in addition, a transforming function $g: [0, 1] \to [0, 1]$ which is continuous, strictly increasing and onto such that

$$U(P) = \int u(x)dg(F_p(x)). \tag{3}$$

The third example is the family of axioms postulating the smoothness of the functional representing the preferences (see, for example, Machina, 1982, 1988, 1989; Chew, Karni and Safra, 1987). As in the second class of axioms this research concentrated on monetary consequences and therefore the preference functional is defined over the space of cumulative distributions on a compact interval. The essential conclusion of this research is that when the functional is smooth[2] then it has a linear approximation which then induces a local (in the space of cumulative distributions) expected utility functional. Thus all the results which depend upon the properties of the von Neumann–Morgenstern utility $u(x)$ in (1) are preserved.

These three examples illustrate the fact that the empirical challenge to the expected utility theory resulted in the weakening of results which depend upon the linearity of the preference functional in the probabilities. On the other hand, this challenge showed that the central applications in areas such as the theory of risk aversion, optimal portfolio, markets for uncertainty, etc. are robust to this criticism and do not depend upon the strong implications (such as (1)) of the independence axiom. Moreover, the extensive debate about the axioms resulted, in our view, in a less rigid view of what constitutes 'rational' behaviour. Contrary to a rather common impression, much of the critical work of writers such as Allais (1953) and Kahneman and Tversky (1979) do not demonstrate irrational behaviour.[3] They do demonstrate that even when individuals are given the structural knowledge represented by the precise description of the probability distribution over consequences, they may *perceive* this description differently, resulting in subjective functionals such as (1), (2) or (3). However, this diversity of functionals is compatible with such universal phenomena as risk aversion, purchase of insurance, optimal portfolio and diversification, etc. Since there are no compelling and generally accepted economic criteria to imply that functionals like (2) or (3) represent irrational behaviour, we must conclude that all the diverse axiom systems should fall into what we have earlier called the *framework* of von Neumann and Morgenstern's analysis. Within this framework there are different modes by which decision-makers perceive probability distributions but all of them are compatible with the central results of uncertainty analysis in economics and finance. We note that the basic assumption that agents choose among completely specified probabilities is an extreme idealization: in most economic applications we do not see or know the 'roulette' which generates the data. Do we know the probabilities which govern the distribution of future prices of common stocks or of the future values of a real-estate investment such as our home? Since we make daily economic decisions whose outcomes depend upon random mechanisms the nature of which we do not know, Savage's (1954) theory of expected utility which addresses the 'horse race' problem[4] becomes applicable.

Savage's (1954) theory aimed to extend the von Neumann–Morgenstern (1944) construction but avoid the assumption of known 'objective' probabilities. Instead, Savage defined actions to be functions from the space Ω of the 'states of the world' to the space of consequences X. The construction was completed by postulating the primitives to be preference orderings on the space of actions. With no explicit probability defined on Ω Savage's expected utility theorem is a striking scientific achievement. The theorem shows that if a preference ordering satisfies a specified set of axioms then there exists not only a utility function measuring the utility of certain outcomes, but also a subjective probability measure on the subsets of Ω such that the selected action maximizes an expected utility functional like (1). Savage's theorem has had a profound impact on the fields of statistics and decision theory in that it firmly established the Bayesian approach in these disciplines. Yet, the theorem has had only a limited impact on economic thinking. This is an important fact which provides the motivation for this chapter and therefore we briefly outline our views for the reasons for this fact. We identify three essential reasons.

(1) *Probabilities and economic theory.* The great controversy about the nature of randomness and the foundations of probability never had an important impact on the thinking of economists. The empirical fluctuations of quantities and prices of economic variables are given scientific explanations based on equilibrium analysis. In such a context the acts of any particular decision-maker do not matter and hence his Savage subjective probabilities may not explain the variability of economic observables. Since such equilibrium magnitudes have well-defined empirical distributions, the modelling of economic variables as stochastic processes with *true* probability has gained widespread acceptance. But then, if equilibrium variables are described as a stochastic process with a specified objective probability, why derive subjective probabilities from abstract axioms about individual preferences?

(2) *Rational Expectations.* The theory of Rational Expectations in economics and finance (and, to some extent, the 'common prior' assumption in the theory of games with incomplete information) took point (1) above one step further. Under Rational Expectations agents know the true, equilibrium, probability distributions of variables and hence all agents hold the same beliefs. It is then obvious that Rational Expectations squarely rejects the relevancy of the subjectivist approach of Savage which is entirely compatible with the heterogeneity of subjective probabilities.

(3) *The crucial role of data.* In this chapter we are concerned only with economic phenomena for which ample past data are available. In fact, it is usually an empirical regularity in such long time series (which could stretch over hundreds of years) that attracts scientific inquiry. Hence, when an economic agent faces a decision in such circumstances, his Savage expected utility incorporates such past information. The Savage axioms obviously do not mention 'data', but since 'information' in Savage's (1954) formulation is represented by subsets of Ω, past data enters the analysis only by identifying a restricted subset of the state space. In this manner past observations induce *conditional* preferences and *conditional* probabilities. Note, however, that such an induced probability is nothing but the conditional probability of the information-free prior probability of the agent induced by Savage's axioms on the entire set Ω for the case of *no* information! Thus, Savage's (1954) subjectivist view leaves no room for real 'learning': the role of information is only to induce a conditioning, via Bayes rule, of the information-free prior. In fact, the idea that a decision-maker will set out to use information in order to learn something about probabilities is intrinsically alien to Savage's vision: preferences are the primitives and probabilities emerge only as consequences. This view of learning was much expanded in the practice of Bayesian statistics where the lack of knowledge of probabilities is modelled as uncertainty about the true parameters $\theta^* \in \Theta$. Thus, if the observations are $\{x_t, t = 0, 1, ...\}$ with $x_t \in R^N$ then each vector of parameters $\theta \in \Theta$ defines a known probability P_θ over infinite sequences of observations $x = (x_0, x_1, ...)$. In this set-up a prior belief is specified by a probability q on the parameter space but this device induces a prior probability P on the observations x (by integrating over Θ). Given $(x_0, x_1, ..., x_t)$ one can compute the posterior $q(\theta | x_0, ..., x_t)$ but integration over Θ leads just to the conditional prior

$P(\bullet \mid x_0, \ldots, x_t)$. In this sense the Bayesian procedure prevents the learning of any probability which is not equivalent to the prior P on the observations.[5] Bayesian learning generically is inconsistent and fails to converge[6] even when the observations are known to be independent identically distributed (i.i.d). This results from the fact that Savage's axioms place no restrictions on the priors. The 'practical' answer of the neo-Baysians is to view 'the prior' as a tool in organizing the data and to ensure that the prior is 'diffused' or 'broad' enough to enable the posterior to converge to the correct distribution. But then the source for determining if a prior is good or bad is the data! That is, if the data can be used as a basis to reject a prior then the Savage axioms must be supplemented by the knowledge about the empirical regularity of the data in order to arrive at a comprehensive conception of rationality. And conversely, one rejects the rationality criteria embodied in the Savage axioms since they lead to subjective probabilities which may be contradicted by the empirical frequency distribution obtained from the data. At the end, the data generate frequency distributions which rational agents should not ignore.

We propose now a new theory to supplement the rationality requirements of Savage. We take the view that economic variables follow a stochastic process with an underlying true probability. However, this probability is a structural knowledge which is not available to agents: they must learn about it as much as they can from the data generated by the economy. With this subjectivist view Savage's (1954) theorem is acceptable to us to the extent that it requires beliefs to be represented by additive probabilities.[7] Our theory applies to economic environments with ample past data so that the rationality of an agent selecting a 'prior' must be judged relative to the known history. The central goals of our development are therefore:

(a) To reject the idea that 'priors' are selected without reference to data and to focus explicitly on the process of selecting a probability belief which is based on the data generated by the system rather than by i.i.d. sampling.
(b) To formulate the criteria of rationality in such a way that the empirical frequencies provide the basis for determining if a belief is rational or not. Although the beliefs of agents are subjective in nature, we shall claim that empirical frequencies cannot be disregarded by rational agents.
(c) To provide an explanation for and a characterization of the diversity of beliefs among rational agents.

3 RATIONAL BELIEFS

3.1 The Theory

The theory of Rational Beliefs aims to characterize the set of probability measures $B(\Pi)$ which qualify as permissible beliefs in an economy where the unknown stochastic law of motion is defined by Π. The data generated by the economy is represented by a stochastic process $\{x_t, t = 0, 1, 2, \ldots\}$ where $x_t \in X \subseteq R^N$ and N is the finite number of observables. We define the state space and the information structure in the natural way:

$$\Omega = X^\infty \subseteq (R^N)^\infty$$

$$\mathcal{F}^t = \sigma(x_0, x_1, \ldots, x_t) - \text{the } \sigma - \text{field generated by } (x_0, x_1, \ldots, x_t),$$

$$\mathcal{F} = \sigma(\overset{\infty}{\underset{t=0}{U}} \mathcal{F}^t).$$

Thus, the true probability space of infinite sequences $x = (x_0, x_1, x_2, \ldots)$ is $(\Omega, \mathcal{F}, \Pi)$. This space is fixed and an agent who adopts the belief Q is, in fact, adopting the *theory* that the true probability space is $(\Omega, \mathcal{F}, Q)$. We shall think of this structure as a 'system' and say that the observations $x = (x_0, x_1, \ldots)$ are generated by the system with a probability Π.

An observing agent takes the system as fixed but he does not know Π; using past data he will try to learn as much as possible about Π. The theory of Rational Beliefs aims to characterize the set of all beliefs which are compatible with the available data. This, obviously, depends upon what we mean by 'compatibility with the data' and what are the data which are available.

From the perspective of principles of statistical inference, the theory of 'Rational Beliefs' is entirely simple. To formulate it consider an economic agent at date t who needs to adopt a belief Q. He starts with the set M of all possible theories one may have about the economic world, and in our case M is simply the set of all probability measures on the underlying space. Next the agent considers the empirical evidence available in order to test which of the theories in M are compatible with this evidence. It is well known that there is a wide spectrum of subjective criteria which agents may employ in accepting or rejecting any hypothesis in M. It follows that the 'rationality' of each agent is defined only relative to his own subjective selection criteria. In order to define an objective concept of rationality there must exist a set of criteria which is common to all individuals and for convenience let us call it the 'overriding evidence'. If the overriding evidence is such that it leads all agents to select a unique member of M, then our problem has a very simple solution. In general, the overriding evidence does not have this property and given the natural diversity among agents such evidence entails only universal rejection criteria rather than universal acceptance criteria. For this reason we propose that the term 'Rational Belief' be only used to identify those members of M which are not rejected by the overriding evidence. This set is denoted $B(\Pi)$.

We turn now to the question of the available data. Suppose first that we consider a two-period economy. With one observation in the first period economic agents have a very limited evidence: any probability belief which contains the observed data in its support cannot be rejected as being irrational.[8] The problem becomes more interesting and far more complex when we consider an infinite horizon systems with extensively long history so that an agent has finite but ample past data. We therefore think of the date $\tau = 0$ as having occurred a long time ago.

Although the data generated by the economy is the infinite vector $x = (x_0, x_1, \ldots)$ we need to introduce a different perspective. In studying complex joint distributions among the observables, econometricians consider blocks of data rather than individual, primitive, observations. For example, if we want to study the joint distribution of x_{today}, $x_{today+1}$, $x_{today+2}$ and $x_{today+3}$ we would consider the following infinite sequence of blocks:

$$(x_0, x_1, x_2, x_3)$$
$$(x_1, x_2, x_3, x_4)$$
$$(x_2, x_3, x_4, x_5)$$

.

.

.

Moreover we would think of these blocks as the data from the perspective of the starting date of each block. It has thus been useful to think of the data *from the perspective of* date 0 to be the infinite vector $x = (x_0, x_1, \ldots)$ and the data *from the perspective of* date 1 as $x^1 = (x_1, x_2, \ldots)$ where

$$x^1 = Tx.$$

T is known as the shift transformation. In general, the data from the perspective of date n is

$$x^n = T^n x.$$

The stochastic dynamical system at hand is denoted by $(\Omega, \mathscr{F}, \Pi, T)$ where $(\Omega, \mathscr{F})$ is the measurable space, Π is the unknown probability and T is the shift transformation.

In order to learn probabilities, agents adopt the natural way of studying the frequencies of all possible economic events. For example, consider the event B

$$B = \left\{ \begin{array}{l} \text{price of commodity 1 today} \leq \$1, \text{ price of commondity 6 tomorrow} \geq \$3 \\ 2 \leq \text{quantity of commodity 14 consumed two months later} \leq 5 \end{array} \right\}$$

Now, using past data, agents can compute for any finite dimensional event B the expression

$$m_n(B) = \frac{1}{n} \sum_{k=0}^{n-1} 1_B(T^k x) = \left\{ \begin{array}{l} \text{The relative frequency that } B \text{ occurred} \\ \text{among } n \text{ observations since date 0} \end{array} \right\}$$

where

$$1_B(y) = \left\{ \begin{array}{l} 1 \text{ if } y \in B \\ 0 \text{ if } y \notin B. \end{array} \right.$$

This leads to a definition of the basic property which the system $(\Omega, \mathscr{F}, \Pi, T)$ is assumed to have:

Definition 1: An economic system is called stable if for any finite dimensional event (i.e. a cylinder) B

$$\lim_{n \to \infty} m_n(B) = \overset{\circ}{m}(B) \ exist.[9] \tag{4}$$

In Kurz (1994a) it is shown that the set function $\overset{\bullet}{m}$ can be uniquely extended to a probability measure m on $(\Omega, \mathscr{F})$. Moreover relative to this probability the system is stationary (or invariant). This leads to two important observations:

(a) Given the property of stability, in trying to learn Π all agents end up learning m which is a stationary probability. In general $m \neq \Pi$: the true system may not be stationary and Π cannot be learned.

(b) Agents know that m may not be Π but with the data at hand m is the only thing that they can learn and agree upon. The invariant probability m is the overriding evidence which we discussed earlier.

Non-stationarity is simply a term which we employ to represent the process of structural change which cannot be explained by the statistical regularity of past data. Hence, a stable but non-stationary system is a model for an economy with structural change but in which econometric work can still be successfully carried out. This is so since all empirical moments will converge. The propositions above say that the use of statistical methods based on laws of large numbers *cannot result in the discovery of the true mechanism which generates the data*. It will result in the discovery of a stationary probability which gives correct average long-term forecasts but may generate wrong forecasts at all dates. It is clear that if all agents knew that the true system is stationary they would adopt m as their belief. The problem is that they do not know if the environment is stationary and hence even if it was stationary, agents may still not adopt m as their belief. It is then clear that the door is open for diverse opinions on the question of the kinds of non-stationarity which are compatible with the data.

It is important to see that m summarizes the entire collection of asymptotic restrictions imposed by the true system with probability Π on the empirical joint distributions of all the observed variables. Our concept of rationality attempts to relate the choice of Q to the evidence represented by the known stationary measure m which was computed from the data. To do this consider the set $T^{-n}B$ which is the preimage of B under T^n defined by

$$T^{-n}B = \{x \in \Omega : T^n x \in B\}.$$

$T^{-n}B$ is the set of points in Ω such that if we shift them by n dates we enter B; $T^{-n}B$ is the event B occurring n dates later in time. Now consider, for any finite cylinder B the set function

$$m_n^\Pi(B) = \frac{1}{n}\sum_{k=0}^{n-1} \Pi(T^{-k}B). \tag{5}$$

It is of central importance to note that $m_n^\Pi(B)$ has nothing to do with data: it is an analytical expression derived from $(\Omega, \mathscr{F}, \Pi, T)$. In Kurz (1994a) we introduce the following concept:

Definition 2: A dynamical system $(\Omega, \mathscr{F}, \Pi, T)$ is said to be *weak asymptotically mean stationary* (WAMS) if for all cylinders $B \in \mathscr{F}$ the limit

$$\overset{\bullet}{m}^\Pi(B) = \lim_{n \to \infty} \frac{1}{n}\sum_{k=0}^{n-1} \Pi(T^{-k}B) \;\; exists. \tag{6}$$

It is *strong asymptotically mean stationary* if the limit in (6) holds for all $B \in \mathscr{F}$. We then prove (see Kurz, 1994a, Proposition 2):

Proposition: A dynamical system $(\Omega, \mathscr{F}, \Pi, T)$ is stable if and only if it is WAMS.

Next it is shown (Kurz, 1994a, Proposition 3) that the set function $\overset{\circ}{m}{}^{\Pi}$ can be uniquely extended to a probability measure m^{Π} on $(\Omega, \mathscr{F})$ which is stationary relative to T.

These propositions are then used to derive the following two conclusions:

(1) Every stable system $(\Omega, \mathscr{F}, Q, T)$ induces a unique stationary measure m^Q which is *calculated analytically* from Q as in (6).
(2) If $(\Omega, \mathscr{F}, \Pi, T)$ is the true system which generated the data on the basis of which m was calculated then $m^{\Pi} = m$.

These two statements together imply that if an agent adopts the belief Q then

(a) Stability implies that Q induces a unique stationary probability m^Q.
(b) Since m was computed from the data if follows that if $m^Q \neq m$ it would constitute an empirical proof that $Q \neq \Pi$.
(c) For a belief Q to be viewed as compatible with the data we must require $m^Q = m$.

This leads to a natural definition:

Definition 3: A selection Q by an economic agent *cannot be contradicted by the data* if

(i) $(\Omega, \mathscr{F}, Q, T)$ is a stable process.
(ii) $m^Q = m$ hence Q induces the same stationary probability as was observed from the data.

Rationality Axioms

A selection Q by an agent is a Rational Belief if it satisfies

(a) Compatibility with the Data: Q cannot be contradicted by the data.
(b) Non-Degeneracy: if $m(S) > 0$, then $Q(S) > 0$.

Now to express his belief in non-stationarity of the environment an agent may select a probability $Q^{\perp}$. This probability is said to be orthogonal with m if there are events S and S^c such that

(i) $S \cup S^c = \Omega$, $S \cap S^c = \emptyset$,
(ii) $m(S) = 1$, $m(S^c) = 0$,
(iii) $Q^{\perp}(S) = 0$, $Q^{\perp}(S^c) = 1$.

We are now ready to characterize the set $B(\Pi)$ of all Rational Beliefs when the data are generated by $(\Omega, \mathscr{F}, \Pi, T)$ and m is calculated from the data.

Theorem (Kurz, 1994a): Every Rational Belief must satisfy

$$Q = \lambda Q_a + (1 - \lambda)Q^{\perp} \tag{7}$$

where $0 < \lambda \leq 1$, Q_a and m are probabilities which are mutually absolutely continuous (i.e. they are 'equivalent') and $Q^{\perp}$ is orthogonal with m such that

(i) $(\Omega, \mathscr{F}, Q, T)$ and $(\Omega, \mathscr{F}, Q^{\perp}, T)$ are both stable
(ii) $m^{Q_a} = m^{Q^{\perp}} = m$.

Moreover, any Q such that λ, Q_a and $Q^{\perp}$ satisfy the above is a Rational Belief.

The probability $Q^{\perp}$ is central since it represents the theory of the agent of how the probability of an event at any date differs from the stationary probability at that date. Moreover, $Q^{\perp}$ permits an agent to place positive probability even on events with zero m probability: these are important but infrequent events. Each one of them is important in the sense that its economic impact is significant and the behaviour of agents can be strongly influenced by the probabilities placed on it by these agents. It is infrequent in the sense that its relative frequencies converge to zero. However, non-stationary systems can give rise to an unbounded number of such events which are different from each other. Consequently, a Rational Belief Q may induce forecasts which are different from the forecasts of m at all dates. Moreover, the difference between the forecasts of Q and m need not converge to zero.

The theorem also says that two economic agents who are equally intelligent and who have *identically the same information* may make two different rational forecasts because they hold two competing theories which are compatible with the data. The agents will disagree on two central questions:

(1) How much weight should be placed on the possibility that the environment is stationary.
(2) What is the nature of the important events over which they put the different non-stationary probabilities $Q^{\perp}$ inducing different forecasts. Disagreement among rational agents must, therefore, arise from their having different theories about the nature of the fluctuations generated by the system rather than about the behaviour of the long-term averages.

Many economic time series exhibit patterns such as long-term growth which violate stability. Moreover, deterministic patterns such as seasonality or regular cycles may be present in the data and a rational agent should take them into account. Violation of stability may be simply resolved by transforming the data, a common practice in time series analysis. Typical transformations include first differencing or detrending the logarithm of the observations. The transformed data may then be stable.

The handling of deterministic patterns requires an examination of subsequences of x. Suppose that $\{x_{t_k}, k = 0, 1, \ldots\}$ is a subsequence. We can compute relative frequencies on the subsequence and if they converge, they may contradict the stationary measure m. We stress that, in general, relative frequencies on subsequences may not converge. Moreover, even if they converge, no general theory exists about the behaviour of the system on subsequences and consequently two rational agents may disagree about the interpretation of such patterns of behaviour. Keep in mind that given a sequence of non-degenerate i.i.d random variables we can find with probability one subsequences which will contradict m. It is then clear that the only relevant subsequences are those which contradict m and are also *predictable*. That is, a subsequence has a *predictable index set* (in short, 'predictable') if there exists a fixed, time invariant, function f such that for all k

$$t_{k+1} = f(t_k).^{10}$$

If a rational agent computes relative frequencies on predictable subsequences and these contradict m, he would supplement m with this knowledge.

The main class of predictable subsequences is the one used to study seasonality and regular cycles. For this class we have a complete theory. The class is characterized by a function f of the linear form

$$t_{k+1} = t_k + n$$

In this case we consider the shift transformations T^n instead of T. For example, quarterly data with seasonality should be studied as a sequence of quadruples $((x_0, x_1, x_2, x_3), (x_4, x_5, x_6, x_7), \dots)$ under the four-shift T^4 rather than under T. It can be shown that if $(\Omega, \mathscr{F}, \Pi, T)$ is stable with a stationary measure m then $(\Omega, \mathscr{F}, \Pi, T^n)$ is stable for all n with the stationary measure $m_{(n)}$. The relationship between m and $m_{(n)}$ is

$$m(A) = \frac{1}{n} \sum_{i=0}^{n-1} m_{(n)}(T^{-i}A) \quad A \varepsilon \mathscr{F}.$$

If $m = m_{(n)}$ then the data contain no seasonality or cycles. If $m \neq m_{(n)}$ then rational agents will use the structure of $m_{(n)}$ instead of m. In this chapter we assume that the data have been adjusted for such patterns.

There could be predictable subsequences which are not linear shifts. For example, let $\{\zeta_t, t = 0, 1, 2, \dots\}$ be an i.i.d. sequence on $[0, 1]$ and let $\{\eta_t, t = 0, 1, 2, \dots\}$ be an i.i.d. sequence on $[2, 3]$. Now consider the composition of these two sequences

$$x_t = \begin{cases} \eta_t \text{ for } t = 2^k \\ \zeta_t \text{ for } t \neq 2^k. \end{cases}$$

The study of the subsequences on $t = 2^k$ can be transformed into the study of the linear shifts T^n in the following way. Let

$$y_\tau = \begin{cases} \eta_{2^k} \text{ for } \tau = 2k & k = 0, 1, 2, \dots \\ \zeta_{2^k} \text{ for } \tau = 2k + 1 & k = 0, 1, 2, \dots \end{cases}$$

Hence

$$y = (\eta_{2^0}, \zeta_{2^0}, \eta_{2^1}, \zeta_{2^1}, \dots, \eta_{2^k}, \zeta_{2^k}, \dots).$$

Treating y as a stochastic sequence we study its asymptotic properties on even and odd dates by comparing the outcomes under T and T^2. If such stationary measures can be defined and they are different, an agent may obtain useful information. From the formal viewpoint this is exactly the same as in the case of linear shifts. The difference is that now there exists no theory to interpret the meaning of the asymptotic frequencies of *y*. Rational agents will discover predictable patterns and supplement the knowledge of *m* with the asymptotic frequencies of *y*. We note, however, that in all applications of this theory we view non-stationarity as a model of *unpredictable* structural change. For this reason predictable subsequences which are not linear shifts are not relevant to these applications.

Our theorem raises some basic questions related to the formation of rational beliefs in non-stationary environments and to the use of econometric techniques in such environments. These are important issues which merit some further comments. However, we also wish to return to the discussion of subjective probabilities and Savage's axioms in Section 2. To accommodate both aims we continue our general discussion in Sections 3.2–3.3. In addition, we study in the Appendix an example of a non-stationary market and discuss the issue of statistical inference in such an environment.

3.2 Rational Beliefs: Relation to Subjective Probabilities

One of the most desirable features of Savage's (1954) theorem is the separation between utilities of sure prospects and probability beliefs. This is entirely compatible with our view: what we called earlier 'risk assessment' emerges in Savage's analysis as a distinct entity out of preferences. Our approach is also compatible with Savage's conclusion that risk assessment is represented by an additive probability measure. Finally, agents with rational beliefs may hold diverse probability assessments in the same manner that Savage's agents have heterogeneous preferences. The main difficulty is that Savage's approach permits all prior probabilities to be permissible beliefs while our approach aims to establish restrictions on the set of allowable probability beliefs. This brings us back to the goals of our development as formulated at the end of Section 2 above.

The difference between our approach and Bayesian learning is centred on the question of how rational agents should use information to formulate beliefs. That is, if a belief is represented by $(\Omega, \mathcal{F}, Q)$ and a long sequence $(x_0, x_1, x_2, \ldots, x_t)$ of past observations is given, then rationality clearly demands that the conditional probability $Q(\cdot \mid (x_0, x_1, \ldots, x_t))$ be the conditional belief given the observed data. To this extent we certainly accept Bayes rule. However, we do not accept the view that a rational agent should select a prior belief $(\Omega, \mathcal{F}, Q)$ without reference to the available information about the past performance of the dynamical system which generated the data.

Our departure from Savage's subjectivist vision is inherent in our view that economic data are generated by the market equilibrium of the economy. This equilibrium is an *objective* stochastic mechanism the nature of which is not fully known to the agents. A 'belief' is therefore a theory about this objective mechanism or is a model of the equilibrium which is adopted by an agent. The economic events of concern are those for which empirical relative frequencies exist and these are represented by the known stationary measure *m*. It is therefore the objectively known empirical frequencies represented by *m* from which we derive the rationality restrictions on beliefs. From the perspective of our theory *it is not rational* to believe that a sequence of random variables is i.i.d. if the data reveals substantial serial correlation! This is somewhat paradoxical since on a deeper level we do accept the subjectivist, heterogeneous, view of Savage but insist that it be supplemented by a *frequentist* criterion of rationality.

3.3 Rational Beliefs: Discussion and Interpretation

Having clarified the relationship between rational beliefs and subjective probabilities we turn now to discuss various aspects of the theory at hand.

(i) Is the Social Environment Stationary?

A central question arises in our theory with respect to the degree of confidence of an agent in the stationarity of his environment. Clearly, if the environment is stationary and *an agent knows that it is stationary* then rationality requires him to adopt $(\Omega, \mathscr{F}, m)$ as his belief. It is obvious, however, that at no time can an agent be certain that his environment is stationary. Moreover, despite the fact that most econometric methods are based on the premise of a stationary social environment, there are compelling reasons to question this. Economic development is strongly influenced by technological changes, inventions and new products, changes in political and organizational structures and other such phenomena which are typical manifestations of non-stationarity. The 'degree of confidence' in the probability derived from the relative frequencies is expressed by λ in the representation (7) of beliefs $Q = \lambda Q + (1 - \lambda)Q^{\perp}$. This interpretation arises from the fact that a rational agent knows that m may not be Π. Moreover, he also knows that the true system $(\Omega, \mathscr{F}, \Pi, T)$ *is not knowable*.

(ii) Structural Change and Rational Beliefs as Models of the Environment.

The rationality requirement that a model selected by an agent be compatible with the data is a minimal one: it restricts the asymptotic moments of the data that would be generated if the model was true. This means that the long-term statistics of the data generated by the models of all rational agents is the same. However, these models do not perform in the same way from the perspective of decision-makers with time preference or discounting. Over any finite interval of time[11] some of them may be good models and others may be poor ones. In many economic environments this may be the difference between great gains and great losses. This issue is important and requires further clarification.

Our basic postulate is that agents do not possess complete structural knowledge and that structural changes are not observable. Moreover, such phenomena as technological innovations, changes in taste, changes in economic institutions or shifts in the international balance of power are typically very difficult to predict. Consequently the argument among competing theories is often reduced to the question whether these changes are purely random variations around the fixed mean value function of a stationary process or whether they reflect changes in the mean value function itself. It is important, however, to note that the fact that past data (using asymptotic moments) do not provide satisfactory statistical forecasts of such changes does not mean that agents may not attempt to profit from utilizing theories or conjectures which we have called 'rational beliefs'. For example, consider a stock market environment in which the real profit process follows a non-stationary process of fluctuating regimes as in the Appendix. It is clear that if one believed that the process has fluctuating regimes, one would then believe that it would be very profitable to identify the switch dates. Theories which attempt to do that cannot be based on the asymptotic properties of the data. Instead they must exploit other sources of knowledge in society. This includes, for example, knowledge about technology, politics and social attitudes as reflected in the daily life of agents. Also, in an economy which undergoes structural changes there are non-recurring and incomplete signals about these changes. The term 'non-recurring' is used here to mean that the signals are unique to each period of change and are not comparable over time. They give only a very limited insight and are therefore subject to conflicting interpretations. Let us consider an illustration. Both Xerox copying and Personal Computing represent major structural changes in their industries. Before the initial introduction of these technologies both Xerox and Apple conjectured that these products would be desired in the future and early market studies provided mixed signals which were interpreted to be relatively encouraging by both companies. Due to the great perceived risks, both inventions (and companies) were offered for sale to IBM who conducted its own examination of office secretaries (for Xerox equipment) and consumer demand (for Apple's PC). IBM's signals and theories about the two markets led it to reject both inventions as having a questionable future. All information was unique to the technologies at hand and no past experience would have enabled any more reliable assessment. Although IBM's decisions have been extensively studied, there is no logical and objective basis to declare them 'irrational'.

The theory of rational beliefs does not aim to explain the differences among the models selected by different rational agents. It proposes that past data alone cannot explain the reasons why investors in the stock market select one decision rule over another, and it holds that market information alone cannot explain why two different inventors will attempt two different approaches to solve the same problem. Variations in qualities such as intuition, insight, persistence and scientific depth lead different rational individuals to arrive at different conclusions given the same information and our theory does not aim to explain these difference. Rather, we claim that the *distribution* of these beliefs in society is an important component in explaining the economic performance of such societies (see Kurz, 1994b, 1993). *The distribution of beliefs is as important a component of market behaviour as the distribution of consumer preferences for spot commodities.*

(iii) Objective and Subjective Selection Criteria

From the perspective of rational expectations the set $B(\Pi)$ of rational beliefs is too large: it permits 'extreme' beliefs to be declared 'rational'. We view this as a central virtue of our theory in that it proposes that *objective* criteria of rationality are not sufficient to ensure that all agents hold the same belief. Each agent employs his own subjective criterion to select specific members of $B(\Pi)$. Some agents may minimize a loss of function (which would differ across agents), some may maximize a likelihood function and many others will use no statistical tools at all to select members from $B(\Pi)$. Instead, they may base their selection in $B(\Pi)$ on theories which incorporate technological and political considerations.

Every large population will surely have individuals with extreme views that would deviate from the 'norm' or the social 'consensus'. However, general equilibrium considerations imply that the extreme beliefs of any one member is relatively unimportant. Instead, as we pointed out above, it is the *distribution* of beliefs in $B(\Pi)$ which matters for economic performance.

4 RATIONAL PREFERENCES

The final step of defining 'rational preferences' is a natural derivation from the theory of rational beliefs. Formally we think of the state space $\Omega = (X^N)^\infty$ as the space of sequences of all observables in the economy. These observables include the endowments of all agents, return on their investments, prices and wage rates, etc. Let Y be the space of desired commodities and let $f: \Omega \to Y$ be a choice function of the agent. Denote by F the set of allowable choice functions. The interpretation of this is that given the resources of the agent and other market conditions (such as wage rates and prices) the agent can select a consumption programme in Y. Given a belief of the agent which is represented by $(\Omega, \mathscr{F}, Q)$ then each choice function f induces a probability distribution on Y. Thus, for a fixed Q, a preference ordering on F is, in fact, a preference ordering on well-specified probability distributions on Y. We now *assume* that this preference ordering on F satisfies the von Neumann–Morgenstern framework. This means (see Section 2 above) that it satisfies a set of axioms that permits its representation by a utility functional; we denote it by $U_Q(f)$. If the set of axioms which are satisfied are the von Neumann–Morgenstern axioms then $U_Q(f)$ has the specific form

$$U_Q(f) = \int u(f(x))dQ(x). \tag{8}$$

We stress, however, that other axioms may be employed leading $U_Q(f)$ to be represented, for example, by functionals which are analogous to (2) or (3). This leads us to our final definition:

Definition 4: Let the economy be represented by the dynamical system $(\Omega, \mathscr{F}, \Pi, T)$. A preference ordering on F is said to be a *rational preference ordering* if it satisfies the von Neumann–Morgenstern framework and if its representation $U_Q(\cdot)$ satisfies the rationality requirement $Q \in B(\Pi)$.

Returning to our discussion in the Introduction, the probability Q is the 'risk assessment' component of the preference and it represents the objective component which is subject to conditions of rationality. On the other hand, the utility function $u(\cdot)$ in (8) represents the purely subjective component of the preference.

It is standard to view the *choices* among risky prospects as the basic empirical implications of a theory of preference orderings on the space of such prospects. Does the concept of 'rational preference' offer any additional empirical implications beyond those actions induced by a preference ordering like (8)? We suggest that the answer is yes, and conclude the chapter by a brief discussion of this point.

In the context of a stochastic dynamical system agents make *choices* among feasible actions as well as *forecasts* about future events. It is true that we may need to ask them to reveal their forecasts, but in most instances their choices are not observable either and therefore we need to ask them to reveal the choices as well. If an agent has rational preferences with probability Q he must also have a very complex set of forecasts which are subject to a specific set of empirical restrictions which we shall now state. Thus let y_{t+k} be the value of any random variable at date $t + k$. Since x_{t+k} is the *vector* of all observables at $t + k$ one may think of y_{t+k} as any m integrable function of $(x_{t+1}, x_{t+2}, \ldots, x_{t+k})$. For $z_j \in R^N$ consider any sequence of $M+1$ vectors $(z_0, z_1, \ldots, z_M) \in R^{N(M+1)}$. Now define

$$E_Q(y_{t+k} \mid x_t = z_0, x_{t-1} = z_1, \ldots, x_{t-M} = z_M) = \bar{y}_{t+k}^Q(z_0, \ldots, z_M) \qquad (9)$$

The function $\bar{y}_{t+k}^Q(z_0, \ldots, z_M)$ is the forecast function of the agent for date $t + k$ given that the past history was the finite vector $(z_0, z_1, \ldots, z_M)$. We can then show that if an agent has rational preferences with probability Q then for all $k > 0$, all random variables y_{t+k} and all finite histories $(z_0, z_1, \ldots, z_M)$ the system of forecasts must satisfy

$$(a) \qquad \lim_{H \to \infty} \frac{1}{H} \sum_{t=0}^{H-1} \bar{y}_{t+k}^Q(z_0, \ldots, z_M) = \bar{y}_k(z_0, \ldots, z_M) \text{ exists,}$$

$$(b) \qquad \bar{y}_k(z_0, \ldots, z_M) = E_m(y_{M+k} \mid x_0 = z_0, \ldots, x_M = z_M). \qquad (10)$$

These two sets of restrictions say that the agent has a system of forecasts and the conditional forecasts over more and more remote horizons must average out to the conditional forecast under m. This also says that the average forecasts *must be equal for all agents and be equal to the stationary forecast under m*.

It is important to note that in the context of our theory it is meaningless to talk about the rationality of any *one* forecast for a specific date (in the sense of (9)). The concept of rationality applies to *the entire system of forecast functions* in (9) which must satisfy the family of conditions in (10). This is analogous to the system of stability conditions implied by the theorem cited in Section 3.1.

A final note about data. We have already stressed the importance of beliefs to the understanding of market performance. Unfortunately, data on individual beliefs are not available, but our analysis implies that extensive data files on individual system of forecasts would be extremely valuable. Such data would also enable a direct testing of our theory.

APPENDIX

The example developed here intends to provide a reasonable approximation for a model of structural change in economics: it allows the mean value function to be fixed for a random length of time. This example, however, is drastically simplified by the assumption that neither the mean value function nor the length of each 'regime' is correlated with other variables or with past values. A more complex model should permit such correlations.

To start with let $a = (a_0, a_1, a_2, \ldots)$ be an infinite sequence of real numbers. The sequence is said to be *stable* if for any finite dimensional set $B \subset R^\infty$ it is true that

$$\lim_{n \to \infty} \frac{1}{n} \sum_{k=0}^{n-1} 1_B(T^k a) \quad \text{exist} \qquad (11)$$

where $T^k a = (a_k, a_{k+1}, a_{k+1}, a_{k+2}, \ldots)$. Consider the following simple example of how to generate a stable sequence. Partition the non-negative integers into two non-predictable index sets R and R^C with equal density. Let $\{z_t^1\}_{t=0}^\infty$ be an i.i.d. sequence taking values on $(b_1^1, b_2^1, \ldots, b_k^1)$ with probabilities $(p_1^1, p_2^1, \ldots, p_k^1)$ and $\{z_t^2\}_{t=0}^\infty$ an i.i.d. (and independent of all z_t^1) on $(b_1^2, b_2^2, \ldots, b_M^2)$ with probabilities $(p_1^2, p_2^2, \ldots, p_M^2)$. Now take the composition

$$z_t = \begin{cases} z_t^1 & \text{for } t\varepsilon R \\ z_t^2 & \text{for } t\varepsilon R^c. \end{cases}$$

Let $a = (a_0, a_1, a_2, \ldots)$ be any realization of the stochastic sequence $\{z_t^1\}_{t=0}^\infty$. Almost all such realizations are stable sequences.

Next, consider the random sequence $\{x_t, t = 0, 1, 2, \ldots\}$ on $(\Omega, \mathscr{F})$ with probability Π. Let $\{\tau_k, k = 1, 2, \ldots\}$ be a non-stationary sequence of random dates on the positive integers. Now define

$$k(t) = k \text{ for } \tau_k \leq t < \tau_{k+1}, \qquad k(0) = 1, \tau_1 = 0 \tag{12}$$

where we note that $k(\tau_k) = k$ but $k(\tau_{k+1}) = k + 1$. We think of k as the index of the regime which prevails at dates t since it satisfies $\tau_k \leq t < \tau_{k+1}$. Define the length of regime k by

$$\ell_k = \tau_{k+1} - \tau_k \quad k = 1, 2, \ldots$$

Our stochastic assumptions are specified relative to the process $\{\ell_k, k = 1, 2, \ldots\}$ as follows:

(a) $\{\ell_k, k = 1, 2, \ldots\}$ is a stable sequence in the sense of the Definition in (11). It has mean $\bar{\ell}$ and asymptotic, unconditional, stationary distribution which is uniform on the integers in $[1, \bar{\ell}]$.

(b) The random sequence $\{\ell_k, k = 1, 2, \ldots\}$ is asymptotically uncorrelated with any observed variable and has asymptotically no autocorrelation. That is, for all $j > 0$

$$\lim_{N\to\infty} \frac{1}{N} \sum_{k=1}^N (\ell_k - \bar{\ell})(\ell_{k+j} - \bar{\ell}) = 0 \quad \text{a.e.}$$

Now, select a sequence of positive, uniformly bounded numbers $\{\delta_j, j = 1, 2, \ldots\}$ which satisfy:

(1) The sequence is stable (in the sense of (11)) and is almost surely asymptotically uncorrelated with anything observable.

(2) The sequence has asymptotically no autocorrelation. That is, for all $j > 0$.

$$\lim_{K\to\infty} \frac{1}{K} \sum_{k=1}^K (\delta_{k+j} - \bar{\delta})(\delta_k - \bar{\delta}) = 0.$$

We can finally define the stochastic process $\{x_t, t = 0, 1, 2, \ldots\}$ by

$$x_t = \delta_{k(t)} + \varepsilon_t. \tag{13}$$

$\{\varepsilon_t, t = 0, 1, 2, \ldots\}$ is an i.i.d. random noise with mean zero and variance σ_ε^2. Assume $\delta_{k(t)}$ to be 'large' so that $x_t \geq 0, \forall t$ with probability 1. The process $\{x_t, t = 0, 1, \ldots\}$ is stable but not stationary since it depends upon a sequence of regimes of length ℓ_k which is assumed to be stable but non-stationary. A typical sample path would look as in Figure 14.1.

Agents do not know the structure which we have postulated. They see the data as in Figure 14.2 and since it is a stable process they can compute moments and relative frequencies with which they can say something about Π. The interest naturally focuses on the autocorrelation structure of the data.

From the assumptions made we have that the time average of x_t satisfies $\bar{x} = \bar{\delta}$ and hence

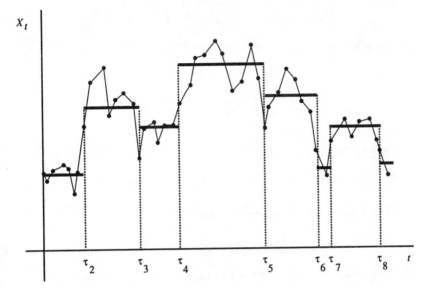

Figure 14.1

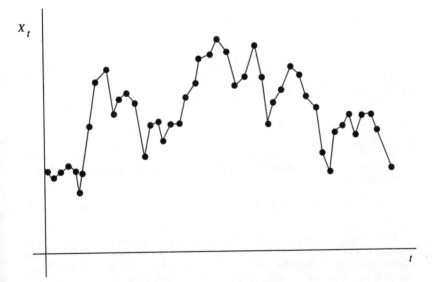

Figure 14.2

$$\frac{1}{T}\sum_{t=0}^{T-1}(x_t - \overline{\delta})^2 = \frac{1}{T}\sum_{t=0}^{T-1}\left[(\delta_{k(t)} - \overline{\delta})^2 + 2(\delta_{k(t)} - \overline{\delta})\varepsilon_t + \varepsilon_t^2\right].$$

We know that

$$\lim_{T\to\infty}\frac{1}{T}\sum_{t=0}^{T-1}(\delta_{k(t)} - \overline{\delta})\varepsilon_t = 0 \quad \text{a.e.}$$

$$\lim_{T\to\infty}\frac{1}{T}\sum_{t=0}^{T-1}\varepsilon_t^2 = \sigma_\varepsilon^2 \quad \text{a.e.}$$

But now compute

$$\sum_{t=0}^{T-1}(\delta_{k(t)} - \overline{\delta})^2 = (\delta_1 - \overline{\delta})^2\ell_1 + (\delta_2 - \overline{\delta})^2\ell_2 + \ldots + (\delta_{k(T)} - \overline{\delta})(T - \tau_{k(T)}).$$

For large T we have that approximately $T = k(T)\overline{\ell}$ hence

$$\frac{1}{T}\sum_{t=1}^{T}(\delta_{k(t)} - \overline{\delta})^2 \approx \frac{1}{\overline{\ell}k(T)}\sum_{j=1}^{k(T)}(\delta_j - \overline{\delta})^2\ell_j.$$

Now recall that the ℓ_j and δ_j are assumed asymptotically uncorrelated, hence

$$\begin{aligned}
\lim_{T\to\infty}\frac{1}{T}\sum_{t=0}^{T-1}(\delta_{k(t)} - \overline{\delta})^2 &= \frac{1}{\overline{\ell}}\left\{\lim_{k\to\infty}\sum_{j=1}^{k}(\delta_j - \overline{\delta})^2 \lim_{k\to\infty}\frac{1}{k}\sum_{j=1}^{k}\ell_j\right\}\\
&= \frac{1}{\overline{\ell}}\sigma_\delta^2\overline{\ell}\\
&= \sigma_\delta^2
\end{aligned}$$

But this shows that

$$\sigma_x^2 = \sigma_\delta^2 + \sigma_\varepsilon^2.$$

In a similar manner it can be shown that for each $1 \le k \le \hat{\ell} - 1$

$$\lim_{T\to\infty}\frac{1}{T}\sum_{t=0}^{T-1}(x_t - \overline{x})(x_{t+k} - \overline{x}) = \sigma_\delta^2\frac{(\hat{\ell} - k)(\hat{\ell} - k + 1)}{(\hat{\ell} + 1)}.$$

It can then be shown that the stationary measure m_x which the agent can learn is a stationary $(\hat{\ell} - 1)$ Markov process. Assume that the transition function can be approximated by the linear equation[12]

$$x_t = \overline{\delta} + \beta_1(x_{t-1} - \overline{x}) + \beta_2(x_{t-2} - \overline{x}) + \ldots + \beta_{\hat{\ell}-1}(x_{t-\hat{\ell}+1} - \overline{x}) + \eta_t. \tag{14}$$

The $(\hat{\ell} - 1)$ vector β is computed from the moments of the data in a well-known way.

Observe that the true stochastic behaviour of x_t is expressed in (13), whereas the 'smoother' model (14) is a representation of the stationary measure which agents can learn from the data. Agents who accept the hypothesis represented by (14) will certainly be adopting a Rational Belief. But there are many other models which are compatible with (14).

Consider an econometrician who looks as the data in Figure 14.2 and postulates that the persistence in the data is a result of the presence of an unobserved permanent component. He could propose a family of non-stationary models of the type

$$x_t = \beta y_t + \xi_t$$
$$y_t = \alpha_0 + \alpha_1 y_{t-1} + \ldots + \alpha_\nu y_{t-\nu} + \zeta_t \tag{15}$$

It is well known from the literature on unobserved components models (see Nerlove, Grether and Carvalho, 1979, particularly ch. 2) that for any specified stochastic structure of the random sequence $\{\eta_t,\ t = 1, 2, \ldots\}$ in (14) there exists an entire family of models of the type specified in (15) such that their asymptotic covariance and (and autocovariance) structure corresponds exactly to the covariance structure in (14). In fact, it is restrictions of this type that enables the identification of the parameters of a model specified in (15). But this means that one can construct a large family of non-stationary models of the type specified in (15) which will be 'compatible with the data' in the exact sense of our basic axiom on Rational Beliefs. The econometrician who accepts any particular member of this collection is, in fact, selecting a Rational Belief represented by the model. This discussion shows that the *basic concept of 'Rational Belief' is entirely standard in the econometric literature*: a model represents a 'Rational Belief' if we can specify a set of restrictions such that given these restrictions, the asymptotic moments of the data implied by the model are the same as the asymptotic moments observed in the data. But then keep in mind that such a model Q is not the true mechanism (13) which generated the data and hence

$$M_t^Q(I_{t-1}) = \delta_{k(t)} - E_Q(x_t \mid I_{t-1})$$

is the 'forecasting mistake' under the belief Q. In the context of the example in (13) the forecasting mistakes of the agents will be most pronounced around the turning points of the sequence $\delta_{k(t)}$.

Notes

1. For extensive review of the literature see Fishburn (1988, ch. 2) and Karni and Schmeidler (1991).
2. In the exact sense of being either Frechet or Gateaux differentiable with respect to the distribution.
3. This impression is particularly enhanced by writers such as Kahneman and Tversky who approach the problem from a psychological perspective which questions the usefulness of rationality as an explanatory principle in human conduct.
4. This is the terminology of Anscombe and Aumann (1963).
5. A simple example will illustrate the point. If the prior at time $t = 0$ is that the x_t are i.i.d. then no matter how much correlation between x_t and x_{t+k} (for some $k > 0$) is computed from the data, a Bayesian procedure will never converge to a distribution which permits such a correlation. The procedure can only select a distribution under which the x_t are distributed independently.
6. See Freedman (1963, 1965), and the survey by Diaconis and Freedman (1986). Feldman (1991) reviews these problems in a market context.
7. This is to be contrasted with recent work on belief functions represented by non-additive probabilities. See Dempster (1967), Shafer (1976) and Schmeidler (1989).
8. This does not preclude different individuals from adopting more stringent selection criteria (e.g. maximum likelihood, minimum loss of diverse loss functions, etc.) but all should be taken as equally 'rational'.
9. As defined, $m_n(B)$ depends on x and should be written $m_n(B)(x)$. In this chapter we assume that $(\Omega, \mathcal{F}, \Pi, T)$ is ergodic in which case the limit in (4) exists Π a.e. and is independent of x.
10. f may also depend upon history of fixed finite length.

11. But such interval of time may last many years!
12. If a linear approximation is not sufficient, use a polynomial approximation and the following argument remains the same.

References

Allais, M. (1953) 'Le comportement de l'homme rational devant le risque: critique des postulats et axiomes de l'école américaine', *Econometrica*, vol. 21, pp. 503–46.

Anscombe, F.J. and R.J. Aumann (1963) 'A Definition of Subjective Probability', *Annals of Mathematical Statistics*, vol. 34, pp. 199–205.

Chew, S.H. (1983) 'A Generalization of the Quasilinear Mean with Applications to the Measurement of Income Inequality and Decision Theory Resolving the Allais Paradox', *Econometrica*, vol. 51, pp. 1065–92.

Chew, S.H. and K.R. MacCrimmon (1979) 'Alpha-Nu Choice Theory: A Generalization of Expected Utility Theory', University of British Columbia Faculty of Commerce and Business Administration Working Paper No. 686.

Chew, S.H., E. Karni and Z. Safra (1987) 'Risk Aversion in the Theory of Expected Utility with Rank Dependent Probabilities', *Journal of Economic Theory*, vol. 42, pp. 370–81.

Dekel, E. (1986) 'An Axiomatic Characterization of Preferences under Uncertainty: Weakening the Independence Axiom', *Journal of Economic Theory*, vol. 40, pp. 304–18.

Dempster, A.P. (1967) 'Upper and Lower Probabilities Induced by a Multivalued Mapping', *Annals of Mathematical Statistics*, vol. 38, pp. 325–39.

Diaconis, P. and D. Freedman (1986) 'On the Consistency of Bayes Estimates', *Annals of Statistics*, vol. 14, pp. 1–26.

Edwards, W. (1962) 'Subjective Probabilities Inferred from Decisions', *Psychological Reviews*, vol. 69, pp. 109–35.

Feldman, M. (1991) 'On the Generic Nonconvergence of Bayesian Actions and Beliefs', *Economic Theory*, vol. 1, pp. 301–21.

Fishburn, P.C. (1983) 'Transitive Measurable Utility', *Journal of Economic Theory*, vol. 37, pp. 293–317.

Fishburn, P.C. (1988) *Nonlinear Preference and Utility Theory* (Baltimore: Johns Hopkins University Press).

Freedman, D. (1963) 'On the Asymptotic Behavior of Bayes Estimates in the Discrete Case I', *Annals of Mathematical Statistics*, vol. 34, pp. 1386–403.

Freedman, D. (1965) 'On the Asymptotic Behavior of Bayes Estimates in the Discrete Case II', *Annals of Mathematical Statistics*, vol. 36, pp. 454–6.

Handa, J. (1977) 'Risk, Probabilities and a New Theory of Cardinal Utility', *Journal of Political Economy*, vol. 85, pp. 97–122.

Kahneman, D. and A. Tversky (1979) 'Prospect Theory: An Analysis of Decision Under Risk', *Econometrica*, vol. 47, pp. 263–91.

Karmarkar, U.S. (1978) 'Subjectively Weighted Utility: A Descriptive Extension of the Expected Utility Model', *Organizational Behavior and Human Performance*, vol. 21, pp. 61–72.

Karni, E. and D. Schmeidler (1991) 'Utility Theory with Uncertainty', ch. 23 in W. Hildenbrand and H. Sonnenschein (eds), *Handbook of Mathematical Economics*, vol. IV (Amsterdam: Elsevier Science).

Kurz, M. (1993) 'Asset Prices with Rational Beliefs', mimeo, Stanford University.

Kurz, M. (1994a) 'On the Structure and Diversity of Rational Beliefs', *Economic Theory*, vol. 4, pp. 877–900.

Kurz, M. (1994b) 'On Rational Belief Equilibria,' *Economic Theory*, vol. 4, pp. 859–876.

Machina, M.J. (1982) '"Expected Utility" Analysis Without the Independence Axiom', *Econometrica*, vol. 50, pp. 277–323.

Machina, M.J. (1988) 'Cardinal Properties of Local Utility Functions', in B.R. Munier, (ed.), *Risk Decision and Rationality* (Dordrecht: Reidel), pp. 339–44.

Machina, M.J. (1989) 'Comparative Statics and Non-Expected Utility Preferences', *Journal of Economic Theory*, vol. 47, pp. 393–405.

Nerlove, M., D.M. Grether and J.L. Carvalho (1979) *Analysis of Economic Time Series* (New York: Academic Press).

Savage, L.J. (1954) *The Foundations of Statistics* (New York: Wiley & Sons).

Schmeidler, D. (1989) 'Subjective Probability and Expected Utility Without Additivity', *Econometrica* vol. 57, pp. 571–87.

Shafer, G. (1976) *A Mathematical Theory of Evidence* (Princeton: Princeton University Press).

von Neumann, J. and O. Morgenstern (1944) *The Theory of Games and Economic Behavior* (Princeton: Princeton University Press).

Yaari, M.E. (1987) 'The Dual Theory of Choice Under Risk', *Econometrica*, vol. 55, pp. 95–116.

Comment

Kenneth J. Arrow

STANFORD UNIVERSITY, USA

Kurz is to be applauded for breaking new ground in defining rationality of belief in terms of some conformity to objective evidence. His aim is to give an objective definition of rational belief rather than the subjective version associated with the name of Thomas Bayes (and, of course, in modern times with Frank P. Ramsey, Bruno de Finetti, and Leonard J. Savage). In that sense, he is associated with the objectivist, frequentist definitions of John Venn and Richard von Mises. But he adds to the latter the view that rational beliefs are *not* necessarily *uniquely* specified by the objective – for example, the time series evidence so typical in economics. Thus different individuals can rationally hold different beliefs, not necessarily attributable to differences in Bayesian priors.

How does the Kurz approach differ from Bayesian analysis? In the usual Bayesian analysis, the belief held at any moment, the posterior, is based on the prior as altered on the basis of a finite amount of information. The simplest way to distinguish Kurz's views is to postulate an infinite amount of information, i.e., a time series has been observed for an infinite number of time periods. To take an example, suppose the observations are a sequence of heads and tails on flips of a coin. In Bayesian terminology, suppose the prior gave zero weight to the possibility of dependence among the tosses. No matter how many tosses occurred, the posterior would still give zero weight to dependence, even if the sequence showed long runs of heads and long runs of tails. But clearly, if one observed an *infinite* sequence of heads and tails, it would hardly be rational to maintain the independence assumption if, in such a sequence, the relative frequency of the conditional event 'heads at time $t + 1$ given heads at time t'', differed from the relative frequency of the event 'heads at time t''.

In other words, even though the limit of the posterior probability of dependence as the number of observations goes to infinity is zero, it would not be rational to deny dependence. This creates a paradox for Bayesian theory. It can of course be overcome by a diffuse prior, in which the probability of dependency is not zero; but this imposes a rationality requirement on *priors*, which is certainly not standard in Bayesian theory.

More specifically, Kurz's approach is to compute the relative frequencies of all possible time-invariant finite-dimensional sets. A belief is *rational* if it implies the observed set of relative frequencies. He does limit himself to the case where these limiting frequencies exist, what he calls *stable* processes (Definition 1). Processes can be stable without being stationary. Then a rational belief is uniquely defined on a set in infinite-dimensional space of relative frequency 1 but may vary off that set.

The restriction to stable processes suggests that observation of even a finite portion of the infinite sequence can restrict the possible rational beliefs. The argument, for which I am indebted to discussions with Kurz, is that if the relative frequencies converge, then the relative frequencies in a sufficiently long finite sequence impose restrictions on the possible limits. From a practical viewpoint, this view certainly has strength. From a theoretical view, it is inconclusive, for even if a sequence is known to converge, we cannot infer anything about the limit unless there is additional information about the rate of convergence.

There is an issue that I do not find completely resolved. It would seem that there is more information in a infinite sequence that can be obtained from looking only at time-invariant finite-dimensional sets. Take the simplest case in discrete time. A sequence is 0 everywhere except at times $t = 2^k$ for all k, when it is 1. Then if B is any finite-dimensional set containing the point $\langle 0, \ldots, 0 \rangle$, the relative frequency of it and its translates is 1; if it does not contain $\langle 0, \ldots, 0 \rangle$, the corresponding relative frequency is 0. Then a belief Q which assigns probability 1 to the infinite sequence of 0's is, in Kurz's terms, compatible with the data and non-degenerate and therefore rational. But it is certainly contradicted by the data.

This argument implies that the set of rational beliefs may be smaller than is suggested by the formal statement of Kurz's Rationality Axiom (a) in conjunction with Definition 3(ii). Kurz does go on to state what may be regarded as a pragmatic interpretation, that the relative frequencies of the translates of finite-dimensional sets should be computed not only for the original sequence but also for all predictable subsequences. The requirements that a belief not be contradicted by the data become correspondingly stronger. This strengthening will certainly handle my counter-example. It will be necessary to state that requirement formally to see if it can be made into a consistent theory.

Postface

Christian Schmidt

UNIVERSITÉ PARIS-DAUPHINE, FRANCE

1 INTRODUCTION

The relationship between rational decision-making and economics has a long and complex history. Utility has been its major point of intersection. A glance towards the past reveals at least three meeting points: the utilitarianist calculation of pleasures and pains which goes back to Bentham and the British utilitarians, the cognitive dimension of economic knowledge which goes back to Menger and the Austrian tradition, and the discrimination between the 'rational' and the 'non-rational' actions which goes back to Pareto. These have remained archaeological layers which sometimes explicitly or, at least, implicitly, are referred to by many contributors of this volume. Viewed from an historical perspective, this volume is no more, but also no less, than an attempt to offer a state of the art of the question in the 1990s. A careful reading of its chapters suggests future developments in the three fields.

Beyond the variety of approaches and the diversity of their background (economics, but also game theory, psychology, philosophy, computer science) several converging ideas emerge from this set of contributions. Putting them together offers the most fruitful element of this survey. First, rationality is not to be understood as an individualistic notion. Its relevance not only concerns the 'self' of every economic agent, but also refers to others, requiring that the rationality of decision-making in economics take into account the decision-maker's knowledge about others. Secondly, choosing an option rationally not only requires well-designed modelling which would identify once and for all the rational choice. It is to be analyzed as a process wherein certain general rules are implemented for computing available data by the decision-maker in actual choice situations. Thirdly, the process of rational decision-making is not a-temporal. Deliberation takes time and the available information most often changes during the dynamics of the choice situation.

2 'SELF' AND OTHERS

Economic situations are generally characterized by dynamic interactions among agents, such that the others are to be taken into account by each individual decision-maker as long as he is assumed to be rational. According to this feature, economic situations can be labelled 'games at large', a specific subset of them being studied by game theory in the narrow sense. It explains both the growing importance of game theory in economics and its limits for examining the meaning of rationality in economic decision-making. The definition of an individual player's rationality necessarily refers to what he knows about the others' rationality. This knowledge becomes very puzzling when the agents are not reduced to the players of a game and when their information on the others is neither complete nor perfect. As soon as the assumption of rationality as a common knowledge begins to be relaxed, the main problem for the decision-maker is no longer about rationality, but about the rational answer to be given to the expected irrationality of the others. The question raised by the knowledge of others' rationality appears closely related to the identification of the interface between rationality and irrationality.

One of the most fascinating consequences of carefully analyzing a decision-maker's belief regarding the others is to open a debate on the foundations of rationality in game theory. A first answer to the question has been already suggested by Harsanyi (1967a, 1967b, 1968) and extensively developed by Aumann in recent years. The Bayesian theory of subjective probabilities· provides a common foundation for modelling individual decision under uncertainty as well as for non-cooperative games with incomplete information. The assumption of a common 'prior' between the players is generally associated with this concept. The interpretation of its probability measure requires reference to a rational outside observer who is assumed to assess the same probabilities as each rational player of the game according to his own private information (Aumann, 1987). Such a condition implies a kind of common knowledge before the beginning of the game which may be consistent with the relaxation of the assumption of rationality as common knowledge during the game. Rationality may be a shared knowledge by the players at level 1, 2, ...n, but not necessarily ad infinitum (Aumann, 1992).

The Bayesian foundations for rationality in game theory are challenged by several game theorists. Binmore criticizes this view on the grounds that the assumption of this common 'prior' is only a device for avoiding the crucial question of how the players come to believe something about the other players (Binmore, 1990b, 1993). He goes further and, in his joint chapter with Samuelson in this volume (Chapter 5), denies that backward induction may be justified by assuming common knowledge of rationality before the game begins. For his part, Mariotti in Chapter 6 suspects some difficulty in combining the private feature of the Bayesian subjective probability with the public nature of common knowledge. Even a consequentialist as active as Hammond (Chapter 2) in supporting the Bayesian interpretation of the subjective probabilities in individual decision-making theory, sympathizes with the view that subjective probability distributions over uncertain states of the world cannot be extended to the players' belief about the other players' strategy. Hammond argues that players' expectations in game theory must be built endogenously and hence suggests for consideration as 'hypothetical probabilities' the distributions attached by each player to the other players on grounds of what he terms a 'conditional rationality'.

All these criticisms tend towards a provocative conclusion: the traditional background of rationality derived from Savage's format for individual decision-making is not relevant for understanding the concept of rationality which operates in the choice situation of non-cooperative game theory. One may note that such a conclusion meets some criticisms which have been expressed on the logical foundations of game theory from a strictly orthodox Bayesian viewpoint. Spohn claimed that game theory cannot be considered as a generalization of the Bayesian theory of individual decision. His main complaints about game theory were of two kinds: the vagueness of the assumptions concerning the players and an unavoidable flirtation with the probabilities of counterfactuals which he considers at least obscure and in the end spurious (Spohn, 1981). The first point is to be related to the arguments developed by the game theorists previously quoted. The second point is the core of the debate which follows the discovery of such paradoxes as the Chain-Store Paradox and Centipede Game which I surveyed in Chapter 3.

Finally, questioning the logical foundations of game theory goes far beyond the debate on its reference to Bayesian rationality. Game theory is basically a code through which some interactive situations between a finite number of decision-makers can be described in a mathematical language. As a mathematical construct, game theory does not really raise problems on that ground. But one can argue that the logical background of these choice situations is to be investigated prior to being shaped into the game theory mathematical format in order to avoid deadlocks and antinomies which have been pointed out (from the many stories of the paradoxical prediction to the Hangman's Paradox discussed by Margalit and Yaari in Chapter 4). Therefore the meaning of terms common in decision theory, such as 'state' and 'world', need revision to take into account several cognitive specificities of these situations from a logical point of view. Two kinds of difficulties must be underlined. First, the understanding of statements such as 'x knows that ...' or 'y believes that ...' requires the use of intentional operators. But the rules of inference are not necessarily the same according to the chosen operator – for instance the property of reflexivity which is verified by agents' knowledge (epistemic logic) but not by their beliefs (doxic logic), a distinction between knowledge and belief which is not clearly made in situations of incomplete and imperfect information (Hintakka, 1962). Second, in the interactive situations, the agents' knowledge as well as their beliefs are generally intricately embedded and often self-referential. Many levels of knowledge and/or belief are then to be identified for each specified agent on the grounds of his own position in the decision-making process. Furthermore, each agent himself meets several levels of knowledge along his reasoning process, as is directly illustrated by me (Chapter 3) and indirectly by Jeffrey (Chapter 1). All these levels co-exist ultimately in the same logical space. Following Lewis (1973) the term 'possible worlds' now designates the worlds which are accessible to the agents according to their specific knowledge. Thus, agents do not generally refer to the same possible worlds when they take their decision. If so, the conventional meaning of a state space becomes *ipso facto* questionable.

Among the responses proposed to such a challenge (Binmore, 1990b; Bacharach, 1992, 1993; Aumann, 1992), Margalit and Yaari in Chapter 4 sound the most radical. Instead of extending, as does Aumann, the domain of the classical proposition calculus in modal logic, the two authors claim that the preliminary step must be to reject the traditional dichotomy between the analytical and the factual statement as the two sole sources of knowledge for the decision-makers. They provide two examples where the postulate of a kind of knowledge, neither strictly analytical nor purely factual, and shared by agents, seems absolutely necessary for the identification of a common state space due to the existence of their different worlds: they name it 'comprehension'. One can be impressed by such an extreme philosophical position, but their thesis, as it is expressed, appears weakened by several oversimplifications. First, factual knowledge is reduced to sensory signals. Secondly, knowledge and information are not clearly differentiated, so that the analytical knowledge overlaps the public information, and the factual knowledge overlaps the private information. However, information belonging to factual knowledge may be public (as, for instance, the focal points of Schelling, 1960). Indeed 'sensory' obviously conveys private information, but why would the set of factual statements be reduced to sensorial information?

To sum up, it is true that what Margalit and Yaari term 'the lowest: knowledge common denominator' implies reference to a rational observer who is analytically omniscient but gets to know only public information. But the state space problem which is for them the consequence of such a general framework can be raised (if not solved) in a quite different way, as suggested by Aumann's 'Comment'. Let us assume that the state space does not belong at all to the agents' knowledge and let us replace the observer by the analyst who is the only one to know it. The meaning of the logical space is then perfectly clear. The question that comes up now is the agents' need for this information, which is a question on the borderline of logic.

3   MODELS AND PROCESSES

Almost all the contributors refer at least implicitly to the notion of 'bounded' and 'procedural' rationality. This seems odd, because, while Simon is one of the most frequently quoted authors in the references, no paper is specifically devoted to these topics. The explanation is very simple. If many features of Simon's analysis are largely accepted today, this acceptance does not imply that Simon's views on rationality are necessarily to be considered as an alternative way for understanding rationality. Therefore, his ingredients are disseminated among many of the contributors. Taking into account the limitation of the information available to the decision-maker and framing rational decision-making in a multi-stage process may be consistent with a weak form of maximization and does nor require any reference to the 'satisficing principle'.

Rational choice is modelled as a complex cognitive process which leads to a revision of our understanding of some basic concepts traditionally considered as given in the classical theory of rational choice (such as the preference order of the decision-maker). Twenty years ago Kahneman and Tversky sought to convince economists that a crucial and most often ignored operation is 'framing' the choice situation in order to choose a rationally justified option. They have finally succeeded. Pursuing the investigation along this line, Tversky (Chapter 8) argues that the system of individual preferences cannot be reduced to an abstract order relation independent of its empirical context. It results from a specific elicitation depending on the framing of the choice situation by the decision-maker ·which frequently violates the underlying 'invariance principle'. This general inspiration is shared by Plott (Chapter 10) who proposes a slightly different analysis. For him, preferences are 'discovered' rather than 'constructed' by the decision-maker, along a process where the search for information plays a central role in the understanding of rational behaviour. His conjecture is illustrated by experimental evidence. Its main advantages to integrate the knowledge of others' rationality into the learning procedure and thus to offer a bridge with game theory, at least in its evolutionary form. More generally, one can question the relationship between the framing of a multi-person choice situation and the knowledge of their mutual beliefs, a problem which puzzled Schelling (1960) a long time ago.

4 DYNAMICS AND TIME

Rationality in choice situations may be static or dynamic, according to the possibility or the impossibility for the decision-makers to know and perhaps to measure all the uncertainty from the beginning to the end of the decision-making process. For the sake of simplicity rationality has been first studied in the former case – for instance the Savagian consequences matrices for individual decision theory and the one-shot games in normal form. Unfortunately the expected utility canvas raises new questions when we shift from static to dynamic applications. Likewise, the Prisoner's Dilemma questions rationality in a different way when it takes the form of a one-shot game or when it is expressed in an iterated game. Most of the contributors agree that choosing rationality belongs to a dynamic process and that rationality in dynamics cannot come from a simple extension of static over-simplified choice situations. Thus, they agree to reconsider the missing link between rationality and time.

The basic schemes of individual decision theory must be profoundly revised to integrate the time dimension. Kahneman in Chapter 9 starts with the general observation that every decision-maker has to formulate an expectation about his future preference to be consistent with his expected outcome evaluation. He focuses his empirical investigation on the cognitive linkage between the memory of past experiments and this expectation at each point in time. The results he obtains suggests two interesting hypotheses. First, a system of individual preferences cannot be viewed as a purely instrumental concept in decision theory of rational choice, because the memory of past experiments implies a more substantial support – as, for example, the pleasure and the displeasure derived from these experiments. Secondly, the individual decision-maker is not always himself in the best position for correctly evaluating his past experiments. According to Kahneman's empirical evidence an outside observer often knows better the real consequences of the decision-makers' experiments than the decision-makers themselves, which is a rather troublesome observation for society. Once again, but for a different reason, rationality requires reference to the knowledge that others have of us.

Time is also relevant for explaining the logical process of rational deliberation even in a Bayesian framework. The subjective probabilities of a rational decision-maker not only may be changed by the observations, but also through the deliberation itself if the available data do not allow him to assess a probabilistic truth value for every proposition of the Bayesian model of decision. Jeffrey in Chapter 1 applies the name 'kinematics' to this kind of mental dynamics. Such a difficulty which restores the role of time in the deliberation process arises paradoxically when too much information is given to the decision-maker. Newcomb's Story supplies a traditional example of this situation. In addition to the knowledge of the possible states of the world, the decision-maker is informed that the providential person is a highly reliable predictor of his behaviour, which is a source of perplexity for choosing rationality in the Bayesian sense.[1]

Rationality in dynamic choice situations with many agents is closely related to the equilibration process of the system which can take the form of a game. Indeed, strategic rationality in game theory is not to be disconnected from the definition of an equilibrium. According to Binmore's terminological distinction, the most fruitful way to study equilibration requires a move away from an 'eductive' to an 'evolutionary' point of view (Binmore, 1990a). Rational behaviour now means an adaptative capacity for the decision-makers to reach collectively a convergence corresponding to an equilibrium point. The question has been experimentally studied by Roth (Chapter 11). One can infer from Roth's results in experimental games that the adaptative rationality of the decision-makers is highly dependent on their environment and that it is not an exclusive property of the individual decision-makers themselves. These observations leave open the question whether we possess a serious theory of the learning process of equilibration.

Must we go further and study rational behaviour from an inductive point of view? This attempt to follow an inductive logic goes back to a philosophical tradition illustrated by Carnap more than forty years ago (Carnap, 1945, 1950). Holland (Chapter 12) and Egidi (Chapter 13) are not that ambitious: both seek a revision of rationality in the light of a computational approach of the decision-making process when considered as a system. What do they really challenge? Implementing rationality in dynamic choice situations characterized by partial information cannot generally be reached by means of purely deductive rules, as in the strict interpretation of the consequentialist programme. A formal apparatus would be needed in order to infer future decision rules from information experienced by the decision-makers (Holland, Holyoak, Nisbett and Thagard, 1986). But these inductive procedures do not work as substitutes for deductive reasoning. Thus, 'forward induction' cannot be understood as a logical alternative to backward induction in game theory.[2] Rather, it seems a way of avoiding difficulties generated by backward induction where its use is not quite relevant, as in the Centipede-type games. The real issue is to know how inductive insights may be utilized to supplement the inadequacy of the purely deductive machinery for modelling temporal evolutionary processes.

Notes

1. This unfamiliar way to present Newcomb's Problem is close to our interpretation. However, according to Jeffrey (1965, 1983), Newcomb's Story cannot be definitely considered as a decision problem.
2. An unfortunate wording because backward induction must not be confused with an inductive inference.

References

Aumann, R.J. (1987) 'Correlated Equilibrium as an Expression of Bayesian Rationality', *Econometrica*, vol. 66, pp. 1–18.

Aumann, R.J. (1992) 'Irrationality in Game Theory', in P. Dasgupta, D. Gale, O. Hart and E. Maskin (eds), *Economic Analysis of Markets and Games* (Cambridge, Mass.: MIT Press).

Aumann, R.J. (1992) 'Notes on Interactive Epistemology', unpublished paper.

Bacharach, M. (1992) 'The Acquisition of Common Knowledge', in C. Bicchieri and B. Skyrms (eds), *Knowledge, Belief and Strategic Interaction* (Cambridge: Cambridge University Press).

Bacharach, M. (1993) 'Variable Universe Games', in K. Binmore, A. Kirman and P. Tani (eds), *Frontiers of Game Theory* (Cambridge, Mass.: MIT Press).

Binmore, K. (1990a) *Essays on Foundations of Game Theory*, (Oxford: Basil Blackwell).

Binmore, K. (1990b) 'Foundations of Game Theory', in 'Foundations of Game Theory', in *Advances in Economic Theory*, Proceedings of the 6th World Congress of the Econometric Society in Barcelona, Spain, vol. 1 (Cambridge: Cambridge University Press).

Binmore, K. (1993) 'De-Bayesing Game Theory', in K. Binmore, A. Kirman and P. Tani (eds) *Frontiers of Game Theory* (Cambridge, Mass.: MIT Press).

Carnap, R. (1945) 'On Inductive Logic', *Philosophy of Science*, vol. 12, pp. 72–97.

Carnap, R. (1950) *Logical Foundations of Probability* (Chicago: Chicago University Press).

Harsanyi, J.C. (1967a) 'Games With Incomplete Information Played by 'Bayesian' Players, Part I', *Management Science*, vol. 14, pp. 159–82.

Harsanyi, J.C. (1967b) 'Games With Incomplete Information Played by 'Bayesian' Players, Part II', *Management Science*, vol. 14, pp. 320–34.

Harsanyi J.C. (1968) 'Games With Incomplete Information Played by 'Bayesian' Players, Part III', *Management Science*, vol. 14, pp. 486–502.

Hintakka, J. (1962) *Knowledge and Belief* (Ithaca, NY: Cornell University Press).

Holland, J.H., K.J. Holyoak, R.E. Nisbett and P.R. Thagard (1986) *Induction: Processes of Inference, Learning and Discovery* (Cambridge, Mass.: MIT Press).

Jeffrey, R.C. (1965; 2nd edn 1983) *The Logic of Decision* (Chicago: Chicago University Press).

Lewis, D. (1973) *Counterfactuals* (Cambridge, Mass.: Harvard University Press).

Schelling, T.C. (1960) *The Strategy of Conflict* (Cambridge, Mass.: Harvard University Press).

Spohn, W. (1981) 'How to Make Sense of Game Theory?', in W. Stegmuller, W. Balzer and W. Spohn (eds), *Philosophy of Economics* (Berlin: Springer-Verlag) pp. 239–70.

Index of Names

Subject Index

ratificationism 20, 21, 75
rationality
  adaptive 1, 370
  beliefs xxv, xxvi, 37, 64, 339–40,
      343–5, 347, 351–4, 358, 359,
      362, 363
  bounded xv, xx, xxiv, 38, 127, 368
  common knowledge of 111, 113,
      114, 116, 122, 125–7, 130, 134,
      147, 149
  conditional 366
  individual 255
  interactive xiii, xvi
  player's 150, 155
  procedural xvii, xxv, 368
  strategic 52, 60, 142, 255, 275, 369
  structural xx, 4, 25, 28, 37
  substantive 4, 43, 203
repeated game 114, 116, 117
risk 186, 207, 339–41, 351
  aversion 187, 223, 340
  neutral 199
  seeking 187, 223
robustness 120, 128, 166

stability
  asymptotic 127, 128, 165–9, 177,
      178
  Lyapunov 158, 165, 166
states of nature, states of the world 3, 11,
      20, 21, 71, 72, 134–6, 139, 144,
      147, 149, 342
stationarity 158, 162, 164, 166
strategy
  dominant 143, 150, 151, 229, 233

dominated 62, 112, 122, 135,
      137–40, 142, 150, 151, 153
  equilibrium xv, xvi, xvii, 36, 70,
      112, 119, 134–6, 140, 141, 143,
      144, 150, 155–69, 173–9, 223, 231,
      247, 263, 271
  iterated elimination 57, 112, 120,
      125, 128, 130, 135, 138, 140,
      142, 145, 150
  iteratively undominated 150, 151
  interior *see* mixed
  mixed 155, 159, 162, 164, 167, 177,
      241
  pure 156–63, 165, 167–8, 261, 263
  rationalizable 35, 36, 38–40, 126,
      137, 152
  strategically stable 166, 168, 177,
      178
  tit-for-tat 114, 294
strategic form game *see* normal form
      game
subjunctive conditional 58, 67, 113,
      122, 130

trajectories 119, 161, 175
truth
  axiom 125
  value 3, 7, 20, 57, 64

utility function xiv, xv, xx, 18, 31, 49,
      128, 134, 194, 200, 201, 205, 206,
      209, 212, 214–16, 220, 222, 272,
      341, 342, 365
  expected 3, 35–7, 51, 52, 55, 56, 59,
      86, 87, 137, 185, 188, 198, 199
  non-expected 46, 59

DATE DUE
